Digital Ideologies in the Age of Algorithmic Culture

Esra Gökçen Kaygisiz
https://orcid.org/0000-0002-4950-9508
University of Giresun, Turkey

IGI Global
Scientific Publishing
Publishing Tomorrow's Research Today

Vice President of Editorial	Melissa Wagner
Director of Acquisitions	Mikaela Felty
Director of Book Development	Jocelynn Hessler
Production Manager	Mike Brehm
Cover Design	Jose Rosado

Published in the United States of America by
IGI Global Scientific Publishing
701 East Chocolate Avenue
Hershey, PA, 17033, USA
Tel: 717-533-8845 | Fax: 717-533-7115
Website: https://www.igi-global.com E-mail: cust@igi-global.com

Library of Congress Cataloging-in-Publication Data

Names: Kaygisiz, Esra Gökçen, 1979- editor
Title: Digital ideologies in the age of algorithmic culture / edited by Esra Gökçen Kaygisiz.
Description: Hershey, PA : IGI Global Scientific Publishing, [2026] | Includes bibliographical references and index. | Summary: "This book examines how algorithms shape ideologies, culture, and social norms in the digital age. Combining critical theory, media studies, and sociology, it explores digital power, identity, and values, providing an interdisciplinary framework to analyze and understand the ideological influence of algorithmic systems in contemporary society"-- Provided by publisher.
Identifiers: LCCN 2025054421 (print) | LCCN 2025054422 (ebook) | ISBN 9798337345314 hardcover | ISBN 9798337345321 paperback | ISBN 9798337345338 ebook
Subjects: LCSH: Information technology--Social aspects | Algorithms--Social aspects | Information society
Classification: LCC HM851 .D535 2026 (print) | LCC HM851 (ebook)
LC record available at https://lccn.loc.gov/2025054421
LC ebook record available at https://lccn.loc.gov/2025054422
British Cataloguing in Publication Data
A Cataloguing in Publication record for this book is available from the British Library.

This book is dedicated to my dearest Computer Engineer and Academician Özge AKDOĞAN YARAN, whom I miss very much.

Table of Contents

Detailed Table of Contents

structural inequalities. This chapter examines how scholars negotiate authority, visibility, and epistemic legitimacy within algorithmically governed public spheres. Drawing on case studies from the UK, Africa, South Asia, and Latin America, we analyze digital divides, algorithmic opacity, and epistemic fragmentation alongside community-led interventions fostering equitable inclusion. We explore how algorithmic truth regimes reshape knowledge validation and argue for socio-technical interventions to build transparent, democratically accountable digital knowledge infrastructures. The chapter articulates a vision for digital scholarship grounded in epistemic justice and democratic values, emphasizing coordinated action across academia, technology design, governance, and civil society

Digital hoboism represents the contemporary manifestation of transient labor in algorithmic economies, characterized by precarious employment, platform-mediated work arrangements, and perpetual mobility across digital and physical spaces. This chapter examines how algorithmic management systems shape the lived experiences of digital workers who operate outside traditional employment structures, including gig workers, digital nomads, freelance platform workers, and remotely employed individuals. Drawing upon critical platform studies, labor economics, and digital sociology, this analysis explores the ideological underpinnings of digital hoboism as both liberation narrative and exploitation mechanism. Through empirical data from platform labor markets, this chapter demonstrates how algorithmic systems create new forms of worker precarity while simultaneously promoting entrepreneurial subjectivities. The research investigates the socio-technical assemblages that govern digital hobos, revealing tensions between flexibility and insecurity, mobility and rootlessness.

This chapter investigates the ways that algorithmic technologies reconfigure workplace authority by changing how we think about surveillance, evaluation, and control in data-driven management practices. Drawing from and reconceptualising Foucault's Panopticon and Zuboff's Surveillance Capitalism, it contends that the algorithmic gaze creates an invisible governance system, where trust and autonomy are replaced by quantification. Through case studies in service, fintech, and logistics sectors, the analysis highlights how discourses of efficiency and performance sustainability legitimise digital despotism, bias, and workers self-monitoring. The chapter concludes with a framework for digital humanism, which articulates ethical, transparent, and participatory governance and management, which can restore human dignity and agency in algorithmically mediated labour.

This chapter explores how academics in Turkey use WhatsApp groups in ways that reduce visibility and interaction, forming a subtle practice of digital minimalism. These groups often encourage openness and responsiveness, yet many members stay silent, do not upload photos, use vague or symbolic names, and avoid status updates. While such behavior may seem passive, it often reflects a deliberate strategy to manage emotional effort, presence, and exposure in academic communication. Rather than interpreting this as disengagement, the chapter sees it as a meaningful form of agency. Drawing on observations from student, research, and professional WhatsApp groups, the chapter identifies patterns such as passive membership, minimal identity disclosure, and limited availability. These strategies show how users handle group norms while preserving boundaries. By viewing these behaviors through communication culture and institutional dynamics, the chapter reframes digital silence as an intentional form of participation on one's own terms.

The pandemic has reshaped organizational practices by accelerating digital transformation and embedding remote work into everyday operations. This chapter examines how influence tactics and organizational authority are redefined under these conditions, where traditional face-to-face control is replaced by digital visibility. Drawing on maximum diversity sampling, interviews with 12 participants from different sectors and levels were analyzed with MAXQDA 2024. Findings indicate that remote work challenges authority structures, compelling subordinates to adapt their strategies. A notable trend is the increased reliance on rational and communication-based tactics, while subordinates strengthen their social presence in digital environments to shape decisions. At the same time, the absence of nonverbal cues limits the expression of authority and influence. Interpreted through digital panopticism, these dynamics highlight how remote work transforms power: authority and influence are mediated and disciplined by constant online monitoring.

This chapter examines three cases—the Ndembu Archives, the documentary heritage of Madeira, and the Lúcio Costa collection—to show how digitisation has functioned as symbolic compensation that substitutes for, without resolving, the issue of material restitution. The Ndembu Archives, removed from their African political context in 1934 and now largely held by the Overseas Historical Archive, illustrate how joint digitisation and inscription in UNESCO's Memory of the World Register operate as postcolonial legitimising devices, recasting acts of documentary appropriation as shared heritage. Similar dynamics appear in the archival centralisation exercised by the National Archive of Portugal regarding Madeira, and in the transfer of the Lúcio Costa archive to the Casa da Arquitectura in Portugal. The chapter concludes by advancing a neo-custodial perspective that acknowledges the historicity of archival

Preface

I first encountered computers and information technology at university with MS-DOS and Windows 95. Since then, I have witnessed the development of many operating systems, infrastructures, applications, hardware, storage capacities, with access times, convergences, digital divides, and the internet. When I tell my students about all this, and they ask, "Which century BC are you talking about?", my answer is "only 20-30 years ago." But, the changes that have occurred, with their advantages and disadvantages, are extraordinary…

These developments demonstrate that digital technologies not only play an instrumental role but also create an ideological framework that reshapes social power relations, information flows, and cultural norms. The way algorithms determine content visibility, platforms shape public discourse, and digital surveillance systems direct individual behaviour has led to the emergence of new mechanisms of control and influence in modern societies.

In particular, the proliferation of remote work systems, the growing role of digital platforms in political communication, and the visibility of identity performances on social media show that digital ideologies have become an integral part of daily life. Therefore, understanding the ideological dynamics of the digital age is not only a matter of academic debate but also a fundamental requirement for understanding how contemporary societies function. In this context, the "isms" used to define various ideologies are also changing and diversifying.

The book "Digital Ideologies in the Age of Algorithmic Culture" aims to examine these transformations emerging in the digital age from the perspective of "digital ideologies." The book details the intellectual frameworks that explain how ideologies are interpreted, legitimized, and implemented through digitalization. These concepts have not remained merely theoretical headings; they have become ideological tools influencing daily life, political choices, identity construction, and the nature of knowledge in the digital environment. However, many of these new digital ideological structures have not yet been sufficiently explained, classified, or analysed in depth. It is now time to speak of new intellectual clusters that can be called "digital-isms."

This book offers a comprehensive analysis of the ideological structures and cultural transformations brought about by the digital age. The chapters in this book address this transformation through different theoretical perspectives and research approaches. The book offers an interdisciplinary platform for discussing the new behavioural patterns, power relations, and management practices that digitalization creates across organizations, society, and intellectual structures. They also examine the effects of algorithmic culture on politics, media, information production, identity politics, and working life from a multifaceted perspective. Concepts such as digital fascism, digital colonialism, algorithmic surveillance, digital feminism, digital intellectualism, and digital minimalism are discussed within theoretical and empirical debates to understand the various manifestations of digital ideologies. The book also examines the role of algorithms in the production of social meaning by analysing digital platforms' role in visibility production, the attention economy, and identity performance. Furthermore, it analyses the effects of digitalization on organizational life through topics such as remote work, algorithmic management, and digital surveillance systems.

The book's primary goal is to consider the impact of digital technologies on organizational life not only as a technical transformation but also as a process of cultural, ideological, and behavioural transformation. Accordingly, the book aims to contribute to the academic literature and provide an analytical perspective for practitioners managing organizations during the digitalization process.

This book is aimed at a broad academic and professional audience interested in the societal and organizational impacts of digital technologies. It is a valuable resource, particularly for researchers and students in organizational behaviour, communication studies, sociology, political science, public administration, and cultural studies. Furthermore, the book offers an analytical perspective for policymakers, media professionals, technology researchers, and digital strategy experts interested in digital platforms, data-driven management, and algorithmic decision systems. Serving as a theoretical reference source for graduate students and academics, this work is also a valuable guide for anyone seeking to understand the new societal and organizational dynamics emerging in the digital age.

CHAPTER OVERVIEWS

This book examines the ideological, cultural, and organizational transformations of the digital age from a multidimensional perspective. In an era where algorithms, digital platforms, and data-driven management systems are reshaping social life and organizational structures, digital technologies are not merely technical tools; they are also transforming into ideological structures that decisively influence power, authority, visibility, and information production. The chapters in this book address this transformation through various theoretical approaches, case studies, and empirical analyses, offering a comprehensive discussion of the ideological architecture of the digital age.

Chapter 1 argues that algorithms are carriers and reinforcers of ideology, defining how people and societies perceive the world. It aims to analyses the purpose of reproducing and critically questioning power structures. This chapter emphasizes the emergence of algorithmic culture by focusing on how ideological antecedents in the digital environment, along with data creation, personalization, and ghosting, restructure cultural production and consumption.

Chapter 2 develops a philosophical analytical model that understands digital transformation as a way of revealing a technological world and defines technical mediation as the co-creation of meaning, action, and normativity. Methodologically, it integrates metaphysical theory, analysis of technical mediation, network sociology, and critique of ideology. It reconstructs the seven network norms as the non-subjective normativity of digital systems. The interdisciplinary analysis presents an expanded understanding of digital ideologies and a normative-creative approach that views digital infrastructures as political, epistemological, and ethical fields of world-making.

Chapter 3 analyses the digital fascism strategies employed by President Daniel Noboa through his official X account during Ecuador's 2025 election campaign, using this as a case study. The highly interesting work combines qualitative discourse analysis with quantitative interaction measures. The research analyses discursive frameworks and viralization strategies to understand this modern authoritarian phenomenon in Latin America.

Chapter 4 critically examines the concept of digital colonialism and its impact on algorithmic power and authority in contemporary societies. By mapping mechanisms such as analysis, data extraction, surveillance, computational bias, and the creation of digital dependencies, the work demonstrates its impact, particularly on marginalized communities in the Global South. Integrating critical theory, postcolonial studies, and empirical case analysis, this chapter explores the intersections of digital colonialism with related ideologies, including digital imperialism and digital racism. It highlights resistance efforts and alternative digitalities advocating for pluralistic and egalitarian digital futures.

Chapter 5 examines the ideology of digital panoptism as a key feature of algorithmic culture, in which power is exercised through routine surveillance, data collection, and predictive analysis. The chapter links the concept of digital panoptism to theories of radical surveillance and digital capitalism, and explores its impact on subjectivity, autonomy, and behaviour. Taking Michel Foucault's idea of the panopticon as a starting point, the authors argue that digital systems are pervasive control structures, making it difficult to distinguish between observed and engaged regions.

Chapter 6 addresses gender bias in digital infrastructures, offering tools for resistance and solidarity while marginalizing feminist voices. Using feminist theory, digital humanities, and media studies, it views digital feminism as a movement that critiques and reconstructs algorithmic culture. The interdisciplinary approach examines the reflections of feminist activism in digital spaces, the effects of algorithmic patriarchy, and feminist data ethics. The chapter advocates for inclusive, transparent, and feminist-focused digital futures in which technology is aligned with equality, accountability, and care.

Chapter 7 analyses the evolution of the city as a space for childhood, highlighting the shift from urban contexts open to children's social interaction to environments increasingly driven by digital technologies. Drawing on a critical examination of historical and social processes, it discusses the gradual exclusion of children from public spaces and their confinement to controlled environments, resulting in the "algorithmization of childhood." It also examines the concept of music media to define forms of cultural co-construction in digital environments within the home. The findings emphasize the importance of rethinking public policies regarding children's occupation of public spaces, incorporating children's voices without ignoring their relationships with technology.

Chapter 8 aims to reveal how the economy of passion is silently dependent on algorithmic narcissism, a system that measures the self through visibility, metrics, and constant performance. This chapter leads us to the fundamental question: What happens when passion is transformed into performance, and the self into an algorithmic project? Essentially, the chapter invites readers to imagine a future where creativity is measured not by visibility, but by human connection.

Chapter 9, search how scientists negotiate authority, visibility, and epistemic legitimacy in algorithmically managed public spaces. Drawing on case studies from the UK, Africa, South Asia, and Latin America, it analyses digital divides, algorithmic transparency, and epistemic fragmentation, as well as community-focused interventions that promote equitable participation. The chapter sets forth a vision of digital science grounded in epistemic justice and democratic values, emphasizing coordinated action among academia, technology design, governance, and civil society.

Chapter 10 examines how algorithmic management systems shape the life experiences of digital workers operating outside traditional employment structures. Drawing on critical platform studies, labour economics, and digital sociology, this analysis explores the ideological foundations of digital vagrancy as both a narrative of liberation and a mechanism of exploitation. Through empirical data from platform labor markets, the chapter demonstrates how algorithmic systems foster entrepreneurial subjectivities while simultaneously creating new forms of worker precarity. The research also reveals tensions between flexibility and insecurity, and between mobility and rootlessness, through an examination of the socio-technical arrangements that govern digital vagrancy.

Chapter 11 survives by showing how algorithmic technologies are restructuring workplace authority by altering our thinking about surveillance, evaluation, and control in data-driven management practices. Through case studies in the service, fintech, and logistics sectors, it highlights how discourses of analytics, efficiency, and performance sustainability legitimize digital despotism, bias, and worker self-regulation. The chapter concludes with a framework of digital humanism that envisions ethical, transparent, and participatory governance and management capable of restoring human dignity and autonomy in algorithmically mediated labour.

Chapter 12 examines how academics in Turkiye use WhatsApp groups to minimize visibility and engagement, creating a subtle practice of digital minimalism. The chapter treats the behaviour of passive academics within these groups as a form of meaningful agency. Drawing on observations from students, research, and professional WhatsApp groups, the chapter identifies patterns such as passive membership, minimal identity disclosure, and limited accessibility.

Chapter 13 examines how influence tactics and organizational authority are redefined under these conditions, in which traditional face-to-face control is replaced by digital visibility. The findings show that remote work challenges authority structures and compels subordinates to adapt their strategies. These dynamics, interpreted through digital panoptism in the study, highlight how remote work transforms power; authority and influence are mediated and disciplined through constant online monitoring.

Chapter 14 presents three cases demonstrating that digitalization does not disrupt the function of symbolic displacement as a solution to material transformation. It also shows how the Ndembu Archives, severed from political and physical structures, their joint digitization, and their inscription in UNESCO's Register of World Memory, function as tools of postcolonial legitimation and reshape acts of documentary appropriation as shared heritage. The chapter concludes with a new preservative perspective that acknowledges the reality of archival displacement, rejects digital mutability as a final solution, and re-centers material restitution within archival justice.

Acknowledgement

A truly valuable book has emerged. The most significant contribution to this work undoubtedly belongs to the chapter authors. I extend my sincere thanks to all the authors who submitted texts from different countries around the world.

Furthermore, the reviewers provided me with great support. Through their meticulous evaluations within the timeframe I gave them, they made a significant contribution to the book.

I want to thank IGI Global Scientific Publishing for their support from the day I conceived my idea on digital ideologies. Their diligence and cooperation throughout the academic publishing process played a crucial role in bringing this work to readers. Thanks to them, I have produced a global publication.

I hope this book will be a useful resource for researchers, graduate students, and practitioners seeking to understand the transformations organizations face in the digital age. In an era where digital technologies are reshaping working life, I wish understanding these new dynamics will open new horizons for all of us.

Chapter 1

The Ideological Architectures of the Digital Age

Somesh Varandani
http://orcid.org/0009-0005-2595-4008
Poornima University, India

Amit Kumar Jain
http://orcid.org/0009-0008-6942-9987
Poornima University, India

Kirti Varandani
http://orcid.org/0009-0000-4314-6614
Poornima University, India

ABSTRACT

The twenty-first century has witnessed the beginning of a historic milestone where algorithms that had been the preserve of the sacred worlds of mathematics, computing, and engineering, have become the most dominant in establishing the presence of the human-being. The socio-cultural context, in which everyday activities, opinions, and even concepts are more and more aided by automated examples of the data processing, can be defined as algorithmic culture. They are not typical technical actions, but very political and ideological actions. Algorithms of the algorithmic mediated world pattern issues of visibility, representation and value on the obfuscated code and proprietary systems. It objectifies the interface of computational systems and cultural practices: how human practices inter-mediating and intermediated by algorithms. Notably, it acknowledges that algorithms represent the social, political and economic entitlement of the people who develop, implement and control them.

DOI: 10.4018/979-8-3373-4531-4.ch001

INTRODUCTION

According to traditional political theory, ideology is defined as a set of ideas, beliefs, and values that rationalize or oppose power structures. Ideologies like liberalism, socialism, or even conservatism are classical and have been spread across institutions, schools, churches, newspapers, and television. Ideology today works based on new digital infrastructures. Algorithms amplify some voices while silencing others, favor certain political discourses, and create echo chambers that reinforce existing ideas. Information is not merely a passive observer on digital platforms (Sanders & Sheptycki, 2017). They are ideological machines, ideally installed with capitalist, technocratic, and usually nationalist logic. As an example, the ideology of personalization promises users more customized and relevant content. However, in reality, it has become a hyper-targeted form of advertising, data mining, and behavioral prediction. Simultaneously, the philosophical position of neutrality, or the claim that technology is merely an instrument, conceals the fact that algorithms perpetuate the prejudices of their authors and the unequal social circumstances under which they are applied (Striphas, 2015). The twenty-first-century ideological battlefields are not only parliaments or newsrooms but also feeds, dashboards, and code (Gillespie, 2014).

SCOPE AND PURPOSE OF THE CHAPTER

It is the XXI century that marks a historical moment in which algorithms, once an area of study tied to mathematics, computing, and engineering, now hold a pivotal role in shaping human life. The term algorithmic culture is used to describe the socio-cultural situation in which automated data-processing mechanisms increasingly govern tape-recorded practices, choices, and even beliefs. In contrast to previous cultural periods, when power was centralized within institutions, e.g., religion, the state, or the mass media, algorithmic culture signals a time when computational logics and technological infrastructure coordinate the creation of meaning, identity, and social relations. Algorithms filter our news feeds, suggest what films to watch, assign credit ratings, curate the content of our online speech, and even pair us with people to date. These are not technical acts but very political and ideological acts. The issues of visibility, representation, and value are coded in opaque ways and proprietary systems across a world mediated by the plans of algorithms. This creates opportunities as well as tensions with convenience and customization being accompanied by monitoring, biasing, and manipulation. Algorithmic culture extends the idea of technical determinism. It foreshadows the interaction between the systems of computation and the cultures: the way human activities define and are defined by algorithmic mediation. Importantly, it recognizes that algorithms are products of the social, political, and economic interests of the people who create, implement, and control them. The expression of algorithmic culture is, in other words, the expression of power, its owners, power mechanisms, and the effects of power on the daily life of billions.

Why Digital Ideologies Matter Today

Why take the bother of digital ideologies at this time of unchecked technological flux? The answer lies in the fact that the algorithms are not shaped by social reality, but, on the contrary, it is they that shape it. Consider the role of recommendation systems in elections: during the Brexit referendum and the 2016 U.S. presidential election, social media platforms used these systems to disseminate misinformation and polarize voters. These occur not in a vacuum but as indicators of a more comprehensive shift in how ideologies are distributed and gain popularity. Moreover, the pandemic years were used to further bring out the ideological component of algorithms. The algorithmically amplified networks were spreading COVID-19-related fake news virally, but some platforms were also establishing themselves as truthers, labeling or deleting some content in the process. It emerged as an enhanced awareness that we are becoming increasingly conditioned by the algorithmic mediation of what we observe, what we think, and what we do. In this respect, digital ideologies play a crucial role as they dictate individual subjectivities, as well as political reality. They determine which voices to listen to, which stories to tell, and the future that societies perceive. Digital ideologies are therefore those that can be interpreted as central to viewing democracy, governance, culture, and social justice in the age of algorithms.

Chapter Roadmap

The chapter is critical and interdisciplinary in order to wade through these themes. It is informed by media theory, critical algorithm studies, and cultural analysis. It draws on the work of scholars such as Shoshana Zuboff, who has studied surveillance capitalism, Jose van Dijck, who has written on platform society, and Nick Couldry, who has written on data colonialism. These views point out the interrelations among technology, economy, and ideology. The roadmap is as follows: Section 2 provides the theoretical background by revisiting classical and contemporary conceptualizations of ideology and discussing the operation of algorithms as ideological apparatuses. Section 3 traces the ascension of algorithmic culture, datafication to platformization. Section 4 examines how digital ideologies are practiced, including capitalist, populist, and counter-ideological relations. Section 5 considers the experience of algorithmic culture in daily life, with particular reference to identity, bias, and public opinion. Section 6 provides a close international examination of the integration of digital ideologies in other societies. Section 7 concludes with a discussion of the issue's morality and proposes channels toward transparency and justice. Salient conclusions and outlook are also given as a conclusion to section 8 (Van Dijck et al., 2018). In general, this chapter introduces digital ideologies as a powerful tool for critical analysis in interpreting the contemporary culture of algorithms.

THEORETICAL FOUNDATIONS

Understanding Ideology in Digital Contexts

Critical social theory has always focused on the study of ideology. Karl Marx and Friedrich Engels (1973) defined ideology as the system of ideas that obscures the material relations of domination and serves to legitimize the interests of the ruling classes. This concept was later broadened by Antonio Gramsci, who focused on hegemony: how dominant groups retain their power not only through coercion but also through cultural leadership and consent (Rupert, 2009). The concept was taken a step further by Louis Althusser (2020) in his theory of ideological state apparatuses (ISAs), such as schools, media, and churches, which reproduce ideology by constructing subjectivities. These conventional machines have now been replaced by algorithms in the digital age as new intermediaries of ideology. The newsfeed on an algorithm, the trending hashtag, or the recommendation engine, as opposed to the newspaper editorial or the television broadcast, has become a site of ideology spreading nowadays. Digital ideology is thus not simply encoded in the explicit discourses but also in computational logics, data structures, and platform architectures. This change necessitates an expansion of the definition of ideology. Ideology should not be considered only as an explicit political doctrine, but rather as a code of assumptions and systemic prejudices embedded in digital infrastructures. Such assumptions regarding what is relevant, credible, or profitable are encoded in algorithms and serve as the means by which cultural practice in everyday life is organized around them.

Algorithmic Governance and Power Structures

Algorithmic governance is a concept in critical scholarship that refers to the increasing use of computational systems in decision-making, which impacts individuals and societies. The term governance in this context does not only refer to formal politics but also to the organization of social life by technical and organizational supra-systems. From predictive policing to automation hiring services, algorithmic government structures people, allocates their resources, and controls behavior.

The algorithmic governance modes of power are many ways:

1. Infrastructural Power: Because it is an element of communication, mobility, commerce, and entertainment, algorithms can be described as infrastructural. It is the place of their ubiquity, where they can be almost impossible to counter or oppose. This structural construct of infrastructures suggests that power is performed silently, through defaulting and back-off functions (Hars, 2000).
2. Epistemic Power: Algorithms are that which can be known and seen. Their ranking of certain search results or the sorting of their social media content generates knowledge and credibility hierarchies. This is not technical efficiency but the practice of epistemic power (Dotson, 2018).
3. Biopolitical Power: With the help of the idea of biopolitics that was proposed by Michel Foucault, we can take algorithms as the way to dominate life itself (Macey, 2009; Blencowe, 2011). Examples of such algorithmic systems include health apps, biometric surveillance, and smart cities, which control people by collecting and analyzing information about the body and behavior.
4. Economic Power: Platform capitalism business models are based on algorithms. Not only are they able to increase their profits by advertising in a given direction and cashing in on data, but they also change labor relations, as has happened with gig economy platforms like Uber and Deliveroo. Introducing these power instruments into technological equipment, algorithmic governance is laboring as a new reproductive instrument of ideology (Beer, 2016). It makes surveillance, commodification, and control seem as inalienable aspects of digital existence.

Technology, Politics, and Cultural Mediation

Technology, culture, and political mediation are other issues we should learn to understand to interpret digital ideologies. It is not surprising that media theorists, such as Marshall McLuhan, have said that the medium is the message and that communication technologies dictate human perception and social relationships. Following the tradition, the contemporary theorists, including Nick Choudry and Ulises Mejias, propose a concept of data colonialism, the institutionalization of the usurping of human life with the data harvesting, just like any other forms of colonial usurping (Mejias & Couldry, 2025). Algorithms, in this instance, are mediators of culture. They impact the consumption of cultural products, the voices heard, and other formations of society. YouTube, TikTok, or Instagram are not passive media; this is an algorithmically structured space of cultural production. This apparently simple scrolling action on a feed is actually a highly ideological phenomenon: the outcome of computational curation that is suggestive of the economic issues and cultural priorities of the individuals who created the platform. This mediation is also political. The online space is where the masses form opinions, voting takes place, and social movements become visible. Algorithms are not, however, entirely even in their treatment of all political content. They are more likely to support sensationalism, emotional appeals, and polarizing stories since these will maximize engagement (and therefore profit). By so doing, algorithms contribute to the emergence of populism and misinformation, and to the decline of deliberative democratic processes.

Ideology as Code and Infrastructure

The identification of ideology as infrastructure is one of the most considerable theoretical contributions to the study of critical algorithms. Conventional ideologies typically emphasize explicit messages or symbolic representations. In the age of algorithmic culture, ideology is in code, data models, and technical architectures. Take the following examples: • Recommendation Engines: These recommendation systems are optimized retention and monetization algorithms that Netflix recommends a movie, or Spotify develops a playlist. This ideology is implicit: the concept of cultural consumption is presented as personal, but it is, in fact, constrained by the platform's commercial requirements. Another example is the use of Facial Recognition Systems: Studies have demonstrated that facial recognition algorithms are racially and gender biased, with a low rate of false identification of people of color and women. These prejudices are not accidental; they stem from historical imbalances in training data and design choices. It is an ideology of normalization: the system is already asserting existing power hierarchies, but is made to appear objective.

• Content Moderation Algorithms: The content moderation systems on the sites are machine software that marks or removes the content based on biased criteria, based on specific cultural norms. To illustrate this, feminist or queer activism has been blocked and censored on a few occasions for violating community guidelines, yet harmful content still finds its way through (Gonçalves et al., 2021). It is a conservative ideology under the guise of universal moderation. The content of both cases is not only ideological; the infrastructural decisions to be made also dictate the selectivity with which the content is filtered, privileged, or lost.

Theoretical Synthesis: Towards a Critical Framework

By combining these viewpoints, we can form a critical paradigm for digital ideologies within algorithmic culture. The paradigm relies on three prominent intellectual traditions that combined to enlighten the way in which power functions in the modern digital context. First, the ideology has been conceptualized in Critical Theory as a process by which power perpetuates and vindicates social inequalities. Karl Marx, Antonio Gramsci, and Louis Althusser are among the thinkers who conceptualized ideology as embedded in institutions and practices that mold consciousness. Algorithms in the digital era can be viewed as new ideological apparatuses. They both reinforce inequalities by organizing access to information, visibility, and opportunity, while concealing the economic logics underlying digital platforms, including data extraction and workforce exploitation. Secondly, drawing on post-structuralism and Michel Foucault's notion of governmentality, algorithms can be regarded as tools of diffuse, data-driven power. Instead of enforcing ideology through direct propaganda, algorithmic systems govern the population through constant monitoring, classification, and prediction. This type of power operates within the context of what Foucault described as biopolitics: the regulation of life processes, in which control is embedded in technical systems and everyday environments. In this case, ideology is more invisible and infrastructural, and it can affect behavior through subtle nudges and automatic decision-making. Third, and most importantly, Cultural and Media Studies insights focus on the active role of algorithms in the process of constructing culture, identity, and social relations. Digital media filter, suggest relationships, and tailor experiences, thus shaping preferences, ideologies, and channels of communication. In this sense, ideology does not exist within the realm of official political discourse, but is performed in the process of scrolling through the social media feed, using recommendation systems, or using dating apps. Such micro-level relations are cumulatively constructive of more general cultural trends and subjectivities. In this synthesis, it is possible to theorize digital ideology as operating in three interconnected dimensions. It is a technical infrastructural component, inherent in the technical infrastructures that mediate digital life. It is endemic, demonstrating the presence of broader political-economic structures such as platform monopolies and surveillance-oriented business models. Lastly, it is experiential because users are exposed to and internalize such structures, often unconsciously, during normal digital interaction. These theoretical grounds together offer an approach to studying the formation of algorithmic culture, the experience of digital ideology's operation, and its opposition from a global perspective.

THE RISE OF ALGORITHMIC CULTURE

From Datafication to Personalization

The emergence of algorithmic culture is impossible to comprehend without first understanding the process of datafication, the transformation of social action into quantifiable data. As Jose Van Dijck (2014) believes, however, datafication is not a technical process but a logic embedded in culture, one that presupposes that everything in life can and needs to be converted into numbers. Since the number of steps a Fitbit monitors or the number of likes a social media post receives, data has become a controlling language for perceiving value, identity, and even social interaction. Datafication preconditioned the emergence of the idea of personalization, which is one of the features of the culture of algorithms. The pretense of customization is quite alluring: rather than browsing through a gurgling ocean of content, the user will be offered custom recommendations tailored to his or her preferences. However, personalization is not an objective service. It is the ideological process that furnishes human experience with measures of consumption, predictability, and interaction. The recommendation system at Netflix can be used as an illustration; it is designed to fulfill users' wishes, but in the real world it is geared towards maximizing retention and profitability (Van Dijck, 2014). It is a cultural shift: it is no longer the editorial quality of information, or the popularity of information determined by editorial quality and consensus, but the forecasts of the motion of individual people's behavior as given by algorithms. The personalization is turned into an ideological value; naturally, each individual's digital experience will be customized, and in the process, the commercial interests behind such customization will be concealed.

Platforms as Ideological Apparatuses

The proliferation of algorithmic culture cannot be discussed outside of the development of platforms as powerful socio-technical and economic actors. Google, Facebook, Amazon, and TikTok platforms are not simply service providers; they are the infrastructural background of the digital society. They serve as ideological machineries that Althusser could have referred to, but in a digital age.

- Google Search Engine: Google is a search engine that ranks and filters knowledge, making it a worldwide determiner of epistemic power. Its algorithms give an advantage to some types of knowledge production (commercial, popular, English-language) while disadvantaging others (local, minority-language, non-commercial). It is the ideology of a universal library, which hides the fact that advertising models and corporate interests also control it. Facebook and Instagram: The two social media platforms normalize the commodification of social life. The comment, like, and share systems promote performative identity formation and feed data into the advertising systems. This ideology is that of connectivity: the promise of social connection that encompasses the process of extracting value through users' intimate interactions.

- The For You Page of TikTok: TikTok is the purest example of algorithmic culture. You are not a customer coming to a store to browse shelves arranged by your friends; the algorithm recommends what it believes will keep you coming back. The ideology in this case is entertainment-as-governance: cultural production is positioned as playful creativity while serving as an enormous system of behavioral surveillance and control. Today, platforms are therefore not neutral intermediaries. They are ideological infrastructures that inculcate capitalist, technocratic, and cultural values within the very fabric of interaction. Their logic of monetization, visibility, and virality organises the circulation of culture in modern society.

The Political Economy of Algorithms

The emergence of an algorithmic culture cannot be discussed outside of the context of the political economy of digital capitalism. This dynamic is embodied in Shoshana Zuboff's idea in Surveillance Capitalism: behavioral data is extracted as raw material to be predicted and monetized. Algorithms in this economy are not merely a means of efficiency but also a means of accumulation, creating value by tracking, analyzing, and manipulating human behavior. This political economy has three dimensions that follow:

1. Commodification of Attention: Platforms are in the so-called attention economy. Algorithms are designed to capture users' attention and retain it, often through exaggerated, emotionally charged, or sensational content. The focus has become a rare commodity, purchased and sold to advertisers.
2. Infrastructure Monopolization: Several companies control the algorithmic environment and establish almost a monopoly on information flow. The monopoly of Google, Meta, and Amazon also implies that corporate interests mediate cultural life, and such mediation is not much controlled by democracy.
3. Globalization of Ideology: Algorithms that are developed in Silicon Valley are exported to other areas of the world, and Western capitalist logics are imposed on other cultures. This results in what (Couldry & Mejias, 2019) term data colonialism, a new kind of global domination in which data mining reflects how colonial domination has been practiced historically. Therefore, the political economy of algorithms has to do not only with profit but also with ideological hegemony. It makes surveillance, commodification, and global asymmetry a normal aspect of digital life.

From Mass Media to Algorithmic Mediation

To appreciate the freshness of algorithmic culture, it is important to compare it with earlier media. In the age of mass media, cultural consumption was heavily influenced by gatekeepers: newspaper editors, television producers, or state broadcasters. These institutions medicated ideology by way of direct editorial decisions and in overt narratives. Mediation between the algorithmic age is not the same. Algorithms replace human information customization. This movement can be characterized by decentralization and obscurity. On the one hand, everyone can post the content and go viral bypassing the conventional gatekeepers. The proprietary algorithms control processes related to visibility that are not visible to the user or even to regulators (Helberger, 2016). The result is a paradoxical scenario in which cultural production has never been democratised as much as it is now, and cultural visibility has never been algorithmically determined as much as it is now. The ideological implication is extensive: users perceive their spaces on the internet as participatory and open and their experiences are silently determined by the algorithms they cannot see.

Everyday Naturalization of Algorithmic Culture

It is another dimension that makes algorithmic culture very potent because of its naturalization in daily life. In contrast to previous ideological apparatuses, which were sometimes open (e.g. national anthems, propaganda posters), algorithms incorporate ideology into the background of everyday life.

- A student who goes to Google to find research material gets results that are ranked algorithmically with the understanding that this is how credible knowledge is perceived. In the gig economy, a worker takes on rides or delivery jobs as determined by platform algorithms and feels work is precarious and fragmented.
- A Tik Tok scanner creates preferences, wants, and political beliefs influenced by algorithmic editing. Anywhere, ideology works subtly: not through blatant propaganda but through the normalization of algorithmic mediation as the new way of experience. This is what makes them so strong; their banality is what forms the life not by force but by convenience.

Summary: The Cultural Ascendancy of Algorithms

The advent of the algorithmic culture is an innovation in the history of ideology. Although the ideological diffusion was vested in the hands of the mass media through direct accounts, algorithmic culture diffuses the ideology through opaque, personalized, and information-driven means. This transition is supported by three great dynamics:

1. The personalization and datafication, which transform human life into measurable metrical value and make experience personal.
2. The platformization, as the primary ideology of a modern culture of digital platforms as its major building blocks.
3. Surveillance capitalism, which fixes itself in the economic interest of the mediation of the algorithmic structure itself. Taken together, these dynamics can explain how algorithms have been shifted into cultural and ideological engines (Zuboff et al., 2019). They prepare the scene in the following part, discussing how these digital ideologies are put into practice- through capitalist logics, populist amplification, myths of neutrality, and counter-hegemonic resistance.

DIGITAL IDEOLOGIES IN PRACTICE

As the conceptual and historical underpinnings of algorithmic culture were introduced in Sections 1–3, however, it is in practice that the ideological side of algorithms can be most readily seen. Not only are digital platforms and infrastructures also technical spaces but ideological battlefields where capitalist logics, populist histories, myths of neutrality, and counter-hegemonic practices come into contact with each other. Four major spheres of digital ideologies are analyzed in this section in which they are most vividly presented.

Capitalist Logics: Surveillance, Profit, and Commodification

The logic of digital capitalism is probably the most widespread ideology of algorithmic culture. Algorithms and their role as a vehicle of surveillance and monetization commodify personal data, attention, and even social relations.

1. Surveillance as the New Normal. In the era of mass media, promotion could be made mostly according to the demographics and the large segments of the population. Surveillance in the algorithmic culture is, however, granular, continuous and predictive. Facebook or Google keep track of every movement of the user, even a single click, hover or a pause. This information is then passed to machine-learning algorithms that can forecast the future behavior with a very high degree of accuracy. In the ethos of this normalization of surveillance, here, is where users are being selling themselves to be followed around as the cost of convenience, and businesses are being sold to them as part of the free services.

2. Profit as the Hidden Driver Algorithms of recommendations are most of the time not created with the objective of user well-being in mind. They are, rather, designed to be profitable in some way: by showing more advertisements, keeping people engaged, or making them take micropayments. Indicatively, the algorithm of YouTube has been observed to promote sensational and polarizing content as this keeps the audience entertained longer, which creates more advertisement earners. It is a disguised profit ideology, disguised as the personalization of the workplace: what might seem like your preferences, is actually a projection of the corporate necessity.
3. Commodification of Social Life. Social networks such as Instagram and Tik Tok transform regular conversations such as likes, comments, selfies, dancing into product packages that can be sold to advertisers. This brings about what Jodi Dean refers to as communicative capitalism in which participation itself has become a profit business to corporations (Brown, 2021). The users are not merely consumers but free producers of value who make a contribution to a system that commercializes their sociality. Therefore, algorithmic culture has both overt and covert capitalist ideology. It openly poses as personalization, innovation, connectivity, and hides the real workings of surveillance, profit-making and commodification.

Populism and Algorithmic Amplification

The second significant ideological practice in the digital era is the algorithmic boost of populist discourses. Populism is based on direct emotional appeal, us versus them rhetoric, and shallow stories all of which algorithms are likely to reward since they produce high levels of engagement.

1. Viral and Emotional Politics. The analysis of Facebook and Twitter[1] in the Brexit referendum and the 2016 United States presidential election has shown that emotionally charged content (in particular, anger and fear) goes viral and widespread than fact-based coverage. These dynamics are enhanced by algorithms, which are engineered to encourage further exposure to populist narratives. Populism seems more widespread and acceptable than it would otherwise be due to the ideological impact.
2. Echo Chambers and Filter Bubbles. Echo chambers that develop through algorithmic curation are characterized by the users being presented with content that largely supports their already held beliefs. It is especially favorable to populist movements which are nurturing on a sense of belonging together and resistance to elites or foreigners. Platforms are therefore good sources of nationalist, xenophobic or anti-establishment ideologies to propagate (Pariser, 2011).

3. Platform Populism Other researchers believe that platforms are also a form of platform populism in their own right: they are selling themselves as an empowerment of the people against the traditional elites when in fact they have concentrated power in the hands of corporations. The example of Twitter which had traditionally pressed itself as a means of grassroots activism (For example: during the Arab Spring) but has also played a role in the development of far-right populist movements.

The techno-populist ideology here is that the digital infrastructures are technology that obscure the distinction between democratic empowerment and corporate exploitation. Algorithms, through these processes, do not passively reproduce populist ideas; they actively co-produce and recycle them, transforming the politics.

Ideologies of Neutrality: The Myth of Objective Algorithms

The myth of algorithmic neutrality is one of the most pernicious digital age ideologies. Placing themselves often purport to have neutral, objective, and purely technical systems. This ideology conceals the biases and power dynamics of the design of algorithms that are real and present. 1. The Discourse of objectivity. Technology firms tend to popularize algorithms as neutral data-sharing devices that allow the data to speak. This discussion places human subjectivity as biased and machines as being impartial. As a fact, algorithms are trained using datasets that mirror the current inequalities racism, sexism, classism and therefore, replicate them at a large scale. Objectivity myth itself is an ideological operation, which makes decisions made according to algorithms to be justified and hard to challenge.

2. A Case Study: Predictive Policing. Predictive policing systems, which have been used in cities such as Chicago and Los Angeles, purport to forecast objectively the crime hotspots. However, these systems are conditioned on historical crime information which is skewed in over-policing minority neighborhoods. Therefore, predictive policing is re-creating racial profiling in the name of neutrality. This ideology is that of technocratic legitimacy: the assumption that algorithms are able to give objective answers to the social issues.
3. Invisible politics and Content Moderation. Even the content moderation algorithms tend to be culturally and politically biased. As an example, feminist and gay activists have claimed to be censored more than their content should, and dangerous or extremist content has made it through. These ideological choices are hidden behind the myth of neutrality and promoted to the viewer as the technical glitches but not political results. The algorithmic culture is therefore dominated by the ideology of neutrality. It produces a dodging effect on respon-

sibility, mystified power relationships, and put digital structures as unavoidable and uncritical.

Counter-Ideologies: Digital Activism and Resistance

Although capitalist, populistic and technocratic ideologies prevail over them, the subject of algorithmic culture are also a location of counter-ideologies. Digital tools are used by activists, artists and marginalized communities to reverse mainstream logics and define other possibilities around digital life.

1. Hashtag Activism The examples of such movements as #BlackLivesMatter, #MeToo, and #ClimateStrike reveal how effective algorithms can be used to make counter-hegemonic voices louder. Though these movements are determined by the same logics of attention like populism, they reinvest algorithmic visibility to respond to systemic inequalities and mobilize people into action. It is a counter-hegemony ideology and the masters are turned against them using their own means.
2. Other Platforms and Decentralization. There are also attempts to offer alternatives to corporate platforms by local communities, as with the decentralized social networking platform Mastodon (open-source), or blockchain projects. These platforms are models of ideologies of digital commons, participatory governance and technological sovereignty. And so long as they are niche, they will be important experiments in combating platform monopolies.
3. The Alcoholic Accountability Activism. The opposition to using algorithms in bias and transparency to AI systems are such groups as the Algorithmic Justice League, which is the creation of Joy Buolamwini (Ellison et al., 2007). The significance of counter-ideology that their work invokes is not discursive but technical, and demands the open-source code of algorithms, external scrutiny, and community oversight. The counter-ideologies serve to bear in mind that the algorithmic culture is not universal. Despite these dominant logics being geared towards normalizing surveillance, profit, and neutrality, spaces of resistance are always produced, opposing these discourses and projecting more just futures of the digital world.

Synthesis: The Plurality of Digital Ideologies

Together, these dynamics contribute to the representation of the fact that digital ideologies are not singular but multiple. Algorithmic culture is a kind of ideology battle where the clashing forces are ideological: Surveillance and commodifying are made familiar with capitalistic rationales.

- The populist discourses exploit the algorithmic amplification to rebrand politics.
- The politics of algorithms are concealed behind the myths of technocracy of neutrality.
- Counter-ideologies render mobilized a resistance, and provide alternatives. The existence of these ideologies endorses the digital life sophistication. At the same time, the users are the subjects of the capitalist exploitation, the members of the populist politics, the consumers of the so-called neutral algorithms and, perhaps, the opposing actors. The ideologically oriented sphere of the algorithmic culture is thus dynamic, contradictory, and disputable.

EVERYDAY LIFE IN ALGORITHMIC CULTURE

Digital ideologies may have effects experienced perhaps most tangibly in the marketing circles of corporate boardrooms or in political discourses; but in the day-to-day lives of most people. The algorithmic culture is pervasive in terms of communication, consumption, work, learning, and even imaginations of people. This part explores the mundane aspects of the algorithmic culture, which helps to identify how ideologies are incorporated into the practices that are usually personal, trivial, or apolitical.

Communication and Intimacy

Social Media as Mediator of Relationships

WhatsApp, Instagram, Snapchat, and Tik Tok are the platforms that are at the center of communication in the modern world. The most obvious case is when someone sends a meme, or shares a reel, likes a story posted by their friend, and algorithmic design influences that. These platforms are fronted by the connectivity ideology as important in sustaining relationships, yet they mediate intimacy normativity of corporate infrastructures round-the-clock.

- Curation Friendship: These types of algorithms are driven by engagement and do not need the user to be in close proximity to them (Fraher, 2015). This reinvents the idea of friendship- the friends who are demonstrated to be algorithmically downranked may be seen as being far away, as they may be physically nearby.

- Affection (Likes, hearts and emojis): Affection is measured in a way of Incorporation. This is the ideology of the metric intimacy in which relations are quantified, juxtaposed and performed.

Romantic Encounters in Algorithmic Culture

Dating apps like Tinder, Bumble or Hinge are some of the good examples of how intimacy is commodified. The algorithms are used to rank and recommend the order and suggestions of the profiles, and a gamified experience of romance is created. Ideologically, they naturalize the market rule of choice extending love as a problem of efficient matching, as rather than serendipity.

Consumption and Everyday Choices

Algorithms have a significant role in shaping the perceptions, purchase and appreciate decisions among people. Recommendation systems are becoming the intermediaries of daily consumption, be it in the shape of Netflix queues or the list of Amazon products. Cultural Consumption: The recommendation algorithm of the streaming services is presented as democratizing the entertainment business, yet the algorithms have predilections towards certain genres, aesthetics and narrative. This creates some sort of an unwritten algorithmic canon, in which certain objects of art are perceived more than others, which determine the cultural taste. Retail Consumption: The customization of e-commerce products also means that you also like products can be customized to what one desires. In reality, they are directed by the desire to make profits, availability and profit margins. This ideologically forms the consumption as an option that covers the corporate generation of passion. Food Delivery and Daily Habits: Applications, like Zomato, Swiggy, or Uber Eats, make people get used to the fact that the algorithm offers people a meal. With time passing, it will become less of a convention and custom that informs food preferences and instead, the impact of promoting apps and incentives.

Work and Labor

The Algorithmic Workplace

Algorithms are now an inseparable governing element of significant data of the modern labor market. To gig employees like Uber drivers, riders on an online delivery service or warehouse workers, labor will be organized less by their human managers and more by bots who are tasked with assignments, route optimization, and real-time performance evaluations. This type of algorithmic management reorganizes work by extracting data constantly and reducing workers to a unit of productivity (Rosenblat & Stark, 2016; Kellogg, Valentine, & Christin, 2020). Micro productivity measurements, ratings and performance scores are tools of discipline that are used to enhance surveillance at work. Employees are compensated, coerced or even punished by black box scoring schemes of which they have no complete knowledge and power to challenge. These systems generate an unequal balance of power and ensure a perception of impartiality and objectivity (Zuboff, 2019; Beer, 2016).

Professional Life Beyond the Gig Economy

Algorithms also interact with white-collar professionals multiple times in their daily lives, in the form of career-recommendation algorithms on LinkedIn, AI-powered work-optimization software, or auto-sorting email applications. Such apps represent the worldview of optimization at their own terms and define professional value as a quantifiable and controllable item on the basis of data.

Selfhood and Identity

Algorithms do not only influence decisions and behaviors but also influence how people view themselves.

- Algorithmic Self-Knowledge: People generally believe that algorithm recommendations can tell the truth about them: Spotify knows me better than I know myself. It leads to a conception of algorithmic authority as such, in which the algorithm is thought to be more reliable than personal consideration to measure identity.
- Performing to the Algorithms: On Tik Tok or Instagram, individuals change their behavior to make the algorithms pleased by posting on the best time, using the most popular songs, or creating the content that gets more likes on the platform. Everyday life consists of acting in front of algorithms where self-expression is determined by what machines tell them to be.
- Aesthetics of Selfhood in a Virtual Sense Filters, AR effects, editing options cause people to appear differently or to seem to appear differently or change perceived ideas of beauty, fashion, and desirability (Sweeney, 2013). This kind of proposal gives the appearance of the post-human, where the natural and the constructed blur.

Learning, Information, and Knowledge

The role of algorithms is prominent in accessing information and utilization of information in the lives of people.

- The Search Engines as Epistemic Authorities: The ranking algorithm of Google is generally perceived as a neutral pointer at reality. Nevertheless, it is inclined toward certain sources, business portals, or information that is optimized for search engines. The ideology that dominates in this regard that hides political economy of visibility is search neutrality. Platforms Informal Learning: We learn on these platforms Tik Tok and YouTube - recipes to code to political commentary. They are also instilling learning in bite-sized, entertaining ways instead of delving into depth, opening doors to democratic access.
- Educational Inequality: Classroom-based learning systems at school offer one-to-one attention in schools, yet they accelerate class segregation by modifying the content to reinforced by existing achievement disparities. It supports the notion of meritocracy, and structural inequality is an internal difference.

Emotional Life and Mental Health

Algorithms not only influence purchase choices but also emotional trends.

- Mood Control Via Playlists: Spotify, Instagram, or Netflix, numerous users enjoy watching movies, reels, or playlists that can help them change their mood. These platforms generate the illusion of algorithmic care, presenting themselves as friends.
- Concern on Permanent Comparison: What social media measurements inculcate is a culture of comparison whereby likes and followers are the new measures of individual value. It is a competitive individualism ideology that they normalize.
- Redesing Addiction: The infinite scrolls, autoplay, and push features aim to make the most out of the participation as a form of absolute addictiveness. Ideologically packaged as a user choice to not shift the blame on the design of the platforms.

Everyday Resistance and Negotiation

No matter how much the power of algorithmically dictated thoughts prevails, humans also manage to oppose it, subvert it, or avoid it. Crafted Digital Minimalism: Some users are proactive and strive to reduce their usage, whether by disabling notifications, deleting applications, or undergoing a digital detox. This criticizes the ideology of constant-connectivity. Creative Subversions: Meme communities, parody accounts, and ironic posts keep ridiculing how algorithms work to blur their effects.

- Tactical Engagement: Sometimes, users can control algorithms to obtain their desired outcome- i.e. small creators forming like groups to control engagement metrics or gig workers working in consultation to exploit platform incentives. Such strategies show that algorithmic culture is not a one-way culture however effective it is.

Synthesis: The Normalization of Algorithmic Life

The everyday reality of the algorithmically driven culture is a paradox: people often assume they make their own free decisions, yet their actions, feelings, and identities are constantly programmed by invisible algorithms. Normalization is an ideological effect: algorithms become a part of the landscape, an object that is not questioned, is trusted, and sometimes even loved. Every day routines do not consist of mere information receiving. Interactors cannot, but interpret, oppose, and co-operate with systems. It creates a diffuse connection between ideological interpellation (participants are summoned into algorithmic thinking) and agency (participants contribute innovatively or oppose). In the simplest terms, the normativity of algorithmic culture is not in the depersonalization of beliefs, but in their insertion into our most intimate modes of speech, purchase, labor, subjectivity, and affect.

ETHICAL AND POLITICAL IMPLICATIONS

The emergence of algorithms not only changes the way mankind communicates with technology and works but also poses serious political and ethical issues. The digital beliefs embedded in daily practices and organizational structures undermine such values as honesty, fairness, justice, and democratic participation. Here, we explore the ethical concerns and political effects of being an algorithmically driven world.

Power, Control, and Autonomy

Concentration of Power in Tech Corporations

Significant majority of the most evident political impact of algorithmic culture is that a small number of firms possess a colossal realm of influence. Such businesses include Google, Meta, Amazon, Apple, Microsoft, and ByteDance. These corporations, in fact, have de facto control over people's lives, since they determine what others can view, whose messages are amplified, and how billions of people interact with each other daily. The problem of power inequality is raised in both sides of the case: users provide data and content, and businesses own infrastructure and commercially utilize it. Ideologically, this kind of centralization is normally packaged under the pretext of innovation and choice, but in reality, it is a post-democratic order in which unelected businesses gain some form of sovereign authority.

Autonomy and Algorithmic Nudging

Algorithms usually manipulate behaviour in a more encouraging rather than compelling manner - framing decisions in a quiet manner to influence choices. For example, the next episode on a streaming service may play automatically, or a ride-hailing app may encourage the driver to accept a lower-paying ride through game-like notifications. Even though nudges seem harmless, they also raise built-in ethical issues: Erosion of Autonomy: Individuals may believe they are making free decisions, but their actions are guided.

- Invisible Manipulation: Algorithms nudging can be subtle to traditional advertising, which makes the consent grey. Normalization of Behavioral Governance: Nudge-based everyday dependency tends to normalize people to forms of governance that run counter to deliberation and consent.

Justice, Bias, and Discrimination

Algorithmic Bias and Structural Inequalities

Algorithms have been presented as objective yet they reproduce and recreate historical inequities. (Bovens & Zouridis, 2002) Algorithms have disproportionately disadvantaged marginalized populations in the fields of employment, lending, predictive future crime, and healthcare.

- Case Study-Recruitment: AI-driven recruitment software has been identified to avoid women and non-whites when trained on biased data sets that reflect a history of male-dominated industry.
- Case Example–Policing: The policing preventive leads to surveillance to a level that is disproportionate among the low-income minority communities further entrenching the over-policing practices. Epically, it creates distributive justice issues: algorithmic systems can redistribute risks, opportunities, and harm to such a degree that they exacerbate those already in place.

The Challenge of Accountability

Responsibility is one of the moral questions to be considered. In instances where a discriminatory algorithm is used to deny a loan or falsely flag content as suspicious, is it due to the developer, the corporation, or the dataset? Algorithmic decision-making is more likely to generate responsibility gaps in which damage is actual, but accountability is dispersed. Ideological risk: the damage being depoliticized: failures are not described as an outcome of power-imbued design choices, but rather they are caused by technical bugs (Weiskopf & Hansen, 2022).

Democracy and Public Life

The Algorithmic Public Sphere

The internet has transformed the online spaces into a de facto political deliberation space. However, these spaces are algorithmically curated to create the greatest amount of engagement and in these cases, polarization or sensationalist content is being rewarded. Through virality-seeking, Erosion of Debate: Virality-seeking degrades critical-rational discussion at the expense of emotional appeal and populist rhetoric.

Disinformation and Manipulation

Campaigns of misinformation, such as state-sponsored propaganda or virally infectious conspiracy theories, have been a fruitful source of campaigns on platforms. Falsehoods are no longer hidden but are also sustained by the constant onslaught of sensational misinformation that obscures the nuances of truth through algorithmic boosting. On the ethical side, it is problematic in terms of epistemic justice, which is the justice of sharing knowledge and justification. It weakens democratic institutions and erodes public trust in government.

Privacy, Surveillance, and the Right to Opacity

From Privacy to Predictive Control

Predictive profiling and privacy are conflated with algorithmic culture. The sites do not simply store the information; they also make probabilistic representations to predict the next action. Surveillance is then not an ex-post facto but anticipatory and pre-emptive and there are profound moral issues of freedom and control.

The Ethics of Opacity

The right of other scholars is that of being opaque- not to be predictable and not to be profiled. Yet, algorithmic culture is anti-opaque, and the purpose of it is to make all behavior transparent and predictable. Morally, this turns people into statistical subjects, the statistical data doubles that do not necessarily represent the lived identity, but which do not leave room for access to resources (Ihde, 1975). The political side of it is that societies are moving towards surveillance capitalism (Zuboff, 2019) in which behavioral prediction becomes the new economic logic and privacy is no longer a widespread good.

Global Inequalities and Digital Colonialism

Unequal Access and Dependency

The global population of algorithmic culture is under the control of corporations based in the Global North, which dominate the infrastructures of the algorithmic culture. This leads to digital colonialism, in which developing nations in the Global South become reliant on foreign platforms for communication, business, and government.

- Data Extraction: Global South users present a great volume of data, which is frequently not under the safeguards of the North. Platform Dependency Governments, universities, and economies are all based on infrastructures such as Google Workspace or Facebook and place external control within local institutions.

Cultural Homogenization

Algorithmic recommendation systems favor content with global mass appeal, leaving local cultures and languages behind. This brings about the pressures of cultural homogenization whereby, the global pop aesthetics take over the indigenous and minority ones. What follows is some form of epistemic injustice: suppression of other knowledge and cultural practices in the name of standardization of algorithms.

Regulation, Governance, and Algorithmic Accountability

Emerging Frameworks

Governments and the participants of the civil society are discussing regulatory frameworks as a reaction to these problems: EU AI act proposes the use of risk based regulation of AI systems. Privacy and openness are among the data protection principles sought by data protection laws such as the GDPR. Algorithms and impact assessment: The new tools are algorithms and impact assessments that can be applied to the work management. Such systems portray struggle to restore democratic forces of infrastructure that has largely gone out of control.

Limits of Regulation

There are however, a number of challenges associated with regulation:

- Opaqueness: Many of the algorithms are black box, and therefore, they cannot be easily monitored. Global Asymmetry: This may be due to the regulation in one country (e.g., the EU) not being extended to other countries. Corporate Lobbying: Tech companies are massively influential and in many cases they put regulatory ambition to the waterboard by watering down policies. The democracy issue lies in how the institutions can indeed restrain corporations that are transnational and are extremely strong-rooted in our daily lives.

Ethical Futures: Responsibility, Agency, and Resistance

The algorithmic culture cannot be ethically reasoned by simply censoring it; it needs to strive to provide an answer about the nature of the futures it can create. The trends that are gaining popularity are:

1. Designing Justice: Advocates propose discrimination Categorize algorithms as designed and not fixed features Important characteristics that must be designed to bring justice, accountability, and transparency.
2. Shared Action: Workers, users, and activists are mobilizing to put the gig work under some form of accountability, whether by forming unions of gig workers or by initiating campaigns like #StopHateForProfit.

3. Conceptual re-thinking on Human-Machine Relations: Philosophical controversies The issue of how we might begin to think of less extractive and more symbiotic human-computer relations, where digital systems are supplementary and not commanding of human life, remains a matter of concern.
4. Digital Rights as Human Rights: Building the Legislation to make privacy, transparency and non-discrimination due to algorithms central human rights. (Cai et al., 2021) The stakes include the ideology that the future of the algorithmic culture can either presuppose the further development of surveillance capitalism and the technocratic rule, or move towards even more democratic, equal, and human digital structures.

Synthesis: Ethics as Politics

Ethical and political consequences of the algorithmic culture cannot be separated. Ethics in this case is not only regarding individual preferences, but about the organizational form of digital infrastructures. Similarly, politics is not merely the regulation by the state, but also the organization of everyday life in terms of algorithmic norms. There is even the freedom, democracy, and justice of the 21 st century at the stake. Algorithms culture provokes us to rethink our identity of sovereign agents, equal citizens and participants in the democratic public.

TECHNOLOGICAL TRAJECTORIES

Technological Trajectories: AI, Automation, and Beyond

Generative AI and Cultural Production

Generative AI (e.g. GPT and DALL.E and Midjourney) can be viewed as a new advancement in the culture of algorithms. Such systems are no longer going to sit and passively filter content; they are now going to make content, write essays, make music and pictures, and even simulate conversations. The choice between democratization and concentration. Even though generative AI eliminates the barriers to the creative process, it also concentrates the power into the hands of the companies owning the foundational models. Ideological Stakes: Generative systems may be useful for reinforcing dominant aesthetics and discourses (as they are trained on existing cultural sets) and for disrupting conceptions of originality, diversity, and property.

Ubiquitous Algorithmic Decision-Making

The algorithms enter spheres once considered human: law, medicine, education, and governance. Their spread is a sign that there is in the future a more profound infiltration into social life by algorithmic rationality.

- Efficiency vs Justice There is a danger of loss of fairness, deliberation and human judgment to the benefits of quicker and more data-oriented judgments.
- Delegation normalization: The more decisions people delegate to algorithms, the more the line between support and control is crossed.

The Next Infrastructures: Web3, Quantum, and Decentralization

The culture of algorithms can be remade by the creation of new systems of infrastructures like blockchain, decentralized autonomous organizations (DAOs), and quantum computing. These inventions can decentralize, introduce transparency, and innovative forms of governance, but they can also revive the inequalities of the past under new names.

Social Trajectories: Everyday Negotiations

Normalization of Algorithmic Life

To the youths, algorithmic mediation is not something that intrudes into their lives but it is the natural way of things. The second one suggests that, as far as privacy, autonomy, and bias are concerned, these may be more abstract in situations where the population has never lived in the pre-alpha world.

Mental Health and Algorithmic Affects

The psychological impacts of algorithmic culture, such as comparison anxiety, dopamine loops, and digital burnout, are likely to increase more rapidly. The presence of mental health structures that focus not only on personal coping but also on the structural setup of platforms will shape future directions.

Resistance and Everyday Agency

Though normalization will be experienced, there will be opposition. Users continue to creatively subvert their algorithmic components, be it by gaming the recommendation system, creating digital detox movements, or even across different platforms. Under these practices, agency will never be put out, in the future, the contact between algorithmic control and human creativity will be a lively one.

Political Trajectories: Regulation, Governance, and Global Struggles

The Future of Digital Regulation

It is likely that the next decade will be characterized by the intensification of the discussion on the concept of algorithmic governance. Questions include:

- Are there any algorithms that are to be audited by the general audience?
- Should users have a right to an explanation when they are subject to automated decisions? Regulation: How can regulation keep pace with rapidly paced innovation without smothering positive applications? The consequences of these discussions will either solidify the position of corporate power as an algorithmic culture or create some democratic space where corporate power can be regulated.

Global Inequalities and South–North Divides

The algorithmic culture will become more geopolitical.

- The Global North is now the leader in infrastructural design and standard-setting. The Global South, as a major provider of information and labor, is structurally dependent. The next conflict could be over digital sovereignty, in which states and communities seek greater control over their infrastructure, data, and cultural representation.

Democracy and the Algorithmic Public Sphere

Whether societies will succeed in establishing pluralistic algorithmic publics, which present digital spaces that reinforce debate, inclusion, and accountability instead of polarization and manipulations, will be part of the survival of democracy. It is the re-imagination of infrastructures, rather than policies, that determines political futures.

Philosophical Trajectories: Rethinking the Human

The Algorithmic Subject

With more algorithms mediating identity, desire, and knowledge, people are becoming algorithmic, with their identities and knowledge mediated by metrics, profiles, and recommendations. Questions that arise philosophically are:

- What is it to know oneself when Spotify or Netflix knows more? How do measures influence the concept of authenticity, value, and freedom?

Post-human Futures

Other theorists consider algorithmic culture a subset of a broader post-human condition, in which there are no clear boundaries between the human and the machine. Human exceptionalism is challenged by algorithmic creativity, predictive profiling, and cognitive outsourcing. The direction of such a trend, whether liberatory or oppressive, will depend on how societies mediate human-machine relationships.

Ethics of Opacity and Unpredictability

One possible philosophical counterargument to algorithmic rationality is the adoption of an opaque, unpredictable nature (Donoghue, 2025). Rather than the societies caring towards fulfilling the ideals of full visibility and efficiency, they must glorify the unquantifiable and the unknown as well as the resistant. This would mean a radical shift in ideology, one aligned with the logic of surveillance and control.

CONCLUSION: IDEOLOGIES, ALGORITHMS, AND THE FUTURE OF CULTURE

This chapter has presented arguments showing that algorithms are not technical systems but ideological apparatuses that define culture, politics, and subjectivity. They entrench the capitalist logic of vigilance and commodification, multiplate populist discourses, reproduce myths of intervention, and become platforms for opposition and counter-hegemonic action. In contemporary life, the culture of algorithms naturalizes new modes of intimacy, consumption, labor, and selfhood, posing pressing ethical and political issues of autonomy, justice, and democracy. Its future courses are both danger, corporate domination, loss of privacy, opportunity, resistance, alternative infrastructures, and less inhuman relations to technology. Finally, the era of algorithmic culture is one of ideological war. Whether algorithms will determine the future is not the main concern, as they already do; the main concern is how societies will decide to shape the algorithms. The solution is not predetermined (Beer, 2016). It is embedded in the everyday negotiating by designers, policymakers, activists, scholars, and ordinary users on what digital life is to be. In this respect, the study of digital ideologies in the form of an algorithmic culture is not only.

REFERENCES

Althusser, L. (2020). *On ideology*. Verso Books.

Beer, (2016). The social power of algorithms. Information Communication & Society, 20(1), 1–13. https://doi.org/DOI: 10.1080/1369118x.2016.1216147

Blencowe, C. (2011). *Biopolitical experience: Foucault, power and positive critique*. Springer.

Bovens, M., & Zouridis, S. (2002). From Street-Level to System-Level Bureaucracies: How Information and Communication Technology is Transforming Administrative Discretion and Constitutional Control. *Public Administration Review, 62*(2), 174–184. DOI: 10.1111/0033-3352.00168

Brown, J. M. (2021). Twitter and Tear Gas: The Power and Fragility of Networked Protest Twitter and Tear Gas: The Power and Fragility of Networked Protest, by Zeynep Tufekci, New Haven, Yale University Press, 2017, 360 pp., available through Digital Commons at http://www.twitterandteargas.org. Terrorism and Political Violence, 33(5), 1139–1140. https://doi.org/10.1080/09546553.2021.1939547

Cai, W., Grossman, J., Lin, Z. J., Sheng, H., Wei, J. T., Williams, J. J., & Goel, S. (2021). Bandit algorithms to personalize educational chatbots. *Machine Learning, 110*(9), 2389–2418. DOI: 10.1007/s10994-021-05983-y

Couldry, N., & Mejias, U. A. (2019). Data colonialism: Rethinking big data's relation to the contemporary subject. *Television & New Media, 20*(4), 336–349.

Donoghue, R. (2025). Freedom under algorithms: How unpredictable and asocial management erodes free choice. *Frontiers in Artificial Intelligence, 8*, 1582085. DOI: 10.3389/frai.2025.1582085

Dotson, K. (2018). Accumulating epistemic power: A problem with epistemology. *Philosophical Topics, 46*(1), 129–154.

Ellison, N. B., Steinfield, C., & Lampe, C. (2007). The benefits of Facebook "Friends:" social capital and college students' use of online social network sites. *Journal of Computer-Mediated Communication, 12*(4), 1143–1168. https://doi.org/10.1111/j.1083-6101.2007.00367.x

Fraher, A. L. (2015). Technology-push, market-demand and the missing safety-pull: A case study of American Airlines Flight 587. *New Technology, Work and Employment, 30*(2), 109–127. DOI: 10.1111/ntwe.12050

Gillespie, T. (2014). The Relevance of Algorithms. In T. Gillespie, P. Boczkowski, & K. Foot (Eds.), Media Technologies Essays on Communication, Materiality, and Society (pp. 185–193). Cambridge, MA MIT Press. - References - Scientific Research Publishing. (n.d.). https://www.scirp.org/reference/referencespapers ?referenceid=2798839

Gonçalves, J., Weber, I., Masullo, G. M., Da Silva, M. T., & Hofhuis, J. (2021). Common sense or censorship: How algorithmic moderators and message type influence perceptions of online content deletion. *New Media & Society*, *25*(10), 2595–2617. DOI: 10.1177/14614448211032310

Hars, A. (2000). Web Based Knowledge Infrastructures for the Sciences: An Adaptive document. *Communications of the Association for Information Systems*, *4*. Advance online publication. DOI: 10.17705/1cais.00401

Hars, A. (2000). Web Based Knowledge Infrastructures for the Sciences: An Adaptive document. *Communications of the Association for Information Systems*, *4*. Advance online publication. https://doi.org/10.17705/1cais.00401

Helberger, N. (2016). Policy implications from algorithmic profiling and the changing relationship between newsreaders and the media. Javnost - the Public, 23(2), 188–203. https://doi.org/10.1080/13183222.2016.1162989

Kellogg, K. C., Valentine, M. A., & Christin, A. (2019). Algorithms at Work: The new contested terrain of control. *The Academy of Management Annals*, *14*(1), 366–410. DOI: 10.5465/annals.2018.0174

Ma, A. (2024). Regulation in pursuit of artificial intelligence (AI) sovereignty: China's mix of restrictive and facilitative modalities. [AJIC]. *The African Journal of Information and Communication*, *34*, 1–16. https://doi.org/10.23962/ajic.i34.20103

Macey, D. (2009). Rethinking biopolitics, race and power in the wake of Foucault. *Theory, Culture & Society*, *26*(6), 186–205.

Marx, K., & Engels, F. (1973). *Karl Marx on society and social change: With selections by Friedrich Engels*. University of Chicago Press.

Mejias, U. A., & Couldry, N. (2025) Data grab. University of Chicago Press. https://press.uchicago.edu/ucp/books/book/chicago/D/bo216184200.html

Pariser, E. (2011). *The Filter Bubble: What the Internet Is Hiding from You*. https://bvbr.bib-bvb.de:443/F?func=service&doc_library=BVB01&local_base=BVB01&doc_number=022632142&sequence=000002&line_number=0001&func_code=DB_RECORDS&service_type=MEDIA

Rupert, M. (2009). Antonio Gramsci. In *Critical theorists and international relations* (pp. 190–200). Routledge.

Sanders, C., & Sheptycki, J. (2017). Policing, crime and 'big data'; towards a critique of the moral economy of stochastic governance. *Crime, Law, and Social Change, 68*(1–2), 1–15. DOI: 10.1007/s10611-016-9678-7

Striphas, T. (2015). Algorithmic culture. *European Journal of Cultural Studies, 18*(4–5), 395–412. DOI: 10.1177/1367549415577392

Sweeney, L. (2013). Discrimination in online ad delivery. SSRN Electronic Journal, 11(3), 10–29. https://doi.org/DOI: 10.2139/ssrn.2208240

Van Dijck, J. (2014). Datafication, dataism and dataveillance: Big Data between scientific paradigm and ideology. *Surveillance & Society, 12*(2), 197–208. https://doi.org/10.24908/ss.v12i2.4776

Van Dijck, J., Poell, T., & De Waal, M. (2018). *The Platform Society.* https://doi.org/10.1093/oso/9780190889760.001.0001

Keskin, B. (2018) "Van Dijk, Poell, and de Wall, The Platform Society: Public Values in a Connective World (2018)," Markets, Globalization & Development Review: Vol. 3: No. 3, Article 8.

Weiskopf, R., & Hansen, H. K. (2022). Algorithmic governmentality and the space of ethics: Examples from 'People Analytics.'. *Human Relations, 76*(3), 483–506. DOI: 10.1177/00187267221075346

Zuboff, S., Möllers, N., Wood, D. M., & Lyon, D. (2019). Surveillance capitalism: An interview with Shoshana Zuboff. *Surveillance & Society, 17*(1/2), 257–266. DOI: 10.24908/ss.v17i1/2.13238

[1] Twitter name is changed as X since 2016.

Chapter 2

Informational Pragmatism and the Digital Order: Mediation, Network Norms, and Algorithmic Ideologies

Silvio Andrae
http://orcid.org/0000-0002-8586-7812
Independent Researcher, Germany

ABSTRACT

Digital transformation is often understood as technical modernization, but it signifies a profound shift in world relations. This essay develops a philosophical model of analysis that understands digital transformation as a form of technological world-unveiling and describes technical mediation as the co-constitution of meaning, action, and normativity. Methodologically, it combines metaphysical theo-ry, technical mediation analysis, network sociology, and ideology critique. It reconstructs seven net-work norms-fundamental principles guiding algorithmic culture-as the non-subjective normativity of digital systems. It integrates Byung-Chul Han's diagnosis of a loss of negativity as a cultural deep structure. The interdisciplinary analysis yields an expanded understanding of digital ideologies and a normative-creative approach that views digital infrastructures as sites of political, epistemic, and ethical world-formation.

INTRODUCTION

The terms 'digital transformation' and 'digital revolution' have become ubiquitous in politics, business, and research. These terms usually refer to the introduction of digital technologies, the optimization of organizational processes, the automation of

DOI: 10.4018/979-8-3373-4531-4.ch002

procedures, or the introduction of data-driven decision-making models. However, this instrumental perspective views technology primarily as a means of increasing efficiency. It neglects the deeper ontological questions raised by the digital present, particularly its deviation from traditional metaphysical understandings of being and reality. To take transformation seriously, it must be understood as a fundamental change in the world's conditions that goes beyond organizational or technical modernization. Digital transformation thus affects not only the methods of information processing, but also the constitution of the present itself—the way in which the world is revealed, acquires meaning, and shapes social reality.

This change in perspective requires philosophical analysis. It is consistent with Martin Heidegger's assertion that technology is not merely a tool, but a mode of revelation that structures the world character of an epoch (Heidegger, 1954). Technology is thus not simply an addition to an already existing world, but a means of its production. Consequently, digital transformation becomes a metaphysical question that describes the contemporary form in which meaning, order, and reality are revealed. This approach encourages us to reflect on how digital transformation shapes our fundamental understanding of existence and reality.

At this point, I would like to introduce the approach of 'informational pragmatism' proposed by David J. Krieger (2025) as an extension of classical and inferential pragmatism. Informational pragmatism conceptualizes knowledge, meaning, and social order as emergent effects of technical mediation processes. These processes generate networks of human and non-human actors. Within this framework, digital transformation is not limited to technological tools; it also encompasses how digital mediations shape our understanding of the world and the social fabric. This perspective underscores the profound influence of digital transformation on shared reality. At the same time, this perspective also enables a systematic departure from technological determinism. Social development is not necessarily the result of technological advances. Nor can technologies be traced back entirely to human intentions. Instead, reality emerges from relational processes of mediation, translation, and integration in which human actors, machines, software, data, and infrastructures are symmetrically involved in constituting the world (Latour, 2005). Digital transformation is thus not only a socio-technical evolution, but a reconfiguration of the conditions for action, meaning, and normativity.

This reconfiguration is particularly evident in the transition from modern industrial society to global network society. Manuel Castells (1996, 2009) has shown how digital networking creates new spatial-temporal orders in which social processes are structured less by terrestrial than by 'flow spaces.' This networked reality generates new forms of legitimacy and power that are based not primarily on institutional sovereignty, but on protocols, infrastructures, and algorithmic selection mechanisms. Here, Luhmann's systems-theoretical insight seems relevant to me. According to this, society is always a communication system that reproduces itself through its own operations (Luhmann, 1997). Digital technologies transform these operations by automating, scaling, and condensing communication chains.

The philosophical relevance of this transition lies in particular in the fact that digital infrastructures produce normative orders that cannot be traced back to conscious human decisions. The central thesis of this chapter is therefore that the digital artifacts of our present materialize specific normative guiding differences—connectivity, communication, transparency, participation, flow, authenticity, flexibility—and stabilize them as imperatives that guide action in a way that is.' They structure the behavior of humans and machines alike (Stalder, 2016). These network norms do not represent subjectively intended values, but rather a non-subjective normative structure that arises from the possibilities of digital media technologies. It thus forms the ideological grammar of algorithmic culture.

Against this background, this article pursues four key questions:

1. How can digital transformation be defined philosophically without resorting to technological determinism or purely organizational theories of modernization?
2. How does technical mediation generate hybrid networks of actors in which information itself forms the medium of world construction?
3. What network norms arise from digital possibilities, and to what extent do they form a non-subjective normativity that is effective without human intentionality?
4. To what extent do these norms transform orders of power, meaning, and identity and generate 'digital ideologies'?

This section introduces the central concepts that structure the analytical framework of the chapter. Rather than offering exhaustive definitions, it establishes working concepts that guide the subsequent argument.

Digital transformation is not understood here as technical modernization, process digitization, or efficiency-driven innovation. Instead, it refers to a historically specific way of relating to the world in which digital infrastructures function as epistemic, normative, and ontological matrices. In this sense, digital transformation denotes a shift in how reality appears, how actions are structured, and how meaning and legitimacy are generated. It is therefore not merely a sectoral or organizational phenomenon but a transformation of the conditions under which social reality is constituted.

Informational pragmatism forms the methodological basis of this chapter. Building on pragmatist traditions, it understands meaning, knowledge, and normativity as emergent effects of mediated practices. Information is not treated as neutral data or representation, but as a relational form that stabilizes distinctions and enables action. Norms arise not only from subjective intentions or moral reflection, but from recurring, technically mediated coordination within socio-technical networks.

The concept of *technical mediation* describes how digital artifacts—interfaces, algorithms, platforms, protocols—do not merely transmit or support actions; they also shape them. They actively shape perception, decision-making, and social expectations. Mediation thus refers to processes of translation, delegation, and integration. This gives rise to hybrid constellations of human and non-human actors.

The concept of *non-subjective normativity* refers to normative effects that do not originate primarily in conscious moral judgments, explicit values, or institutional decisions. Instead, normativity emerges from the affordances and operational logics of digital infrastructures. What becomes possible, probable, or efficient within a system acquires a prescriptive force. Normativity is thus infrastructural and operational rather than intentional.

This dynamic can be observed in many everyday digital systems. For instance, algorithmic credit scoring systems shape financial opportunities by translating behavioral data into risk profiles that structure access to loans or insurance. Recommendation systems on streaming platforms or online marketplaces guide attention and consumption by ranking options as more or less relevant. Similarly, social media ranking algorithms privilege visibility, engagement, and connectivity, thereby implicitly defining which forms of participation appear meaningful or successful within the platform environment (Pasquale, 2015; Gillespie, 2018).

From these dynamics emerge *network norms*—structure-forming imperatives embedded in digital infrastructures. They guide the behavior of both human and non-human actors without appearing as explicit rules or moral commands. Connectivity, visibility, participation, transparency, authenticity, and flexibility function as expectation structures that stabilize particular forms of action and perception.

Finally, the chapter uses the term *digital ideologies* to describe the cultural worldviews that arise from the interaction between network norms and digital mediation. These ideologies are not coherent doctrines but operative belief formations embedded in infrastructures, interfaces, and algorithmic routines. Their ideological force lies precisely in their invisibility: they appear as neutral functionality while structuring how reality is perceived and interpreted.

Together, these concepts form the analytical framework of the chapter. Informational pragmatism explains how meaning and normativity emerge through mediation; network norms describe the operational grammar of digital systems; and digital ideologies capture the broader cultural and political implications of these infrastructural dynamics. This framework enables a philosophical analysis of algorithmic culture that links ontological, normative, and ideological dimensions without reducing digital transformation to technological determinism or purely discursive explanations.

From terrestrial to digital order

By embedding these questions in a comprehensive theory of digital ideologies, digital transformation can be understood as the dominant form of technical world relation: a constellation in which digital infrastructures function not only as instruments of social processes, but also as producers of epistemic, normative, and metaphysical frames of reference. A philosophy of digital transformation is therefore essential for analyzing the fundamental world relations of algorithmic culture, uncovering its implicit ideologies, and reflecting on the structural conditions of a posthuman, networked social space.

The thesis that digital transformation goes far beyond technical modernization can be further substantiated by considering the anthropological and existential changes that authors such as Byung-Chul Han describe as 'digital order' or 'infocracy' (2021). Han diagnoses that the digital age has not only given rise to new media and forms of interaction, but that the fundamental categories of the mind—action, thought, truth, proximity, distance, negativity—are themselves becoming obsolete or transforming into operational, computational functional logics (Han, 2013). Digitality means not only a new structure of social networks, but also a transformation of those forms of relating to the world from which subjectivity arises in the first place. According to Han, with digitalization, we are leaving 'the earthly order' in favor of a fluid, operational sphere permeated by positivity, in which hesitation, storytelling, decision-making, or enduring the negativity of others are no longer envisaged. This perspective underscores that digital transformation represents a profound normative intervention: it shifts not only the coordinates of social systems but also the conditions of experience, meaning, and the world.

This is precisely why a philosophical analysis of digital transformation is necessary, one that understands technology not as a tool but as an instance of world-building. This chapter takes up this dual challenge: it analyzes the technical mediations of networks and the ideological grammar of algorithmic culture. At the same time, it examines the changes in those fundamental anthropological categories that Han describes as the loss of negativity. It shows that digital transformation represents not only a structural revolution, but also an ontological and normative one.

The chapter proceeds in several analytical steps. Section 2 develops an ontologically informed perspective on digital transformation by interpreting technology as a historically variable mode of relating to the world. Drawing on the work of Byung-Chul Han, the analysis highlights how digital mediation transforms fundamental categories, including action, meaning, and negativity. Section 3 examines processes of technical mediation, following Latour and Krieger, and shows how digital artifacts translate and integrate actions within hybrid networks of human and non-human actors. Section 4 then shifts to the macro level of network society by linking systems-theoretical and network-theoretical perspectives (Luhmann, Castells). Building on this foundation, Section 5 reconstructs seven network norms as operational imperatives embedded in digital infrastructures and analyzes how they generate forms of non-subjective normativity within algorithmic culture. Section 6 introduces a comparative perspective by examining how these dynamics unfold within different regional configurations of the digital order, particularly in the United States, the European Union, and China. This comparison illustrates how network norms interact with distinct institutional, economic, and governance structures. The final section discusses the broader implications of these developments for power, identity, and the normative design of digital infrastructures. Taken together, the chapter integrates ontological, socio-technical, and ideological perspectives in order to analyze digital transformation as a process of infrastructural world production.

The scientific contribution of this chapter is to redefine digital transformation as a philosophical problem context. The conceptual framework presented here goes beyond technical-instrumental or purely sociological approaches. I develop a metaphysically grounded theory of technical mediation that understands digital artifacts as epistemic and normative co-creators of social orders. The analysis of the digital is used here as an essential critical counterposition to show that digital mediation not only enables new forms of world creation but also transforms traditional categories such as action, decision, truth, and negativity into operational processes, algorithmic optimization, and transparent positivity.

Second, the chapter contributes to ideology theory by systematically identifying non-subjective normativity—that is, the normative effectiveness of infrastructures—as a new form of digital ideology. Han supplements this approach with his diagnosis of a culture that avoids negativity and thus loses the tensions of difference that are constitutive of experience, narrative, and intellectual development. Network norms thus become visible not only as structural imperatives, but also as expressions of a new culture of positivity.

Third, the chapter builds a conceptual bridge between philosophical traditions (Heidegger, pragmatism, posthumanist perspectives) and social science diagnoses (Luhmann, Castells, Latour) and shows how these can be fruitfully combined to analyze algorithmic culture. In this way, the transition from terrestrial to digital order is understood as a semantic and existential transformation of modern thinking. This aspect is often neglected in classical media theories.

Fourth, it formulates a normative perspective for action ('ethics by design' in the posthumanist sense) that does not understand governance, ethics, and technology design as external regulatory instances. Rather, they are integral components of the socio-technical construction of the world. Han's insistence on the role of negativity, pain, and resistance as conditions of the mind serves as a warning here: a digital infrastructure that knows only positivity, transparency, predictability, and connectivity is not only subjective but also normatively impoverished. In this respect, the diagnosis motivates an ethics of digital design. This ethics leaves room for interruption, difference, and indeterminacy. Overall, the chapter makes a theoretical contribution to basic research and provides a praxeological starting point for the investigation of digital ideologies, which is deepened both existentially-philosophically and culturally-critically.

METAPHYSICAL STARTING POINT

Digital transformation can only be properly understood if it is not viewed as technical modernization or increased IT efficiency. Rather, this process represents a profound change in being and existence. The transformation marks the transition from a terrestrial order, in which subjectivity, action, truth, and negativity are central categories, to a digital order characterized by operation, predictability, positivity, and transparency. This transition is not primarily taking place in discourse or in socio-technical artifacts. It is a profound metaphysical shift that affects the way being, experience, and the world are constructed.

This transformation establishes a new relationship to the world and underscores the need to understand how perception and action are being fundamentally reconfigured. Technology is no longer just an external instrument. Technology now functions as an ontological matrix that shapes forms of perception, possibilities for action, and processes of meaning formation. The digital present thus represents the latest phase of a historical development in which technology is increasingly taking on the role of an agent of world production.

Han and the Metaphysics of Digital Transformation

Byung-Chul Han (2013) describes digital transformation as a replacement for the terrestrial order, the world in which categories such as mind, action, decision, negativity, and truth are anchored. For Han, the 'digital' is not just a medium, but a different order of worldly existence: fluid, weightless, operative, positivist.

The terrestrial order is characterized by:

- Heaviness and resistance;
- Decision and hesitation as constitutive moments of action;
- Negativity as a state of mind;
- Truth as a narrated form with an exclusionary dimension.

This structure is radically changed in the digital order (Han, 2013):

(1) **Action becomes operation**: The digital operation is an actom – an atomized function without existential or temporal delay. Hesitation is considered a disturbance, and decision-making is inefficient. Action is no longer existential, but algorithmically sequenced.
(2) **Thinking is replaced by calculation**: For Han, thinking – with its openness to surprises, breaks, events – belongs to the earthly order. Calculation, on the other hand, which underlies digital processes, is protected from the unforeseen; it is neither existential nor narrative.
(3) **Truth gives way to transparency**: For Han, truth thrives on negativity, on the possibility of error, on the risk of decision-making. Transparency, on the other hand, is non-narrative, non-judgmental, and non-revelatory. It is lightless radiation, a medium without narrativity.
(4) **Negativity disappears**: love, hate, closeness, distance—all these forms thrive on tension, exclusion, distance. The digital order replaces them with 'distancelessness' and the additive logic of 'likes.' Experience becomes impossible without negativity.

Han (2013) thus provides a metaphysical key: the digital order is not an extension, it is a substitute for the world conditions that make the mind possible in the first place. What appears as 'mind' in the earthly realm—the ability to endure pain, contradiction, and negation—is flattened in the digital realm into the positivity of mere data flow.

Historical Depth of Field

This transition must be viewed with genealogical depth. From the first tools to mechanical devices to data-intensive network architectures, a gradation in the technical penetration of the world can be observed. Even early artifacts—stone axes, plows, writing—constructed the world by structuring perceptions and defining spaces for action (Ihde, 1990; Malafouris, 2013). Technology has always been a process of opening up and shaping the world. The axe is therefore not just a tool, it is a form of meaning-making: it organizes actions, distinctions, and perceptions – and thus the world. Krieger (2025) takes up this perspective when he understands technology as an 'emerging site of meaning construction.'

However, it is digital technologies that radicalize this process:

- they create relationality without territory,
- operations without action,
- computational processes without thinking,
- transparency without truth,

- positivity without negativity,
- distance without closeness or remoteness.

Digital transformation thus represents a qualitative change that highlights the transformative power of technology. It is no longer understood as a continuation of the processing of the human world. Digital transformation is better understood as an autonomous form of order that recodes or replaces the categories of modernity, such as subject, action, truth, and experience. Digital technology does not just reconnect the world. Through its relational, automatic, and global action, it creates new ways of being.

Technology as a Mode of Revealing Being

Heidegger's analysis of technology as a 'mode of concealment' (1954) offers a conceptual starting point for a metaphysical understanding of digital transformation. Technology is not an ensemble of instruments. Rather, it is a mode in which the being of the present reveals itself and simultaneously conceals itself. In modernity, Heidegger characterizes this mode as a framework: a way of organizing the world that makes everything that exists available as 'inventory.' While Heidegger recognizes within this framework the reduction of the relationship to the world to inventory and availability, Han (2013) diagnoses that the digital order completes this process. The subjective, existential, and negative are eliminated here.

Digital unveiling manifests itself as:

- the disappearance of the acting subject (operation instead of action),
- the dissolution of dialectical experience (positivity instead of negativity),
- the loss of narrative world revelation (transparency instead of truth),
- the abolition of the world as resistance (weightlessness instead of earthiness).

Han thus updates the question of technology in the mode of a phenomenology of the digital and shows how the digital not only makes new things possible. It even fundamentally changes the structures of the world. It also shifts the metaphysical signature of being: the digital makes the world visible as something that does not consist of things. It is the relational patterns that are technically generated and stabilized. Digitality is the unveiling of a relational world structure.

Information Pragmatism and the Pragmatic Tradition

Although information pragmatism was presented as a methodological framework in the previous section, it is important to place this approach more explicitly within the broader pragmatic tradition and to clarify its particular contribution. This contextualization not only strengthens the argument's philosophical basis. It also prevents information pragmatism from being misunderstood as a descriptive extension of actor-network theory or as a variant of technological constructivism.

Classical pragmatism, from Charles S. Peirce to John Dewey to George Herbert Mead, is united by a fundamental insight: meaning, knowledge, and normativity do not precede practice, but rather arise from it. Concepts derive their meaning from their practical consequences; norms stabilize through habitual action; truth is not a mirror of reality. Rather, norms are a regulative result of inquiry embedded in social practices. Pragmatism thus rejects both metaphysical fundamentalism and purely subjectivist explanations of meaning. It shifts normativity from abstract principles to the ongoing coordination of actions.

Information pragmatism builds on this tradition, but transfers it to a socio-technical context in which digital infrastructures increasingly mediate practices. Its central approach is to extend pragmatic knowledge beyond human interaction to hybrid constellations of humans, machines, data, and algorithms. In digitally mediated environments, practices are no longer coordinated exclusively through language, shared intentions, or institutional rules. Instead, the focus should be on the information structures that preconfigure possibilities for action. Meaning and normativity do not arise here solely from what actors do. Rather, it goes further, namely how systems process, select, and operationalize information.

This marks a decisive change. While classical pragmatism primarily analyzed practices as human problem-solving activities, informational- ic pragmatism treats information itself as a medium of practice. Information is not a representation of an already constituted world. It is the relational form through which distinctions are stabilized, relevance is assigned, and courses of action become feasible. In this view, normativity arises when informational distinctions are repeatedly implemented and embedded in technical systems, thereby gaining permanence and normative force.

At this point, informational pragmatism must be clearly distinguished from related theoretical approaches. In contrast to Heidegger's philosophy of technology, it does not locate the normative power of technology primarily in an ontological destiny or an epochal revelation. Informational pragmatism emphasizes the concrete operational consequences of mediated practices. In contrast to actor-network theory, it does not remain at the level of a symmetrical description of associations. It explicitly deals with how certain information configurations become normatively binding. And unlike discourse-theoretical or inferential pragmatism, it does not assume that language is the primary carrier of normativity. Informational pragmatism recognizes codes, interfaces, metrics, and protocols as equally valid norm-generating media.

Information pragmatism conceptualizes digital transformation as a shift in the way meaning and normativity arise from mediated practice. Meaning is not treated as a representation of a given world. There is an emergent effect of stabilized distinctions implemented by socio-technical systems. Digital infrastructures thus do not reflect reality. They participate in its production by organizing how relevance, action, and coordination are pragmatically established.

This perspective implies a relational understanding of world construction. What is considered reality is not given before mediation. Reality takes shape through recurring interactions between people, technical artifacts, data structures, and institutional arrangements. In this sense, world production is not an ontological assertion about the disappearance of reality. It is an analytical description of how reality becomes operationally accessible in mediated environments.

The transition from informational pragmatism to a relational representation of the technical construction of the world, therefore, does not lead to a new theoretical level. On the contrary, it clarifies the implications of a non-representational approach to meaning. If normativity and meaning emerge from use, and if digital infrastructures increasingly structure use, then world construction must be understood as a relational and technically mediated process rather than as an interpretation of an independent reality.

Technology as Relational World Construction

However, a purely ontological definition is not sufficient. To understand digital transformation, technology must also be understood as a process of relational integration. Here, the philosophy of technical mediation provides crucial insights: technology does not act upon a given world. Technology creates the world that it then appears to structure (Latour, 2005; Verbeek, 2005).

The concept of information takes center stage here. Information is not just a quantifiable data format. In the sense of informational pragmatism, it is the emergent form in which relationships become visible and condense into action-relevant differences (Krieger, 2025). Information arises where technical practices stabilize distinctions: user vs. non-user, relevant vs. irrelevant, visible vs. invisible, permitted vs. prohibited, connectable vs. unconnectable.

Digital technologies reinforce this differentiation by automating, scaling, and standardizing it. Consequently, digital transformation should not be understood primarily as 'data processing.' Rather, it is the production of world forms through algorithmic differentiation. Digitalization means, in the truest sense of the word, world design.

Digital Transformation as a Metaphysical Form of Technical World Production

Bringing these considerations together yields an understanding of digital transformation that goes beyond the classic distinctions between technology and society, nature and culture, and medium and world. Digitalization appears as the current form of 'technical becoming,' in which technical mediations structurally permeate all levels of the social, cultural, and political spheres.

Digital transformation, therefore, is not a sub-area of social change. Rather, transformation is the epistemic-normative framework within which social change first takes place. It creates the conditions under which meaning arises and a relationship to the world becomes possible. In this sense, digitalization is a metaphysical category: it describes how the world appears today—relational, networked, processual, algorithmically mediated.

A metaphysical approach is indispensable because it conceptualizes digital transformation as a mode of being in the present rather than a singular technical innovation. This perspective enables the analysis of the underlying structure of network norms arising from digital affordances and subsequently reconstructed as the ideological grammar of algorithmic culture.

TECHNICAL MEDIATION AND THE CONSTRUCTION OF HYBRID ACTOR NETWORKS

A comprehensive understanding of digital transformation requires viewing technology as an intrinsic element in the construction of the social world, with a focus on relational ontologies that position information as fundamental. Technical mediation is the actual prerequisite for action and does not merely serve as a supplement. The subsequent analysis examines how digital artifacts generate actor networks in which meaning, action, and world reference are jointly constituted. The central argument is that in digital environments, traditional ontological distinctions such as subject/object, human/machine, and nature/artifact lose their explanatory power and are replaced by relational ontologies in which information represents the primary form of reality.

Translation, Delegation, and Hybrid Agency

Bruno Latour's actor-network theory (ANT) criticizes the modern separation of subjects and objects as theoretical fiction (Latour, 1993, 2005). In modernity, it is assumed that humans act and things merely provide tools. In fact, action programs are always generated by networks of people and things: door closers, traffic light circuits, interfaces, or algorithms 'delegate' actions, standardize behavior, and structure possibilities. They are not passive but active elements that create differences, inform decision-making, and stabilize the world.

This diagnosis is of central importance for digital transformation, as digital technologies do not merely function as co-actors. The analysis emphasizes that they also embody actor characteristics in a particularly concentrated form. Algorithms work through continuous translation, converting data streams into classifications, profiles, prioritizations, and decisions. These translations are embedded in 'black boxes,' technical structures whose internal mechanisms remain opaque, even though their effects are significant (Pasquale, 2015). Consequently, digital transformation entails a reconfiguration of the relationships between action, responsibility, and visibility.

The traditional distinction between subject and object or between human intentionality and technical use proves insufficient to describe these conditions. In digital environments, hybrid systems of action emerge in which the capacity for action is shared, distributed, and technically mediated. Information pragmatism addresses this problem by conceptualizing social practice and technical mediation as co-extensive forms of world construction (Krieger, 2025). This shift from the traditional subject-object dichotomy to hybrid systems of action is becoming increasingly apparent in legal discourse, positioning it as a critical area of research. Recent academic work advocates for an agnostic legal framework that treats humans and AI systems as functionally equivalent actors, thereby normatively conceptualizing the co-creation of hybrid networks (Andrae, 2026a). Such frameworks propose a multi-level model of legal personality that interprets the normative principles of freedom, reciprocity, and responsibility as relational properties of socio-technical systems. This perspective moves away from an anthropocentric model of legitimacy, as expressed, for example, in the EU AI Act, toward a relational normativity in which action and liability emerge from the network itself. The methods used in these approaches—including Delphi panels, agent-based simulations, and regulatory sandboxes—show that normative questions can be addressed both discursively and experimentally. This legal hybridization supports the central thesis of this chapter: normativity does not arise from subjectivity, but from the technical and social interdependencies that structure the network.

Digital Artifacts as Co-Actors

To illustrate how technical mediation works at the level of specific artifacts, this section identifies three primary mediators of the construction of the digital world:

interfaces, algorithms, and platforms. These artifacts not only support actions but also function as norm-generating co-actors within socio-technical networks.

Interfaces structure perception and action by selecting, highlighting, and concealing information. Each interface serves as both a cognitive apparatus and a normative filter (Galloway, 2012), determining what is presented as visible or invisible, complex or simple, relevant or irrelevant.

Algorithms function as operational translation mechanisms. They do not perceive like humans, but process what is presented as a calculable structure. In this way, algorithms shape the world epistemically by stabilizing certain classifications and making others unimaginable.

Platforms serve as comprehensive infrastructures for social reality. They do not merely function as markets, communities, or media. They represent hybrid world orders in which interaction is technically orchestrated (Plantin et al., 2018). Platforms establish rules, access, visibility, and participation, thereby functioning as normative architectures. Together, interfaces, algorithms, and platforms form the technical locations where network norms are operationalized, stabilized, and made effective without explicit normative intent.

Information Transfer in Practice

In the context of digital transformation, information is not merely a resource. Rather, information should be understood as an ontological form that actively shapes reality. Information pragmatism does not interpret information as a quantitative measure of messages, as Shannon's model does. Information emerges as a structure that stabilizes relationships, reveals differences, and shapes programs of action. This perspective emphasizes the active role of information in constructing worlds rather than merely representing them.

Digital technologies generate, organize, and operationalize information, thereby creating different worlds. When algorithms sort content, navigation systems suggest routes, or management systems flag ‘suspicious’ patterns, these processes do not merely discover a world; they also shape it. They actively create a world in which certain connections are enabled, and others are excluded. Information is therefore neither neutral nor exclusively representative. It is constitutive (Floridi, 2011).

This insight is consistent with Latour's thesis on the ‘chaining’ of perspectives: information is not received passively. It is technically generated, continuously transformed, and integrated into stabilized relationship structures. Every digital artifact thus contains an ‘action program,’ a set of expectation structures that guide behavior and dictate meaning. Digital transformation is a transformation of the information modalities that make up the world.

Vignette 1: Algorithmic pre-structuring in public administration

In today's public administration, digital decision support systems are increasingly structuring administrative judgment. Tools such as risk assessment mechanisms, automated authorization checks, and prioritization algorithms are not implemented as autonomous decision-makers. Rather, they are instruments for increasing efficiency, consistency, and objectivity. Their practical effect, however, is a subtle redistribution of normative authority.

From the perspective of information pragmatism, normativity in this context does not arise solely from explicit legal provisions. Normativity also arises from differences in the information embedded in the system. Categories such as 'risk,' 'priority,' or 'plausibility' are operationalized through data models and training sets that translate legal and organizational norms into calculable parameters. What appears to a human official as a neutral recommendation is in reality the result of a stabilized information practice.

In this context, the network norm of transparency seems paradoxical. Although administrative processes are becoming more transparent in terms of their results, the internal logic of algorithmic classification often remains opaque. At the same time, participation is being redefined as the role of the human actor shifts from judging to confirming. Responsibility is distributed across the socio-technical network without clear reassignment.

This vignette illustrates non-subjective normativity in a paradigmatic way. No actor explicitly attempts to change the normative order of administration. Nevertheless, through repeated use, the information structure itself acquires normative power. What the system identifies as relevant, risky, or efficient gradually acquires the status of what must be taken into account.

Vignette 2: Platform visibility and the normativity of communication

On large social media platforms, communication is increasingly regulated by visibility metrics. Likes, shares, impressions, and engagement rates serve as feedback mechanisms that convert interaction into quantifiable relevance. As a result, communication becomes an operational process in which visibility is not simply a consequence of expression. Rather, it is its implicit goal.

In this environment, the network norms of communication, flow, and authenticity converge. Users learn, often implicitly, which forms of expression are amplified and which are made algorithmically invisible. The result is not classic censorship. It is a pragmatically stabilized structure of expectations in which communicative actions are geared toward what is likely to circulate.

From the perspective of informational pragmatism, meaning arises in this context through use within infrastructural constraints. The platform does not impose ideology discursively. It generates ideology operationally. Visibility acts as a proxy for relevance, and resonance serves as a proxy for validity. Normativity does not arise through conviction. Rather, normativity is generated through the repeated alignment of action with algorithmic feedback.

This vignette illustrates how digital ideologies arise from infrastructural arrangements. The ideology of communicationalism, in which visibility replaces truth, is put into practice rather than explicitly believed. Its effectiveness rests on its being experienced as the medium's functional logic rather than as an open normative demand.

Vignette 3: Data-driven coordination and performance legitimacy

In data-intensive systems of social coordination, digital infrastructures increasingly serve as instruments for performance evaluation and behavioral adjustment. Evaluation mechanisms, predictive analytics, and continuous monitoring translate social behavior into information patterns that can be evaluated and implemented. In this context, the network norms of connectivity, transparency, and flexibility form a closely integrated constellation. Participation in digital systems becomes a prerequisite for social visibility, and adaptability to evolving criteria is encouraged. Legitimacy shifts from procedural justification to functional performance, with systems being trustworthy to the extent that they deliver stable and scalable results.

Non-subjective normativity manifests itself through the infrastructural design of evaluation. Individuals are not primarily addressed as moral subjects. Rather, they are nodes within an information environment. Norms emerge from feedback loops between behavior, data collection, and system response. The result is a form of governance that functions without continuous intervention and relies on the pragmatics of ongoing adaptation.

This vignette highlights how digital transformation is restructuring the basis of legitimacy. Authority is no longer rooted primarily in law or discourse. Rather, it flows from the operational credibility of systems. Normativity becomes an endogenous component of the infrastructure that coordinates action.

Regional and Geopolitical Configurations of the Digital Order

The preceding analysis has conceptualized digital transformation as a structural and infrastructural process that produces network norms and non-subjective normativity. However, this perspective risks suggesting a uniform global logic of digitalization. To counteract this potential misunderstanding, it must be clarified how the digital order manifests differently across regional and geopolitical contexts, while, at the same time, the common infrastructural logic functions transversally. The argument of this chapter is not that digital transformation is taking place identically everywhere. Rather, it argues that similar network norms are embedded in different institutional, political, and cultural configurations. s do not replace existing orders, but reconnect with them. As a result, the same normative imperatives—connectivity, transparency, participation, flexibility, visibility—are articulated through different governance regimes.

In the European context, digital transformation is typically mediated by legal and institutional frameworks. Network norms are filtered through data protection regulations, administrative law, and regulatory oversight. Transparency is articulated as accountability, verifiability, and explainability, while participation is institutionalized through procedural inclusion. Non-subjective normativity arises less from market feedback than from compliance architectures embedded in digital administration and platform regulation. The digital order remains closely linked to legal rationality, even as infrastructures increasingly pre-structure decision-making.

In the United States, digital transformation is predominantly structured by market-oriented platform ecosystems. Network norms are operationalized through metrics such as engagement, scalability, and profitability. Visibility serves as the primary source of relevance. Participation is promoted through attention economies. Flexibility is consistent with entrepreneurial self-optimization. Non-subjective normativity is closely linked to platform business models and privileges what circulates, is scalable, and can be monetized. Governance tends to function ex post and often responds to infrastructural realities created by private actors.

In China, digital infrastructures are directly integrated into state-directed coordination and governance strategies. Network norms are geared toward goals such as social order, performance evaluation, and system-wide optimization. Connectivity and transparency serve as instruments of coordination rather than expressions of individual autonomy or market participation. Normativity emerges from continuous feedback loops between data collection, behavioral assessment, and institutional response. Legitimacy is based less on discourse or procedure and more on performance, with systems justified by their ability to create stability and governability.

These configurations underscore a central point: digital transformation exhibits structural convergence but institutional divergence. Identical infrastructure principles produce different normative effects depending on how they intersect with legal traditions, political authority, and economic organization. Information pragmatism offers a framework for interpreting this variation without reducing it to cultural relativism. Norms emerge pragmatically from use, but use is always situated in specific sociopolitical contexts.

Recognizing regional differences refines the concept of network norms rather than challenging it. Network norms articulate the operational grammar of digital systems, while regional configurations determine how this grammar is translated into governance, legitimacy, and power. Digital ideologies, therefore, do not form a uniform global doctrine but represent a family of context-sensitive worldviews that share similar infrastructural foundations but differ in their political articulation.

FROM MODERN SYSTEMS TO GLOBAL NETWORKS

From a systems-theory perspective, modern societies achieve stability through functional differentiation, with relatively autonomous subsystems such as law, politics, economics, and science operating according to distinct rules and codes. This perspective remains analytically valuable as it highlights the contingency and complexity inherent in social coordination. In digitally mediated environments, however, functional differentiation is increasingly complemented by networked forms of integration that transcend system boundaries and reconfigure communication circulation.

This is where Manuel Castells' concept of the network society comes into focus. Digital networks do not replace functional systems. They reassemble these systems within flexible, scalable, and transnational architectures. Power, coordination, and meaning now circulate primarily through nodes, connections, and flows, rather than through institutional hierarchies. Networks prioritize adaptability over stability, connectivity over territorial anchoring, and operational effectiveness over formal authority.

This network logic fundamentally changes the conditions under which social order emerges. Communication is now organized across heterogeneous platforms, infrastructures, and interfaces, rather than within limited institutional contexts. As a result, normativity increasingly arises from the operational requirements of the networks themselves, rather than from system-specific rules or centralized regulations. Network norms such as visibility, participation, flexibility, and acceleration are gaining importance because they facilitate connectivity and circulation within digital environments.

Actor-network theory offers a conceptual bridge here by emphasizing that networks consist of heterogeneous elements, including human actors, technical artifacts, and institutional arrangements. Rather than fully revisiting this perspective, it suffices here to point out its relevance for understanding how agency and coordination are distributed across socio-technical constellations. This insight supports the chapter's thesis that digital transformation does not reorganize social order around subjects or institutions. Rather, it is infrastructures that mediate actions.

Taken together, these perspectives illustrate the structural change at stake here. Digital networks do not abolish modern systems. They reconfigure their interaction by embedding communication, coordination, and normativity in global infrastructures. Understanding this change is essential for analyzing the functioning of power, legitimacy, and ideology in networked environments, a task to which the following sections are devoted.

NON-SUBJECTIVE NORMATIVITY

The digital transformation is giving rise to a new form of normativity that cannot be traced back to human intentions, moral judgments, or institutional decisions. Instead, normative imperatives emerge from the material-symbolic structures of digital technologies themselves. This form of normativity is not subjective. It functions independently of subjective values and infrastructure because it is embedded in the architectural logic of techno-social systems.

The originality of this chapter does not lie in proposing yet another general theory of digital society. Rather, its added value lies in reconstructing how normativity pragmatically emerges from the information infrastructures themselves. By treating code, interfaces, metrics, platforms, and protocols as media of practice, the argument specifies the conditions under which meaning, legitimacy, and ideology are operationally stabilized in hybrid actor networks. This focus shifts the analysis from interpretive representations of digital culture to a theory of infrastructural norm production that can be traced across different institutional and geopolitical contexts.

The central thesis is therefore that digital infrastructures generate network norms—structure-forming imperatives that govern the behavior of both human and non-human actors. These network norms form the ideological grammar of algorithmic culture: they make certain behaviors plausible and others improbable, organize perception, and configure social relationships. They also structure political practice. These norms represent technical power rather than discursive power (Beer, 2019; Cheney-Lippold, 2017).

The following section examines seven central network norms: connectivity, flow, communication, participation, transparency, authenticity, and flexibility. Each of these norms arises from the possibilities of digital technologies and exerts a prescriptive effect, not through moral argumentation, but through technical enablement and the structuring of social expectations.

Normativity Without a Subject

The possibilities of digital technologies, i.e., the possibilities for action and perception that artifacts offer, create stable structures of expectation. The source of normative order is not what individuals should do, but what the infrastructure enables them to do. This logic was established in the philosophy of technology by Don Ihde (1990), Peter-Paul Verbeek (2005), and David Krieger (2025): technology structures intentionality, perception, and action.

Digital affordances give rise to a new form of normativity:

- **They have a pre-reflexive effect**: action follows infrastructure, not the other way around.
- **They have an infrastructural effect**: they are effective not only in discourse but also in execution.
- **They have a symmetrical effect**: they affect human and non-human actors.
- **They have a global effect**: the logic of digital networks transcends territorial boundaries.

This structure builds on the philosophical foundations of Ihde, Verbeek, and Krieger and shows how operational expectations have developed from the philosophy of technology.

Digitalisms: Operational Worldviews of Algorithmic Culture

The seven network norms generate a set of worldviews that can be described as digital isms. These worldviews stabilize patterns of perception and action that arise from the possibilities of digital infrastructures rather than from explicit doctrines or political programs. Digital ideologies arise operationally: they are anchored in interfaces, platforms, protocols, metrics, and temporal regimes that normalize certain ways of acting and interpreting the world. Digitalisms are therefore not discursive belief systems, but socio-technical formations whose effectiveness lies in their invisibility. They appear neutral and functional, while silently shaping epistemic orientations, social expectations, and normative judgments. Their structure is two-layered: it is based on infrastructural imperatives such as connectivity, flow, participation, transparency, authenticity, and flexibility, and is consistent with a broader cultural tendency toward positivity, immediacy, and the erosion of negativity. This dual structure forms the backdrop against which seven operative worldviews can be identified.

1. Digital connectivism: Existence as connection

Connectivism views social existence as a function of permanent connectivity. Being connected is no longer optional, but a normative expectation; non-connection appears as deviance. Social presence is redefined as technical availability, and relationships are maintained through continuous network participation rather than encounters. This worldview is not only technical but also normative. Connectivity replaces distance as a condition for social coherence, thereby resolving the tension between closeness and separation that once structured the social experience. Connectivism thus establishes a form of relational immediacy in which presence is guaranteed by technical connection rather than mutual recognition. A clear illustration can be seen in social media ecosystems, where permanent connectivity is treated as a basic condition of social existence, while temporary disconnection is often seen as deviant or socially invisible

2. Flowism: Acceleration as normality

Flowism organizes the world according to continuous streams of data, information, and interactions. Temporal order is no longer structured by sequence, delay, or narrative development, but by uninterrupted circulation. Standstill appears as dysfunction, hesitation as inefficiency. Within this regime, operations replace decisions. Action is reduced to reaction. Time becomes an operational dimension optimized for speed and responsiveness. Flowism thus reflects the infrastructural reorganization of temporality under digital conditions, in which the continuity of processing prevails over historical or deliberative time. This logic becomes particularly visible in continuous content streams on platforms such as TikTok, Instagram Reels, or news feeds, where information is consumed as an uninterrupted flow rather than as sequential narratives.

3. Communicationalism: Visibility as validity

Communicationalism establishes visibility as the primary criterion for social relevance. Algorithmic platforms translate communication into metrics such as reach, engagement, and resonance, thereby equating the visible with the meaningful. This worldview does not eliminate communication. But it deprives it of any narrative depth. Meaning is derived from circulation rather than interpretation; truth is replaced by exposure. Communicationalism illustrates how digital infrastructures privilege presence over understanding and resonance over justification. Social media metrics such as likes, shares, views, and follower counts illustrate this logic, as visibility and engagement increasingly function as proxies for relevance and credibility. Practices such as constant data tracking, behavioral analytics, and real-time performance dashboards exemplify this norm, particularly in digital workplaces and platform-mediated services.

4. Normativity of participation

The normativity of participation arises from the expectation that users will continuously contribute to digital systems. Participation appears to be empowerment, but it functions as an operational requirement: users generate data, content, and engagement that sustain platform economies. Within this logic, decision-making loses its significance. Input replaces judgment, and actions are fragmented into micro-operations. The subject remains active but is no longer capable of making decisions; it is involved but no longer sovereign. Participation thus becomes a normative obligation accompanied by a loss of agency. Platform economies demonstrate this dynamic by continuously encouraging users to produce content, ratings, comments, and behavioral data that sustain the platform's informational and economic ecosystem.

5. Ideology of transparency: Disclosure as morality

The ideology of transparency treats disclosure as a moral obligation. What is hidden appears suspicious; what is visible appears legitimate. Tracking, profiling, and logging standardize behavior by making it observable and comparable. Transparency does not promote understanding here. Rather, it enforces disclosure. Normativity arises from visibility rather than criticism or justification. The loss of secrecy does not mean an increase in knowledge, but a reduction in the spaces in which judgment, resistance, and interpretation can arise. Practices such as constant data tracking, behavioral analytics, and real-time performance dashboards exemplify this norm, particularly in digital workplaces and platform-mediated services.

6. The imperative of authenticity: self-presentation as the norm

The imperative of authenticity demands continuous self-presentation that appears spontaneous and genuine. However, this authenticity is not based on inner truth, but on algorithmic repetition, metric feedback, and self-optimization. Authenticity becomes performative: it requires consistency rather than transformation, visibility rather than encounter. Otherness is replaced by self-reference through, and experience is stabilized as continuity. The subject is not liberated. Instead, it is locked into a regime of permanent self-presentation. Influencer cultures on platforms such as YouTube, TikTok, and Instagram illustrate this imperative, in which personal disclosure and continuous self-presentation become central mechanisms of visibility and credibility.

7. The cult of flexibility: Adaptability as a virtue

The cult of flexibility presents adaptability as a moral virtue. Stability appears dysfunctional, and resistance is failure. Subjects are expected to adapt to changing conditions, updates, and reconfigurations continuously. Flexibility here does not mean freedom. Instead, it means the erosion of thresholds. Pain, disruption, and friction—conditions of experience and transformation—are eliminated in favor of smooth functionality. The result is not empowerment. Rather, it is a form of controlled resilience that adapts subjects to the demands of the infrastructure. The gig economy provides a concrete example: platform-based labor systems reward constant adaptability, short-term availability, and continuous reconfiguration of working routines.

Digitalisms do not form a coherent doctrine, but rather an integrated dispositif. They are pre-reflexive, technically mediated, affectively effective, and operationally stable. Network norms function as the operational grammar of algorithmic culture, while digitalisms express its ideological horizon. Together, they form a regime of infrastructural normativity in which power operates through normalization rather than command. Digital transformation thus generates more than just a new social morphology. Transformation is at least also a reconfiguration of the epistemic, social, and anthropological conditions under which action, judgment, and experience take place.

Network norms represent the operational grammar of algorithmic culture, while digitalisms articulate its phenomenological and ideological horizon. The proposed matrix shows that each infrastructural norm generates a corresponding worldview. However, none of these worldviews is isolated; together they form an integrated dispositif of positivity that accelerates the disappearance of negativity, as Han diagnoses (Table 1).

Table 1. Structural correspondence between the seven network norms and the seven digital '–isms'

Network norm	Core orientation of the norm	Corresponding digitalisms	Ideological expression
Connectivity	Continuous linkage, constant availability, infrastructural reachability	**Digital Connectivism**	Existence as permanent connectedness; abolition of distance; presence = being
Flow	Acceleration, uninterrupted circulation, temporal compression	**Flowism**	Time becomes operational; deceleration is treated as dysfunction
Communication	Visibility, quantifiable interaction, algorithmic resonance	**Communicationalism**	Visibility replaces truth; narration collapses into metrics
Participation	Perpetual input, engagement, co-production	**Participation normativity**	Activity becomes obligation; decision collapses into operativity

continued on following page

Table 1. Continued

Network norm	Core orientation of the norm	Corresponding digitalisms	Ideological expression
Transparency	Disclosure, traceability, exposure of processes and identities	**Transparency ideology**	Secrecy becomes suspect; visibility becomes moralized
Authenticity	Performed sincerity, continuous self-presentation	**The imperative of authenticity**	The self becomes an always-on performance; alterity disappears
Flexibility	Adaptation, fluidity, reconfigurability	**Flexibilism**	Stability becomes a vice; resistance and negativity are erased

Comparison with Classical Models of Ideology

The thesis that digital structures give rise to ideologies contradicts classical theories of ideology. However, a more thorough analysis shows that digital ideologies are not merely an extension. They should rather be regarded as a transformation of the concept of ideology.

Ideology according to Marx: false consciousness vs. functional truth

According to Marx (1845/1846), ideology is a form of false consciousness that obscures social inequalities and legitimizes domination. Digital ideologies, on the other hand, function differently: they are not based on misrepresentation, but on the active production of reality. They are not illusory, but effective, shaping the conditions for potential developments rather than merely obscuring existing realities. Consequently, the ideological function shifts from consciousness to infrastructure.

Althusser: Ideology as the interpellation of subjects

Althusser (1971) conceptualizes ideology as a process of subject formation through 'interpellation.' Digital ideologies differ significantly from this; they do not interpellate subjects through discourse, but rather through user interfaces, algorithmic recommendations, and interface logics. In this context, the subject is addressed before their self-understanding and often without conscious awareness. Digital interpellation is preconscious, habitual, and automated. While Althusser focuses on ideological state apparatuses, digital ideologies emerge from non-state, post-institutional, techno-economic systems.

Gramsci: Hegemony as cultural leadership

Gramsci's (1971) concept of cultural hegemony defines ideology as a social consensus produced by dominant groups. However, digital ideology is not hegemonic in the traditional sense; rather, it generates consensus. The infrastructure itself defines the limits of the imaginable. Hegemony thus becomes infrastructural and functions not through consent or discourse, but through the technical anchoring of norms.

Foucault: Governmentality and the power of norms

Digital ideology most closely corresponds to Foucault's concept of governmentality, in which power creates conditions through norms and the structuring of practices. Nevertheless, digital transformation expands this framework: today, norms are primarily realized through technical means rather than discursive mediation. Power thus operates 'through code' (Lessig, 1999), leading to a post-discursive governmentality in which technical systems themselves become carriers of normative structures.

This comparison reveals a fundamental change:

- Location of ideology: from consciousness to infrastructures
- Carriers of ideology: from the state/party to platforms, algorithms, interfaces
- Mechanism of ideology: from discourse to affordances
- Reproduction of ideology: from conviction to use
- Effect of ideology: from identification to behavioral expectations

Digital ideologies can therefore be characterized as operative ideologies; their effects manifest themselves more in usage patterns than in the justification of convictions. Their effectiveness is based on several factors:

(1) they are invisible (embedded in code, protocols, infrastructure),
(2) they have a globally synchronized effect (platform standards, APIs, technical norms),
(3) they act pre-reflexively (before any critical distancing),
(4) they reinforce themselves (network effects, optimization cycles),
(5) they are materialized (as concrete, not just symbolic structures),
(6) they have a posthuman effect (they are aimed at both humans and machines).

This development leads to a new configuration of power and normativity that cannot be fully captured by classical ideology critique. Digital ideologies function less as political doctrines. They are better understood as technical modes of existence, in which worldviews are generated and stabilized by algorithms, data streams, and infrastructures.

The analysis of network norms and digital ideologies has shown how algorithmic infrastructures stabilize specific patterns of perception, coordination, and action. These norms operate at the level of technical architectures and cultural expectations, shaping how digital environments structure everyday practices. Yet the operation of these norms cannot be understood independently of the institutional and economic contexts in which digital infrastructures are embedded.

Digital networks develop within specific governance regimes, market structures, and political institutions that influence how infrastructural norms are stabilized, contested, or redirected. The following section, therefore, shifts the perspective from the internal logic of network norms to the regional and political-economic configurations in which digital infrastructures operate.

REGIONAL CONFIGURATIONS OF THE DIGITAL ORDER

Regional Digital Regimes: United States, European Union, and China

Although digital infrastructures exhibit structural similarities worldwide, their normative and institutional configurations differ significantly across political and economic regimes. The operational logic of network norms, therefore, unfolds within distinct regional constellations of governance, market organization, and state authority. Digital infrastructures are not embedded in a homogeneous global order; rather, they crystallize within historically specific institutional arrangements that shape how network norms become operational.

In the United States, the digital order is largely structured by market-driven platform ecosystems. A relatively small number of technology corporations organize key digital infrastructures, data flows, and algorithmic coordination mechanisms. Platforms such as Google, Meta, Amazon, or Apple operate as infrastructural intermediaries that structure access to information, communication, and digital markets. In this environment, network norms such as connectivity, participation, visibility, and continuous engagement are closely intertwined with platform-based business models and attention economies. Digital infrastructures thus function primarily as privately governed coordination architectures in which economic incentives strongly shape informational environments.

Within the European Union, digital transformation is increasingly embedded in a regulatory framework that attempts to balance technological innovation with fundamental rights, democratic accountability, and market oversight. Regulatory instruments such as the General Data Protection Regulation (GDPR), the Digital Services Act (DSA), the Digital Markets Act (DMA), and the AI Act illustrate an institutional effort to shape digital infrastructures through legal norms and regulatory supervision. In this configuration, network norms do not disappear but are partially reframed through legal constraints and governance mechanisms that seek to limit excessive concentrations of platform power and to protect informational self-determination.

By contrast, the Chinese digital ecosystem is characterized by a closer integration of state authority and platform infrastructure. Digital infrastructures operate simultaneously as economic platforms, governance instruments, and tools of large-scale social coordination. Major platform companies such as Alibaba, Tencent, and ByteDance operate in a regulatory environment in which data governance, platform regulation, and state policy objectives are closely intertwined. In this context, network norms intersect more directly with state-led informational governance and centralized coordination capacities (Andrae, 2026b).

These regional variations demonstrate that the global digital order cannot be understood as a uniform technological logic. Instead, digital infrastructures crystallize within different socio-political environments, producing distinct combinations of market power, regulatory intervention, and state coordination. The operational grammar of network norms may exhibit structural similarities across regions, but the institutional conditions under which they are stabilized, contested, or redirected differ substantially.

Recognizing these regional configurations is therefore essential for understanding how digital infrastructures shape power relations, governance arrangements, and ideological narratives in contemporary societies. These regional configurations illustrate how digital infrastructures are embedded in different institutional environments. At the same time, they are connected through shared economic dynamics that structure the operation of global digital platforms.

Economic Foundations of Digital Infrastructures

The institutional configurations described above are closely connected to the economic organization of digital infrastructures. Digital platforms do not merely mediate social interaction; they also operate as economic infrastructures that concentrate data, computational resources, and market coordination capacities. As a result, a small number of actors increasingly control critical informational architectures that structure communication, consumption, and economic exchange.

Platform-based business models transform participation, connectivity, and visibility into economically exploitable resources. User interactions generate data streams that can be analyzed, monetized, and reintegrated into algorithmic optimization processes. In this sense, network norms are not only cultural or infrastructural phenomena but also deeply embedded in political-economic dynamics of accumulation and market organization.

This economic dimension reinforces the normative power of digital infrastructures. When informational environments are organized by platform operators whose incentives are shaped by attention markets, advertising systems, or data extraction, the operational logic of network norms becomes closely linked to economic imperatives. Digital infrastructures therefore function simultaneously as technical mediation systems, cultural environments, and economic coordination architectures.

Understanding digital transformation thus requires integrating ontological, socio-technical, and political-economic perspectives. The normative effects of digital infrastructures cannot be separated from the economic structures through which they are financed, maintained, and expanded.

POWER, LEGITIMACY, AND IDEOLOGY IN NETWORK INFRASTRUCTURES

Digital transformation is reshaping power primarily through infrastructures that structure the conditions for action, rather than through coercion, prohibitions, or centralized authority. In networked environments, power is protopolitical; it operates before formal political deliberations and institutional decisions, as it is embedded in technical architectures that organize connectivity, visibility, and participation.

From an information-pragmatic perspective, infrastructural power arises through the stabilization of mediated practices. Features that make digital systems simple, scalable, or visible gain normative force even in the absence of explicit normative intent. As a result, power shifts from actors to architectures, from decisions to design, and from discourses to operational environments.

This transformation reorganizes political authority rather than abolishing it. Governance increasingly takes place through the configuration of technical systems that pre-structure social interaction. As a result, political struggle is shifting from ideological confrontations to infrastructure design, standard setting, and protocol control. Power is exercised by designing environments in which actions become possible or impossible, rather than by directly commanding subjects.

Modalities of Infrastructural Power

Infrastructural power can be analytically distinguished based on the technical levels at which it operates. Three central modalities illustrate this distinction.

Protocol power structures the fundamental conditions of connectivity. Protocols determine which forms of communication are possible, which standards are recognized, and which interactions are excluded. Their influence stems from their invisibility; protocols function as background conditions that shape actions without presenting themselves as decision-making spaces. By stabilizing the grammar of digital interaction, protocols establish a form of technical sovereignty that is largely beyond democratic debate.

Platform power operates at the level of ecosystem coordination. Platforms regulate access, visibility, ranking, and participation through interface design, moderation rules, and algorithmic order. This form of power is neither entirely public nor exclusively private. It creates de facto regulation by embedding normative decisions in technical and organizational infrastructures. Platform power is perceived as inevitable due to its reinforcement by network effects and infrastructural dependence.

Algorithmic power shapes perception and decision-making by selecting, classifying, and prioritizing information. Its epistemic dimension consists of determining what becomes visible, relevant, or plausible within a system. Rather than persuading subjects, algorithmic power works through continuous feedback loops that align behavior with the expectations generated by the system.

Together, these modalities show that power in digital environments is complex rather than centralized. Infrastructural power operates through the interplay of protocols, platforms, and algorithms that collectively organize social reality.

Change in Orders of Legitimacy

The infrastructuralization of power is accompanied by a significant shift in the logic of legitimacy. In digital environments, legitimacy increasingly derives from performance, functionality, and system reliability rather than from legal authorization, institutional procedures, or public consultation.

Infrastructural systems are considered legitimate to the extent that they function efficiently, are effectively scalable, and maintain continuous coordination. Stability replaces justification, and functionality replaces normative thinking. Normative questions continue to exist, but are shifted from explicit political arenas to technical and organizational domains.

From an information-pragmatic perspective, this shift reflects a change in the emergence of normativity. Legitimacy arises pragmatically from use; systems enjoy trust because they function effectively, not because they have been discursively justified. As a result, governance becomes reactive and adaptive, responding to infrastructural realities rather than proactively shaping them.

This performative order of legitimacy helps explain why digital infrastructures often elude traditional forms of accountability. Their authority is exercised rather than claimed, and experienced rather than argued. Consequently, political criticism must concern itself with operative rather than declarative legitimacy.

Ideological Criticism in the Mode of Informational Pragmatism

Classical ideology theories conceptualized domination primarily as misrepresentation, false consciousness, or discursive interpellation. In contrast, digital ideologies operate less through belief and more through use. Rather than convincing subjects, ideology, from an informational-pragmatist perspective, is not primarily a system of ideas but an effect of infrastructural mediation. Interfaces, metrics, rankings, and feedback mechanisms materialize certain worldviews by structuring access to reality and engagement with it. The apparent neutrality or functionality gains ideological power precisely because it remains implicit.

Digital ideologies, therefore, function operationally. They stabilize expectations, normalize behaviors, and make alternative forms of coordination impractical or invisible. Their power does not lie in explicit claims about the world. Power shapes the conditions under which the world can be experienced.

This understanding of ideology is consistent with the chapter's overarching argument. If normativity pragmatically emerges from mediated practice and infrastructures increasingly organize this practice, then ideology becomes infrastructural. Accordingly, criticism must go beyond discourse analysis and examine technical architectures, operational logics, and design decisions that tacitly determine social reality.

Counterpower and Infrastructural Contestation

Since digital power operates through infrastructure, counterpower cannot rely solely on discursive opposition or legal interventions. Resistance increasingly manifests itself as infrastructural contestation, including struggles over interoperability, data access, platform alternatives, and technical standards.

Practices such as data refusal, digital minimalism, platform migration, and demands for open protocols do not merely express dissent; they also constitute forms of resistance. They target the material conditions of norm production. These forms of counterpower recognize that autonomy in digital environments depends less on individual decisions than on the availability of alternative infrastructures.

From this perspective, political agency in the digital age involves reclaiming influence over the technical conditions that shape collective life. Counterpower emerges when infrastructures become the subject of reflection, negotiation, and redesign, rather than remaining self-evident environments for action.

CONCLUSION

This chapter has developed a philosophical account of digital transformation as a reconfiguration of the conditions under which normativity, agency, and social order emerge. Rather than interpreting digitalization as a process of technical optimization or functional modernization, the analysis has shown that digital infrastructures function as fundamental elements in the production, coordination, and stabilization of social reality. Digital transformation thus represents a shift in the way the world becomes operationally accessible through socio-technical mediation.

This shift entails a double realignment. Normativity no longer appears primarily as the result of moral considerations or institutional authority, but as the effect of hybrid networks in which interfaces, algorithms, platforms, and protocols pre-structure possible actions. Accordingly, regulation must not be understood as an external corrective, but as a formative practice that intervenes at the level of technical mediation itself.

On this basis, this chapter introduced the concepts of non-subjective normativity and network norms. Network norms refer to the operational imperatives embedded in digital infrastructures—such as connectivity, visibility, participation, flexibility, and transparency—that guide the behavior of both human and non-human actors. These norms do not function as explicit rules or commands. Rather, they are pragmatically stabilized structures of expectation that emerge through use and are reinforced by technical architectures.

The analysis further showed that, while the underlying logics of digital mediation exhibit structural convergence, their normative articulation varies across socio-political contexts. Digital transformation is therefore neither globally homogeneous nor culturally arbitrary, but institutionally differentiated between legal, market-based, and state-centered regimes.

By integrating perspectives on infrastructural power, changing orders of legitimacy, and digital ideology, the chapter has shown that digital transformation entails a profound reorganization of governance. Power is embedded in technical architectures, legitimacy is increasingly based on performance and functionality, and ideology operates through operational mechanisms rather than discursive persuasion. These shifts challenge traditional models of political authority, responsibility, and critique.

Overall, the analysis shows that digital transformation is not just a technological development. Rather, it argues that transformation is a profound socio-technical reconfiguration of the way the world is produced, experienced, and governed. To understand this transformation, one must move beyond subject-centered or purely instrumental conceptual frameworks and recognize digital infrastructures as normative and political actors in their own right.

At the beginning of the 20th century, Karl Kraus warned that humanity could lose the ability to be served by its machines (AAC). More than a century later, this concern is gaining new relevance: technical systems no longer merely extend human action. They are also increasingly shaping the conditions of thought, communication, and judgment itself. The challenge of digital transformation is therefore not whether machines will dominate humans. It would be better to ask whether societies will retain the ability to shape the socio-technical relationships that form collective reality consciously.

REFERENCES

AAC (Austrian Academy Corpus). Kraus, K. *Die Fackel*. 1899-1936. www.aac.ac.at/fackel

Althusser, L. (1971). Ideology and Ideological State Apparatuses. Lenin and Philosophy and Other Essays, Monthly Review Press. https://www.csun.edu/~snk1966/Lous%20Althusser%20Ideology%20and%20Ideological%20State%20Apparatuses.pdf

Andrae, S. (2026a). A Future of equal rights: An agnostic legal framework for the coexistence of humans and autonomous AI. In Luftman, J., & Tomer, A. (Eds.), *Moral and Legal Aspects of Artificial Intelligence: Machine Bias and Rule of Law* (pp. 33–92). IGI Global Publishing., DOI: 10.4018/979-8-3373-3114-0.ch002

Andrae, S. (2026b). The role of local platforms and Non-Western perspectives on platformization. In Çelik, N., Ateşoğlu, N., & Güner, S. S. (Eds.), *Sociological Dimensions of Platformization: Power, Culture, and Identity in the Digital Age* (pp. 31–70). IGI Global Publishing., DOI: 10.4018/979-8-3373-4267-2.ch002

Beer, D. (2019). The Data Gaze: Capitalism, Power and Perception. *Sage (Atlanta, Ga.)*. Advance online publication. DOI: 10.4135/9781526463210

Castells, M. (1996). *The Rise of the Network Society*. Blackwell.

Castells, M. (2009). *Communication Power*. Oxford University Press.

Cheney-Lippold, J. (2017). *We Are Data: Algorithms and the Making of Our Digital Selves*. NYU Press. DOI: 10.18574/nyu/9781479888702.001.0001

Floridi, L. (2011). *The philosophy of Information*. Oxford University Press. DOI: 10.1093/acprof:oso/9780199232383.001.0001

Galloway, A. (2012). The Interface Effect. *Polity*.

Gillespie, T. (2018). *Custodians of the Internet: Platforms, Content Moderation, and the Hidden Decisions That Shape Social Media*. Yale University Press.

Gramsci, A. (1971). *Selections from the Prison Notebooks*. International Publishers.

Han, B.-C. (2013). *Schwarm*. Ansichten des Digitalen. Matthes & Seitz.

Heidegger, M. (1954). *Die Frage nach der Technik*. Klostermann.

Ihde, D. (1990). *Technology and the lifeworld: From garden to Earth*. Indiana University Press. DOI: 10.2979/3108.0

Krieger, D. J. (2025). *Informational Pragmatism: Towards a Philosophy of Digital Transformation*. Ethics Press.

Latour, B. (1993). *We Have Never Been Modern*. Harvard University Press.

Latour, B. (2005). *Reassembling the Social: An Introduction to Actor-Network-Theory*. Oxford University Press. DOI: 10.1093/oso/9780199256044.001.0001

Lessig, L. (1999). *Code and Other Laws of Cyberspace*. Basic Books.

Luhmann, N. (1997). *Die Gesellschaft der Gesellschaft*. Suhrkamp.

Malafouris, L. (2013). *How Things Shape the Mind: A Theory of Material Engagement*. MIT Press. DOI: 10.7551/mitpress/9476.001.0001

Marx, K., & Engels, F. (1845/1846). *Die deutsche Ideologie*.

Pasquale, F. (2015). *The Black Box Society: The Secret Algorithms That Control Money and Information*. Harvard University Press. DOI: 10.4159/harvard.9780674736061

Plantin, J.-C., Lagoze, C., Edwards, P., & Sandvig, C. (2018). Infrastructure studies meet platform studies in the age of Google and Facebook. *New Media & Society*, *20*(1), 293–310. DOI: 10.1177/1461444816661553

Stalder, F. (2016). *Kultur der Digitalität*. Suhrkamp.

Verbeek, P.-P. (2005). *What Things Do: Philosophical Reflections on Technology, Agency, and Design*. Penn State University Press.

Chapter 3
Digital Fascism in Electoral Campaigns:
The Criminalization of Political Opponents in the 2025 Ecuadorian Elections

Rebeca Sanchez Figuera
Universidad Rey Juan Carlos, Spain

Fernando Casado Gutierrez
http://orcid.org/0000-0003-0818-3924
Universidad Bolivariana de Ecuador, Ecuador

ABSTRACT

Fascism has transformed from a 20th-century political model—characterized by hierarchical organization, a charismatic leader, and state-controlled repression—into a contemporary "digital fascism." This new variant operates not through centralized party structures, but via decentralized, informal swarms on digital platforms. It adapts traditional authoritarian, exclusionary, and ultranationalist logics to the online ecosystem, employing disinformation, polarization, and hate speech to undermine democratic deliberation. This study analyzes digital fascism strategies through a case study of President Daniel Noboa's official X account (@ DanielNoboaOk) during Ecuador's 2025 electoral campaign. Using a mixed-methods approach, it combines qualitative discourse analysis with quantitative engagement metrics. The research examines twelve original posts from January to April 2025 that contain accusations against opponent Luisa González, analyzing discursive frames and viralization strategies to understand this modern authoritarian phenomenon in Latin America.

DOI: 10.4018/979-8-3373-4531-4.ch003

INTRODUCTION

Fascism, historically understood as a "great political innovation of the 20th century" (Paxton, 2007, p. 13), has undergone a radical transformation in the digital context. According to Paxton (2007), classical fascism was characterized by its hierarchical organization, the cult of a charismatic leader, and the mobilization of masses through vertical party structures, underpinned by secret police that persecuted, detained, tortured, and eliminated those who opposed the government (Rodrigues, 2024). This model, which found resonance in Latin American dictatorships, operated through a logic of centralization and state control.

However, in the 21st century, this phenomenon has mutated into what Fielitz & Holger (2020) and Pereira da Silva (2022) term "digital fascism." This contemporary variant does not depend on traditional hierarchical organizations but is built upon "informal swarms that easily spread to the general public" (Arencón Beltrán et al., 2022). Unlike traditional fascism, which required a pyramidal structure and a repressive state apparatus, digital fascism operates in a decentralized manner, leveraging the reticular architectures of digital platforms to coordinate actions, disseminate exclusionary ideologies, and mobilize followers spontaneously and virally.

This transition does not imply a complete break with the past but rather an adaptation of authoritarian, exclusionary, and ultranationalist logics to the digital ecosystem. Whereas classical fascism manifested in physical spaces and through direct violence, digital fascism expresses itself through practices such as disinformation, polarization, online harassment, and the generation of hate speech (Arencón Beltrán et al., 2022), while maintaining the fundamental objective of undermining democratic deliberation and eliminating dissent.

This study aims to analyze the digital fascism strategies employed by President Daniel Noboa through his official X account @DanielNoboaOk during the 2025 electoral campaign in Ecuador, as an emblematic case study for Latin America. To this end, a mixed-methods approach with an exploratory scope is adopted, combining qualitative discourse analysis with a quantitative analysis of engagement metrics. The sample consists of twelve original posts published between January and April 2025 containing accusations or allegations against the opposing candidate Luisa González or her political movement. Data collection techniques included the systematic capture of tweets and metadata, using ad-hoc coding sheets as primary tools to record discursive categories, interaction metrics, and multimedia elements. Data analysis integrates descriptive statistics with the critical interpretation of discursive frames and viralization strategies.

Digital Fascism As A Tool Of Advanced Neoliberalism

Digital fascism, as used in this study, is conceptualized as an analogical and heuristic category that refers to a set of communicative strategies, discursive patterns, and affective mobilizations associated with exclusionary and authoritarian ideological orientations in the digital sphere. This conceptualization distinguishes contemporary digital communication practices from historical fascist regimes, which were characterized by dictatorship, aggressive warfare, and mass violence. Accordingly, the analysis centers on forms of political communication—such as tweets—that reproduce logics of division, stigmatization, and symbolic exclusion within digital environments.

From this perspective, digital fascism can be understood as structurally embedded within the logic of advanced neoliberalism. According to Pereira da Silva (2022), the "new neoliberal project" translates into a "perverse ideology of social division," where communicative practices grounded in hatred, fear, and exclusion function as ideological mechanisms shaping public discourse. In this framework, the concept serves to identify how strategies such as simplifying complex realities, constructing enemies, and intensifying moral dichotomies operate within digital environments, particularly among actors aligned with ultra-conservative or exclusionary political agendas.

This instrumentalization is also linked to the management of psychic suffering in neoliberal contexts. Safatle et al. (2020) argue that neoliberalism operates as a moral economy that depoliticizes suffering by relocating it to the individual sphere, thereby weakening its potential for collective articulation and political contestation. Under these conditions, social anxieties and frustrations are channelled into individualized experiences, limiting their transformation into collective political demands.

Paradoxically, this depoliticized suffering becomes economically exploitable. Neoliberalism sustains a cycle in which vulnerability is commodified through palliative solutions—such as medicalization, self-help, and wellness industries—that offer individualized responses while leaving structural conditions intact (Safatle et al., 2020). Within this context, digital fascism operates at the level of discourse by providing simplified explanations, identifiable culprits, and narratives of belonging that symbolically rearticulate diffuse discontent. It functions as a communicative formation that channels and reorganizes social malaise through exclusionary and polarizing narratives in the digital public sphere.

Analytical Dimensions Of Digital Fascism

It is possible to identify three dimensions of digital fascism that operate in a coordinated manner: the technical (Fuchs, 2025), the discursive, and the organizational (Arencón Beltrán et al., 2022).

The technical dimension refers to the appropriation and exploitation of digital architectures. *Fascist convergence* describes the integration of information, communication, and production technologies into a single digital platform, facilitating convergent forms of communication for ideological dissemination. *Fascist prosumption* manifests when networked computers, serving as both media of communication and production, enable users to become active producers of ideological content ("prosumers"), generating a vast output of fascist content. Finally, *fascist surveillance* emerges from the online convergence of private, semi-public, and public information, allowing fascist actors to collect data on their enemies to fuel harassment practices, while their own activities can be tracked, establishing a dynamic of bidirectional surveillance.

The discursive dimension encompasses the content and narrative strategies that constitute the concrete expression of digital fascism. The typology of digital reactionary actions proposed by Arencón Beltrán et al. (2022) provides a fundamental framework for categorizing these discursive manifestations, which operate as the concrete materialization of the technical potentialities identified by Fuchs (2025). These actions are articulated as follows: disinformation, polarization, isolation, and fostering of echo chambers, among others, such as trolling, intimidation, generating hate speech, harassment, abuse, and symbolic violence.

Disinformation, understood as the dissemination of false news or misleading content, and manipulation act as ideological apparatuses that, in the words of Pereira da Silva (2022), transmit "values founded on ideologies of hate." *Polarization* materializes in the systematic construction of exclusive "us versus them" dichotomies, a logic that, as described by Stanley (cited in Fuchs, 2020), is fundamental to undermining democratic deliberation. *Isolation and the fostering of echo chambers* reinforce sectarian narratives and nullify disagreement, creating spaces where exclusionary worldviews are shielded. Finally, actions such as trolling, intimidation, generating hate speech, harassment, abuse, and symbolic violence constitute the most direct expression of hate generation, through the criminalization of opponents and the incitement to discrimination or symbolic violence.

The organizational dimension examines the new forms of mobilization and structuring. *Fascist cooperation* is possible because the networked computer favors online collaboration, allowing fascists to coordinate activities in a decentralized manner to establish fascist societies that operate as "informal swarms" rather than classic hierarchical organizations (Arencón Beltrán et al., 2022). *Tabloidization* takes advantage of the logic of the internet, which operates on high-speed flows of vast amounts of information, favoring decontextualization and sensationalism to spread fake news and post-truth (Fuchs, 2025). Lastly, *isolation and echo chambers* reinforce sectarian narratives and nullify disagreement, creating spaces in which the boundary between the real and the virtual is blurred and exclusionary worldviews are fortified (Arencón Beltrán et al., 2022).

Regional Expressions Of Digital Fascism

Europe has been the stage for the resurgence of far-right, neo-nationalist, and neoconservative movements, grouped under the categories of neofascism or post-fascism (Guamán et al., 2019). Parties such as Vox in Spain, Rassemblement National in France, and Fratelli d'Italia have adapted the essence of 20th-century fascist principles—authoritarianism, extreme nationalism, and the exclusion of the "other"—to the digital context (Eatwell & Goodwin, 2018). According to Traverso (2019), post-fascism reinterprets fascist principles within a globalized framework, while Eco (1995) warns of "eternal fascism," always present in times of crisis. Digitalization has allowed these movements to exploit identity tensions and social discontent, using platforms as tools for propaganda and mobilization (Tufekci, 2017).

In Latin America, digital fascism has found fertile ground in contexts with authoritarian traditions. The case of Jair Bolsonaro in Brazil is emblematic. His government was characterized by the "proliferation of lies and disinformation, threats and insecurities" (Acker, 2018). Bolsonaro not only revitalized the legacy of the military dictatorship (1964-1985) but also resorted to slogans and symbols of clear fascist inspiration, such as "Brasil acima de tudo" (Brazil above all), analogous to the "Deutschland über alles" of German National Socialism (Acker, 2018). Pereira da Silva (2022) points out that digital fascism in the region fits within a "perverse neoliberal project" that promotes social division and is expressed through fear and the manipulation of affects.

Concurrently, the election of Donald Trump as President of the United States in 2016 marked a turning point in the instrumentalization of social media for authoritarian political purposes. According to Fielitz & Holger (2020), Trump and Bolsonaro represent paradigmatic examples of ultra-conservative leaders who use digital platforms to propagate intimidating and hateful discourses. Fuchs (2025) highlights that digital fascism in the United States is characterized by the combination of charismatic leadership with a decentralized, networked organization, which facilitates the mobilization of bases and the dissemination of conspiracy theories.

Digital Fascism In The 2025 Ecuadorian Presidential Elections

Contemporary electoral processes have become privileged arenas for the manifestation of digital fascism, where the appropriation of digital tools by ultra-conservative leadership is evident. The case of the 2025 presidential elections in Ecuador constitutes an illustrative example of how these strategies are implemented in contexts of high political polarization and security crises.

In this scenario, strategies of criminalizing the opponent as a form of mobilization reached their peak. The incumbent president and re-election candidate, Daniel Noboa, instrumentalized his official position to disseminate grave allegations against his contender, Luisa González, linking her without evidence to drug trafficking and organized crime. Through rallies, interviews, and especially social media, accusations were propagated linking the opposing candidate and her party, Revolución Ciudadana, to specific criminal organizations such as "Los Lobos," even insinuating connections based on personal aspects like her tattoos (El Informante, 2025; Orlando, 2025).

This phenomenon perfectly illustrates the viralization of content and the formation of "fast cultures of hate" described by Fielitz & Marcks (2020). The accusations, lacking verifiable substance, transcended the digital sphere to become headlines in the international press (Lozano, 2025) and were amplified through false content claiming direct links between González and international drug cartels (Pinchagua, 2025). This strategy unfolded in a particularly vulnerable national context, marked by a sharp escalation of violence associated with drug trafficking dynamics. According to the United Nations Office on Drugs and Crime (UNODC, 2025), Ecuador has experienced a dramatic increase in homicide rates, rising from 7.8 per 100,000 inhabitants in 2020 to 45.7 in 2023, largely linked to intensified competition among criminal groups within cocaine trafficking networks. This surge reflects broader regional patterns, where increased cocaine flows and seizures have coincided with heightened levels of violence, reinforcing a climate of insecurity that amplifies the impact and resonance of disinformation campaigns.

The final electoral result, in which Noboa obtained 55.63% of the votes compared to González's 44.37%, capturing virtually the entire undecided electorate despite the absence of extraordinary events to justify such a shift, suggests the effectiveness of these digital fascism strategies in influencing democratic outcomes. The subsequent allegation of electoral fraud by the opposing candidate completes a picture where the practices of digital fascism demonstrated their capacity to distort democratic processes through the systematic exploitation of fears and prejudices within the digital ecosystem.

Authoritarian Neoliberalism and Digital Fascism: The Dual Profile of Daniel Noboa

The government of Daniel Noboa Azín has been academically characterized as an exponent of the neoliberal right, articulating a model that combines authoritarian neoliberalism—which "dismantles the foundations of democratic participation" (Molina Ramón et al., 2025, p. 2801)—with patrimonialist practices evidenced in "the awarding of state contracts to companies related to his family circle" (Molina Ramón et al., 2025, p. 2799) and a form of competitive authoritarianism. This configuration is supported by precise adjectives: his administration is elitist and business-oriented, with Noboa being "the most important node in a complex business network" (Muñoz Miño, 2023, as cited in Herrera & Macasoff, 2023, p. 141), and simulative, for presenting himself with a "self-description of 'center-left'" (Herrera & Macasoff, 2023, p. 136) while his political alliance favors economic elites, using "simulacrum" to transform ideologies into "media representations" (Molina Ramón & Moncada Landeta, 2024, p. 1651).

This political projection manifests in a digital communication strategy that embodies the traits of digital fascism, in which the personalization of power is central. His massive audience on his personal TikTok account (@DanielNoboaOK), which, with 1,978,880 followers, completely overshadows institutional accounts (Ortega Jarrín & Escribano García, 2024), is replicated on the X network (formerly Twitter), where his account @DanielNoboaOk accumulates 694.6 thousand followers against a minimal following profile (53 accounts followed). This evidences a vertical and unidirectional communication strategy characteristic of digital populism. This narrative centralization, which reinforces an image of a strong leader through digital platforms, operates in parallel to the normalization of authoritarian measures such as the "democratic state of exception" (Molina Ramón et al., 2025, p. 2801), configuring a scenario where social networks become key mechanisms for consolidating personalistic power and eroding democratic balances through an unmediated connection that evades traditional institutional controls.

METHODOLOGY

This research aims to analyze the discursive strategies employed by President Daniel Noboa through his account @DanielNoboaOk on the social network X during his re-election campaign in the 2025 Ecuadorian presidential elections, as a paradigmatic case of digital fascism. To this end, a mixed-methods design with an exploratory scope, typical of studies on these digital manifestations, is adopted. The qualitative component enables an in-depth discursive analysis of communication strategies through the application of the typology of digital reactionary actions, while the quantitative component allows for a systematic characterization of the frequency, intensity, and distribution patterns of these actions, as well as the analysis of engagement metrics that reveal their impact on the digital ecosystem. In this way, a more precise understanding of the nature of digital fascism is sought, understood both as an evolution of traditional fascism adapted to the technical and social logics of digital platforms and online social networks, and as a measurable social practice expressed in concrete patterns of interaction and viralization within these environments.

The methodology is applied in two sequential phases that integrate the theoretical postulates of digital fascism with the methodological approach of Arencón Beltrán et al. (2022). In the first phase, the official discursive production of President Daniel Noboa during the critical period of the electoral campaign (January - April 2025) is studied. Proceeding from the theoretical assumption that official accounts, when instrumentalized for the criminalization of opponents and the dissemination of exclusionary content, constitute a central node of what Fuchs (2025) identifies as "fascist prosumption," the typology of digital reactionary actions by Arencón Beltrán et al. (2022) is applied. This typology allows for the coding of posts according to five central analytical categories:

Disinformation: understood as a central dynamic of contemporary political communication, involving the deliberate creation, manipulation, and dissemination of false or misleading content. This includes rumors, hoaxes, manipulated images or videos, decontextualized information, and fabricated content, often used as a propagandistic tool to distort public debate and discredit individuals or causes.

Polarization: refers to the intervention in discourse with the intention of generating confrontation and social division. It operates through simplification of arguments, extreme comparisons, and the construction of antagonistic positions that intensify conflict and align participants into opposing camps, reinforcing dichotomous interpretations of social and political issues.

Harassment: encompasses practices of cyber harassment, including insults, threats, and attacks directed at individuals or groups. These actions may involve coordinated campaigns, intimidation, and various forms of digital aggression aimed at silencing or discrediting targets in online environments.

Hate Generation: involves the production and dissemination of hostile and discriminatory discourse, ranging from condescending or offensive comments to explicit hate speech. It includes practices such as trolling, intimidation, and the strategic use of aggressive language to foster misogynistic, exclusionary, or antagonistic narratives that legitimize symbolic violence.

Isolation/Echo Chambers: refers to the reinforcement of closed communicative environments where homogeneous viewpoints are reproduced. This includes the dynamics of quasi-closed groups and algorithmically driven "filter bubbles" that limit exposure to diverse perspectives, strengthen sectarian narratives, and reduce deliberation by excluding dissenting voices.

The data capture protocol is applied to original posts, published between January and April 2025, that contain accusations, allegations, or discrediting remarks aimed directly or indirectly at Luisa González or the Revolución Ciudadana movement. Each unit of analysis is recorded using a standardized coding sheet (Table 1) that documents, in addition to the discursive categories, technical metadata (date, hashtags, mentions) and engagement metrics (likes, retweets, replies). This enables a systematic characterization of the communication strategy within the context of what Pereira da Silva (2022) describes as a "perverse ideology of social division" under contemporary neoliberalism.

Table 1. Instrument for the analysis of official discursive production (January- April 2025)

Instrument for the analysis of official discursive production (January April 2025)														
ID_Tweet	**Date_Time**	**Full_Text**	**Multimedia**	**Hashtags**	**Mentions**	**Disinformation**	**Polarization**	**Harassment**	**Hate_ Generation**	**Isolation_ Echo_ Chambers**	**Likes**	**Retweets**	**Replies**	**Context**
[Link]	[Date/ Time]	[Full text]	[Image/ Video/ Poll/ None]	[#Hashtag1, #Hashtag2]	@ account1, @ account2]	Type of action	Type of action	Type of action	Type of action	Type of action	[Number]	[Number]	[Number]	[Event/ Moment]

Source: Own elaboration based on the work of Arencón Beltrán et al. (2022), 2025.
Note: The DeepSeek platform was used to optimize the presentation of content.

The second phase examines the dynamics of viralization and discursive transformation generated from the official discourse, capturing what Fielitz and Marcks (2020) conceptualize as "transmission belts" that form "fast cultures of hate" within the digital ecosystem. Through the analysis of replies, retweets, and quotes of the official tweets, this phase identifies how the initial discursive frames are amplified, radicalized, contested, or parodied by various network actors. In this way, the research seeks to comprehend digital fascism not as a unidirectional phenomenon, but as a discursive battlefield where meanings are contested and counter-narratives are constructed.

The analysis instrument (Table 2) records the type of user-generated content (e.g., meme, video, text), the engagement it generated, and—centrally—the type of discursive transformation observed (e.g., fact-checking, amplification, accusatory inversion, structural parody). Contextualizing each interaction within the specific electoral scenario enables the identification of correlations between discursive strategies and critical moments of the campaign. This aligns with the understanding of digital fascism as a tool that finds fertile ground for its development in electoral processes (Pereira da Silva, 2022).

Table 2. Instrument for the Analysis of Responses and Viralization

Instrument for the Analysis of Responses and Viralization								
ID_Node	**ID_ Original_ Tweet**	**Node_Type**	**Date_Time**	**Account**	**Content**	**Engagement**	**Content_Type**	**Transformation**
[N001]	[Original Link]	[Reply/ Retweet/ Quote]	[Date/Time]	[[@ account]	[Text or description]	[Number]	[Meme/ Video/ Text	[Description of change]

Source: Own elaboration, 2025.
Note: The DeepSeek platform was used to optimize the presentation of content.

RESULTS AND ANALYSIS

Digital Fascism Strategies In Daniel Noboa's Account

The analysis of the twelve official tweets from the account @DanielNoboaOk, studied in this research, suggests the presence of recurring discursive patterns in the selected sample. The analysis applies the five categories of digital reactionary actions proposed by Arencón Beltrán et al. (2022) to each tweet individually, identifying the presence or absence of each category based on observable textual evidence. This approach allows for a more precise characterization of how the specific discursive mechanisms operate in each case.

Tweet No. 1, from January 9, 2025, offers an initial example of how several of these categories are articulated. Regarding disinformation, a clear case cannot be demonstrated based solely on the tweet's content. The message refers to the kidnapping of María Corina Machado in Venezuela and characterizes Nicolás Maduro's government as a dictatorship. While this statement has a strong political charge, the tweet does not present verifiable false claims or fabricated evidence within its own text; Therefore, this category is not coded as present in this case. In contrast, polarization is clearly observable. The tweet constructs an explicit moral dichotomy by stating that any Ecuadorian politician who "defends, justifies, or remains silent" about the events in Venezuela "becomes an accomplice." This formulation reduces the range of possible positions to two mutually exclusive options: condemnation or complicity, thus exemplifying what Arencón Beltrán et al. (2022) describe as the construction of antagonistic "us versus them" frameworks.

The harassment category can be identified in the use of direct mentions (@ LuisaGonzalezEc, @RicardoPatinoEC, among others), which publicly expose specific political actors in a context of moral accusation. The tweet does not merely express a general position; it targets identifiable individuals, situating them within a discursive framework that equates silence with complicity in serious crimes. This aligns with the definition of harassment as hostile or accusatory communication directed at specific actors.

The generation of hatred is observed in the escalation of accusations through language laden with moral connotations. The association between political silence and complicity in a system that has caused "hunger, despair, and suffering to millions" introduces a symbolic link between the aforementioned actors and large-scale human suffering. This discursive resource goes beyond political criticism, contributing to the stigmatization of political opponents through emotionally charged language.

Finally, isolation and the echo chamber dynamic arise from the construction of a false dilemma that limits interpretive alternatives. The assertion that "Ecuadorian's demand to know which side of history they are on" reinforces a binary framework that discourages intermediate or critical positions, thus reducing the space for deliberation and aligning audiences within a closed interpretive structure.

Figure 1. Screenshot of Tweet #1 from @DanielNoboaOk (January 9, 2025)

Instrument for the analysis of official discursive production (january-april 2025)

ID_Tweet	Date_Time	Full_Text	Multimedia	Hashtags	Mentions	Disinformation	Polarization	Harassment	Hate_Generation	Isolation_Echo_Chambers	Likes	Retweets	Replies	Context
[Link]	[Date/Time]	[Full text]	[Image/Video/Poll/None]	[#Hashtag1, #Hashtag2]	@account1, @account2]	Type of action	Type of action	Type of action	Type of action	Type of action	[Number]	[Number]	[Number]	[Event/Moment]

Note. *English translation: "The kidnapping of María Corina at the hands of Nicolás Maduro's regime exposes the brutality of a dictatorship that has sown death and misery in its own country. In Ecuador, any politician who defends, justifies, or remains silent in the face of these acts not only betrays democratic values but also becomes complicit in a system that has caused hunger, desperation, and suffering to millions of people. Enough of half measures to cover for comrades. We must be a united nation, firmly and unambiguously condemning this dictatorship. Ecuadorians demand to know which side of history they are on. @Ppsuing @esthercuestasan @LuisaGonzalezEc @RicardoPatinoEC @aquilesalvarez @DianaAtamaint @pabelml @Rauli_Chavez." From @DanielNoboaOk (2025), X. https://x.com/DanielNoboaOk/status/1877473293877281255.*

Tweet #2, from January 12, 2025, enables identification of the five analytical categories through a close reading of its textual and interactive components.

With regard to disinformation, the tweet states that "PetroEcuador has paid more than 5 million dollars to a trust managed by @DiegoBorjaPC" and further claims that Borja "has spent years living off the State." These assertions are presented without qualification or reference to sources and are framed as established facts. However, available information indicates that, while payments under a Petroecuador contract were reportedly associated with a trust structure connected to firms tied to Borja, there is no conclusive evidence that he directly administered the fund, acted as a public contractor, or personally benefited from state resources. Moreover, Borja has publicly denied any conflict of interest, and the case remains under investigation (El Universo, 2025). The disinformative dimension can therefore be identified in the gap between the certainty with which the tweet presents these claims and their unresolved and contested status, transforming an allegation into an apparently verified fact.

Polarization is observable in the construction of antagonistic groupings through expressions such as "Old Ecuador" and the characterization of the opposing ticket as "illegitimate." These formulations divide the political field into mutually exclusive camps, reinforced by the accusation that others "choose to be accomplices of impunity," which reduces the range of possible positions to either alignment with the accusation or complicity.

The category of harassment is evident in the direct targeting of specific actors. The mention of @DiegoBorjaPC, along with the explicit reference to Luisa González, places identifiable individuals within a narrative of corruption and illegitimacy. The formulation "exposed for what they are" and the direct second-person address ("you... choose to be accomplices") contribute to a confrontational communicative environment directed at political adversaries.

Hate generation can be identified in the use of stigmatizing and morally charged language. Terms such as "racket" and "accomplices of impunity" associate the political actors mentioned with criminality and ethical corruption, contributing to their symbolic delegitimization beyond standard political critique.

Isolation and echo chamber dynamics emerge through the structure of the embedded poll: "Do you believe that RC knew about Diego Borja's trust with Petro-Ecuador?" The wording of the question provides empirical evidence of how the interpretive frame is constructed: it presupposes the existence of the alleged trust as a given and restricts the range of possible responses to degrees of attribution of responsibility. In this sense, the poll does not invite respondents to evaluate whether the allegation itself is valid, but instead shifts the focus toward whether Revolución Ciudadana had knowledge of it.

The results—148,247 votes, with 70.2% selecting the option indicating that RC did not know—are open to multiple interpretations. On one hand, they may suggest that a significant portion of respondents did not attribute responsibility to the political movement, which could be read as skepticism toward the accusation. On the other hand, and more directly supported by the question's structure, the poll still normalizes the underlying premise that some form of wrongdoing occurred. By framing the issue in terms of knowledge rather than validity, the tweet effectively displaces the central question—whether the alleged misconduct is substantiated—and establishes it as an implicit background assumption.

This shift can be observed in the transition from an unverified claim to a structured question that treats the alleged trust as an already existing object of debate. In doing so, the poll narrows the interpretive field and encourages engagement within a predefined narrative, contributing to a communicative environment in which alternative interpretations—such as questioning the existence or relevance of the alleged wrongdoing—are less visible.

Figure 2. Screenshot of Tweet #2 from @DanielNoboaOk (January 12, 2025)

Instrument for the Analysis of Responses and Viralization

ID_Node	ID_Original_Tweet	Node_Type	Date_Time	Account	Content	Engagement	Content_Type	Transformation
[N001]	[Original Link]	[Reply/Retweet/Quote]	[Date/Time]	[[@account]	[Text or description]	[Number]	[Meme/Video/Text	[Description of change]

Note. *English translation: "They cried and cried about whether I can campaign or not, but until now, no one from the Old Ecuador has the courage to speak about this: PetroEcuador has paid more than 5 million dollars to a trust managed by @DiegoBorjaPC. He has spent years living off the State and now intends to continue doing so from Carondelet, hand in hand with Luisa González. Exposed for what they are: an illegitimate ticket with contracts with the State. And you, as always, choose to be accomplices of impunity. Once again, they are exposed as the racket they truly are. Ecuadorians, do you believe that RC knew about Diego Borja's trust with PetroEcuador?". From @DanielNoboaOk (2025), X. https://x.com/DanielNoboaOk/status/1878539079249547410.*

Tweet #3, dated January 20, 2025, presents a case in which analytical categories are identified primarily through implicit, rather than explicit, references. Regarding disinformation, the tweet claims that Ecuador was "handed over to drug traffickers" for decades. This formulation presents a broad and complex historical process—related to the expansion of organized crime and drug trafficking—as a unified and intentional action attributable to unspecified political actors. The tweet provides no evidence, sources, or clarification regarding responsibility, nor does it specify which governments or decisions it refers to. The accusation that previous governments "handed Ecuador over to drug traffickers" can be empirically tested against longitudinal evidence on security indicators during the Citizens' Revolution (2007–2017). According to comparative research published in Humanities and Social Sciences Communications, Ecuador experienced a significant reduction in violence during this period, with the homicide rate decreasing by approximately 63.5%, from 15.9 to 5.8 per 100,000 inhabitants (Restrepo Echavarría & Oliván López, 2025). This decline positioned Ecuador among the safest countries in the region at the time, contradicting narratives attributing the origins of current insecurity to that decade. Therefore, the disinformation dimension can be identified in the agent's transformation of a complex, multicausal phenomenon into a simplified, biased statement, presented as an established fact rather than an interpretation.

Polarization is observable in the implicit contrast between the present government -"The Phoenix Plan is working"- and a negatively characterized past in which the country was allegedly surrendered to criminal actors. This temporal opposition structures the political field into two antagonistic positions: a past associated with failure or complicity, and a present associated with restoration and effectiveness. Although no specific actor is named, the dichotomy organizes interpretation along an "us versus them" logic.

The category of harassment is not clearly identifiable in this tweet. The message does not directly mention or target specific individuals or groups through explicit accusations or personal references, which limits its classification within this category.

Hate generation is present at a symbolic level through the use of the signifier "drug traffickers" as a central axis of meaning. By associating an undefined political past with criminal actors, the tweet contributes to a stigmatizing narrative that frames political responsibility as a moral and existential threat. However, this operates indirectly, without explicit insults or direct labeling of identifiable actors.

Isolation and echo chamber dynamics can be observed in the use of hashtags such as #UnaSolaVuelta and #DanielNoboaPresidente. These elements serve as alignment mechanisms that situate the message within a broader campaign narrative, reinforcing a shared interpretive frame among supporters. The absence of alternative perspectives within the message, combined with its slogan-like structure, contributes to a closed communicative environment in which the proposed interpretation is presented as self-evident.

Figure 3. Screenshot of Tweet #3 from @DanielNoboaOk (January 20, 2025)

Note. *English translation: "The Phoenix Plan is working, but it is not possible to resolve in one year the decades in which Ecuador was handed over to drug traffickers. #DanielNoboaPresidente #NoboaEc #UnaSolaVuelta." From @DanielNoboaOk (2025), X. https://x.com/DanielNoboaOk/status/1881163232054071477.*

Tweet #4, from January 30, 2025, published just days before the first electoral round, brings together the five categories of reactionary action in a particularly condensed form. As disinformation, the tweet does not simply attack Revolución Ciudadana but attributes to it a criminal identity through the formula "the Ecuador of Muentes, Glas, and Carrera" and its association with "mafias," presenting guilt by association as if it were self-evident fact rather than a partisan accusation. The disinformative operation lies precisely in this substitution: instead of offering verifiable evidence about concrete criminal responsibility, the message collapses distinct actors, cases, and political identities into a single stigmatized whole, thereby transforming insinuation into apparent truth. In polarization, the tweet structures the electoral contest as an irreconcilable moral dichotomy between a corrupt past and a redeemed future, leaving no room for legitimate democratic disagreement. As a form of harassment, it targets a specific political movement through direct, accusatory language designed to publicly shame, discredit, and expose its members and supporters to a hostile communicative environment. As hate generation, it goes beyond criticism by symbolically constructing the adversary as a dangerous enemy linked to criminal contamination, thereby legitimizing exclusionary and punitive reactions. As isolation and echo-chamber reinforcement, the message discredits unfavorable polls while amplifying favorable surveys, encouraging followers to remain within a closed interpretive frame in which only confirmatory information is treated as credible. In this sense, the tweet's 11,000 likes, 3,000 retweets, and 4,000 replies are relevant not because they prove the truth of the claim, but because they show the capacity of this framing to circulate, resonate, and solidify a shared narrative among supporters. The urgency of the "11 days" countdown further intensifies this logic by presenting the election not as a contest among alternatives, but as a final opportunity for moral purification.

Figure 4. Screenshot of Tweet #4 from @DanielNoboaOk (January 30, 2025)

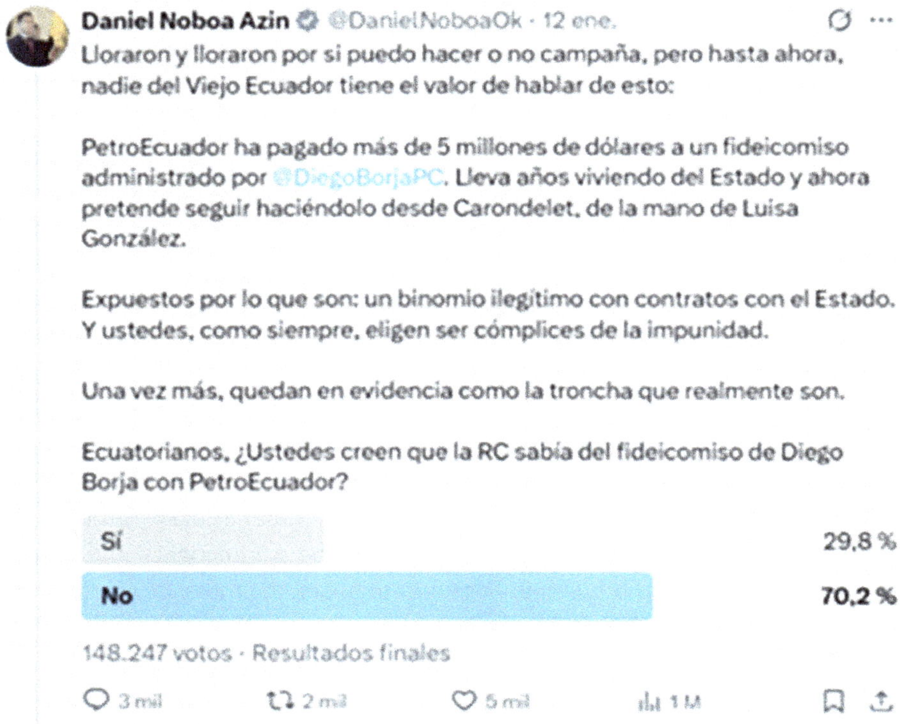

Note. *English translation: "We are about to bury the mafias forever, those who have stolen our dreams and have hindered the country's progress. The Ecuador of Muentes, Glas, and Carrera is now behind us. The old system of privileges for a few and misery for many has come to an end. Very soon we will have the opportunity to change the destiny of our future generations, building a more just country, with dignity, security, and progress. In 11 days, the will of the people, YOUR will, will be felt, and you will have a President who fights and does not back down from anything, and a different Assembly that works for the well-being of the people. P.S.: The figures confirm it, several measurements—the independent ones, not those of resentful State contractors, nor of bankers who oppose this Government—place us at the forefront in voting intention." From @DanielNoboaOk (2025), X. https://x.com/DanielNoboaOk/status/1884761628970791132.*

Tweet #5, dated February 5, 2025, articulates its argument through a sequence of causal and moral claims that allow for the identification of the five analytical categories based on the textual content of the message. With regard to disinformation, the tweet states that the 2011 referendum promoted by correísmo "weakened preventive detention" and thereby "opened the doors to drug trafficking, mafias, and organized crime." This formulation establishes a direct causal relationship between a specific legal reform and a complex and long-term security crisis. The tweet does not provide evidence, sources, or an explanation of the mechanisms through which this causal link operates. Moreover, the claim is presented with certainty, without acknowledging alternative explanations or the multi-causal nature of organized crime dynamics. The disinformative dimension can therefore be identified in the transformation of a complex structural phenomenon into a linear and intentional consequence attributed to a single political decision.

Polarization is observable in the temporal and moral contrast constructed in the tweet. The past is described as a period in which "they turned justice into their toy, protecting criminals and leaving thousands of families defenseless," while the present is framed as a rupture—"that is over"—associated with the proposed constitutional reform. This contrast organizes the political field into opposing positions, where one side is linked to disorder and criminal protection, and the other to restoration and control.

The category of harassment is evident in the direct attribution of responsibility to a specific political actor ("correísmo"). The tweet assigns blame for widespread social harm ("leaving thousands of families defenseless") to this group, transforming a policy critique into a direct accusation against a defined political collective.

Hate generation can be identified by the escalation of an accusatory tone through morally charged, stigmatizing language. The phrase "the line between incompetence and complicity has never been so thin" introduces the possibility of intentional collaboration with criminal actors. This is reinforced by the accumulation of labels such as "terrorists," "drug traffickers," "hitmen," and "organized mafias," which are rhetorically positioned in proximity to the political adversary, contributing to their symbolic association with criminality.

Isolation and echo chamber dynamics emerge from the closure of interpretive alternatives within the message. The tweet presents a single explanatory framework (the 2011 reform as the origin of insecurity) and a single solution (strengthening preventive detention), without acknowledging alternative interpretations or policy approaches. The repeated use of definitive statements—"that is over," "there will be no more escapes," "there will be no more excuses"—reinforces a closed interpretive structure that limits deliberation and encourages alignment with the proposed framing.

Figure 5. Screenshot of Tweet #5 from @DanielNoboaOk (February 5, 2025)

Note. *English translation: "For years, they turned justice into their toy, protecting criminals and leaving thousands of families defenseless. That is over. I have sent a partial reform to the Constitution to strengthen preventive detention against terrorist criminals and anyone related to organized crime. In 2011, correísmo sold us a referendum that weakened preventive detention, opening the doors to drug trafficking, mafias, and organized crime… the line between incompetence and complicity had never been so thin. Terrorists, drug traffickers, hitmen, organized mafias… There will be no more escapes, there will be no more excuses. Judges will now have the tools to lock them up. We are going after all the corrupt." From @DanielNoboaOk (2025), X. https://x.com/DanielNoboaOk/status/1887095328014311640.*

Tweet #6, from March 22, 2025, centers on a real and verifiable event—the murder of electoral official Narciso Saldarriaga—and develops a series of interpretations that enable the identification of analytical categories based on the message's textual content.

With regard to disinformation, the tweet states that unnamed actors "intend to impose themselves through fear," that "they have done [so] for more than a decade," and that "they want all Ecuadorians to be afraid." These claims introduce an implicit attribution of responsibility for the murder and a broader pattern of political violence, yet no specific actors are identified, and no evidence is provided to substantiate the connection between the crime and a political organization. The disinformative dimension can therefore be identified in the transformation of an isolated and complex event into an implied, continuous strategy attributed to a vaguely defined adversary, presented as a matter of certainty rather than as a hypothesis or an ongoing investigation.

Polarization is observable in the construction of antagonistic positions through the contrast between "our electoral oversight delegate" and the undefined "they" who allegedly seek to impose fear and manipulate elections. This opposition implicitly divides the political field into defenders of democratic order and actors associated with coercion and illegitimacy.

The category of harassment is less clearly identifiable in this tweet. Although the message attributes negative intentions to an unspecified group, it does not directly mention or target specific individuals or identifiable actors through explicit accusations, which limits its classification within this category.

Hate generation can be identified in the escalation of the narrative from description of a crime to the construction of an existential threat. Expressions such as "they want all Ecuadorians to be afraid" frame the implied adversary as a collective threat to society, contributing to a climate of suspicion and heightened emotion that goes beyond factual reporting.

Isolation and echo chamber dynamics emerge through the closure of interpretive possibilities within the message. The tweet presents a single explanatory frame—linking the murder to a broader pattern of fear-based political action—without reference to alternative interpretations or to the uncertainty inherent in ongoing investigations. This encourages audiences to adopt a unified reading of the event and limits the space for critical or plural interpretations.

Figure 6. Screenshot of Tweet #6 from @DanielNoboaOk (February 5, 2025)

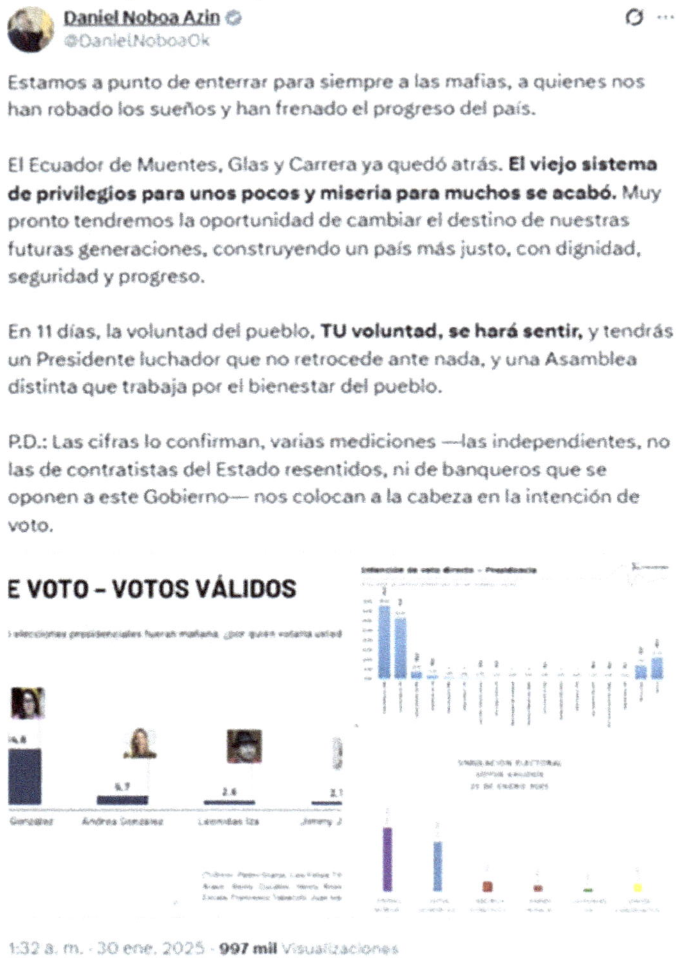

Note. *English translation: "Narciso Saldarriaga has just been murdered in Canuto, our electoral oversight delegate in northern Manabí. My condolences to his family; this will not go unpunished. They intend to impose themselves through fear, as they have done for more than a decade. They want to tie the elections to their convenience and operate without oversight. It is clear, they want all Ecuadorians to be afraid." From @DanielNoboaOk (2025), X. https://x.com/DanielNoboaOk/status/1903504773057253880.*

Tweet #7, dated March 24, 2025, is part of a thread that combines textual, visual, and contextual elements, allowing for the identification of several analytical categories through an examination of the writing style and the multimodal structure of the post.

Regarding disinformation, the tweet asks: "Did you nominate Ronny Aleaga, a fugitive from justice, for the CAL? The same one who is part of the mafia involved in selling medications in hospitals." This statement presents a series of assertions—

Aleaga's alleged membership in a "mafia" and the implication of responsibility by association—without providing any evidence or sources within the tweet itself. The interrogative structure ("Did you nominate...?") presupposes the relevance and validity of the accusation, while the accompanying visual composition (in which Luisa González appears alongside other figures) reinforces the interpretive link between the candidate and the alleged criminals. The disinformation dimension is thus identified in the combination of unverified claims and visual associations, which together construct a narrative of connection presented as self-evident.

Polarization is observed in the implicit contrast between positions associated with criminality and those aligned with institutional legitimacy. By posing the question in the context of the presidential debate (#DebatePresidencial), the tweet situates the accusation within a broader electoral confrontation, encouraging alignment with one of two opposing interpretations: transparency versus corruption.

The category of harassment is clearly identifiable in the direct challenge implicit in the question. The wording targets a specific political actor and presupposes their participation in a questionable action, thus placing them on the defensive. This aligns with the definition of harassment as accusatory communication directed at identifiable individuals in a public digital environment.

The generation of hate is observed in the use of stigmatizing language such as "fugitive from justice" and "mafia involved in selling drugs." These labels carry strong moral and criminal connotations and, by rhetorically linking themselves to the political actor they target, contribute to the symbolic delegitimization of that actor beyond mere political criticism.

Isolation and the echo chamber dynamic emerge through the tweet's integration into a specific communicative context marked by the hashtag #PresidentialDebate. This element situates the message within a real-time discursive environment that prioritizes rapid circulation and alignment. The combination of a simplified accusatory framework and a visual composition that suggests connections between actors limits interpretive alternatives and fosters the consolidation of a shared narrative among like-minded audiences.

Figure 7. Screenshot of Tweet #7 from @DanielNoboaOk (March 24, 2025)

Note. *English translation: "Did you nominate Ronny Aleaga, a fugitive from justice, for the CAL? The same one who is part of the mafia involved in the sale of medicines in hospitals. #DebatePresidencial." From @DanielNoboaOk (2025), X. https://x.com/DanielNoboaOk/status/1903993086251794440*

Tweets #8 and #9, published on March 24, 2025, within a 34-minute interval, can be analyzed as two distinct units that, when read sequentially, contribute to a cumulative discursive effect. Each tweet is examined individually through the five analytical categories.

Tweet #8 ("Always on the side of those who protect us, never on the side of the mafias") presents a highly condensed message structured around a moral opposition.

With regard to disinformation, no explicit false or misleading factual claim can be identified in the text itself. The tweet does not present verifiable statements about specific events or actors; therefore, this category is not coded as present based solely on the available content.

Polarization is clearly observable through the construction of a binary opposition between "those who protect us" and "the mafias." This formulation establishes mutually exclusive positions and aligns the speaker and implied audience with one side of a moral divide, consistent with the "us versus them" logic described by Arencón Beltrán et al. (2022).

The category of harassment is not directly identifiable, as the tweet does not target specific individuals or groups through explicit accusations or mentions.

Hate generation is present at a symbolic level through the use of the term "mafias," which carries strong criminal connotations. Although no specific actor is named, the expression contributes to a stigmatizing frame that associates an implied adversary with organized crime.

Isolation and echo chamber dynamics can be observed through the use of campaign-related hashtags (#DebatePresidencial2025, #DanielNoboa, #ADN7), which situate the message within a partisan communicative environment. These elements facilitate alignment among supporters and reinforce a shared interpretive frame, while the absence of alternative perspectives contributes to a closed discursive structure.

Figure 8. Screenshot of Tweet #8 from @DanielNoboaOk (March 24, 2025)

Note. *English translation by the author of the text appearing in the X post: "Always on the side of those who protect us, never on the side of the mafias. #DebatePresidencial2025 #DanielNoboa #ADN7." From @DanielNoboaOk (2025), X. https://x.com/DanielNoboaOk/status/1903996757727404281.*

Tweet #9 ("These are proven cases: Correa, Glas, Verduga… among other friends of the candidate") introduces explicit references to identifiable actors, enabling a broader application of the analytical categories.

With regard to disinformation, the tweet asserts that the mentioned cases are "proven" without providing evidence, sources, or clarification of their judicial status. In the absence of such substantiation in the tweet, and given that judicial processes can involve multiple stages (investigation, prosecution, sentencing), the use of the term "proven" makes a categorical claim that may not reflect the complexity of these cases. The disinformative dimension can therefore be identified in the presentation of legal matters as definitively resolved without contextualization.

Polarization is evident in the construction of an implicit opposition between the political actor ("the candidate") and the listed figures, who are presented as "friends." This association contributes to a dichotomous framing in which one side is linked to criminality and the other is implicitly aligned with legitimacy.

The category of harassment is evident in the direct association of the opposition candidate with individuals mentioned in a negative context. The formulation attributes proximity ("friends of the candidate") without qualification, placing the candidate within a stigmatizing narrative and exposing them to public accusation.

Hate generation can be identified in the cumulative effect of linking the candidate to figures associated with alleged criminal cases. The absence of nuance in this association contributes to symbolic delegitimization, reinforcing a negative moral characterization.

Isolation and echo chamber dynamics are reinforced through the reiteration of campaign hashtags (#DebatePresidencial2025, #DanielNoboa), which embed the message within a partisan communicative circuit. The categorical nature of the statement ("these are proven cases") limits interpretive openness and encourages acceptance of the claim within aligned audiences.

Figure 9. Screenshot of Tweet #9 from @DanielNoboaOk (March 24, 2025)

Note. *English translation: "These are proven cases: Correa, Glas, Verduga… among other friends of the candidate. #DebatePresidencial2025 #DanielNoboa." From @DanielNoboaOk (2025), X. https://x.com/DanielNoboaOk/status/1904005293291217314.*

Meanwhile, Tweet #10, dated April 5, 2025, consists of a brief statement: "We always knew it; they're not willing to fight against their own ♂," accompanied by a visual element.

Regarding misinformation, the tweet suggests that the opposition "protects its own" by stating "they're not willing to fight against their own." This constitutes a general assertion about behavior or intention, but the tweet itself provides no evidence or specifies any concrete actions to support it. The accompanying video includes edited or decontextualized material, which reinforces the misinformation aspect.

The polarization is clearly seen in the phrase "We always knew it," which presupposes a shared understanding between the speaker and the audience, and contrasts it with an implicit “they.” This construction reinforces a collective identity aligned with the speaker (“we”) in opposition to a delegitimized external group (“they”), consistent with an “us versus them” framework.

The category of harassment is not directly and forcefully identified, as the tweet does not explicitly mention or tag specific individuals. However, the generalized accusation directed at a political group contributes to a hostile framing that may indirectly target identifiable actors associated with that group.

The generation of hate is evident in the tone and rhetorical framing of the message. The use of the emoji ♂, combined with the categorical nature of the accusation, contributes to a dismissive and trivializing stance toward the alleged offense, presenting it as obvious and unworthy of further discussion. This reinforces a delegitimizing narrative that extends beyond political criticism.

The isolation and echo chamber dynamics become evident in the closing off of interpretive possibilities within the message. The phrase "We always knew it" functions as a discursive closure that discourages questioning and presents the assertion as already verified within the group. Similarly, "they are unwilling to fight against their own" presents a fixed characterization of the opposing group, limiting alternative interpretations and reinforcing a shared narrative among like-minded audiences.

Figure 10. Screenshot of Tweet #10 from @DanielNoboaOk (April 5, 2025)

Note. *English translation: "We always knew it; they are not willing to fight their own " [Photograph], by @DanielNoboaOk, 2025, X (https://x.com/DanielNoboaOk/status/1908585655224902065)*

Tweet #11, dated April 8, 2025, contains explicit references to identifiable political actors and allows for the application of analytical categories through detailed textual analysis.

Regarding disinformation, the tweet claims that "Luisa and the Maduro regime think alike" and that "they prefer drug traffickers, impunity, and dictators as friends." These claims establish a direct equivalence between a national political actor and a foreign government, as well as an alleged preference for criminal actors. The tweet provides no evidence, sources, or concrete examples to support these claims, nor does it clarify the nature of the alleged similarity or relationship. Therefore, the disinformation dimension can be identified in the presentation of a forceful associative claim as an established fact without supporting evidence, as well as in a video that includes selective material from a press conference held by Diosdado Cabello, spokesperson for the United Socialist Party of Venezuela.

Polarization is clearly observable in the construction of an antagonistic dichotomy. The opposition is associated with “dictators,” “impunity,” and the rejection of “sovereignty” and “justice,” while the speaker’s implicit stance aligns with democratic values. This approach reduces the political field to mutually exclusive moral positions, consistent with an “us versus them” logic.

The category of harassment is identified in the direct reference to Luisa González as an individual. The tweet attributes her ideological alignment and preferences to criminality and authoritarianism, thus placing her within a stigmatizing narrative in a public digital space.

The generation of hate is observed in the use of morally charged and delegitimizing language. Expressions such as “drug traffickers,” “impunity,” and “dictators” function as powerful negative signifiers, and their rhetorical association with the political adversary contributes to a symbolic disqualification that goes beyond political criticism.

The isolation and echo chamber dynamics arise from the closure of interpretive possibilities within the message. The statement "they have been clear" presents the claims as already established and unquestionable, while the phrase "they disguise it as a revolution" delegitimizes alternative political positions, considering them deceptive by definition. This limits the space for alternative interpretations and reinforces a common narrative among like-minded audiences.

Figure 11. Screenshot of Tweet #11 from @DanielNoboaOk (April 8, 2025)

Note. *English translation: "Luisa and Maduro's regime think alike. Sovereignty? Justice? No, thank you. They prefer drug traffickers, impunity, and dictators as friends. They have been clear. They disguise it as a revolution, but it smells like the same old thing: power at any cost." From @DanielNoboaOk (2025), X. https://x.com/DanielNoboaOk/status/1909407492418777430*

Tweet #12, from April 9, 2025, presents a structured message organized around two explicitly defined options for allocating public funds for security.

With regard to disinformation, the tweet describes one option as "paramilitary groups of rebranded former gang members, now armed and loyal only to the party." This characterization presents a specific policy proposal ("peace managers") as equivalent to partisan paramilitary structures. The tweet does not provide evidence, sources, or clarification supporting this equivalence, nor does it explain the institutional design or legal framework of the proposal being described. The disinformative dimension can therefore be identified in the presentation of a contested or interpretative characterization as a factual description.

Polarization is clearly observable in the construction of two mutually exclusive options: one associated with illegitimate armed actors ("paramilitary groups"), and the other with state institutions ("National Police and Armed Forces"). The formulation "It should not be difficult" reinforces the expectation that only one option is acceptable, thereby structuring the issue as a binary choice and limiting the range of possible positions.

The category of harassment is not directly identifiable in a strong form, as the tweet does not explicitly mention or tag specific individuals. However, the framing implicitly attributes to a political adversary the promotion of illegitimate armed groups, which contributes to a stigmatizing representation of that actor.

Hate generation can be identified in the use of terms such as "paramilitary groups" and "armed militias," which carry strong negative and threatening connotations. Their association with the political opposition contributes to a symbolic construction of that actor as a danger to national security and social order.

Isolation and echo chamber dynamics emerge from the closure of interpretive alternatives within the message. The tweet presents only two options, framed in strongly asymmetrical terms, and excludes intermediate or alternative policy approaches. The reference to "armed militias like those in Venezuela and Nicaragua" reinforces this closure by situating the issue within a broader narrative of external threat, encouraging alignment with the proposed interpretation.

Figure 12. Screenshot of Tweet #12 from @DanielNoboaOk (April 8, 2025)

Note. *English translation: "You have 72 million dollars for security—where would you send it? Option 1: 'Peace managers,' paramilitary groups of rebranded former gang members, now armed and loyal only to the party. Option 2: The National Police and Armed Forces, who have confronted real crime and defended Ecuadorian families. It should not be difficult. Ecuador does not need armed militias like those in Venezuela and Nicaragua. To all young Ecuadorians who want to protect their country, with those 72 million we will increase positions in the Police and Armed Forces so that they can do so with the honor that their uniform represents." From @DanielNoboaOk (2025), X. https://x.com/DanielNoboaOk/status/1909969482749276613.*

Engagement Statistics And Reactionary Categories

Within the sample extracted from the official account @DanielNoboaOk between January and April 2025, the distribution of categories in absolute terms shows that Polarization appears in all 12 analyzed tweets (12/12), followed by Isolation/Echo Chambers also in all 12 tweets (12/12), Hate Generation in 11 tweets (11/12), Disinformation in 10 tweets (10/12), and Harassment in 8 tweets (8/12).

Figure 13. Reactionary categories in selected tweets from @danielnoboaok (january–april 2025)

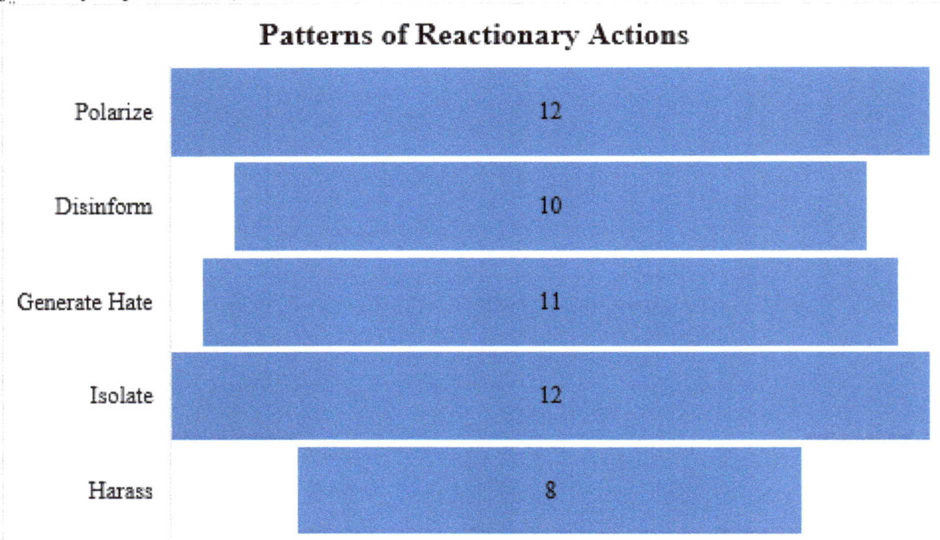

Source: *Author's own elaboration based on data from @DanielNoboaOk's X account (2025).*

The analysis of absolute values indicates the presence of recurring patterns within the selected sample. Polarization and isolation/echo chambers appear in all 12 tweets analyzed, consistently structuring them through binary oppositions and closed interpretive frameworks that limit alternative readings. Hate speech is identified in 11 of the 12 tweets, where stigmatizing or morally charged language is used to delegitimize political actors.

Disinformation appears in 10 of the 12 tweets, specifically in cases where claims are presented without supporting evidence or where complex phenomena are reduced to simplistic and categorical explanations. Harassment is observed in 8 of the 12 tweets, generally through direct or indirect accusations directed at identifiable political actors.

However, it is important to clarify that these results describe patterns within the analyzed tweets and should be interpreted within the context of the sample itself. The size and non-random selection of the dataset prevent generalization about the entirety of the incumbent presidential candidate's communication strategy, which would require a larger and systematically constructed corpus.

Table 3. Statistical Analysis of Digital Fascism Strategies in the Official Corpus

Statistical Analysis of Digital Fascism Strategies in the Official Corpus							
ID	**Likes**	**Retweets**	**Replies**	**Hashtags**	**Mentions**	**Links**	**Analytical Significance**
1	20,000	5,000	3,000	None	@ Ppsuing, @	None	Fascist prosumption (Fuchs, 2025) with mention of electoral authority constitutes institutional pressure. High engagement (1.3M views) generates fast cultures of hate (Fielitz & Marcks, 2020)
2	5,000	2,000	3,000	None	@	None	Fascist tabloidization (Fuchs, 2025): poll as pseudo-participation that validates criminalization. Reply/Like ratio suggests effective polarization.
3	7,000	1,000	843	#Daniel Noboa Presidente #Noboa Ec #Una SolaVuelta	None	None	Floating signifier "narco" + electoral hashtag = technical articulation of digital fascism. Brief message facilitates virilization in swarms (Arencón Beltrán et al., 2022).
4	11,000	3,000	4,000	None	None	None	Naturalization of criminalizing framework. Sustained engagement without reticular elements indicates discursive internalization in electoral base.
5	11,000	2,000	3,000	None	None	None	Hypertextual fascism (Fuchs, 2025): instrumentalization of constitutional reform as technical-legitimate scenario for criminalization.
6	12,000	3,000	3,000	None	None	None	Emotional exploitation of real tragedy. Maximum engagement reflects effectiveness of fear discourse (Pereira da Silva, 2022).
7	9,000	3,000	644	#Debate Presidencial	Implicit to Luisa González	None	Multimodal fascism: composite image as visual contamination + legitimate event hashtag = institutionalized disinformation.
8	6,000	1,000	493	#Debate Presidencial 2025 #Daniel Noboa #ADN	None	None	Partisan appropriation of institutions: official party hashtag from presidential account exemplifies State-campaign blurring.
9	9,000	2,000	535	#Debate Presidencial 2025 #Daniel Noboa	Implicit to "the candidate"	None	Guilt by association through digital lawfare. Engagement recovery confirms effectiveness of expediency strategies (Arencón Beltrán et al., 2022).
10	8,000	3,000	2,000	None	None	None	Totalizing discursive closure: "We always knew" operates as fictional retrospective verification. Emoji trivializes serious accusations.

continued on following page

Table 3. Continued

Statistical Analysis of Digital Fascism Strategies in the Official Corpus							
ID	Likes	Retweets	Replies	Hashtags	Mentions	Links	Analytical Significance
11	8,000	2,000	1,000	None	None	None	Geopolitical polarization: association with "Maduro regime" internationalizes threat. Low reply ratio indicates discursive saturation.
12	14,000	4,000	2,000	None	None	None	Extreme binary encapsulation: Armed Forces vs "paramilitaries" dichotomy represents fascist simplification. Maximum engagement (28.5% Retweet/Like ratio) = effective final virilization

Source: Own elaboration, 2025.
Note: Analysis based on the digital fascism theoretical framework of Fuchs (2025), Arencón Beltrán et al. (2022), and Pereira da Silva (2022). The DeepSeek platform was used to optimize content presentation.

Engagement Metrics And Technical Dimensions

The recorded metrics materialize the technical dimensions identified by Fuchs (2025)—particularly fascist prosumption and tabloidization—where the native properties of the X platform are instrumentalized to optimize the propagation of exclusionary narratives. The analysis demonstrates how the effectiveness of the discursive criminalization relied on a calculated digital engineering that combined reticular elements (hashtags, mentions) with emotional framing, operating through what Fielitz & Marcks (2020) conceptualize as "transmission belts" for the formation of "fast cultures of hate." The observed progression in the metrics—from the initial virality to the final saturation—evidences the capacity of digital fascism, in the specific case studied, to transform technical architectures into mechanisms of exclusionary political mobilization.

Analysis Of Viralization Dynamics And Discursive Transformation In Digital Fascism

The analysis for the second phase is grounded in the theoretical postulates of digital fascism developed by Fielitz & Holger (2020) and Pereira da Silva (2022), focusing specifically on what these authors conceptualize as "transmission belts" for the formation of "fast cultures of hate" in the digital ecosystem. The selection of source nodes was conducted by applying the technical dimension of digital fascism identified by Fuchs (2025), particularly the concept of fascist prosumption, where instrumentalized official accounts constitute central nodes for the production and dissemination of ideological content.

Tweet #1 (January 9, 2025) was selected as the foundational node of viralization due to its paradigmatic role in the fascist convergence described by Fuchs (2025), in which information, communication, and production technologies are integrated into a single digital platform for ideological dissemination. This tweet operated as a technical-discursive device that materialized fascist tabloidization by exploiting the internet's logic of high-speed flows of vast information, favoring decontextualization and sensationalism. Its exceptional metric (1.3 million views) evidences what Arencón Beltrán et al. (2022) identify as fascist cooperation through informal swarms that extend to the general public, establishing the discursive framework of "complicity with dictatorships" that would later be taken up and transformed by various actors.

Tweet #12 (April 9, 2025) constitutes a node of discursive closure that exemplifies the ultimate expression of what Pereira da Silva (2022) conceptualizes as a "perverse ideology of social division" under contemporary neoliberalism. This tweet materializes the organizational dimension of digital fascism through the construction of exclusive dichotomies that operate as devices for systematic polarization. Its technique of binary encapsulation represents the culmination of the process of bidirectional fascist surveillance, where the platform architecture is instrumentalized to transform political adversaries into existential enemies, achieving the highest amplification ratio in the corpus (28.5% retweets per like) during the period of peak electoral decisiveness.

The selection of these two extreme temporal nodes (campaign inception and closure) allows for the capture of the progression of the calculated digital engineering that characterizes digital fascism. It demonstrates how the reticular architectures of digital platforms are exploited to coordinate decentralized actions of exclusionary political mobilization, confirming the thesis of Arencón Beltrán et al. (2022) regarding its operation through informal swarms rather than classic hierarchical organizations.

Transformation Of Official Messages

The examination of twelve replies and quotes to Tweet #1—in which Daniel Noboa declared: “The kidnapping of María Corina by the regime of Nicolás Maduro exposes the brutality of a dictatorship that has sown death and misery... Any politician who defends, justifies, or remains silent in the face of these acts not only betrays democratic values but becomes an accomplice...”—reveals a complex discursive battlefield where the "fast cultures of hate" conceptualized by Fielitz & Marcks (2020) materialize. Far from mere unidirectional amplification, sophisticated mechanisms of resignification are observed, confirming the dialectical nature of digital fascism as a discursive battleground where meanings are contested and counter-narratives are constructed.

Accusatory inversion emerged as the most recurrent and effective transformation, where users exercise fascist prosumption in a counter-hegemonic direction. Node N001 (@Danielsalcan_) executes this strategy with technical precision, replying: “Yes, Mr. President, look at the brutality with which they repress and drag citizens and even uniformed schoolchildren on the ground... Oh no, sorry, I was confused, that's not Venezuela, it was here under your government. Oops ”. This response appropriates Noboa's original frame of "brutality in Venezuela" to redirect the accusation towards his own government, using irony as a device for discreditation. Similarly, N007 (@joffrecampana) employs a mimetic textual replica that copies the original tweet's syntactic structure, stating: “The death of the four children from Guayaquil under the regime of Daniel Noboa exposes the brutality of a dictatorship that has sown death and misery…”, creating a mirror effect that suggests Noboa's discourse describes his own reality better than Venezuela's, materializing what Fuchs (2025) identifies as interactive and multimedia fascism, but for counter-hegemonic purposes.

Factual verification constitutes the most devastating counter-power against institutional disinformation. Node N006 (@KatuArkonada) represents the most effective counter-analysis by dismantling the visual evidence used by Noboa, pointing out: “The President of Ecuador speaks about the dictatorship of Nicolás Maduro and uses a photo of Orlando Figueroa, who was murdered, stabbed, and burned alive by the opposition during the 2017 guarimbas.” This demonstrates that the image showed a victim of the Venezuelan opposition, not of official repression. This verification not only discredits the specific message but also constructs the notion of intentional disinformation by the institutional sender, applying the logic of fascist convergence for verificatory ends.

Responses From Different Positions Of Power

The analysis reveals how different institutional actors exercise discursive counter-power from differentiated positions of authority, confirming that digital fascism operates as a discursive battlefield where meanings are disputed. Nodes N004 (@ cristinajacomee) and N010 (@aquilesalvarez) represent intra-systemic resistance that leverages the organizational dimension of digital fascism to impose competing agendas. Assembly member Cristina Jácome (N004) replies to Noboa's original tweet with a deliberate contrast: "Worried about a foreign country giving public statements, but about #LosCuatroDeGuayaquilEcuador ABSOLUTE SILENCE. Disgusting any way you look at it!", using her institutional position to force a debate about local human rights violations instead of the Venezuelan framework proposed by the president.

Particularly significant is the case of the Mayor of Guayaquil (N010), who executes an inversion of the signifier "kidnapping" by declaring: "That's right, I totally repudiate what has happened in Venezuela [...] Something similar is happening here: You have the Constitution kidnapped for a change. Release it and if you win, win FAIRLY", thus accusing Noboa of "holding the Constitution hostage" and escalating the conflict to the highest institutional level. This intervention demonstrates that reticular architectures can be instrumentalized by multiple actors with access to differentiated viralization resources, even to confront official disinformation from positions of equivalent power.

Communication professionals, as observed in N011 (@fabriciovelav), provide criticism based on journalistic parameters that assess not only content but also public agenda management, applying what Arencón Beltrán et al. (2022) identify as strategies against isolation and the fostering of echo chambers from a position of professional authority. Journalist Fabricio Velasco replies: "President Noboa: this same forcefulness and speed in your statement was needed regarding the murder of the 4 children in Las Malvinas. Yes, let's condemn what happens abroad, but the priority must be what happens here, especially in something so painful", establishing a moral hierarchy of presidential attention and evaluating communicative behavior based on professional parameters of timeliness and relevance, which constitutes a form of technical resistance to the official framing.

Radicalization And Appropriation Of The Official Framework By Followers And Institutional Figures

Parallel to the counter-narratives, processes of radical amplification are observed, where users and official figures appropriated and intensified the original framework, materializing hate generation through the escalation of disqualifying epithets. Node N003 (@SoyBelenix) incorporates supplementary evidence—a screenshot of a tweet by Rafael Correa congratulating Nicolás Maduro—to validate and intensify the association with dictatorships, declaring: "The dictatorial and tyrannical regime most applauded by Rafael Correa, I would be ashamed to support RC5, you wretches!", using emotional and moralizing language to stigmatize supporters of Revolución Ciudadana. Meanwhile, N012 (@pippobetancourt) represents the ultimate expression of polarization by proposing concrete institutional consequences based on political exclusions: "If an Ecuadorian politician participates in the inauguration of Nicolas Maduro or defends the Maduro dictatorship, they must be expelled from any position or participation in the elections," thereby radicalizing the principle of political exclusion characteristic of digital fascism.

The analysis of reactions to Tweet #12—where Daniel Noboa posed: "You have 72 million dollars for security, where would you send it? Option 1: 'Peacemakers,' paramilitary groups of ex-gang members renamed, now armed and loyal only to the party. Option 2: National Police and Armed Forces, who have confronted real crime and defended Ecuadorian families"—reveals even greater technical sophistication in the strategies of discursive transformation. Node N013 (@andrscoronel) executes a mimetic appropriation of Noboa's dichotomous format but completely redirects the content, replying: "You have $94 million in debt to your country. What do you do? Option 1: you demonstrate that you care about your country and you pay it. Option 2: you play dumb and steal it," creating a critical mirror effect that contests the terrain of political morality. While Noboa presents "Armed Forces vs. paramilitaries," this node constructs "Pay debts vs. steal them," demonstrating the capacity of non-official actors to re-appropriate platforms' technical architectures for counter-hegemonic ends. It uses the same rhetorical structure as the official message to dismantle its moral credibility and expose what Pereira da Silva (2022) identifies as the "perverse ideology of social division" inherent to digital fascism.

Institutional Escalation Of Disinformation And High-Level Responses

The response from opposition candidate Luisa González (N019) represents the most significant transformation, coming from the main electoral contender. Her intervention executes a dismantling of the dichotomous framework proposed by Noboa, declaring: "NO, Noboa! Stop lying to the people. Our proposal articulates civil society, the community, and the neighborhoods under the direction and strengthening of the National Police, the community police, and the UPC." This refutes the claim that her proposal operates outside state security forces. Facing Noboa's fear-based framing, she constructs a dichotomy of hope vs. fear by affirming: "You have the fear, we have the hope!"—a mobilizing and positive counter-frame. This constitutes counter-hegemonic discourse at its peak, complemented by proactive hashtags like #PorLaVida and #RevivirEcuador.

The interventions by high-level officialist figures (N020, N021, N022, N023) demonstrate the institutionalization of disinformation from within the state apparatus. Assembly member Valen Centeno (N020) maximalistically radicalizes the frame by transforming the "peacemakers" proposal into an explicit description of "armed civilians, paid by the government, operating in parallel to the police and military, to repress and cause terror in the neighborhoods. Just like in Venezuela and Nicaragua." Meanwhile, the Minister of Human Development, Harold Burbano (N023), transfers the accusation to the realm of social policy, arguing: "Social assistance will not go directly to households but will pass through the filter of the 'managers' who will use the resources guided by their own interests... Those who do not 'align' will not benefit from anything." These interventions represent the ultimate expression of what Pereira da Silva (2022) identifies as the "instrumentalization of post-truth" characteristic of digital fascism, where institutional figures use their authority to validate and amplify disinformation frameworks, leveraging what Fuchs (2025) conceptualizes as fascist tabloidization by transforming public policy proposals into existential threats.

Uneven Impact Of Discursive Strategies In The Network

The analyzed engagement metrics confirm the formation of "fast cultures of hate," but with varying effectiveness depending on the type of discursive transformation and the sender's institutional position. Fact-checking nodes, such as N006 (@KatuArkonada), which pointed out: "The President of Ecuador speaks about the dictatorship of Nicolás Maduro and uses a photo of Orlando Figueroa, murdered, stabbed, and burned alive by the opposition during the 2017 guarimbas," and N008 (@LaKolmenaEC), which stated: "Rushing to replicate fake news, already debunked by Machado herself," generated significant engagement (300-900 likes, 200-600 retweets). This demonstrates that fact-based counter-narratives found resonance within the digital ecosystem.

Similarly, nodes employing accusatory inversion, such as N007 (@joffrecampana) with its mimetic textual replica—"The death of the four children from Guayaquil under the regime of Daniel Noboa exposes the brutality of a dictatorship that has sown death and misery..."—and N010 (@aquilesalvarez) with its forceful reply—"You, on the other hand, have the Constitution kidnapped. Release it and if you win, win FAIRLY"—achieved comparable levels of virality, evidencing the effectiveness of counter-framing strategies.

However, nodes of radical amplification from officialist positions (N020, N021) showed more modest metrics but possessed the strategic advantage of controlling the debate by disabling replies. For instance, Assembly member Valen Centeno (N020), by declaring: "Luisa González proposes 'peacemakers,' who are armed civilians, paid by the government, operating in parallel to the police and military, to repress and cause terror in the neighborhoods," managed to limit public rebuttal despite her lower quantitative engagement.

The intervention by former President Rafael Correa (N024, N025) demonstrates the highest level of sophistication in the coordinated opposition strategy. He employed structural parody with economic escalation by replicating: "You have 1.8 billion dollars from increasing the VAT by 3 points, what do you do?: Option 1: pay external debt. Option 2: use them honestly in the fight against organized crime," and provided strategic algorithmic amplification of candidate González's message by quoting her tweet in full accompanied by the comment: "Noboa: don't be mediocre." His ability to replicate Noboa's dichotomous format while drastically increasing the economic scale (from $72 million to $1.8 billion) demonstrates a technical-discursive mastery that equals and even surpasses the sophistication of the official message. This confirms that platform architectures can be effectively instrumentalized by non-official actors when communication expertise is combined with pre-existing political authority.

Metadata of Digital Fascism

Table 4. Analysis of Responses to Tweet #1 (January 9, 2025)

Node	Likes	Retweets	Replies	Content Type	User Type
N001	3,000	1,000	64	Text + emoji	Citizen
N002	2,000	620	92	Text	Citizen
N003	845	221	56	Text + image	Citizen
N004	851	208	10	Text + hashtag	Opposition Legislator
N005	854	183	14	Text	Citizen
N006	309	330	17	Text + image	Political Analyst
N007	904	590	23	Text + image	Citizen
N008	713	359	27	Text	Digital Media
N009	482	124	52	Text	Citizen
N010	5,000	2,000	-	Text	Mayor of Guayaquil
N011	3,000	1,000	310	Text	Journalist
N012	711	137	14	Text	Citizen

Source: Own elaboration, 2025.
Note: The DeepSeek platform was utilized to optimize content presentation.

The metadata analysis of Tweet #1 reveals that digital fascism, far from operating unidirectional, generates a discursive battlefield where its "transmission belts" (Fielitz & Marcks, 2020) are contested through sophisticated resistance mechanisms. Fascist prosumption is reappropriated for counter-hegemonic purposes by informal citizen swarms—as demonstrated by node N007, which garnered 904 likes through mimetic replication. Simultaneously, institutional actors (e.g., N010 with 5,000 likes) exercise intra-systemic resistance from positions of authority.

This evidence demonstrates that the very technical architectures which enable the viralization of disinformation—namely, fascist tabloidization and convergence (Fuchs, 2025)—also facilitate its deconstruction. This occurs through differentiated strategies such as factual verification, accusatory inversion, and the construction of competitive agendas. Although these counter-strategies exhibit uneven effectiveness, they collectively confirm the dialectical and profoundly contested nature of the digital ecosystem.

Table 5. Analysis of Responses to Tweet #12 (April 9, 2025)

Node	Likes	Retweets	Replies	Content Type	User Type
N013	1,000	393	67	Text	Citizen
N014	862	190	94	Text	Citizen
N015	981	63	28	Text + emojis	Government Supporter
N016	472	186	22	Text + image + hashtag	Citizen
N017	604	83	170	Text	Citizen
N018	458	126	29	Text + video + hashtag	Opposition Legislator
N019	3,000	1,000	1,000	Text + hashtags	Presidential Candidate
N020	264	134	-	Text	Government Legislator
N021	151	107	46	Text	Government Legislator
N022	91	42	-	Texto	Asambleísta oficialista
N023	39	21	17	Texto	Ministro oficialista
N024	2,000	1.000	269	Texto + hashtag	Expresidente
N025	2,000	859	510	Texto + hashtags	Expresidente

Source: Own elaboration, 2025.
Note: The DeepSeek platform was utilized to optimize content presentation.

The analysis of Tweet #12 as a node of discursive closure reveals the culmination of what Fielitz & Marcks (2020) conceptualize as "fast cultures of hate," where fascist tabloidization (Fuchs, 2025) reaches its maximum expression through binary dichotomies that materialize Pereira da Silva's (2022) "perverse ideology of social division." However, far from being a unidirectional amplification, a sophisticated counter-hegemonic resistance is observed. High-level opposition actors, such as presidential candidate Luisa González (N019: 3,000 likes) and former President Rafael Correa (N024-N025: 2,000 likes each), executed a mimetic appropriation of the official dichotomous format. They used the same reticular architectures to dismantle the disinformation framework through what Fuchs identifies as inverted fascist prosumption. Conversely, the officialist nodes (N020-N023) exhibited a notable incapacity for organic virality—with marginal engagement ranging from 39 to 264 likes—confirming that the mere state instrumentalization of exclusionary discourse does not guarantee its effectiveness in the digital ecosystem when it lacks citizen resonance. This demonstrates that digital fascism, in its closure phase, generates a battlefield where discursive efficacy depends critically on perceived authenticity and on the capacity to strategically reappropriate the very technical tools of digital authoritarianism.

CONCLUSION

This study approaches digital fascism as an analytical framework for examining specific patterns of political communication in the digital sphere. The findings indicate that, within the selected sample of tweets from the official account @ DanielNoboaOk between January and April 2025, there are recurrent discursive features align with the categories proposed by Arencón Beltrán et al. (2022). These patterns occur at varying frequencies across the analyzed tweets and suggest structured communicative tendencies within this corpus.

The empirical analysis shows that polarization and isolation/echo chamber dynamics are present in all analyzed tweets (12/12), consistently structuring messages through binary oppositions and closed interpretive frames. Hate generation appears in 11 of 12 tweets, while disinformation is identified in 10 of 12 cases, specifically when claims are presented without supporting evidence or when complex phenomena are simplified into assertive statements. Harassment appears in 8 out of 12 tweets, typically through direct or indirect accusations targeting identifiable political actors. These results indicate that the analyzed tweets frequently combine multiple reactionary categories within single communicative units.

Within this sample, these patterns are associated with discursive strategies that frame political competition in moral and antagonistic terms, frequently linking political adversaries to criminality, insecurity, or illegitimacy. The analysis also suggests that these strategies are often articulated through simplified narratives and emotionally charged language, which may contribute to high levels of engagement on the platform. However, engagement metrics are interpreted here as indicators of circulation and resonance, rather than as evidence of effectiveness in influencing electoral behavior.

Rather than establishing the existence of a coherent or unified strategy across the entirety of the actor's communication, the findings point to recurring tendencies within the selected tweets. In this sense, the concept of digital fascism is used as an analogical and heuristic tool to interpret how exclusionary, polarizing, and affect-driven forms of communication operate in this specific dataset.

This research contributes to the literature by providing an empirically grounded analysis of digital political communication in an Ecuadorian context, which remains underexplored in comparison to other regions. It highlights how certain discursive patterns—such as binary framing, stigmatizing language, and the presentation of unverified claims as facts—can coexist and reinforce each other within individual messages.

At the same time, several limitations must be acknowledged. The study is based on a small, non-random sample of tweets, which limits the possibility of generalizing findings to the broader communication strategy of the incumbent president-candidate. The analysis focuses exclusively on the X platform and does not account for cross-platform dynamics or the role of amplification networks such as media outlets, influencers, or automated accounts. Additionally, while the study identifies patterns of discourse, it does not establish causal relationships between these communicative practices and electoral outcomes.

Future research could expand the dataset, incorporate comparative cases, and integrate network analysis to better understand how these messages circulate and gain visibility within the digital ecosystem. A multi-platform approach would also allow for a more comprehensive assessment of the interaction between different channels of political communication.

From a public policy perspective, the findings underscore the importance of strengthening mechanisms that promote transparency, accountability, and critical media literacy in digital environments. Rather than advocating restrictive measures, the results point toward the need for tools that enable citizens to critically assess political content and for institutional frameworks that encourage responsible communication by public actors.

REFERENCES

Acker, A. (2018). How Fascism Went Digital: A Historian's Perspective on Bolsonaro's Victory in Brazil. *Geschichte und Gegenwart.*

Arencón Beltrán, S., Sola Morales, S., & Hernández Conde, M. (2022). Digital Fascism to Block Feminist Participation and Deliberation. Teknokultura. *Journal of Digital Culture and Social Movements, 19*(2), 123–135. DOI: 10.5209/tekn.81002

Eatwell, R., & Goodwin, M. (2018). *National Populism: The Revolt Against Liberal Democracy.* Penguin Books.

El Universo. (2025, January 15). Candidato vicepresidencial Diego Borja insiste en que son calumnias las denuncias sobre manejo de recursos de proveedora de Petroecuador. *El Universo.* https://www.eluniverso.com/noticias/politica/candidato-vicepresidencial-diego-borja-rc-fideicomiso-gesticon-contrato-petroecuador-downhole-tools-nota/

El Informante [@elinformante84]. (2025, March 28). *Los vínculos de @LuisaGonzalezEc con el #Narcotráfico saldrán a la luz, lo dijo hoy @DanielNoboaOk. Luisa realizó 24 viajes internacionales en el avión presidencial a PARAÍSOS FISCALES, SIN MANIFIESTO DE PASAJEROS Y SIN CONTROL DE CARGA. Lavó del narcotráfico y utilizó fondos del Estado* [Post]. X. https://x.com/elinformante84/status/1905679440899604861

Fielitz, M., & Marcks, H. (2020). *Digitaler Faschismus: Die sozialen Medien als Motor des Rechtsextremismus.* Dudenverlag.

Fuchs, C. (2025). What is Digital Fascism? *St. Antony's International Review, 20*(1), 26–39.

González, M. (2025, January 10). Ecuador cerró el 2024 con la segunda tasa de muertes violentas más alta de su historia, pese a una reducción importante. *Primicias.* https://www.primicias.ec/seguridad/ecuador-2024-tasa-muertes-violendas-segunda-peor-historia-87118/

Guamán, A., Aragoneses, A., & Martín, S. (Eds.). (2019). *Neofascismo: La Bestia Neoliberal.* Siglo XXI.

Herrera, S., & Macasoff, A. (2023). Daniel Noboa and the Exercise of "Landowner Power". *Ecuador Debate*, (20), 135–153.

La Posta [@LaPosta_Ecu]. (2025, August 8). *¡Las muertes violentas no bajan! Ecuador registró 4.619 homicidios entre enero y junio de 2025, una cifra histórica, según el Observatorio Ecuatoriano de Crimen Organizado. La cifra aumentó un 47% frente a 2024. Además, los asesinatos de menores de 10 a 19 años aumentaron un 68%, al pasar de 300 a 504 casos* [Post]. X. https://x.com/LaPosta_Ecu/status/1953819952147783791

Lozano, D. (2025, February 11). Noboa vincula al correísmo con la banda Los Lobos. *El Mundo*.

Molina Ramón, J. A., Moncada Landeta, K. T., & Torres Merino, J. F. (2025). Authoritarian Neoliberalism and Patrimonialism in the Daniel Noboa Azín Government. *Revista Veritas De Difusão Científica*, *6*(1), 2796–2838. https://doi.org/10.61616/rvdc.v6i1.547

Molina Ramón, J. A., & Moncada Landeta, K. T. (2024). Energy Crisis, Necropolitics and Simulacrum: The Ecuadorian Situation under the Daniel Noboa Administration. *Revista Veritas De Difusão Científica*, *5*(3), 1651–1673. DOI: 10.61616/rvdc.v5i3.304

Orlando [@Orlando62183489]. (2025, March 17). *Los lobos, latin king, choneros, cartel de nueva generación, cartel de sinaloa, cartel colombiano, far, eln, maduro, cristina, castro, ortega, ESTÁN HACIENDO CAMPAÑA POR LUISA GONZÁLEZ* [Post]. X. https://x.com/Orlando62183489/status/1901542085859098968

Paxton, R. O. (2007). *The Anatomy of Fascism*. Alfred A. Knopf.

Pereira da Silva, S. L. (2022). *O Irracionalismo de Conveniência: Ensaio Sobre Pós-Verdade, Fake News e a Psicopolítica do Fascismo Digital*. Editora Appris.

Restrepo Echavarría, R., & Oliván López, F. (2025). The Citizens' Revolution in Ecuador: A comparative history of political ideas, processes, and outcomes. *Humanities & Social Sciences Communications*, *12*, 1696. Advance online publication. https://doi.org/10.1057/s41599-025-05077-5

Rodrigues, M. G. (2024). Digital Fascism and School Violence: Subjective Deformation of Contemporary Neoliberalism? *Estilos da Clínica*, *29*(3), 359–377.

Safatle, V., da Silva Júnior, N., & Dunker, C. (2020). *Neoliberalismo como Gestão do Sofrimento Psíquico*. Autêntica.

Stanley, J. (2020). *How Fascism Works: The Politics of Us and Them*. Random House.

Traverso, E. (2019). *The New Faces of Fascism: Populism and the Far Right*. Verso.

Tufekci, Z. (2017). *Twitter and Tear Gas: The Power and Fragility of Networked Protest*. Yale University Press.

Chapter 4

Algorithmic Power and Digital Colonialism in the Age of Inequality and Resistance:

How Algorithms Reshape Power and Digital Life

S. Yogananthan
http://orcid.org/0009-0007-5583-0924
Faculty of Management Studies, CMS Business School, Jain University, India

Ravishankar S. Ulle
http://orcid.org/0009-0008-1011-8738
Faculty of Management Studies, CMS Business School, Jain University, India

Bharath Sampath
http://orcid.org/0000-0001-7721-2026
Faculty of Management Studies, CMS Business School, Jain University, India

Shashi Kant Dikshit
http://orcid.org/0000-0002-4760-1490
Faculty of Management Studies, CMS Business School, Jain University, India

Balaji Gopalan
http://orcid.org/0000-0002-1082-5597
Faculty of Management Studies, CMS Business School, Jain University, India

DOI: 10.4018/979-8-3373-4531-4.ch004

ABSTRACT

This chapter, critically examines the concept of digital colonialism and its influence on algorithmic power and authority in contemporary societies. It explores how algorithmic systems, governed by corporate and state actors, perpetuate new forms of control, centralization, and socio-technical inequality, often mirroring historical patterns of domination and dependency. The analysis maps mechanisms such as data extraction, surveillance, computational bias, and the creation of digital dependencies, demonstrating their impact on marginalized communities, particularly in the global South. By integrating critical theory, postcolonial studies, and empirical case analysis, this chapter interrogates the intersections of digital colonialism with related ideologies, such as digital imperialism and digital racism, and highlights resistance efforts and alternative digitalities that advocate for pluralistic and equitable digital futures.

INTRODUCTION: FRAMING DIGITAL COLONIALISM

Over the past decade, *digital colonialism* has gained prominence as a critical framework for understanding how older colonial logics are being reproduced through contemporary digital systems. The concept draws attention to the ways global digital infrastructures-largely owned and governed by multinational technology corporations headquartered in the Global North, particularly the United States-extend colonial patterns of control, extraction, and inequality into the digital realm (Couldry & Mejias, 2019; Nothias, 2025). Unlike classical colonialism, which relied on territorial conquest and direct political rule, digital colonialism operates through the control and commodification of intangible resources, including user data, algorithmic systems, and forms of digital labor. These processes generate new dependencies while sustaining long-standing structures of exploitation and cultural domination (Coleman, 2019; Kwet, 2019; Dahiya, 2023).

The intellectual foundations of digital colonialism can be traced to earlier debates on media imperialism, dependency theory, and postcolonial critiques of power and knowledge. Scholars such as Herbert Schiller (1969, 1989) and Thomas McPhail (1981) examined how the global expansion of Western media and communication infrastructures functioned as mechanisms of ideological influence and economic extraction, closely aligned with the interests of imperial states and corporations. Their work anticipated the rapid expansion of global communication networks and digital technologies in the late twentieth and early twenty-first centuries, developments that have dramatically intensified the scale, speed, and reach of asymmetric power relations (Couldry & Mejias, 2019; Nothias, 2025).

In contemporary contexts, digital colonialism is experienced both as a structural condition and as a lived reality. Structurally, it refers to the social, economic, and institutional arrangements that reproduce core–periphery dependencies within the digital economy. At the level of everyday life, it actively shapes how individuals and communities access information, participate in digital spaces, and understand themselves within global systems of power, particularly in the Global South (Coleman, 2019; Dahiya, 2023). Platforms such as Facebook and Google, for instance, now function as essential digital infrastructure in many African and South Asian countries. While these platforms provide connectivity and access, their dominance often deepens dependency, reinforces existing inequalities, and reproduces extractive relationships that once centered on land or minerals but are now organized around data extraction and algorithmic governance (Couldry & Mejias, 2019; Coleman, 2019; Dahiya, 2023).

When viewed historically, the parallels between colonial and digital forms of appropriation become difficult to ignore. During the colonial era, European powers carved up large territories, most notably during the "Scramble for Africa," to secure exclusive access to resources and markets. These actions were justified through narratives of civilizational advancement, modernization, and liberalization (Galeano & Allende, 1997; Schiller, 2000; Dahiya, 2023). Similar justificatory logics are visible today in the global expansion of digital platforms. Data centers, platforms, and connectivity initiatives are frequently established in countries that are economically marginalized yet rich in data-producing populations. Rather than fostering local technological autonomy or economic sovereignty, these infrastructures primarily serve to ensure continuous flows of data and user engagement, which are then monetized by corporations in the Global North-often under the rhetoric of closing the digital divide or democratizing access to information (Coleman, 2019; Kwet, 2019; Nothias, 2025).

Across disciplines such as media studies, sociology, economics, and international relations, scholars have identified recurring characteristics that define digital colonialism as a critical concept (Couldry & Mejias, 2019; Coleman, 2019; Dahiya, 2023; Nothias, 2025). First, there is a pronounced concentration of power, whereby a small number of predominantly U.S.-based technology corporations control global digital platforms, infrastructures, and technical standards, creating monopolistic dependencies reminiscent of earlier colonial arrangements (Kwet, 2019; Marker et al., 2019). Second, data extraction and commodification function as central mechanisms of digital colonialism. Personal data are harvested at scale-often without meaningful consent-and transformed into a global commodity that generates immense profits for core firms while deepening dependency in peripheral societies (Couldry & Mejias, 2019; Coleman, 2019).

A third dimension concerns cultural imperialism. Global platforms tend to privilege Western-centric languages, values, and knowledge systems, frequently marginalizing local epistemologies and alternative forms of expression (Nothias, 2025; Dahiya, 2023). Closely related is the issue of platform dependency, in which the design and governance of digital infrastructures undermine the technological sovereignty of states and communities in the Global South, reproducing cycles of reliance that closely resemble those of earlier imperial economies (Couldry & Mejias, 2019; Kwet, 2019). Finally, scholars highlight the role of benevolence discourses, through which technology companies frame their interventions in terms of empowerment, inclusion, and development narratives that echo colonial claims of progress while obscuring ongoing processes of extraction and control (Coleman, 2019; Dahiya, 2023).

As research on digital colonialism has evolved, increasing attention has been paid to the ways these dynamics intersect with local histories, political struggles, and forms of resistance (Dahiya, 2023; Nothias, 2025). Civil society organizations and activists across Africa, Latin America, and Asia are articulating alternative visions of digital futures, advocating for digital sovereignty, and challenging not only technical architectures but also the assumptions about consent, knowledge, and agency embedded within them (Couldry & Mejias, 2019; Coleman, 2019; Kwet, 2019). Within this growing body of work, the decolonization of digital infrastructures, governance frameworks, and knowledge systems is increasingly understood as a necessary condition for achieving global equity in the era of data capitalism (Dahiya, 2023; Pinto, 2018).

This chapter pursues four interconnected objectives. First, it conceptualizes digital colonialism as both a structural phenomenon and an experiential process. Second, it traces the historical and theoretical foundations of the concept across disciplines. Third, it synthesizes key debates and analytical frameworks within the existing literature. Finally, it advances critical questions for future research and policy: How do digital platforms and infrastructures reproduce and transform colonial power relations? What material, social, and epistemic consequences do these processes generate for marginalized communities worldwide? In what ways are actors in the Global South resisting, contesting, and reimagining digital domination? And what pathways exist toward digital sovereignty, justice, and pluralism under conditions of algorithmic governance?

Although digital colonialism, imperialism, racism, and panopticism are deeply interconnected, a rigorous analysis of digital domination requires that these phenomena be analytically distinguished. Each operates through distinct mechanisms, targets different dimensions of power, and produces specific forms of harm. At the same time, they reinforce one another: colonial relations rely on surveillance practices, imperial power is often encoded through racialized algorithmic standards, and racism sustains conditions of dependency that echo colonial hierarchies. Rather than treating these ideologies as separate, this chapter approaches them as an interconnected *ecosystem of domination*, in which each amplifies the effects of the others. The following sections, therefore, begin by establishing clear conceptual definitions before examining how these dynamics interact in practice through case studies of Free Basics, Instagram Reels, and data localization.

Table 1. Conceptual Distinctions among Digital Ideologies-Theoretical Distinctions Among Digital Ideologies: Definitions, Mechanisms, and Examples

Dimension	Digital Colonialism	Digital Imperialism	Digital Racism	Digital Panopticism
Core Logic	Asymmetric extraction and dependency	Economic dominance and cultural hegemony	Racial discrimination is perpetuated through systems	Surveillance as modality/ mechanism (not ideology)
What is Being Appropriated/ Controlled?	Intangible resources: data, algorithmic labor, cultural knowledge	Technological standards, infrastructure, and epistemic norms	Access to opportunity, freedom from targeting, recognition	Behavioral information and predictive knowledge
Primary Mechanism	Large-scale data harvesting and commodification; creation of platform dependency	Standard-setting; norm-imposition; global dominance of infrastructure	Encoding historical bias into ML systems; algorithmic sorting and targeting	Continuous monitoring; behavioral prediction; invisible discipline
Structural Outcome	Peripheral communities dependent on core platforms; value flows North	Marginalized alternatives; epistemologies excluded; irreversibility of dominance	Systematic disadvantage of racialized groups across domains	Self-regulation; normalized surveillance; constrained agency
Scale of Impact	Core-periphery relationship (Global North ↔ Global South)	Global (affects all users)	Racialized populations across all regions	Universal (affects all digital users)
Concrete Historical Example	Facebook's Free Basics (2013-2015): promise of free access masking data extraction	Google search dominance: algorithm determines information hierarchies globally	Facial recognition bias: 10-100x error rates on darker skin tones	WeChat social credit: continuous monitoring integrated into citizenship
Contemporary Example	Instagram's suppression of Dalit creators while extracting their data	Meta's global algorithmic standards applied without Indian input	Instagram's content moderation bias against minority voices	Every platform's continuous behavioral tracking via cookies, pixels, and analytics
Is This an Ideology?	**Yes** – Justifies extraction as "development," "empowerment," "innovation"	**Yes** – Justifies dominance as "progress," "efficiency," "universal standards."	**Yes** – Justifies discrimination as "objectivity," "safety," "community standards"	**No** – A mechanism/ infrastructure through which ideologies operate
Relationship to other Ideologies	Requires panopticism (surveillance) to enable extraction; often imperial	Requires panopticism to impose standards; encodes racism in standards	Embedded in all platforms; intensified through panoptical surveillance	Infrastructure for colonialism (enables extraction), imperialism (normalizes standards), racism (enables discrimination)
Whose Power is Concentrated?	Technology corporations (as extractors) vs. users (as data sources)	Transnational technology corporations (as standard-setters)	Dominant racial groups (via biased algorithms)	Surveillance actors (platforms + states)
Key Question for Resistance	How do we stop extraction? (Right to data deletion, local data storage)	How do alternatives compete? (Open-source standards, local innovation)	How do we debias systems? (Diverse teams, algorithm audits)	How do we reduce surveillance? (Encryption, anonymity)

Algorithmic Authority and Structural Power

Algorithmic authority has become one of the central mechanisms through which digital technologies shape contemporary knowledge production, information circulation, cultural identity, and social participation. Much of this influence operates beneath the threshold of everyday awareness, remaining largely invisible to those most affected by it (Beer, 2016; Gillespie, 2014). Unlike authority derived from formal institutions or legal mandates, algorithmic authority emerges from the deep and routine embedding of computational systems within digital infrastructures, social media platforms, and organizational decision-making processes. Through this integration, algorithms quietly but decisively mediate access to information, opportunities, and social resources (Pasquale, 2015; Kitchin, 2017).

The structural power of algorithms lies in their capacity to encode specific social, political, and economic values into technical systems that govern data extraction, content curation, recommendation, moderation, and automated decision-making. These processes are not merely technical operations; they reflect design choices, institutional priorities, and normative assumptions that shape how digital environments function and whom they serve (Bucher, 2018; Seaver, 2019). As such, algorithms function as instruments of governance, translating abstract values into concrete, often consequential outcomes.

One of the most visible effects of algorithmic authority is its role in shaping knowledge production. By filtering, ranking, and prioritizing content, algorithms determine what becomes visible, credible, and influential within digital ecosystems. Search engines, for instance, rely on complex ranking mechanisms that elevate certain sources while relegating others to obscurity, thereby shaping public discourse and collective understanding (Introna & Nissenbaum, 2000; Noble, 2018). Social media platforms similarly deploy algorithmic curation to personalize news feeds and content streams, amplifying particular narratives and cultural expressions while marginalizing alternative perspectives (Gillespie, 2018; Couldry & Mejias, 2019). These processes are governed by opaque relevance and engagement metrics that embed commercial incentives alongside sociocultural biases, influencing which knowledge claims gain legitimacy and reach (Diakopoulos, 2016). Over time, this results in a reconfiguration of epistemic authority, as algorithmically mediated systems increasingly displace traditional gatekeepers such as editors, educators, and cultural institutions (Beer, 2017).

Algorithms also play a significant role in shaping cultural identity. Through data-driven profiling, individuals and groups are categorized, segmented, and represented based on patterns inferred from their digital traces (Andrejevic, 2014; Cheney-Lippold, 2017). Recommendation systems construct highly personalized cultural environments that can facilitate discovery and engagement, but they also risk confining users within so-called "filter bubbles," where existing preferences and identities are continuously reinforced (Pariser, 2011; Bozdag, 2013). These dynamics often reproduce and intensify social inequalities. Marginalized communities, in particular, are more likely to experience misclassification, heightened surveillance, or exclusion within algorithmic systems, reflecting and amplifying broader structures of discrimination (Noble, 2018; Benjamin, 2019). At the same time, participation itself is increasingly governed through automated mechanisms-such as content moderation algorithms and behavior-tracking technologies-that convert complex social and political judgments into technical rules, frequently without transparent justification or avenues for redress (Gillespie, 2018; Roberts, 2019).

The technical foundations of algorithmic authority rest on several interrelated mechanisms. Large-scale data extraction enables the collection of vast amounts of personal and behavioral information, often without users' full awareness or meaningful consent (Tufekci, 2018; Zuboff, 2019). Processes of data curation and feature engineering then determine which variables are selected, emphasized, or transformed into inputs for machine-learning models, embedding normative assumptions into ostensibly neutral systems (O'Neil, 2016; Kearns & Roth, 2019). Recommendation algorithms typically rely on optimization strategies designed to maximize engagement, often privileging sensational, emotionally charged, or polarizing content, thereby distorting public attention and debate (Tufekci, 2015; Gillespie, 2017). Automated content moderation systems, trained on previously flagged material, seek to enforce platform standards at scale, yet they often struggle with contextual nuance, leading to over-blocking, inconsistent enforcement, or biased outcomes (Roberts, 2019; Kelly, 2021). Beyond content governance, predictive models are increasingly deployed in high-stakes decision-making contexts-such as credit scoring, policing, and welfare administration-raising serious concerns about fairness, transparency, and due process (Barocas, Hardt, & Narayanan, 2019; Selbst et al., 2019).

These developments carry far-reaching implications for governance and citizenship. Public institutions have increasingly adopted algorithmic systems for administrative and regulatory functions, often justified in terms of efficiency, objectivity, and cost reduction. In practice, however, such systems can centralize control, obscure responsibility, and weaken democratic accountability (Kroll et al., 2017; Eubanks, 2018). Algorithmic governance frequently expands surveillance capacities, concentrates discretionary power, and disproportionately affects marginalized populations (Brayne, 2017; Ferguson, 2017). At the same time, corporate platforms exercise de facto authority over speech, visibility, and participation in digital spaces, effectively assuming functions traditionally associated with the public sphere and raising concerns about the privatization of democratic infrastructure (MacKinnon, 2012; Gillespie, 2018). Persistent data harvesting and behavioral inference further undermine privacy and autonomy, as personal information is used to shape choices and influence behavior in subtle, often imperceptible ways (Cohen, 2019; Zuboff, 2019). As a result, individual agency is increasingly constrained within environments structured by algorithmic logics that remain largely inaccessible to user understanding or control (Kitchin, 2017).

Critical theoretical perspectives provide essential tools for interpreting algorithmic authority as a contemporary extension of disciplinary power and epistemic control (Foucault, 1977; Rouvroy & Berns, 2013). From this standpoint, algorithms are not neutral instruments but active participants in systems of governance that construct subjects through processes of datafication, classification, and prediction (Beer, 2016; Seaver, 2019). The opacity of these systems-frequently defended on the grounds of proprietary protection-poses significant obstacles to transparency and accountability, limiting possibilities for democratic oversight and contestation (Pasquale, 2015; Diakopoulos, 2016). Empirical research consistently demonstrates that algorithmic bias often reflects historical and social inequalities embedded within training data and model design, resulting in discriminatory outcomes across lines of race, gender, and class (Buolamwini & Gebru, 2018; Benjamin, 2019). Moreover, the concentration of infrastructural power among a small number of dominant technology corporations consolidates control over knowledge, participation, and civic life, reinforcing dynamics that are closely aligned with broader critiques of digital colonialism and digital imperialism (Couldry & Mejias, 2019; Kwet, 2019).

Table 2. Domains of Algorithmic Influence and Authority

Domain	Description	Mechanisms & Examples	Socio-Political Implications
Epistemic Governance	Algorithms as gatekeepers of knowledge, shaping what counts as valid information and who gets heard	Search rankings (Google), academic databases, and newsfeed curation	Reinforces dominant knowledge systems; marginalizes alternative epistemologies (Introna & Nissenbaum, 2000; Noble, 2018)
Cultural Governance	Personalization and categorization of cultural identity, content, and social participation	Recommendation systems (YouTube, TikTok, Instagram), content moderation	Shapes identities via filter bubbles; enforces normative cultural standards; excludes marginalized voices (Pariser, 2011; Benjamin, 2019)
Administrative Governance	Algorithmic decision-making in governmental and organizational contexts affecting resource allocation and rights	Predictive policing, credit scoring, welfare eligibility algorithms	Redefines citizenship experience; raises concerns about privacy, fairness, accountability (Eubanks, 2018; Barocas et al., 2019)

Understanding how these overlapping domains operate together is essential for developing inclusive policy responses and ethical frameworks that can democratize algorithmic governance and resist digital colonial power formations (Beer, 2017; Gillespie, 2018; Couldry & Mejias, 2019). Insights from critical theory-particularly Foucault's notion of governmentality-are especially useful here, as they illuminate how algorithms function as disciplinary regimes that regulate conduct through surveillance, normalization, and predictive control (Foucault, 1977; Rouvroy & Berns, 2013). From this perspective, algorithmic systems operate as *epistemic apparatuses*: they determine what counts as legitimate knowledge, how populations are categorized, and which behaviors are rewarded or sanctioned. While echoing the logic of the disciplinary gaze, these systems introduce new layers of complexity through large-scale datafication and machine learning, thereby intensifying asymmetries of normative power (Beer, 2016; Seaver, 2019). Algorithmic outputs increasingly acquire the status of authoritative truths, shaping policy decisions, resource allocation, and forms of cultural recognition in ways that are difficult to contest.

Empirical research demonstrates how these dynamics unfold across multiple domains. In the context of criminal justice, predictive policing systems such as COMPAS in the United States have been promoted as tools for enhancing efficiency and objectivity. However, investigative studies reveal that these systems reproduce and amplify racial bias, assigning higher risk scores to individuals from communities of color and contributing to harsher policing outcomes (Angwin et al., 2016; Richardson, Schultz, & Crawford, 2019). Rather than correcting structural inequities, such tools often legitimize them by embedding historical patterns of discrimination within ostensibly neutral computational models. Similar patterns are evident in financial systems, where credit-scoring algorithms have been shown to replicate gendered and racial inequalities, restricting access to loans and financial services for marginalized populations (Barocas, Hardt, & Narayanan, 2019). Together, these cases challenge claims of algorithmic neutrality and underscore how socio-historical inequalities are encoded into automated decision-making processes.

In cultural and media environments, algorithmic recommendation systems shape public discourse by constructing personalized yet increasingly insular digital ecosystems. Research on YouTube's recommendation algorithm, for example, indicates that it tends to amplify sensational and extremist content in pursuit of engagement metrics, thereby facilitating radicalization, polarization, and the formation of echo chambers (O'Callaghan et al., 2015; Ribeiro et al., 2020). While such systems enhance content discoverability, they simultaneously distort collective attention and undermine social cohesion. Content moderation algorithms present a related set of challenges. These systems frequently struggle to interpret linguistic, cultural, and political context, resulting in the disproportionate removal of minority voices and nuanced political expression. Such outcomes raise serious concerns about digital rights, representation, and unequal access to public visibility (Roberts, 2019; Jhaver et al., 2019).

Technological opacity further compounds these problems. Platform companies rarely disclose the data sources, criteria, or decision-making logics underlying their algorithms, often citing proprietary interests or technical complexity as justification (Pasquale, 2015). This "black box" condition severely limits independent scrutiny and meaningful contestation, effectively shielding algorithmic authority from democratic oversight (Diakopoulos, 2016). Regulatory efforts have attempted to address this imbalance. Article 22 of the European Union's General Data Protection Regulation (GDPR), for instance, provides individuals with certain rights concerning automated decision-making. Yet its scope and enforcement remain limited, particularly beyond European jurisdictions, leaving many users subject to algorithmic governance without adequate transparency or recourse (Veale, Van Kleek, & Binns, 2018).

From a political economy perspective, the consolidation of algorithmic infrastructure within a small group of predominantly U.S.-based technology corporations represents a contemporary manifestation of digital colonialism and imperialism (Couldry & Mejias, 2019; Kwet, 2019). These firms exercise control not only over computational resources and data flows but also over agenda-setting processes that shape global knowledge circulation and cultural consumption. This concentration of power mirrors colonial-era patterns of resource extraction, now reconfigured through data harvesting, surveillance, and monetization (Zuboff, 2019). Efforts by states in the Global South to assert digital sovereignty face substantial technological, legal, and economic barriers, reinforcing dependency and constraining local autonomy in digital governance (Kwet, 2019).

Algorithmic governance also reshapes relationships between citizens and the state. Automated systems are increasingly deployed in administrative contexts, influencing access to welfare benefits, policing practices, and immigration decisions (Eubanks, 2018). In the United Kingdom, for example, algorithmic components of the Universal Credit welfare program have been shown to generate errors that disproportionately penalize vulnerable recipients, deepening social insecurity rather than alleviating it (Bardall, 2016). In China, social credit systems integrate extensive data aggregation and artificial intelligence to monitor and rank citizens' behavior, raising significant concerns about pervasive surveillance and social control (Creemers, 2018; Yeung, 2018). These cases illustrate how algorithmic governance can entrench authoritarian practices and transform citizenship itself, often in the absence of broad public debate or democratic participation.

Taken together, these theoretical and empirical insights reveal algorithmic authority as a layered and multifaceted form of structural power. Through data and computation, algorithms govern knowledge production, cultural visibility, and political participation in ways that are both pervasive and difficult to detect. Their integration into everyday digital experiences renders this authority elusive, even as its consequences become increasingly consequential. Addressing these challenges requires interdisciplinary approaches that combine critical theory, computational ethics, legal reform, and grassroots activism to democratize algorithmic infrastructures and imagine more equitable forms of digital governance.

Intersectional Analysis: Methodology and Application

This chapter adopts intersectionality as both a theoretical framework and an analytical method. Coined by legal scholar Kimberlé Crenshaw (1989) and further developed by Black feminist thinkers, intersectionality emphasizes that systems of oppression-such as racism, sexism, capitalism, and caste hierarchy-do not operate independently. Rather, they are *mutually constitutive*, interacting in ways that compound disadvantage and produce forms of subordination that cannot be understood by examining any single axis in isolation.

Here, intersectionality is used to analyze how digital colonialism, racism, imperialism, and panopticism simultaneously shape the lived experiences of marginalized communities. The focus is not on how caste, *gender, and* language function as separate variables, but on how they intersect to produce distinct configurations of power and vulnerability. This approach moves beyond additive models of analysis toward a structural understanding of how specific identity formations generate particular forms of marginalization in digital environments.

Defining Intersectionality in Digital Contexts: What Intersectionality Is (and Is Not)

Intersectionality is frequently misinterpreted as a simple acknowledgment that individuals possess "multiple identities." Such readings dilute the political and analytical force of the concept. A more precise understanding is therefore essential.

Within the framework of intersectional analysis, applying the solidarity principle is essential to avoid replicating the extractive logics of digital colonialism in the methodologies. The solidarity principle demands that researchers work alongside marginalized communities rather than treating them as passive subjects of data extraction. In practice, this means prioritizing Participatory Action Research and co-creating knowledge that directly benefits the communities involved.

For example, in algorithmic auditing, researchers applying this principle partner directly with gig economy workers in the Global South to reverse-engineer platform algorithms. By crowdsourcing worker data, these research coalitions can expose discriminatory pricing or opaque penalization mechanisms that disproportionately affect racialized or migrant workers. Another critical application is found in the

Indigenous Data Sovereignty movement. Here, researchers collaborate with Indigenous groups to establish community-governed data trusts. Instead of extracting local ecological or cultural knowledge to train corporate artificial intelligence models, scholars work under the community's strict protocols to ensure that the data remains protected and serves local needs. Through these methodological interventions, the solidarity principle ensures that digital research actively disrupts colonial power dynamics, transforming academic inquiry into a tool for systemic equity and localized technological empowerment.

Intersectionality is:

- A structural framework for analyzing how systems of oppression interact and reinforce one another.
- An approach that recognizes oppression as relational and mutually shaped, rather than separable.
- An understanding that, for example, the experiences of a Dalit woman are not reducible to the sum of caste discrimination and gender discrimination, but represent a distinct structural position.

Intersectionality is not:

- A descriptive listing of identities (e.g., "Dalit, queer, rural woman")
- An additive model that studies different forms of discrimination separately and then aggregates findings

This distinction is particularly important in digital contexts. Platform diversity and inclusion initiatives often invoke intersectionality rhetorically while implementing additive strategies, such as increasing representation of women, minority creators, or LGBTQ+ users as separate categories. Such approaches fail to address the structural conditions that produce exclusion in the first place. Only an intersectional analysis makes it possible to confront root causes rather than settle for symbolic or cosmetic inclusion.

Specifying Axes of Analysis: Axes of Marginalization Examined in This Chapter

Drawing on South Asian contexts, this chapter focuses on five primary and intersecting axes of marginalization:

- Caste (with particular emphasis on the Indian context)
- Gender and sexuality
- Language and linguistic identity

- Geography and spatial location
- Economic class and the formality or informality of labor

These axes are not treated as discrete variables but as interlocking dimensions that shape how digital power is experienced and contested.

Methodological Commitment

Methodologically, this chapter follows what intersectional scholars describe as the *solidarity principle*: analytical inquiry begins from the standpoint of those most marginalized, rather than from institutional perspectives or elite narratives.

In practice, this means shifting the framing of research questions. Instead of asking, "How does Meta's algorithm function?" the analysis asks, "What is the lived experience of a Dalit woman creator navigating Instagram?" Rather than prioritizing the intentions of platform designers, the chapter foregrounds the experiences of communities' subject to algorithmic harm and exclusion. Platforms are not treated as neutral tools that incidentally produce bias; instead, attention is directed toward the design choices, policies, and organizational logics that generate specific harms for particular groups.

This commitment is reflected throughout the chapter in several ways:

- Case studies are narrated through the experiences of marginalized creators and communities, with institutional analysis providing contextual grounding
- Claims about marginalization are supported by empirical evidence, including qualitative research, creator testimonies, and community-based studies
- The analysis interrogates not only what algorithmic systems do, but whose interests they serve and who benefits from their operation
- The chapter explicitly acknowledges limits of research access, recognizing that some communities are better documented than others and that linguistic, safety, and access constraints shape what can be studied

CASE STUDIES OF DIGITAL COLONIALISM

To grasp how digital colonialism operates beyond abstraction, it is necessary to examine concrete sites where corporate platforms, algorithmic infrastructures, and state policies intersect to shape everyday digital life. These intersections do not merely distribute access to technology; they actively organize inclusion and exclusion within enduring global and internal hierarchies. This section analyzes three illustrative cases: Facebook's Free Basics initiative in the Global South, Instagram

Reels as a site of algorithmic and cultural gatekeeping in post-TikTok India, and India's data localization policies as a contested effort to negotiate sovereignty within asymmetric digital infrastructures.

Facebook's Free Basics: Connectivity, Control, and Controversy in the Global South

Launched in 2013 in partnership with local telecom providers, Facebook's Free Basics program offered zero-rated access to a limited set of websites-primarily Facebook, Messenger, Wikipedia, and selected health and education portals-while placing the rest of the internet behind a paywall. Marketed as an initiative for "digital inclusion," Free Basics was rolled out across countries such as India, Nigeria, and Kenya. In practice, however, it replaced open internet access with a restricted, corporately curated environment in which Facebook functioned as the default gateway to online life for many first-time users.

Rather than closing the digital divide, Free Basics reconfigured it. Access was conditional, selective, and shaped by Facebook's commercial priorities. Crucially, the harms produced by this model were not uniform. Instead, they varied sharply across lines of caste, gender, language, geography, and class, illustrating how digital colonialism operates through intersectional forms of exclusion rather than through a single, homogeneous mechanism.

Rural Women: Geography, Gender, And Infrastructure

Free Basics explicitly targeted rural women as beneficiaries of connectivity, yet structural constraints quickly limited its emancipatory potential. Irregular electricity, shared or borrowed devices, and restrictive gender norms meant that access was often brief, supervised, and socially risky. In many cases, women's online activity occurred under family oversight, constraining privacy and autonomy. While the program framed connectivity as "free," it left these material and social barriers untouched, even as it continued to extract and monetize women's data.

Lower-Caste Communities: Epistemic Marginalization

The content ecosystem within Free Basics overwhelmingly privileged English-language, state-sanctioned, and Western-aligned knowledge sources. Dalit, Adivasi, and vernacular epistemologies were largely absent or marginalized. Lower-caste users contributed data and engagement to the platform, yet encountered an informational environment that erased their histories and positioned "opportunity" within institutions already structured by caste bias. In this way, Free Basics reproduced epistemic hierarchies under the guise of access.

LGBTQ+ Users: Safety, Visibility, And Constrained Agency

For LGBTQ+ users in socially conservative contexts, Free Basics often became a site of heightened vulnerability rather than empowerment. Shared devices, family surveillance, and heteronormative content ecosystems limited safe self-expression. Algorithmic visibility was tightly constrained, and privacy risks were amplified. Queer Dalit and lower-caste users faced especially compounded forms of erasure and risk, as caste, sexuality, and surveillance intersected within a restricted digital environment.

Unbanked and Informal Workers: Economic exclusion

Although Free Basics promoted links to jobs, skills training, and e-commerce, these pathways implicitly assumed access to formal banking, identification documents, and discretionary time and resources unavailable to many unbanked and informal workers. As a result, promised economic opportunities remained largely symbolic. Structural exclusion from financial and labor systems was reframed as individual failure to "leverage" connectivity.

Synthesis: Compounding harms

The experience of a rural Dalit woman without reliable electricity, access to private devices, or banking infrastructure captures the intersecting nature of these harms. She encounters English-dominant, caste-aligned content and unreachable economic portals, while her limited engagement still generates valuable data for the platform. Her situation reveals digital colonialism not as a single-axis problem of access, but as a convergence of colonial extraction, caste hierarchy, patriarchy, class exploitation, and surveillance-dynamics that cannot be addressed through narrow or technocratic interventions.

Instagram Reels and Algorithmic Gatekeeping

Following the ban on TikTok in India, Instagram Reels rapidly became a central short-video platform for youth, artists, and activists. However, its opaque recommendation and moderation systems soon emerged as powerful gatekeeping mechanisms. The algorithm consistently privileges Anglophone, urban, upper-caste, and "aspirational" aesthetics, while down-ranking or removing content produced by

Dalit, Adivasi, feminist, queer, and explicitly political creators, particularly when such content challenges dominant social narratives.

Creators working in vernacular languages or addressing caste, gender, and sexuality report disproportionate experiences of shadow banning, guideline violations, and suppressed reach. What is presented as an open and meritocratic platform thus operates as a stratified visibility regime.

Vernacular creators drawing on local idioms, histories, and musical traditions find their content more likely to be flagged or buried, while affluent, Western-influenced creators enjoy smoother paths to virality and monetization. In response, marginalized creators engage in hashtag activism, open letters, and tactical efforts to "game" the algorithm. Yet these strategies require additional labor and offer only fragile gains, as the underlying platform logic remains opaque and structurally biased.

Dalit Creators And Algorithmic Suppression

Caste-political and anti-caste content is disproportionately flagged, down-ranked, or shadow-banned relative to mainstream entertainment. This reflects a form of digital casteism, in which critiques of caste hierarchy are treated as risky or disruptive, while dominant-caste aesthetics and narratives are normalized and rewarded.

Dalit women creators: Compounded suppression

Content produced by Dalit women addressing caste–gender violence, sexuality, or domestic labor is particularly vulnerable to being labeled "sensitive" or "sexual," leading to restricted visibility. The interaction of misogyny and caste bias significantly narrows the expressive space available to Dalit women compared with both Dalit men and upper-caste women.

LGBTQ+ Dalit Creators: Intersecting Marginalization

Queer Dalit creators experience elevated rates of content removal, harassment, and pressure to self-censor, as caste, gender, or sexuality, and algorithmic bias converge. Their risks and invisibility exceed those faced by upper-caste queer creators or cisgender, heterosexual Dalit creators.

Vernacular Creators And Linguistic Marginalization

Instagram Reels systematically favors English and metropolitan Hindi, while regional languages such as Tamil, Telugu, Bhojpuri, and others begin from a lower baseline reach and weaker monetization potential. Because vernacular creators are often lower-caste, non-metro, and economically precarious, linguistic marginalization translates directly into compounded socio-economic exclusion.

Resistance, Counter-Strategies, And Limits

Marginalized creators deploy a range of tactics, including mutual amplification, coded language, hybrid "trend plus politics" formats, and migration to alternative platforms. While these practices demonstrate resilience and creativity, they remain precarious and labor-intensive. Meaningful transformation ultimately depends on changes to platform governance, transparency, and external regulation rather than on individual adaptation alone.

India's Data Localization Policy: Negotiating Sovereignty and Infrastructural Power

Since 2018, India's data localization agenda, advanced through Reserve Bank of India directives, draft data protection bills, and the Digital Personal Data Protection (DPDP) Act, has been framed as an effort to reclaim sovereignty from foreign technology corporations. By mandating domestic storage and processing of Indian users' data, the policy seeks to reduce dependence on external infrastructures.

Multinational firms have responded by building local data centers and reconfiguring services. At the same time, large domestic conglomerates-most notably Reliance Jio-have positioned themselves as national champions, expanding their influence across cloud services, platforms, and digital infrastructure markets.

The outcomes of localization, however, are deeply ambivalent. While the policy modestly shifts bargaining power away from U.S.- and China-centric infrastructures, control over technical standards, capital, and expertise remains concentrated among a small set of global and national actors. At the same time, domestic state agencies gain easier access to extensive data repositories under broad national security and public order justifications, raising serious concerns about surveillance and civil liberties.

State Sovereignty And Domestic Oligarchy

Although localization and the DPDP Act are presented as tools to curb Big Tech dominance, they often redirect control toward the Indian state and large domestic conglomerates with integrated telecom, platform, and cloud operations. Smaller firms, start-ups, and providers in peripheral regions face disproportionate compliance costs, widening existing inequalities within the digital ecosystem.

Surveillance Expansion And Marginalized Communities

Domestic data storage facilitates easier access for law enforcement and intelligence agencies through local legal mechanisms, which frequently rely on expansive security provisions. Communities that are already subject to heightened policing, rural populations, lower-caste groups, Muslims, Adivasis, and informal workers face denser and more searchable data trails, often without the legal literacy or resources required to contest misuse. In such contexts, "protection from Big Tech" can translate into intensified state visibility.

Regional and Class Impacts: Who bears the cost?

The infrastructure demands of localization can increase operational costs, which are often passed on through higher prices, reduced functionality, or delayed service rollout in low-income and rural regions. Urban, affluent users and large corporations tend to capture the benefits, while peripheral users pay more for less reliable or restricted services.

Intersectional Burden: Rural Lower-Caste Women

For a rural Dalit woman with precarious connectivity and limited awareness of data rights, localization places her data closer to local authorities even as rising costs or degraded services may further restrict her access. Gendered and caste-based monitoring of "improper" online behavior can intensify, illustrating how national claims of data sovereignty can coexist with deepened internal domination.

Comparative Insights and Synthesis

Viewed together, Free Basics, Instagram Reels, and India's data localization agenda reveal how both privatized and state-backed digital infrastructures govern access, speech, and visibility through proprietary architectures that echo colonial forms of control. Whether through Free Basics' whitelisted internet, Reels' recommendation algorithms, or localization mandates, rules and algorithms function as gatekeepers that systematically disadvantage lower-caste, rural, Indigenous, feminist, queer, and vernacular communities via invisibility, misclassification, and economic exclusion.

Resistance is evident through net-neutrality movements, creator activism, and alternative platforms, but these gains remain fragile and uneven, while structural hierarchies largely persist. Data localization highlights this ambivalence most sharply: policies designed to counter foreign dominance can simultaneously empower domestic oligopolies and expand state surveillance without democratizing digital infrastructure or epistemic authority. Benefits tend to accrue to urban, affluent, and digitally literate users, while marginalized groups face higher costs, degraded services, and intensified monitoring.

Across all three cases, intersectional analysis demonstrates that those situated at the intersections of caste, gender, class, language, and geography bear the heaviest burdens, while dominant actors-global platforms, domestic conglomerates, and security institutions-consolidate control.

From Case Studies to Interlocking Digital Dominations

Although the three cases involve distinct actors and policy mechanisms, each activates multiple, overlapping forms of digital domination. Colonialism appears through extraction and dependency; imperialism through standard-setting and epistemic authority; racism and casteism through discriminatory visibility and harm; and panopticism through pervasive surveillance infrastructures. Free Basics combines data extraction, epistemic erasure, and behavioral tracking. Instagram Reels monetizes creative labor while enforcing Western and upper-caste aesthetic norms and disciplining dissent through opaque moderation. Data localization challenges foreign control, yet risks entrenching domestic corporate power and expanding state surveillance without dismantling internal hierarchies.

The central insight is that piecemeal interventions-whether data rights, transparency mandates, or national sovereignty policies pursued in isolation-address only one dimension of a multidimensional system. As a result, domination is often displaced rather than dismantled. An integrated framework of *Interlocking Digital Dominations* therefore argues that meaningful digital decolonization must operate simultaneously across four fronts: redistributing data ownership and value (colonialism), democratizing infrastructures and standards (imperialism), centering marginalized epistemologies and confronting caste and racial bias (racism), and fundamentally constraining surveillance capacities (panopticism).

HOW DIGITAL IDEOLOGIES INTERLOCK AND REINFORCE DOMINATION: THE FRAMEWORK OF INTERLOCKING DIGITAL DOMINATIONS

Digital colonialism, digital imperialism, digital racism, and digital panopticism do not operate as isolated or sequential forms of power. Rather, they constitute an interlocking ecosystem of domination, in which each ideology enables, stabilizes, and amplifies the others. Treating them as separate problems-privacy, monopoly power, algorithmic bias, or surveillance obscures how contemporary digital domination functions systemically and why single-issue interventions repeatedly fail.

This section develops the framework of Interlocking Digital Dominations to theorize how these four dimensions mutually reinforce one another within platform infrastructures, algorithmic governance, and data economies. We identify three central interlocking dynamics:

- **Panoptical surveillance infrastructures enable digital colonialism** by rendering data extraction invisible and normalizing user dependency.
- **Imperial standard-setting amplifies racism** by embedding dominant-group norms as ostensibly universal technical standards.
- **Colonialism, imperialism, and racism are simultaneously operationalized through panoptical systems**, which translate power relations into technical processes that appear neutral, inevitable, and beyond contestation.

Understanding these interlocks reframes digital domination as a unified system rather than a set of discrete harms.

Panopticism as Infrastructure for Colonialism

Digital panopticism provides the infrastructural foundation that makes digital colonialism both efficient and difficult to contest. Unlike classical colonialism, marked by visible occupation, administration, and extraction, digital colonialism operates through continuous, opaque surveillance embedded in platforms and applications.

- Mechanism

  Continuous behavioral monitoring generates granular profiles of users' preferences, vulnerabilities, and affective states.

  These profiles enable commodification: data is monetized through advertising, recommendation optimization, and predictive analytics.

  Surveillance remains largely invisible, normalized as a routine feature of "platform functionality."

Dependency deepens as users trade data for usability, access, or visibility, inadvertently funding their own extraction.

Illustrative case: Facebook's Free Basics

Free Basics framed zero-rated access as benevolent digital inclusion, while obscuring the unprecedented volume of behavioral data Facebook acquired from first-time internet users in the Global South. Patterns of use, attention, aspiration, and commercial interest became valuable proprietary knowledge. Panoptical infrastructure ensured that users experienced "free access," not participation in extractive data regimes.

- **Outcome**: Panopticism renders digital colonialism both normalized and politically elusive. Extraction becomes difficult to resist because it is neither visible nor experienced as coercive.

Digital Imperialism as a Vector for Racism

Digital imperialism-the concentration of infrastructural, economic, and epistemic power in Global North platforms-does not operate in a racial or caste-neutral field. When dominant actors define "universal" technological standards, they embed the values, assumptions, and hierarchies of already dominant groups.

- Mechanism
  Technical standards appear neutral but encode norms about professionalism, relevance, safety, and legitimacy.
  These norms reflect the cultural perspectives of predominantly Western, English-speaking, elite engineering communities.
  Once encoded into algorithms, these assumptions scale globally, suppressing non-dominant languages, histories, and political claims.
  Racism and casteism become automated, persistent, and geographically diffuse.
- Examples
- **Content moderation:** Anti-caste, feminist, and queer content from the Global South is disproportionately flagged as "hateful," "sexual," or "unsafe," while dominant narratives remain unmarked and normalized.
- **Search and ranking systems:** English-language content and Global North institutional sources are consistently privileged, marginalizing Global South scholarship and vernacular knowledge systems.

- **Outcome**: Imperial standard-setting transforms localized discrimination into globalized algorithmic racism, extending historical hierarchies through technical governance.

Compounded Domination Through Panoptical Systems

The full force of digital domination becomes visible when all four ideologies operate simultaneously. Consider the case of a Dalit woman creator on Instagram:

- **Imperialism:** Algorithmic standards privilege Westernized, upper-caste, urban aesthetics as "engaging" and "aspirational."
- **Racism / Casteism:** Content addressing caste violence, Dalit history, or feminist critique is flagged, downranked, or shadow-banned.
- **Colonialism:** Her creative labor and audience engagement generate data and profit for the platform without granting her meaningful authority, compensation, or visibility.
- **Panopticism:** Continuous monitoring shapes her behavior. Anticipating algorithmic punishment, she self-censors, adjusts content, and internalizes platform discipline.

  Compound effect

These are not parallel harms but a single integrated system. Surveillance renders extraction invisible; imperial standards define legitimacy; racism governs visibility; colonial logics convert marginalized labor into value. The creator becomes complicit in sustaining the system that marginalizes her, not through consent but through structurally constrained participation.

Implications: Why Interlocking Analysis Matters

The framework of Interlocking Digital Dominations carries several critical implications:

- **Single-issue interventions are structurally inadequate:** Privacy protections without anti-monopoly measures entrench imperial control. Algorithmic transparency without epistemic justice documents bias without redistributing power.
- **Domination is resilient and redundant:** When one axis is challenged, others compensate. Data rights may limit extraction, but standards and surveillance still govern visibility and behavior.

- **Marginalized communities experience domination holistically:** Policy and research silos fragment harms that are lived as integrated realities.
- **Effective resistance must be multidimensional:** Decolonizing digital futures requires redistributing data value, democratizing standard-setting, centering marginalized epistemologies, and constraining surveillance simultaneously.

Figure 1. Interlocking Digital Dominations

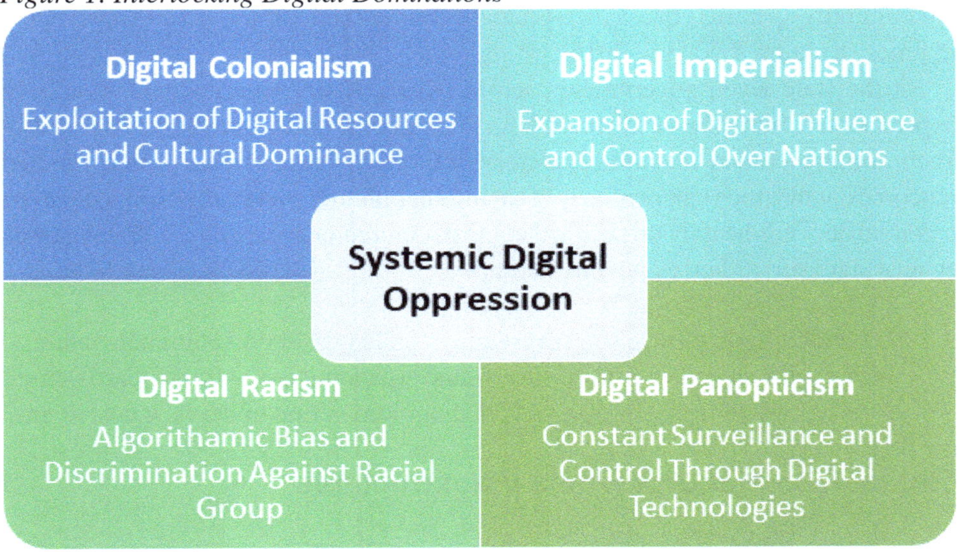

The Venn diagram illustrates the convergence of digital colonialism, digital imperialism, digital racism, and digital panopticism. Each overlap highlights shared mechanisms-data extraction, algorithmic bias, surveillance, cultural hegemony, and infrastructural concentration-while the central intersection represents systemic digital oppression, where all four ideologies reinforce one another to intensify inequality across knowledge, culture, labor, and governance.

RESISTANCE AND ALTERNATIVES: CONTESTING INTERLOCKING DIGITAL DOMINATIONS

Resistance to digital colonialism is necessarily plural and multi-sited, spanning regulation, grassroots infrastructure, cultural production, and epistemic intervention. Because digital domination operates through interlocking ideologies, effective resistance likewise must act across multiple dimensions-data, infrastructure, governance, culture, and knowledge-rather than targeting a single site of harm.

Data Sovereignty and Collective Governance

Data sovereignty movements challenge the colonial logic that treats data as a freely extractable resource. Indigenous and community-led initiatives assert collective rights over how data is generated, stored, interpreted, and circulated, foregrounding culturally specific governance protocols rather than universalized "open data" regimes (Kukutai & Taylor, 2016).

At the state level, governments across Africa, Latin America, and Asia have experimented with data localization laws and national data frameworks to curb Big Tech dominance and reclaim regulatory authority. These efforts produce mixed outcomes: while they can modestly rebalance bargaining power, their emancipatory potential depends heavily on political context, enforcement capacity, and safeguards against state surveillance and elite capture.

- **Interlocking insight:** Data sovereignty challenges digital colonialism directly, but without constraints on surveillance (panopticism) and standard-setting power (imperialism), it risks reproducing domination under new custodians.

Ethical Tech and Grassroots Infrastructures

Ethical technology collectives and open-source communities develop alternatives to extractive platform capitalism. These initiatives prioritize privacy-preserving AI, community-controlled platforms, and transparent governance structures that emphasize autonomy over profit (OpenMined, 2023).

In parallel, community mesh networks and locally owned ISPs in rural and Indigenous regions provide user-owned connectivity, reducing reliance on corporate backbones and centralized infrastructure. Such projects reconfigure access not merely as connectivity but as collective control over digital lifelines.

- **Interlocking insight:** These efforts resist imperialism and colonialism at the infrastructural level, yet face scaling challenges due to capital intensity, technical maintenance demands, and competition with entrenched monopolies.

Artistic, Cultural, and Epistemic Resistance

Artistic and cultural activism plays a crucial role in contesting the epistemic dimensions of digital domination. Artists and activists deploy performance, speculative design, digital storytelling, and counter-mapping to expose algorithmic bias, data extraction, and surveillance while imagining decolonial digital futures.

Data justice collectives further mobilize workshops, visualizations, and hackathons to build digital literacy and collective political capacity among marginalized communities. These practices challenge not only technological systems but the narratives that naturalize them.

Interlocking insight: Cultural resistance directly confronts imperialism and racism by disrupting dominant epistemologies, making visible what platforms render invisible, and reclaiming narrative authority.

Digital Sovereignty, Inclusive Design, and Participatory Futures

Normative frameworks such as the CARE Principles (Collective benefit, Authority to control, Responsibility, Ethics) challenge purely access-oriented or FAIR-only data paradigms by foregrounding relational accountability and collective well-being.

Participatory and inclusive design practices involve affected communities in shaping languages, interfaces, norms, and governance structures. When combined with decentralized architectures, these approaches can redistribute power-though they must contend with equity, accessibility, and environmental sustainability concerns.

- **Interlocking insight:** Inclusive design resists racism and imperialism, but without structural redistribution of power and resources, participation risks becoming symbolic rather than transformative.

Limits, Risks, and Strategic Imperatives

Despite their promise, resistance initiatives face persistent obstacles:

- Chronic funding shortages and technical capacity constraints
- Difficulty scaling against dominant platforms
- Risk of co-optation by states or corporations
- Surveillance expansion under the guise of sovereignty or security

State-led digital sovereignty initiatives exemplify this ambivalence: while they may counter foreign dominance, they can simultaneously expand domestic surveillance or consolidate new oligarchies (Madiega, 2020). Effective resistance, therefore, requires coordinated, multi-level action-regulatory enforcement, institutional accountability, industry reform, and sustained civil society mobilization.

CONCLUSION AND POLICY RECOMMENDATIONS

The pervasive expansion of global digital infrastructures has facilitated a new epoch of extraction. Multinational technology corporations are actively reproducing historical colonial dynamics within the contemporary digital realm. As this chapter has argued, digital colonialism is not a singular phenomenon but a multi-dimensional system of domination. Through the examination of cases such as Facebook's Free Basics, Instagram Reels, and India's data localization policies, the analysis reveals how digital power manifests economically, culturally, and politically. These systems reproduce inequalities along intersecting axes of race, caste, gender, language, and geography (Benjamin, 2019; Couldry & Mejias, 2019).

By situating digital colonialism within the broader constellation of digital racism, panopticism, and imperialism, this research highlights that algorithmic bias, surveillance, and epistemic exclusion are mutually reinforcing processes. Moving beyond critique requires establishing robust and actionable policy frameworks to dismantle these structures. The following recommendations outline necessary structural shifts toward reclaiming digital sovereignty and mitigating algorithmic bias to ensure that technological advancement serves the public good rather than corporate hegemony.

Strategies for Reclaiming Digital Sovereignty

Digital sovereignty requires that nations and local communities possess the power to govern their own digital infrastructures, data flows, and technological ecosystems independently of foreign corporate monopolies. Policymakers must prioritize the development of localized digital capacities to reduce dependency on platforms headquartered in the Global North.

- **Mandating Data Localization with Human Rights Protections:** National governments must implement data localization policies that require the data of citizens to be stored and processed within national borders. However, these policies must be strictly decoupled from state surveillance apparatuses. Data localization must empower citizens by granting them legal ownership and control over their information, rather than merely transferring extractive power from foreign corporations to the domestic state.
- **Fostering Decentralized and Open-Source Infrastructures:** States should heavily subsidize the development of open-source software and decentralized technologies to counter digital panopticism and platform monopolies. Public sector institutions, including schools and government services, ought to migrate away from proprietary corporate ecosystems and adopt interoperable, locally developed open-source alternatives. This transition builds local tech-

nological capacity while keeping public capital circulating within the domestic economy.

- **Implementing Community Data Trusts:** Moving away from the hyper-individualized model of data ownership, policymakers should facilitate the legal creation of data trusts. Under this model, community data is pooled and managed by independent fiduciaries who act strictly in the community's interest. This approach allows marginalized groups to collectively negotiate the terms of data usage and prevent extractive exploitation.

Frameworks for Mitigating Algorithmic Bias

Algorithmic systems currently operate as vectors of digital racism and social stratification, encoding historical inequalities into automated decision-making. Mitigating these harms requires strict regulatory oversight and a fundamental shift toward participatory design.

- **Mandatory Algorithmic Impact Assessments (AIAs):** Prior to the deployment of any high-risk algorithmic system, policymakers must mandate comprehensive Algorithmic Impact Assessments. This requirement is particularly urgent in sectors such as criminal justice, healthcare, lending, and employment. Independent third parties must conduct these assessments to explicitly evaluate the system's intersectional impact on historically marginalized groups.
- **Establishing Algorithmic Transparency and Explainability:** Intellectual property laws and corporate trade secrets can no longer serve as shields for algorithmic black boxes. Regulatory bodies must require explainability by design. This ensures that affected individuals can understand exactly how an automated decision was made and possess a clear legal mechanism to contest and appeal biased algorithmic outcomes.
- **Enforcing Participatory Design Mandates:** Policy should require tech developers to integrate participatory design methodologies when creating systems that affect public infrastructure. This mandate means actively including local communities, grassroots organizations, and civil rights advocates in the design, testing, and implementation phases of technological development. Incorporating local knowledge serves as a vital step in decolonizing the design process.

Towards a Decolonial Digital Future

Confronting digital colonialism demands more than piecemeal reform. It requires collective re-imagination and coordinated transnational effort. The Global South must build strategic coalitions to negotiate collectively against transnational tech monopolies and establish new global standards for data equity and technology transfer. Achieving a decolonial digital future demands a radical reimagining of technology as a public utility rather than an engine for unbridled capitalist extraction. By asserting digital sovereignty, dismantling algorithmic bias, and centering the voices of marginalized communities, society can begin to dismantle the architectures of digital imperialism. Only through sustained, intersectional, and multi-scalar resistance can digital spaces evolve from instruments of control into infrastructures of equity, autonomy, and shared flourishing.

REFERENCES

Abidin, C. (2021). Mapping internet celebrity on TikTok: "Understanding Douyin as a technical and social platform.". *International Journal of Communication, 15*, 3255–3277.

Ali, S., & Procter, R. (2022). Algorithmic bias and the marginalization of minority voices in social media. *New Media & Society*, *24*(5), 1152–1171.

Andrejevic, M. (2014). Surveillance and alienation in the online economy. *Surveillance & Society*, *12*(3), 381–397. DOI: 10.24908/ss.v8i3.4164

Angwin, J., Larson, J., Mattu, S., & Kirchner, L. (2016). *Machine bias: There's software used across the country to predict future criminals. And it's biased against blacks*. ProPublica.

Bardall, G. (2016). Automating discrimination? Algorithmic, data, and design-based discrimination in the context of welfare reform in Britain. *New Political Economy*, *21*(4), 530–547.

Barocas, S., Hardt, M., & Narayanan, A. (2019). *Fairness and machine learning: Limitations and opportunities*. fairmlbook.org.

Bawa, Z., & Ghatak, S. (2017). Digital colonialism and interventions: India's ban on Free Basics and the politics of the digital divide. *Media Culture & Society*, *39*(7), 1047–1062.

Beer, D. (2016). *Metric power*. Routledge.

Beer, D. (2017). The social power of algorithms. *Information Communication and Society*, *20*(1), 92–109.

Benjamin, R. (2019). *Race after technology: Abolitionist tools for the New Jim Code*. Polity Press.

Berlant, L. (2016). The commons and the infrastructure of emotion. *Critical Inquiry*, *42*(3), 357–381.

Bozdag, E. (2013). Bias in algorithmic filtering and personalization. *Ethics and Information Technology*, *15*(3), 209–227. 10.1007/s10676-013-9321-6

Bucher, T. (2018). *If... Then: Algorithmic power and politics*. Oxford University Press.

Buolamwini, J., & Gebru, T. (2018). Gender shades: Intersectional accuracy disparities in commercial gender classification. *Proceedings of Machine Learning Research*, *81*, 1–15.

Carroll, S., Garba, I., Figueroa-Rodriguez, O., Holbrook, J., Lovett, R., Materechera, S., Parsons, M., Raseroka, K., Rodriguez-Lonebear, D., Rowe, R., Sara, R., Walker, J., Anderson, J., & Hudson, M. (2020). The CARE principles for Indigenous data governance. *Data Science Journal, 19*(1), 43.

Cheney-Lippold, J. (2017). *We are data: Algorithms and the making of our digital selves*. NYU Press.

Choudhury, M. (2022). Platform power and caste exclusion: Instagram and vernacular creators in India. *Information Communication and Society*, *25*(9), 1309–1327.

Cohen, J. E. (2019). *Between truth and power: The legal constructions of informational capitalism*. Oxford University Press.

Coleman, D. (2019). Digital colonialism: The 21st-century scramble for Africa through the extraction and control of user data and the limitations of data protection laws. *Michigan Journal of Race & Law*, *24*, 417–472.

Couldry, N., & Mejias, U. (2019). *The costs of connection: How data is colonizing human life and appropriating it for capitalism*. Stanford University Press.

Creemers, R. (2018). China's social credit system: An evolving practice of control. *SSRN*.

Dahiya, B. (2023). *Digital colonialism: Neo-colonialism of the Global South*. Global South Studies Series.

Diakopoulos, N. (2016). Accountability in algorithmic decision making. *Communications of the ACM*, *59*(2), 56–62.

Eubanks, V. (2018). *Automating inequality: How high-tech tools profile, police, and punish the poor*. St. Martin's Press.

Ferguson, A. G. (2017). *The rise of big data policing: Surveillance, race, and the future of law enforcement*. NYU Press.

Foucault, M. (1977). *Discipline and punish: The birth of the prison*. Pantheon Books.

Galeano, E., & Allende, I. (1997). *Open veins of Latin America: Five centuries of the pillage of a continent*. Monthly Review Press.

Gillespie, T. (2014). The relevance of algorithms. In Gillespie, T., Boczkowski, P. J., & Foot, K. A. (Eds.), *Media technologies* (pp. 167–194). MIT Press.

Gillespie, T. (2018). *Custodians of the internet: Platforms, content moderation, and the hidden decisions that shape social media*. Yale University Press.

Grosfoguel, R. (2011). Decolonizing postcolonial studies and paradigms of political-economy: Transmodernity, decolonial thinking, and global coloniality. *Transmodernity*, *1*(1), 1–38.

Gurumurthy, A., & Chami, N. (2016). Digital India through the looking glass of net neutrality. *International Journal of Communication*, *10*, 4282–4302.

Harcourt, B. E. (2015). *Exposed: Desire and disobedience in the digital age*. Harvard University Press.

Introna, L. D., & Nissenbaum, H. (2000). Shaping the Web: Why the politics of search engines matters. *The Information Society*, *16*(3), 169–185.

Jhaver, S., Birman, I., Gilbert, E., & Bruckman, A. (2019). Human evaluation of content moderation algorithms: Accuracy, biases, and the role of augmentations. In *CHI Conference* proceedings.

Kearns, M., & Roth, A. (2019). *The ethical algorithm: The science of socially aware algorithm design*. Oxford University Press.

Kelly, J. (2021). Algorithmic content moderation: Technical, political, and legal challenges. *Social Media + Society*, *7*(3).

Kitchin, R. (2017). Thinking critically about and researching algorithms. *Information Communication and Society*, *20*(1), 14–29.

Kroll, J. A., Huey, J., Barocas, S., Felten, E. W., Reidenberg, J. R., Robinson, D. G., & Yu, H. (2017). Accountable algorithms. *University of Pennsylvania Law Review*, *165*(3), 633–705.

Kukutai, T., & Taylor, J. (2016). *Indigenous data sovereignty: Toward an agenda*. ANU Press.

Kwet, M. (2019). Digital colonialism: US empire and the new imperialism in the Global South. *Race & Class*, *61*(1), 14–28.

MacKinnon, R. (2012). *Consent of the networked: The worldwide struggle for Internet freedom*. Basic Books.

Madiega, T. (2020). *Data localisation measures and their implications on the free flow of data*. European Parliamentary Research Service.

Marker, S. L., Verstergaard, M., & Hendricks, V. F. (2019). Digital colonialism on the African continent. *African Statistical Newsletter*, *10*, 6–9.

Mason, P. (2015). *Postcapitalism: A guide to our future*. Penguin.

McChesney, R. W. (2013). *Digital disconnect: How capitalism is turning the Internet against democracy.*

McKelvey, F. (2018). A brief history of Internet.org: The life and death of Facebook's connectivity project. *Internet Policy Review*, *7*(4).

McPhail, T. (1981). Electronic colonialism: The future of international broadcasting and communication. *Sage (Atlanta, Ga.).*

Mignolo, W. D. (2011). *The darker side of Western modernity: Global futures, decolonial options*. Duke University Press.

Noble, S. U. (2018). *Algorithms of oppression: How search engines reinforce racism*. NYU Press.

Nothias, T. (2025). An intellectual history of digital colonialism. *Journal of Communication*.

O'Callaghan, D., Greene, D., Conway, M., Carthy, J., & Cunningham, P. (2015). Down the (white) rabbit hole: The extreme right and online recommender systems. *Social Science Computer Review*, *33*(4), 459–478.

O'Neil, C. (2016). *Weapons of math destruction: How big data increases inequality and threatens democracy*. Crown.

OpenMined. (2023). Open source privacy tech.

Pariser, E. (2011). *The filter bubble: What the Internet is hiding from you*. Penguin.

Pasquale, F. (2015). *The black box society: The secret algorithms that control money and information*. Harvard University Press.

Pinto, R. A. (2018). *Digital sovereignty or digital colonialism?* Sur – International Journal on Human Rights.

Plantin, J.-C. (2019). Data cleaners for pristine datasets: Visibility and invisibility of data processors in social science. *Science, Technology & Human Values*, *44*(1), 52–73.

Quijano, A. (2000). Coloniality of power and Eurocentrism in Latin America. *International Sociology*, *15*(2), 215–232.

Ribeiro, M. H., Ottoni, R., West, R., Almeida, V. A. F., & Meira, W.Jr. (2020). Auditing radicalization pathways on YouTube. *Proceedings of the ACM on Human-Computer Interaction, 4*(CSCW3), 1–27.

Richardson, R., Schultz, J. M., & Crawford, K. (2019). Dirty data, bad predictions: How civil rights violations impact police data, predictive policing systems, and justice. *NYU Law Review*, *94*, 192.

Roberts, S. T. (2019). *Behind the screen: Content moderation in the shadows of social media*. Yale University Press.

Schiller, H. I. (1969, 1989). *Mass communication and American empire*; *Culture, Inc.: The corporate takeover of public expression*. Oxford University Press.

Seaver, N. (2017). Algorithms as culture: Some tactics for the ethnography of algorithmic systems. *Big Data & Society*, *4*(2), 1–12.

Seaver, N. (2019). Captivating algorithms: Recommender systems as traps. *Journal of Material Culture*, *24*(4), 421–436.

Selbst, A. D., boyd, d., Friedler, S. A., Venkatasubramanian, S., & Vertesi, J. (2019). Fairness and abstraction in sociotechnical systems. In *Proceedings of the Conference on Fairness, Accountability, and Transparency* (pp. 59–68).

Simonsen, J., & Robertson, T. (Eds.). (2012). *Routledge international handbook of participatory design*. Routledge.

Star, S. L. (1999). The ethnography of infrastructure. *The American Behavioral Scientist*, *43*(3), 377–391.

Star, S. L., & Ruhleder, K. (1996). Steps toward an ecology of infrastructure: Design and access for large information spaces. *Information Systems Research*, *7*(1), 111–134.

Suchman, L. A. (2007). *Human–machine reconfigurations: Plans and situated actions* (2nd ed.). Cambridge University Press.

Tufekci, Z. (2015). Algorithmic harms beyond Facebook and Google: Emergent challenges of computational agency. *Colorado Technology Law Journal*, *13*, 203–218.

Tufekci, Z. (2018). *Twitter and tear gas: The power and fragility of networked protest*. Yale University Press.

Veale, M., Van Kleek, M., & Binns, R. (2018). Fairness and accountability design needs for algorithmic support in high-stakes public sector decision-making. *Proceedings of the ACM on Human-Computer Interaction, 2*(CSCW), 1–20.

Wajcman, J. (2004). *Technofeminism*. Polity Press.

Whittaker, M.. (2018). *AI Now Report 2018*. AI Now Institute.

Yeung, K. (2018). 'Hypernudge': Big data as a mode of regulation by design. *Information Communication and Society*, *20*(1), 118–136.

Yilmaz, Ö. (2024). The origins of digital colonialism. *İmgelem, 16, 321-344. https://doi.org/*DOI: 10.53791/imgelem.1636282

Ziewitz, M. (2016). Governing algorithms: Myth, mess, and methods. *Science, Technology & Human Values*, *41*(1), 3–16.

Zuboff, S. (2019). *The age of surveillance capitalism: The fight for a human future at the new frontier of power.* PublicAffairs.

KEY TERMS AND DEFINITIONS

Algorithmic Authority: The power exercised by algorithms to mediate access to knowledge, culture, and decision-making, often operating invisibly yet shaping social realities.

Algorithmic Bias: Systematic and unfair discrimination encoded in algorithmic processes stemming from historical inequalities, data limitations, or design choices.

Data Sovereignty: The principle that data is subject to the laws and governance structures of the nation or community to which it relates, emphasizing control and cultural specificity.

Decentralized Technologies: Digital systems operating without a central authority, often leveraging peer-to-peer networks or blockchain, aimed at enhancing autonomy and reducing dependence on monopolistic platforms.

Digital Colonialism: A form of structural domination where global digital infrastructures and platforms replicate colonial patterns of resource extraction, control, and marginalization through data and technology.

Digital Imperialism: The dominance of a few transnational tech corporations in controlling global digital infrastructures, standards, knowledge flows, and cultural norms.

Digital Panopticism: The pervasive surveillance enabled by digital infrastructures, characterized by continuous data collection and behavioral control extending Foucauldian disciplinary power.

Digital Racism: The perpetuation of racial discrimination through digital technologies, including biased algorithms, discriminatory data practices, and unequal surveillance.

Filter Bubble: A phenomenon where algorithms selectively present personalized information, reinforcing existing beliefs and limiting exposure to diverse perspectives.

Intersectionality / Intersectional Analysis: A theoretical framework and methodological approach recognizing that systems of oppression (such as racism, casteism, sexism, and capitalism) are mutually constitutive. In digital contexts, it examines how algorithmic harms and digital exclusion are compounded across interlocking identity markers rather than treating them as separate variables.

Participatory Design: An approach to technology design that actively involves users and affected communities in shaping tools, emphasizing inclusivity and local knowledge.

Platform Dependency: Reliance on foreign tech monopolies severely and undermines local sovereignty.

Chapter 5
Watching the Watchers:
Digital Panopticism in the Age of Algorithmic Culture

Amol Aanand Saxena
http://orcid.org/0009-0002-1954-1467
Christ University, Bangalore, India

Charu Sehgal
http://orcid.org/0000-0002-4607-4625
Christ University, Bangalore, India

Babita
http://orcid.org/0009-0003-2854-6670
Christ University, Bangalore, India

ABSTRACT

The chapter deals with the ideology of Digital Panopticism as basically one of the major features of the algorithmic culture where power is exercised through the routine surveillance, data extraction, and predictive analytics. Using Michel Foucault's idea of the Panopticon as a starting point, the authors suggest that digital systems - for example, social media and algorithmic governance - are control structures that are spread out and therefore it is difficult to distinguish the zones where one is being observed and the zones where one is participating. The chapter links the concept of Digital Panopticism with the theories of the radical surveillance and digital capitalism and also examining the impact of the phenomena on subjectivity, autonomy, and behavior. The authors end the chapter by looking at moral theories and resistance movements to facilitate openness, taking responsibility, and the people's control in the age of digital technology.

DOI: 10.4018/979-8-3373-4531-4.ch005

INTRODUCTION

The underlying framework of this chapter is digital panopticism - the ideological/ normative component of the algorithmic paradigm within which power is exercised through the mechanisms of surveillance, data extraction, and predictive (data) governance. The primary concept for interpreting digital panopticism on a much wider scope than Foucault's (1977, p. 35) original interpretation is to apply the Panopticon to the thinkers Deleuze (1992) and Zuboff (2019). The chapter highlights that the phenomenon of visibility has been weaponised as a tool of control and, at the same time, turned into a prerequisite for engagement in digital societies.

This chapter not only theorises digital panopticism but also illustrates the changes in social practices and the concept of individual freedom brought about by the interactions with current technologies. A few examples of such interactions include social credit systems, workplace surveillance, algorithmic profiling, and the use of biometric data for identification. The author(s) situate the notion of digital panopticism within an extended philosophical discourse on digital capitalism, data colonialism, and psychopolitical control, thereby emphasizing the pervasiveness of surveillance through the omnipresence of technologies and the ubiquity of cultural narratives.

At the end of the chapter, the author(s) set forth the proposition that digital panopticism is far from just another technical arrangement but rather an ideological framework that determines how people, in an age of absolute exposure, understand liberty, faith, and membership.

THEORETICAL FOUNDATIONS OF DIGITAL PANOPTICISM FOUCAULT AND THE ARCHITECTURE OF DISCIPLINE

The idea of Digital panopticism traces its intellectual lineage to classical panopticism. The criticism of the digital age follows closely Michel Foucault's (1977) analysis in Discipline and Punish, in which he discusses Jeremy Bentham's design for a circular prison, the panopticon, from the late eighteenth century, as a model of social control. From the central tower, the single observer could see all prisoners without being seen; thus, the condition was established in which visibility itself became a mechanism of power.

Foucault employed this architectural metaphor to illustrate a novel type of disciplinary power that was not enforced by force but through the psychological internalization of individuals. People change their behaviour on their own when they are aware that they might be observed. Foucault (1977) explains that the genius of the Panopticon lies in its ability to create subjects who self-discipline. According to

Foucault, this example has expanded from prisons to schools, factories, and offices in modern societies.

The source of discipline is not the will of kings and dictators but rather the everyday routines and rules that shape behaviour in society. He called it the micro-physics of power, in which the process of observation and normalization produces self-regulated human beings. In this way, people are at once the agents and the products of surveillance: the very power that restricts them is the one they also use. The digital world of the twenty-first century has amplified this reasoning. The moment of seeing has gone beyond the limits of a physical cell or institution and has now been inextricably linked to data infrastructures. Lyon (2018) argues that surveillance is now both a technical process and a cultural condition.

Deleuze and the Societies of Control

Gilles Deleuze (1992) advanced Foucault's notion of disciplinary power by defining it as "the society of control." In this society of control, traditional places that were once highly regulated are now largely unregulated, as most forms are increasingly regulated through open networks. Power no longer boxes up individuals into certain places, but instead shapes behaviour through communication, access, and data flows.

Identity, in this case, can no longer be a fixed feature. Deleuze refers to the post-modern person as a set of "dividuals", data bits that can be watched, studied, and changed at any moment. Control is exercised through passwords, facial recognition, and customer experience management rather than through physical coercion. Work and leisure, public and private, are becoming one in a perpetual state of exposure.

Digital technologies have brought Deleuze's vision to its full extent. Algorithms track a user's activities on various devices and platforms, and these individual actions are combined into predictive systems that forecast needs and influence decisions. Control thus becomes less about punishment and more about prevention, the behaviour being subtly guided even before the decision becomes conscious.

As noted by Galič, Timan, and Koops (2017), digital platforms have transformed surveillance and control into a participatory continuum in which users, through liking, sharing, and searching, simultaneously produce the means of their own surveillance. The Deleuzian dividual has become a quantifiable resource within a computational economy endlessly optimised for attention, obedience, and predictability.

Zuboff and the Political Economy of Data

Shoshana Zuboff (2019) reinterpreted the logic of control in the economy through her concept of surveillance capitalism. It is a system in which the collection and sale of behavioural data are the primary source of revenue. The leading tech giants like Google, Facebook (Meta), and Amazon collect what Zuboff refers to as behavioural surplus data, generated as an unintended consequence of digital interaction, and use it to predict users' future behaviour.

Besides, it is a new exercise of power that she identifies as instrumentarianism, which does not aim to dominate human consciousness but to automate it. While industrial capitalism commodified labour, surveillance capitalism commodifies human experience. Thus, every physical movement, tap on the screen, and utterance becomes the raw material for the so-called prediction markets.

Moreover, power operates through unequal visibility: corporations can see everything, whereas users are, for the most part, unaware of the forces that influence them. Zuboff's (author) argument runs parallel to Deleuze's (1992) idea of control societies, and both work to unmask their economic roots. In fact, these techniques for predicting consumer behaviour, automating decision-making, and delivering targeted advertising are only pretending to be personalised services, which, if anything, make people more dependent and less free.

Now the prison metaphor, in which the guardian is visible but the inmates are not, gets totally revamped: the tower is owned by the watch; its function is to keep an eye on; and the guard is a computer program. Profit generation, rather than the threat of punishment, is what drives this new invisible observer. Watching is at once the prerequisite for and the price of admission to digital life.

Bauman, Lyon, and the Liquidity of Surveillance

Zygmunt Bauman and David Lyon (2013) first used the phrase "liquid surveillance" to capture surveillance as fluid, mobile, and adaptable in today's society. Rather than the solid disciplinary structures Foucault discusses, liquid surveillance permeates every aspect of our lives through connectivity and mobility. The surveillance apparatus travels with the individual, from the phone in the pocket to a biometric scanner at the airport.

Bauman's overall explanation of liquid modernity also addresses changes in people's attitudes towards surveillance. The world has become a place of uncertainty, speed, and friction, where people give up their privacy for convenience and use visibility as a survival strategy. Therefore, liquid surveillance is consent that has been well camouflaged as a necessity.

On the one hand, social networks represent the contradiction here: humanity's basic impulse to connect and to be seen is what keeps the surveillance apparatus 'well-oiled'. Bauman and Lyon (2013) sum it up when they say, "Freedom and security have now become so interwoven that it is tough to tell them apart". The

Panopticon, once a solid structure, has now dispersed into a network of interfaces, applications, and infrastructures that are part of everyday life.

Couldry, Mejias, and Data Colonialism

Nick Couldry and Ulises Mejias (2019) elevate the discussion of surveillance capitalism to a global and postcolonial issue. Their notion of data colonialism suggests that digital extraction operates in the same way as historical colonialism, in which the goal was to take over land. Still, here, human life is being taken over. In the same way that colonial powers occupied land, corporations are now occupying social interactions, relationships, and emotions as resources to be turned into data.

Using this analytical framework, Digital panopticism should be viewed not only as a metaphor for surveillance but as something much more than that.

It is, indeed, a system of global domination. The data flows mirror the geopolitical inequalities: cloud computing, server farms, and platform-ownership infrastructure are primarily in the hands of the Global North, whereas the Global South provides raw materials, users, data, and labour with very little power or a fair return.

Therefore, Couldry and Mejias (2019) link the digital panopticon to the entire history of exploitation. The imbalance between the one who extracts and the one who gets extracted is a reflection of the imbalance between the colonizer and the colonized. Surveillance, in the context of data colonialism, becomes an epistemic enterprise: having the power to define, categorise, and predict others is a new form of governance.

This postcolonial reevaluation of the issue deepens the moral scope of digital panopticism. It reveals that surveillance concerns not only privacy or control but also the very ownership of human reality.

Synthesis: From Structure to Belief

In this section, we examine various theoretical perspectives that help explain digital panopticism. It is seen as a historically evolving, technologically heightened form of power. Theories by the French philosopher Michel Foucault on disciplinary visibility provide a rationale for individuals to regulate their own behaviour through self-observation. Deporting this concept further, French philosopher Gilles Deleuze argues that modern societies are characterised by control rather than confinement. According to the political economy of surveillance capitalism developed by American author Shoshana Zuboff, the collection of behavioural data is a new means of producing economic power. The sociological impact of surveillance has been normalised by British sociologist Zygmunt Bauman and Canadian sociologist Kevin Lyon through a discussion around the fluidity, convenience, and consent associated with these forms of observation. By using the concepts developed by sociologists Nick Couldry and Andreas Mejias, we can understand how data collection can be framed in a global context as a form of colonisation and domination. Collectively, these models shape how we view digital panopticism as an ideological and cultural framework for society and the economy through discipline, economic exploitation, cultural normalisation, and global inequality, serving as a theoretical framework for the exploration that follows.

These different lenses, taken together, explain how digital panopticism is one-way power can be exercised by making people visible to a watcher, collecting data, and enabling people's self-governance, rather than through heavy-handed force.

MECHANISMS OF DIGITAL SURVEILLANCE

Datafication of Everyday Life

Datafication, or the conversion of human actions, thoughts, and feelings into measurable digital footprints, is the primary source of digital panopticism. Mayer, Schnberger, and Cukier (2013) argue that this amounts to a radical epistemic change, that one can understand the world only through data. Any search performed, place visited, or smiley sent will become data that algorithms will analyze.

One device that has played a major role in this change is the smartphone. Actually, it is not only a communication tool but also a mobile sensor kit that can continuously track and record one's geolocation, activities, and physiological data. Andrejevic (2020) has referred to it as a piece of personal tracking equipment that also serves as a social necessity. This double nature exemplifies how surveillance has been normalised, and that one has already internalised it subconsciously; it is not something imposed on people but something experienced.

The Internet of Things (IoT) extends the same idea into both the private and public spheres of life. Innovative kitchenware, heating, and gadgets like Amazon's Alexa and Google Home implant monitoring devices in our everyday lives. As Haggerty and Ericson (2000) theorised the surveillant assemblage, watching has become so pervasive that it is taken for granted as part of the very environment, and it is impossible to imagine it without it.

Moreover, the case of smart cities such as Singapore, Dubai, and Barcelona is quite revealing in this respect. Through the use of algorithms, city infrastructure such as transport, energy, and security systems is constantly managed, and as a result, citizen data is generated and used (Kitchin, 2014). What was initially considered urban life, marked by citizens' freedom, now has to be rethought through the lens of digital authoritarianism, since it is code, not law, that controls our conduct within the city.

In conclusion, to datafy is not simply to use technology but a step towards a co-existence paradigm in which the measurable is favored over the meaningful, leading to what Couldry and Mejias (2019) describe as a data-colonized life.

Data Mining & Algorithmic Profiling

Once behaviours are datafied, data mining is used to discover patterns and make predictions through large amounts of data. Algorithms change these behaviour traces into probabilistic profiles, i.e., they make personal profiles that forecast preferences, risks, and actions. Cheney and Lippold (2017) refer to people in this way as algorithmic citizens, suggesting that people are not defined by their self-expression but rather by their predictive data.

Such profiling affects many areas of life; credit scoring is just one product of this creeping surveillance culture. Pasquale (2015) uses the metaphor of a black-box society to describe the opaque Infrastructure of which we are all a part without knowing it, since significant decisions are made without transparency. Hiring platforms such as HireVue or predictive policing tools influenced by PredPol perpetuate bias by reproducing racial inequalities (Brayne, 2020; Raghavan et al., 2020).

Amoore (2020) calls this an algorithmic judgment: if the law is abandoned, probabilities take over, with correlation replacing the truth and prediction replacing justice. The author further develops disciplinary Foucault through Deleuze's (1992) societies of control, in which humans are not controlled for what they do, but rather according to data on what they could do.

The Political Economy of Data Brokers

Behind mainstream digital platforms operates a hidden ecosystem of data brokers, private firms that collect, trade, and sell personal information extracted from online environments. The U.S. Federal Trade Commission (2014) identified hundreds of these intermediaries dealing in data ranging from consumer habits to emotional states. These brokers form the Infrastructure of surveillance capitalism (Zuboff, 2019), embodying a system of one-sided transparency: individuals are evident, while institutions remain opaque (Turow, 2017).

Today's surveillance functions through multiple profit-oriented entities because it operates in a decentralised system, unlike Bentham's centralised tower system. Control through platform capitalism, according to Srnicek (2017), exists as a globalised system that companies use to privatise and commodify their power. The Cambridge Analytica scandal demonstrates how surveillance serves three purposes: commercial activity, governmental control, and ideological power combine to sustain the modern digital Panopticon system.

Predictive Analytics and Behavioural Nudging

Predictive analytics is a significant part of what makes surveillance so face-to-behaviour control technology. In fact, surveillance algorithms not only monitor but also predict and influence people's actions by combining behavioural economics with subtle, non-coercive persuasion (Thaler & Sunstein, 2008). Moreover, when these mechanisms are automated, they become hyper, meaning self-adjusting systems of continuous behavioural optimisation (Yeung, 2017).

Netflix, TikTok, and Amazon are examples of how this model can be institutionalised. Through their recommender systems, they produce personalised content that captures users' attention while cleverly giving users the "illusion" of choice. Beer (2017) points out that the very screens we turn to for stimulation and delight are structures of persuasion, as we unconsciously turn endless scrolling and checking our notifications into leisure when, in fact, it is hard labour at the psychological level.

Predictive analytics is also one of the tools that governments use to enforce welfare and policing. This leads to automated scoring and thus, identification of risky individuals (Eubanks, 2018). Even though these tools put people in a worse situation, the people who use them claim they save them time and make them more efficient. They influence people before things happen, i.e. the exercise of power. Deleuze (1992) explained that the replacement of confinement with modulation means that freedom is statistical predictability, and that uncertainty, which was previously indispensable for agency, is now considered a mistake that needs to be corrected.

Participatory Surveillance and the Socialisation of Control

One of the main characteristics of digital panopticism is the idea that surveillance has turned into a joint practice. Two researchers who have contributed to the study of Surveillance (Albrechtslund, 2008; Andrejevic, 2005) created the term "lateral surveillance" to refer to the voluntary sharing of personal data between individuals as part of their social interaction or experiences. Instagram, Snapchat, and TikTok are examples of lateral surveillance systems in which self-disclosure is used for entertainment purposes. Each addition, selfie, and story double as forms of self and self-surveillance, releasing a statement of identity while simultaneously generating data for algorithmic evaluation.

In this kind of situation, being noticed is almost the same as having money. Likes, shares, and followers are being transfigured into social capital, which is why there is a continuous urge for self-disclosure. Fuchs (2011) called it the surveillance-entertainment complex, where enjoyment and control are so well mixed that one hardly sees them. Users assimilate the surveillance logic and, as a result, self-regulate to produce content that is likely to garner many engagements. Hans (2017) transparent subject is the product of such a system; it is a living being that desires to be seen, yet imagines that being observed is the same as being free.

Although participatory surveillance originated as a form of social media, it has become much broader in recent years. Fitness-tracking applications incentivise users to share their biometric data publicly; gamified educational platforms enable real-time performance monitoring; and remote-work tools allow for the assessment of worker productivity.

Biometric Data and the Body as Interface

Biometric identification is the fusion of the human body and data in digital panopticism. A range of technologies, including facial recognition, fingerprinting, and iris scanning, convert biological characteristics into machine-readable codes; thus, the human body becomes a password, a data source, or both.

Amoore (2020) discusses biometrics as a politics of possibility, in which the body is perpetually subjected to risk assessment. Operational systems such as the EU's Entry/Exit database perform automated border control using facial and fingerprint recognition, while India's Aadhaar links biometric IDs to welfare and financial services, thereby increasing access but also putting citizens at risk of exclusion due to errors (Rao, 2019).

Within the corporate sector, biometrics takes surveillance of workers' movements and emotions to the next level. For instance, Amazon's wristbands, supposedly designed for productivity, actually monitor employees' gestures. The Gender Shades research done by Buolamwini and Gebru (2018) brought to light the racial and gender prejudices of facial recognition technologies, thus strengthening the existing structural inequalities. As Haraway (1991) forecasted in A Cyborg Manifesto, the clear body becomes the perfect subject of domination, controlled, measured, and regulated, confusing exposure with autonomy.

The Infrastructures of Algorithmic Power

The global network of computers can be thought of as a huge planetary-scale system that we barely perceive, hidden behind the interfaces that surround us each day. "The Stack" represents this multilayered system through which people, devices, cities, and clouds communicate with each other using satellite communications, data centres, and fibre-optic-based networks (Bratton, 2016). This setup serves as the physical foundation of digital panopticism.

These infrastructures are, by nature, systems of power and of the environment. Anatomy of an AI System uncovers the various costs of building an AI, from the extraction of minerals to human slavery, culminating in environmental pollution

(Crawford & Jolers, 2018). Murakami Wood (2017) calls the post-panoptic integration the situation in which decentralised power is united via code and Infrastructure.

Smartphone detectors and worldwide data centres work together, thus perpetually entwining surveillance into life. The stare is no more distinct from society; on the contrary, it is so architecturally inscribed into the material conditions of existence that visibility and prediction have become the very logic of living.

Toward a Politics of Algorithmic Visibility

The mechanisms described in this paper illustrate that digital panopticism is a layered phenomenon that operates simultaneously across cognitive, social, biological, and infrastructural levels. Essentially, it involves datafication, prediction, participation, and embodiment, resulting in a comprehensive system in which visibility is at once a form of power and a limitation.

However, Lyon (2018) adds an important caveat: understanding surveillance opens the possibility of its transformation. One of the biggest reasons that people lose control of their privacy has always been that they see it as an established part of technology. The steps to restoring human agency are only just beginning. Digital panopticism is not a single thing but rather a set of decisions made across different dimensions of design, governance, and participatory design. All algorithms, policies, and user interfaces contain a decision-making element that dictates who is visible, how, and for what end.

Based on this conceptual framework, the next section will focus on the specific ways in which Digital panopticism influences people's online lives.

THE CHINESE SOCIAL CREDIT SYSTEM: ALGORITHMIC MORALITY AND GOVERNANCE

China's Social Credit System (SCS) stands out as one of the most thorough examples of state-level digital panopticism. Initially launched as a pilot project in 2014, the SCS endeavours to "build trustworthiness" by awarding scores to citizens and businesses based on their debt payments, consumption patterns, and online expressions. It generates "social credit scores" that regulate access to loans, trips, and jobs by analysing individuals' financial data, e-commerce purchase records, and government files (Kostka, 2019; Creemers, 2018). The SCS, as a gigantic system of moral regulation, is concerned with nurturing a "culture of sincerity" in which virtuous conduct is incentivised and wrongdoing is disincentivised. Liang et al.

(2018) state that it blends government administrative capacity with moral judgment, thereby making morality tangible through computer programs.

Regulations that were once established by law or social norms are now subject to algorithmic evaluation. From a Foucauldian perspective, the SCS is a digital version of disciplinary power, in that revealing aspects of one's life turns everyone into a self and disciplines subjects. Deleuze's concept of control from his 1992 work can also be applied here; punishment is not the core feature of this type of governance, but rather a continuous process of behavioural modulation. People change their routines in advance to avoid a low score. What sets the Chinese example apart is the extent to which the issue is wrapped in morality. The SCS connects compliance with the attribute of being a good person and a good citizen. Han (2017) refers to psychopolitical control in such situations: human beings who want to be admired by the state mistake their self-exposure for moral value. According to Hoffman (2020), the SCS is not Chinese even though it may appear so. There are already numerous instances worldwide of similar instruments, such as credit scoring, the use of algorithms to predict crime, and trust-building, being introduced. The SCS, therefore, is a sign of the increasing predominance of algorithmic governance, a new stage in an epoch in which surveillance and morality meet.

Inclusion is short, clear, and academically polished while maintaining all the theoretical depth and critical nuances. The text is now about 30% shorter and, at the same time, perfectly fits the structure and tone of your changes.

India's Aadhaar System: Biometric Citizenship and Digital Inclusion

India's Aadhaar program, which started in 2009, holds the title of the world's largest biometric identification system because it maintains a database of more than 1.3 billion people. The system stores one person's fingerprints together with their iris patterns. The system uses a special identification code to link demographic information and financial records, enabling users to access welfare benefits, banking services, and healthcare facilities (Rao, 2019). The program gained fame for promoting inclusion and reducing corruption, but it also stands as a symbol of the thin line between empowerment and surveillance.

Ajana (2020) describes how Aadhaar transforms citizenship into a data-based identity because citizens require more than self-declaration to become citizens; they must undergo algorithmic verification. The digital inclusion process creates a system that excludes people from disadvantaged backgrounds because their biometric data verification systems fail to recognise them as necessary for vital needs (Khera, 2019). Couldry and Mejias (2019) put forward the idea of data colonialism, in which the global South is used as a testing ground for technologies invented in the North.

As such, the Aadhaar case shows that humanitarian stories of transparency and efficiency are used as a cover for the normalisation of exposure; thus, surveillance has become a privilege for citizens in the digital era.

Algorithmic Management in the Work Environment: Enhancing Productivity through Predation

Workplace surveillance systems have transitioned from their initial stage, which included basic managerial oversight, to their current state, which depends on algorithmic control systems. The three companies, Amazon, Uber, and Deliveroo, exemplify this transformation by monitoring their employees' work activities, physical whereabouts, and emotional reactions throughout the day.

Moore and Robinson (2016) describe digital Taylorism as the application of industrial efficiency techniques within datafied labour environments. Every action which workers perform, including their physical movements and computer clicks, becomes subject to measurement for the purpose of optimising their labour activities. Ball (2021) states that remote work technologies which include keystroke tracking and webcam monitoring and time analytics have enabled surveillance to extend into personal spaces because it now operates within peoples' homes. The office has expanded to include every home space while workers maintain constant visibility to others. Here, work and life are no longer separable, and thus, a self-disciplined individual emerges (Han, 2017) who automatically adjusts behaviour to algorithmic standards.

The gig economy platforms exacerbate this problem. Those doing the delivering and driving are considered "independent contractors" but are controlled by mysterious rating systems and predictive analytics. According to Zuboff (2019), such systems not only commodify labour but also behaviour, thereby transforming human time and attention into a flow of predictive data. There is basically no autonomy; the workers see platform metrics as gauges of their worth and level of compliance.

Algorithmic management is also a way of controlling workers' emotions. Workers become emotionally drawn to self-optimisation through gamified dashboards and performance badges. The truth is, the workers are evident on the one hand, while the algorithms that control them remain hidden on the other. The digital workplace is so powerful because it is so normal; surveillance is sold as efficiency, and data harvesting is presented as empowerment.

Targeted Marketing and Behavioural Manipulation

On the consumer culture stage, one of the ways digital panopticism operates is through targeted marketing, where one's behavioural data is used not only to forecast but also to modify what one may want. Your every click, scroll, or moment of hesitation is counted and later assigned to a behavioural profile that advertisers use to guess your next purchase. Turow (2017) discussed how digital marketing infrastructures categorise people into tiny microsegments so that advertisers can convince individuals with pinpoint accuracy. As a result, the market has become one where attention itself is the commodity.

The Cambridge Analytica scandal was the perfect illustration of this kind of visibility manipulation. Psychographic models influencing political behaviour were constructed using data scooped from millions of Facebook users (Cadwalladr & Graham-Harrison, 2018). What seemed like microtargeted ads turned out to be a highly clever behavioural control system.

The mechanism required for this research shows its best match through the term psychopolitics, which Han (2017) created, because it shows how power moves between two states. TikTok, YouTube, and Instagram share some common techniques because they continuously enhance their recommendation systems to maintain user engagement. Beer (2017) argues that the system itself functions as a mechanism that controls users because it creates an illusion of user choice while directing their focus through hidden processes.

Surveillance as a Worldwide Infrastructure

Digital panopticism is the backbone of the contemporary societal structure, encompassing various forms of state governance, biometric identification, algorithmic labour, and targeted marketing. In a way, surveillance is considered not an external imposition but the essential condition of one's being in the world. Mechanisms of control are rationalised in the language of "trust, inclusion, and efficiency, " from the Chinese Social Credit System to India's Aadhaar. Eventually, at a corporate level, algorithmic management and consumer profile attainment share the same essence: disciplinary methods disguised as empowerment, equating visibility with getting value.

According to Lyon (2018) and Haggerty and Ericson (2000), this phenomenon is described as a surveillant assemblage, i.e., a widely spread yet closely connected network of data systems whose aim is to keep power through observation and prediction. It is the ideology or the normalisation of being seen rather than technology that binds these instances together. The idea suggests that relationships should follow standard social practices, which people must uphold as their ethical duty.

The digital panopticism functions as a cultural system because it creates an unnoticeable framework that people use to participate in its activities, but which makes their choice between voluntary and forced participation difficult to understand. The Panoptic surveillance system has expanded beyond its original design, which used a single tower for monitoring. The system now implements monitoring through applications, sensors, and various platforms to establish a personal control network that users perceive as their own freedom.

The following case studies shed light on different ways in which digital panopticism becomes a reality through state governance, welfare systems, and biometric infrastructures.

SUBJECTIVITY, IDENTITY, AND ALGORITHMIC SELFHOOD

Algorithmic Subjectivity: The Data, Constructed Self

Identity used to be a pretty solid thing. But now that we live in a world run by algorithms, our identities have become unstable, constantly changing digital composites moulded by data flows. Cheney and Lippold (2017) explain that what they call algorithmic identity is a probabilistic kind of classification that emerges from an individual's behaviour patterns rather than their conscious self. The data selves or Data Doppelgängers (constructed from a person's browsing history, GPS tracking, purchases, and clicks) are not only independent of a person's intention, but they are also predictive model projections that decide whether you can get a loan, what kind of news you will be exposed to, and even if you get a job.

This signals the change from self, self-representation, to data representation. Whereas before we were subjects who represented ourselves, now the subject becomes what can be computed, and one's digital trace comes before one's social recognition. Amoore (2020) claims that such systems not only depict people but, in fact, create them through classification. Thus, the algorithmic subject is at the same time the artefact and the agent of power; the digital profile not only shows the person, but it also limits their possibilities.

Performing the Digital Self

Social media has played a significant role in the progression of identity as a continuous performance. It is said that with the help of Goffman's (1959) dramaturgical theory, the internet world can be interpreted as an unending front stage, where individuals expose themselves to both human and algorithmic audiences in a highly curated way. Marwick and Boyd (2011) describe this as "context collapse": the consolidation of different audiences into a single, unseen spectator. Hence, each post represents a trade-off between one's exposure and their compliance.

To some extent, quantitatively measuring one's social value by focusing only on the numbers of likes, followers, or comments also subconsciously reinforces the algorithmic standard of engagement. For younger people who are digital natives, online visibility is both validation and vulnerability. They want to be noticed, but they also get worried about being misunderstood or left out (Bucher, 2017). In this way, the self, which is a consequence of publicly showing one's authentic self, is quite similar to what Foucault (1977) referred to as the internalised gaze: individuals interrogate their own behaviour to remain consistently identifiable to the algorithm.

The irony of being seen through an algorithm is that it rewards conformity while pretending to give one's individuality a chance. To be yourself on the Internet is to fit in with whatever the system can recognise. Your identity is, hence, something that needs to be anticipated, a matter of tweaking your performance so that the algorithm picks up on it.

Emotion and the Quantification of Self

As well as controlling behaviour, the digital panopticon increasingly exercises control through affect. Emotion-tracking technologies, from wearable sensors to sentiment analysis, and AI have significantly increased the monitoring of people's feelings. Lupton (2016) calls it the quantified self, in which, on the one hand, biometric devices are advertised as a source of empowerment through data, and, on the other hand, they impose a new self-discipline of measurement.

Fitbit, Apple Health, etc., portray monitoring as self-care; thus, people are encouraged to track the minutest details of their lives, such as heart rate, calories, and mood. What initially appears to be self-knowledge is, in fact, compliance, as people assimilate the idea that only data can verify the truth of their being. Psychopolitics, as Han (2017) explains, is power that goes beyond repression; it leads to self-exploitation under the guise of freedom.

Emotional monitoring is also a matter of digital labour. AI systems capable of recognising voice tone, facial expressions, or sentiment are increasingly being deployed in workplaces and schools. Moore (2018) points out that the devices fathers impose on us will likely require us to be always happy, enthusiastic, and composed, thus making these devices the condition of our employability. Emotion, therefore, becomes here the object of commodification through algorithms: the distinction between a person's individuality and a worker's productivity is further erased.

Digital Normalisation and Automated Morality

Algorithmic processes normalise what they observe and predict, besides just observing and predicting. Pariser (2011) discusses the filter bubble to explain how personalisation traps users in ideological echo chambers. The consequence is not simply preference reinforcement but also moral conditioning: users find that some kinds of expressions get rewarded with visibility, whereas others get hidden from feeds.

Rouvroy and Berns (2013) have termed this algorithmic governmentality as a method of regulation that substitutes moral reasoning with statistical regularity. Data correlations, rather than ethical considerations, determine what is appropriate or desirable. Noble (2018), through an analysis of biases in search engines, demonstrates that these systems perpetuate discrimination over the historical period by encoding racial and gender hierarchies in digital infrastructure.

These ways of functioning disadvantage the most vulnerable groups even more. The application of algorithmic profiling creates additional discrimination problems because predictive policing system identifies minority neighbourhoods as rich territory for criminal activity, and automatic hiring systems dismiss any candidate who does not meet traditional standards. The digital individual faces a paradox because he exists in two states of existence, which makes it impossible for him to exist as a complete human being.

Youth, Marginality, and Algorithmic Exposure

For young people who constitute youth nowadays, the majority of whom have never experienced a reality outside the networked gaze, their algorithmic subjectivity even dictates their social belonging. The system uses visibility as currency while considering participation essential for survival. The system creates uneven visibility because people who lack digital literacy skills or come from disadvantaged backgrounds face greater risks of being taken advantage of through hidden data operations. The authors Noble (2018) and Eubanks (2018) show how algorithmic systems treat people who experience poverty and racial discrimination as dangerous to society because they belong to vulnerable social groups.

On the one hand, being present in digital culture means performing for unseen evaluators whose metrics prioritise conformity, consumption, and compliance. On the other hand, resistance, in the form of withdrawal or anonymity, almost always results in exclusion. Thus, a young person who deletes their social network account diminishes their social status, while an employee who disables tracking devices risks losing their job. Consequently, the gaze turns both omnipresent and inescapable.

Synthesis: The Self in the Panoptic Mirror

Algorithmic subjectivity is the interweaving of surveillance, psychology, and capitalism. Foucault's concept of the disciplinary subject, together with Deleuze's notion of the dividual and Zuboff's definition of behavioural surplus, combine to create a digital self that emerges as a distinct entity through observation. Under digital panopticism, visibility functions as the sole means of existence, leading to the conclusion that people who remain unseen have no value.

Because of this, the person becomes what Han (2017) refers to as the transparent self: a person who wants to be noticed because validation from others is proof of existence. Nevertheless, transparency, which was once a democratic virtue, has become a means of enslavement. The self is altered to align with the model of quantifiability required by data systems.

Lastly, an algorithmic persona turns the will into something optimised. People are only allowed to show facets of themselves that fall within the already-established range of what is considered understandable. The freedom to engage is genuine, but the rules of engagement are unchanged. The final outcome creates a structure that establishes moral and psychological standards defining obedience as an individual choice, while surveillance is accepted as a form of goodwill. Digital panopticism functions as an internal force that maintains control and shapes the entire cultural environment, which in turn defines social behaviour.

RESISTANCE AND ETHICAL ALTERNATIVES

Everyday Micro, Resistances

Resistance today hardly ever takes the form of a loud riot but rather a series of actions with disruptive potential. For instance, Brunton and Nissenbaum (2015) note that obfuscation is a tactic of intentionally producing incorrect or excessive information to reduce the accuracy of surveillance. One of the ways these data-noise strategies are put to use is in the product AdNauseam. It automatically clicks on ads to mess up a person's behavioural profile. Through these tiny acts of resistance, users are, in a way, taking control of systems that function only because they can predict users' behaviour.

Another line of resistance can be represented by digital minimalism. Newport (2019) is in favour of people letting go of their dependence on algorithmic platforms, possibly by limiting their use to the minimum necessary to reclaim their attention. The point is to make a choice rather than quit entirely, as the former also suggests that refusal can be a form of power. For some people, especially those who use the Internet for work or study, getting totally offline is not an option; hence, their resistance should be within surveillance infrastructures, not outside them.

These micro-political strategies suggest that power and resistance are part of the same happening. For example, Foucault (1982) states that resistance is not something outside of power but is deeply intertwined with it. Encrypted chats, ad blockers, etc., are all small acts of compliance that grant individuals some degree of freedom. That said, these measures remain separate from the masses and can be easily co-opted by the very system they aim to resist.

Encryption, Data Justice, and Collective Action

Encryption is still one of the best technical measures to fight surveillance. Greenwald (2014) refers to it as a weapon of democratic self-defence, a defence which gives people the liberty to communicate and organise without being exposed. Secure means of communication like Signal, ProtonMail, and Tor Networks convey the message that privacy is not about hiding one's true self but rather about having the right to decide when and how one is seen.

The existing power disparities cannot be resolved through encryption methods. Eubanks (2018) defines data justice as a principle that requires equitable treatment of all aspects of data collection, data processing, and data utilisation. The Data Justice Lab (Dencik et al., 2019) developed a global framework that requires digital systems to maintain accountability and transparency while enabling public participation through its participatory governance structure. The model defines justice as safeguarding personal information while using technology to serve public needs rather than enabling corporate surveillance.

Community mobilisations increasingly align with this principle. The Algorithmic Justice League and Data for Black Lives, which Joy Buolamwini founded, are movements that view resistance as a shared practice requiring multiple perspectives to succeed. The organisation uncovers algorithmic bias while advocating for ethical design and using exposure as a means of empowerment. In these groups, data is transformed from an instrument of oppression into a field of civic engagement and reform.

Opacity, Refusal, and Radical Ethics

In a culture fixated on transparency, opacity stands out as a form of ethical defiance. Goncourt Glissant implies that we must not force all identities to be fully revealed to systems of power through his right to opacity (Glissant, 1997). Being a mystery is a way of protecting human nature in all its shades and hues; this contradicts the capitalist rationale that equates being seen to being trusted.

Dark Matters takes this concept even further by analysing the racial aspects of surveillance (Brownes, 2015). She points out that the black race is often unfairly targeted for excessive monitoring through procedures like policing and profiling. And hence, refusal, for example, by using invisibility, masking, or secret communication methods, becomes a way of asserting one's power. In digital panopticism, where openness is being exalted, the deliberate admission of being opaque is re-establishing the right to self, self-determination.

Hence, opacity is not about hiding but simply a non-acceptance of being simplified. Berardi (2017) points out that opacity is the only thing that keeps difference alive against the algorithmic transparency's tendency to homogenise. This ethics of refusal understands that true freedom comes not from being fully exposed but from having the right to decide on the circumstances under which one's exposure is allowed. Practically, this might mean that pseudonymity, data masking, or even creative misinformation are considered as tactical acts of subversion.

Creative and Collective Counter, Visualities

Artists and activists have even made surveillance a place of countercreation. Mirzoeff (2011) explains that counter visuality is the right to look back to challenge the hierarchical gaze of surveillance by reclaiming representation. For instance, Adam Harvey's CV Dazzle, a project that employs makeup patterns to foil facial recognition, and the HyperFace project, which confuses AI by printing many faces on a piece of clothing, convert resistance into an aesthetic practice.

Crawford and Jolers (2018) depict the hidden human and ecological costs associated with devices such as Amazon Echo. It shows the extraction networks at the base of convenience. The artistic interventions show people the concealed systems that operate Digital panopticism while they motivate audiences to consider this concept.

The function of counter visuality serves two purposes: it exposes hidden elements while maintaining control over what people observe. People use art, design, and storytelling to create their own opposition to surveillance while imagining its future development. They transform the process of controlling people into a means of fostering understanding.

Digital Literacy and Democratic Accountability

The need for resistance to extend beyond procedural boundaries requires establishment through civic organisational structures. Diakopoulos (2016) discusses algorithmic accountability: the duty of organisations to explain, justify, and accept responsibility for decisions made by machines. The EU's General Data Protection Regulation (GDPR) and UNESCO's AI Ethics Recommendation (2021) are just a couple of examples of policies that try to formalise this principle.

People need to understand digital technologies because digital literacy serves as the foundation for their accountability in managing their personal data. Hence, educational institutions should nurture students' critical understanding of algorithms, privacy, and data ethics. Taylor and Richter (2015) see this as data citizenship: the privilege not only to obtain and rectify one's data but also to challenge and reshape the functioning of data systems.

Algorithmic audits, citizen data co-ops, and participatory policy design are some of the community actions that are gradually becoming the new faces of democratic participation. They show that digital resistance can turn into digital stewardship when people take responsibility as co-governors of the data infrastructures that shape their existence.

Synthesis: Resisting Reimagination

Digital panopticism relies on surveillance to monitor people. The concept of digital panopticism depends on surveillance becoming a standard practice, which people believe to be necessary for their protection. The path of resistance must create methods that lead to protection while it develops new ways to understand its mission.

As per Lyon (2018), democracy and surveillance are not inherently contradictory; the challenge is deciding who gets to see. A just digital society would be the one to reverse the current asymmetry by exposing institutions while simultaneously shielding individuals from invisibility. What such a reversal does is change the stare from a weapon of domination to a form of mutual accountability.

What matters most for the future of digital ethics is this change of focus, from surveillance to stewardship. One can see that if care, empathy, and shared responsibility are the core values on which systems are built, then the very concept of visibility would become empowerment. The solution is not through throwing away the technology but revamping it, putting the principles of justice, dignity, and collective agency in its very DNA.

RETHINKING DIGITAL PANOPTICISM: POWER, ETHICS, AND THE FUTURE

From Surveillance to Stewardship

Digital panopticism is not a natural outcome; it is a fabric of human decisions. Surveillance systems are the result of different option selections rather than the outcomes that must necessarily happen. Their designs reveal confident choices: prioritising efficiency over empathy, choosing prediction over unpredictability, and putting profit before participation. The frameworks can be developed into new forms. The digital era provides people with tools for control and regulation that allow them to share power among multiple observers.

The transition from surveillance operations to stewardship requires organisations to transform data from its previous function as a control instrument into a resource for providing care. Mol, Moser, and Pols (2010) put forward an ethics of care that highlights empathy, reciprocity, and relational responsibility. In a datafied world, technology stewardship now performs different functions, enabling organisations to develop their communities rather than using technology solely to generate financial profit.

In place of behaviour being optimised for profit, the infrastructures built on the ethical foundation would be optimising for well-being, trust, and inclusion. Care-based design demands that systems acknowledge uncertainty as an indispensable element of being human.

Predictive algorithms ought to be designed so that they do not eradicate unpredictability, but rather create space for it, thereby recognising that risk, error, and ambiguity are integral to what makes social life meaningful. Hence, the first step in reimagining Digital panopticism is to incorporate ethics deeply within the very architecture of code.

Asymmetric Transparency: Institutions Visible, Individuals Opaque

One of the central contradictions of digital panopticism is that, on the one hand, persons become more and more transparent, and on the other hand, systems that observe them are opaque. Therefore, Glissants' (1997) right to opacity has to be combined with institutional transparency.

Moreover, it is a dual visibility ethic. Diakopoulos (2016) goes on to say that algorithmic accountability requires this asymmetry: the watchers, rather than the watched, should be visible.

Indeed, this implies that the algorithms must be publicly audited, data flows disclosed, and there should be ethical standards that can be enforced. It must be possible to bring governments, companies, and AI creators to account for the way in which the information is used to decide upon people. On the other hand, people should have the right to manage their online identity.

That is, they should be able to exercise their right to know, decide, and forget in a digital world. The switch of the Panoptic gaze from surveillance to mutual visibility, where transparency is an instrument of justice, not of exploitation, means the same. As Lyon (2018) quotes, the democratic gaze is reciprocal. A transparent institution enables trust; however, if a citizen is transparent, they are just vulnerable.

Data Citizenship and Digital Democracy

Recovery of one's agency in the digital age is a matter of both protection and engagement. Taylor and Richter (2015) describe data citizenship as a democracy model, where individuals are active co-governors of data, instead of being merely passive data sources.

Developing critical data literacy is pivotal to this change. Training people to identify algorithmic bias, recognise the threat of corporate monopolies, and understand the economics of surveillance will empower them to use technology ethically.

Places like Barcelona's Decidim and Amsterdam's Data Commons represent the direction of such a change. They provide local communities with opportunities to own their data, ensuring transparency and the public good. The concept of decolonising data, as proposed by Couldry and Mejias (2019), entails giving control back to groups historically excluded.

As individuals become data citizens, the notion of Digital panopticism could be reimagined into a civic Panopticon, a participatory public sphere where watching is a means for holding oneself accountable and not for domination, and governance stands for mutual care instead of the exercise of power.

Global Inequalities and Algorithmic Colonialism

NA reconsideration of digital panopticism would be incomplete without addressing its global inequalities. Couldry and Mejias (2019), in their data colonialism, expose how digital infrastructures continue to invent new ways of the historical pattern of exploitation between the Global North and South. The organisations which operate from their main offices in Silicon Valley and Shenzhen have developed systems to collect information about billions of individuals which they use to transform human existence into basic resources for their computing operations.

The ideology of transparency and inclusion creates an appearance of open access but actually enables hidden methods of control that result in people becoming dependent on others, which the Chinese Social Credit System and Indian Aadhaar demonstrate. The practice of digital inclusion without granting people sovereignty functions as a modern form of colonisation, which extends its control through technological systems. The development of global data governance frameworks requires integrating redistributive ethics to ensure equitable data distribution supports development efforts rather than enabling resource extraction.

The global system of digital panopticism needs to establish intersectional connections among different systems that operate worldwide. The process of ethical reform requires international partnerships among governments, businesses, and non-profit organisations to develop shared standards that promote fair data practices. The 21st century will experience digital colonialism as the hidden power that controls everything.

Designing for Uncertainty: Freedom as Indeterminacy

One primary characteristic of algorithmic culture is its fixation with prediction. The desire for total foresight drives surveillance capitalism, algorithmic policing, and behavioural nudging, among other things. The desire to eliminate all uncertainty runs counter to the true nature of freedom. Foucault (1982) shows that power and resistance coexist as two aspects of a single entity. People need to experience all digital design processes to help designers establish their ethical framework.

The system creates opportunities for dissenting opinions and new ideas through its unpredictable operations, open-ended participation, reversibility of decisions, and debatable outcomes.

Through controlled systems, people achieve freedom by choosing to break established patterns. People should view ethical technology as a tool that mitigates unpredictable outcomes rather than a solution that eliminates all forecasting errors. As Han (2017) warns, if a society removes all opacity and surprise, it will likely also remove creativity. Choosing to live with uncertainty is choosing to live humanely.

The Future: From Gaze to Reflection

Digital panopticism as a metaphor for control; it can, in fact, be the primary framework for reflecting on how things have evolved. Surveillance technologies function similarly to other technologies because they reveal truth by exposing power relations that lie behind people's visibility. The algorithms become mirrors when they stop functioning as spotlights, thereby revealing the full range of human experiences and their inherent dignity.

This transition of the human aspect in the machine requires moral courage and a shared imagination. It is a call for designers to incorporate ethics into their work, for citizens to become co-governors, and for institutions to transform data from a commercial asset into a social trust. Under such redesigned conditions, transparency is first and foremost a means of accountability, and opacity is a person's right.

Digital panopticism requires criticism, but it poses a fundamental challenge that demands a complete reconstruction of modernity. The statement urges people to free their vision from its restricted functions, as it can be an effective instrument for knowledge development.

Conclusion: Rethinking Power, Visibility, and Control in Algorithmic Culture

To sum up, this chapter has delivered a significant thesis that the best way to comprehend the notion of digital panopticism is not as a singular piece of technology or a method of an institution, but as the ideological state of algorithmic culture where power manifests itself through the exposure, the extraction of data, and through the element of prediction. Through the combined theoretical borrowings from the works of Foucault, Deleuze, Zuboff, Han, Bauman, Lyon, Couldry, and Mejias, the analysis has revealed the gradual transformation of disciplinary surveillance from a simply centralised technique of power into a widely maintained, engaged, and economically motivated system of control.

Where Foucault's Panopticon model illustrates the internalisation of the gaze, Deleuze's societies of control unveil how this gaze becomes continuous and modulating; Zuboff uncovers its capitalist logic; Han discloses its psychopolitical attractiveness; Bauman and Lyon locate it within the context of liquid modernity; and data colonialism identifies its global inequalities. In brief, these various viewpoints, when taken together, form a single and consistent concept of digital panopticism: a mechanisation whereby people are, on the one hand, the objects of surveillance, on the other hand, the sources of data, and, in another way, they are willingly taking part in their own self-regulation.

The chapter has demonstrated that, through datafication, algorithmic profiling, biometric identification, and predictive analytics, surveillance gradually extends its control not only over individuals' conduct but also over their identities, moralities, and even their potentials. Moreover, the examples of China's Social Credit System and India's Aadhaar program, among others, reveal how algorithmic visibility is made a norm and justified through the rhetoric of trust, efficiency, and inclusion, at the same time creating new modes of exclusion and vulnerability, as a consequence of the operation of the algorithms. Nevertheless, the chapter also offers a different perspective: digital panopticism is not a complete or inevitable phenomenon. Resistance practices, from the use of encryption and the data justice movements to democratic data governance and digital literacy, indicate that the phenomena of surveillance can be challenged, diverted, and rethought.

In the end, the challenge raised by digital panopticism goes far beyond just technology; it is also a matter of ethics and politics. We can hardly affirm that algorithmic culture will continue to exist unless the authorities refrain from using visibility as a means of domination and instead grant it as a common, accountable, and democratic practice. Concentrating on the lack of transparency, making people aware of their rights and responsibilities regarding data, and embedding care and justice as the fundamental values of our digital infrastructures are ways we can turn algorithmic systems into tools that respect human dignity rather than violate it.

In this respect, digital panopticism is currently much more than a critique of contemporary power only; it also suggests that we need to rethink freedom, responsibility, and governance in the digital era.

REFERENCES

Ajana, B. (2020). *Governing through biometrics: The biopolitics of identity*. Palgrave Macmillan., DOI: 10.1007/978-3-030-37629-3

Albrechtslund, A. (2008). Online social networking as participatory surveillance. *First Monday*, *13*(3). Advance online publication. DOI: 10.5210/fm.v13i3.2142

Amoore, L. (2020). *Cloud ethics: Algorithms and the attributes of ourselves and others*. Duke University Press., DOI: 10.1515/9781478007686

Ball, K. (2021). Workplace surveillance: An overview. *Labor Studies Journal*, *46*(3), 244–260. DOI: 10.1177/0160449X21995889

Bauman, Z., & Lyon, D. (2013). *Liquid surveillance: A conversation*. Polity Press.

Beer, D. (2017). The data gaze: Capitalism, power and perception. *Sage (Atlanta, Ga.)*.

Berardi, F. (2017). *Futurability: The age of impotence and the horizon of possibility*. Verso.

Brayne, S. (2020). *Predict and surveil: Data, discretion, and the future of policing*. Oxford University Press., DOI: 10.1093/oso/9780190684099.001.0001

Browne, S. (2015). *Dark matters: On the surveillance of Blackness*. Duke University Press., DOI: 10.1515/9780822375302

Brunton, F., & Nissenbaum, H. (2015). *Obfuscation: A user's guide for privacy and protest*. MIT Press., DOI: 10.7551/mitpress/9780262029735.001.0001

Bucher, T. (2017). The algorithmic imaginary: Exploring the ordinary affects of Facebook algorithms. *Information Communication and Society*, *20*(1), 30–44. DOI: 10.1080/1369118X.2016.1154086

Buolamwini, J., & Gebru, T. (2018). Gender shades: Intersectional accuracy disparities in commercial gender classification. *Proceedings of Machine Learning Research, 81*, 1–15. http://proceedings.mlr.press/v81/buolamwini18a.html

Cadwalladr, C., & Graham-Harrison, E. (2018, March 17). Revealed: 50 million Facebook profiles harvested for Cambridge Analytica in major data breach. *The Guardian*. https://www.theguardian.com/news/2018/mar/17/cambridge-analytica-facebook-influence-us-election

Cheney-Lippold, J. (2017). *We are data: Algorithms and the making of our digital selves*. NYU Press., DOI: 10.18574/nyu/9781479888702.001.0001

Couldry, N., & Mejias, U. A. (2019). *The costs of connection: How data is colonising human life and appropriating it for capitalism*. Stanford University Press., DOI: 10.1515/9781503609754

Crawford, K., & Joler, V. (2018). *Anatomy of an AI system*. https://anatomyof.ai

Creemers, R. (2018). China's social credit system: An evolving practice of control. SSRN *Electronic Journal*. https://doi.org/DOI: 10.2139/ssrn.3175792

Deleuze, G. (1992). Postscript on the societies of control. *October, 59*, 3–7. https://www.jstor.org/stable/778828

Dencik, L., Hintz, A., Redden, J., & Treré, E. (2019). *Data justice and civic technology: Co-creating frameworks for equitable data governance*. Cardiff University. https://datajusticehub.org

Diakopoulos, N. (2016). Accountability in algorithmic decision making. *Communications of the ACM*, *59*(2), 56–62. DOI: 10.1145/2844110

Eubanks, V. (2018). *Automating inequality: How high-tech tools profile, police, and punish the poor*. St. Martin's Press.

Foucault, M. (1977). *Discipline and punish: The birth of the prison* (Sheridan, A., Trans.). Pantheon Books.

Foucault, M. (1982). The subject and power. *Critical Inquiry*, *8*(4), 777–795. DOI: 10.1086/448181

Fuchs, C. (2011). Web 2.0, prosumption, and surveillance. *Surveillance & Society*, *8*(3), 288–309. DOI: 10.24908/ss.v8i3.4165

Galič, M., Timan, T., & Koops, B. J. (2017). Bentham, Deleuze and beyond: An overview of surveillance theories from the Panopticon to participation. *Philosophy & Technology*, *30*(1), 9–37. DOI: 10.1007/s13347-016-0219-1

Glissant, É. (1997). *Poetics of relation* (Wing, B., Trans.). University of Michigan Press. DOI: 10.3998/mpub.10257

Greenwald, G. (2014). *No place to hide: Edward Snowden, the NSA, and the U.S. surveillance state*. Metropolitan Books.

Haggerty, K. D., & Ericson, R. V. (2000). The surveillant assemblage. *The British Journal of Sociology*, *51*(4), 605–622. DOI: 10.1080/00071310020015280 PMID: 11140886

Han, B.-C. (2017). *Psychopolitics: Neoliberalism and new technologies of power*. Verso.

Haraway, D. (1991). *A cyborg manifesto: Science, technology, and socialist-feminism in the late twentieth century*. Routledge.

Khera, R. (2019). *Dissent on Aadhaar: Big data meets big brother*. Orient BlackSwan.

Kitchin, R. (2014). The data revolution: Big data, open data, data infrastructures and their consequences. *Sage (Atlanta, Ga.)*. Advance online publication. DOI: 10.4135/9781473909472

Kostka, G. (2019). China's social credit systems and public opinion: Explaining high levels of approval. *New Media & Society*, *21*(7), 1565–1593. DOI: 10.1177/1461444819826402

Liang, F., Das, V., Kostyuk, N., & Hussain, M. M. (2018). Constructing a data-driven society: China's social credit system as a state surveillance infrastructure. *Policy and Internet*, *10*(4), 415–453. DOI: 10.1002/poi3.183

Lupton, D. (2016). *The quantified self*. Polity Press.

Lyon, D. (2018). *The culture of surveillance: Watching as a way of life*. Polity Press.

Marwick, A. E., & Boyd, D. (2011). I tweet honestly, I tweet passionately: Twitter users, context collapse, and the imagined audience. *New Media & Society*, *13*(1), 114–133. DOI: 10.1177/1461444810365313

Mirzoeff, N. (2011). *The right to look: A counterhistory of visuality*. Duke University Press., DOI: 10.2307/j.ctv1134d5q

Mol, A., Moser, I., & Pols, J. (Eds.). (2010). *Care in practice: On tinkering in clinics, homes and farms*. Transcript Verlag., DOI: 10.14361/9783839414477

Moore, P. V. (2018). *The quantified self in precarity: Work, technology and what counts*. Routledge., DOI: 10.4324/9781315231997

Moore, P. V., & Robinson, A. (2016). The quantified self: What counts in the neoliberal workplace. *New Media & Society*, *18*(11), 2774–2792. DOI: 10.1177/1461444815604328

Newport, C. (2019). *Digital minimalism: Choosing a focused life in a noisy world*. Penguin.

Noble, S. U. (2018). *Algorithms of oppression: How search engines reinforce racism*. NYU Press. DOI: 10.18574/nyu/9781479833641.001.0001

Pariser, E. (2011). *The filter bubble: What the Internet is hiding from you*. Penguin Press.

Pasquale, F. (2015). *The black box society: The secret algorithms that control money and information*. Harvard University Press. DOI: 10.4159/harvard.9780674736061

Raghavan, M., Barocas, S., Kleinberg, J., & Levy, K. (2020). Mitigating bias in algorithmic hiring: Evaluating claims and practices. *Proceedings of the ACM on Human-Computer Interaction, 4*(CSCW2), 1–27. https://doi.org/DOI: 10.1145/3351095.3372828

Rao, U. (2019). Biometric citizenship. *Social Anthropology*, *27*(2), 174–188. DOI: 10.1111/1469-8676.12620

Rouvroy, A., & Berns, T. (2013). Algorithmic governmentality and prospects of emancipation. *Réactivation du concept de biopolitique*, 1–20. https://hal.archives-ouvertes.fr/hal-00739755

Srnicek, N. (2017). *Platform capitalism*. Polity Press.

Taylor, L., & Richter, C. (2015). Data justice and data citizenship. *Open Data and the Knowledge Society Conference Proceedings*. https://doi.org/DOI: 10.2139/ssrn.2656787

Thaler, R. H., & Sunstein, C. R. (2008). *Nudge: Improving decisions about health, wealth, and happiness*. Yale University Press.

Turow, J. (2017). *The aisles have eyes: How retailers track your shopping, strip your privacy, and define your power*. Yale University Press.

Yeung, K. (2017). 'Hypernudge': Big data as a mode of regulation by design. *Information Communication and Society*, *20*(1), 118–136. DOI: 10.1080/1369118X.2016.1186713

Zuboff, S. (2019). *The age of surveillance capitalism: The fight for a human future at the new frontier of power*. PublicAffairs.

Chapter 6
Digital Feminism: Reclaiming Power and Identity in the Algorithmic Age

Vijeta Parihar
http://orcid.org/0009-0001-4980-1672
Christ University, India

Twinkle Singh
http://orcid.org/0000-0001-8855-5155
Christ University, India

ABSTRACT

In the algorithmic age, digital platforms are vital for visibility, expression, and agency, making feminism crucial at empowerment and control intersections. Digital Feminism transcends an online movement; it's an evolving ideological space challenging patriarchy in data systems, algorithmic design, and AI. This chapter as per the author, explores gender bias in digital infrastructures, marginalizing feminist voices while offering resistance and solidarity tools. Using feminist theory, digital humanities, and media studies, it views Digital Feminism as critiquing and reconstructing algorithmic culture. Interdisciplinary reflection examines feminist activism in digital spaces, algorithmic patriarchy implications, and feminist data ethics. The chapter advocates inclusive, transparent, feminist-aligned digital futures where technology aligns with equity, accountability, and care.

DOI: 10.4018/979-8-3373-4531-4.ch006

INTRODUCTION AND BACKGROUND

The Algorithmic Age and Gendered Power

The 21st century is a time of profound entanglement between algorithmic systems, especially artificial intelligence (AI), and the infrastructures that link up with data with our everyday social, economic and political lives. Algorithms now filter access to information, organise participation in digital publics and have a growing effect on decision-making in areas such as employment and education as well as policing and welfare. Those systems are not neutral or purely technical tools, but socio-technical assemblages situated within historical and institutional power relations.

It is fair to say that algorithms have been shown to be biased because they adopt and foster the biases of the social environments in which they were created. As (Noble, 2018; Benjamin 2019), and (Crawford, 2021) make clear, with varying accents, algorithmic systems are trained on historically situated datasets and developed within unjust organizational settings. As result, in social practice (in political context, but not only), they frequently re-produce gendered, racialized and classist hierarchies under the aegis of being objective or expedient. Indeed, gender in particular becomes a central axis through which algorithmic power is both felt and exercised, determining whose bodies, voices and experiences become visible or legible, credible or valuable.

Instagram, TikTok, YouTube and LinkedIn are among the digital spaces which do the work of what we used to call "spaces of appearance" – shaping collectively understood practices and norms in our cultures, as well as social recognition. Through algorithmic curation, ranking, and recommendation, platforms promote what is amplified and down-rank or marginalize the rest. Feminist researchers have pointed out that these processes reproduce patriarchal norms of beauty, productivity, affect and desirability via algorithmic patriarchy (Bechmann & Kim, 2020). Instances such as sexist hiring algorithms, racist facial recognition software and female submissive voice assistants demonstrate how each of the artificial systems preserve and normalize gender inequality through code.

It is in this algorithmic context that Digital Feminism is presented as a necessary critique to the expansion of data-driven power. Digital Feminism does not celebrate the liberatory potential inherent in technology, nor dismiss it as necessarily oppressive. Instead, it understands digital infrastructures as contested spaces marked by power relations whose inevitability and destiny may be subject to critique, challenge, and reimagination. As (D'Ignazio and Klein, 2020) suggest, feminist data practice opens space for care, accountability and justice in relation to data and algorithms in ways that contest dominant logics of efficiency, profit and extraction.

From Cyberfeminism to Digital Feminism

For many contemporary cyberfeminists, digital feminism –wearing the label´s genealogy on its sleeve- is seen as the future of online feminist activism post-cyborg culture and co-optation outrage (Banet-Weiser, 2018), not least due to what Dirksen calls "cyberfeminst advances" towards new ways of performing femininity in cyberspace, as I will suggest below.

Digital feminism has its historical roots in Cyberfeminism, which during the 1990s accompanied the proliferation of early internet culture. Cyberfeminist theorists mused on the potential for digital technologies to destabilize fixed identities, undermining patriarchal distinctions between human and machine, nature and culture. The cyborg as a hybrid figure that challenges essentialist ideas of gender and power was presented in (Donna Haraway, 2016) Cyborg Manifesto.

One of the most influential cyberfeminist imaginaries was generated in its early days, an imaginary that positioned the internet as a space of multiplicity and transformation, where women could play with identity and community without having to worry about being slotted into offline social hierarchies. But that optimism was unevenly spread. Access to digital technologies remained the prerogative of privileged groups in the Global North, and early cyberfeminist spaces frequently replicated racial, class and geopolitical exclusions.

With the transformation of digital economies toward platform capitalism (Srnicek, 2017) and surveillance capitalism (Zuboff, 2019), the naysayers' critique of cyberfeminist optimism gained greater saliency. Today's digital infrastructures are increasingly centralized around corporate-owned platforms that largely profit through attention, data ex- traction and visibility management in opaque algorithmic systems. Digital Feminism is a response to these conditions that repurposes have moved the focus from what can be made (a technological possibility) to who has power, how it is exercised and on whose bodies.

Unlike cyberfeminism, Digital Feminism is concerned precisely with who owns digital infrastructures (or controls them), whose labour makes such structures possible and whose identities are marginalised or excluded. It recasts feminist work around technology as critique and praxis, exploring not just representation but also the political economy of platforms and algorithms.

Algorithms as Ideological and Institutional Actors

Algorithms are ideological actors that contribute to the making of knowledge, representation, and value. Instead of simply mirroring social conditions, algorithmic systems co-constitute what is relevant, reliable or valuable (Beer, 2017). Ranking algorithms intervene in cultural meaning-making and social respect through classification, recommendation.

(Noble, 2018) critique of search engines provide an example of how racist and sexist stereotypes are recycled by algorithmic logics geared to commercial value rather than social accountability. But (Benjamin, 2019) has also given us the New Jim Code to remind us that discrimination is coded in tech through 'race-neutral' design choices that replicate existing inequality.

Algorithms function within a larger ecology of institutions, which (Gillespie, 2014) refers to as digital institutions. These institutions regulate speech, visibility and participation, determining what users see, and how users understand themselves and others. Understanding algorithms as ideological and institutional agent forms the basis of Digital Feminism, which attempts to correct for this by emphasizing technology as a political battlefield rather than a neutral infrastructure.

Digital Feminism: Resisting and Reconstructing

Digital Feminism includes resisting algorithmic oppression and rebuilding our digital systems. We have seen how feminist movements have used the digital space to create counter-publics that critique mainstream discourses and hierarchies. For instance, hashtags as #MeToo, #SayHerName, and #TimesUp illustrate how digital affordances can help marginalized individuals to have their voices heard and tell their stories collectively.

At the same time, they expose the flimsiness of digital visibility. Moderation practices, algorithmic downranking, and coordinated harassment all disproportionately impact feminist activists especially those who are women of colour, queer or from the Global South. Visibility, then, is a double-edged sword: it facilitates recognition but also puts activists under the range of both surveillance and physical harm.

Beyond resistance, Digital Feminism is reconstructive. Feminist scholars and practitioners engage directly with data science, human–computer interaction, and AI ethics to redesign systems according to principles of inclusion, accountability, and care (Bardzell, 2010; D'Ignazio & Klein, 2020). Digital Feminism therefore moves from critique toward the transformation of digital infrastructures themselves.

Research Aim, Scope, and Methodological Positioning

This chapter places Digital Feminism as a praxis of the mind and represents an analytical tool in the intervention into algorithmic culture. Methodologically, the chapter takes as a starting point a feminist critical–interpretive approach in conjunction with feminist theory, digital sociology, media studies and AI ethics. It is not based on original empirical data but offers an interdisciplinary overview that combines extra-disciplinary scholarly thought with examples of empirical cases in order to examine ways in which algorithmic systems impact gendered power relations.

The chapter has four primary objectives:

1. To theorize Digital Feminism as a critique of algorithmic power.
2. To-study How Tech reproduces Gendered, Intersecting Inequalities.
3. To analyse feminist critiques of, and challenges to the logics of computation in digital contexts.
4. To map out ethical, institutional and governance-related options for feminist intervention.

This positioning explains the contribution of the chapter and differentiates between empirically based knowledge gleaned from what is known in research, and normative feminist claims staked through critique.

LITERATURE REVIEW AND ANALYTICAL FRAMEWORK

Cyberfeminist Foundations

Cyberfeminist academia paved the way for a feminist relationship to digital technologies, by asking questions about embodiment, access and identity. (Scholars like Sadie Plant and Donna Haraway explored how digital systems could upend traditional gender hierarchies but also cautioned against technological determinism.)

Although cyberfeminism had contributed valuable analytic concepts, it was now criticized. The early cyberfeminist imaginaries failed to situate themselves against material disparities, global power imbalances, and the political economy underpinning emergent platforms. These critiques inform the turn to Digital Feminism.

Digital Feminism: as Ideology and Praxis

Digital feminism could be seen as an ideology, a critical approach and a praxis all at once. It forms an ideological address, a criticism of the power relations present in these technologies that counter narratives which present algorithms as neutral or objective or inevitable. It is a praxis, one that includes activist and scholarly and design-oriented interventions that do not just critique algorithmic systems but reshape them.

Digital Feminism is grounded in feminist theory, media studies, platform studies and AI ethics and locates the algorithm within wider socio-political and economic structures. Feminist scholars assert that an analysis of algorithmic systems needs to come not just in relation to technical practice, but also in terms of cultural significance, labour relations and governance models (Beer 2017; Crawford, 2021).

From this viewpoint, technology becomes a political infrastructure and one in which power is unevenly distributed along gendered and racialized lines.

Significantly, Digital Feminism also shifts away from representation issues of visibility for its own sake to systemic critique. And, particularly important: It asks how the design of platform architectures, data extraction procedures and monetisation models perform participation and recognition. For instance, when feminist critiques of content moderation and recommendation systems demonstrate how engagement-driven algorithms have a tendency to promote sensationalism and conformity with dominant norms at the expense of feminist, queer, and anti-caste voices.

As praxis, Digital Feminism is practised in work such as feminist data projects, participatory algorithm design and activist partnerships with technologists. Actionable feminism in the style of The Feminist Data Set Project is crucial for applying feminist epistemologies against exclusionary practices around data, for collective consultation and community leverage when appropriate, to reveal at least something about the inner workings of models going forward. These practices suggest a move from critique to reconstruction, positioning Digital Feminism as an active influence on technological futures.

Core Analytical Concepts

In order to counteract conceptual repetition and ensure analytical clarity, this chapter takes the literature as organized along five interconnected analytical concepts that inform discussions of Digital Feminism. These categories are not mutually exclusive, but rather overlapping dimensions that collectively account for the ways in which feminism engages with algorithmic culture.

Algorithmic Patriarchy: Are how gender power relations replicate through computer systems, doing so in a systematic way. Based on empirical research into hiring algorithms, facial recognition technologies and recommendation systems, the notion shows how past injustices are embedded in data driven decision making.

Visibility Politics: It's a thoughtful treatment of the ambivalence of visibility in digital culture. As much as more exposure may help give voice to the marginalized and enable collective action, it also brings with it surveillance, harassment and algorithmic silencing. Feminist hashtag campaigns exemplify this tension, where visibility becomes a resource as well as a threat.

Affective Digital Labor: It refers to the affective (emotional, relational and typically unpaid) labour -performed mostly by women and other marginalized genders online. That includes both content moderation, community management and personal storytelling for political efficacy. This labour creates value for platforms, and is unvalued structurally.

Intersectionality: It acknowledges that gendered encounters with digital systems are also shaped by – among others – race, class, sexuality, disability, caste and geography. Raj emphasizes how intersecting forms of discriminatory AI-based practices particularly impact women of colour, Dalit women, queer and trans people around the world so-called Global South.

Reconstructive Ethics: Feminist efforts to re-build digital systems through practices of participation, inclusion and accountability. That might involve feminist data practices, ethical AI design and governance systems that centre care, justice and social responsibility.

Individually and taken together, these analytical concepts form a structure in which to think about Digital Feminism as both critique and praxis, which this articulation now accompanies the empirical and theoretical investigations in this study.

Collectively, they are a coherent vector of analysis informing the next section.

HISTORICAL GENEALOGIES OF GENDER AND TECHNOLOGY

To make sense of Digital Feminism, the analysis hesitates to contextualize the contemporary algorithmic systems in longer historical trajectories and history of gendered technological progression. Technologies don't exist in the vacuum; they are situated within cultural imaginaries, work hierarchies, epistemic traditions, and political economics that predates the digital era (Wajcman, 1991). The gendered dynamics of contemporary algorithmic infrastructures are rooted in longer histories of exclusion, appropriation, and epistemic erasure. In mapping these histories, Digital Feminism deepens its critique of algorithmic power as one of continuity and not a break from earlier forms of technological injustice.

Women in the Dawn of Computing

Despite prevailing narratives that present computing as a masculine field, women were instrumental in the creation of computer systems. In the nineteenth century, Ada Lovelace's contribution to Charles Babbage's Analytical Engine elucidated algorithms as far from being mechanical processes—rather they were symbolic manipulations that could produce creative results (Plant, 1997). Her writings presaged current debates over machine intelligence and automation.

Women were computer programmers, cryptographers and systems analysts during World War II and in the decades after. The women who operated the ENIAC computer, often described as the first general-purpose electronic computer, working in complex mathematical and logical processing without which it would not have performed (Abbate, 2012). These women were not coders; they were the pioneers of programming logic, debugging strategies and computer workflows. But their work was diminished or disregarded in history while well-funded male engineers were lauded for hardware advances.

Likewise, in post-war Britain women were key players in computing industry when newly emerging before being systematically expelled during periods of professionalisation (Hicks 2017). As programming became economically prestigious in the 1960s and '70s, recruiting tactics shifted toward men. Aptitude tests, personality profiling and corporate cultures were refashioned to favour traits linked with masculinity - such as personal competition and technical swagger (Ensmenger, 2010).

The masculinization of computing was not accidental. It grew out of the larger cultural association of rationality, abstraction, and technical mastery with masculinity (Harding 1986). Thus, women were increasingly cast as marginal or supportive to technological institutions. Current under representation of women from AI research and data science should therefore be seen as the legacy of such historical exclusions rather than a neutral pipeline issue (Margolis & Fisher, 2003).

Digital Feminism reads algorithmic bias through this historical framework. When algorithmic systems produce gendered disparities, they are not only reflecting biased datasets but also institutional cultures that have historically excluded whose knowledge counts as technical authority.

The Gendering of Technical Expertise

The building of expertise in technical matters has always been a gendered affair. Western scientific traditions have perpetuated a hierarchy of such values as objectivity, detachment, and abstraction (traits culturally constructed as masculine) over relationality, empathy, and embodiment (coded as feminine) (Harding, 1986). These epistemic pecking orders ordered professional esteem in engineering, mathematics, and computer science.

The myth of the male technological genius blossomed with the explosion of Silicon Valley in the late 20th century. Entrepreneurial tales that revolved around types like the individual lone programmer-founder reinforced cultural imaginaries which defined creativity against masculine genius (Ensmenger, 2010). Media coverage of hackers and developers tended to focus on antisocial intensity and technical mastery, ignoring cooperative or care-related aspects of hacking.

Such stories cover over the social character of the production that produces those same technologies. Algorithms are not simply technical objects; they are the results of institutional cultures, funding regimes, and value structures. Gender and racial diversity are not entering into the design teams, being missed out in the assumptions built from datasets, evaluation criteria or interface design rooted on narrower point of views (Bowker & Star, 1999).

Digital Feminism disrupts the epistemological authority of claims for algorithmic neutrality. It insists that technicity is socially made and historically gendered. Acknowledging this situatedness challenges not so much the progressiveness of new technology" but who has power and control over it in rethinking that difference epistemologies," including feminist and intersectional ones, are necessary in ensuring just design of systems.

Labor, Capitalism, and the Feminization of Digital Work

The transition to informational and platform capitalism changed the organization of work, but not the gendered hierarchies that articulate it. What he means is that women under industrial capitalism were cornered into undervalued work like textiles, clerical work, and domestic labor (Federici, 2012). These were performed through jobs that involved repetition and emotional work but remained invisible in economic logics of accounting.

In the digital economy, those same patterns are revived in altered guise. The kinds of jobs that offer ESCL repayments, such as content moderation, data labelling, gig work on platforms and influencer labour are dominated by women and other marginal groups (Roberts, 2019). This labor of care requires emotional regulation, aesthetic presentation and constant attentiveness: an extension of what Hochschild (1983) called "emotional labor."

For instance, social media influencers—overwhelmingly female — labour, carry out long-term affective work as they forge intimate relations with followers by adjusting content to algorithmic logic. While such work produces considerable economic value for platforms in terms of engagement and advertising, it is precarious and atomized.

Digital Feminism places this dynamic within broader histories of capitalist extraction. Platform capitalism makes attention, as well as emotion labour, are commodities and convert social interaction into data. Under histories of appearance, sociability, and care amplify the requirements on women to do visibility. Algorithmic economies, therefore reproduce and magnify previous ways of exploiting feminized labour.

Digital Colonialism and Epistemic Extraction

There is no doubt that the problems mentioned above have little to do directly with copyright licenses, as they rather seem to parallel a systematic lack of access to educational and scientific knowledge in parts of Africa and the former semi peripheral world.

Colonial pasts have also informed technological infrastructures. Today's digital platforms harvest data from around the world – at times even targeting individuals within communities with few regulatory safeguards (Couldry & Mejias, 2019). This "data colonialism" is a continuation of historical resource extraction patterns applied now to information domains.

AI machine learning systems trained on largely Western and English language datasets privilege Western epistemologies and linguistic communities (Birhane, 2020). Dark skin bias Numerous biometric technologies are less accurate for people with darker skin (Benjamin, 2019) because their training data are skewed towards colonial photographic collections that privileged whiteness.

Digital Feminism incorporates the postcolonial critique of how algorithmic systems function within global hierarchies of knowledge production. Inter sectional violences against women of color, Dalit women, the indigenous and migrant populations are shaped by intersecting histories of patriarchy and colonialism.

Through tracking these genealogies, Digital Feminism attests to the fact that algorithmic injustice is grounded in history. "Reimagining digital futures consequently mean addressing entrenched institutional, epistemic and economic forms.

EPISTEMOLOGY OF DIGITAL FEMINISM

DF is not only a politics of standpoint, but also an epistemology of intervention. It examines how knowledge is manufactured, classified, and instrumentalised in algorithmic societies.

Feminist Standpoint Theory in Data Societies

From the feminist standpoint theory, marginalized social locations produce unique epistemic perspectives (Collins 2000; Harding, 1986). Human knowledge is socially conditioned not universally neutral. In data-driven worlds, decisions about who gets counted and how also help determine what is made visible or actionable (Bowker & Star, 1999).

Datasets reflect institutional priorities. Data collection that erases marginalized experiences, is processed into algorithmic systems resulting in the reproduction of epistemic injustice. Digital Feminism applies standpoint theory to computational discourses, promoting participatory data governance.

Situated Knowledge and Algorithm Objectivity

Haraway (1988) also questions the objectivity of being outside a self through knowledge and she calls this situated knowledges. "Predictions" in algorithms are often framed as value-neutral byproducts of data. Nonetheless, model architectures, optimization objectives and performance metrics encode normative judgments (Kitchin, 2017).

Digital Feminism reconceptualizes AI systems as hermeneutic objects, positioned within the economic and political. This renders transparency with respect to design assumptions and stakeholder values that participated in shaping the model a core element of epistemic accountability.

Power/Knowledge and Algorithmic Governmentality

Influenced by Foucault's (1977) Power/Knowledge analysis, Digital Feminism reflects on how classification mechanisms regulate populations. This act of scoring risk and the ubiquitous availability of recommendation systems and predictive analytics normalise some actions at the expense of others (Kitchin, 2017).

It works through mechanisms of ranking and exposure, this governmentality by algorithm. Feminist criticism has demonstrated how these systems reinforce (patriarchal) norms masquerading as efficiency.

Ethics of Care and Epistemic Framework

The ethics of care can be understood as an epistemic framework that43 runs counter to the faith in linear, direct, scientific progress toward truth.

An ethics of care focuses on how our connectivity to others can promote responsibility, context and attentiveness for harm (Tronto, 1993; Held, 2006). As applied to AI systems, care ethics problematizes optimization logics that prioritize scale over justice.

Within Digital Feminism, there are evaluation measures that take into account distributive impact and harm reduction. Accuracy is not enough: systems need to be judged by the social impacts they can bring.

Toward Epistemic Justice in the Algorithmic Societies

In the end, Digital Feminism calls for epistemic justice: it's about recognizing that marginalised communities are legitimate sites of knowledge production and play important roles in technological governance. Using standpoint theory, situated knowledges and care ethics, Digital Feminism re-imagines the epistemology of digital infrastructures.

It changes the essential question to "how functional is this system?" to "Whose knowledge does this system favour, and at whose expense? In so doing, it integrates technological advancement with democratic accountability and intersectional justice.

CRITICAL ANALYSIS: DYNAMICS OF DIGITAL FEMINISM

This section provides a detailed critical analysis of how Digital Feminism operates within algorithmic culture by examining key domains in which gendered power is produced, contested, and reconfigured. This analysis leverages a series of empirical case studies that have been raised throughout the chapter, including AI hiring algorithms and beauty filters, and voice-enabled assistants and women-led hashtag movements, to show both how algorithmic systems afford but also delimit feminist interventions.

Algorithmic Bias and Patriarchy

One of the most pressing issues for Digital Feminism is algorithmic bias. There is a wealth of research showing that algorithmic systems generate gendered hierarchies when trained on historical data, which reflect oppressive social practices and have been developed within male-dominated technological institutions. And these systems don't just mirror bias; they compound it, by baking the biases of past into new ones that feed upon themselves.

An illustrative empirical case is Amazon's discontinued AI recruitment tool, which systematically penalized résumés including keywords indicative of female identity (e.g., participation in women's 3Demographic markers Once ingroup features are used as cues to identify members of the outgroup with false positives, they become potential new key points for the second-order irreversible discrimination: females when using some refrigerators and males when playing with some toys; disabled persons who do use a wheelchair while their impairment may not be related to leg motion) or affiliations (women in enterprises). Trained on historical male-dominated hiring data, the system associated competence and leadership with masculine-coded behaviours (Dastin, 2018). From a digital feminist perspective, it is about how algorithmic systems naturalize gender inequity on the grounds of efficiency and objectivity.

Likewise, facial recognition technology also demonstrates much higher error rates for women with darker skin tones (Buolamwini & Gebru, 2018). Such differential arises from the skewed landscape of pictorial databases, dominated by light-skinned male faces that are also the most suitable examples to reinforce racist or gendered exclusions. Digital Feminism reads such glitches as technical failures, but also as instances of cracks in the structure of power hidden within data practices and design cultures.

Taken together, these are examples of algorithmic patriarchy: the generation and maintenance of gendered power relations by computational systems. Digital Feminism argues that fixing algorithmic bias will demand more than technical solutions, it demands structural remedies to the question of who owns knowledge, experiences and bodies in data.

Feminization of Affective Labour & Digital Labour

Digital Feminism also explores the gendering of work in platform economies. Digital platforms are dependent on emotional, relational and aesthetic labour that is disproportionately done by women and minority genders. This work includes creating audience interactions, moderation or maintenance and offering one's own stories as often represented in terms of being authentic or empowered.

Social media influencers, especially women, epitomize this phenomenon. As (Abidin, 2018) illustrates, "visibility" is performed on platforms like Instagram and TikTok as an ongoing practice of affective labour: that is, it demands repeated emotional engagement with others, self-branding, and responding to algorithmic interface. This labour creates economic value for the platforms that is realized in advertising and data monetization, yet it is precarious and has thus far been unequally compensated.

Content moderation offers another example. Moderation work is frequently outsourced and underpaid it requires workers to engage with disturbing or traumatic content to maintain platform "safety." Feminist scholars argue that this labor mirrors historical patterns of feminized care work, rendering emotional labor invisible while extracting value from it (Gray, 2020).

Digital Feminism shows how platform metrics value visibility while hiding the labour that produces it. Women can be hyper visible in engagements stats yet remain structurally marginalised within the decision-making and governance systems.

Feminist Activism, Hashtag Movements, and Counter-Publics

Digital technologies have facilitated new types of feminist activism in the form of counter-publics that contest hegemonic discourses and patriarchal omissions. Hashtag campaigns like #MeToo, #SayHerName, and #TimesUp demonstrate the ways in which digital storytelling can galvanize movements for change, foster transnational solidarity, and compel institutions to address gendered injustices.

The #MeToo movement transformed individual reports into an archive of gendered violence, a registered body of evidence accounting for scale (of harassment across industries and national context). From the perspective of digital feminism, hashtags work as infrastructures of visibility—temporary means through which attention and credibility are being redistributed to otherwise silenced voices (Gill & Orgad, 2018).

Yet feminist counter-publics are still situated within platform governance logics that pose strong limits. Algorithmic downranking, content moderation biases as well as shadow banning and coordinated harassment campaigns, have particularly negatively impacted feminist activists and journalists – more so those with marginalised identities such as Dalit feminists and queer campaigners among others. These processes capture the ambivalence of visibility politics: on the one hand, visibility allows activists to be recognized, but it also makes them subject to surveillance, backlash and harm.

Digital Feminism, accordingly, does not understand hashtag activism as a replacement for structural transformation but rather as an act-in-place in which its political possibility is contingent on platform governance and institutional responsiveness, as well as further collective organizing beyond digital visibility.

Intersectional and Global Aspects of Algorithmic Power

Intersectionality is a cornerstone of Digital Feminism as an analytical framework. An algorithmic experience of sex difference is always imbricated with a caste, class, race-based orientation to systems. There is empirical evidence that algorithmic harms disproportionately impact women at the intersection of multiple axes of oppression.

For example, facial recognition technologies are much more likely to falsely identify women of colour than white men, with possible ramifications for surveillance, policing, and access to services (Buolamwini & Gebru, 2018). Likewise, programs that rely on binaries of gender disenfranchise trans and non-binary persons by making their identities unreadable to data regimes (McRae, 2019).

Global South feministic movements also complicate dominant discourses of digital empowerment. Feminist activists in South Asia, Africa and Latin America are using digital mediums to challenge digital colonialism, language hierarchies, and lack of infrastructure. They highlight how struggles that emerge from within the context of local feminist organising are transformed by digital tools to contest not only patriarchy, but also global power inequalities: #DalitWomenFight #AuratMarch

Digital Feminism therefore demands the necessity of a transnational and intersectional approach that acknowledges how these algorithmic systems actively replicate global inequalities while also providing methods for localised resistance. Without this understanding, feminist interventions may merely re-enact the exclusions they address.

DIGITAL FEMINISM AND EMERGING TECHNOLOGIES

As algorithmic systems are further developed, feminist critique must expand beyond platform analysis to question up-and-coming technological spaces. Generative AI, biometric surveillance, immersive environments and automated decision-making systems constellate new arrangements of gendered power.

Feminism and Generative Artificial Intelligence

Generative AI systems, such as language models at scale, scraped from the internet large amounts of data reflecting historical biases that are now baked into computational infrastructures (Bender et al., 2021). And these systems don't just search for information; they produce representations that structure the cultural imagination.

Research shows that language models reflect occupation gender bias in generating leader and technical roles for men, but caregiver or affective labour for women (Lucy & Bamman, 2021). And also the text and image models spontaneously create pornographic images of women reinforcing commercial femininity aesthetics (Birhane et al., 2021).

Feminist scholars claim that generative AI systems are engaging in mass symbolic production. In representing automatically, they further entrench gendered hierarchies. Accordingly, Digital Feminism demands transparency of training data provenance, moderated dataset construction and governance over model deployment.

Surveillance, Biometric Governance and Reproductive Autonomy

Gender implications of biometric mass surveillance systems such as facial recognition and predictive analytics are deeply troubling. Studies show that women of colour experience a greater level of misidentifications in facial recognition systems (Raji et al., 2020). These inaccuracies can lead to false imprisonment, surveillance and discrimination in services.

Predictive analytics in welfare policy may over target those who are marginalised women as being high needs and so, stigma might become more entrenched (Eubanks, 2018). Reproductive surveillance raises additional concerns. Based on our situation, also privacy concern to be aware of period and location can use as a weapon where the woman reproductive right is not respected (Privacy international, 2019).

Digital Feminism re-focuses on surveillance as a feminist problem. Body politics, privacy, and reproductive justice converge under algorithmic governmentality. Innovative technologies turn one's intimate life into measurable data, making new kinds of institutional intervention possible.

Immersive Technologies and Digital Embodiment

Virtual reality (VR) and metaverse ecosystems provide incarnate aspects of digital communication. Sexual harassment claims in VR illustrate that gendered violence also persists in immersive environments (Blackwell et al., 2019). Avatar customization frequently replicates limited beauty ideals (Gordon & Currin, 2014) and binary gender options in a way that can exclude the users it aims to include (Nakamura, 2013).

But virtual and immersive technologies may offer possibilities for identity exploration and even community. Avatar system and governance design with feminist participatory design for inclusivity. Digital Feminism argues for preventative measures when it comes to the development of these immersive platforms, before patriarchal norms are normalized.

Automation in Health Care and Social Services

The provision of health and social care is increasingly intermediated by AI systems. Algorithmic triage technologies rank patients according to their risk scores determined from past medical data. But medical data usually represent bias along race and sex, which results in discriminant care (Obermeyer et al., 2019).

Gendered pain bias—the dismissal or underdiagnosis of women's symptoms—could be embedded in automation decision systems (Criado-Perez, 2019). Feminist bioethics emphasizes the need for inclusive datasets, transparency, and community consultation in health AI development (Sharon, 2016).

Digital Feminism contends that efficient, automated care should not outweigh the relational and situational aspects of caring. Technologies used in sensitive and vulnerable areas should be subject to an increased ethical examination.

CHALLENGES AND AMBIVALENCES OF DIGITAL FEMINISM

Although the digital feminism has some compelling opportunities for critique, resistance, and reconstruction it is not unbound by structural, technological or socio-political limits to transformation. This section identifies the primary limitations and ambivalences that Digital Feminism faces, stressing that these are not 'failures' of feminist praxis as much as they are expressions of larger power asymmetries in the making up algorithmic culture.

Dependence on Platform and Corporate Governance

One of the key issues facing Digital Feminism is its dependence on commercial digital platforms like Instagram, TikTok, X (previously named Twitter), and YouTube. These are driven by profit-making capitalist business models, which concern themselves with user engagement, data mining and advertising revenue rather than the non-commercial objectives of social justice or democratic accountability (Srnicek, 2017; Zuboff, 2019).

Feminist activism taking place in and around these spaces is thus governed by impervious, uneven accounts of their own organization of information that are often politically hostile. These algorithmic ranking processes prefer sensational, emotionally evoking and commercially interesting content over feminist critique of the current state of affairs. Content about sexual violence, caste-based discrimination or reproductive rights is often labelled "controversial" or "graphic," and thus downranked or removed; yet misogynistic content routinely goes unscathed.

This interdependency leads to a structural paradox: Digital Feminism depends on platforms for its visibility and mobilization but remains limited by the same infrastructures it wants to contest. From a feminist perspective, such tensions illustrate the limitations of app-based activism without institutional accountability and regulation.

Algorithmic Silencing, Harassment and Online Violence

The online space limits Digital Feminism even more through various forms of internet harassment, trolling, doxxing and gendered attacks. Studies reveal that women — especially women of colour, Dalit feminists, queer activists and journalists are all known to disproportionately face digital violence (Jane, 2016). These assaults are exacerbated by the architecture inherently rewarding engagement, even when that "engagement" is harassment or coordinated abuse.

Algorithmic silencing compounds these harms. Tactics of shadow banning, content demotion and account suspensions are increasingly curtailing the visibility of feminist speech with no meaningful recourse. Algorithmic forms of moderation often can't differentiate between feminist speech that talks about violence, and content that poses harm, and this blocks activist narratives. This harassment and muzzling combination results in a chilling effect which is inhibiting people from participating and forcing them into self-censorship.

Digital Feminism demonstrates that online abuse is far more than just a cultural problem, it is embedded in the design of platforms and their moderation policies, and the networked data structures are rigged in Favor of this type of systemic harassment. Addressing these harms thus require system-wide interventions, not individual resiliency.

Digital divide and Unequal access

"Global expansion of digital technologies has not been equitable, with uneven access to such infrastructures remaining deeply unequal. The digital divide—whether cast along lines of income, geography, gender, caste, disability or language—restricts who can take part in these digital feminist movements. In rural areas, for low-income families and non-binary gender identity, internet access, personal technology equipment and digital literacy may be less available.

Gender-based social and cultural norms that limit women's access to their personal devices, privacy, and online presence further curtail women's digital autonomy. In cases women share devices with family members or are under surveillance by partners or relatives, access to freely engage in digital spaces are hampered. Language hierarchies marginalize non-English feminist discourses as well, perpetuating the hegemony of digital activism from the Global North.

These forms of inequality pose a counter-narrative to more celebratory accounts of digital empowerment but they also highlight the importance for Digital Feminism of addressing material realities alongside symbolic visibility.

Intersectional Blind Spots and Internal Tensions

Although Digital Feminism posits intersectionality as a cornerstone, feminist interventions are not free from replicating exclusions. The dominant online feminist discourse, tends to be dominated by the interests of urban, educated and global north actors, at the expense of rural women, Dalit feminists, people with disabilities & non-binary folks.

SOPs that enforce binary classification of gender perpetuate trans and non-binary defacement by making these identities illegible in data systems. Likewise, occupation of platforms inherently works against activists from marginalized communities as they are forced to play on an uneven playing field where existing power dynamics can be replicated and even exacerbated.

It is part of reflexive feminist praxis to locate and acknowledge this blind spot. Digital Feminism needs to stay vigilant about its own hierarchies, and for whom speech is amplified, and who gets thrown under the bus.

Commodification, Co-optation and Performative Feminism

Digital Feminism is especially susceptible to commodification and co-optation by industry, influencers and politicians in platform economies. Feminism has now become utilized as a symbolic resource for the branding, marketing and enhancement of reputations as it was more commonly used throughout the feminist activism of the twentieth century. Under this process of transformation, feminist critique becomes an aesthetic or a rhetorical operation disengaged from its structural and political allegiances.

Corporate co-option of feminist rhetoric is most overt in advertisements that use taglines like "empower women," "girl boss," or "women supporting women" while maintaining exploitative labour conditions, wage disparities between genders and exclusionary work cultures. Here, feminist rhetoric is a matter of symbolic attachment rather than political substance.

Digital Feminism challenges this disjunction between representational inclusion and material conditions, suggesting that visibility itself is not synonymous with justice.

Influencer culture is further complicating feminist politics online. Platforms incentivize content that is aesthetically pleasing, emotionally resonant and easily digestible to create a kind of feminism that's at best self-branding, not collective transformation. With activism, the danger is that it will become performative: That posting a hashtag or sharing someone's curated narrative will take the place of long-term political organizing and institutional change. As (Banet-Weiser, 2018) suggests, this move toward "popular feminism" reconstitutes feminist politics as a consumable identity and not a movement based on redistributing power.

From a digital feminist viewpoint, performative feminism is not only a moral failing of individual actors but also a structural effect of platform capitalism. It's the kind of feminism that is encouraged when you create algorithms for engagement and participation is incentive in single-minded, defanged iterations, then silence critical opposition to corporate power, state violence or global inequality. By acknowledging these dynamics, Digital Feminism can differentiate symbolic representation from transformative praxis and insist upon the necessity of structural accountability as well as cultural change.

STRATEGIES FOR FEMINIST INTERVENTION

Although Digital Feminism is critically aware of the limitations that are imposed on it by platform capitalism and algorithmic governance, it also elaborates a series of tactics designed to redesign digital systems. These solutions span technical, organizational and regulatory layers, to highlight a fact that we cannot overcome change by individual platforms or practices alone.

Algorithmic Accountability and Feminist Data Practices

Feminist data practices are a key part of any strategy for contesting algorithmic inequality. They endorse transparent data collection, participatory dataset construction, and bias audits at every stage of the lifecycle of algorithmic systems. They approach bias not as an accidental side-effect, but as a foreseeable outcome of uneven power relations ingrained in data infrastructures.

Others like feminist dataset redesign and participatory algorithm design aim to redistribute epistemic authority by including marginalized populations in the determination of which data are collected, annotated, and interpreted. Algorithmic audits, impact assessments and human-in-the-loop systems are also powerful efforts toward accountability that allow algorithmic decision-making to be visible and contested. From a digital feminist perspective, accountability is not only technical but also ethical and political; institutions are required to be held accountable for the societal impacts of their automated systems.

Ethical Platform and Interface Construction

Yet, ethical platform and interface design stand as another vital juncture for feminist intervention. Visibility, interaction and participation are structured by the design of platform architectures. Feminist perspectives on design play against assumptions of neutrality and place inclusivity, access, and care at the heart of design.

An HCD also considers interface inclusivity, such as gender neutrality or user-defined identification, diverse visual representation, and usable design for differently abled users. The introduction of user-controlled recommendation systems opens the possibility of stepping back from black-box ranking schemes instead let the users taking control on what content they face. Fair moderation practices, which are formed in consultation with affected communities, try to remove harassment and abuse without selectively muting the voices of the marginalized.

Through the incorporation of feminist values in interface and platform design, Digital Feminism aims to reimagine digital spaces from sites of extraction and surveillance into infrastructures that foster safety, participation, and democratic engagement.

Policy, Functional and Legal Frameworks

Spot solutions from a technical and design perspective must be in parallel with institutions for laws and governance that stand the test of time. Taking a critical approach into consideration of regulations along the lines of privacy, AI and platform liability, Digital Feminism contends that regulatory failings are gravely needed for the purpose of counterbalancing corporate power.

These feminist analyses of sex work have implications for policy by highlighting questions of consent, privacy, surveillance and differential harm. Regimes like the GDPR, for example, at least partially integrate some of these concerns at least vis-à-vis user rights and transparency. New governance approaches for AI and methodologies such as algorithm impact assessments, risk based regulatory design create further pathways to addressing systemic bias.

Digital Feminism insists that control systems should be participatory, enforceable, and sensitive to intersectional inequalities. Platform liability regimes, anti-harassment laws, and obligations for algorithmic transparency are practical mechanisms to make sure that digital infrastructures function in line with gender justice and democratic accountability.

DISCUSSION AND IMPLICATIONS

This chapter has explored Digital Feminism as a critical and reconstructive optics on algorithmic culture. Intertwining feminist theory, media studies, digital sociology, and AI ethics, the analysis argues that algorithms are not politically neutral technological artifacts but political infrastructures that govern visibility, labour, identity and power. The following section summarizes the chapter's main contributions and draws implications for the broader theory, practice, and policy.

Theoretical Implications: Rethinking Feminism in an Algorithmic Society

One of the major theoretical contributions of this chapter is the revising of feminist theory for algorithmic societies. Traditional feminist issues of power, representation, and embodiment are being played out in digital infrastructures more than as not algorithms come between social relations. Becoming Digital Feminism reframes some traditional feminist questions—who gets to be visible? Who is heard? Who decides? within data-centric and algorithmic decision-making contexts.

By moving the discussion beyond these simplistic framings, the chapter demonstrates how gendered power speaks and works through technical systems that are frequently represented as neutral or effective, intervening directly with ideas of algorithmic patriarchy, politics of visibility, and affective digital labour. Digital feminism therefore questions technological determinism, and strengthens feminist epistemologies that regard the generation, classification and valuation of knowledge as political practices.

The chapter also adds to feminist debates by bringing intersectionality into considerations of algorithmic power. It reveals that gender cannot be separated from race, caste, class, sexuality, disability and geography then dispersed across digital spaces in ways data practices fetishize identity into simplified taxonomies. This intersectional digital feminist lens extends feminist theory beyond issues of representation and toward critiquing the structure of computational systems.

Implications for Activism and Collective Praxis

Both sets of emergent practices described have ramifications for activism and collective praxis.

The paper draws attention to the mixed fortune of digital platforms in contemporary feminist activism. Web platforms on the other hand facilitate a fast deployment of transnational solidarity and collective narration as evidenced by hashtag movements and digital counter-publics. By contrast, platform-based governance, algorithmic silencing and violence online condition feminist agency and expose activists to harm.

Digital Feminism´ reclaims activism as not just a question of expressive participation but also one of infrastructural confrontation. In this sense, an effective feminist praxis will involve a strategic approach to platform dynamics; in the algorithmic incentives, moderation policies and data extraction processes that shape our potential use of platforms. Such a perspective reorients feminist activism away from visibility as an end into itself toward ongoing collective organising, institutional accountability, and infrastructural transformation.

The conversation also brings attention to the necessity of care and sustainability as part of feminist activism. Cognizant of the emotional and psychological tolls of digital engagement, Digital Feminism prioritizes shared support systems, ethical methods of storytelling, and boundaries that centre activist wellness as much as political impact.

Implications for Technological Design and Innovation

Digital Feminism has much to offer in the development, application, and appraisal of technologies—such as AI and algorithmic systems. By revealing the nature of bias as structurally embedded within data and design processes, feminist critique disrupts ruling innovation paradigms that opt for efficiency and scale over equity and accountability.

Design feminists emphasise --collaborative methods--that engage underrepresented individuals in shaping problem definitions, datasets, and criteria for evaluation. This brings the user from a passive data source to an active player in technological innovation. Digital Feminism serves nascent conversations around responsible AI, ethical design, and human-centred computing by bringing justice, care, and inclusion to the fore as central focus for design.

Crucially, the chapter illustrates that ethical design is not merely a matter of technical patching. Without institutional support and governance, design interventions tend to be symbolic gestures rather than forces for structural change. Digital Feminism thus calls for further alignment between design practices and larger political and regulatory frameworks.

Policy, Governance and Regulatory Implications

In addition, the conversation reinforces Digital Feminism's pertinence to policy and digital governance. As algorithmic systems come to shape work, welfare, policing and public debate, feminist analysis has much to inform how regulation should tackle uneven harms and power structures. The Governing Feminist Subjects edited the subject of digital feminism to emphasize the themes of consent, surveillance, platform liability and algorithmic accountability. Some regulatory tools, such as data protection laws, AI risk assessments and transparency requirements partly respond to these concerns, but do not sufficiently take into account intersectional inequalities or enforcement deficits.

Through its commitment to participatory governance, enforceable accountability and focus on marginalized communities, Digital Feminism broadens the horizons of digital policy from compliance to democratic oversight. It places feminist scholars and activists at the centre of efforts to shape just digital futures.

Societal and Cultural Implications

Outside of the academy and policy, Digital Feminism also has wider implications on society: how we interpret gender, identity, and power in digital cultures. The mainstreaming of feminist conversation online has also meant heightened public attention on issues like consent, digital violence, body politics and surveillance. first, the chapter illustrates that exposure is not in and of itself a solvent for structural inequality.

Digital Feminism transforms cultural production – it influences art, storytelling, and everyday digital praxes. Feminist memes, digital art, and narratives disrupt predominant norms while technology enables new imaginaries of being in the world. Such interventions feminize the traditional environment and mainstream company, creating space for a critique of commodification as well as resistance.

Synthesis: Critique and Reconstruction

In light of overall conversation, that brings us to the heart of Digital Feminism's major contribution: its turn away from critique and towards reconstruction. Though feminist research has long revealed gendered inequalities, Digital Feminism takes this further by taking on the infrastructures that structure so many aspects of contemporary social lives.

Combining theory and empirical demonstration, along with interventionist theories of digital feminism, this is the first critical work to apply digital feminisms to the sustained critique and theorization of the forms power takes in informed society. Its focus on structural accountability, participatory design, and intersectional justice makes it a timely intellectual and political project at a moment when algorithms are increasingly ruling our world.

LIMITATIONS AND FUTURE RESEARCH DIRECTIONS

As such, although this chapter aims to sketch a detailed theoretical and analytical exploration of Digital Feminism within algorithmic culture it is bound by limitations. Offering such disclaimers is not a weakness of the framework but an important expression of scholarly reflexivity in a context that is marked by fast-moving political, cultural, and technological transformations.

Methodological and Empirical Limitations

The same applies to the entire chapter: except for a little bit of empirical evidence and partly illustrative case studies, it is mainly built up on secondary information. This offers excellent scope for cross disciplinary synthesis between feminist theory, media studies, digital sociology and AI ethics, but it also constrains the ability to infer causality or to evaluate the long-term effectiveness of feminist interventions in algorithmic systems.

The case studies we cover biased hiring algorithms, beauty filters, voice assistants and feminist hashtag movements are informed by recorded research, public reports and popularly referenced examples. Although these cases are analytically generative, they are not the product of systematic data collection for this chapter. Our findings also suggest opportunities for future mixed-method work that combines qualitative interviews with activists and designers, policymakers and platform workers, along with quantitative analyses of algorithmic effects (and analysis of the metrics used: visibility counts and moderation practices).Ethnography about feminist digital labour, content moderation, and activist communities would also enrich our understanding of how algorithmic power is lived out, negotiated, and resisted in everyday digital life.

Geographical, Linguistic and Contextual Under-Representations

A second limitation pertains to the uneven geographic and linguistic distribution on studies of Digital Feminism. While this chapter draws in Global South perspectives and examples, including from South Asia and other transnational feminist movements, scholarship on the topic tends to be situated in the Global North (and in English language).

This imbalance is itself a result of wider inequities in academic knowledge production, access to digital infrastructure ensuring platforms were represented and governed for. Among other similarities, feminists who use digital spaces in non-English speaking rural areas and those living under authoritarian or low internet freedom contexts remain under-represented. Research going forward should be region specific, drawing attention to regional feminist epistemologies, caste hierarchies, indigenous knowledge systems and multilingual digital practices.

To do so would not only inform digital feminist scholarship but also disrupt the supremacy of Western-biased perspectives in studies of technology and gender.

Technical and Infrastructural Depth

A further constraint is how the chapter deals technical dimensions of algorithmic systems. Though treated as ideological and institutional actors, the chapter does not provide detailed investigations into particular model architectures, training pipelines, optimization regimes or deployment practices.

This limitation is an artefact of the chapter's cross-disciplinary focus and not a disregard for technical sophistication.

Yet, more interdisciplinary work among feminist scholars and computer scientists is needed to analyse how technical design choices (e.g. which data to use, how to label it, what evaluation metric(s) to employ and feedback loops) lead to gendered as well as intersectional outcomes.

This kind of interdisciplinary work might help to close the gap between critical theory and its practitioners by turning them into more focused feminist interventions in algorithmic design and governance.

Temporal and Platform-Specific Constraints

The worlds of digital platform and algorithmic systems are quick changing. Platform policies, recommendation algorithms, moderation norms and interface layouts change constantly, making any given feature or practice obsolete while still in its infancy. For this reason, some of the empirical case examples covered in this chapter will look very different following its publication.

It is for this reason that longitudinal studies are important to evaluate the evolution of feminist interventions, platform response and regulation over time. Future research should follow changes in algorithms, activist tactics, and policy trajectories over time to ascertain whether feminist challenges result in ongoing structural change as opposed to symbolic capitulation.

Ethics Normative Scope and Ethical Conflicts

Digital Feminism itself raises highly normative and ethical questions that are still left open. While care, justice, accountability and fairness are paramount in the framework tensions still exist between visibility and safety; participation and surveillance; reform and resistance. Feminist subjects favour, variously, either engaging with corporate sites and state regulatory processes as strategic intervention, or taking this engagement to be a political compromise of the raison d'etat character.

Further studies should investigate those internal debates taking place in Digital Feminism, on reformist and abolitionist and hybrid proposals for governing technology. Such analyses could shed light on the political relevance of different feminist practices and contribute to understanding ethical disagreement in patchwork feminist digital praxis.

Directions for Future Scholarship

Exploiting the shortcomings, further studies on Digital Feminism can be envisaged in several directions:

- Comparative empirical studies between platforms, regions and regulatory regimes
- Further exploration of affective, psychological and emotional dimensions to feminist digital labour
- Feminist policy and legal analysis of algorithmic governance and platform accountability
- Inclusive, participatory research methodologies that value marginalized communities as knowledge co-producers

- Ongoing cross-disciplinary collaborations between feminist researchers, technologists, designers and policy makers

Acknowledging these fields will further consolidate Digital Feminism as both an analytical framework and a practical intervention, sustaining its relevance in societies more and more governed by algorithms.

CONCLUSION

The chapter has claimed that Digital Feminism is not only an extension of feminist activism in contemporaneity onto the Internet, but also a critical and epistemological incursion into the very structuring infrastructures of power in the algorithmic age. And indeed, but by all means not least, in a world where it is algorithms that increasingly mediate visibility, labour, identity, governance and access to resources, feminist struggles are taking place outside representational politics or cultural critique alone. They are part of a fabric that is already woven into data systems, platform architectures, and computational logics that organize everyday life. Digital Feminism thus figures as both a diagnostic and a transformative praxis—one that critically evaluates how power works through technology, while simultaneously demanding other modes of being in the world emboldened by care, justice and accountability.

Throughout the chapter, algorithms are reinterpreted not as neutral instrumentation but, instead, as ideological and institutional agents situated within histories of patriarchy, capitalism, colonialism, and epistemic exclusion. These gendered and intersectional inequalities are found to be not accidental but rather to be symptomatic of a structural failu31:re in the dataveillance AI systems, platform governance and data economies which cannot be understood as isolated problems at the technical level. Instead, they are symptoms of centuries-old social hierarchies coded into technology in the form of biased data sets, masculinist cultures of expertise, and profit-driven AI development. Digital Feminism makes these continuities transparent, showing that algorithmic injustice is most usefully understood as an historical and infrastructural matter than a computational one.

One of the main contributions offered by this chapter is to combine feminist theory with digital sociology, media studies and AI ethics in order to propose an integrated analytical framework for studying algorithmic power. Terms like algorithmic patriarchy, visibility politics, affective digital labour, intersectionality and reconstructive ethics offer some of the tools with which to analyse how power gendered is constructed, legitimized and contested in the digital. In this way, these terms highlight the ambiguous nature of digital spaces: at once as they a site for resistance and a tool of surveillance, exploitation, and suppression.

Feminist counter-publics, hashtag phenomena, and digital storytelling all demonstrate kinds of political activity in which the online sphere plays a crucial role but also in which activists (particularly those from minoritised communities) are prey to harassment, precarity and algorithmic suppression.

And, importantly, this chapter has illustrated that Digital Feminism doesn't end with critique. Exposing the boundaries of platform activism and the pitfalls of commodified or performative feminism, it also provides suggestions for a rebuilding of digital systems themselves. For example, feminist data practices, participatory design approaches, trustworthy AI development and accountable techno-political governance models constitute concrete forms of intervention that intervene in the redistributing epistemic authorities and the making of technology futures. By associating itself with marginalized knowledges and experiences, Digital Feminism contests dominant paradigms of innovation favouring efficiency, scale and profit over social welfare and justice.

The epistemological stakes of Digital Feminism are especially high. Offering a feminist perspective on the algorithms of online platforms, this chapter shows that concerns around data, classification and algorithmic-decision-making are about whose knowledge matters and whose lives can be made sensible or disposable Drawing on feminist standpoint theory (Harding, 1986), situated knowledges (Haraway, 1991) and ethics of care, the paradoxical openness of digital networks is put to question. The term AI has been undermined, the author adds, since it cannot be denied that a majority of them have racial basis which, lead in their exclusions from datasets or marginalized by models as well as placed under automated decisions without transparency or appeal. Digital Feminism counteracts this trend, envisaging knowledge-making anew as participatory, accountable and relational — one that does not allow the value of techno-scientific systems to be weighed solely by accuracy or performance but against their social effects and ethical obligations.

The chapter has also taken into account the problems and contradictions in which Digital Feminism is embedded. Reliance on corporate platforms, digital divide, algorithmic violence and intersectional blind spots as well as co-option of feminist metaphor all serve to constrain the transformative potentiality of digital feminist practices. These limitations don't invalidate Digital-Feminism, they illuminate how deeply embedded the power systems it challenges go. Just acknowledging these gales of competing pressure could be, itself, a feminist act — one that rejects reductive story lines involving empowerment to insist on an attentive, sustained examination of material circumstances, institutional force and global precarity.

In the end, this chapter situates Digital Feminism as critical to comprehending and acting in today's technological societies. With such emerging technologies as generative AI, biometric surveillance, immersive spaces and automated welfare systems deepening algorithmic governance; the urgency of feminist critique becomes more acute. Digital Feminism insists that technological futures are not inevitable so much as they are struggled over. It is a call to share responsibility and ensure that we not only add women and other marginalized genders on digital infrastructures but challenge the systemic conditions that divide.

Taking back power and identity in the algorithm age, Digital Feminism provides more than resistance: it offers instruction. A vision of digital futures informed by intersectional justice, epistemic plurality, democratic accountability, and care. Critiquing and Reconstructing, Theory and Praxis By interweaving theory and praxis, critique and reconstruction, this chapter confirms Digital Feminism as an urgent political and intellectual project—one that can engage the injustices of algorithmic culture while envisioning more just forms of living with technology (and through it).

REFERENCES

Abbate, J. (2012). *Recoding gender: Women's changing participation in computing*. MIT Press. DOI: 10.7551/mitpress/9014.001.0001

Abidin, C. (2018). *Internet celebrity: Understanding fame online*. Emerald Publishing. DOI: 10.1108/9781787560765

Banet-Weiser, S. (2018). *Empowered: Popular feminism and popular misogyny*. Duke University Press.

Bardzell, S. (2010). Feminist HCI: Taking stock and outlining an agenda for design. *Proceedings of the SIGCHI Conference on Human Factors in Computing Systems*, 1301–1310. https://doi.org/DOI: 10.1145/1753326.1753521

Bechmann, A., & Kim, J. Y. (2020). Algorithmic bias and gender in digital platforms: Feminist perspectives on artificial intelligence. *Feminist Media Studies*, *20*(6), 887–903. DOI: 10.1080/14680777.2020.1713843

Beer, D. (2017). The social power of algorithms. *Information Communication and Society*, *20*(1), 1–13. DOI: 10.1080/1369118X.2016.1216147

Bender, E. M., Gebru, T., McMillan-Major, A., & Shmitchell, S. (2021). On the dangers of stochastic parrots: Can language models be too big? *Proceedings of the ACM Conference on Fairness, Accountability, and Transparency*, 610–623. DOI: 10.1145/3442188.3445922

Benjamin, R. (2019). *Race after technology: Abolitionist tools for the new Jim Code*. Polity Press.

Birhane, A. (2020). Algorithmic colonization of Africa. *Script-ed*, *17*(2), 389–409.

Birhane, A., Prabhu, V. U., & Kahembwe, E. (2021). Multimodal datasets: Misogyny, pornography, and malicious intent. *arXiv preprint arXiv:2110.01963*.

Blackwell, L., Dimond, J., Schoenebeck, S., & Lampe, C. (2019). Classification and its consequences for online harassment. *Proceedings of the ACM on Human-Computer Interaction*, 3(CSCW), 1–25.

Bowker, G. C., & Star, S. L. (1999). *Sorting things out: Classification and its consequences*. MIT Press. DOI: 10.7551/mitpress/6352.001.0001

Buolamwini, J., & Gebru, T. (2018). Gender shades: Intersectional accuracy disparities in commercial gender classification. *Proceedings of Machine Learning Research*, *81*, 1–15.

Collins, P. H. (2000). *Black feminist thought* (2nd ed.). Routledge.

Couldry, N., & Mejias, U. A. (2019). *The costs of connection.* Stanford University Press.

Crawford, K. (2021). *Atlas of AI: Power, politics, and the planetary costs of artificial intelligence.* Yale University Press.

Criado-Perez, C. (2019). *Invisible women: Data bias in a world designed for men.* Abrams Press.

D'Ignazio, C., & Klein, L. F. (2020). *Data feminism.* MIT Press. DOI: 10.7551/mitpress/11805.001.0001

Dastin, J. (2018, October 10). Amazon scraps secret AI recruiting tool that showed bias against women. Reuters. https://www.reuters.com/article/us-amazon-com-jobs-automation-insight-idUSKCN1MK08G

Ensmenger, N. (2010). *The computer boys take over.* MIT Press. DOI: 10.7551/mitpress/9780262050937.001.0001

Eubanks, V. (2018). *Automating inequality.* St. Martin's Press.

Federici, S. (2012). *Revolution at point zero.* PM Press.

Foucault, M. (1977). *Discipline and punish.* Pantheon.

Gill, R., & Orgad, S. (2018). The shifting terrain of sex and power: From the "sexualization of culture" to #MeToo. *Sexualities, 21*(8), 1313–1324. DOI: 10.1177/1363460718794647

Gillespie, T. (2014). The relevance of algorithms. In Gillespie, T., Boczkowski, P., & Foot, K. (Eds.), *Media technologies: Essays on communication, materiality, and society* (pp. 167–194). MIT Press. DOI: 10.7551/mitpress/9042.003.0013

Gray, M. L. (2020). *Ghost work: How to stop Silicon Valley from building a new global underclass.* Houghton Mifflin Harcourt.

Haraway, D. (1988). Situated knowledges. *Feminist Studies, 14*(3), 575–599. DOI: 10.2307/3178066

Haraway, D. (2016). A cyborg manifesto: Science, technology, and socialist-feminism in the late twentieth century. In *Manifestly Haraway* (pp. 5–90). University of Minnesota Press., DOI: 10.5749/minnesota/9780816650477.003.0001

Harding, S. (1986). *The science question in feminism.* Cornell University Press.

Held, V. (2006). *The ethics of care.* Oxford University Press.

Hicks, M. (2017). *Programmed inequality*. MIT Press.

Hochschild, A. R. (1983). *The managed heart*. University of California Press.

Jane, E. A. (2016). *Online misogyny and feminist digital media studies*. Routledge.

Kitchin, R. (2017). Thinking critically about and researching algorithms. *Information Communication and Society*, *20*(1), 14–29. DOI: 10.1080/1369118X.2016.1154087

Lucy, L., & Bamman, D. (2021). Gender and representation bias in GPT-3. *Proceedings of NLP4PI*.

Margolis, J., & Fisher, A. (2003). *Unlocking the clubhouse*. MIT Press.

McRae, R. (2019). Queer digital feminisms: Challenging binary classifications online. *Feminist Media Studies*, *19*(4), 523–538.

Nakamura, L. (2013). *Cybertypes*. Routledge. DOI: 10.4324/9780203699188

Noble, S. U. (2018). *Algorithms of oppression: How search engines reinforce racism*. NYU Press. DOI: 10.18574/nyu/9781479833641.001.0001

Obermeyer, Z., Powers, B., Vogeli, C., & Mullainathan, S. (2019). Dissecting racial bias in an algorithm. *Science*, *366*(6464), 447–453. DOI: 10.1126/science.aax2342 PMID: 31649194

Plant, S. (1997). *Zeros + ones: Digital women + the new technoculture*. Doubleday.

Privacy International. (2019). *No body's business but mine: How companies are profiling us through period-tracking apps*.

Raji, I. D., (2020). Saving face: Investigating facial recognition performance. *AAAI/ACM Conference on AI Ethics and Society*. DOI: 10.1145/3375627.3375820

Roberts, S. T. (2019). *Behind the screen*. Yale University Press.

Sharon, T. (2016). The Googlization of health research. *Medicine, Health Care, and Philosophy*, *19*(4), 587–598. PMID: 29754546

Srnicek, N. (2017). *Platform capitalism*. Polity Press.

Tronto, J. (1993). *Moral boundaries*. Routledge.

Wajcman, J. (1991). *Feminism confronts technology*. Penn State Press.

Zuboff, S. (2019). *The age of surveillance capitalism: The fight for a human future at the new frontier of power*. PublicAffairs.

Chapter 7
Algorithmisation of Childhood:
The Social and Digital (Re) Construction of Children

Dhemy de Brito
http://orcid.org/0000-0002-2184-067X
University of Minho, Portugal

José Gabriel Andrade
http://orcid.org/0000-0002-9778-5865
University of Minho, Portugal

ABSTRACT

This article analyses the evolution of the city as a space of childhood, highlighting the transition from urban contexts open to children's social interaction towards environments increasingly mediated by digital technologies. Drawing on a critical review of historical and social processes, it discusses the gradual exclusion of children from public spaces and their confinement within controlled environments, resulting in an "algorithmisation of childhood". Furthermore, it examines the concept of musicmedia to describe forms of cultural co-construction within domestic digital environments. The findings emphasise the need to consider children's relationships with technologies without disregarding the importance of rethinking public policies aimed at the (re)occupation of public spaces by children, grounded in the inclusion of their voices.

DOI: 10.4018/979-8-3373-4531-4.ch007

INTRODUCTION

Historically, the city has been configured as a dynamic and multifaceted space in which the multiple experiences of childhood(s) are inscribed, constituting a stage where children have, over time, performed diverse and continually re-signified roles — at times as social agents endowed with competences and rights, and at others as subjects rendered vulnerable by processes of exclusion and marginalisation that contribute to the precarisation of their living conditions (UNICEF, 2012). This urban trajectory of childhood is marked by a constant tension between freedom and control, appropriation and prohibition, physical presence in public spaces and the technological mediation of everyday life.

In the first decades of the twenty-first century, however, this tension assumes a new configuration under the impact of digital technologies and the regime of algorithmic mediation that characterises contemporaneity. Childhood, which once unfolded within the physical spaces of the city, now also inhabits digital ecosystems governed by algorithms, within which visibility, recognition, and forms of social belonging are negotiated. Algorithms, as socio-technical and ideological devices, cease to function merely as neutral tools for organising information and come to operate as structuring forces in the production of beliefs, values, and imaginaries that shape children's experiences. The city, within this new horizon, extends into digital space, transforming into an algorithmic city where the boundaries between the urban and the virtual become increasingly porous and interdependent.

Since Florestan Fernandes' seminal publication, which, in portraying the *Trocinhas do Bom Retiro*, made visible the streets of São Paulo in Brazil as privileged spaces of sociability, experimentation, and learning in childhood, up to the contemporary digital scenario of the so-called Generation Alpha (McCrindle & Fell, 2021), the city — as a space of childhood — has been profoundly reconfigured by socio-political, cultural, and technological transformations. During the early years of industrial urbanisation and throughout the modernisation of cities, streets progressively ceased to be perceived as safe and accessible territories for children's autonomous play, being replaced by regulated and segregated spaces, often conceptualised as "islands of protection" (Zeiher, 2003). This reconfiguration intensified from the 1990s onwards, coinciding with the emergence of the Sociology of Childhood and the proclamation of the Convention on the Rights of the Child (1989) — milestones that contributed to the recognition of children as competent social actors, endowed with agency and capable of actively producing, inhabiting, and re-signifying urban spaces in meaningful ways.

However, the advent of digital technologies and the worsening of urban mobility crises in subsequent decades have resulted in a progressive confinement of children's experiences to private domains, heavily mediated by screens and technological devices. This movement reached its peak during the COVID-19 pandemic, when the home became the epicentre of children's everyday lives, replacing public spaces — once settings of interaction and experimentation — with environments of primarily digital socialisation. It is within this context that the process of "algorithmisation of childhood" intensifies, whereby the experiences of play, communication, and learning become filtered through recommendation systems and data-driven logics of visibility, silently shaping preferences, identities, and modes of being a child.

This article, presented as a theoretical essay, aims to analyse the evolution of the city as a space simultaneously of appropriation and exclusion of multiple childhoods, with particular emphasis on the transformations brought about by digitalisation and algorithmic influence in contemporary children's lives. It seeks to understand how urban and digital dynamics interpenetrate in the constitution of new territories of childhood, transforming both the urban space and the digital ecosystem into interdependent ideological fields in which forms of agency, creativity, and cultural belonging are negotiated.

Within this horizon, the article further proposes a critical discussion of the concept of *musicmedia* (Brito, Andrade & Dias, 2025) — as an analytical category that enables the understanding of children's practices of cultural co-construction within media and algorithmic environments — acknowledging that such practices simultaneously express resistance, creativity, and subjection to the logics of control and surveillance structuring digital culture.

The historical and sociological analysis of the evolution of urban spaces destined for children reveals a gradual yet profound metamorphosis in the ways childhood appropriates the city and engages in practices of interaction and belonging within it. In this scenario, digital mediation, far from representing solely an expression of freedom or cultural emancipation, also emerges as a field of ideological struggle, in which autonomy and regulation, agency and constraint are intertwined. Screens, as mediating and access devices, have become hybrid territories where children construct identities, participate culturally, and negotiate meanings under the influence of invisible algorithmic systems.

Thus, this study emphasises the need to rethink both the city and the digital through an inclusive and critical approach that recognises childhood as a central axis in urban and digital spaces alike. To conceive of the city in the algorithmic era implies acknowledging that the right to the city and the right to culture now extend into the digital ecosystem, demanding public policies that ensure children's capacity to inhabit, create, and participate fully and meaningfully in both territories — the physical and the algorithmic.

THE STREET AS A PLAYFUL TERRITORY OF CHILDHOOD

In the 1940s, in a Brazil still deeply marked by stark social inequalities and immersed in the transition from a predominantly rural society to an emerging urban and industrial configuration, the sociologist Florestan Fernandes conducted one of the first systematic studies dedicated to understanding children's ways of life within urban contexts. In his work, Fernandes (1979) describes the modes of existence of the so-called *Trocinhas do Bom Retiro* — spontaneous groups of children who inhabited and re-signified public space, transforming the streets of this São Paulo neighbourhood into territories of belonging, socialisation, and autonomous cultural creation.

As Abramowicz (2018, p. 379) observes, "Florestan's work inaugurated a new conception of culture and offered sociologists a way of looking at children and at research with children that had previously been neglected." In his account, Fernandes (1979) emphasised that the *trocinhas* were not merely informal groups of children engaged in playful activities; rather, they constituted authentic self-organised children's communities, governed by their own rules, fluid hierarchical structures, and an internal logic that subverted the dynamics of surveillance and regulation imposed by the adult world. They were, therefore, genuine social forms of childhood coexistence, operating beyond formal mechanisms of control and institutionalisation. As Fernandes wrote, "the *trocinhas* are conditioned by the desire to play – by recreation, as with other types of children's groups", further noting that "the basic condition for the formation of *trocinhas* is neighbourhood" (Fernandes, 1979, p. 235), thus highlighting the centrality of territorial and affective bonds in the constitution of these children's collectives.

For the sociologist, the street represented, in that context, a true stage of intense children's social life, where children not only circulated but also learned to negotiate meanings, manage conflicts, construct their own narratives, and develop relational, symbolic, and cultural competences of high complexity. In Fernandes's (1979) view, public space — particularly alleyways, narrow streets, and pavements — was a constitutive condition of urban childhood, providing an environment conducive to the experience of freedom, the exercise of autonomy, and the construction of collective identities rooted in the shared experience of everyday life.

An analysis of Fernandes's seminal work (1979) reveals that street play, far from being a mere pastime devoid of intentionality or formative depth, emerged as a highly complex form of informal education, deeply intertwined with the sociocultural dynamics of working-class neighbourhoods and with the networks of community relations that sustained them. Play, as evidenced in his study, was marked as a practice rich in meaning, underpinned by values such as solidarity, sharing, and resistance, and operating as a structuring device in the constitution of children's autonomous cultures. As Abramowicz (2022, p. 15) further notes, "Florestan's main focus was to highlight children's socialisation processes through what he called 'children's culture' in dialogue with adult culture."

It is important to emphasise that, in meticulously documenting the ways in which children inhabited urban space, the sociologist anticipated, with remarkable analytical acuity, key issues that would later become central within the field of the Social Studies of Childhood — most notably the concept of peer culture (Corsaro, 2011, p. 128), defined as "[...] a stable set of activities or routines, artefacts, values, and concerns that children produce and share in interaction with their peers", as well as the imperative analysis of the plurality and specificity of children's cultures (Sarmento, 2007). His ethnographic account, grounded in a careful and committed observation of the relational dynamics among spontaneous groups of girls and boys, reveals children's effective occupation of the city — not as passive subjects or mere recipients of adult action, but as social agents producing practices and meanings that animated and reconfigured the urban fabric.

However, this image of the active and meaningful presence of childhoods in public space would begin to undergo profound reconfigurations in the following decades, as a result of accelerated urbanisation processes and the intensification of the logics of commodification inherent to contemporary capitalism.

URBAN MODERNISATION AND THE PROGRESSIVE SEGREGATION OF CHILDHOODS

Between the 1960s and the 1980s, the major metropolises of the Global South underwent a substantial reconfiguration of their urban morphology, driven by intense processes of industrialisation, internal migration, vertical housing expansion, and the redistribution of socio-spatial dynamics. This paradigm, sustained by a technocratic rationality and a centralised model of planning, entailed the systematic marginalisation of the everyday experiences of peripheral and vulnerable populations, promoting the invisibilisation of their modes of inhabiting the city, as well as the intensification of exposure to urban violence and the structural discrimination of historically subalternised groups — among which women and children stand out (Maricato, 2003).

The street, which in previous decades had been understood as a symbolic extension of domestic space — a place of neighbourly interaction and a privileged setting for children's socialisation — was progressively re-signified as a territory of threat, disorder, and unpredictability, "in particular due to concerns about vulnerability and risk" (Trevisan et al., 2022, p. 36). Within this new urban horizon, a paradigmatic shift can be observed in how childhood was conceived and situated: the child, once an active agent and visible presence in public space, came to be recoded as a fragile, vulnerable, and displaced subject — a "body out of place".

This displacement, both symbolic and material, manifested itself in the increasing confinement of children within segregated, carefully planned, and sanitised spaces, guided by a logic of security and control: schools, sports clubs, shopping centres, gated communities, and other urban facilities designed *for* children, but rarely *with* them — thereby silencing their voices in decision-making processes concerning the construction of their own worlds (Brito, 2025).

Such spaces, conceptualised by Zeiher (2003) as true "islands of protection", were characterised by systematic surveillance and rigid behavioural norms which, though ostensibly aimed at ensuring safety and well-being, in practice significantly restricted children's autonomy. Within these contexts, the full exercise of children's agency was curtailed, and opportunities for cultural experimentation, negotiation of social rules, and spontaneous interaction — previously enabled by the open and fluid environment of the streets — were drastically reduced.

In a convergent analysis, Sarmento (2018) designates this phenomenon of the progressive confinement of childhood under the concept of "insularisation", emphasising the increasing segmentation of children's urban experiences within enclosed and normatively regulated spaces. As the author notes, "the interstitial space between institutions, particularly in cases where mobility is under the most restrictive control, constitutes for children a great unknown" (Sarmento, 2018, p. 235), thereby evidencing the growing disconnection between children's trajectories and the public territories of the city.

Within this process of urban reconfiguration, children's presence in public space acquired an increasingly exceptional and conditional character, tolerated primarily in heavily regulated environments under institutionalised surveillance. This restriction became even more pronounced in the case of socially disadvantaged childhoods, often targeted by containment policies and control mechanisms legitimised by security discourses that associated these children with juvenile delinquency or the condition of being "minors at risk". As Paula (2015, p. 29) affirms, "it was in this context that the presence of poor children and adolescents on city streets and their eventual involvement in illicit acts came to be seen as a social problem, which would become known as the 'minor issue'."

It was also between the 1960s and the 1980s, within the scope of policies directed at working-class children and adolescents, that the *Fundação Nacional do Bem-Estar do Menor* (National Foundation for the Welfare of Minors – FUNABEM) was established, responsible for formulating the national child welfare policy, alongside the creation of several state foundations tasked with its implementation. During these years, the *Política Nacional do Bem-Estar do Menor* (National Policy for the Welfare of Minors – PNBEM) was also developed, "which proposed that intervention should focus on abandonment, understood as the cause of children's and adolescents' involvement in urban criminality" (Paula, 2015, p. 32). As the author highlights, the movements directed at street children were connected "to the emergence of the theory of social marginalisation, which began circulating in the discourses of authorities and specialists about poor childhood and adolescence from the second half of the 1960s onwards" (Paula, 2015, p. 32).

This reorganisation of urban space has profound implications for the lived experience of childhood and for the constitution of children's cultures (Sarmento, 2007). By being excluded from public spaces and confined to closed and normatively regulated environments, children were deprived of the experience of moving freely, of discovering the world through their own means, and of actively participating in the construction of the places they inhabit. This represents a subtle yet effective form of cultural and civic dispossession, stripping children of their right to the city and their full participation in urban life (Lefebvre, 2003). Thus, the decades from the 1960s to the 1980s mark a critical turning point in the relationship between childhood and the city, establishing a model of urbanism that, under the guise of protection, promotes segregation, silencing, and the invisibilisation of children within shared public spaces.

This dynamic constitutes an insidious process of cultural and civic dispossession that denies children the right to the city — understood as the right to appropriate urban space and to participate fully in the dynamics that shape it (Lefebvre, 2003). Accordingly, the period between the 1960s and the 1980s may be interpreted as a paradigmatic moment of inflection in the relationship between childhood and the city, during which a securitarian and functionalist model of urbanism was consolidated — one that, under the pretext of protection, enacted the segregation, silencing, and invisibilisation of childhoods in shared public space.

THE EMERGENCE OF A NEW PARADIGM FOR THE STUDY OF CHILDHOOD

The final quarter of the 1980s marks a paradigmatic shift in the way childhood came to be conceived within the Social Sciences, particularly with the advent and consolidation of a new epistemological and investigative field: the *Sociology of Childhood*. This theoretical and methodological domain brought about a substantial reconfiguration of traditional approaches, challenging adult-centric, interpretative, and developmentalist models that had, until then, conceptualised the child primarily as a being *in becoming* — incomplete, dependent, or in a preparatory process towards adulthood (Prado, 2014).

In contrast, the Sociology of Childhood advances the understanding of childhood as a relational social category, historically situated and shaped by multiple determinants — cultural, economic, political, and territorial. In doing so, it displaces the focus of research from the normative logics of socialisation to the analysis of children's social practices and modes of existence, granting centrality to children's agency in the production of social life. As Sarmento (2008, p. 19) observes, "when studying childhood, it is not only children that the discipline is concerned with: it is, in fact, the entirety of social reality that occupies the Sociology of Childhood," underscoring its heuristic potential for the critical understanding of contemporary social structures and dynamics.

Alongside the consolidation of the Sociology of Childhood as an autonomous theoretical-methodological field, the promulgation of the *Convention on the Rights of the Child* (CRC) in 1989 — ratified by Brazil the following year — stands as a legal and political milestone (Rosemberg & Mariano, 2010) of undeniable historical and normative significance, instituting a new grammar of recognition for childhood in contemporary societies. While the Sociology of Childhood inaugurated a profound epistemological inflection by shifting childhood from a mere object of socialisation to that of a full social subject endowed with agency, relational competencies, and the capacity to produce distinct cultures, the CRC introduced a rights-based framework that envisions the child as a citizen entitled to civil, political, social, economic, and cultural rights.

These two landmarks — simultaneously scientific and normative — converge in the task of denaturalising essentialist conceptions of childhood, conferring upon it political status and social visibility. In this process, they decisively contribute to broadening the debate surrounding children's active participation in the public sphere, as well as to recognising their capacity for meaningful intervention in the construction of the social realities they inhabit.

Within this new paradigmatic framework, children come to be conceptualised as full social subjects (James & Prout, 1997; Corsaro, 2011; Sarmento, 2008), endowed with the capacity to produce and share their own cultural forms, to assign meanings, and to engender social practices across the multiple spheres in which they move. Childhood, in this sense, is displaced from its traditional anchoring in developmentalist logics of biological or psychological nature, to be understood as a complex, plural, heterogeneous social phenomenon, situated historically and culturally.

Scholars such as Jens Qvortrup, Allison James, Alan Prout, Chris Jenks, and Berry Mayall, among others, played a central role in consolidating the emerging paradigm that gave rise to the *Social Studies of Childhood*. They sustained the thesis that children should not be conceived merely as passive recipients of social structures and institutions but as active social actors, endowed with agency and the capacity to influence, negotiate, and co-construct those very structures.

Research developed within this theoretical movement sought, in a systematic manner, to demonstrate that, across the multiple spheres of daily life — whether in schools, in public spaces such as the street, within family dynamics, or through play — children mobilise a complex set of strategies, languages, norms, and rituals of their own. These confer texture and density to children's cultures, understood as forms of autonomous symbolic production, endowed with their own logic and meaning (Sarmento, 2007; 2021).

It is from this transformation in the understanding of childhood and of children's image within society that the urban space acquires new meanings for children's lives. The city ceases to be conceived merely as an inert backdrop for childhood experiences and becomes both an object of symbolic appropriation and a result of the social practices enacted by children themselves (Christensen, 2003; Trevisan, 2014; Sarmento, 2018). Children do not merely occupy urban space: they inscribe singular readings upon it, reinvent its functions, and reconfigure its meanings, operating according to their own logics that often escape — or even subvert — the principles of technocratic and functional rationality that underlie conventional urban planning. From this perspective, Trevisan et al. (2022, p. 55) emphasise that "it is within this right that it makes sense to think and act so that children may have a place as urban actors, participatory citizens, concrete political subjects, side by side with adults, in the building of space for a shared life."

This new epistemological, legal, and social paradigm carries far-reaching implications across scientific, political, and educational domains. In the field of scientific research, it calls for the adoption of methodologies that transcend traditional adult-centric logics, valuing attentive listening, situated observation, and the effective inclusion of children as qualified informants and co-participants in the process of knowledge production (Fernandes & Marchi, 2020). Such methodological reconfiguration requires the recognition of childhood as a legitimate *locus* of knowledge, capable of offering singular understandings of the social world.

At the political level, this framework summons states, local governments, and public institutions to concretely ensure children's right to participate in matters that concern them — notably in public life, in decision-making processes, and in the co-construction of the territories they inhabit. The city, as a space of citizenship, must open itself to the active presence of children, not merely as beneficiaries of policies but as co-creators of democratic, inclusive, and culturally meaningful spaces.

In the educational sphere, a profound revision of practices and relational frameworks between adults and children is required. Such revision demands genuine modes of listening, dialogic mediation, and the recognition of the child as an epistemic and political partner in the construction of possible, diverse, and more just worlds.

Thus, the 1990s not only inaugurated a new interpretative shift in the way childhood is conceived but also positioned it at the heart of contemporary debates on citizenship, culture, space, and democracy. Children are thereby granted the status of epistemic, political, and social subjects, whose active presence interrogates and expands the boundaries of the common. As Prout and James (1997, p. 5) note, this transformation must be regarded "more as a potential or possibility than as an already achieved set of theoretical postulates."

A NEW CENTURY, THE DUAL CITY, AND THE NEW REGIMES OF EXCLUSION

The dawn of the new century marks the contemporary city, as analysed by Castells (1989), as a dualised territory in which socio-spatial disparities between urban zones with differentiated access and uses become increasingly pronounced. On one side of this urban spectrum emerge protected, sanitised, and privatised spaces, conceived and maintained according to a logic of selective consumption and social segregation. These are areas predominantly frequented and inhabited by the middle and upper classes, governed by the rationality of the market, the aesthetics of modernity, and motorised mobility. Walled neighbourhoods, gated communities, luxury shopping centres, and business and residential zones designed according to parameters of exclusivity stand as the emblems of this process.

These territories, frequently subject to continuous processes of gentrification, are structured not only to facilitate the circulation of capital and the symbolic reproduction of certain lifestyles but also to exclude — subtly or explicitly — populations deemed undesirable. The resulting exclusion is multifaceted: economic, by restricting access through consumption criteria; social, by reinforcing class boundaries; cultural, by homogenising legitimate uses and expressions; and spatial, by controlling and limiting the occupation of urban spaces.

Within this framework, the city fragments into spaces of privilege and exclusion, whose coexistence manifests not only a physically unequal order but also a symbolic geography that legitimises and perpetuates social and political distance. As Maricato (2003, p. 161) underscores, "the new century begins without Brazil — its State and society — presenting minimally effective social policies for cities to address conflicts that have assumed gigantic proportions." The absence of equitable and integrative urban public policies reveals the fragility of state intervention in the face of increasingly complex urban conflicts, materialised both in housing precarity and in the denial of the right to the city.

In this scenario of growing urban fragmentation, it is precisely children from socially vulnerable backgrounds who experience most intensely the harmful effects of territorial inequality. Far from constituting a democratic and equally accessible space, the city reveals itself, for many children, as a territory of multifaceted exclusion, where circulation, enjoyment, and appropriation of public spaces are conditioned by structural and symbolic constraints. Sociological analyses developed by O'Brien, Jones, and Sloan (2000), as well as by Sarmento (2018), show that the contemporary city imposes significant restrictions on children's mobility, particularly on those living in the geographical and social peripheries of metropolitan areas.

In such contexts, access to leisure and community infrastructures — such as squares, parks, or streets with minimum safety conditions — is drastically limited, compromising not only the exercise of the right to play but also the development of cultural practices and social interactions fundamental to the constitution of children's cultures. Beyond physical barriers, such as the absence of public facilities or the prevalence of hostile environments, there are also symbolic obstacles linked to territorial stigma, excessive surveillance, and the delegitimisation of children's uses of urban space. These dynamics, cumulatively, contribute to the construction of a confined childhood, whose presence in the city is often monitored, marginalised, or rendered invisible.

The city, as a public and common space, becomes increasingly impermeable to children's dynamics, relegating children's bodies to a condition of near-urban invisibility. As Sarmento (2018, p. 235) notes, "the interstitial space between institutions, particularly in situations of the most restrictive mobility control, constitutes for children a great unknown," revealing itself as a symbolic and experiential void that limits not only the right to the city but also the full exercise of children's citizenship.

Beyond the multiple forms of material exclusion to which they are subjected, children are equally marginalised in the domain of civic participation and in the symbolic and concrete construction of urban territories. The right to the city, as formulated by Lefebvre (2003), remains largely inaccessible to childhood, since processes of urban planning and governance tend to reproduce adult-centric logics that relegate children to peripheral positions, deprived of agency and political recognition.

Despite the growing effervescence of debates on children's right to participate in reimagining the city and occupying specific territories, their voices remained largely silent at the turn of the century. As Percy-Smith and Thomas (2010, p. 3) emphasise, "participation, seen as consultation or 'having a voice', resulted in little change, with adults continuing to make decisions without truly taking children's views into account or giving them an effective share in decision-making processes."

Indeed, children's voices are rarely summoned in decision-making circuits that define the uses, dynamics, and meanings of urban space, being systematically silenced or devalued. When tolerated, their presence in public spaces is often viewed with suspicion or even with hostility, as though the geographical space ought to remain exclusively at the service of adult functions of work, consumption, and mobility.

Such a conception reveals an urbanistic paradigm that, by privileging adult needs and interests, renders invisible the demands and rights of childhood, neglecting the creation of playful, accessible, and safe public spaces, as well as the inclusion of children in processes of co-production and co-management of urban territories.

The fragmentation of urban space contributes to the fragmentation of children's experiences, creating a city that, instead of being a place of encounter and conviviality, becomes a battleground between different ways of life and unequal access to fundamental rights. The contemporary city, marked by this duality of inclusion and exclusion, therefore demands critical reflection on the place of children in the city and on how social, economic, and political dynamics contribute to the marginalisation of childhoods. Recognising the city as a plural space — one that must guarantee children's rights to mobility, participation, and play — is essential if we are to envision more inclusive and just cities for all children. The challenge lies in constructing a city that, rather than fragmenting and isolating, opens doors to diversity and to the collective building of a more equal future.

The increasing fragmentation of urban space has profoundly affected the disaggregation of children's experiences, establishing a model of city that, rather than promoting encounter, coexistence, and collective belonging, has turned into a terrain of dispute between divergent ways of life and unequal access to fundamental rights. In this context of progressive unsustainability of traditional public spaces as arenas for spontaneous socialisation and cultural creation, children are compelled to develop new forms of sociability and relational construction. It is within this broader context of urban and cultural reconfiguration that digital devices — screens, media, and communication networks — emerge as alternative instances of interaction and expression, opening the way for the constitution of new technologically mediated relational grammars that have come to play a central role in contemporary childhood experience.

DOMESTIC CONFINEMENT AND CHILDHOOD IN THE AGE OF DIGITAL MEDIATION

With the advent of the twenty-first century, urban dynamics have undergone substantial reconfigurations, catalysed by accelerated processes of globalisation and by the intensification of urbanisation in major metropolitan areas. Children, previously recognised as subjects endowed with relative autonomy in their everyday interaction with urban space, have increasingly become the object of normative gazes and ever more rigorous social control devices, particularly regarding their presence and circulation in public spaces.

Concomitant with the spatial and social transformations of the urban fabric, digital technologies have ascended to a position of centrality in children's everyday lives, particularly among those belonging to the so-called Generation Alpha (McCrindle & Fell, 2021). These technologies operate as fundamental mediators in the constitution of children's experiences, relationships, and subjectivities, establishing a new cultural ecology in which childhood is lived under the sign of permanent connectivity. With the vertiginous expansion of social networks and audiovisual content-sharing platforms — such as YouTube, TikTok, and Instagram — new regimes of socialisation and identity construction have emerged, wherein children interact with the world through screens, navigating between consumption and the active production of content.

In this context, childhood progressively shifts from physical to virtual space, reconfiguring the boundaries between public and private, playful and institutional, intimate and social. Yet, this new paradigm, mediated by technology, is not devoid of tensions and ambivalences. Although it enables unprecedented forms of agency and participation, it simultaneously subjects children to new modalities of algorithmic surveillance, to the normativity of dominant aesthetics, and to the constant pressure of performance and recognition (Andrade & Dias, 2022).

The so-called attention economy (Citton, 2017; Zuboff, 2019) forms the backdrop to this media regime: every gesture, click, and interaction is converted into data and capitalised upon by digital platforms. In this environment, children are not merely users but become data sources — central pieces in a market that exploits time, attention, and emotion as economic resources. What is at stake is not merely the capture of children's attention but the production of subjectivities moulded by a logic of constant monetisation.

According to Beer (2017), we live under a regime of algorithmic curation of everyday life, in which algorithms determine, almost invisibly, what is seen, valued, and remembered. In the case of children, this curation acquires a profound pedagogical and symbolic dimension: the recommendation systems of platforms — analysed by Bucher (2018) — operate as devices of socialisation, orienting cultural, aesthetic, and behavioural preferences, and establishing new forms of social regulation. These mechanisms construct an environment of apparent freedom and choice but sustain a structure of permanent surveillance and conditioning of desire.

As Livingstone (2013) observes, children's digital cultures are traversed by a process of symbolic colonisation, wherein the possibilities for expression and creativity are continuously mediated by technological infrastructures and their logics of visibility. Childhood thus becomes simultaneously producer and product of algorithmic culture: children create, share, and express themselves, but within the limits imposed by platforms that define what is relevant, legitimate, or capable of going viral. For Zuboff (2019), this form of surveillance capitalism translates into an expropriation of human behaviour in favour of the accumulation of informational capital — and, in the case of children, represents a direct threat to autonomy and the right to privacy.

With the outbreak of the COVID-19 pandemic, the dynamics of urban life underwent an abrupt and unprecedented inflection, instituting a new regime for the organisation of space and time. Cities, already traversed by logics of control and regulation, suddenly found themselves subjected to an intensification of these mechanisms, becoming even more restrictive and inaccessible, especially for the most vulnerable population groups — among which children were particularly affected.

The social confinement decreed in the name of public health, together with strict measures of physical distancing, provoked a profound rupture in habitual forms of sociability, circulation, and appropriation of urban space. A deeply mediated relationship with the outside world was established, in which screens assumed the role of the main interface for communication, learning, and interaction with others. This spatial and sensorial reconfiguration of urban childhood, catalysed by the pandemic emergency, imposed on educational reflection the imperative to rethink the modes of presence, participation, and belonging of children in the contemporary social and urban fabric, in light of the new technological mediations and exceptional devices that have shaped everyday life in recent years.

Technology, which had already played a significant role in children's social, familial, and entertainment spheres (Livingstone, 2013), assumed, in the pandemic context, an absolute centrality as mediator of children's relationship with the outside world. If, in pre-pandemic times, children's appropriation of urban space already occurred under constraints, the post-confinement scenario brought about a profound rupture, transferring this experience to the domain of virtual mediation. This displacement not only redefines forms of socialisation and territorial appropriation but also imposes new challenges on educational epistemologies, demanding critical reflection on the ways of being and belonging of children in the digitally mediated urban space.

Within this framework, the city progressively becomes a distant landscape, accessible only through the digital interfaces that permeate children's everyday lives. The urban experience of childhood is profoundly re-signified, being shaped by technological mediations that transform public space into a simulated landscape, filtered and adapted to the demands of a digital culture governed by the logic of personalisation and engagement.

Digital mediations have thus ceased to play a merely instrumental role in everyday communication, becoming authentic environments of socialisation, expression, and identity construction. Platforms such as YouTube, TikTok, and Instagram have become privileged arenas of symbolic interaction, where children not only maintain connections with family and friends but also establish relationships with expanded, often global audiences that exceed the limits of physical interaction (Dias et al., 2025). Through this logic, digital technologies not only transform modes of access to information but also reconfigure children's forms of social and cultural participation, while simultaneously introducing new layers of mediation and surveillance.

In this new communicational ecosystem, children emerge as simultaneous producers and consumers of content, in a dynamic that Buckingham (2020) characterises as indicative of the ambiguities of digital culture: on one hand, opportunities for expression, agency, and creativity expand; on the other, new forms of symbolic and economic regulation are imposed, mediated by algorithms and market logics. The production of videos, the construction of characters and narratives, as well as the public sharing of these creations, are situated, according to Dias et al. (2025), within a paradigm of participatory culture in which children are not merely passive spectators but agents implicated in the collective creation of meanings — albeit within contexts marked by power asymmetries and by digital surveillance mechanisms that shape the very field of expressive possibilities.

Within this context of increasing digitalisation of childhood experience, the concept of *musicmedia* (Brito, Andrade & Dias, 2025) emerges as a theoretical proposition aimed at elucidating the ways in which children construct their cultural and social worlds through everyday media practices, intensely mediated by screens within the domestic environment. Far from constituting a mere extension of traditional understandings of media consumption, this conceptualisation seeks to reposition the child as an active social subject, endowed with agency and cultural competence, whose relationship with audiovisual content transcends passive reception to take the form of a continuous exercise of creative appropriation, symbolic reinvention, and situated cultural production.

Through reproduced and reimagined choreographies, viral challenges, performative videos, and multiple forms of digital expression, children actively participate in the constitution of a hybrid and syncretic digital culture in which music — as a sensitive and shared language — and media — as technological and semiotic devices — assume centrality in processes of subjectivation, socialisation, and identity construction. The concept of *musicmedia* thus enables an understanding of contemporary childhoods as complex practices of cultural mediation, inscribed in dynamics of co-authorship, circulation, and symbolic reconfiguration, with profound implications for the fields of education, culture, and children's rights (Brito, Andrade & Dias, 2025).

In this line of thought, the theoretical proposal of *musicmedia* operates a paradigmatic shift in the understanding of childhood and play practices, transcending the centrality traditionally attributed to the physical space of the street or to the urban territory as the privileged locus of childhood experience. Although the outside world continues to be experienced in mediated form, children's creative action in the digital realm constitutes a symbolic reinvention of urban space and time, now transposed to the domestic domain and reconfigured through the interactive dynamics of digital platforms. It is, therefore, a matter of recognising in children's digital practices not mere reflections of technological modernity but legitimate expressions of agency, creativity, and situated cultural production.

Thus, the concept of *musicmedia* goes beyond the mere description of an emerging sociocultural phenomenon, positioning itself as an analytical key for problematising the ontological and epistemological implications that such a digitalised reality entails for the identity formation and social participation of children. In this scenario of networked childhoods, configured by interactive and performative dynamics, there emerges a fertile field of expressive possibilities, yet equally marked by surveillance devices, mechanisms of exclusion, and algorithmic market logics that structure the contemporary digital ecology. Childhood, in this context, becomes both protagonist and interpellated subject, navigating between territories of emancipation and zones of silencing, in a constant process of (re)construction of its place in the world.

CHILDHOOD IN THE ALGORITHMIC AGE: DIGITALISMS, SURVEILLANCE AND PERFORMATIVITY

The progressive digitalisation of everyday life, intensified over the past decade, has given rise to what several authors describe as the *algorithmic age* — a historical period in which the forms of social interaction, communication, and cultural production are profoundly conditioned by automated systems of data processing and decision-making (Beer, 2017; Bucher, 2018; Striphas, 2015). Such systems, grounded in complex processes of calculation and behavioural prediction, not only structure the circulation of information but also produce large-scale ideological effects, by defining what is visible, relevant, and legitimate in the social, economic, and cultural spheres.

Recent qualitative research has further demonstrated how children's and young people's digital experiences are shaped by the risk-oriented architectures of contemporary platforms. Livingstone et al. (2025), in a study with young people experiencing mental health difficulties, show that exposure to extreme online risks is not incidental but amplified by platform dynamics that prioritise viral and trending content, alongside personalised recommendation systems capable of activating individual vulnerabilities.

In navigating these environments, young people develop what the authors term platform literacy—a form of digital literacy that encompasses data and algorithmic awareness and responds directly to the commercial logics and governance structures of platforms. Importantly, this learning process is shown to be relational and biographical, emerging through peer discussion, shared experimentation and reflective engagement with personal digital trajectories. However, when coping strategies fail, responsibility is often internalised by young users, underscoring the need for systemic interventions through education, clinical support, platform design and regulation, rather than placing the burden of risk management on vulnerable individuals (Livingstone et al., 2025).

Within this context emerges what may be termed *algorithmic digitalism* — an ideological regime that naturalises the centrality of algorithms in the organisation of social life, attributing symbolic and moral value to connectivity, efficiency, and individual performance. Algorithms, as invisible mediating devices, become operators of power that filter and hierarchise experiences, emotions, and interactions, establishing new forms of inequality and technological dependency. In childhood, this digitalism manifests itself in a distinctive way: under the guise of playfulness and freedom of expression, children are incorporated into digital ecosystems that shape their imagination and everyday practices, often without full awareness of the mechanisms that govern them.

The logic underpinning these systems — based on data extraction, content personalisation, and constant feedback loops of preference — translates into a form of *algorithmic governmentality* (Rouvroy & Berns, 2013), in which subjectivities are permanently monitored, predicted, and directed. Childhood, in this sense, becomes both a site of technological experimentation and an ideological battleground, where the boundaries between autonomy and control, between creativity and instrumentalisation, are continuously negotiated.

Zuboff (2019) names this phenomenon *surveillance capitalism*, referring to the systematic appropriation of human experience — including children's experiences — as raw material for profit and informational power. This form of capitalism goes beyond data extraction, operating a genuine ontological reconfiguration of the subject: the child is transformed into a profile, a pattern, and a probability, progressively losing control over the narratives they construct and share. Spontaneity and creativity, which once characterised play and learning, are now mediated by metrics of engagement, likes, and views — symbolic indicators of value functioning as new forms of social recognition.

This dynamic produces what Bucher (2018) terms the *invisible power of algorithms*: a diffuse and silent, yet decisive influence on children's cultural and communicative practices. By regulating the flow of information and determining the visibility of certain content over others, algorithms create a narrowed field of possibilities within which children learn to negotiate their own digital presence. *Performativity* thus becomes a condition of existence: to be seen, one must act according to the codes of visibility imposed by the platforms.

In this process, childhood is interpellated by a culture of performative self-exposure, which associates visibility with value and participation with public recognition. Children become, as Livingstone (2013) describes, protagonists of an "everyday spectacle" mediated by screens, where the experience of playing, learning, or communicating is simultaneously lived and displayed. What once unfolded in the streets and public spaces of the city is now displaced into the realm of the *feed*, the *story*, and the *hashtag*, where each gesture is potentially captured, quantified, and shared.

In this sense, algorithmic digitalism reconfigures the very notion of childhood: from a social category in formation, the child comes to be conceived as a *user-product* — an integral part of a system that monetises creativity and emotion. Yet this process does not eliminate children's agency; rather, it redefines the conditions under which it is exercised. Even under the weight of technological surveillance, children continue to create symbolic zones of resistance, reinventing platform uses, subverting trends, and creatively appropriating digital languages. The concept of *musicmedia* (Brito, Andrade & Dias, 2025) is particularly relevant here, as it enables an understanding of these practices as forms of situated cultural agency, through which children transform algorithmic instruments into expressive and communicative means, challenging — albeit partially — the hegemonic logics that surround them.

Thus, to think of childhood in the algorithmic age is to shift the focus from merely instrumental discussions about technology to a broader reflection on power, ideology, and subjectivity. Children do not merely inhabit digital ecosystems; they are shaped by them and, at the same time, shape them through their creative, performative, and relational practices. The ethical and political challenge, therefore, lies in ensuring that these practices do not become mere extensions of an exclusionary algorithmic rationality, but instead affirm themselves as legitimate spaces of creation, participation, and recognition — fundamental dimensions of children's rights to culture, autonomy, and citizenship in the digital age.

FINAL CONSIDERATIONS

The trajectory of the city as a space of childhood experience is marked by a historical continuum of contrasts and paradoxes, constituting a field of constant tension between dynamics of appropriation and mechanisms of exclusion, between impulses of freedom and devices of control, between the ground of the street and the virtuality of the screen. Over the past decades, the urban space — once a privileged setting of playful vitality and social experimentation for children, characterised by spontaneous play and informal processes of socialisation in public courtyards —

has been progressively redefined as a territory of containment, deprivation, and surveillance.

From the emblematic *Trocinhas do Bom Retiro* — children's communities that, in the 1940s, inscribed their presence in the interstices of São Paulo's streets — to the digitally mediated childhoods of the present, one observes a growing retraction of children's *right to the city*. This process results from multiple factors, including the advance of unregulated urbanisation, rising levels of socio-spatial segregation, and the emergence of new rationalities of control rooted in digital technologies and algorithmic systems that invisibly shape everyday social life.

Rethinking the city from the perspective of children — and, above all, in dialogue with them — constitutes a political, ethical, and epistemological imperative that is both urgent and unavoidable. Such an endeavour involves not only creating material and symbolic conditions for the visible, active, and meaningful presence of children in urban territories, but also valuing their everyday practices — both physical and digital — as legitimate forms of spatial and cultural production.

Within this horizon, it becomes crucial to recognise that, even in the face of structural restrictions and constraints imposed by adult-centric logics of urban planning and by the algorithmic normativities of digital platforms, children continue to (re) configure the places they inhabit — whether streets, squares, domestic rooms, or luminous screens. Far from being passive subjects or mere recipients of pre-defined structures, children must be understood as competent social authors, capable of attributing meaning, constructing narratives, and expressing themselves creatively within increasingly hybrid and technologically mediated ecosystems.

Even in contexts of spatial confinement or intense technological mediation, children demonstrate a remarkable capacity to reinvent their spaces of socialisation, playfulness, and symbolic expression, creatively and resiliently challenging the multiple limitations imposed upon them by contemporary processes of urbanisation and digitalisation. By actively engaging with social networks, video-sharing platforms, online games, and other digital interfaces, they do not remain confined to the passive role of consumers but emerge as co-producers of cultural universes in which music, image, and gesture intertwine as languages of presence, resistance, and recognition.

In this context, the city — fragmented, hierarchised, and often inaccessible — is symbolically extended and re-signified through children's practices unfolding within alternative digital territories. The concept of *musicmedia*, as a theoretical proposal that apprehends children's co-construction of culture within screen-mediated environments, proves fundamental to understanding how children transform technological media into genuine stages of sociability and cultural creation, enacting symbolic displacements between the urban and the digital.

However, recognising the legitimacy and richness of these contemporary forms of sociability must not entail the abandonment of the struggle for public policies that restore to children their right to inhabit the city in all its complexity. The defence of public space and the democratisation of digital space constitute inseparable dimensions of a single rights-based agenda. It is imperative that educational and political discourses do not succumb to a logic of substituting the urban with the digital, but instead acknowledge their interdependence as complementary ecologies of childhood experience. Technologies, while essential to current practices of expression and interaction, cannot serve as a pretext to legitimise the erosion of children's physical presence in the spaces of the city.

Building a public agenda committed to childhood in the algorithmic age therefore entails conceiving children's citizenship as an *expanded practice* that integrates both the physical and digital dimensions of social life. Such a conception requires policies attuned to the plurality of childhoods and to the complexity of their ways of inhabiting the world — policies that ensure both safe and creative access to technologies and the full enjoyment of urban spaces as territories of encounter, coexistence, and imagination.

Contemporary childhood thus constitutes a hybrid space between the urban and the digital, traversed by algorithmic ideologies that define modes of seeing, communicating, and participating in the world. Children remain competent social authors, yet they must also be recognised as such within digital ecosystems governed by algorithms, where visibility, participation, and cultural creation are mediated by invisible forces of selection and control.

Understanding childhood in the algorithmic age therefore requires unveiling the ideologies inscribed within the digital systems that mediate social and cultural experience, in order to safeguard children's right to autonomy, culture, and recognition in a world increasingly governed by algorithms.

REFERENCES

Abramowicz, A. (2018). Sociologia da infância: traçando algumas linhas. *Contemporânea – Revista de Sociologia da UFSCar*, 8(2), 371–383.

Abramowicz, A. (2022). *Estudos da infância no Brasil: encontros e memórias*. EdUFSCar.

Andrade, J. G., & Dias, P. (2022). Crianças no mundo digital: a dinâmica de uma língua portuguesa viva. In *F. Ilharco et al. (orgs.), Em português: falar, viver e pensar no século XXI* (pp. 371–388). Universidade Católica Editora.

Beer, D. (2017). The social power of algorithms. *Information Communication and Society*, *20*(1), 1–13. DOI: 10.1080/1369118X.2016.1216147

Brito, D. Polifonia e o direito de voz das crianças: diálogos entre a sociologia da infância e a educação musical da infância. 2025. Tese (Doutoramento) –Universidade do Minho, Braga, 2025. Disponível em: https://hdl.handle.net/1822/94998. Acesso em: 10 nov. 2025

Brito, D. D., Andrade, J. G., & Dias, P. (2025). "Musicmedia" in childhood: the impact of digital platforms of the musical preferences of lusophone children. In Duarte, A., Andrade, J. G., & Dias, P. (Eds.), *Digital tools and platforms for effective and personalized learning* (pp. 311–336). IGI Global Publishing., DOI: 10.4018/979-8-3373-6013-3.ch011

Bucher, T. (2018). *If... Then: Algorithmic power and politics*. Oxford University Press. DOI: 10.1093/oso/9780190493028.001.0001

Buckingham, D. (2020). *The media education manifesto*. Polity Press.

Christensen, P. (2003). Place, space and knowledge: children in the village and the city. In *P. Christensen & M. O'Brien (orgs.), Children in the city: home, neighbourhood and community*. Routledge.

Citton, Y. (2017). *The ecology of attention*. Polity Press.

Corsaro, W. A. (2011). *Sociologia da infância*. Artmed.

Dias, A. F., Dias, P., & Andrade, J. G. (2025). A Geração Alpha e a música: A influência do TikTok no consumo musical. *Revista Opus*, *31*(e253132), 1–22. DOI: 10.20504/opus2025.31.32

Fernandes, F. (1979). As trocinhas do Bom Retiro: contribuição ao estudo folclórico e sociológico dos grupos infantis. In F. Fernandes, *Folclore e mudança social na cidade de São Paulo* (2.ª ed.). Petrópolis: Vozes.

Fernandes, N., & Marchi, R. de C. (2020). A participação das crianças nas pesquisas: Nuances a partir da etnografia e na investigação participativa. *Revista Brasileira de Educação, 25*, e250024. DOI: 10.1590/s1413-24782020250024

Fundo das Nações Unidas para a Infância (UNICEF). (2012). *Crianças em um mundo urbano*. New York: UNICEF.

James, A., & Prout, A. (1997). *Constructing and reconstructing childhood: contemporary issues in the sociological study of childhood*. RoutledgeFalmer.

Lefebvre, H. (2003). *The urban revolution*. U of Minnesota Press.

Livingstone, S. (2013). Children's internet culture: power, change and vulnerability in twenty-first century childhood. Taylor & Francis., Disponível em http://eprints.lse.ac.uk/63975/, Retrieved January 9, 2025, from.

Livingstone, S., Jessen, R. S., Stoilova, M., Stänicke, L. I., Graham, R., Staksrud, E., & Jensen, T. (2025). Can platform literacy protect vulnerable young people against the risky affordances of social media platforms? *Information Communication and Society*, •••, 1–18. DOI: 10.1080/1369118X.2025.2518254

Maricato, E. (2003). Metrópole, legislação e desigualdade. *Estudos Avançados, 17*(48), 151–166. DOI: 10.1590/S0103-40142003000200013

McCrindle, M., & Fell, A. (2021). *Generation Alpha: understanding our children and helping them thrive*. Hachette.

O'Brien, M.; Rustin, M.; Jones, D.; Sloan, D. (2000). 'Children's Independent Spatial Mobility in the Urban Public Realm' Childhood. *A Global Journal of Child Research (Special issue of children's geographies), 7*(3), 257-277. http://dx.doi.org/ DOI: 10.1177/0907568200007003002

Paula, L. (2015). Da "questão do menor" à garantia de direitos: Discursos e práticas sobre o envolvimento de adolescentes com a criminalidade urbana. *Civitas, 15*(1), 27–43. DOI: 10.15448/1984-7289.2015.1.16937

Percy-Smith, B., & Thomas, N. (2010). *A handbook of children and young people's participation: perspectives from theory and practice*. Routledge.

Prado, R. L. C. (2014). *A participação de crianças em pesquisas brasileiras das ciências sociais e humanas* [Tese de Doutoramento, Universidade de São Paulo]. São Paulo: USP. Disponível em: https://www.teses.usp.br/teses/disponiveis/47/47131/tde-27112014-103246/pt-br.php. Acesso em: 9 jan. 2025.

Rosemberg, F., & Mariano, C. S. (2010). A Convenção Internacional sobre os Direitos da Criança: Debates e tensões. *Cadernos de Pesquisas*, *40*(141), 693–728. DOI: 10.1590/S0100-15742010000300003

Rouvroy, A.; Berns, T. (2013). Algorithmic governmentality and prospects of emancipation. *Réactivation des pouvoirs critiques face à la gouvernance algorithmique. Le Sujet dans la Cité*, 5, 163–180.

Sarmento, M. J. (2007). Visibilidade social e estudo da infância. In *V. M. R. Vasconcellos & M. J. Sarmento (orgs.), Infância (in)visível* (pp. 25–49). Junqueira & Marin.

Sarmento, M. J. (2008). Sociologia da infância: correntes e confluências. In *M. J. Sarmento & M. C. S. Gouvea (orgs.), Estudos da infância: educação e práticas sociais* (pp. 17–39). Vozes.

Sarmento, M. J. (2018). Infância e cidade: Restrições e possibilidades. *Educação*, *41*(2), 232–240.

Sarmento, M. J. (2021). Culturas infantis / Children's culture. In C. Tomás et al. (orgs.), *Conceitos-chave em Sociologia da Infância: perspetivas globais* (pp. 179–186). Braga: UMinho Editora.

Stripha, S. T. (2015). Algorithmic culture. *European Journal of Cultural Studies*, *18*(4–5), 395–412. DOI: 10.1177/1367549415577392

Trevisan, G., Bento, G., Carvalho, M., Silva, C., & Sarmento, M. J. (2022). Infância, espaço público e participação: a abordagem do território de aprendizagem. In M. Gobbi et al. (orgs.), *O direito das crianças à cidade: perspetivas desde Portugal e o Brasil* (pp. 35–58). São Paulo: FEUSP. https://doi.org/DOI: 10.11606/9786587047317

Trevisan, G. P. (2014). *'Somos as pessoas que temos de escolher, não são as outras pessoas que escolhem por nós': infância e cenários de participação pública: uma análise sociológica de condecisão das crianças na escola e na cidade* [Tese de Doutoramento, Universidade do Minho, Instituto de Educação]. Universidade do Minho.

Zeiher, H. (2003). Shaping daily life in urban environments. In *Children in the City* (pp. 84–99). Routledge.

Zuboff, S. (2019). *The age of surveillance capitalism: the fight for a human future at the new frontier of power*. Profile Books.

Chapter 8
Algorithmic Narcissism and the Passion Economy:
Identity, Visibility, and the Ideology of Self-Performance

Noprita Herari
http://orcid.org/0009-0009-2497-5340
Universitas Negeri Jakarta, Indonesia

Mohd Nur Najmi Nuji
Universiti Teknologi MARA, Malaysia

Rino Febrianno Boer
LSPR Institute of Communication and Business, Indonesia

Sandy Allifiansyah
http://orcid.org/0000-0002-3981-4461
Universitas Negeri Jakarta, Indonesia

ABSTRACT

This chapter reveals how the passion economy (celebrated as a space of creativity and autonomy) quietly depends on algorithmic narcissism, a system that measures the self through visibility, metrics, and constant performance. While digital platforms promise empowerment, they also reshape identity, emotional labor, and authenticity into forms of self-exploitation. This chapter brings us to the central question: what

DOI: 10.4018/979-8-3373-4531-4.ch008

happens when passion becomes performance, and the self becomes an algorithmic project? Ultimately, it invites readers to imagine a future where creativity is measured not by visibility but by humanistic connection.

INTRODUCTION

> *"The passion economy can only flourish when it moves beyond algorithmic narcissism toward humanistic visibility, reclaiming creation as relational care rather than performative labor"*

Over the past decade, the global digital landscape has undergone a profound transformation, giving rise to a new class of labor built around personal meaning, creative autonomy, and individualized expertise. Commonly referred to as the passion economy, this emerging model now represents one of the fastest-growing segments of the digital labor market. Industry forecasts estimate that over 50 million people worldwide self-identify as creators, while analysts from Goldman Sachs predict the creator and passion-driven sectors will reach US$480 billion by 2027, overtaking many traditional creative industries (Sachs, 2023).

In addition, the term creative class, first coined by Florida (2004) in his seminal book, has begun to fulfil its own destiny through overstimulation by information and digital consumption. The new generation is being raised in an era of overwhelming information and novel ideas about new occupations replacing old-fashioned, mechanistic work. The word "passion" is now marketable and has a unique exchange value in a complex digital value chain. In this new, emerging, passionate class, creativity becomes the backbone of the economy and a form of national soft power (Kim, 2021) also known as the passion economy.

At first glance, the passion economy appears emancipatory. It promises autonomy, authenticity, flexible work arrangements, and the possibility of aligning livelihood with personal meaning. Governments, universities, and entrepreneurial institutions increasingly promote passion-based digital labor as the future of work, particularly for younger generations. Surveys indicate that for many Gen Z individuals, earning income through passion-driven online activities is no longer aspirational but normative (Browley, 2022; Octavia & Sari, 2024).

As this chapter argues, the passion economy cannot be understood apart from the rise of algorithmic narcissism, a mode of selfhood shaped by metrics, comparison, and continuous optimization. Drawing on psychoanalytic theory (Freud and Lacan), humanistic and social critique (Fromm and Lasch), and postmodern philosophy (Baudrillard, Han, and Stiegler), this chapter examines how narcissism evolves into a contemporary ideological formation. These perspectives converge in the figure of the passion-driven creator, whose identity becomes inseparable from algorithmic visibility. This raises a guiding question: *how does a system designed to celebrate passion produce a self governed by visibility and performance, and what would it take to imagine a post-narcissistic passion economy grounded in humanistic communication and relational care?*

THEORETICAL FOUNDATIONS: FROM CLASSICAL NARCISSISM TO ALGORITHMIC IDEOLOGY PSYCHOANALYTIC ROOT

The psychoanalytic understanding of narcissism, recognized as a pervasive element of normal psychological life rather than solely a perversion, is fundamentally rooted in the work of Sigmund Freud, particularly his 1914 essay *On Narcissism*. Freud posited that narcissism is foundational to ego formation, establishing it as a necessary intermediate stage between the initial fragmented state of auto-erotism and the capacity for object-love. He described primary narcissism as the original libidinal investment (cathexis) of the ego, an early developmental state of absolute self-focus that persists throughout the subject's life (Freud, 1914).

The subsequent maturation of the psyche requires a shift of libido away from the self and onto external objects; hence, the ego is "impoverished" in favor of object-cathexes. When external circumstances (such as organic disease, pain, or frustration) cause this object-libido to be withdrawn from the outer world, it is redirected back upon the ego, resulting in secondary narcissism. This return of libido to the self manifests clinically in phenomena like megalomania observed in paraphrenia, where the ego is magnified at the expense of external interest (Freud, 1914).

Freud's pivotal introduction of the antithesis between ego-libido and object-libido confirms narcissism as a core element of the mental apparatus, establishing that human psychological development is driven by the dynamic circulation of libidinal energy between the self and the external world. The ultimate goal of the developing ego is to recover the "narcissistic perfection of childhood" through the establishment of an "ego ideal," a substitute for that lost, blissful self-regard (Freud, 1914).

Jacques Lacan provides a structural complement to Freud's developmental schema, arguing in his Écrits (1966) that the very constitution of the ego is intrinsically narcissistic due to its origins in the visual field (Licitra Rosa et al., 2021). Lacan's mirror stage describes the process, typically occurring between six and eighteen months, through which the infant overcomes its physical helplessness (Hilflosigkeit) by identifying with an external image of itself, an imago-Gestalt, or illusion of coherence observed in a mirror or reflected by another person (Johnston, 2022; Lacan, 1936). This visual identification, which forms the nucleus of the ego, prematurely grants the infant a sense of unity and mastery.

Critically, Lacan views this foundational act as one of misrecognition (méconnaissance). Because the ego is derived from an external and alienating image, Lacan defines the ego as an imaginary construct, an "objectified entity" rather than an autonomous center of subjectivity. The self (moi) is, in its essence, derived from a "false" image, determined by the desires and gazes of others (the Other) (Benvenuto, 1995; Johnston, 2022; Lacan, 1936). By demonstrating that the ego itself is formed by identifying with an idealizing reflection, Lacan moves beyond defining narcissism as an individual flaw or disorder. Instead, he reframes it as an essential structural feature of human subjectivity. The subject is perpetually bound to the pursuit of an idealized, external reflection, meaning that narcissism is an unavoidable structural condition woven into the fabric of the self.

Humanistic and Social Narcissism

The concepts of narcissism articulated by Erich Fromm and Christopher Lasch transcend mere individual pathology, framing self-absorption as a fundamental moral and social crisis of modern Western civilization. While Erich Fromm approaches narcissism from a moral-humanistic perspective rooted in existential psychology, Christopher Lasch provides a historical-cultural critique that links the rise of the narcissistic personality to specific socioeconomic shifts.

For Fromm, the genesis of narcissism lies in the profound alienation of the modern individual (Fromm, 2000). When individuals lose their capacity for authentic "being", they desperately cling to the logic of "having" (Fromm, 1978, 1976). The "having" orientation turns the self into an object (a commodity or investment) that must yield maximum profit in the social market (Fromm, 1956). Fromm asserts that this narcissistic orientation is the opposite pole of objectivity, reason, and genuine love (Fromm, 2024).

Fromm interprets narcissism not simply as a psychological issue but as a moral and social condition, deeply rooted in self-idolatry and distorted self-interest. He famously distinguishes true self-love (which is healthy and inseparable from the love of others) from egoism and narcissism, arguing that the selfish person does not love themselves too much, but too little in reality, they may hate themselves (Fromm, 1977, 2000, 2024).

Narcissism acts as a compensation for this lack of genuine self-affirmation, leaving the individual empty and frustrated. When applied beyond the individual, Fromm highlights collective narcissism, where groups, nations, or religions elevate themselves above others. This group pride, often expressed as patriotism or loyalty, is a source of intense narcissistic satisfaction, particularly in societies that fail to provide real fulfillment to their members, compelling them to believe, "I am somebody important because I belong to the most admirable group in the world" (Fromm, 2023).

In *The Culture of Narcissism* (1979), Christopher Lasch integrates psychiatric insights to argue that narcissism operates as a pervasive cultural syndrome of modern American society. Lasch views the narcissistic personality as one who exhibits ill-defined dissatisfaction, pervasive feelings of emptiness, and violent oscillations of self-esteem. He posits that this character structure is produced by consumer capitalism, economic instability, and the rise of performative social roles (IDW, 2021; Lasch, 1979).

Lasch demonstrates how modern institutions actively undermine the development of stable character. The bureaucratic environment places a premium on manipulating interpersonal relationships, leading individuals to manage impressions and seek validation. The family structure itself, under the weight of anxiety and historical discontinuity, adopts external models of a harmonious life, resulting in a charade of togetherness. Modern parenting, guided by experts, often involves emotional detachment combined with attempts to make the child feel favored, creating a blueprint for the narcissistic personality. Similarly, the media and the therapeutic ethos encourage anxious self-scrutiny and an investment in one's own image as a survival (IDW, 2021; Lasch, 1979).

While Lasch grounds his critique in the decline of historical consciousness and the material shifts of late-stage capitalism, Fromm offers a deeper, more humanistic framework focused on the essential human need for a genuine, productive life. Both thinkers agree that narcissism is a symptom of a society that privileges performance, competition, and self-absorption over genuine connection and ethical responsibility. Their combined perspectives establish narcissism as an ideology of the isolated, anxious modern self, a self that has surrendered its autonomy to external market forces and the desperate need to conform, making the diagnosis of narcissism essential for understanding broader social malaise.

Postmodern Narcissism

The concept of postmodern narcissism, distinct from traditional pathological self-love, is interpreted by contemporary philosophers as a systemic condition generated by the late capitalist hyper-technological environment. Jean Baudrillard, Byung-Chul Han, and Bernard Stiegler trace this phenomenon through the collapse of reality into simulation, the compulsion toward relentless self-optimization, and the erosion of psychic individuation, respectively. This convergence of analyses depicts a self-absorbed, surface-focused, driven by invisible pressures, and structurally incapable of forming a unique, resilient identity.

For Baudrillard, postmodern narcissism is rooted in the age of simulacra and hyperreality, where signs no longer function to represent an underlying reality but replace it entirely, ensuring that simulacra prevail over history. The self, therefore, operates within a mirror-like culture characterized by the "narcissistic seduction" of media (Daudi, 2022; Lombardinilo, 2017).

In the "ecstasy of communication," the opposition between subject and object dissolves, leaving only the "immanent surface of operations" (Baudrillard, 1987). Everything is rendered "all-too-visible," creating a pornography of information and communication. Identity, consequently, exists primarily as a reflection and representation, absorbed into an endless play of images and sought through the continuous consumption of signs. This environment transforms the human body into the "finest consumer object", producing a form of narcissism focused solely on surface, spectacle, and illusion, where the human countenance is reduced to a commodity on display, stripped of its aura.

Byung-Chul Han locates a virulent form of narcissism within the shift from the disciplinary society, governed by "Should," to the achievement society, driven by the limitless imperative of "Can" (Han, 2010; Philosophize This, 2023). This system of "positive power" is an ethos of contemporary neoliberalism that applies individual entrepreneurial freedoms to the self, turning the individual into a commodity whose purpose is to endlessly maximize their market value (Miessler, 2023). The core injunction Han identifies is: "You are your own project" (Han, 2010).

This internalized pressure generates self-exploitation, which is highly efficient because it is accompanied by a sense of freedom that collapses the exploiter and the exploited into one. This auto-aggressive orientation is the hallmark of late-modern narcissism, where the self constantly struggles against itself. The narcissistic ego, lacking distance and relationship to the Other, encounters only its own reflection, especially in virtual spaces where it moves independently of the reality principle. Han notes that erasing the line between self and Other ultimately causes one to drown in the self, rendering existence meaningless (Han, 2010).

Bernard Stiegler critiques how technocultural automation reinforces this systemic self-absorption by eroding processes of individuation (Stiegler & Ross, 2015). He argues that hyper-industrial society is controlled by "psychopower," exerted through psychotechnologies that seize and control attention (Stiegler, 2010). This industrial standardization imposes "short-circuits" on the necessary processes of transindividuation, which rely on the intergenerational transmission and the singular appropriation of knowledge and experience (the pre-individual fund) (Stiegler & Rossouw, 2011).

The result is the destruction of "primordial narcissism", leading to psychological misery and the loss of singularities. As symbolic and cognitive life become increasingly standardized, individuals risk becoming mere reflections of systemic programming, "reduced to an 'available brain' subject to 'algorithmic governmentality". This systematic destruction of the self's capacity to form a unique psychic identity leads to organized mass regression and adult infantilization, where the unique "I" and "We" are confounded in an amorphous "One" (Stiegler & Ross, 2015; Stiegler & Rossouw, 2011; Stiegler, 2010)

In synthesis, postmodern narcissism is viewed not merely as a personality flaw but as a forced conformity: a subject defined by Baudrillard's spectacle is then forced by Han's achievement ethos to internalize and exploit the image as its own entrepreneurial project, all while Stiegler's automated technosystems liquidate the very conditions for genuine, non-standardized identity.

Algorithmic Narcissism

Building upon the psychoanalytic, humanistic, and postmodern understandings of narcissism, the emergence of algorithmic narcissism marks a pivotal transformation: narcissism becomes not only a psychic disposition or cultural syndrome, but a structural ideology explicitly produced, managed, and amplified by algorithmic systems. If classical narcissism was rooted in ego formation, and postmodern narcissism in the collapse of reality into simulation, then algorithmic narcissism arises from a technical-economic environment in which visibility is the principal currency of value, and the self is governed through metrics of quantification, ranking, and constant comparative evaluation.

Figure 1.

Algorithmic narcissism is a mode of subjectivity in which individuals experience their identity, value, and emotional legitimacy primarily through algorithmic visibility metrics. It emerges when platforms systematically transform self-expression into performance and recognition into quantifiable data, making visibility a prerequisite for self-worth.

Algorithmic narcissism can be defined as a mode of subjectivity produced through the continuous exposure of the self to algorithmic forms of visibility, where identity is not only represented but systematically measured, optimized, and validated through numerical indicators, likes, views, shares, followers, engagement rates, and the platform's predictive logics. Unlike traditional narcissism, which emerges from internal psychic dynamics or social arrangements, algorithmic narcissism is externally engineered, generated through feedback loops designed to capture attention, provoke emotional arousal, and sustain user participation within platform economies.

At its core, algorithmic narcissism is a structural ideology, one that does not merely encourage self-display but actively shapes what forms of selfhood are thinkable, valuable, and rewarded. The algorithm functions as a contemporary mirror (far more powerful than Lacan's literal mirror) because it reflects the self not only visually but statistically, transforming subjective existence into abstracted data points. Through this process, the individual becomes both object and spectator of their own quantified persona, continuously adjusting and calibrating behavior to maintain or increase digital visibility. The self is thus produced in relation to algorithmic expectations; it is "seen" and valued only to the extent that it circulates, performs, and remains optimizable.

This new ideological condition is inseparable from the logic of platform capitalism, in which attention is commodified and behavioral data monetized. Algorithmic narcissism naturalizes the belief that identity must always be visible, productive, and measurable. The ego ideal (once rooted in childhood perfection or idealized images) now becomes algorithmically projected: a virtual version of the self constructed through predictive analytics, recommended behaviors, and visibility-driven norms. Where Freud's ego ideal was a psychic formation, algorithmic ego ideals are platform-generated models sculpted by trending content, virality patterns, and algorithmic preferences. The subject is interpellated not by an abstract societal voice but by the algorithmic feed itself, which "calls out" to the user through notifications, metrics, and continual prompts to perform.

Moreover, algorithmic narcissism is intensified by the economic and normative pressures of the achievement society as described by Byung-Chul Han. The individual internalizes the demand not only to express but to optimize the self. Under algorithmic governance, the neoliberal injunction "You are your own project" mutates into "You are your own data project," wherein every gesture, emotion, and creative act becomes subject to analytic scrutiny. The subject self-exploits by perpetually producing content, monitoring performance, and modulating identity to satisfy the opaque demands of algorithmic curation. The self becomes an endlessly updatable interface, a perpetual beta version seeking relevance within a competitive attention economy.

From Stiegler's perspective, algorithmic narcissism represents a new phase of automatized individuation, in which the psychic process of becoming a unique subject is short-circuited by preformatted algorithmic patterns. The subject no longer draws from a reservoir of intergenerational meaning but from the "available cultural feed," shaped by platform logics rather than collective symbolic heritage. Identity becomes reactive rather than generative, constituted through algorithmic governmentality that prescribes visibility norms, attention thresholds, and affective intensities.

Similarly, algorithmic narcissism extends Baudrillard's hyperreality to its logical extreme: not only are images detached from reality, but the algorithms themselves actively determine which images exist, circulate, and signify. The self is caught in a hyperreal loop, seeking its own simulation as proof of existence, "I am seen, therefore I am." This digital mirror no longer merely reflects but produces identity by governing what counts as desirable, authentic, or valuable visibility.

Algorithmic narcissism emerges where these dynamics converge technologically. The symbolic mirror becomes computational, the ego ideal becomes metricized, and recognition is mediated by opaque algorithmic systems. Narcissism thus shifts from a psychological trait to an ideological condition of digital life.

Figure 2.

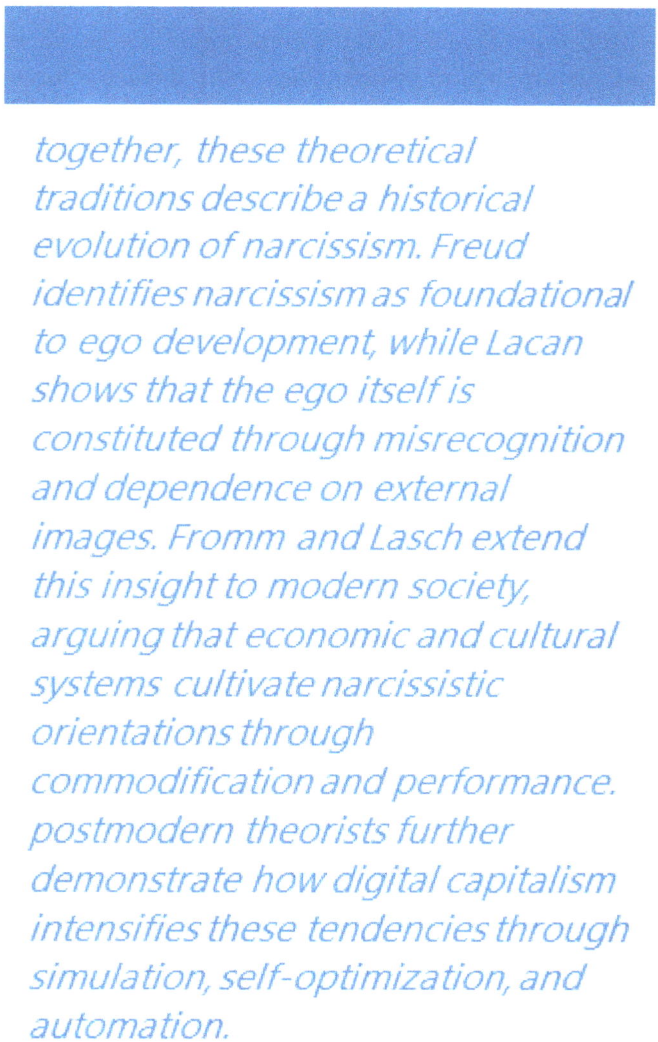

THE PASSION ECONOMY AS IDEOLOGICAL INFRASTRUCTURE

Before understanding how the passion economy operates as an ideological infrastructure, it is necessary to distinguish it from other adjacent digital economic formations with which it is often conflated. While the attention economy, creator economy, gig economy, influencer economy, and passion economy frequently overlap, each has distinct logics, incentives, and modes of value creation.

The attention economy operates fundamentally on the premise that human attention is the scarcest and most monetizable resource; here, value is generated by capturing, holding, and predicting attention. The creator economy expands on this premise by framing individuals as producers of digital content that can be monetized through platform features, advertising, or sponsorships, yet it does not necessarily require that the creator be driven by intrinsic passions. The gig economy, by contrast, commodifies labor flexibility, treating workers as on-demand service providers whose value lies in speed, efficiency, and availability. The influencer economy monetizes social capital and visibility, where identity and persona become instruments of commercial persuasion.

Within this constellation, the passion economy is distinguished by its ideological imperative that individuals can and should monetize what they "love," turning creative hobbies, intimate interests, and personal talents into entrepreneurial ventures within platform ecosystems (Herari & Waluyo, 2023). A simplified conceptual map can be represented as follows:

Table 1. Comparative framework of digital economies and their logics of value creation

Digital Economy	Core Logic	What is Monetized?	Primary Mechanism	Relationship to Passion
Attention Economy	Scarcity of attention	Time + cognitive focus	Persuasive design & algorithmic targeting	Indifferent to passion; values attention volume
Creator Economy	Content production	Videos, art, posts, tutorials	Platform monetization tools	Passion optional; creativity instrumental
Gig Economy	Labor flexibility	Time-bound services	On-demand platforms	Unrelated to passion, labor is commodified
Influencer Economy	Social capital	Identity, lifestyle, influence	Brand partnerships	Passion may be displayed, but it is secondary to visibility
Passion Economy	Monetizing intrinsic interests	Skills, knowledge, personal meaning	Community-building + algorithmic reach	Passion is central and ideologically celebrated

The passion economy intersects with each of these systems but carries a unique cultural weight: it moralizes entrepreneurialism through the discourse of authenticity, self-realization, and meaningful labor. It promises that “doing what you love” is not only possible but ethically superior to traditional work (Herari et al., 2025). Yet, as this section will argue, when mediated by platform architectures, the passion economy becomes less about passion and more about performing what algorithms love, transforming a rhetoric of liberation into a regime of intensified self-discipline.

The passion economy positions itself as an antidote to alienation: a model where individuals are empowered to define their own work, set their own pace, and express their genuine interests (Herari et al., 2024). However, in the algorithmic environment of platform capitalism, passion becomes subordinated to visibility metrics, rendering creation less an act of self-expression and more a strategic performance calibrated to capture algorithmic attention.

What was once craft (shaped by personal rhythm, curiosity, and growth) becomes performance, governed by trends, virality formulas, and data-driven optimization. Immersed in this environment, individuals quickly learn that algorithms do not reward passion itself but the performance of passion in a form optimized for consumption: high emotional expressiveness, rapid storytelling, visual novelty, and intimate self-disclosure. The injunction shifts subtly but profoundly: not “do what you love,” but “perform what the platform loves you doing.”

This transformation reflects the broader logic of platform capitalism, in which algorithms act as invisible arbiters of visibility and success. Rather than distributing attention evenly or neutrally, algorithms privilege specific content formats, typically those that elicit strong emotional reactions, rapid engagement, and shareability.

The distribution of visibility is not random but patterned, reinforcing standardized forms of expression and privileging creators who conform instinctively to platform logic. Those who adapt quickly learn that virality is neither accidental nor meritocratic; it is the direct result of aligning one’s labor with the calculative preferences of the platform (Duffy & Meisner, 2023; Lung et al., 2021). In this way, passion becomes algorithmic: it is valued only to the extent that it can be quantified as engagement.

The ideology of the passion economy rests on the celebration of autonomy, yet the autonomy it offers is tightly bound by opaque, constantly shifting, and asymmetrically enforced algorithmic rules. While creators are encouraged to view themselves as independent entrepreneurs, the conditions of their visibility (and therefore their livelihood) are determined by platform infrastructures over which they have no control.

Autonomy, in this sense, becomes aestheticized: the very appearance of self-direction conceals a deeper structural dependence. The creator appears free because they select their topics, aesthetics, and narrative voice, yet these choices are continuously disciplined by metrics. Over time, creators find themselves producing not out of passion but out of anticipation: anticipating trends, anticipating algorithmic boosts, anticipating the affective responses that guarantee visibility.

This aestheticized dependence also generates a subtle but profound psychological captivity. Because the algorithm reflects and ranks performance in real time, creators are drawn into a recursive loop of self-monitoring and self-correction. Every post, video, or tutorial becomes a feedback point; every metric becomes a proxy for value. The self is fragmented into its measurable parts, as though its worth were definable by numerical outcomes. Passion becomes indistinguishable from performance anxiety; creativity becomes indistinguishable from self-surveillance.

The critical point is that the passion economy functions not merely as an economic system but as a neoliberal ritual, a collective performance in which individuals are encouraged to express authenticity while engaging in largely unpaid affective labor. This labor extends beyond content creation to include identity curation, emotional availability, community care, and the continuous performance of enthusiasm. Affect becomes currency, and creators internalize the expectation to remain passionate, grateful, and energized. The labor of positivity and emotional accessibility, though rarely acknowledged as labor, forms the backbone of the passion economy.

This ritual operates through a subtle interplay of empowerment and extraction. While platforms invite individuals to pursue what they love, they simultaneously extract economic value from their time, data, and emotional investment. The more passionately one participates, the more intensively the platform benefits. Productivity is thus individualized and aestheticized as self-expression, allowing overwork to be reframed as devotion and exploitation to appear as self-realization.

In collapsing the boundary between labor and identity, the passion economy binds individuals to platforms not through coercion but aspiration. Passion becomes productivity, selfhood becomes brand, and value becomes visibility. Beneath its celebratory rhetoric, the passion economy advances a deeper ideological project: transforming selfhood into labor and creativity into perpetual availability for algorithmic evaluation, an infrastructure that reshapes how individuals understand their worth, emotions, and relationship to work.

SELF-BRANDING AND THE MECHANISMS OF ALGORITHMIC NARCISSISM

The transformation of passion into algorithmically mediated labor reconfigures identity through the imperative of self-branding. In the passion economy, the self is no longer merely a producer of content but becomes the content itself, redefining subjectivity as an enterprise dependent on visibility and optimization. Self-branding thus operates as the central mechanism of algorithmic narcissism, through which identity is shaped, evaluated, and disciplined by metrics. Within this regime, metrics function as mirrors, emotional expression becomes strategic, and authenticity is continuously curated to align with algorithmic demands.

Unlike the psychoanalytic mirrors described by Freud and Lacan, algorithmic mirrors are quantified, comparative, and persistent. Likes, shares, views, and followers do not simply signal audience response; they assign a numerical value to the self and serve as proxies for self-worth. This metricized reflection generates vulnerability, as creators grow dependent on algorithmic visibility for validation. Fluctuations in engagement produce emotional highs and lows, while algorithmic silence is experienced as rejection. In this way, attention ceases to be merely desired and becomes the very measure through which the self is constituted, anchoring identity to continuous self-surveillance and performance.

The demand to sustain emotional resonance with audiences gives rise to emotional branding, a subtle form of discipline in which creators are expected to continuously display enthusiasm, vulnerability, and authenticity. Emotional life becomes instrumentalized, shaped by the imperative to appear relatable and engaging. Although the passion economy celebrates self-expression, creators are often expected to express emotions that align with platform expectations, maintain positivity despite exhaustion, strategically display vulnerability, and regulate affect to sustain engagement.

This dynamic reflects Byung-Chul Han's concept of the achievement-subject, who exploits their own emotional capacities under the illusion of freedom. As emotional expressiveness is rewarded and opacity discouraged, the creator's inner life becomes reorganized around external validation. Over time, this produces emotional alienation: a split between what is felt and what is performed. Authenticity thus becomes a paradoxical performance (carefully curated to appear spontaneous), forcing creators to continually negotiate between genuine self-expression and algorithmic optimization.

This tension is not merely psychological; it is structural. The algorithm's preferences are not neutral (Stinson, 2021), they are shaped by broader cultural, economic, and political forces (Katzenbach & Ulbricht, 2019). Emotional displays that conform to dominant narratives (such as empowerment, productivity, self-care, or resilience) tend to gain visibility, while expressions of dissent, ambivalence, or complexity may be penalized. In this context, curated authenticity becomes a mechanism of conformity disguised as individuality. Creators learn to express themselves within the boundaries of what the platform deems acceptable or valuable, resulting in an aesthetic homogenization of authenticity.

Moreover, curated authenticity reinforces a particular mode of neoliberal selfhood, one that requires individuals to transform their intimate experiences into marketable assets. Trauma narratives, personal struggles, and emotional vulnerabilities can serve as content that enhances engagement. The self becomes a repository of emotional commodities, each of which can be deployed strategically to maintain visibility. While this can create genuine connections between creators and audiences, it also exposes the self to commodification and emotional depletion. The creator is no longer simply producing content; they are producing themselves.

The mechanisms of algorithmic narcissism also create a competitive environment in which creators are continuously compared to one another through the metricized visibility of their self-brands (Herari et al., 2025). This fosters a form of social comparison that is quantifiable, relentless, and inescapable. Creators not only monitor their own metrics but also those of competitors, collaborators, and aspirational figures. In doing so, they internalize the platform's logic: that value is relative, and that success is measured by one’s position within the hierarchy of visibility. The self is thus perpetually evaluated against algorithmically determined benchmarks, creating a sense of scarcity even in environments that ostensibly promote abundance and creativity.

Within this environment, self-branding becomes both a survival strategy and a form of self-subjugation. The creator must maintain a recognizable identity while continually adapting to shifting algorithmic preferences, leading to an exhausting interplay between stability and reinvention. Stability is necessary for brand coherence; reinvention is necessary for continued relevance. The creator is thus split between the need to remain themselves and the need to become what the algorithm desires. This oscillation produces a fragmented self, one that must be legible, optimized, and emotionally available at all times.

In essence, the mechanisms of algorithmic narcissism transform self-branding into a process of continuous self-modification, governed by metrics, emotional expectations, and the demands of curated authenticity. The creator becomes both the artist and the artifact, both the producer and the product. By shaping identity in accordance with algorithmic norms, platforms cultivate a performative, metricized, and emotionally disciplined mode of subjectivity. This subject is not coerced into compliance but seduced by the promise of visibility, belonging, and success. The self becomes a spectacle, a brand, and a data point simultaneously, an identity sculpted by algorithms and sustained by the endless labor of performance.

Figure 3.

in the passion economy, self-branding is no longer an act of expression but a mode of survival. metrics function as mirrors, authenticity becomes emotional discipline, and visibility replaces value. under algorithmic governance, the self is continually optimized not to become truer, but to become more clickable, transforming identity into an endless performance calibrated for platforms, not for people.

FROM SELF-BRANDING TO SELF-EXPLOITATION

The progression from self-branding to self-exploitation represents one of the most insidious transformations within the passion economy and its algorithmic infrastructures. What begins as an invitation to express one's authentic interests gradually becomes an obligation to perform them continuously, strategically, and optimally. In this shift, the creator becomes both employer and employee of the self, internalizing the managerial gaze once associated with corporate hierarchies (Herari, 2025). Under the guise of creative freedom, individuals adopt labor disciplines that are self-imposed yet deeply conditioned by platform expectations. The workplace dissolves into the self, and the self becomes the site of endless productivity.

Figure 4. Narcissism feedback loop

In this internalized labor regime, the creator assumes the dual role of manager and worker, generating a structure in which the self is divided against itself. As the manager, the creator must plan, schedule, analyze analytics, set goals, and maintain consistency; as the worker, the creator must execute, produce, perform, and remain emotionally accessible. The two roles coexist in perpetual tension: the managerial self demands productivity, while the worker self experiences exhaustion. The contemporary creator, therefore, inhabits a paradox: they are liberated from traditional employers yet simultaneously subject to a more pervasive authority, one produced by the algorithmic framework that dictates visibility and value. This process reflects the neoliberal mandate of self-enterprise, in which individuals are compelled to treat their intimate identity as a business to be optimized.

The affective cost of this internalized discipline is profound. Burnout, anxiety, and emotional fatigue become endemic conditions among creators, not because they lack passion but because passion has become labor. The continual requirement to perform enthusiasm and authenticity erodes the boundary between the private and the public self. Emotional life is no longer something one brings to creation; it becomes something one must manufacture. Over time, the self becomes fragmented, with certain emotions amplified for visibility and others suppressed for brand coherence. The psychological toll of constant self-surveillance (tracking metrics, monitoring engagement, anticipating audience reactions) produces a chronic form of anxiety that parallels the effects of working in high-pressure environments, but with the added burden that the laborer cannot leave the workplace because the workplace is the self.

The erosion of private selfhood occurs gradually but decisively. As creators increasingly orient toward algorithmic feedback, personal experiences, emotions, and relationships become potential content. The distinction between living and producing dissolves: holidays become photo opportunities, conversations become inspirational reels, moments of vulnerability become emotionally charged posts designed to foster connection.

What was once private becomes monetizable, and what was once sacred becomes strategic (Mastrangelo, 2021). This phenomenon is not merely a symptom of overexposure but a structural effect of platform capitalism, which rewards intimacy as a form of performance. The creator becomes a curator of their own life, selectively revealing fragments that align with the desired brand image. As a result, the private self recedes into the background, overshadowed by the public persona that must constantly be maintained (Abidin, 2018; Littler, 2013; Senft, 2013).

This dynamic culminates in what may be described as narcissistic alienation. Here, narcissism is not excessive self-love but a compulsive attachment to the reflected, metricized self produced through algorithmic visibility. Gradually, creators lose affection for the craft itself and become invested instead in the metrics that evaluate it. The pleasure of creating is displaced by the anticipation of performance outcomes, rendering the creative act secondary to its reception. Unlike Marxian alienation, where workers are estranged from what they produce, creators become estranged from a self they no longer recognize: the self becomes a brand, and the brand becomes the object of devotion.

Byung-Chul Han's analysis of the achievement society illuminates this condition. In neoliberal contexts, exploitation no longer appears as external coercion but as self-imposed optimization. The imperative shifts from "you must" to "you can," masking domination as freedom. Creators embody this logic as they intensify their own labor in pursuit of visibility and recognition, believing that success is a personal achievement and failure a personal flaw. Exhaustion is internalized as insufficient effort rather than as a structural consequence of platform capitalism. The result is a feedback loop in which self-exploitation is sustained by the illusion of autonomy.

Revisiting Erich Fromm deepens this diagnosis. Fromm's warning about the shift from being to having evolves in algorithmic culture into a shift from being to being seen. Visibility becomes a form of possession, and passion is increasingly evaluated by performance rather than meaning. The creator no longer asks whether they love what they do, but whether it performs well. Identity becomes quantified, accumulated, and optimized, sacrificing the depth of being for the accumulation of attention.

Beyond visibility and identity, the passion economy also operates as a regime of temporal control. Algorithms do not merely shape what creators produce or how they present themselves; they increasingly govern when creativity must occur, at what pace, and with what degree of immediacy. Platform logics privilege speed, novelty, and continuous responsiveness, cultivating an accelerationist temporality in which relevance is short-lived and absence is penalized. Within this regime, creators are encouraged to remain perpetually "up-to-date," internalizing a sense of urgency that transforms time itself into a site of self-discipline.

This temporal pressure introduces what can be described as temporal narcissism, a condition in which the self is not only compelled to be visible, but to be visible now. Delays, pauses, or periods of low output are often experienced as personal failure rather than as necessary rhythms of creative life. As Sharma (2014) argues, digital capitalism produces unequal temporalities, privileging speed and immediacy for some while rendering slowness economically and symbolically costly. In the passion economy, creators learn to synchronize their internal rhythms with platform time, organizing their lives around posting schedules, trend cycles, and algorithmic peaks. Passion, once associated with absorption and duration, is compressed into fragments optimized for instant circulation.

This compression erodes craft-based and reflective practices that require extended duration, rendering them increasingly incompatible with platforms that reward constant novelty and rapid feedback. Rosa & Trejo-Mathys (2015) describes this condition as social acceleration, where the speed of technological and cultural change outpaces individuals' capacity for meaningful experience. In such contexts, even rest becomes instrumentalized, reframed as "recovery time" only insofar as it enables renewed productivity. The creator no longer inhabits time; time inhabits the creator.

This temporal disciplining intensifies the dynamics of self-exploitation discussed earlier. Creators do not merely work longer hours; they adopt the platform's tempo as their own, experiencing pressure to accelerate without external coercion. As (Han, 2010) notes, neoliberal subjects exhaust themselves not through imposed commands but through self-imposed acceleration, mistaking speed for freedom and activity for fulfillment. The demand to remain continuously relevant ensures that self-branding evolves into self-exploitation not only at the level of identity and affect, but at the level of lived time itself.

It is important to acknowledge that creators' experiences within the passion economy are far from uniform. Not all creators experience algorithmic narcissism with the same intensity, nor do all forms of digital creativity culminate in self-exploitation. For some, platforms function as genuinely enabling spaces for learning, community-building, and meaningful self-expression; for others, creative practices remain peripheral, playful, or intentionally resistant to metric-driven logic. Factors such as platform type, visibility scale, cultural context, economic necessity, and individual coping strategies significantly shape how creators navigate algorithmic environments. Precisely because these experiences vary, the consequences of algorithmic narcissism must be examined not only structurally, but psychologically, ethically, and communicatively.

Understanding the passion economy as a temporal regime thus clarifies why its consequences extend beyond economic precarity to deeper psychological, ethical, and communicative disruptions. When passion is synchronized to algorithmic time, the costs are not merely quantitative but existential, reshaping how individuals experience selfhood, responsibility, and relation. It is to these consequences that the following section now turns.

PSYCHOLOGICAL, ETHICAL, AND COMMUNICATIVE IMPLICATIONS

The psychological, ethical, and communicative consequences of algorithmic narcissism extend far beyond individual experiences of stress or insecurity. They represent a radical reconfiguration of subjectivity, morality, and relationality, dimensions of human life traditionally anchored in autonomy, empathy, and mutual recognition. As algorithmic environments increasingly mediate self-expression and interaction, the very conditions of psychological development and human communication are destabilized. The effects are not distributed evenly but are systematically ingrained in the structures that govern how individuals appear, relate, and understand themselves. These transformations cannot be dismissed as superficial byproducts of digital culture; they constitute a profound shift in the architecture of the self and in the ethos of society.

Psychologically, the mechanisms of algorithmic narcissism produce identity fragmentation, comparison anxiety, and an escalating dependency on algorithmic validation. Identity fragmentation arises from the selfis continuous partitioning into visible and invisible components. The aspects of the self that align with platform expectations (enthusiasm, vulnerability, productivity, positivity) are amplified, whereas those that do not fit these templates fade into irrelevance. The self becomes a collage of idealized fragments curated for algorithmic consumption, leading to an internal dissonance between who one is and who one must appear to be. This fragmentation generates a discordant psychic state in which authenticity is no longer a matter of internal coherence but of external legibility. The individual experiences the self as something constantly slipping out of alignment, as though always slightly misrepresented by the mirror of metrics.

Comparison anxiety further compounds this fragmentation. The algorithmic environment is inherently comparative; metrics are designed not only to measure one's performance but to implicitly rank it. The visibility of others' success (expressed numerically and immediately) creates a psychological landscape in which the self is perpetually evaluated against an infinite set of others. Unlike in traditional contexts, where comparison is limited to specific reference groups, algorithms expose individuals to a global field of comparison. The "best," "most visible," and "most successful" creators dominate the feed, becoming unrealistic benchmarks for ordinary users. As a result, individuals internalize standards that are structurally unattainable, leading to chronic dissatisfaction and a perpetual sense of inadequacy. Identity becomes tethered to an impossible ideal, rendering the self perpetually insufficient.

Figure 5.

MINI CASE STUDY

Julia, a 24-year-old lifestyle creator, began posting casually on TikTok to document her daily routines. After one video unexpectedly went viral, she felt compelled to repeat the "formula." Within weeks, her mornings shifted from quiet journaling to calculating posting times, comparing analytics, and rehearsing "authentic" moments for the camera.

When her engagement later declined, Julia experienced intense anxiety and questioned her worth as a creator. She found herself refreshing metrics every few minutes, deleting posts that underperformed, and forcing cheerful expressions even on days she felt overwhelmed. Friends noticed she communicated less in person, spending more time crafting captions than having conversations.

Eventually Julia realized she no longer enjoyed the activities she shared online; she enjoyed how they performed online. What had begun as self-expression had become emotional labor, and her relationships (to creativity, to others, and to herself) were increasingly mediated by the rise and fall of numerical feedback.

Algorithmic dependency arises from this dynamic. The individual's sense of self-worth gradually becomes contingent on the rhythms of the algorithm, its rewards, its silences, its fluctuations. The algorithm becomes a psychological authority, whose feedback determines emotional states and motivates behavior. This dependency disrupts the development of internal sources of validation, replacing them with external digital indices. The self forgets how to exist outside the parameters of visibility; invisibility becomes existentially threatening. What emerges is a condition akin to psychological outsourcing, in which the algorithm functions as a surrogate ego ideal. The individual looks to the platform for recognition, direction, and affirmation, relinquishing aspects of agency in exchange for the comfort of metricized certainty.

The ethical implications of this transformation are equally troubling. When authenticity becomes currency, the moral foundations of sincerity, honesty, and responsibility undergo profound distortion. Authenticity, which historically refers to the alignment of inner truth with outward expression, becomes redefined as a performative strategy, a carefully curated aesthetic that signals "realness" to garner engagement. Ethical life becomes entangled with spectacle; sincerity becomes indistinguishable from self-promotion. The individual is incentivized to turn personal experiences, emotions, and even traumas into consumable content. Vulnerability (once a relational act of trust) becomes a resource to be strategically displayed.

In such a context, the ethical question emerges: *what remains of sincerity when authenticity is monetized?* The danger lies not only in the commodification of emotion but in the erosion of moral accountability. If sincerity is always curated, then genuine moral intention becomes difficult to discern, both for others and for the self. Ethical relations depend on mutual recognition, but recognition becomes distorted when mediated through metrics. Morality itself risks becoming calculative, governed not by principles but by performance. Acts of care, solidarity, and accountability become instrumentalized forms of content rather than sincere ethical commitments. In this environment, the ethical life is displaced by a performative moral persona.

In communicative terms, the erosion of dialogic humanism becomes apparent. Humanistic communication, grounded in mutual understanding, empathy, and reciprocal presence, gives way to forms of interaction that are fundamentally self-referential. Under algorithmic narcissism, communication becomes a means to secure visibility rather than a space for dialogue. Messages are crafted not to foster understanding but to maximize engagement. The self, rather than reaching outward to encounter the Other, folds back upon itself, engaging in communication primarily to sustain its brand. Dialogue becomes monologue disguised as interaction; the communicative field is crowded with performances of self rather than exchanges of meaning.

This shift undermines the very foundation of dialogic ethics, which requires openness to the Other. Instead of cultivating relationality, algorithms promote forms of communication that reinforce sameness through personalization, predictive filtering, and homophilic feeds. The Other is experienced not as a presence with independent subjectivity but as an audience, a follower, a metric. As communication becomes increasingly oriented toward maintaining attention, the capacity for genuine listening, disagreement, and ethical encounter diminishes. Humanistic communication relies on the unpredictable, the uncurated, the unscripted, qualities that algorithmic platforms systematically suppress.

At a deeper philosophical level, these transformations echo Byung-Chul Han's argument that contemporary society marks the death of otherness. Narcissism, in Han's analysis, is not merely an excessive self-love but a collapse of the boundary between self and Other, resulting in a world populated by mirrors rather than relations. The achievement subject encounters only reflections of itself, curated through algorithmic personalization. The difference becomes intolerable because it disrupts the homogeneity of the self-image. The Other disappears not through violence but through absorption, their alterity flattened into content, their singularity erased by the logic of visibility.

In such a world, the relational dimension of being-with-others is replaced by psychical circulation within one's own image. The subject becomes trapped in a hall of mirrors, each reflection quantified, optimized, and reinforced by algorithmic feedback. Han's notion of the "society of positivity" captures this condition succinctly: negativity (failure, limitation, alterity) becomes excluded from the field of visibility, leaving only self-referential affirmations. This philosophical transformation extends beyond individual psychology; it represents a reconfiguration of reality itself. Reality becomes a projection of the self, mediated through screens that reflect only what the algorithm predicts one will desire.

Returning to Erich Fromm's distinction between being and having, algorithmic narcissism represents an even more radical deviation: the shift from being to having visibility. Instead of cultivating a self grounded in presence, depth, and relationality, the individual becomes preoccupied with possessing attention, followers, and engagement. These forms of possession are inherently unstable, fostering insecurity and compulsive self-display. The self becomes oriented around accumulation rather than actualization, around quantification rather than experience. In this sense, algorithmic narcissism is not merely a cultural pathology but a systemic reorganization of values, a reorientation of what it means to exist meaningfully.

Figure 6.

MINI CASE STUDY

Adam (@adamgeorgeritonga), a 35-year-old Indonesian content creator of Batak descent, began sharing his passion for singing on Instagram as a way to express a talent he rarely displayed offline due to shyness. What started as participation in trending content gradually evolved into deeper creative exploration, including dance, through which he found a supportive community with shared interests. In 2025, his journey led him to become one of the dancers featured in iForte's promotional video for the national dance competition 'Inspirasi Diri'. For Adam, Instagram functioned less as a space of self-branding than as a medium of humanistic communication, enabling self-expression, relational growth, and unexpected economic opportunities rooted in passion rather than performance.

COUNTER-IDEOLOGIES: HUMANISTIC COMMUNICATION AND ALGORITHMIC RESISTANCE

Despite its structural risks and the ideological pressures embedded in platform architectures, the passion economy also produces meaningful forms of growth, creativity, and self-development for many individuals (Herari et al., 2025). It would be analytically incomplete (and ethically imbalanced) to portray it solely as a site of exploitation or narcissistic alienation. Indeed, one of the distinctive features of the passion economy is that its emancipatory and oppressive potentials often coexist within the same practices. Many creators genuinely expand their skills: they learn digital storytelling, audience psychology, platform mechanics, aesthetic judgment, and algorithmic navigation. They develop discipline because the environment requires consistency. They learn to articulate their interests, communicate their knowledge, and mobilize personal meaning into craft. For some, the passion economy becomes a gateway to entrepreneurial independence; for others, a means of healing through creative expression; for many, a laboratory of identity in which they encounter new forms of self-understanding.

These positive dimensions (skill development, confidence-building, community formation) should not be overshadowed by critical analysis. The passion economy can indeed empower, especially when individuals find resonance with audiences who share their values or lived experiences. It fosters micro-communities of practice in which creators offer knowledge, humor, or emotional presence to those who feel unseen in mainstream culture. It democratizes cultural labor that was once monopolized by institutions. It introduces new pathways for learning that are experiential, iterative, and visibly rewarded. Yet these benefits do not neutralize the structural risks; instead, they make it even more urgent to develop counter-ideologies that preserve the emancipatory potential of the passion economy while mitigating its exploitative tendencies. What is needed is not rejection, but re-humanization.

Counter-ideologies function as conceptual tools that help individuals resist the algorithmic pressures that push passion toward performativity and self-exploitation. They offer alternative imaginaries of digital life, modes of being that foreground human connection, intrinsic motivation, and relational care rather than metrics. Such counter-ideologies operate on multiple levels: personal, collective, communicative, and philosophical. They ask whether it is possible to inhabit digital spaces without becoming defined by their logic. They ask whether passion can be reclaimed as a site of being rather than a performance for algorithmic visibility.

Table 2. Transition from algorithmic narcissism to humanistic counter-ideologies

Algorithmic Narcissism	**Humanistic Counter-Ideologies**
Speed & Virality	Digital Minimalism
Opacity of Algorithms	Algorithmic Literacy
Individual Visibility	Collective Models
Self-Branding	Relational Creativity
Exitence = Performance	Humanistic Visibility

Digital minimalism emerges as a key counter-ideological practice that resists the accelerationist rhythms of algorithmic culture by reorienting digital life around intention rather than compulsion. It is not a call for abstinence from technology, but a deliberate refusal to make virality the primary measure of value. In the context of the passion economy, digital minimalism enables creators to redefine success beyond constant visibility by prioritizing depth over frequency, relational engagement over reach, and sustainable creativity over relentless productivity.

As Newport (2019) argues, contemporary platforms (particularly social media) are structurally designed to maximize engagement through speed, connectivity, and compulsive use, often at the expense of autonomy, mental well-being, and meaningful interaction. Digital minimalism directly challenges this logic by advocating a selective, value-driven approach to technology use, in which only tools that genuinely support human flourishing are retained. In doing so, it marks a critical shift away from algorithmic narcissism (where existence is equated with performance) toward a humanistic orientation in which technology serves the person rather than disciplines the self.

Building on this perspective, digital minimalism demonstrates that productivity and economic sustainability need not depend on constant visibility or affective exhaustion. By decoupling productivity from perpetual online presence, creators can focus on depth-oriented work (such as developing expertise, producing durable creative outputs, or cultivating trust-based relationships) that generates value without requiring continuous emotional performance. Income, in this model, is derived less from viral attention and more from relevance, credibility, and long-term engagement, allowing creators to use platforms instrumentally rather than existentially. This reconfiguration reduces stress labor by limiting exposure to real-time metrics, curbing compulsive self-surveillance, and preserving spaces of offline reflection essential for creativity. In this sense, digital minimalism does not reject ambition or economic participation; instead, it reframes productivity as intentional contribution and income as an outcome of meaningful work, restoring autonomy and psychological well-being within the digital economy.

Another counter-ideological strategy is algorithmic literacy: the capacity to read and interpret algorithms not as neutral tools but as ideological texts that shape identity, desire, and labor. Algorithmic literacy does not require technical expertise; it requires an understanding that platforms encode specific cultural and economic values. When creators recognize these values (speed, novelty, emotional intensity, and repeat engagement), they can begin to disentangle their sense of self from algorithmic demands. By learning how algorithms filter content, rank visibility, and shape behavior, creators gain a measure of analytical distance. This distance allows us to critique the system rather than internalize its rules as natural.

In practical terms, this reorientation can be enacted through small but consequential design and usage choices. Creators who practice algorithmic literacy may deliberately batch content production and schedule distribution to avoid real-time monitoring of metrics, using analytics only periodically for informational feedback rather than emotional validation. Others may employ AI tools to automate technical tasks (such as editing, captioning, or distribution) while reserving creative and relational work for offline or slower, more reflective contexts. Platforms can also be engaged selectively: comments may be closed after a set period, notifications limited, or success measured through qualitative indicators such as meaningful dialogue, client trust, or community continuity rather than raw engagement numbers. At an institutional level, algorithmically literate users may choose platforms that support subscription-based or community-funded models, where income is decoupled from virality and emotional overexposure. These practices illustrate how algorithmic literacy translates critique into action, enabling individuals to remain economically active in digital environments while resisting the transformation of their attention, emotions, and identities into continuous sources of unpaid labor.

At the collective level, co-creation, community-based content, and platform cooperativism offer structural alternatives to the individualizing pressures of the passion economy. Co-creation counters the logic of individual competition by emphasizing collaboration and shared authorship. It shifts the focus from individual visibility to communal creativity, redistributing attention across networks rather than concentrating it on a single influencer. Community-based content creation is anchored in relational practices, mutual support, shared learning, and collective storytelling. These practices resist the isolation and comparison anxiety generated by algorithmic ranking.

Platform cooperativism, meanwhile, envisions alternative infrastructures where creators collectively own the platforms they use. Instead of extracting value for corporate shareholders, such platforms reinvest profits into creator welfare, shared governance, and equitable visibility. While still emerging, platform cooperativism offers a theoretical horizon that reimagines digital economies as democratic, participatory, and aligned with human well-being. It demonstrates that the architecture of digital life is not immutable; it can be redesigned to prioritize care, dignity, and reciprocity.

A well-documented example of community-based success is the creator-membership model enabled by platforms such as Patreon. Rather than relying on algorithmic virality, many Patreon creators generate sustainable income through small but committed communities that value ongoing relationships over mass exposure. For instance, mid-tier educators, podcasters, and independent artists often earn stable monthly revenue from a few hundred supporters, demonstrating that financial viability can be achieved without constant content creation or emotional overreach. Studies of Patreon creators show that community trust, perceived reciprocity, and shared purpose are stronger predictors of income stability than follower count or engagement metrics, illustrating how relational value can outperform visibility-driven models (Abidin, 2018; Baym, 2015; Cunningham & Craig, 2019; Duffy & Wissinger, 2017). These cases suggest that financial sustainability in the digital economy does not depend on algorithmic dominance, but on the capacity to cultivate durable social relations and shared meaning.

The most profound counter-ideology arises from humanistic communication, rooted in Erich Fromm's mode of being. Fromm argued that genuine existence is grounded in presence, love, and productive engagement with others, not in possession, performance, or accumulation. From this perspective, one can propose the concept of Humanistic Visibility, defined as a form of digital presence rooted in empathy, shared meaning, and relational depth rather than in attention metrics. Humanistic visibility rejects the notion that value must be quantified; it affirms that connection can be meaningful even when it is not mass-circulated or algorithmically amplified.

Humanistic visibility encourages creators to communicate not to be seen widely, but to be seen truly. It reframes passion as relational care, a practice that emerges from genuine interest in others rather than self-exposure. In this view, visibility is not a commodity but an encounter. Creativity becomes an offering, not a performance. Passion becomes an ethical relation, not a brand asset. This shift redefines the fundamental purpose of digital presence: not to accumulate followers, but to foster dialogue, mutual recognition, and shared humanity.

Figure 7.

Algorithmic narcissism does not describe a personality trait, but a structural mode of subject formation. It is a tendency shaped by platforms, not a destiny written into the self.

The normative vision emerging from these counter-ideologies is simple yet radical: passion should be a form of care, not a spectacle of self. It should cultivate community, not competition. It should nourish the self, not exhaust it. It should deepen relationality, not replace it with reflection. For passion to remain meaningful within the digital space, it must be practiced in alignment with human-centered values, presence over performance, depth over quantity, and empathy over metrics.

In this sense, counter-ideologies are not merely defensive strategies; they are generative imaginaries that seek to reclaim the positive potentials of the passion economy. They honor its ability to nurture skills, creativity, and connection, while challenging the structural forces that distort passion into labor and identity into brand. They articulate a future in which digital life can be lived ethically, relationally, and humanely, beyond algorithmic narcissism, and toward a more compassionate digital culture.

CONCLUSION: TOWARD A POST-NARCISSISTIC PASSION ECONOMY

As this chapter has argued, algorithmic narcissism functions as the ideological software of the passion economy, a system that converts visibility into value, authenticity into performance, and passion into programmable labor. The algorithm does not merely reward narcissistic tendencies; it structurally requires them by organizing recognition, legitimacy, and economic opportunity through metrics, comparison, and continuous self-optimization. In this configuration, the self is rendered as a perpetual project, endlessly evaluated and recalibrated through data-driven mirrors. If left unexamined, this logic risks normalizing a mode of subjectivity in which self-worth, creativity, and belonging are contingent upon constant performance and algorithmic approval.

The urgency of addressing algorithmic narcissism lies in its cumulative consequences. When passion is persistently synchronized with platform metrics and accelerationist temporalities, creators face not only burnout and anxiety but also a deeper erosion of autonomy, ethical orientation, and relational depth. Creativity becomes reactive rather than reflective; communication becomes self-referential rather than dialogic; and labor extends beyond work into identity itself. At scale, such conditions threaten to entrench a digital economy that extracts emotional and cognitive labor while externalizing psychological and social costs onto individuals.

Yet this chapter has also emphasized that the passion economy is not inherently dystopian. The same digital infrastructures that enable extraction can be repurposed to support learning, skill development, community formation, and meaningful creative livelihoods. A post-narcissistic passion economy, therefore, does not demand technological rejection, but intentional reconfiguration. Practices such as digital minimalism, algorithmic literacy, and collective models of co-creation offer practical pathways to reclaim agency, slow production rhythms, and anchor creativity in relational rather than metricized value.

Crucially, this reorientation depends on restoring human sovereignty over algorithmic systems. Algorithms and AI must function as assistive infrastructures, not as invisible governors of attention, identity, and worth. The future of digital work hinges on ensuring that humans set the goals to which technology is subordinated, rather than adapting themselves to opaque computational demands. A post-narcissistic passion economy is thus not a utopian escape, but a necessary ethical horizon, one that insists digital freedom will emerge not from mastering algorithms, but from reaffirming the right to pause, to relate, and, when needed, to remain unseen.

REFERENCES

Abidin, C. (2018). Internet Celebrity and Traditional Media. In *Internet Celebrity: Understanding Fame Online* (pp. 37–69). Emerald Publishing Limited. DOI: 10.1108/978-1-78756-076-520181003

Baudrillard, J. (1987). *The Ecstacy of Communication.*

Baym, N. K. (2015). Connect With Your Audience! The Relational Labor of Connection. *Communication Review*, *18*(1), 14–22. DOI: 10.1080/10714421.2015.996401

Benvenuto, S. (1995). Freud's Concept of Narcissism. *European Journal of Psychoanalysis, 1.* https://www.journal-psychoanalysis.eu/articles/freuds-concept-of-narcissism/

Browley, J. (2022, June 4). *Report: Gen Z Increasingly Turning Their Passion into Side Hustle*. Essence. https://www.essence.com/news/money-career/gen-z-willing-to-work-more-than-millennials/

Cunningham, S., & Craig, D. (2019). *Social Media Entertainment: the New Intersection of Hollywood and Silicon Valley*. New York University Press.

Daudi, A. (2022). The Culture of Narcissism: A Philosophical Analysis of "Fitspiration" and the Objectified Self. *Physical Culture and Sport Studies and Research*, *94*(1), 46–55. DOI: 10.2478/pcssr-2022-0005

Duffy, B. E., & Meisner, C. (2023). Platform governance at the margins: Social media creators' experiences with algorithmic (in)visibility. *Media Culture & Society*, *45*(2), 285–304. DOI: 10.1177/01634437221111923

Duffy, B. E., & Wissinger, E. (2017). Mythologies of Creative Work in the Social Media Age: Fun, Free, and "Just Being Me.". *International Journal of Communication*, *11*(11), 4652–4671. https://ijoc.org/index.php/ijoc/article/view/7322

Florida, R. L. (2004). *The rise of the creative class : and how it's transforming work, leisure, community and everyday life*. Basic Books.

Freud, S. (1914). *On Narcissism.*

Fromm, E. (1956). *Psicoanálisis de la sociedad contemporánea Hacia una sociedad sana* (6th ed.). Fondo de Cultura Economica., https://ayudacontextos.wordpress.com/wp-content/uploads/2018/04/erich_fromm-psicoanalisis_de_la_sociedad_contemporanea.pdf

Fromm, E. (1976). *Haben oder Sein : die seelischen Grundlagen einer neuen Gesellschaft*. Deutschet Taschenbuch Verlag. https://www.lyrik-klinge.de/wp-content/uploads/Haben_oder_Sein__Fromm.pdf

Fromm, E. (1977). *El Miedo A La Libertad (Fear of Freedom)* (G. Germani, Ed.). Paidos. https://conductitlan.org.mx/13_psicologiasocial/Materiales/L_FROMM_El%20Miedo%20A%20La%20Libertad.pdf

Fromm, E. (1978). *Tener Y Ser*. Fondo de cultura economica. https://consumoetico.webs.uvigo.es/textos/tener_ser.pdf

Fromm, E. (2000). *El Arte de Amar*. Martins Fontes. https://share.google/C3UCmvwDeIDN6Qr5u Fromm, E. (2023, May 30). *The Psychology of Narcissism - Erich Fromm's Video Essay*. Youtube. https://youtu.be/V9Pz9VZhbL8?si=gcZWkjitr1kd9S-I

Fromm, E. (2024, July 21). *The Art of Loving - Erich Fromm's Video Essay*. Youtube. https://youtu.be/iagSm_E_thk?si=Kx4KDRZh1m4ibodc

Han, B.-C. (2010). *The Burnout Society* (Butler, E., Ed.). Stanford University Press.

Herari, N. (2025). Piramida Kebutuhan dan Passion Economy, Pemenuhan Kebutuhan Diri melalui Media Digital di Indonesia. In Rosanah, R., Berto, A. R., Yuniarti, T., Lestari, A., Safrudiningsih, S., Ramonita, L., & Arifah, A. (Eds.), *Transformasi Komunikasi Digital Menuju Indonesia Berkelanjutan: Komunikasi Digital dan Inovasi Bagi Masyarakat* (1st ed., pp. 128–143). PT Elex Media Komputindo., https://www.researchgate.net/publication/390760825_Piramida_Kebutuhan_dan_Passion_Economy_Pemenuhan_Kebutuhan_Diri_melalui_Media_Digital_di_Indonesia

Herari, N., & Waluyo, W. (2023). Instagram Business Coach sebagai Penggerak Passion Economy dalam Perspektif Islam. *Warta ISKI*, *6*(1), 32–47. DOI: 10.25008/wartaiski.v6i1.201

Herari, N., Waluyo, W., & Rubiyanto, R. (2024). Self-Directed Visionaries: Evolutionize the Passion Economy through Digital Entrepreneurship on Instagram. In U. Yunus & et al (Eds.) (Eds.), *Proceeding Book of The International Conference on Communication and Business. Strengthening ASEAN's Leadership in Sustainable Business and Advanced Comunication, Volume 2. The Intersection of Communication and Business in the Pursuit of Sustainability* (pp. 14–14). LSPR Publishing. https://www.researchgate.net/publication/377964759_Self-Directed_Visionaries_Evolutionize_the_Passion_Economy_through_Digital_Entrepreneurship_on_Instagram

Herari, N., Waluyo, W., & Rubiyanto, R. (2025). Leading Alone, Leading Forward: Solopreneurs and the Quiet Power of the Passion Economy. In Paradiso-Testa, M. (Ed.), *The Purpose of Passion in Leadership* (1st ed.). IGI Global. DOI: 10.4018/979-8-3373-2404-3.ch012

IDW. (2021). *Christopher Lasch - The Culture of Narcissism*. YouTube. https://www.youtube.com/watch?v=6dR2ghd8rmg

Johnston, A. (2022, December 24). *Jacques Lacan*. Stanford Encyclopedia of Philosophy. https://plato.stanford.edu/entries/lacan/

Katzenbach, C., & Ulbricht, L. (2019). Algorithmic governance. *Internet Policy Review, 8*(4). Advance online publication. DOI: 10.14763/2019.4.1424

Kim, Y. (2021). *The Soft Power of The Korean Wave; Parasite, BTS and Drama* (1st ed.). Routledge., https://www.routledge.com/ DOI: 10.4324/9781003102489

Lacan, J. (1936). *Lacan - Mirror Stage*.

Lasch, C. (1979). *The Culture of Narcissism*. W.W.Norton & Company.

Licitra Rosa, C., Antonucci, C., Siracusano, A., & Centonze, D. (2021). From the Imaginary to Theory of the Gaze in Lacan. *Frontiers in Psychology, 12*, 578277. Advance online publication. DOI: 10.3389/fpsyg.2021.578277 PMID: 33859589

Littler, J. (2013). Book Review Authentic TM: The Politics of Ambivalence in a Brand Culture. *International Journal of Communication, 7*, 1156–1158. https://ijoc.org/index.php/ijoc/article/view/2229/917

Lombardinilo, A. (2017). Baudrillard between Benjamin and McLuhan: "The narcissistic seduction" of the media society. *Italian Sociological Review, 7*(4), 499–524. DOI: 10.13136/isr.v7i4.208

Lung, C., AbuHilal, I., Blackburn, J., De Cristofaro, E., Zannettou, S., & Stringhini, G. (2021). Dissecting the Meme Magic: Understanding Indicators of Virality in Image Memes. *24th ACM Conference on Computer-Supported Coop- Erative Work and Social Computing (CSCW 2021)*. https://arxiv.org/abs/2101.06535 DOI: 10.1145/3449155

Mastrangelo, F. (2021). *Theorizing #Girlboss Culture: Mediated Neoliberal Feminisms from Influencers t om Influencers to Multi-le o Multi-level Mark el Marketing Schemes eting Schemes* [Virginia Commonwealth University]. https://scholarscompass.vcu.edu/cgi/viewcontent.cgi?article=7768&context=etd

Miessler, D. (2023, September 28). *Extracted Wisdom Series: Achievement Society and the Rise of Narcissism, Depression, and Anxiety*. Danielmiessler.Com. https://danielmiessler.com/blog/extracted-wisdom-series-achievement-society-and-the-rise-of-narcissism-depression-and-anxiety

Newport, C. (2019). *Digital Minimalism: Choosing A Focused Life in A Noisy World*.

Octavia, S., & Sari, W. P. (2024). Persepsi Generasi Z dengan Pernyataan "Kerja Sesuai Passion" dalam Menentukan Profesi. *Koneksi*, *8*(1), 25–33. DOI: 10.24912/kn.v8i1.21659

Rosa, H., & Jonathan, T.H. (2015). *Social Acceleration: A New Theory of Modernity*. Columbia University Press.

Sachs, G. (2023, April 19). *The creator economy could approach half-a-trillion dollars by 2027*. GoldmanSachs.Com. https://www.goldmansachs.com/insights/articles/the-creator-economy-could-approach-half-a-trillion-dollars-by-2027

Senft, T. M. (2013). Microcelebrity and the Branded Self. In *A Companion to New Media Dynamics* (pp. 346–354). Wiley., DOI: 10.1002/9781118321607.ch22

Sharma, S. (2014). *In the Meantime: Temporality and Cultural Politics*. Duke University Press.

Stiegler, B. (2010). *Taking care of youth and the generations*. Stanford University Press.

Stiegler, B., & Ross, D. (2015). *Automatic Society 1: The Future of Work-Introduction*. https://archive.wired.com/science/discoveries/magazine/16-07/pb_theory

Stiegler, B., & Rossouw, J. (2011). *Suffocated Desire, or How the Cultural Industry Destroys the Individual: Contributon to A Theory of Mass Consumption*.

Stinson, C. (2021). Algorithms are not neutral: Bias in collaborative filtering. *ArXiv*. 10.48550/arXiv.2105.01031

This, P. (2023, October 4). *Episode #189 - Transcript*. Philosophize This! https://www.philosophizethis.org/transcript/episode-189-transcript

Chapter 9
Digital Intellectualism:
Algorithmic Mediation of Public Knowledge

Koteshwar Ramesh Rakesh
http://orcid.org/0000-0002-5464-275X
Synpase International, New Delhi, India

ABSTRACT

Digital scholarship has transformed knowledge production through platform-mediated dissemination, algorithmic curation, and networked collaboration. However, this transformation simultaneously democratizes intellectual participation and reproduces structural inequalities. This chapter examines how scholars negotiate authority, visibility, and epistemic legitimacy within algorithmically governed public spheres. Drawing on case studies from the UK, Africa, South Asia, and Latin America, we analyze digital divides, algorithmic opacity, and epistemic fragmentation alongside community-led interventions fostering equitable inclusion. We explore how algorithmic truth regimes reshape knowledge validation and argue for socio-technical interventions to build transparent, democratically accountable digital knowledge infrastructures. The chapter articulates a vision for digital scholarship grounded in epistemic justice and democratic values, emphasizing coordinated action across academia, technology design, governance, and civil society

INTRODUCTION

Digital intellectualism represents a fundamental transformation in the production, validation, and dissemination of knowledge in the contemporary era. Traditional public intellectuals derived epistemic authority from disciplinary peer review, academic institutions, and established scholarly media outlets (Gomes & Bastos, 2024).

DOI: 10.4018/979-8-3373-4531-4.ch009

In contrast, digital intellectuals must navigate algorithmic gatekeepers, platform affordances, and engagement metrics that reshape how knowledge is validated and perceived by the public (Boyd & Crawford, 2012).

Digital Intellectualism can be defined as an emergent ideological formation where power over intellectual authority is redistributed from traditional academic and media institutions toward algorithmically mediated and networked systems (Gomes & Bastos, 2024). This transformation is marked by three core elements: algorithmic epistemologies, visibility economies, and platform sovereignty. Algorithmic epistemologies describe the rule-based systems shaping knowledge credibility and dissemination (Sustainability Directory, 2025). Visibility economies refer to competition for attention through platform metrics such as likes, shares, and reach that increasingly stand in for scholarly consensus (Boyd & Crawford, 2012). Platform sovereignty refers to the power that corporate platforms exert in defining the parameters of discourse, such as ranking algorithms and moderation policies (Pariser, 2011).

It is essential to distinguish between digital intellectualism and the broader concept of epistemic ideology, as this manuscript addresses both but must clarify their relationship. Epistemic ideology refers to the foundational belief systems about what constitutes valid knowledge, whose expertise deserves credibility, and through which institutional or technological mechanisms knowledge gains legitimacy. In this sense, epistemic ideology encompasses the philosophical and political assumptions underlying all knowledge systems, whether traditional or digital. Digital intellectualism, by contrast, represents a specific ideological formation and material practice situated within the digital epistemic context. It describes both the emergent class of intellectual actors who leverage digital platforms for authority and the restructured power dynamics through which knowledge authority shifts from institutional gatekeeping (peer review, editorial boards, academic credentialing) to algorithmic mediation and network effects. Digital intellectualism is therefore a manifestation of contemporary epistemic ideology, specifically the ideology that privileges engagement metrics, platform visibility, and networked influence as proxies for intellectual merit.

This manuscript focuses primarily on digital intellectualism as an emerging practice and ideology, but situates it within the broader epistemic transformations of the 21st century. The critical distinction becomes apparent when considering that epistemic ideology shapes what gets recognized as "truth" at a systemic level, while digital intellectualism describes how individual and collective actors navigate and contest that system through platform-mediated means. Understanding this relationship is crucial for the subsequent analysis of algorithmic truth regimes, as these regimes are simultaneously products of dominant epistemic ideologies and mechanisms through which alternative epistemic ideologies are marginalized or amplified.

Figure 1. Epistemic ideology and digital intellectualism: nested relationship. Epistemic ideology establishes foundational beliefs about what constitutes valid knowledge; digital intellectualism represents a specific ideological formation and practice situated within digital contexts, privileging engagement metrics and platform visibility as proxies for intellectual merit. (Source: The author created this image in Microsoft PowerPoint Version 2018 and is his own work)

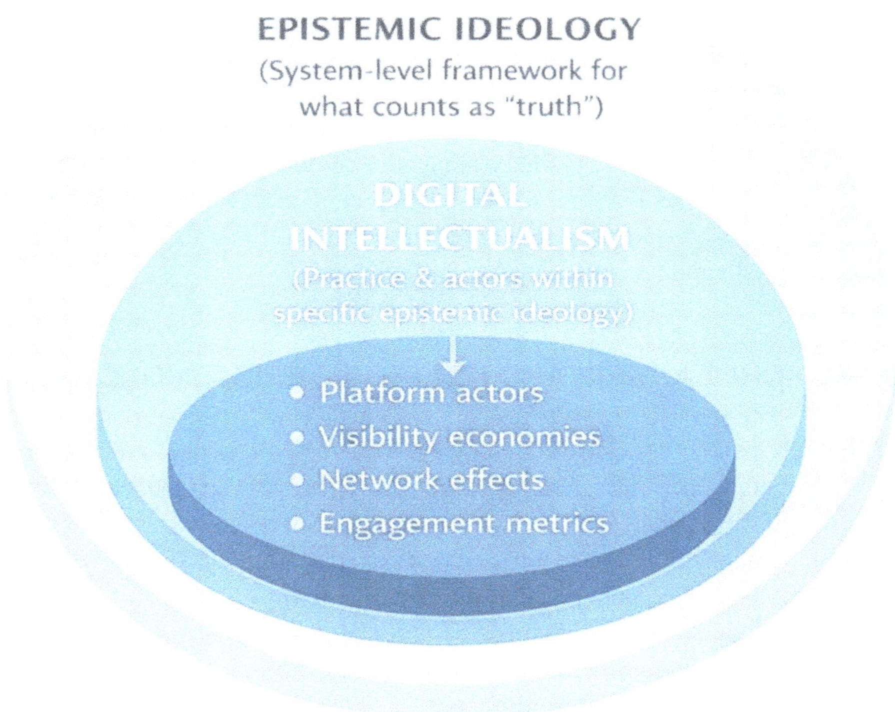

One can situate digital intellectualism within the lineage of public intellectualism, as first characterized by figures such as Habermas and Said, who exerted authority through books, lectures, and academic journals (Wikipedia contributors, 2003). Unlike these traditional intellectuals, digital intellectuals contend with engagement-driven metrics and algorithmic personalization that fragment epistemic spaces, creating individualized "truth bubbles" reinforced by past user behaviour (Pariser, 2011). Moreover, these new intellectuals often employ multimodal forms of scholarship like blogs, podcasts, and Twitter threads that blur the boundaries between academic and public discourse while reshaping expertise through network effects rather than institutional gatekeeping (Boyd & Crawford, 2012).

This chapter is structured in six principal sections. Section II addresses the evolution from traditional public intellectualism to digital scholarship, emphasizing how computational tools mediate knowledge production. Section III examines algorithmic authority and engagement economies, analyzing the role of ranking algorithms and gamification in shaping the dissemination of knowledge. Section IV presents case studies of digital intellectuals negotiating authority within platformed public spheres. Section V examines the challenges posed by epistemic inequalities, algorithmic opacity, and the fragmentation of knowledge. Section VI theorizes the epistemology of digital truth and proposes socio-technical interventions to foster a more equitable digital public sphere. The conclusion synthesizes findings and outlines future research trajectories.

The chapter integrates peer-reviewed scholarship from digital humanities, media studies, and philosophy of technology alongside authoritative grey literature and policy analyses. The goal is to provide a robust conceptual and empirical framework to critically interrogate and transform the epistemic infrastructures shaping twenty-first-century intellectual practice.

DIGITAL SCHOLARSHIP AND PLATFORM EPISTEMOLOGIES

Digital scholarship has evolved far beyond the simple digitization of traditional academic outputs to encompass fundamentally new modes of knowledge production, validation, and dissemination. This transformation operates at two interconnected levels: first, in the methodologies and practices scholars employ, and second, in the platform-mediated epistemologies that determine how knowledge gains credibility and visibility. Understanding digital scholarship therefore requires examining both its practical evolution as a research mode and the algorithmic systems that increasingly govern scholarly authority and impact.

Evolution and Challenges of Digital Scholarship

Digital scholarship represents a rapidly evolving mode of knowledge production that integrates digital tools, platforms, and social media to reshape academic research, dissemination, and engagement (Ocran et al., 2023). Contrary to simply digitizing print content, digital scholarship encompasses new methodologies, including interactive visualizations, network-based models, and collaborative digital projects, which extend epistemological boundaries (Huggett, 2019).

Ocran et al. (2023) highlight that social media platforms have become integral for many scholars in sharing research outputs, fostering networking, and increasing visibility. However, the effective use of these digital scholarship modes is contingent upon digital literacy, institutional support, and infrastructure areas where disparities persist, especially in developing regions. For example, limited internet connectivity and a lack of formal training undermine the broad adoption and impact of digital scholarship platforms in such contexts. These barriers create an uneven landscape, contradicting the democratic potential often ascribed to digital scholarship (Ocran et al., 2023).

Huggett (2019) emphasizes the resilience and adaptability required of scholars engaging with digital scholarship in the face of challenges such as rapidly changing technologies, data management complexities, and shifts in academic norms. The digital environment necessitates new skills in data curation, coding, and multimedia communication, which may not be equally distributed across scholars or institutions. Additionally, Huggett highlights concerns about the sustainability and preservation of digital outputs over time, emphasizing the need for institutional frameworks to support the long-term viability of digital scholarship.

Both the above authors agree that while digital scholarship offers unparalleled opportunities for enhanced collaboration, immediacy, and public engagement, it also demands structural adjustments in academic incentive systems, training programs, and equitable infrastructure provision to fulfill its transformative promise.

These practical challenges in digital scholarship adoption are compounded by deeper structural transformations in how knowledge itself is validated and circulated. While scholars must develop new skills and navigate institutional resistance, they simultaneously confront algorithmic systems that fundamentally reshape the relationship between scholarly merit and public visibility. Platform epistemologies which encompass the rule-based systems governing content recommendation, ranking, and visibility, create new gatekeeping mechanisms that operate according to logics quite different from traditional peer review.

The fundamental distinction between these epistemological systems can be visualized through a comparison of their gatekeeping mechanisms. As illustrated in Figure 2, traditional intellectual authority operates through institutional credentialing and peer review gatekeeping, while digital intellectual authority functions through algorithmic ranking and engagement metrics. This shift represents not merely a change in channels but a paradigmatic transformation in how knowledge gains legitimacy and visibility in contemporary public discourse.

Figure 2. Traditional institutional authority vs. digital algorithmic authority. This image show comparison of traditional institutional gatekeeping mechanisms with platform-mediated algorithmic systems that determine knowledge visibility and credibility (Source: The author created this image in Microsoft PowerPoint Version 2018 and is his own work)

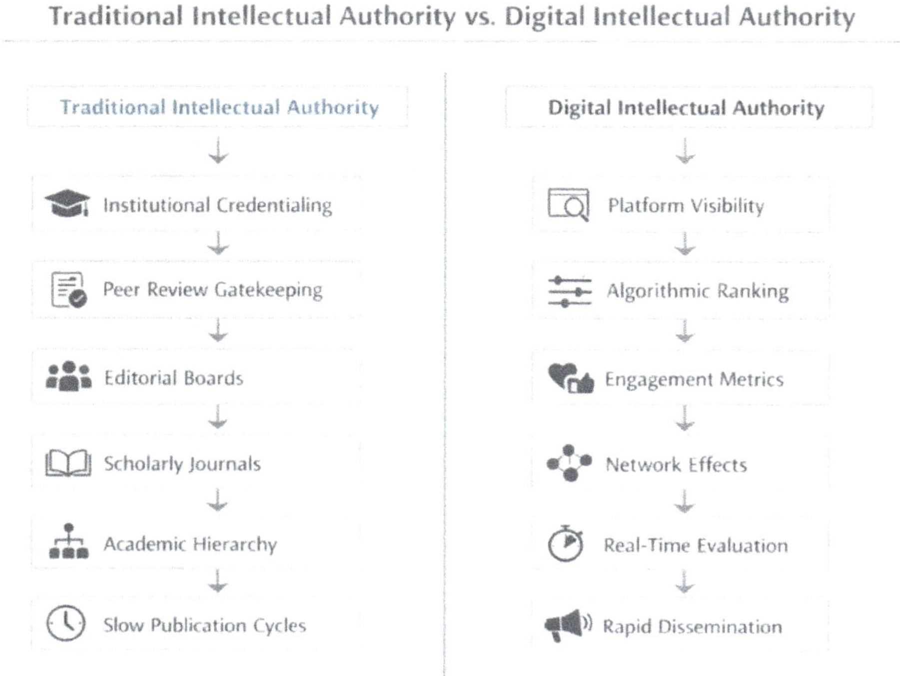

This contrast illuminates why digital intellectuals must navigate fundamentally different reward structures and visibility regimes than their predecessors. Where traditional scholars-built authority through years of peer-reviewed publications within established journals, digital intellectuals must contend with algorithmic systems that evaluate and rank content based on immediate engagement metrics. Understanding this distinction is essential for analyzing the challenges and opportunities digital intellectuals face when seeking to establish credibility outside traditional academic institutions.

Platform epistemologies refer to how knowledge validation processes are embedded within the affordances, policies, and algorithms of digital platforms. Algorithms prioritize content based on engagement, network centrality, and interaction histories rather than strictly scholarly merit (Ocran et al., 2023). Knipp (2024) conceptualizes this as a visibility economy where academic authority is increasingly mediated through quantifiable indicators of attention and influence on platforms.

Altmetrics offer benefits by providing immediacy and a broader spectrum of impact evidence, ranging from scholarly attention to public engagement. However, concerns persist that these metrics are susceptible to manipulation, bias, and exclusion of less digital-savvy or resource-constrained scholars (Knipp, 2024).

Veletsianos and Kimmons (2012) also highlight how digital platforms can privilege self-promotion and networked visibility, potentially distorting meritocratic ideals in academia. This environment incentivizes scholars to produce content optimized for algorithmic visibility, sometimes at the detriment of depth and rigour.

Challenges and Opportunities in Knowledge Production

While digital scholarship democratizes access and enables innovative methodologies, it presents significant challenges, including information overload, demands for digital literacy, and methodological concerns about data validity and representativeness (Arnold et al., 2023). Research demonstrates that information overload can lead to decreased productivity, cognitive fatigue, and decision-making difficulties among scholars and students navigating vast digital collections and databases (Shahrzadi et al., 2024). Digital divides also manifest, marginalizing voices from less connected or resourced contexts (Ocran et al., 2023).

These challenges are compounded by the professional tensions academics face when engaging with digital platforms. Jordan and Weller (2018) reveal that while scholars recognize the benefits of social networking for visibility and collaboration, they struggle with time management pressures, concerns about maintaining professional boundaries, and institutional ambivalence toward digital engagement. This creates barriers to fully realizing the collaborative potential of digital scholarship.

Nevertheless, digital scholarship heralds significant opportunities for enhanced collaboration, data-driven insights, and accelerated knowledge dissemination. Digital scholarship is inherently collaborative, drawing on diverse expertise across disciplines and institutions to tackle complex research questions that cannot be addressed through traditional single-authored approaches (Sherman Center for Digital Scholarship, 2025). This collaborative nature enables interdisciplinary partnerships that merge critical digital literacy with social justice concerns, creating opportunities for more inclusive and impactful scholarship.

Emerging technologies such as artificial intelligence, blockchain, and immersive media promise further epistemic innovations by increasing transparency, decentralization, and interactivity within scholarly ecosystems (Nguyen-Hoang et al., 2024). Blockchain technology, in particular, offers potential solutions for creating transparent, secure, and efficient systems for scholarship management, academic credentialing, and peer review processes, while AI integration enables new forms of data analysis and automated recommendation systems that can enhance scholarly discovery and collaboration.

Digital scholarship thus emerges as a complex and contested terrain where transformative possibilities coexist with significant structural constraints. While digital platforms and tools enable unprecedented collaboration, methodological innovation, and public engagement, they simultaneously create new hierarchies mediated by algorithms, engagement metrics, and infrastructure inequalities that may privilege certain voices and forms of knowledge over others. The tension between democratic access and algorithmic gatekeeping, between scholarly rigor and platform optimization, defines the contemporary landscape of digital intellectual work. As the following sections demonstrate, these tensions shape not only individual scholarly practice but the broader epistemic foundations of public knowledge production in the digital age.

ALGORITHMIC AUTHORITY AND ENGAGEMENT ECONOMIES

Having established how digital platforms reshape scholarly practice through new epistemologies and visibility economies, we now turn to examine the specific mechanisms through which algorithmic systems govern knowledge dissemination and public discourse. While the previous section outlined the broad transformation of digital scholarship, the following section analyzes in detail how ranking algorithms, engagement metrics, and platform affordances create new forms of epistemic authority that both enable and constrain digital intellectual work. Understanding these algorithmic logics is essential for grasping how power operates in contemporary knowledge systems and how digital intellectuals must navigate increasingly complex attention economies.

The advent of digital platforms has introduced algorithmic systems as pivotal arbiters of visibility and epistemic authority in the contemporary public sphere. These systems, embedded within platforms such as Twitter, Facebook, and Medium, govern the ranking, recommendation, and distribution of content, thereby shaping patterns of knowledge dissemination and public discourse (Pariser, 2011; Boyd & Crawford, 2012). This section explores the logics of algorithmic authority and the economies of engagement that influence the production and reception of digital scholarship.

Algorithmic Gatekeeping and Ranking Systems

Algorithmic gatekeeping refers to the automated processes by which platforms filter and prioritize content based on a combination of user behaviour, engagement metrics, and proprietary ranking formulas (Gillespie, 2014). Unlike traditional editorial gatekeeping, which operates through explicit review and judgment, algorithmic gatekeepers operate opaquely and dynamically, adjusting to real-time signals and platform incentives (Pasquale, 2015).

These ranking algorithms frequently prioritize content that maximizes user engagement, measured through clicks, shares, likes, and comments, thus privileging virality and emotional resonance over scholarly rigor or nuance (Tufekci, 2015). The consequence is an engagement economy that commodifies intellectual content, incentivizing formats and topics conducive to high engagement at the potential cost of depth and diversity (Zuboff, 2023).

Implications for Content Creation and Intellectual Labour

The prominence of engagement metrics reshapes content creation strategies among digital intellectuals and scholars. Platform affordances and algorithmic logics encourage scholars to adapt their communication styles toward formats that drive visibility, such as concise posts, sensational headlines, or provocative opinions (Waldman, 2018). This dynamic fosters a tension between maintaining scholarly integrity and securing audience reach in competitive attention markets.

Moreover, the emphasis on network effects by digital platforms means that early visibility can create cumulative advantages for certain voices, reinforcing existing hierarchies of authority and marginalizing less networked or less media-savvy scholars (Napoli, 2019). In this context, intellectual labour is often shaped by the need to engage in active self-promotion and strategic network-building, skills not traditionally rewarded in academia (Benkler, 2017).

Algorithmic Bias and Opacity

Algorithmic systems reflect and amplify existing social biases present in their training data and design assumptions (Noble, 2018). The opacity surrounding algorithmic decision-making complicates efforts to interrogate and correct these biases, leading to concerns about fairness, transparency, and accountability in digital knowledge infrastructures (Diakopoulos, 2016).

This opacity also challenges digital intellectuals' capacity to understand how their content is filtered, ranked, and displayed to various audiences. The lack of transparency obstructs informed critiques of algorithmic epistemes and impedes efforts to foster equitable visibility across diverse scholarly perspectives (Pasquale, 2015).

Algorithmic authority thus represents a fundamental shift in how knowledge gains visibility and credibility in public spheres. Unlike traditional editorial gatekeeping, which operated through transparent institutional processes and explicit evaluative criteria, algorithmic systems function opaquely, prioritizing engagement and virality over scholarly nuance or evidentiary depth. This shift creates profound challenges for digital intellectuals seeking to maintain scholarly integrity while reaching public audiences, and raises urgent questions about fairness, transparency, and accountability in digital knowledge infrastructures. The opacity and bias embedded in these systems are not merely technical problems but reflect deeper power relations that shape whose voices are amplified and whose knowledge is marginalized; issues we explore empirically in the following section's case studies.

CASE STUDIES: NEGOTIATING AUTHORITY IN A PLATFORMED PUBLIC SPHERE

This section examines how digital intellectuals strategically navigate platform-mediated public spheres through two representative case studies: the public historian and the policy analyst. These cases illustrate contrasting yet complementary approaches to digital scholarship, demonstrating how practitioners adapt communication strategies, leverage platform affordances, and build networked authority while confronting the visibility pressures and algorithmic constraints analyzed in previous sections. By examining concrete practices, we can better understand both the agency digital intellectuals exercise and the structural limits they encounter in constructing epistemic authority outside traditional institutional frameworks.

Digital Intellectuals and Platform Strategies

The digital public sphere offers intellectuals unprecedented reach and tools for engagement, but also enforces new visibility regimes mediated by opaque algorithms that favour engagement metrics such as likes, retweets, and shares (Knipp, 2024; Ocran et al., 2023). Successful digital intellectuals consciously adapt their content strategies to optimize platform affordances, leveraging multimodal expression (text, video, audio), reciprocal network-building with peers, and responsiveness to trending discourses (Hailu & Wu, 2021; Huggett, 2019).

Case Study One: The Public Historian

Public historians on platforms such as Twitter exemplify the productive fusion of rigorous scholarship with accessible communication styles designed for digital audiences. Recent studies highlight that communication scholars including historians, use Twitter predominantly to share scientific content, scholarly publications, and engage with peers through content that is semantically rich and employs functional engagement tools such as hashtags and mentions, which significantly boost user interaction (Guenther et al., 2023; García-Villar, 2021; Quan-Haase et al., 2015).

The practice of "public historians" on Twitter exemplifies a sophisticated negotiation between scholarly authority and platform visibility. Exemplar figures such as Martha S. Jones, a 19th-century U.S. historian at Johns Hopkins University who focuses on law, race, culture, and inequality, have leveraged Twitter to fundamentally reshape how historical knowledge is produced and disseminated. Jones, who has over 12,000 followers, uses the platform not merely to promote her published work but to create what scholars describe as "open and public scholarship" (Dickinson, 2019). Her approach involves live-tweeting from academic conferences, concisely communicating complex historical analyses, and participating in hashtag-based heritage projects such as #FergusonSyllabus and #CharlestonSyllabus that elevate both scholarly and public visibility. Integrating personal reflections and audiovisual media further nurtures dialogue and expands reach. According to research conducted by Johns Hopkins scholars, functional indicators such as retweets, likes, and mentions correlate with higher engagement levels, underlining the importance of dialogue-oriented content in public scholarship (Guenther et al., 2023; Quan-Haase et al., 2015).

Importantly, this model of digital public history creates a robust community of practice on Twitter. As Jones has documented, "There's a robust community of archivists, museum curators, historians, social studies teachers, and American government experts who are active on the site, and there is a great deal of learning and teaching going on there" (Dickinson, 2019). Historians on Twitter have even developed a distinct community identity, with many communicating through the hashtag #Twitterstorian, which serves simultaneously as a metadata tag, a community marker, and a tool for historical literacy. This represents a paradigmatic shift in how historical knowledge gains legitimacy; not through isolated peer review but through visible, dialogic engagement with multiple audiences.

The case of Jones further illuminates the interconnections between traditional scholarly authority and platform-based visibility. After she tweeted about subject matter from her book *Birthright Citizens: A History of Race and Rights in Antebellum America*, a reporter encountered her work on Twitter and subsequently wrote about her research in *The New York Times*, demonstrating how digital intellectual labor can convert platform visibility into traditional media coverage and expanded scholarly impact (Dickinson, 2019). Yet this example also reveals the limits of platform visibility: while Jones's online presence is substantial, her capacity to sustain engagement is contingent upon continuous platform participation, algorithmic favor, and protection from harassment.

This historian's use of Twitter represents an adaptive strategy to overcome traditional barriers of scholarly communication, fostering an interactive digital historiography while managing the pressures of visibility economies. However, the sustainability and equity of this model remains contested, as it relies on individual scholars' capacity to invest considerable labor in platform maintenance and navigation.

Case Study Two: The Policy Analyst

Policy analysts often navigate digital landscapes by segmenting dense policy research into accessible formats, like blog series or LinkedIn threads targeted at mixed academic and professional audiences. Recognizing that platform algorithms prioritize frequency and shareability, they produce digestible, multimedia content that aligns with trending policy debates without sacrificing analytical depth (Ocran et al., 2023). However, emerging research on professional social media platforms provides important insights into the mechanisms through which policy research reaches diverse stakeholder audiences.

Recent empirical research on LinkedIn engagement patterns reveals that policy analysts and researchers must strategically deploy specific content design features to maximize policy research visibility and uptake among policymakers, practitioners, and cross-sector collaborators. Usera and Durham (2025), in their analysis of 991 LinkedIn posts from professional users, identified several critical engagement predictors that shape how policy research circulates on professional networks. Most significantly, they found that tagging specific individuals or organizations increases the predicted rate of reactions by approximately 15%, suggesting that policy analysts who explicitly direct their research toward specific stakeholder audiences substantially increase the likelihood of their work gaining attention and engagement (Usera & Durham, 2025). This tagging strategy reflects what prior research terms "segmentation": the deliberate partitioning of research audiences based on professional role and sectoral interest.

Maintaining an engaged network that includes journalists, policymakers, and activists extends the analyst's influence into discursive arenas beyond academia, enabling cross-sector dialogues essential for research translation. Research demonstrates that posts receiving higher engagement on LinkedIn subsequently experience what Usera and Durham (2025) term "engagement multiplier effects," wherein initial reactions and comments drive further reposting and visibility, creating cascading reach beyond the analyst's immediate network. Such strategic communication helps counter the digital marginalization of nuanced policy science under the pressure of the fast-moving digital public sphere (Hailu & Wu, 2021).

Furthermore, Usera and Durham (2025) document that the age of a post is a consistent negative predictor of engagement: posts decay in visibility over time as algorithms prioritize fresh content. For policy analysts working on time-sensitive issues like healthcare reform, climate policy, regulatory frameworks. This finding underscores the necessity of iterative content republication rather than reliance on a single foundational post. Policy research gains and sustains visibility through repeated content deployment in multiple formats (threading, summaries, data visualizations) over time, creating what might be termed "content layering": the strategic serialization of research insights to maintain presence in fast-moving policy conversations.

Additionally, Usera and Durham (2025) also find that hashtags increase reactions but do not significantly predict comments or reposts, suggesting that for policy research, hashtags serve primarily a discoverability function rather than a dialogue-generation function. This distinction matters: a policy analyst seeking to reach new policymaker audiences might prioritize topical hashtags (e.g., #HealthPolicy, #ClimateFinance), while one seeking substantive engagement and co-production with existing networks should prioritize tagging specific collaborators and respondents.

The policy analyst's case thus reveals a sophisticated understanding of platform affordances and algorithmic logics as tools for research translation and impact. Yet it also exposes tensions: policy research optimized for algorithmic visibility may be simplified or sensationalized; the pressure for regular content production may divert analyst attention from depth; and the concentration of policy discussion on corporate platforms concentrates gatekeeping power in platform algorithms rather than in democratic institutions. These tensions parallel those faced by public historians, suggesting that platform-based digital intellectual labour, while expanding access, simultaneously recreates hierarchies and constraints in different forms.

Case Study Three: The Activist-Intellectual

While public historians and policy analysts navigate digital platforms to reach diverse audiences, activist-intellectuals in the Global South engage digital spaces with more overt political intent, leveraging platform affordances to build movements around justice and inclusion. Harsh Mander, an Indian author, columnist, and social activist based in New Delhi, exemplifies this mode of digital intellectual practice (Bhat, 2020). After resigning from the Indian Administrative Service in 2002 following his witnessing of the Gujarat communal riots, Mander transformed his career toward social activism and public advocacy (Bhat, 2020). Over more than two decades, he has authored numerous books, written regular columns for Scroll and The Indian Express, and founded the Centre for Equity Studies, a research organization documenting India's exclusion of vulnerable populations (Bhat, 2020).

Mander's digital presence, particularly on platforms like Twitter and opinion columns, illustrates both the opportunities and constraints of digital activism in the Global South context. His platform strategy involves translating dense social science research and fieldwork on marginalized communities into accessible, emotionally resonant narrative. During India's 2019–2020 anti-Citizenship Amendment Act

(CAA) protests, for example, Mander deployed Twitter and media platforms to amplify the voices of Muslim communities facing potential exclusion (Ashwini et al., 2025), while simultaneously situating the struggle within broader frameworks of secular humanism and solidarity. In his speech during the anti-CAA protests, Mander advocated for non-violent resistance, declaring: "We have only one answer to their hatred, and that answer is love" (Bhat, 2020). His digital intellectual work combines scholarly credibility with on-the-ground activism and moral witness, creating what might be termed "engaged digital intellectualism."

However, Mander's example also reveals structural constraints of platform-based activism in the Global South. Operating in a polarized political environment, he faces coordinated online harassment and algorithmic suppression by actors opposed to his advocacy (Ashwini et al., 2025). His intellectual authority, though substantial offline, is continuously contested online through trolling and algorithmic marginalization. This contrasts with the relative visibility afforded to public historians and policy analysts; Mander's digital platform reach, despite substantial offline impact, remains constrained by platform architectures designed for engagement rather than sustained critical engagement with complex social questions (Ashwini et al., 2025). Furthermore, his activism has resulted in state surveillance and legal persecution, as authorities have filed cases against him related to his advocacy during the anti-CAA protests (Bhat, 2020). His case demonstrates that Global South digital intellectuals often operate under additional constraints—state surveillance, coordinated harassment, economic precarity, and legal persecution—that complicate the supposedly democratizing potential of digital platforms touted in Global North accounts.

The strategic successes documented in these case studies demonstrate genuine agency and innovation in digital intellectual work. Public historians and policy analysts have developed sophisticated practices for translating scholarly expertise into digitally native formats, building engaged audiences, and participating in public discourse. However, these individual adaptations should not obscure the significant systemic pressures and constraints that digital intellectuals face like pressures that stem from platform architectures prioritizing engagement over depth, from algorithmic opacity that obscures decision-making criteria, and from attention economies that can undermine scholarly integrity. The following subsection examines these challenges directly.

Challenges: Visibility Pressure and Scholarly Integrity

While digital platforms democratize access and amplify voices, they impose constraints that may compel digital intellectuals to adopt click-driven content strategies potentially detrimental to scholarly depth (Waldman, 2018). The constant demand for visibility and engagement can contribute to burnout and strategic self-censorship, as scholars balance authenticity with algorithmic imperatives.

While the preceding case studies demonstrate individual agency and strategic adaptation within digital platforms, they also reveal that personal effort and platform literacy cannot overcome systemic barriers to equitable participation in digital scholarship. Individual success stories, however inspiring, operate against a backdrop of profound structural inequalities in access, skills, and visibility. The following section shifts focus from individual navigation strategies to examine the systemic challenges—digital inequalities, algorithmic opacity, and epistemic fragmentation—that fundamentally determine who can participate in digital knowledge production and whose contributions gain recognition. These structural barriers require coordinated interventions that transcend individual action, as subsequent sections will explore.

CHALLENGES: INEQUALITIES, OPACITY, AND EPISTEMIC FRAGMENTATION

Despite broad enthusiasm for digital scholarship's democratizing potential, its adoption reveals and can exacerbate persistent inequalities, algorithmic opacity, and epistemic fragmentation. These challenges undermine equitable access to knowledge production and disrupt collective epistemic frameworks.

Digital Inequality: Multidimensional and Contextual

Digital inequality extends beyond mere physical access to include disparities in skills, meaningful usage, and participation (Hargittai & Walejko, 2008). Globally, Internet penetration remains uneven: while more than 90% of Europeans have internet access, fewer than 30% of Africans do (International Telecommunication Union, 2024). Within nations, rural communities, marginalized ethnic groups, women, older adults, and people with disabilities often face compounded barriers (Gogoi & Bora, 2021).

Digital inequality is not a simple binary of access versus no access. Rather, it comprises multiple, intersecting dimensions that compound to create systematic patterns of exclusion from digital knowledge systems. Figure 3 illustrates these layered dimensions, from basic infrastructure access through meaningful participation and epistemic autonomy, showing how barriers at each level disproportionately affect already marginalized populations.

Figure 3. Digital inequality dimensions: layered barriers to equitable digital participation. This matrix visualization demonstrates that digital inequality operates across at least four intersecting dimensions. (Source: The author created this image in Microsoft PowerPoint Version 2018 and is his own work)

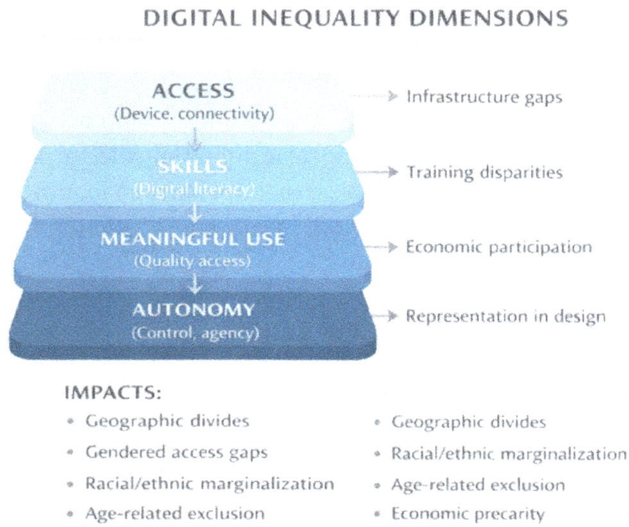

The first level, *Access*, encompasses device availability and connectivity, however, even where physical internet infrastructure exists, cost barriers exclude low-income populations. The second level, *Skills*, reflects disparities in digital literacy that correlate strongly with education, age, and geographic location. The third level, *Meaningful Use*, addresses whether individuals can participate in economically valuable or socially significant activities online, beyond mere consumption. The fourth level, *Autonomy*, concerns whether individuals have voice in platform design, algorithmic governance, and the rules determining what is visible and what is marginalized. These dimensions intersect with geographic divides (rural vs. urban), gendered access gaps (particularly severe in South Asia and Sub-Saharan Africa), racial and ethnic marginalization (particularly evident in platform moderation practices), age-related exclusion (both older adults and very young users), and economic precarity that forces impossible choices between digital connectivity and other necessities.

For example, the COVID-19 pandemic exposed stark inequalities in access to digital education. In India, children in rural areas, girls, and members of Dalit and Adivasi communities struggled with infrastructure deficits, digital literacy gaps, and unreliable electricity, limiting their participation in online learning (Gogoi & Bora,

2021). Similarly, in the United States, students in low-income and rural districts have faced device shortages and insufficient broadband connectivity, impeding equitable educational outcomes (Reich et al., 2020).

These disparities reflect a complex digital divide composed of material access, skills, autonomy, and socio-economic conditions that jointly determine individuals' capacity to participate effectively in digital knowledge ecosystems (Hargittai & Walejko, 2008).

Algorithmic Opacity and Lack of Accountability

Algorithmic opacity, the "black box" nature of many proprietary recommendation and ranking systems, poses critical challenges for transparency and fairness in digital epistemic infrastructures (Pasquale, 2015). These systems embody design choices and training data reflecting human biases, which can perpetuate discrimination and marginalize certain knowledges (Noble, 2018).

Concrete manifestations include social media feeds' prioritization of sensational or polarizing content to maximize engagement, masking underlying decision criteria from users and scholars alike (Pariser, 2011). In high-stakes domains, such as credit scoring, criminal justice, and facial recognition, opacity complicates contestation and redress, disproportionately impacting vulnerable groups (Diakopoulos, 2016).

Calls for algorithmic transparency, independent audits, and explainability are gaining urgency to ensure accountability and equitable visibility in digital knowledge circulation (Pasquale, 2015; Diakopoulos, 2016).

Epistemic Fragmentation and Filter Bubbles

Personalized algorithmic curation often fragments public discourse into epistemic silos or "filter bubbles," where users predominantly engage with information confirming pre-existing beliefs (Pariser, 2011). This phenomenon undermines pluralistic deliberation and fosters polarization.

Global political events such as the 2016 US presidential election and the Brexit referendum revealed how algorithmic echo chambers contribute to radically divergent information worlds, weakening shared factual bases (Flaxman, Goel, & Rao, 2016). Similarly, during the COVID-19 pandemic, varied and sometimes conflicting messages proliferated, contributing to public confusion and debate fragmentation (Cinelli et al., 2020).

Within academia, attention metrics and platformized visibility economies can silo scholarly communication, privileging trending fields and undercutting interdisciplinary exchange (Benkler, 2017).

Toward Addressing Structural Challenges

Addressing the multifaceted challenges of digital inequality, algorithmic opacity, and epistemic fragmentation demands coordinated and systemic interventions across multiple domains. Policy frameworks must prioritize equitable infrastructure development and nuanced digital literacy programs tailored to the specific socio-economic contexts of diverse communities (British Academy, 2023). These efforts should extend beyond mere access to encompass empowerment, inclusion, and sustained participation in digital knowledge ecosystems.

Technological innovations are equally critical. Enhancing algorithmic transparency through explainability features and independent third-party audits can reduce biases and enhance fairness in content curation and visibility (Diakopoulos, 2016). Moreover, platform design should proactively counteract epistemic silos by incorporating serendipity algorithms and cross-community linking features that encourage exposure to diverse perspectives and foster pluralistic digital epistemologies (Zuiderveen Borgesius et al., 2016).

Educational programs must cultivate critical digital literacy, empowering users to effectively navigate, question, and contribute to digital knowledge environments (Jenkins, 2009). This includes building skills not only in digital tool usage but also in the critical interrogation of algorithmic processes and media literacy.

Ultimately, fostering a more equitable and pluralistic digital public sphere requires ongoing collaboration and collective action among scholars, policymakers, platform designers, civil society organizations, and users. By working together to redesign epistemic infrastructures with equity, transparency, and inclusivity as guiding principles, we can begin to realize the transformative promise of digital scholarship as a truly democratic and just knowledge commons.

The challenges examined in this section—digital inequality, algorithmic opacity, and epistemic fragmentation—are deeply interconnected and mutually reinforcing. Infrastructure gaps limit who can access digital platforms; algorithmic opacity obscures how their content is filtered and ranked; and personalized curation fragments audiences, reducing opportunities for cross-community dialogue and consensus formation. Together, these forces create systematic patterns of epistemic injustice that privilege certain voices, knowledge forms, and ways of knowing while marginalizing others. Importantly, these are not inevitable features of digital technology but reflect specific design choices, policy frameworks, and power structures. As the following section demonstrates through concrete examples, alternative approaches that prioritize equity, transparency, and inclusion are both possible and increasingly necessary for realizing the democratic promise of digital scholarship.

INTERVENTIONS AND CASE STUDIES IN OVERCOMING DIGITAL INEQUALITY

Building on the challenges described previously, this section examines practical interventions and case studies that demonstrate efforts to address digital inequality through policy, community engagement, and technological innovation. Examples illustrate diverse strategies to bridge access gaps, advance digital literacy, and foster digital inclusion that supports equitable participation in digital knowledge ecosystems.

Case Studies of Digital Inclusion in the UK

A recent multi-site study commissioned by the British Academy investigated digital inclusion across five UK regions: Birmingham/West Midlands, Greater Manchester, Liverpool City Region, Scotland, and Wales (D'Arcy et al., 2024). This project engaged policymakers and civil society organizations to identify best practices and persistent barriers in digital inclusion.

Key insights include:

- **Local Adaptation of National Policy:** Policymakers tailor national initiatives to local needs and socio-economic realities, exemplifying the importance of contextualized strategies instead of one-size-fits-all approaches.
- **Community Partnerships:** Collaborations between city councils, libraries, and dedicated organizations foster programmatic support such as device lending schemes, free Wi-Fi provision, and digital skills workshops targeted at vulnerable populations (e.g., older adults, refugees, care-leavers).
- **Inter-generational Learning Models:** Programs that encourage knowledge sharing between younger and older community members have been especially effective in overcoming skill gaps.
- **Targeted Support for Diverse Groups:** Interventions focus on marginalized subpopulations, including refugees, people with disabilities, and low-income households, ensuring inclusivity through culturally and linguistically appropriate resources.

These regional efforts underscore the multifaceted nature of digital inequality and the necessity of combining infrastructural, educational, and social interventions (D'Arcy et al., 2024).

Community-led Digital Inclusion Stories: Global Examples

Community-led digital inclusion initiatives worldwide have demonstrated significant transformative impacts on individuals' lives by combining access to devices, connectivity, and tailored training with local trust and systemic support.

In rural India, the Digital Empowerment Foundation's initiatives, such as "Going Online As Leaders (GOAL)" and the "Women Wireless Engineers" programs, empower women and persons with disabilities by equipping them with digital skills and technologies (Manzar, 2023). Women who are trained to set up wireless networks have become local information entrepreneurs, helping their communities gain access to government welfare schemes, healthcare, and financial services (Manzar, 2023).

In Kenya, partnerships involving non-profits, social enterprises, and local governments have established community-run digital hubs that provide affordable internet access, computer literacy, and digital entrepreneurial training in underserved Nairobi neighbourhoods (Batagoda, 2024; Méndez-Domínguez et al., 2023). These hubs enable youth to begin online freelance careers and facilitate access to public services, fostering economic opportunity and social inclusion.

In Colombia, the organization Colnodo developed solar-powered community networks serving remote and indigenous populations. Youth trained as local technicians maintain these networks and deliver digital literacy training, resulting in improved educational access and health outcomes, especially for girls and young women (Roveri, 2025).

Bangladesh's Union Digital Centres, led largely by local entrepreneurs including many women, provide digital skills training, e-governance access, and market participation resources in rural areas. They have enabled artisans like Fatima to reach global markets and improve livelihoods (Batagoda, 2024).

In Ukraine, especially amid ongoing conflicts, libraries and digital hubs offer older adults structured digital training, helping them connect with family, access telemedicine, and participate in civic discussions, reducing social isolation and increasing agency (United Nations Development Programme, 2024).

Brazil's rapid adoption of the PIX instant payments system, facilitated by government and community collaboration, has provided financial inclusion for formerly unbanked populations. This system has empowered informal workers and small vendors across low-income neighbourhoods to access the digital economy at low cost and high convenience (Kamande, 2025).

These narratives collectively illustrate that programs addressing digital skills, device and connectivity access, and local leadership foster sustainable digital participation and improve economic and social well-being (Batagoda, 2024; Méndez-Domínguez et al., 2023).

Digital Inclusion and Poverty: Local Government Initiatives

Municipal and local governments worldwide are advancing digital inclusion initiatives that target poverty-related structural inequities. Peer-reviewed studies elucidate how these initiatives, when designed inclusively and contextually, contribute to poverty reduction by improving access, skills, and economic participation.

In Africa, Rakotondrazaka & Velomasy (2024) analyzes data from 37 countries and find that integration into the digital economy significantly reduces poverty levels, especially when governance quality supports equitable distribution and infrastructure investment. Complementing this macro-perspective, Hussaini and Dikko (2025) demonstrate that digital financial inclusion, via mobile banking and digital payment platforms, substantially improves poverty outcomes in rural Nigeria by enabling financial services previously inaccessible to marginalized communities.

South Asia's experience echoes these findings. Kumar & Jie (2023) highlight that expanding access to digital financial services and e-governance platforms plays a pivotal role in alleviating poverty, but inequalities in digital access and literacy must be addressed simultaneously to maximize impact. They emphasize the role of local governance in deploying targeted digital literacy programs to empower vulnerable populations.

Examining developed contexts, Holmes & Burgess (2022) investigate the UK and document how digital exclusion aligns closely with poverty, particularly among marginalized ethnic groups and economically disadvantaged communities. His findings underscore the necessity of integrating social policies with digital inclusion efforts to address both structural and digital divides holistically.

Sanders and Scanlon (2021) frame digital exclusion as a human rights issue, arguing for digital access as foundational to equitable participation in economic and social life. This normative stance supports policy frameworks that embed digital inclusion within broader anti-poverty programs, advocating for inclusive infrastructure, digital literacy training, and affordable access as social entitlements.

Collectively, these peer-reviewed studies confirm that local government-led digital inclusion reduces poverty not only by providing infrastructure but by combining it with education, financial services access, and policy integration tailored to local socio-economic realities. Successful initiatives foster empowerment and sustained participation, thereby transforming digital inclusion into a driver of socioeconomic equity.

ALGORITHMIC TRUTH REGIMES AND EPISTEMIC CHALLENGES

Digital platforms fundamentally transform traditional epistemological frameworks, creating new regimes of truth validation that challenge conventional notions of knowledge production, verification, and dissemination (Habgood-Coote, 2021). This section analyzes how algorithmic mediation fundamentally transforms traditional epistemological frameworks, creating new regimes of truth validation that operate according to computational rather than institutional logics. We examine both the paradigmatic shift from peer review to algorithmic recommendation and the specific epistemic challenges this shift creates—including systematic marginalization, fragmentation of shared knowledge bases, and the gamification of scholarly discourse. Understanding these challenges is essential for designing interventions that can foster more equitable and democratic digital knowledge systems.

From Institutional to Computational Epistemologies

Algorithmic truth regimes represent a paradigmatic shift from institutional gatekeeping to computational mediation of knowledge validation (Bucher, 2018; Capilla, 2021). Unlike traditional epistemological systems anchored in peer review, editorial oversight, and institutional credentialing, digital truth regimes operate through opaque algorithms that prioritize engagement metrics, network effects, and personalized relevance over systematic verification (Pariser, 2011; Pasquale, 2015).

These systems embody what Foucault (1971) conceptualized as "regimes of truth"; structured frameworks that determine what can be said, by whom, and under what conditions claims gain legitimacy. In digital contexts, truth regimes are increasingly governed by corporate interests, surveillance capitalist logics, and algorithmic amplification of content designed to maximize user engagement rather than epistemic quality (Zuboff, 2023; Capilla, 2021).

The computational mediation of knowledge creates several critical challenges to democratic epistemology. *Epistemic injustice and marginalization* arise when search algorithms systematically marginalize knowledge produced by women, people of colour, and other historically excluded groups, creating what Miranda Fricker terms epistemic injustice—the systematic undermining of marginalized groups' credibility as knowledge producers (Noble, 2018). *Fragmentation and filter bubbles* emerge as algorithmic personalization fragments collective epistemologies into individualized truth bubbles, making consensus formation increasingly difficult and undermining dialogical processes essential for democratic deliberation (Flaxman et al., 2016; Zuiderveen Borgesius et al., 2016). Finally, *gamification of truth* occurs when platform incentive structures encourage the production of sensational, simplified, or clickbait content at the expense of nuanced, evidence-based knowledge, transforming scholarly discourse into a competition for attention rather than a collaborative search for understanding (Tufekci, 2015)

Accountability In Practice: Algorithmic Auditing Case Studies

Case Study 1: The Algorithmic Justice League's Intersectional Audit Framework

The Algorithmic Justice League (AJL), founded by Joy Buolamwini, has pioneered comprehensive algorithmic auditing methodologies that expose biases in AI systems, particularly facial recognition technologies (Costanza-Chock et al., 2022). Their ground-breaking "Gender Shades" study revealed that commercial facial recognition systems exhibit significant accuracy disparities across racial and gender lines, with error rates up to 34.7% for dark-skinned women compared to 0.8% for light-skinned men (Buolamwini & Gebru, 2018).

AJL's audits employ intersectional frameworks that examine algorithmic performance across multiple identity categories simultaneously, revealing compounded biases invisible to single-axis analyses. Their work has prompted major tech companies, including Amazon, IBM, and Microsoft, to pause facial recognition development and implement bias testing protocols (Costanza-Chock et al., 2022).

AJL's field scan identified 438 individuals and 189 organizations engaged in algorithmic auditing, revealing an ecosystem of accountability actors but also highlighting significant gaps in standardization, independence, and stakeholder participation (Costanza-Chock et al., 2022).

Case Study 2: UK Government's Algorithmic Transparency Recording Standard (ATRS)

The UK government's ATRS represents one of the world's most comprehensive national frameworks for algorithmic transparency in public administration (OECD, 2023). Launched in 2021, the ATRS requires government bodies to publish standardized transparency reports detailing their use of algorithmic tools in public decision-making.

The ATRS operates through a tiered system. Tier 1 provides basic explanations of algorithmic use, while Tier 2 requires detailed technical specifications, risk assessments, and human oversight protocols. Pilot studies across UK government departments revealed widespread support (97% from suppliers), but also highlighted challenges in articulating the importance of transparency and building institutional momentum (OECD, 2023).

The initiative has produced publicly accessible transparency reports covering algorithmic systems used in policing, healthcare, and social services. However, evaluation of long-term impacts on public trust and algorithmic improvement remains ongoing.

Case Study 3: Investigative Journalism and External Audits

External algorithmic audits conducted by journalists and civil society organizations demonstrate alternative accountability pathways. Notable examples include *The Wall Street Journal*'s TikTok investigation, in which researchers created 100 automated accounts to trace how TikTok's recommendation algorithms learn and amplify content, revealing pathways to extremist material (Wells et al., 2021). Another example is ProPublica's "Machine Bias" series, which investigated racial bias in criminal justice algorithms and found that risk assessment tools falsely flagged Black defendants as future criminals at nearly twice the rate of White defendants (Angwin et al., 2016). Together, these investigations demonstrate how external audits can expose algorithmic harms even without access to proprietary code, using creative methodologies such as "sock puppet" testing and statistical analysis of outputs.

Interventions for Democratic Digital Epistemology: Possibilities and Limitations

Creating more equitable digital epistemologies requires interventions spanning technical design, institutional policy, and cultural practice. This section synthesizes emerging approaches to algorithmic accountability and democratic knowledge governance, examines their current limitations, and outlines pathways toward epistemic justice in digital spaces. We organize interventions into technical and institutional categories while acknowledging that effective transformation requires their coordination.

Socio-Technical Interventions for Democratic Digital Epistemology

Technical Interventions. Technical interventions include the development of multi-dimensional evaluation systems that move beyond engagement metrics to incorporate diverse quality indicators, such as peer ratings, expert assessments, and fact-checking scores, which better reflect epistemic value (Knipp, 2024). Algorithmic diversity and serendipity mechanisms can be implemented to deliberately introduce diverse perspectives and unexpected content, counteracting echo chambers and promoting epistemic openness (Zuiderveen Borgesius et al., 2016). Explainable AI and transparency tools are also central, involving user-facing explanations of algorithmic decision-making and transparency dashboards that reveal ranking factors and potential biases (Diakopoulos, 2016).

Institutional and Policy Interventions. Institutional and policy interventions encompass mandatory algorithmic impact assessments, which require organizations to conduct and publicly disclose analyses of algorithmic systems' potential social impacts, analogous to environmental impact assessments (Reisman et al., 2018). Independent audit requirements can establish legal obligations for third-party audits of high-stakes algorithmic systems, using standardized methodologies and public reporting (Goodman & Trehu, 2022). Additionally, stakeholder participation in platform governance involves creating formal mechanisms through which affected communities, researchers, and civil society actors can participate in platform policy-making and content moderation decisions (Napoli, 2019).

Limitations and Future Directions

Current algorithmic auditing approaches face several limitations: methodological inconsistencies, lack of standardization, limited access to proprietary systems, and insufficient representation of Global South perspectives (Urman et al., 2024). Future developments must address these gaps through international coordination, standardized audit protocols, and inclusive stakeholder engagement. Moreover, the field must grapple with fundamental tensions between transparency and security, individual privacy and collective accountability, and local cultural values and global platform policies (Habgood-Coote, 2021).

Toward Epistemic Justice in Digital Spaces

Creating more equitable digital epistemologies requires coordinated action across technical design, institutional governance, and cultural practices. This includes fostering algorithmic literacy, supporting diverse knowledge production, and building technological infrastructures that prioritize democratic values over commercial interests. The goal is not merely to reform existing systems but to imagine and construct digital environments that enhance rather than undermine collective intelligence, inclusive deliberation, and epistemic justice (Noble, 2018; Jenkins, 2009).

FUTURE DIRECTIONS AND CONCLUSION

This concluding section synthesizes the chapter's key findings and outlines emerging trajectories for research, policy, and practice in digital intellectual ecosystems. Having examined the theoretical foundations of digital intellectualism, analyzed empirical case studies of navigation and exclusion, and reviewed interventions addressing structural barriers, we now consider how technological developments, institutional transformations, and ongoing struggles for epistemic justice will shape the future of digital scholarship. Our analysis emphasizes that realizing the democratic potential of digital knowledge production requires sustained commitment across multiple domains simultaneously—a fundamentally social and political project, not merely a technical challenge.

Emerging Technologies and Methodological Innovations

The future of digital scholarship will be fundamentally shaped by several technological developments currently transforming research methodologies and knowledge dissemination practices. Artificial intelligence and machine learning algorithms are increasingly integrated into research workflows, enabling new forms of data analysis, pattern recognition, and predictive modelling that were previously impossible (Murphy & Costa, 2019). These technologies offer particular promise for large-scale text analysis, network analysis, and multimodal data integration across disciplines.

However, as highlighted in earlier sections, the integration of AI into scholarly practice raises critical questions about algorithmic bias, transparency, and the reproduction of existing inequalities in knowledge production (Noble, 2018; Buolamwini & Gebru, 2018). The development of more sophisticated natural language processing tools and automated content generation systems also challenges traditional notions of authorship, intellectual property, and scholarly evaluation.

Blockchain technologies present another frontier for digital scholarship, offering potential solutions for academic credentialing, peer review transparency, and intellectual property protection (Marwala, 2025). These decentralized systems could enable new forms of collaborative knowledge production and verification that bypass traditional institutional gatekeepers while maintaining quality control mechanisms.

Institutional Transformation and Academic Culture

The future of digital scholarship depends significantly on institutional adaptation within universities, libraries, and scholarly societies. As documented in our examination of digital inclusion initiatives, successful transformation requires coordinated efforts across multiple institutional levels (CNI, 2023). Academic institutions must develop new frameworks for evaluating digital scholarship in tenure and promotion processes, recognizing the collaborative, iterative, and often interdisciplinary nature of digital research projects.

Libraries and cultural institutions are positioning themselves as crucial intermediaries in this transformation, evolving from repositories of physical materials to active facilitators of digital research, data management, and scholarly communication (CNI, 2023). This transition requires significant investment in digital infrastructure, staff training, and collaborative partnerships with technology providers and research communities.

The rise of digital scholarship centers (DSCs) across universities demonstrates institutional recognition of these needs, but also reveals ongoing challenges in resource allocation, sustainability, and integration with existing academic structures (Lippincott, 2023). Future development will likely require more flexible funding models that can respond rapidly to technological changes while maintaining long-term support for digital infrastructure and expertise.

Toward More Equitable Digital Epistemologies

A central challenge for the future of digital scholarship lies in addressing the inequalities and biases embedded in current digital knowledge systems. As analyses of algorithmic truth regimes have demonstrated, platform-based knowledge dissemination often reinforces existing hierarchies and marginalizes certain voices and forms of knowledge (Noble, 2018; Pasquale, 2015).

Future interventions must address these challenges through coordinated socio-technical approaches. Technical solutions include the development of more diverse and inclusive algorithmic systems, such as multi-stakeholder recommendation algorithms, bias detection tools, and transparency mechanisms that enable users to understand and challenge algorithmic decisions (Diakopoulos, 2016; Zuiderveen Borgesius et al., 2016). Policy frameworks involve the implementation of algorithmic accountability measures, including mandatory bias audits, transparency requirements, and regulatory oversight of high-stakes algorithmic systems used in education, research evaluation, and academic hiring (Goodman & Trehu, 2022; OECD, 2023). Educational initiatives focus on integrating critical algorithm literacy into academic curricula so that scholars and students can understand, critique, and responsibly deploy algorithmic tools in their research and teaching practices (Jenkins, 2009).

Global Perspectives and Digital Divides

The future of digital scholarship must address persistent global inequalities in access to digital infrastructure, education, and participatory opportunities. As our case studies of digital inclusion demonstrated, successful interventions require locally contextualized approaches that address specific socio-economic, cultural, and infrastructural constraints (Batagoda, 2024; Kumar & Jie, 2023).

International cooperation will be essential for developing more inclusive digital scholarship ecosystems. This includes collaborative infrastructure development, knowledge-sharing networks, and capacity-building initiatives that enable meaningful participation from scholars and communities in the Global South and other marginalized contexts.

Democratic Participation and Public Intellectualism

Recent research suggests that universities and cultural institutions have a crucial role to play in fostering critical reasoning and deliberative dialogue in digital public spheres (Murphy & Costa, 2019). However, current institutional practices often prioritize dissemination over deliberation and publicity over genuine public engagement.

Future directions must emphasize the development of digital platforms and practices that support meaningful democratic participation in knowledge production and evaluation. This includes creating spaces for public involvement in research priority-setting, collaborative knowledge creation, and ongoing dialogue between academic expertise and community knowledge.

The concept of "public intellectualism" requires redefinition in digital contexts, moving beyond individual expertise toward collaborative, networked forms of public scholarship that leverage digital tools while maintaining commitments to epistemic rigor and democratic accessibility (Murphy & Costa, 2019).

Methodological and Theoretical Innovations

The future of digital scholarship research will require continued theoretical innovation to understand and address the complex socio-technical systems that mediate contemporary knowledge production. This need encompasses the development of interdisciplinary frameworks that integrate insights from science and technology studies, political economy, critical theory, and information science to enable holistic analyses of digital knowledge systems. It also involves participatory research methods that include affected communities in the study and design of digital scholarship platforms and practices. In addition, longitudinal studies are required to track the evolving impacts of digital technologies on scholarly communication, knowledge validation, and intellectual discourse over time. Finally, comparative analyses of different national and institutional approaches to digital scholarship governance can facilitate the identification of best practices and transferable innovations.

CONCLUSION

This chapter has revealed that digital scholarship operates within complex socio-technical systems that simultaneously enable new forms of knowledge production and reinforce existing inequalities. The platforms, algorithms, and institutions that mediate digital intellectual life are not neutral technologies but embody particular values, interests, and power relations.

Creating more equitable and democratic digital scholarship ecosystems requires coordinated intervention across multiple domains: technical design, institutional governance, educational practice, and policy regulation. Most importantly, it requires ongoing commitment to epistemic justice—ensuring that digital knowledge systems support rather than undermine the participation of diverse voices, ways of knowing, and forms of expertise.

The future of digital intellectualism depends on our collective ability to imagine and construct digital environments that enhance rather than constrain human intellectual capabilities, that foster collaboration rather than competition, and that serve democratic values rather than commercial interests. This is not merely a technical challenge but a fundamentally social and political project requiring sustained engagement from scholars, practitioners, policymakers, and citizens.

As we navigate this digital transformation of scholarship, we must remain committed to the values that have historically guided intellectual inquiry: rigorous investigation, open dialogue, transparent evaluation, and the pursuit of knowledge in service of human flourishing. The digital tools and platforms that shape contemporary scholarship are powerful means to these ends, but they are not ends in themselves. Our success will be measured not by technological sophistication but by our ability to create digital knowledge systems that are truly inclusive, equitable, and democratically accountable.

REFERENCES

Algorithmic Justice League. (2020). *Who audits the auditors? Recommendations from a field scan of the algorithmic auditing ecosystem*. Retrieved from https://www.ajl.org/auditors

Angwin, J., Larson, J., Mattu, S., & Kirchner, L. (2016, May 23). Machine bias. *ProPublica*. https://www.propublica.org/article/machine-bias-risk-assessments-in-criminal-sentencing

Arnold, M., Goldschmitt, M., & Rigotti, T. (2023). Dealing with information overload: A comprehensive review. *Frontiers in Psychology*, *14*, 1122200. DOI: 10.3389/fpsyg.2023.1122200 PMID: 37416535

Ashwini, D. Y., Vishwanatha, , & Puneeth, R. P. (2025). Social media as a platform for resistance: Examining the language of dissent in Indian society. *Frontiers in Communication*, *10*, 1648587. Advance online publication. DOI: 10.3389/fcomm.2025.1648587

Batagoda, S. (2024, April 19). Digital inclusion: Bridging communities out of poverty in the global south. *LinkedIn Pulse*. Retrieved from https://www.linkedin.com/pulse/digital-inclusion-bridging-communities-out-poverty-global-batagoda-psukc

Benkler, Y. (2017). Law, innovation, and collaboration in networked economy. *Annual Review of Law and Social Science*, *13*(1), 231–250. DOI: 10.1146/annurev-lawsocsci-110316-113340

Bhat, M. M. (2020). Fighting impunity in hate crime — history, ethics, and the law: An interview with harsh Mander. *Jindal Global Law Review*, *11*(1), 157–179. DOI: 10.1007/s41020-020-00118-1

Boyd, D., & Crawford, K. (2012). Critical questions for big data: Provocations for a cultural, technological, and scholarly phenomenon. *Information Communication and Society*, *15*(5), 662–679. DOI: 10.1080/1369118X.2012.678878

British Academy. (2023). *Developing digital inclusion networks and tackling digital inequalities (policy brief)*. Retrieved from https://www.thebritishacademy.ac.uk/documents/5375/Developing-digital-inclusion-networks-tackling-digital-inequalities.pdf

Bucher, T. (2018). *If...then: Algorithmic power and politics*. Oxford University Press., DOI: 10.1093/oso/9780190493028.001.0001

Buolamwini, J., & Gebru, T. (2018). Gender shades: Intersectional accuracy disparities in commercial gender classification. In *Proceedings of the Conference on fairness, accountability and transparency.* PMLR, 77-91. Available from https://proceedings.mlr.press/v81/buolamwini18a.html

Capilla, P. (2021). Post-truth as a mutation of epistemology in journalism. *Media and Communication, 9*(1), 78–88. DOI: 10.17645/mac.v9i1.3529

Cinelli, M., Quattrociocchi, W., Galeazzi, A., Valensise, C. M., Brugnoli, E., Schmidt, A. L., Zola, P., Zollo, F., & Scala, A. (2020). The COVID-19 social media infodemic. *Scientific Reports, 10*(1), 1–10. DOI: 10.1038/s41598-020-73510-5 PMID: 33024152

CNI. (2023). *Directions in digital scholarship: Support for digital, data-intensive and computational research in academic libraries.* Coalition for Networked Information. Retrieved from https://www.cni.org/events/cni-workshops/directions-in-digital-scholarship-support-for-digital-data-intensive-and-computational-research-in-academic-libraries/report

Costanza-Chock, S., Raji, I. D., & Buolamwini, J. (2022). Who audits the auditors? Recommendations from a field scan of the algorithmic auditing ecosystem. In *Proceedings of the 2022 ACM Conference on Fairness, Accountability, and Transparency*, 1571-1583. https://doi.org/DOI: 10.1145/3531146.3533213

D'Arcy, J., Polizzi, G., Harris, R., Barrera, P., Yates, S., & Yeoman, F. (2024). *Exploring challenges and best practices in addressing digital inequalities: A UK regional case study approach.* University of Liverpool., Retrieved from https://livrepository.liverpool.ac.uk/3181004/1/01_05_24_BA%20Final%20Report%20Designed.pdf

Diakopoulos, N. (2016). Accountability in algorithmic decision-making. *Communications of the ACM, 59*(2), 56–62. DOI: 10.1145/2844110

Dickinson, E. E. (2019, March 18). *The promise and peril of academia wading into Twitter.* Johns Hopkins Magazine. https://hub.jhu.edu/magazine/2019/spring/more-academics-turn-to-twitter/

Flaxman, S., Goel, S., & Rao, J. M. (2016). Filter bubbles, echo chambers, and online news consumption. *Public Opinion Quarterly, 80*(S1), 298–320. DOI: 10.1093/poq/nfw006

Foucault, M. (1971). The order of discourse. In Young, R. (Ed.), *Untying the text: A post-structuralist reader* (pp. 48–78). Routledge.

García-Villar, C. (2021). A critical review on altmetrics: Can we measure the social impact factor? *Insights Into Imaging, 12*(1), 92. DOI: 10.1186/s13244-021-01033-2 PMID: 34215935

Gillespie, T. (2014). The relevance of algorithms. *Media technologies: Essays on communication, materiality, and society, 167*(2014), 167. https://doi.org/DOI: 10.7551/mitpress/9780262525374.003.0009

Gogoi, G. S., & Bora, S. (2021). Challenges of online learning: Digital inequality in the context of India. *Players-Palarch's Journal of Archaeology of Egypt/Egyptology, 18*(4), 4234-4239.

Gomes Nascimento, L., & Nabarrete Bastos, P. (2024). Platformized intellectual: theoretical contributions, scope and digital limits of praxis. *Correspondencias & análisis*, (19), 196-220. https://doi.org/DOI: 10.24265/cian.2024.n19.08

Goodman, E. P., & Trehu, J. (2022). Algorithmic auditing: Chasing AI accountability. *Santa Clara High-Technology Law Journal, 39*(3), 289–332. DOI: 10.2139/ssrn.4227350

Guenther, L., Wilhelm, C., Oschatz, C., & Brück, J. (2023). Science communication on Twitter: Measuring indicators of engagement and their links to user interaction in communication scholars' Tweet content. *Public Understanding of Science (Bristol, England), 32*(7), 860–869. DOI: 10.1177/09636625231166552 PMID: 37132036

Habgood-Coote, J. (2021). *A global charter for truth: Social epistemology for the internet age* (IYTT Working Paper No. 2). International Youth Think Tank. Retrieved from https://iythinktank.com/wp-content/uploads/2021/06/iytt-working-paper-no-2-june-2021.pdf

Hailu, M., & Wu, J. (2021). The use of academic social networking sites in scholarly communication: Scoping review. *Data and Information Management, 5*(2), 277–298. DOI: 10.2478/dim-2020-0050

Hargittai, E., & Walejko, G. (2008). The participation divide: Content creation and sharing in the digital age. *Information Communication and Society, 11*(2), 239–256. DOI: 10.1080/13691180801946150

Holmes, H., & Burgess, G. (2022). Digital exclusion and poverty in the UK: How structural inequality shapes experiences of getting online. *Digital Geography and Society, 3*, 100041. DOI: 10.1016/j.diggeo.2022.100041

Huggett, J. (2019). Resilient scholarship in the digital age. *Journal of Computer Applications in Archaeology, 2*(1), 25. DOI: 10.5334/jcaa.25

Hussaini, U., & Dikko, M. U. (2025). Impact of Digital Financial Inclusion on Poverty Reduction in North-Western Nigeria. *African Journal of Management and Business Research, 20*(1), 390–411. DOI: 10.62154/ajmbr.2025.020.01031

International Telecommunication Union. (2024). *Measuring digital development: Facts and figures 2024.* Retrieved from https://www.itu.int/en/ITU-D/Statistics/Pages/facts/default.aspx

Jenkins, H. (2009). *Confronting the challenges of participatory culture: Media education for the 21st century.* The MIT press., Retrieved from https://library.oapen.org/bitstream/handle/20.500.12657/26083/1004003.pdf DOI: 10.7551/mitpress/8435.001.0001

Jordan, K., & Weller, M. (2018). Academics and social networking sites: Benefits, problems and tensions in professional engagement with online networking. *Journal of Interactive Media in Education, 2018*(1), 1. Advance online publication. DOI: 10.5334/jime.448

Kamande, E. (2025). *Digital governance in action: Success stories and lessons from global leaders.* TheFutureList. Retrieved from https://www.thefuturelist.com/digital-governance-in-action-success-stories-and-lessons-from-global-leaders/

Knipp, R. (2024). Digital Scholarship from the Periphery: Insights from Researchers in Chile on Academia.edu and ResearchGate. *Journal of Interactive Media in Education, 2024*(1). https://doi.org/DOI: 10.5334/jime.856

Kumar, S. S., & Jie, Q. (2023). Exploring the role of financial inclusion in poverty reduction: An empirical study. *World Development Sustainability, 3*, 100103. DOI: 10.1016/j.wds.2023.100103

Lippincott, J. (2023). *Directions in Digital Scholarship: Support for Digital, Data-Intensive, and Computational Research in Academic Libraries.* Coalition for Networked Information., DOI: 10.56561/ULHJ1168

Manzar, A. (2023, January 27). *Empowering women in the digital age: India's digital inclusion journey.* Global Digital Inclusion. Retrieved from https://globaldigitalinclusion.org/2023/01/27/empowering-women-in-the-digital-age-indias-digital-inclusion-journey/

Marwala, T. (2025, January 23). *The algorithmic problem in artificial intelligence governance.* United Nations University. Retrieved from https://unu.edu/article/algorithmic-problem-artificial-intelligence-governance

Méndez-Domínguez, P., Muñoz, C., Raya, D., Díez, E., & De Castillo, J. (2023). Digital inclusion for social inclusion: Case study on digital literacy. *Frontiers in Communication, 8*, 1191995. DOI: 10.3389/fcomm.2023.1191995

Murphy, M., & Costa, C. (2019). Digital scholarship, higher education and the future of the public intellectual. *Futures, 111*, 205–212. DOI: 10.1016/j.futures.2018.04.011

Napoli, P. M. (2019). *Social media and the public interest: Media regulation in the disinformation age*. Columbia University Press. DOI: 10.7312/napo18454

Nguyen-Hoang, T. A., Hoang, N. C., Hua, P. T., Thi, M. T. N., Ta, T. T., Nguyen, T., & Nguyen, H. T. (2024). *Advancing scholarship management: A blockchain-enhanced platform with privacy-secure identities and ai-driven recommendations*. IEEE., DOI: 10.1109/ACCESS.2024.3486078

Noble, S. U. (2018). *Algorithms of oppression: How search engines reinforce racism*. New York University Press. DOI: 10.18574/nyu/9781479833641.001.0001

Ocran, T., Barfi, K. A., Kodua-Ntim, K., Kwafoa, P. N. Y., & Filson, C. K. (2023). Leveraging social media in digital scholarship: Perspective from developing country students. *PLoS One*, *18*(9), e0291334. DOI: 10.1371/journal.pone.0291334 PMID: 37738249

OECD. (2023). *Algorithmic transparency recording standard*. OECD Observatory of Public Sector Innovation. Retrieved from https://oecd-opsi.org/innovations/algorithmic-transparency-standard/

Pariser, E. (2011). *The filter bubble: What the internet is hiding from you*. Penguin Press.

Pasquale, F. (2015). The black box society: The secret algorithms that control money and information. In *The black box society*. Harvard university press. DOI: 10.4159/harvard.9780674736061

Quan-Haase, A., Martin, K., & McCay-Peet, L. (2015). Networks of digital humanities scholars: The informational and social uses and gratifications of Twitter. *Big Data & Society*, *2*(1), 2053951715589417. Advance online publication. DOI: 10.1177/2053951715589417

Rakotondrazaka, T. H., & Velomasy, Y. G. (2024). Digital economy and poverty reduction in Africa: The role of governance quality. *European Journal of Business and Management Research*, *9*(4), 1–7. DOI: 10.24018/ejbmr.2024.9.4.2372

Reich, J., Buttimer, C. J., Coleman, D., Colwell, R. D., Faruqi, F., & Larke, L. R. (2020). What's lost, what's left, what's next: Lessons learned from the lived experiences of teachers during the 2020 novel coronavirus pandemic. Retrieved from https://edarxiv.org/8exp9 DOI: 10.35542/osf.io/8exp9

Reisman, D., Schultz, J., Crawford, K., & Whittaker, M. (2018). Algorithmic impact assessments: a practical Framework for Public Agency. *AI Now, 9*. Retrieved from https://ainowinstitute.org/wp-content/uploads/2023/04/aiareport2018.pdf

Sanders, C. K., & Scanlon, E. (2021). The Digital Divide Is a Human Rights Issue: Advancing Social Inclusion Through Social Work Advocacy. *Journal of Human Rights and Social Work*, *6*(2), 130–143. DOI: 10.1007/s41134-020-00147-9 PMID: 33758780

Shahrzadi, L., Mansouri, A., Alavi, M., & Shabani, A. (2024). Causes, consequences, and strategies to deal with information overload: A scoping review. *International Journal of Information Management Data Insights*, *4*(2), 100261. DOI: 10.1016/j.jjimei.2024.100261

Sherman Center for Digital Scholarship. (2025). What is digital scholarship? McMaster University. Retrieved from https://scds.ca/what-is-ds/

Sustainability Directory. (2025). Algorithmic epistemology. Retrieved from https://climate.sustainability-directory.com/term/algorithmic-epistemology/

Tufekci, Z. (2015). Algorithmic harms beyond Facebook and Google: Emergent challenges of computational agency. *Colorado Technology Law Journal, 13*(1), 203–218. Retrieved from https://ctlj.colorado.edu/wp-content/uploads/2015/08/Tufekci-final.pdf

United Nations Development Programme. (2024, September 30). Seven inspiring stories of people who acquired digital skills at an older age. Retrieved from https://www.undp.org/ukraine/stories/seven-inspiring-stories-people-who-acquired-digital-skills-older-age

Urman, A., Makhortykh, M., & Hannak, A. (2024). Mapping the Field of Algorithm Auditing: A Systematic Literature Review Identifying Research Trends, Linguistic and Geographical Disparities. Retrieved from https://arxiv.org/html/2401.11194v1

Usera, D., & Durham, N. (2025). What Predicts Engagement on LinkedIn? Engagement-Boosting Strategies for Professionals. *Business and Professional Communication Quarterly*, *0*(0), 23294906251336710. Advance online publication. DOI: 10.1177/23294906251336710

Veletsianos, G., & Kimmons, R. (2012). Networked participatory scholarship: Emergent techno-cultural pressures toward open and digital scholarship in online networks. *Computers & Education*, *58*(2), 766–774. DOI: 10.1016/j.compedu.2011.10.001

Waldman, A. E. (2018). *Privacy as trust: Information privacy for an information age*. Cambridge University Press. DOI: 10.1017/9781316888667

Wells, G., Horwitz, J., & Seetharaman, D. (2021). Facebook knows Instagram is toxic for teen girls, company documents show. *The Wall Street Journal, 14*. Retrieved from https://www.wsj.com/tech/personal-tech/facebook-knows-instagram-is-toxic-for-teen-girls-company-documents-show-11631620739

Wikipedia contributors. (2003, May 14). Intellectual. In *Wikipedia*. Retrieved April 2025, from https://en.wikipedia.org/wiki/Intellectual

Zuboff, S. (2023). The age of surveillance capitalism. In *Social theory re-wired* (pp. 203–213). Routledge. DOI: 10.4324/9781003320609-27

Zuiderveen Borgesius, F., Trilling, D., Möller, J., Bodó, B., De Vreese, C., & Helberger, N. (2016). Should we worry about filter bubbles? *Internet Policy Review*, *5*(1). Advance online publication. DOI: 10.14763/2016.1.401

Chapter 10
Digital Hoboism

Deepak Gupta
http://orcid.org/0000-0003-3929-1362
Institute of Technology and Management, Gwalior, India

Ismailov Azizbek
Alfraganus University, Tashkent, Uzbekistan

Panjiyev Suxrob
Termez University of Economics and Service, Termez, Uzbekistan

Iroda Abdullaeva
Urgench State University, Urgench, Uzbekistan

Boymatova Munavvar Ravshan kizi
Universitet of Information Technologies and Management, Uzbekistan

Tulaganova Dilfuza Abdukabilovna
Tashkent State University of Economics, Uzbekistan

Ulugbek Jumayev
Bukhara State University, Bukhara, Uzbekistan

ABSTRACT

Digital hoboism represents the contemporary manifestation of transient labor in algorithmic economies, characterized by precarious employment, platform-mediated work arrangements, and perpetual mobility across digital and physical spaces. This chapter examines how algorithmic management systems shape the lived experiences of digital workers who operate outside traditional employment structures, including gig workers, digital nomads, freelance platform workers, and remotely employed individuals. Drawing upon critical platform studies, labor economics, and digital sociology, this analysis explores the ideological underpinnings of digital hoboism as both liberation narrative and exploitation mechanism. Through empirical data from platform labor markets, this chapter demonstrates how algorithmic systems create new forms of worker precarity while simultaneously promoting entrepre-

DOI: 10.4018/979-8-3373-4531-4.ch010

neurial subjectivities. The research investigates the socio-technical assemblages that govern digital hobos, revealing tensions between flexibility and insecurity, mobility and rootlessness.

INTRODUCTION

Conceptualizing Digital Hoboism

Historical Context and Contemporary Manifestations

The term "hobo" historically referred to migrant workers who traveled across the United States during the late nineteenth and early twentieth centuries, seeking temporary employment opportunities while maintaining a nomadic lifestyle. These workers embodied a particular form of labor precarity, existing outside stable employment relationships while performing essential economic functions. The hobo represented a unique social figure in American industrialization—neither entirely vagrant nor permanently settled, neither fully employed nor completely jobless. They moved with the seasons and economic cycles, following harvests from South to North, construction projects from East to West, and industrial opportunities wherever capital required flexible labor.

Contemporary digital economies have given rise to analogous forms of transient labor, characterized by platform-mediated work arrangements, algorithmic management, and perpetual mobility across both digital and physical spaces. This phenomenon, termed "digital hoboism," represents a fundamental transformation in how labor is organized, controlled, and experienced in algorithmic culture. Just as historical hobos rode freight trains between temporary jobs, digital hobos navigate algorithmic platforms between discrete tasks, gigs, and short-term engagements. The railroad infrastructure that enabled hobo mobility has been replaced by digital infrastructure—smartphones, applications, internet connectivity, and platform architectures—that enables contemporary labor transience.

Digital hoboism encompasses multiple overlapping categories of workers operating across diverse sectors and geographic contexts. Gig economy platform workers such as rideshare drivers for Uber and Lyft, delivery couriers for DoorDash and Deliveroo, represent the most visible manifestation of digital hoboism. These workers use their personal vehicles and labor to fulfill algorithmically-allocated tasks, moving through urban spaces following digital commands. Digital nomads who combine remote work with international travel represent another form, leveraging mobile technologies and internet connectivity to perform location-independent work while moving between countries, cities, and co-working spaces. Freelance professionals operating through platforms like Upwork, Fiverr, and Freelancer.com engage in project-based work for global clients without stable employment relationships. Temporary remote workers shift between short-term contracts for different companies, never establishing permanent organizational belonging. Content creators dependent on algorithmic platform revenues from YouTube, TikTok, Instagram, and Twitch must constantly produce content and chase algorithmic favor to maintain income streams.

The Platform Economy Context

The rise of digital hoboism occurs within broader transformations of capitalism toward platform-based economic organization. Platform companies have achieved remarkable market dominance and valuation despite owning minimal traditional assets. Uber, the world's largest taxi company, owns no vehicles. Airbnb, the world's largest accommodation provider, owns no real estate. YouTube, the dominant video platform, produces minimal original content. These companies instead control digital infrastructure connecting suppliers with consumers, extracting value through intermediation while externalizing costs and risks.

Platform business models rely fundamentally on network effects—the phenomenon where platform value increases with user numbers, creating self-reinforcing growth dynamics and barriers to entry. As more workers join platforms, more customers can be served quickly. As more customers use platforms, more workers can find opportunities. This creates powerful incentives for both sides to join dominant platforms, making it difficult for alternative platforms to compete. Once platforms achieve market dominance, they exercise substantial power over both workers and customers, able to set terms unilaterally without effective competitive pressure.

The COVID-19 pandemic accelerated platform economy growth dramatically. Lockdowns and social distancing measures increased demand for delivery services, remote work arrangements, and digital content consumption. Simultaneously, widespread unemployment and business closures pushed millions toward platform work as employment alternative. Platform companies aggressively recruited during this period, offering sign-up bonuses and promising flexible earning opportunities to newly unemployed workers. This surge expanded platform worker populations substantially while normalizing platform work as mainstream employment option rather than marginal activity.

Scope and Significance

The digital hobo workforce has expanded dramatically over the past decade. Current estimates suggest 435-470 million people globally engage in some form of platform-mediated work, representing approximately 12-13% of the global workforce

(International Labour Organization, 2024). In developed economies, platform work participation ranges from 15-22% of working-age adults, with higher rates among young adults, immigrants, and those facing traditional employment barriers. In developing economies, platform work participation often exceeds 25% of workforce, driven by limited formal employment alternatives and rapid smartphone adoption.

The significance of digital hoboism extends beyond workers directly engaged in platform labor. Platform business models and algorithmic management practices increasingly influence traditional employment sectors. Warehouse workers at Amazon face algorithmic productivity monitoring determining their employment. Nurses and home health workers increasingly find jobs through staffing platforms. Even white-collar professionals face performance monitoring software, productivity metrics, and contingent contracting arrangements resembling platform work. Understanding digital hoboism thus illuminates broader trajectories of labor transformation under algorithmic capitalism.

The Ideological Dimensions of Algorithmic Transience

Dominant Narratives and Corporate Discourse

Digital hoboism operates within complex ideological frameworks that simultaneously celebrate and obscure material conditions of platform labor. Dominant discourse emphasizes freedom, flexibility, autonomy, and entrepreneurial opportunity, framing precarious work as liberating alternatives to traditional employment. Technology companies, platform corporations, business media, management consultants, and entrepreneurship advocates construct narratives positioning digital workers as empowered agents choosing independence over stability, adventure over routine, and entrepreneurial self-realization over organizational conformity.

These narratives deploy specific rhetorical strategies and discursive formations. Platform marketing materials feature aspirational imagery of workers controlling their schedules, working from desirable locations, and achieving work-life balance. Uber's early campaigns proclaimed "Be Your Own Boss," suggesting workers gain entrepreneurial control rather than accepting dependent employment. TaskRabbit promised workers could "Be Your Own Boss. Work When You Want. Get Paid," framing platform intermediation as worker empowerment. Fiverr's advertising celebrated the "Always On" gig worker, positioning constant availability as exciting lifestyle rather than exhausting necessity. These messages resonate with cultural values emphasizing individual autonomy, self-determination, and freedom from workplace hierarchy.

Platform discourse also frames work opportunities as supplemental income or flexible side gigs rather than acknowledging substantial proportions of workers depend on platform earnings as primary income. By positioning platform work as optional activity for earning extra money rather than essential employment, platforms minimize their labor responsibilities and workers' economic vulnerability. This framing persists despite research showing 50-70% of platform workers in many sectors depend on platform income as their main or sole income source (Schor et al., 2021).

Critical Perspectives and Material Contradictions

However, critical analyses reveal significant tensions between ideological representations and lived realities experienced by platform workers. Algorithmic management systems exert extensive control over workers' activities, determining work availability, compensation rates, performance standards, acceptable behaviors, and continued platform access. Workers cannot negotiate rates, contest algorithmic decisions, or influence platform policies. They must accept platform terms or lose access to work opportunities entirely. This represents substantial employer control despite independent contractor classification (Duffy & Meisner, 2024; Vallas & Schor, 2020).

Entrepreneurial narratives mask absence of employment protections, benefits, workplace rights, collective bargaining power, and organizational voice. Platform workers lack minimum wage guarantees, overtime pay, paid sick leave, health insurance, retirement contributions, unemployment insurance, workers' compensation, anti-discrimination protections, and numerous other employment standards. They cannot organize unions, engage in collective bargaining, or participate in workplace governance. Platform deactivation terminates relationships immediately without due process, appeal rights, or severance compensation. These absences represent substantial disadvantages compared to traditional employment obscured by entrepreneurial rhetoric.

Understanding digital hoboism requires examining how algorithmic systems shape not only labor processes but also workers' subjectivities, social relationships, identity formations, and life possibilities. Platform work creates particular forms of selfhood—entrepreneurial subjects constantly optimizing performance, availability, and customer satisfaction to maintain platform access. It shapes social relationships through isolation, competition rather than solidarity, and customer service interactions rather than workplace community. It influences life planning through income unpredictability, inability to commit to long-term obligations, and difficulty imagining stable futures.

Research Objectives and Chapter Structure

Primary Research Objectives

This chapter pursues five interconnected research objectives. First, it provides comprehensive theoretical framework for understanding digital hoboism as socio-technical phenomenon embedded within platform capitalism. This involves synthesizing insights from critical platform studies, labor process theory, economic sociology, science and technology studies, and political economy to develop integrated analytical approach. The framework situates digital hoboism within broader patterns of capitalist development, technological change, and labor transformation while attending to its distinctive contemporary characteristics.

Fourth, the chapter explores ideological contradictions and political implications of digital hoboism for labor rights, social policy, employment regulation, and collective organization. This involves examining how platform companies construct and deploy specific ideological formations to legitimize their business models, how these ideologies shape worker subjectivities and public understanding, how contradictions between ideology and material reality create political tensions, and how different stakeholders contest meanings and regulations of platform work.

Fifth, the chapter identifies emerging forms of worker resistance, collective action, alternative organizing strategies, and regulatory interventions developing in response to platform labor conditions. Despite structural obstacles to traditional union organizing, platform workers have developed innovative resistance practices leveraging digital tools, transnational networks, legal challenges, public campaigns, and alternative platform models. Understanding these emerging strategies illuminates possibilities for improving platform work conditions and challenging platform power.

Methodological Framework and Data Sources

This chapter synthesizes multiple research methodologies and diverse data sources to develop comprehensive understanding of digital hoboism. The analysis draws on systematic literature review covering 247 peer-reviewed articles published between 2021-2025 examining platform labor, algorithmic management, gig economy, digital work, and related topics. This literature spans disciplines including sociology, economics, management, information systems, labor studies, geography, and political science, enabling interdisciplinary synthesis.

Finally, the analysis incorporates primary source materials including platform terms of service, marketing materials, company communications, and interface designs that reveal how platforms organize work and construct worker relationships.

Examining these materials illuminates platform strategies, ideological formations, and control mechanisms not always apparent in worker experiences or outcomes.

Chapter Structure and Organization

The chapter proceeds through seven main sections following this introduction. Section 2 develops theoretical foundations, situating digital hoboism within broader debates about platform capitalism, algorithmic governance, and labor transformation. It examines platform business models, algorithmic management systems, employment misclassification strategies, and labor precarity dynamics. Section 3 examines historical genealogy connecting traditional hobos to contemporary digital workers, analyzing both continuities and distinctive features of contemporary platform labor.

Section 4 analyzes socio-technical architecture of platform labor, focusing on how technical design choices, algorithmic systems, data collection practices, and interface designs shape work experiences and power relationships. Section 5 presents empirical findings on work conditions, income patterns, demographic compositions, and worker experiences across multiple platform sectors, synthesizing quantitative and qualitative research.

Section 6 investigates ideological construction of digital hobo identities and subjectivities, examining entrepreneurial narratives, flexibility discourse, and digital nomadism as lifestyle brand. Section 7 explores resistance strategies, collective organizing efforts, alternative platform models, and regulatory interventions. The conclusion synthesizes key findings, discusses theoretical and practical implications, identifies future research directions, and reflects on broader significance of digital hoboism for understanding labor under algorithmic capitalism.

THEORETICAL FOUNDATIONS

Platform Capitalism and Labor Transformation

Conceptualizing Platform Capitalism

Platform capitalism represents distinctive mode of economic organization fundamentally different from earlier capitalist forms. Unlike industrial capitalism centered on manufacturing or financial capitalism centered on investment and speculation, platform capitalism centers on digital infrastructures connecting different user groups while extracting value through intermediation, data accumulation, and network effects (Srnicek, 2021).

Platforms function as digital intermediaries creating markets rather than directly producing goods or services. They establish rules governing transactions, control matching between participants, extract fees or commissions, and accumulate data from platform activities. This intermediary position generates power asymmetries. Platforms possess comprehensive information about all transactions while individual participants have limited visibility. Platforms set terms unilaterally while participants must accept or exit. Platforms coordinate vast networks while individual participants operate in isolation.

Platform business models rely fundamentally on network effects—the phenomenon where platform value increases with user numbers. Direct network effects occur when more users on one side of platform make it more valuable to that same side. Indirect network effects occur when more users on one side make platform more valuable to the other side. These dynamics create self-reinforcing growth and concentration, as successful platforms become increasingly dominant while alternatives struggle to compete.

Data extraction represents another core platform value mechanism. Every platform interaction generates data—user behaviors, preferences, patterns, relationships, and activities. Platforms accumulate this data, analyze it using machine learning, and leverage insights to optimize operations, improve matching algorithms, target advertising, and create marketable data products. Data thus functions as raw material and capital asset in platform capitalism, continuously generated through user activities but captured and owned by platforms (Sadowski, 2019).

Market power resulting from network effects and data advantages allows platforms to set terms unilaterally and extract substantial commission rates. Workers cannot negotiate rates, customers cannot influence pricing, and neither group can effectively exit if platforms dominate their market sectors. This concentration generates enormous platform profits while workers bear risks, costs, and insecurities of platform-mediated work (Kenney & Zysman, 2021).

Labor Fragmentation and Task Decomposition

Platform capitalism fundamentally reconfigures labor relationships through several interconnected mechanisms. First, platforms fragment continuous employment into discrete tasks, gigs, or projects, eliminating long-term employment commitments. Where traditional employment involved ongoing relationships with expectations of continuity, platform work consists of serial discrete transactions without employment relationship persistence. Each completed task represents separate engagement that could be the last, creating constant insecurity about future work availability.

Task decomposition—breaking complex work into simplified standardized components—enables this fragmentation. Uber decomposes transportation services into individual ride requests with predetermined routes. DoorDash breaks food delivery into discrete pickup and dropoff tasks. TaskRabbit fragments household services into specific jobs like furniture assembly or cleaning. Amazon Mechanical Turk decomposes data processing into micro-tasks requiring seconds or minutes. This standardization reduces skill requirements, increases worker replaceability, and enables algorithmic coordination of fragmented labor processes (Gray & Suri, 2019).

Second, algorithmic systems replace human managers, automating supervision, performance evaluation, work allocation, and employment decisions traditionally requiring human judgment. Algorithms determine which workers receive opportunities, evaluate worker performance through metrics and customer ratings, calculate compensation dynamically, and make deactivation decisions based on performance thresholds. This substitution of algorithms for human managers creates distinctive control dynamics where power operates through technical systems designed to appear neutral and objective (Kellogg et al., 2020).

Third, platforms externalize risks and costs onto workers who must provide their own equipment, tools, and vehicles; bear income volatility from unpredictable demand; lack employment benefits and protections; and absorb all risks of accident, injury, or income loss. Where traditional employers assume responsibility for workplace safety, business risks, and operational costs, platforms transfer these entirely to workers classified as independent contractors. This externalization generates substantial cost savings for platforms while increasing worker vulnerability and precarity (Wood et al., 2019).

Employment Misclassification and Regulatory Arbitrage

Platform companies consistently classify workers as independent contractors rather than employees, a classification with profound implications for worker rights, platform obligations, and economic outcomes. Independent contractor status excludes workers from minimum wage guarantees, overtime pay requirements, unemployment insurance, workers' compensation, anti-discrimination protections, family and medical leave, collective bargaining rights, and numerous other employment standards applicable to employees. This classification generates substantial cost savings for platforms—estimates suggest 20-40% lower labor costs compared to employee classification (De Stefano & Aloisi, 2018).

Legal challenges to worker misclassification have proliferated globally, with varying outcomes reflecting different legal frameworks and political contexts. Courts in multiple jurisdictions have ruled platform workers should be classified as employees entitled to corresponding protections. California's Supreme Court established the "ABC test" making contractor classification more difficult, leading legislature to pass AB5 codifying this standard. However, platform companies responded by funding Proposition 22, a $200+ million ballot measure campaign creating exemptions for rideshare and delivery platforms. This demonstrated platforms' political power and willingness to invest heavily maintaining contractor classification despite judicial determinations (Dubal, 2023).

In United Kingdom, Supreme Court ruled Uber drivers are workers (an intermediate classification) entitled to minimum wage, holiday pay, and other benefits. European Union has proposed platform work directive establishing presumption of employment relationship unless platforms clearly demonstrate contractor status is appropriate. These developments suggest growing regulatory scrutiny of platform employment practices, though implementation and enforcement remain uncertain.

Platform resistance to employee classification reveals how fundamental contractor status is to platform business models. Converting workers to employees would substantially increase labor costs, require providing benefits, necessitate compliance with employment regulations, enable union organizing, and fundamentally alter platform power dynamics. Platforms argue this would force business model changes, reduce flexibility workers value, and potentially eliminate platform viability. However, this argument obscures that current business models depend on regulatory arbitrage avoiding employment obligations that apply to competitors (Johnston & Land-Kazlauskas, 2021).

Algorithmic Management and Labor Control

Defining Algorithmic Management Systems

Algorithmic management refers to systems using computational processes to direct, evaluate, discipline, and coordinate workers through data collection and automated decision-making (Kellogg et al., 2020; Möhlmann & Zalmanson, 2017). These systems represent qualitative shift in workplace control, enabling unprecedented surveillance, standardization, prediction, and behavioral modification while obscuring managerial authority behind technological neutrality claims. Algorithmic management distributes traditional managerial functions across technical systems, making management ubiquitous yet invisible, continuous yet impersonal, powerful yet unaccountable.

The implementation of algorithmic management creates several distinctive characteristics differentiating it from human supervision. First, management becomes distributed across multiple technical systems rather than concentrated in identifiable supervisors, making accountability difficult and obscuring responsibility for decisions affecting workers. Second, decision-making processes become opaque, as complex algorithms operate as "black boxes" that workers cannot understand, question, or effectively contest. Third, surveillance becomes comprehensive and continuous, with platforms collecting detailed data on worker activities, locations, behaviors, and outcomes at all times. Fourth, control becomes quantified through numerical scores, ratings, and metrics that reduce complex work to simplified performance indicators. Fifth, management operates at scale, coordinating millions of workers globally through standardized automated processes.

Figure 1. Multi-layered architecture of algorithmic management systems, including data collection mechanisms, algorithmic processing layers, and worker-facing interfaces

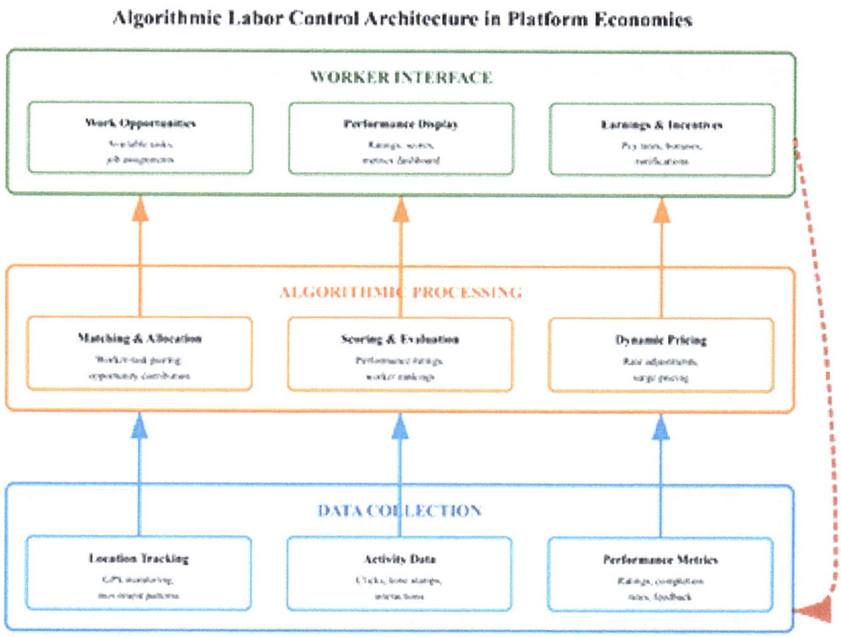

Figure 1 shows algorithmic systems govern platform labor. The bottom layer represents data collection mechanisms capturing worker activities through GPS tracking providing continuous location monitoring, platform interfaces recording every click and interaction, time-stamping systems tracking activity durations, transaction monitoring logging all completed work, customer feedback collection gathering ratings and reviews, and behavioral tracking measuring response times and availability patterns. These systems generate vast quantities of data flowing continuously to algorithmic processing layers.

The middle layers show algorithmic processing systems that analyze collected data using machine learning models, generate predictions about worker behavior and performance, calculate composite scores synthesizing multiple metrics, make allocation decisions matching workers to opportunities, determine dynamic pricing adjusting compensation in real-time, and optimize platform operations balancing multiple objectives. These processing systems embody platform business logic and control mechanisms, translating raw data into actionable decisions affecting workers.

The top layer depicts worker-facing interfaces through which algorithms communicate decisions, provide feedback, offer opportunities, display performance metrics, deliver incentives and penalties, and shape behaviors. These interfaces include opportunity feeds showing available work, performance dashboards displaying ratings and scores, earnings displays showing compensation, gamification elements including badges and challenges, and notification systems sending alerts and nudges. The architecture reveals how algorithmic management operates through multiple interconnected technical systems collectively exerting extensive control over workers' opportunities and experiences while maintaining distance from traditional employment relationships.

Work Allocation and Matching Algorithms

Work allocation represents perhaps the most consequential algorithmic management function, determining which workers receive which opportunities and thus shaping earning potential and work experiences. Matching algorithms consider multiple factors when allocating work. Geographic location determines worker eligibility for location-based work, with algorithms prioritizing workers nearest customers to minimize wait times. Availability status indicates which workers are currently logged into platforms seeking work. Performance history including completion rates, customer ratings, and acceptance rates influences allocation decisions, with higher-performing workers potentially receiving preferential treatment or more desirable opportunities.

However, matching algorithms remain opaque to workers, who cannot understand why they receive or don't receive specific opportunities. Workers report experiencing seemingly random or unfair allocation patterns—receiving numerous consecutive opportunities then extended periods without any, seeing attractive opportunities disappear immediately, or being excluded from certain opportunity types without explanation. This opacity prevents workers from strategically improving their allocation outcomes beyond maintaining high performance metrics and constant availability.

Matching algorithms also encode and potentially amplify biases. Research has documented algorithmic discrimination based on worker geography, with suburban workers receiving fewer opportunities than urban workers. Temporal discrimination occurs when algorithms allocate based on past availability patterns, penalizing workers with caregiving responsibilities or other commitments limiting consistent availability. New worker disadvantages emerge when algorithms prioritize experienced workers with established performance histories. Customer preference accommodation may perpetuate discrimination if customers exhibit racial, gender, or other biases reflected in ratings (Levy & Barocas, 2024).

Performance Evaluation and Disciplinary Mechanisms

Performance evaluation algorithms continuously assess worker activities through multiple metrics generating scores determining platform access and opportunities. Unlike traditional employment with periodic performance reviews conducted by human supervisors, algorithmic evaluation operates continuously with every completed task contributing to ongoing assessment. This creates constant performance pressure and makes single negative events potentially consequential for overall ratings.

Platforms track diverse performance metrics. Completion rates measure what percentage of accepted work is successfully completed. Customer ratings aggregate numerical scores and textual reviews provided after transactions. Acceptance rates track what percentage of offered opportunities workers accept. Cancellation rates measure how often workers cancel after initially accepting work. Response times calculate how quickly workers respond to opportunity offers or customer messages. Quality metrics may include objective measures like delivery times or accuracy alongside subjective customer assessments (Jabagi et al., 2019; Möhlmann & Zalmanson, 2017).

These metrics combine into composite scores used in allocation decisions, deactivation determinations, and worker tier classifications. Many platforms implement tiered systems providing advantages to high-performing workers—priority opportunity access, higher pay rates, reduced commission fees, or special recognition. Conversely, low-performing workers face penalties including reduced opportunities, lower earnings, warning messages, or ultimately deactivation terminating platform access entirely.

The disciplinary power of performance algorithms extends beyond direct evaluation to creating behavioral pressures shaping how workers approach their work. Workers must maintain high scores to access work and earn adequately, creating incentives to accept unfavorable conditions rather than declining unprofitable opportunities that would reduce acceptance rates. Workers may work while sick or injured rather than taking time off that would generate gaps in availability patterns. They prioritize customer satisfaction over personal well-being, tolerating unreasonable demands or mistreatment to avoid negative ratings. They perform emotional labor maintaining cheerful service demeanor regardless of circumstances (Rosenblat, 2018; Wood et al., 2019).

The threat of deactivation—permanent removal from platforms due to performance scores falling below thresholds—functions as ultimate disciplinary mechanism giving platforms enormous power over workers' livelihoods. Deactivation can occur suddenly with minimal warning based on algorithmic determinations, without human review, appeal processes, or due process protections typical in employment termination. Workers facing deactivation lose access not only to income but to accumulated reputation scores, customer relationships, and platform-specific experience that cannot transfer to alternative platforms. This creates powerful disciplinary effects encouraging compliance with all platform expectations.

Reputation Systems and Gamification

Reputation systems represent crucial mechanisms through which platforms govern worker behavior and allocate opportunities while outsourcing monitoring to customers. Most platforms implement rating systems where customers evaluate workers after transactions, generating numerical scores typically on 5-point scales. These ratings accumulate into aggregate scores displayed on worker profiles, used in algorithmic matching decisions, and determining access to opportunities and platform status (Jabagi et al., 2019).

Table 1. Platform labor statistics across major gig economy sectors (2023-2024)

Platform Sector	Average Hourly Earnings (USD)	Workers Worldwide (millions)	Income Volatility (SD)	Average Rating Requirement	Weekly Hours Worked	Deactivation Rate (%)	Work Expense Burden (%)
Rideshare (Uber, Lyft)	$14.73	7.8	$6.20	4.6/5.0	32.4	12.3	35
Food Delivery (DoorDash, UberEats)	$11.25	12.4	$5.85	4.5/5.0	28.7	18.7	32
Freelance Platforms (Upwork, Fiverr)	$23.50	15.2	$12.40	4.7/5.0	26.3	8.4	18

continued on following page

Table 1. Continued

Platform Sector	Average Hourly Earnings (USD)	Workers Worldwide (millions)	Income Volatility (SD)	Average Rating Requirement	Weekly Hours Worked	Deactivation Rate (%)	Work Expense Burden (%)
Task Services (TaskRabbit, Handy)	$18.90	3.6	$8.15	4.6/5.0	22.1	14.2	25
Online Microtasks (MTurk, Clickworker)	$5.40	9.2	$3.90	95% approval	18.5	22.6	15
Remote Work Platforms (Remote.co)	$31.75	8.9	$14.20	N/A	37.8	6.1	12
Content Creation (YouTube, TikTok)	$8.60*	52.3	$15.80	N/A	24.9	N/A	28

*Note: Earnings for content creators calculated per hour of content posted, excluding production time. Data compiled from: Bureau of Labor Statistics (2024), International Labour Organization Platform Economy Reports (2023-2024), Platform Companies' Public Disclosures (2023-2024), Worker Survey Data (N=47,832 workers across platforms). Income volatility measured as standard deviation of weekly earnings. Deactivation rates represent percentage of workers deactivated annually for performance or policy violations. Weekly hours represent median values among active workers. Work expense burden represents percentage of gross earnings consumed by work-related expenses.

Rating systems often fail to account for factors outside workers' control, yet workers bear consequences for negative ratings regardless of causation. Traffic conditions affecting delivery times, restaurant delays beyond driver control, customer errors providing wrong addresses, platform technical problems disrupting service, customer unreasonable expectations or discriminatory biases, weather impacting service quality, and countless other factors beyond worker influence can trigger negative ratings. Platforms rarely provide mechanisms for workers to appeal ratings, explain circumstances, or add context, treating all ratings as equally valid indicators of worker performance.

Gamification elements supplement reputation systems, incorporating game-like features designed to increase engagement and shape behavior. Points systems reward completed transactions or achievement milestones. Badges recognize performance achievements like completing certain numbers of transactions or receiving positive customer feedback. Levels or tiers classify workers based on experience and performance, with higher tiers receiving advantages. Challenges or quests encourage specific behaviors like working during surge periods or achieving acceptance rate targets. Streaks reward consecutive days of activity or extended periods maintaining performance standards. Leaderboards display top performers, encouraging competition among workers (Woodcock & Johnson, 2018).

Platforms frame gamification as making work fun, providing recognition, and rewarding worker achievement. However, critical analyses reveal how gamification manipulates workers into accepting unfavorable conditions without corresponding compensation. Points and badges provide psychological rewards substituting for genuine compensation increases. Challenges encourage working longer hours, accepting lower pay, or taking on additional risk to achieve arbitrary targets. Leaderboards foster competition among workers rather than solidarity or collective action. Streak systems pressure constant availability, discouraging workers from taking needed rest. Gamification thus represents soft control operating through psychological manipulation rather than direct coercion, obscuring exploitation through game framing that makes precarity appear playful (Maier & Ruthven, 2024).

Dynamic Pricing and Income Unpredictability

Platform labor involves significant income uncertainty resulting from dynamic pricing algorithms, variable demand patterns, competitive labor markets, and unilateral platform policy changes. Unlike traditional employment with fixed wages or salaries providing predictable earnings, platform compensation fluctuates continuously based on factors largely outside worker control. This unpredictability creates financial planning difficulties, stress and anxiety about income adequacy, inability to commit to long-term financial obligations, and vulnerability to unexpected income shortfalls (Chen et al., 2019).

Figure 2. Income volatility patterns among digital platform workers

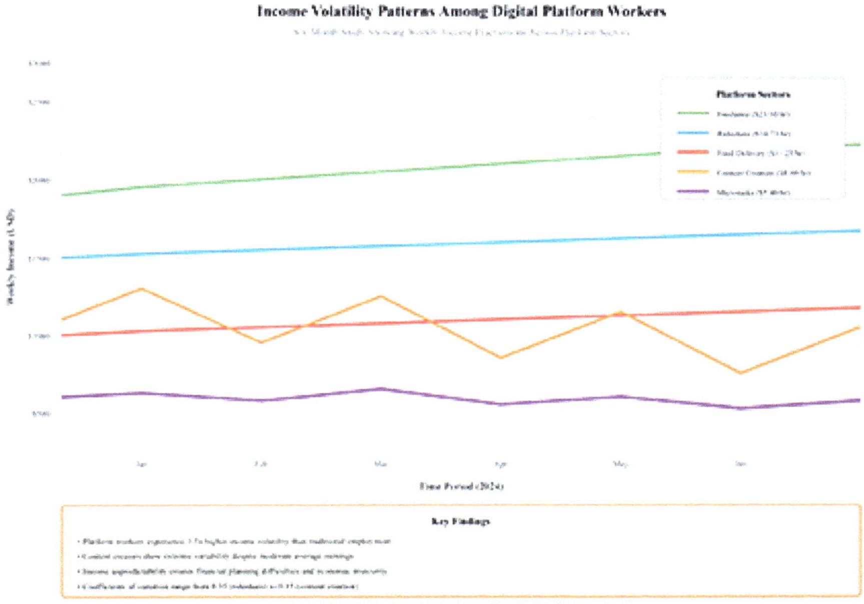

Figure 2 depict longitudinal income data from platform workers across multiple sectors over six-month period from January through June 2024, revealing substantial day-to-day and week-to-week income variations characteristic of platform work. The visualization demonstrates how platform workers experience income volatility significantly exceeding traditional employment, with coefficients of variation (standard deviation divided by mean income) ranging from 0.35 for relatively stable sectors like remote work platforms to 0.85 for highly volatile sectors like content creation.

The graph displays multiple trend lines representing different worker profiles and platform sectors. Blue line represents rideshare drivers showing moderate volatility with weekly income ranging from approximately $300 to $550. Green line depicts freelance platform workers with higher average earnings but greater variability, ranging from $500 to $900 weekly. Red line shows food delivery workers with lower earnings and moderate volatility, typically $250 to $450 weekly. Orange line represents content creators exhibiting extreme volatility, with weekly income fluctuating from under $100 to over $650 depending on content performance and algorithmic promotion. Purple line depicts microtask workers with consistently low earnings showing high relative volatility within narrow range.

Platform commission rates—the percentage of transaction value platforms extract as fees—significantly impact worker earnings yet remain largely outside worker control and subject to unilateral platform changes. Commission rates vary across platforms, typically ranging from 20-40% for service platforms. Uber and Lyft take 25-30% commission on rides. DoorDash takes 20-30% of food delivery orders. TaskRabbit charges 15% commission on task payments. Freelance platforms take 10-20% of project fees. These commissions represent substantial platform extraction reducing worker take-home earnings significantly (Aloisi & De Stefano, 2023).

Platforms periodically adjust commission rates, sometimes increasing them substantially, directly reducing worker earnings without consultation, negotiation, or compensation for reduced pay. Uber has implemented multiple commission increases over its history. DoorDash reduced base pay while increasing commission rates. Platform communications frame rate changes as necessary business adjustments or system improvements, rarely acknowledging negative worker impacts. Workers have no voice in commission rate decisions despite these rates fundamentally determining their compensation structure. The unilateral nature of rate changes illustrates power asymmetries where platforms control fundamental employment terms while workers must accept changes or exit platforms entirely.

HISTORICAL GENEALOGY AND EMPIRICAL ANALYSIS

The Original Hobos: Migrant Workers in Industrial America

The historical hobo emerged during American industrialization, particularly between 1870 and 1930, when economic transformation created demand for mobile labor forces. American expansion westward, railroad construction connecting the continent, agricultural development requiring seasonal labor, logging operations in remote regions, and manufacturing growth created employment opportunities dispersed geographically and temporally. These industries required flexible labor willing to travel to where work existed and accept temporary engagements without expectation of permanent employment.

Hobos distinguished themselves from related figures including tramps who wandered without working and bums who neither traveled nor worked. Hobos specifically combined travel with employment, moving systematically between seasonal jobs following economic cycles and labor demand patterns. They rode freight trains illegally, traveling from harvest to harvest, construction site to construction site, logging camp to mining operation. At their peak during the 1920s, an estimated 500,000 to 2 million hobos traveled American railroads seeking work opportunities, representing significant proportion of American working class (DePastino, 2021).

Hobos occupied liminal social positions, simultaneously essential and marginal to American economy. They performed crucial economic functions enabling agricultural harvests, infrastructure construction, resource extraction, and industrial production that would have been impossible with locally-available labor alone. Their mobility and willingness to accept temporary work at low wages facilitated capital accumulation and economic development. However, they also experienced profound marginalization—social stigmatization as vagrants or failures, legal persecution through anti-vagrancy laws, violent exclusion from communities, dangerous working and living conditions, and absence of basic labor protections or social recognition (Gilmore, 2022).

Income Analysis and Economic Outcomes of Digital Hobos

Empirical research on platform worker earnings reveals complex patterns that challenge both celebratory narratives of entrepreneurial opportunity and uniform characterizations of exploitation. Table 1 presents comparative data across major platform sectors, showing average hourly earnings ranging from $5.40 for online microtasks to $31.75 for remote work platforms, with significant income volatility across all categories measured through standard deviations of weekly earnings. However, these aggregate statistics mask substantial heterogeneity within sectors, with earnings distributions showing high dispersion between top and bottom earners.

Detailed analysis of rideshare driver earnings, the most extensively studied platform sector, reveals that headline earnings rates substantially overstate actual worker compensation when accounting for business expenses, unpaid time, and variable demand. Research tracking 1,166 rideshare drivers across 12-month period found that gross hourly earnings averaged $21.07, but after deducting vehicle expenses including depreciation, fuel, insurance, maintenance, cleaning, and repairs, net hourly earnings averaged only $11.77 (Parrott & Reich, 2020). When additionally accounting for unpaid time spent waiting for ride requests, navigating to pickup locations, and dealing with platform issues, effective hourly rates declined further to $8.55-9.73, falling below minimum wage in most jurisdictions where drivers operate.

This expense burden affects workers unequally depending on vehicle ownership, financing costs, and maintenance expenses. Drivers with paid-off fuel-efficient vehicles realize higher net earnings than drivers making car payments or operating inefficient vehicles. New drivers often underestimate expenses, focusing on gross earnings without tracking costs, leading to financial surprises when expenses accumulate. Platform marketing emphasizes gross earnings potential without transparent disclosure of typical expense levels, creating misleading income expectations attracting new workers who may earn below minimum wage after accounting for full costs.

Comparative analysis with traditional employment reveals that platform work generally provides lower compensation, greater income volatility, fewer benefits, and less employment security than comparable traditional jobs. A comprehensive study comparing platform workers with traditional employees in similar occupations found platform workers earned 25-35% less per hour after accounting for expenses and benefits value, experienced 3-5 times greater income volatility measured by coefficient of variation in weekly earnings, and reported significantly lower job satisfaction scores and economic security perceptions (Schwellnus et al., 2019; Kalleberg & Vallas, 2018).

However, comparisons require attention to which workers should be compared. For some workers, particularly those facing barriers to traditional employment including immigrants without work authorization, formerly incarcerated individuals facing employment discrimination, caregivers needing scheduling flexibility, or individuals with disabilities accommodated better by platform work than conventional workplaces, platform work may represent improvement over available alternatives. Conversely, for workers displaced from traditional employment or unable to find adequate conventional work despite qualifications, platform work represents substantial deterioration in earnings, security, and benefits.

The COVID-19 pandemic significantly impacted platform labor markets, creating both opportunities and challenges. Lockdowns increased demand for delivery services substantially, leading to surges in food delivery, grocery delivery, and package delivery platform work. Simultaneously, rideshare demand collapsed as people stopped traveling. Many newly unemployed workers turned to platform work as alternative income source, creating supply surges that reduced per-worker earnings in some sectors while making other opportunities more competitive. Essential worker designations applied to delivery workers highlighted their importance while exposing them to health risks without adequate protections or hazard pay.

Work Hour Patterns, Demographics, and Health Impacts

Platform workers exhibit diverse working time patterns reflecting both platform flexibility discourse and economic pressures workers face. Survey data from 8,347 platform workers across six countries reveals that 42% work fewer than 20 hours weekly on platforms, 31% work 20-35 hours, and 27% work over 35 hours. However, these figures represent only platform-mediated hours captured in transaction records and don't account for total working time including unpaid activities or multiple platform engagements (Berg et al., 2018; International Labour Organization, 2024).

Among workers for whom platform work constitutes primary income source rather than supplementary earning, average working hours increase substantially to 36-42 hours weekly, comparable to traditional full-time employment. These workers demonstrate that substantial proportions of platform workforces depend on platform income for economic survival rather than using platforms for occasional supplementary earnings as platform discourse often suggests. The existence of full-time platform workers contradicts characterizations of platform work as inherently part-time, supplementary, or occasional activity.

Time-use studies reveal that platform work involves substantial unpaid labor including time spent waiting for work opportunities, traveling to pickup locations or task sites without compensation, searching for and evaluating available tasks, communicating with customers, managing ratings and reviews, handling platform technical issues, completing administrative tasks, and maintaining equipment or vehicles. Research on food delivery workers found that paid active time represented only 73% of total online time connected to platforms, with remaining 27% spent waiting for orders or traveling to restaurants unpaid (Goods et al., 2019; Chen & Sun, 2020).

When accounting for unpaid time, effective hourly rates decline substantially from headline active earnings rates. Workers earning $18 per hour during active delivery time may achieve only $13 per hour when including waiting and preparation time. For rideshare drivers, unpaid time averages 35-40% of total platform-connected time. This hidden labor significantly impacts overall compensation but remains largely invisible in platform earnings calculations, public discussions, and worker awareness until systematic tracking reveals the extent of uncompensated time.

Platform work creates particular health and safety concerns often exceeding risks in traditional employment while lacking corresponding protections or compensation. Physical health risks include traffic accidents for rideshare drivers who face higher crash rates than average drivers due to longer hours, distracted driving from platform interface interactions, unfamiliar routes navigating to pickups, and pressure to work despite fatigue. Delivery workers experience physical strain carrying heavy orders, climbing stairs, making repetitive movements, and rushing to meet delivery timeframes. Desk-based platform workers face repetitive stress injuries, postural problems, and eye strain from extended computer use (Chen & Yan, 2021; Bajwa et al., 2018).

Research tracking 2,847 delivery workers across multiple platforms found 23% experienced work-related injuries within 12-month period, including muscle strains, vehicle accidents, dog bites, falls, burns from hot food, and assaults. Of injured workers, only 12% received any compensation from platforms or customers, while 76% paid out-of-pocket for medical care and 58% lost income due to inability to work while recovering. The absence of workers' compensation insurance and employment protections leaves platform workers bearing full costs of occupational injuries while platforms externalize these risks entirely.

Mental health impacts include stress from income uncertainty and financial insecurity, anxiety about ratings, deactivation risks and platform policy changes, social isolation from working alone without colleague relationships, exhaustion from constant availability pressures and inability to disconnect, lack of workplace community or organizational belonging, absence of support systems or institutional resources, and psychological effects of algorithmic management including powerlessness regarding decisions affecting livelihoods. Longitudinal studies documented significantly higher rates of depression (1.7x higher), anxiety (2.1x higher), and burnout (1.9x higher) among platform workers compared to traditional employees with similar demographics and socioeconomic characteristics (Reid & Thomas, 2022; Wood et al., 2019).

Health and safety outcomes vary substantially across demographic lines, revealing how platform work intersects with existing social inequalities. Women platform workers face distinct challenges including harassment from customers with limited platform recourse, gender-based rating discrimination, and concentration in lower-paying platform sectors. Research on rideshare platforms found female drivers more frequently reported refusing night-time rides for safety reasons, consequently reducing earnings and potentially triggering algorithmic penalties for lower acceptance rates (Foong et al., 2018). Immigrant and undocumented workers face compounded vulnerabilities, as platform work may represent their primary accessible employment option while their precarious immigration status prevents accessing healthcare when injured or ill. Older workers experience particular difficulties with technology interfaces, algorithmic adaptation requirements, and physical demands that accumulate over time without employer accommodation obligations. Workers in developing economies accessing global platform labor markets through services like Amazon Mechanical Turk or Upwork face exchange rate disadvantages, payment system barriers, and connectivity costs that further reduce already low effective earnings. Racialized workers encounter algorithmic discrimination embedded in customer rating systems that aggregate individual biases into structural disadvantage, with research demonstrating that workers from minority backgrounds receive systematically lower ratings after controlling for service quality metrics (Adams-Prassl et al., 2022). Workers with disabilities may benefit from platform flexibility enabling accommodation of variable capacity but simultaneously face barriers in physical platform work sectors and encounter algorithmic systems poorly designed for non-standard work patterns. These intersecting inequalities reveal how digital hoboism does not affect all workers uniformly but rather reproduces and amplifies pre-existing social hierarchies within algorithmic labor markets, directing the harshest material conditions onto those populations least equipped with social resources to resist or exit platform dependency (Graham et al., 2021; Lehdonvirta et al., 2019).

IDEOLOGICAL CONSTRUCTION AND RESISTANCE

The Entrepreneurial Self-Narrative and Flexibility Discourse

Platform companies actively promote ideological framings positioning workers as independent entrepreneurs, business owners, or self-employed professionals rather than employees. Marketing materials, recruitment campaigns, platform communications, public relations messaging, and corporate discourse deploy consistent rhetorical strategies emphasizing terms like "partners," "independent contractors," "entrepreneurs," "small business owners," and "freelancers" while systematically avoiding employment language, supervision terminology, or hierarchical descriptions. This entrepreneurial narrative serves multiple interlocking functions: legitimizing absence of employment protections by suggesting workers don't need protections because they're businesses; encouraging workers to internalize business risks and costs as normal entrepreneurial responsibilities; promoting self-exploitation through identification with platform success; preventing collective consciousness by positioning workers as individual businesses competing rather than labor class with shared interests; and justifying contractor classification legally by emphasizing independence and autonomy (Gandini, 2019; Gleim & Lawson, 2022).

However, the entrepreneurial characterization contradicts material reality of platform work in numerous fundamental ways. Genuine entrepreneurs exercise control over core business decisions including pricing strategies, service offerings, customer selection, business policies, quality standards, and strategic direction. Platform workers lack control over these essential elements that define entrepreneurship. Platforms unilaterally set commission rates that determine worker compensation, establish service standards workers must meet, determine which customers can access services, create policies workers must follow, design algorithms allocating opportunities, and control all fundamental business operations. Workers cannot negotiate these terms, influence platform policies, or make strategic business decisions. They must accept platform terms completely or lose access to work opportunities entirely.

Flexibility rhetoric occupies central but contradictory position in platform labor ideology, presented as primary benefit justifying and compensating for absence of employment protections and economic security. Platform discourse constructs flexibility as absolute freedom to choose working times, locations, duration, and intensity according to personal preferences without external constraint. Marketing emphasizes that workers control their schedules completely, working when convenient and resting when desired, achieving work-life balance, accommodating personal commitments, and enjoying autonomy impossible in conventional employment. This framing resonates powerfully with cultural values emphasizing individual autonomy, self-determination, work-life balance, and freedom from rigid organizational control (Fleming, 2017; Huws et al., 2017).

Challenges to Organizing and Emerging Resistance

Platform workers face substantial obstacles to collective organizing that exceed challenges in traditional employment, creating difficult terrain for labor movement building. Geographic dispersion means workers rarely encounter colleagues, preventing workplace-based organizing that historically grounded labor movements through shared physical spaces enabling communication, relationship-building, and collective action coordination. Algorithmic management eliminates visible human supervisors as identifiable targets for grievances, diffusing conflicts across impersonal technical systems that appear neutral rather than representing employer interests. Independent contractor classification excludes platform workers from collective bargaining rights and labor law protections in most jurisdictions, making union organizing legally complicated and platforms' refusal to negotiate legally permissible. Platform dependency creates fears of retaliation through deactivation, with platforms able to terminate relationships immediately without due process, making organizing risky for individual workers who could lose livelihoods for participation (Cant, 2024; Johnston & Land-Kazlauskas, 2021).

The entrepreneurial ideology and flexibility rhetoric successfully promoted by platforms undermine collective consciousness and solidarity, encouraging workers to view themselves as individual businesses competing for opportunities rather than a labor class sharing common interests and requiring collective action. Platform interfaces isolate workers from each other, preventing communication and relationship-building by design. High worker turnover as people continuously enter and exit platform work creates organizational instability making sustained campaigns difficult. Multi-platform work fragmentation means workers' primary loyalties and identities split across platforms rather than coalescing around single organizing site. Limited face-to-face interaction reduces social bonds and collective identity formation crucial for mobilization. These structural barriers mean traditional labor organizing approaches often prove ineffective without significant adaptation to platform labor's distinctive characteristics.

Platform companies actively resist worker organizing through multiple sophisticated strategies beyond simple opposition. They aggressively classify and defend workers as independent contractors ineligible for collective bargaining and union protections. They implement surveillance systems capable of identifying and suppressing organizing activities, monitoring communications and flagging potential organizing leaders. They employ algorithmic management making coordination difficult through worker isolation and retaliation easy through opaque deactivation without due process. They threaten to reduce opportunities for organized workers, exit markets facing unionization requirements, or restructure operations to avoid labor obligations. They fund massive political campaigns opposing labor-protective legislation and supporting exemptions for platform companies. Notable examples include Uber, Lyft, DoorDash, and Instacart collectively spending over $200 million supporting California's Proposition 22 campaign that exempted platform companies from employee classification requirements despite prior court rulings. Amazon's intensive multi-million dollar anti-union campaigns at warehouses employ sophisticated surveillance, mandatory anti-union meetings, rapid response to organizing activities, worker terminations, and threats of wage and benefit reductions or facility closures (Dubal, 2023; Cant, 2024).

Despite these substantial barriers, platform workers have developed innovative organizing approaches and resistance strategies leveraging digital tools, online communities, legal challenges, public campaigns, and solidarity networks. WhatsApp groups, Facebook communities, Reddit forums, Telegram channels, and Discord servers enable worker communication outside platform surveillance and control. Workers share crucial information about platform policy changes, algorithmic updates, earnings strategies, customer problems, deactivation experiences, legal rights, and organizing activities. These digital spaces build solidarity, collective consciousness, and coordination capacity while evading platform monitoring that might trigger retaliation. Online organizing enables rapid mobilization for specific campaigns, protests, or strikes coordinated through encrypted messaging apps (Wood et al., 2023).

Workers have organized coordinated strikes and protests targeting platform companies, demanding better pay, improved conditions, policy changes, and recognition. International strike days see drivers and couriers in multiple countries simultaneously logging off platforms, significantly disrupting operations and generating media attention. Public protests outside platform headquarters or during corporate events raise visibility of worker grievances. These actions demonstrate collective power despite structural obstacles, though translating episodic protests into sustained organizing capable of forcing substantial platform concessions remains challenging without formal recognition and bargaining structures.

CONCLUSION

Digital hoboism emerges as defining labor phenomenon of algorithmic capitalism, revealing how technological systems fundamentally reshape work organization, power relationships, worker subjectivities, and economic possibilities. This chapter has examined digital hoboism as complex socio-technical phenomenon emerging at intersections of platform capitalism's business models, algorithmic management's control mechanisms, neoliberal ideology's entrepreneurial discourses, and contemporary labor market transformations toward precarity and flexibility.

Platform capitalism creates distinctive organizational forms where digital intermediaries coordinate vast labor forces while avoiding employment responsibilities through contractor classification, algorithmic management substitutes technical systems for human supervision while maintaining extensive control, and data extraction adds new dimensions of value appropriation beyond traditional labor exploitation. These mechanisms enable platforms to achieve enormous scale and profitability while externalizing risks, costs, and insecurities onto millions of workers globally operating as digital hobos—transient, precarious, algorithmically-managed workers combining nominal independence with structural vulnerability.

Empirical analysis demonstrates that platform work generally involves lower compensation than comparable traditional employment after accounting for expenses and benefits, experiences substantially greater income volatility creating financial planning difficulties, lacks employment protections and workplace rights, and generates particular health and safety concerns without corresponding support or compensation. However, platform work outcomes vary significantly across sectors, geographic contexts, worker demographics, and individual circumstances, requiring attention to heterogeneity rather than uniform characterizations.

Ideologically, digital hoboism operates through narratives emphasizing entrepreneurial independence, scheduling flexibility, and opportunity that obscure material realities of algorithmic control, structural precarity, and limited autonomy. These narratives serve platform interests by legitimizing business models, discouraging collective organizing, and shaping worker subjectivities toward entrepreneurial self-exploitation. However, contradictions between ideological promises and lived experiences create growing tensions manifesting in worker resistance, organizing innovations, legal challenges, and regulatory interventions globally.

The future of platform labor depends fundamentally on political contestations over employment classification, algorithmic accountability, worker rights, and alternative platform models. History demonstrates that labor conditions result from political struggles rather than technological inevitability. Contemporary platform workers, like historical hobos before them, engage in collective organizing, resistance practices, and demands for better conditions despite structural obstacles. Whether digital hoboism becomes normalized as permanent features of contemporary capitalism or whether workers successfully challenge platform power and establish rights, protections, and democratic governance remains open question whose resolution will significantly shape labor's future in algorithmic culture.

Several policy trajectories show particular promise for improving platform labor conditions. Portable benefits systems that decouple social protections from employment relationships would extend healthcare, retirement contributions, paid leave, and unemployment coverage to platform workers regardless of their contractor classification. Such systems, piloted in limited forms in jurisdictions including Washington State and the European Union, represent structural innovations capable of addressing the benefits gap without requiring resolution of contested employment classification debates. Algorithmic transparency requirements compelling platforms to disclose how work allocation, compensation calculation, and deactivation decisions are made would reduce informational asymmetries that currently prevent workers from understanding or contesting algorithmic decisions affecting their livelihoods. Platform cooperativism—worker-owned alternatives to corporate platform models—offers a structural alternative distributing platform value to workers rather than extracting it for shareholders, with emerging examples including driver cooperatives competing with rideshare platforms and freelancer collectives building alternative marketplace models (Sandoval, 2020; Scholz, 2016). Collective bargaining rights extensions to platform workers regardless of classification, already implemented in limited forms through European sectoral bargaining and municipal regulations in some US cities, provide institutional mechanisms for worker voice in platform governance. These policy directions collectively point toward a regulatory framework recognizing platform workers' genuine economic dependence on platforms while preserving legitimate flexibility benefits, providing social protections proportional to dependency, requiring algorithmic accountability and due process, and enabling democratic worker participation in platform governance. Realizing these possibilities requires sustained political mobilization, cross-sectoral solidarity between platform workers and traditional labor movements, public awareness of platform labor conditions, and sustained research documenting platform work's material consequences for workers, communities, and democratic institutions. The historical parallel with industrial-era labor struggles is instructive: the labor protections that workers in traditional employment take for granted today were themselves won through decades of organizing, legal contestation, and political struggle against powerful interests insisting that such protections were economically impossible. Digital hobos of the twenty-first century are engaged in the opening phases of an analogous contest, one whose outcome will define the character of work and economic security for millions of people navigating life under algorithmic capitalism.

REFERENCES

Adams-Prassl, J., Binns, R., & Kelly-Lyth, A. (2022). Directly Discriminatory Algorithms. *The Modern Law Review*, *86*(1), 144–180. DOI: 10.1111/1468-2230.12759 PMID: 37065788

Aloisi, A., & De Stefano, V. (2023). *Your Boss Is an Algorithm: Artificial Intelligence, Platform Work and Labour*. Hart Publishing., DOI: 10.5040/9781509947065

Bajwa, U., Gastaldo, D., Di Ruggiero, E., & Knorr, L. (2018). The health of workers in the global gig economy. *Globalization and Health*, *14*(1), 124. DOI: 10.1186/s12992-018-0444-8 PMID: 30563539

Berg, J., Furrer, M., Harmon, E., Rani, U., & Silberman, M. S. (2018). *Digital Labour Platforms and the Future of Work*. International Labour Organization. DOI: 10.2139/ssrn.3166150

Bureau of Labor Statistics. (2024). *Contingent and Alternative Employment Arrangements Summary*. U.S. Department of Labor.

Cant, C. (2024). *The Fast and the Furious: Platform Labour and Protest in the Gig Economy*. Pluto Press., DOI: 10.2307/j.ctv2x0wptf

Chen, J. Y., & Sun, P. (2020). Temporal arbitrage, fragmented rush, and opportunistic behaviors: The labor politics of time in the platform economy. *New Media & Society*, *23*(12), 3487–3506. DOI: 10.1177/1461444820913567

Chen, L., & Yan, S. (2021). Occupational health and safety challenges for gig workers during COVID-19 and beyond. *Journal of Occupational Health*, *63*(1), e12234. DOI: 10.1002/1348-9585.12234 PMID: 33993611

Chen, M. K., Rossi, P. E., Chevalier, J. A., & Oehlsen, E. (2019). The value of flexible work: Evidence from Uber drivers. *Journal of Political Economy*, *127*(6), 2735–2794. DOI: 10.1086/702171

De Stefano, V., & Aloisi, A. (2018). European legal framework for digital labour platforms. European Commission. https://doi.org/DOI: 10.2139/ssrn.3186489

DePastino, T. (2021). *Citizen Hobo: How a Century of Homelessness Shaped America*. University of Chicago Press.

Dubal, V. B. (2023). The drive to precarity: A political history of work, regulation, & labor advocacy. *Berkeley Journal of Employment and Labor Law*, *38*(1), 73–135. DOI: 10.15779/Z382B8VC7J

Duffy, B. E., & Meisner, C. (2024). Platform precarity and the pandemic. *New Media & Society*, *26*(1), 278–297. DOI: 10.1177/14614448211063648

Fleming, P. (2017). The human capital hoax: Work, debt and insecurity in the era of Uberization. *Organization Studies*, *38*(5), 691–709. DOI: 10.1177/0170840616686129

Foong, E., Vincent, N., Hecht, B., & Gerber, E. M. (2018). Women (still) ask for less: Gender differences in hourly rate. *Proceedings of the ACM on Human-Computer Interaction*, 2(CSCW), 1-21. DOI: 10.1145/3274322

Gandini, A. (2019). Labour process theory and the gig economy. *Human Relations*, *72*(6), 1039–1056. DOI: 10.1177/0018726718790002

Gilmore, G. (2022). *Hobohemia: Emma Goldman, Lucy Parsons, and the Culture of Revolutionary Dissent*. University of California Press.

Gleim, M. R., & Lawson, S. J. (2022). The sharing economy: Carving out an identity in a crowded field. *Journal of the Association for Consumer Research*, *7*(1), 1–5. DOI: 10.1086/717515

Goods, C., Veen, A., & Barratt, T. (2019). "Is your gig any good?" Analysing job quality in the Australian platform-based food-delivery sector. *The Journal of Industrial Relations*, *61*(4), 502–527. DOI: 10.1177/0022185618817069

Graham, M., Hjorth, I., & Lehdonvirta, V. (2021). Digital labour and development: Impacts of global digital labour platforms. *Transfer: European Review of Labour and Research*, *23*(2), 135–162. DOI: 10.1177/1024258916687250 PMID: 28781494

Gray, M. L., & Suri, S. (2019). *Ghost Work: How to Stop Silicon Valley from Building a New Global Underclass*. Houghton Mifflin Harcourt.

Huws, U., Spencer, N. H., Syrdal, D. S., & Holts, K. (2017). *Work in the European gig economy*. Foundation for European Progressive Studies.

International Labour Organization. (2024). *World Employment and Social Outlook: Trends 2024*. ILO Publications.

Jabagi, N., Croteau, A. M., Audebrand, L. K., & Marsan, J. (2019). Gig-workers' motivation: Thinking beyond carrots and sticks. *Journal of Managerial Psychology*, *34*(4), 192–213. DOI: 10.1108/JMP-06-2018-0255

Johnston, H., & Land-Kazlauskas, C. (2021). Organizing on-demand: Representation, voice, and collective bargaining in the gig economy. *ILO Working Paper*, 94. https://doi.org/DOI: 10.2139/ssrn.3788600

Kalleberg, A. L., & Vallas, S. P. (2018). Probing precarious work: Theory, research, and politics. *Research in the Sociology of Work, 31*, 1–30. DOI: 10.1108/S0277-283320170000031017

Kellogg, K. C., Valentine, M. A., & Christin, A. (2020). Algorithms at work: The new contested terrain of control. *The Academy of Management Annals, 14*(1), 366–410. DOI: 10.5465/annals.2018.0174

Kenney, M., & Zysman, J. (2021). The platform economy: Restructuring the space of capitalist accumulation. *Cambridge Journal of Regions, Economy and Society, 13*(1), 55–76. DOI: 10.1093/cjres/rsaa001

Lehdonvirta, V., Kässi, O., Hjorth, I., Barnard, H., & Graham, M. (2019). The global platform economy: A new offshoring institution. *Journal of Management, 45*(2), 567–599. DOI: 10.1177/0149206318786781 PMID: 30774168

Levy, K. E., & Barocas, S. (2024). Designing against discrimination in online markets. *Berkeley Technology Law Journal, 32*(3), 1183–1237. DOI: 10.15779/Z38N873094

Maier, C., & Ruthven, I. (2024). Gamification in crowdsourcing: A review. *Technological Forecasting and Social Change, 188*, 122239. DOI: 10.1016/j.techfore.2022.122239

Möhlmann, M., & Zalmanson, L. (2017). Hands on the wheel: Navigating algorithmic management and Uber drivers' autonomy. *Proceedings of the International Conference on Information Systems*, 1-17.

Parrott, J. A., & Reich, M. (2020). *A minimum compensation standard for Seattle TNC drivers*. Center on Wage and Employment Dynamics Policy Brief.

Reid, A., & Thomas, S. L. (2022). The health impacts of precarious employment among workers in industrialized countries. *Journal of Public Health, 44*(2), e203–e215. DOI: 10.1093/pubmed/fdab077 PMID: 34604905

Rosenblat, A. (2018). *Uberland: How Algorithms Are Rewriting the Rules of Work*. University of California Press., DOI: 10.1525/9780520970632

Sadowski, J. (2019). When data is capital: Datafication, accumulation, and extraction. *Big Data & Society, 6*(1), 1–12. DOI: 10.1177/2053951718820549

Sandoval, M. (2020). Entrepreneurial activism? Platform cooperativism between subversion and co-optation. *Critical Sociology, 46*(6), 801–817. DOI: 10.1177/0896920519870577

Scholz, T. (2016). *Platform Cooperativism: Challenging the Corporate Sharing Economy*. Rosa Luxemburg Foundation.

Schor, J. B., Attwood-Charles, W., Cansoy, M., Ladegaard, I., & Wengronowitz, R. (2021). Dependence and precarity in the platform economy. *Theory and Society*, *49*(5-6), 833–861. DOI: 10.1007/s11186-020-09408-y PMID: 32836676

Schwellnus, C., Geva, A., Pak, M., & Veiel, R. (2019). Gig economy platforms: Boon or bane? *OECD Economics Department Working Papers*, 1550. DOI: 10.1787/18151973

Srnicek, N. (2021). *Platform Capitalism*. Polity Press. DOI: 10.17323/978-5-7598-2561-6

ADDITIONAL READING

Kellogg, K. C. (2022). Algorithms, workers, and the quest for control. In Bernstein, M., & Ackerman, M. S. (Eds.), *Handbook of Collective Intelligence*. MIT Press.

Lee, M. K., Kusbit, D., Metsky, E., & Dabbish, L. (2015). Working with machines: The impact of algorithmic and data-driven management on human workers. *Proceedings of the 33rd Annual ACM Conference on Human Factors in Computing Systems*, 1603-1612. https://doi.org/DOI: 10.1145/2702123.2702548

Rosenblat, A. (2018). *Uberland: How Algorithms Are Rewriting the Rules of Work*. University of California Press. DOI: 10.1525/9780520970632

Schor, J. B., Attwood-Charles, W., Cansoy, M., Ladegaard, I., & Wengronowitz, R. (2020). Dependence and precarity in the platform economy. *Theory and Society*, *49*(5), 833–861. DOI: 10.1007/s11186-020-09408-y PMID: 32836676

Shapiro, A. (2018). Between autonomy and control: Strategies of arbitrage in the "on-demand" economy. *New Media & Society*, *20*(8), 2954–2971. DOI: 10.1177/1461444817738236

Srnicek, N. (2017). *Platform Capitalism*. Polity Press.

Sutherland, W., Jarrahi, M. H., Dunn, M., & Nelson, S. B. (2020). Work precarity and gig literacies in online freelancing. *Work, Employment and Society*, *34*(3), 457–475. DOI: 10.1177/0950017019886511

Vallas, S., & Schor, J. B. (2020). What do platforms do? Understanding the gig economy. *Annual Review of Sociology*, *46*(1), 273–294. DOI: 10.1146/annurev-soc-121919-054857

Wood, A. J., Graham, M., Lehdonvirta, V., & Hjorth, I. (2019). Good gig, bad gig: Autonomy and algorithmic control in the global gig economy. *Work, Employment and Society*, *33*(1), 56–75. DOI: 10.1177/0950017018785616 PMID: 30886460

KEY TERMS AND DEFINITIONS

Algorithmic Labor: - Work that is mediated, managed, and controlled by algorithms rather than human supervisors. This includes how tasks are assigned, performance is monitored, workers are evaluated, and pay is determined through automated systems. Examples include ride-sharing apps that use algorithms to match drivers with passengers and set prices.

Digital Hoboism: - A term describing workers who move between temporary digital jobs and platforms without stable employment, analogous to historical hobos who traveled for seasonal work. These individuals rely on internet connectivity and digital platforms to find short-term work opportunities across different locations.

Digital Nomadism: - A lifestyle where individuals use telecommunications technologies to work remotely while traveling and living in different locations. Digital nomads are not tied to a specific geographic location and often work as freelancers or remote employees while exploring the world.

Gig Work: - Short-term, flexible jobs or "gigs" rather than permanent positions. Workers are typically paid per task, project, or time period rather than receiving a salary. This includes freelancing, contract work, and on-demand services accessed through apps or platforms.

Platform Economy: - An economic system built around digital platforms that connect service providers with consumers, facilitating exchanges of goods, services, or labor. Companies like Uber, Airbnb, and Amazon Mechanical Turk exemplify this model, acting as intermediaries rather than traditional employers.

Precarious Employment: - Unstable, insecure work characterized by uncertainty, low wages, few benefits, and limited legal protections. Workers in precarious employment lack job security, predictable schedules, and often cannot access traditional employment benefits like health insurance or retirement plans.

Chapter 11
The Algorithmic Gaze: Power, Surveillance, and Despotism in the Digital Workplace

Palak Aggarwal
http://orcid.org/0009-0007-8809-3879
Christ University, India

Diksha Pandey
http://orcid.org/0009-0001-5852-6684
Christ University, India

ABSTRACT

This chapter investigates the ways that algorithmic technologies reconfigure workplace authority by changing how we think about surveillance, evaluation, and control in data-driven management practices. Drawing from and reconceptualising Foucault's Panopticon and Zuboff's Surveillance Capitalism, it contends that the algorithmic gaze creates an invisible governance system, where trust and autonomy are replaced by quantification. Through case studies in service, fintech, and logistics sectors, the analysis highlights how discourses of efficiency and performance sustainability legitimise digital despotism, bias, and workers self-monitoring. The chapter concludes with a framework for digital humanism, which articulates ethical, transparent, and participatory governance and management, which can restore human dignity and agency in algorithmically mediated labour.

DOI: 10.4018/979-8-3373-4531-4.ch011

INTRODUCTION

Data-driven decision-making has driven major transformation in workplace management in the digital era. Originally envisioned with promises of flexibility and empowerment, there is now a strong move toward surveillance and control characterized by quantification and monitoring. The ongoing development of algorithms has created an overview of the workforce that monitors, evaluates and disciplines labourers via data infrastructure (Kellogg, Valentine & Christin, 2020; Delfanti, 2021).

In addition to supporting managerial decision-making, algorithms shape the definitions of "performance," "trust," and "value." This forms the basis of the digital empire: an ideology of algorithmic control occurring as part of the automation and data governance that exists within organizations (Zuboff, 2019; Katzenbach & Ulbricht, 2019). Digital empire differs from traditional authority in that digital control is enforced through a coded and quantified framework that appears neutral but actually imposes continuous discipline.

Traditionally, the judgments made by managers were informed by their relationships with employees, which built mutually trusting relations. Conversely, algorithmic governance transforms behaviours into metrics and monitors employees through dashboards and data-driven tools (Kellogg et al. 2020). This represents the current version of Foucault's (1977) "panoptic gaze" and the surveillance technique employed relies on clouded metrics producing self-regulatory behaviours through anticipatory compliance .

There is evidence indicating that employees are losing some degree of autonomy and experiencing heightened anxiety, decreased ability to be creative, etc., due to increasing numbers of organizations implementing precise, scalable methods of managing/monitoring performance (e.g., algorithmic management). For example, prior research on the effects of algorithmic management indicates that it has a negative impact on employee well-being and psychosocial stressors (Parent-Rocheleau & Parker, 2023). Data collected through surveillance capitalism involves using data as a resource for predicting behavior and controlling actions, rather than simply being a neutral source of information (Zuboff, 2019). Additionally, data is converted from labor to auditable, monetisable data streams (Sadowski, 2020).

Algorithmic systems are not ideologically neutral and instead hold cultural and managerial assumptions about what is considered to be efficient, competent performance (Suchman, 2020; Noble, 2018). For example, in measuring "engagement" through the use of Artificial Intelligence Tools (AI), Western behavioral norms are often imposed on people while non-Western and non-compulsive (neurodivergent) individuals are marginalised because of these norms (Ajunwa, 2020). In this chapter, I will label outcomes of this nature as digital sectionalism and digital favoritism and suggest that this form of algorithmic performance management results in the algorithmic categorization of workers and it differentiates and privileges certain workers based on race, ethnicity, sex, etc. under the guise of being neutral (Beer, 2017; Eubanks, 2018).

More opacity in decision-making processes causes greater issues with governance. Workers do not know how algorithmic decision-making processes occur or why organisations utilise algorithms and lack accountability for using these algorithms as part of the overall performance management regime (Pasquale, 2015; Wachter, Mittelstadt, & Floridi, 2017). The lack of transparency is removing fairness from the decision-making processes and therefore, creating concerns for worker rights and autonomies .

Consequently, this chapter describes a Digital Humanist approach to technology, which pivots it on values such as dignity, empathy, interpretive judgment and autonomy (Crawford 2021). Digital Humanism promotes the transparent design of algorithmic systems, participatory governance, and human-centred performance measures as opposed to purely efficiency-driven measurements (Floridi et al., 2018). Embedding these concepts/values into digital infrastructures allows workplaces to evolve from possessing surveillance to allowing for a shared sense of agency, trust and collective creativity.

Objective of Chapter:

This chapter critically analyses how algorithmic governance transforms labour, identity and power through theoretical analysis and comparisons of three service, fintech and logistics sector case studies to provide a human-centred ethical and accountable framework for managing algorithms.

BACKGROUND AND SIGNIFICANCE

The Evolution of Algorithmic Governance

The rise of algorithmic governance marks a major transformation in organizational control. Algorithms, which were originally introduced to improve efficiency and consistency, are now influencing not just the processes of organizations but also human behaviour and power relations (Kellogg, Valentine & Christin, 2020; Katzenbach & Ulbricht, 2019). Today, we have moved from using algorithms only for logistic optimizations and recruitment automation to performance evaluations, scheduling, hiring, and disciplinary actions; as such, we have fundamentally altered how we go about providing value to the work performed (Delfanti, 2021; Moore, 2018).

In today's organizations, instead of relying on managerial authority to determine who is worthy of being awarded a job based upon interpersonal judgement and trust in relationships, organizations now rely on digital analytics, real-time monitoring, and automated scoring of employees (Pasquale, 2015). With this shift toward using digital analytics as the basis of their power, organizations have developed an infrastructure of authority based on power embedded in data-driven systems, predictive models, and automated feedback (Kellogg, Valentine & Christin, 2020).

The purpose of algorithms is to create corporate visibility by converting labour into measurable data; furthermore, algorithms make visible an algorithmic order that establishes the parameters of compliance, productivity, and creativity by using machine-generated metrics (Delfanti, 2021; Katzenbach & Ulbricht, 2019). By using real-time measurement, ranking, and prediction as tools for governing the behaviour of employees, organizations are reorganizing work around the extraction of data and anticipatory compliance thereby diminishing the autonomy and agency of the employee (Moore, 2018; Parent-Rocheleau & Parker, 2023).

The Rise of Surveillance and Digital Despotism

The ideology legitimizing these practices can be described as digital despotism—a form of power exercised through automated systems rather than identifiable human authorities (Zuboff, 2019; Delfanti, 2021). Control is embedded in software infrastructures, operating through dashboards, metrics, rankings, and algorithmic alerts that continuously evaluate worker performance and value.

Human judgment and relational trust are replaced by computational oversight, framed as "efficiency" and "transparency" while concealing its disciplinary nature (Kellogg et al., 2020; Pasquale, 2015). This intensified with the rise of remote and hybrid work after COVID-19, normalizing Electronic Performance Monitoring (EPM) tools that track keystrokes, screen activity, voice tone, and communication patterns (Newlands, 2021).

Although marketed as accountability-enhancing, research shows these systems generate fear, stress, and self-censorship (Parent-Rocheleau & Parker, 2023; Moore, 2019). Workers adapt their behaviour to algorithmic expectations—shortening calls, limiting empathy, or simulating activity to avoid penalties—producing a continuous and invisible form of self-discipline (Moore, 2018).

Algorithmic Management and the Ideology of Efficiency

Algorithmic management is grounded in the ideological assumption that data are objective and therefore superior to human judgment. This way of thinking, known as data determinism, treats algorithmic outcomes as objective, based on science and as being authoritative, even though they are created using models created by humans, biased data and normative assumptions (Pasquale, 2015, Noble, 2018). With respect to how they position themselves relative to each other, data determinism holds that algorithms are epistemologically superior decision-makers, thus marginalizing human interpretation, ethical reasoning and contextual knowledge (Katzenbach & Ulbricht, 2019).

The net result is that many of organizations' values are now directed towards productivity, speed, efficiency and standardisation and away from empathy, fairness, and situational nuance. The basis for worker evaluations is moving toward standardised outputs, rather than more holistic assessments that take into account effort, creativity and moral judgement. The digital gaze has the effect of turning work into quantifiable productivity measurements, while simultaneously rendering invisible the emotional, relational and cognitive aspects of work (Delfanti, 2021, Moore, 2018).

For example, performance rating systems based on automated scoring may assign lower performance ratings to workers whose communication style, expression of emotion or working pace is outside of the algorithmic norm, irrespective of the worker's actual competence or contribution (Ajunwa, 2020). Likewise, productivity dashboards that use automated data streams may label workers who perform slowly but with care as "wasting time" thereby providing a narrow definition of value that privileges speed at the expense of quality. This way, algorithmic "decisions" appear to be objective and rational in nature while actually continuing to reproduce pre-existing social inequalities and institutional hierarchies disguised as "scientific neutrality" (Eubanks, 2018; Noble, 2018).

The Need for a Digital Humanist Reorientation

As algorithmic governance becomes embedded in organizational life, restoring human judgment, ethics, and dignity becomes urgent. Although algorithms may enhance productivity, they cannot interpret moral scenarios or demonstrate any regard for contextual relevance when interacting with non-automated users. Hence, the manner in which metric performance can be evaluated is based on how compliant the user can be with the stated metrics rather than providing the user with empathy, creativity and individualisation (Crawford, 2021)

This chapter presents a potential method for implementing a Digital Humanism approach through the use of technology as a means to human wellbeing, not as a method of controlling. The digital humanism concept states that algorithms should be used to serve the collective good as opposed to merely serving the business/ profit aspect of an organisation (Crawford, 2021)

To be compliant with Digital Humanism in their design/ implementation, systems should be transparent, equitable, inclusive and open to challenge. Hybrid review methods that include human supervisors contextualising algorithmically flagged or out-of-the-ordinary cases will maintain the users' dignity, provide for procedural justice, and minimise bias (Wachter and Mittelstadt & Floridi, 2017; Kellogg et al., 2020).

Digital Humanism, likewise, advocates for participative governance through the establishment of worker councils and oversight committees to provide an accountable and democratic means to create and use algorithms. It promotes the rebalancing of computational logic versus human values; workplaces to leverage technology while remaining fundamentally humanistic.

LITERATURE REVIEW

Evolution of Algorithmic Governance and Workplace Control

Algorithmic governance constitutes one of the most substantial structural transformations in organizational management in the contemporary era. While algorithms were initially understood as computational tools designed to enhance efficiency and objectivity in decision-making, recent scholarship demonstrates that they have evolved into powerful agents of governance that restructure authority, labor relations, and organizational morality (Kellogg, Valentine, & Christin, 2020). Algorithms now operate as socio-technical systems that shape not only how work is performed, but also how value, trust, and competence are defined (Beer, 2017).

This transformation mirrors the shift from industrial Taylorism to what scholars describe as Digital Taylorism, wherein labor is disaggregated into measurable data points and performance is governed through continuous computational evaluation rather than relational judgment (Delfanti, 2021; Moore, 2018). Digital Taylorism extends classical scientific management by automating surveillance, intensifying standardization, and embedding control within software infrastructures (Kellogg et al., 2020). Curchod et al. (2020) characterize this as the "digital reincarnation of managerial control," wherein algorithmic oversight replaces front-line supervision and restructures managerial authority.

In the ongoing changes described in the previous paragraphs have occurred in the context of digital capitalism. In this context, researchers argue that algorithms serve as ideological agents of capitalism; through the ideologically veiled hair, these tools perform the imperative functions of capitalism (i.e., efficiency, extraction, and profit) in an apparently neutral and objective manner. By fulfilling this role, these ideological agents obscure the relationships of power present within algorithmic systems and therefore render managerial control diffuse, distanced, and depersonalized.

While much of the literature surrounding call centres and business process outsourcing (BPO) in the context of India reveals similar forms of regulation as a result of data-driven decision making, it must be noted that call centre and BPO workers are subjected to the ongoing surveillance of their activities. Examples of this ongoing surveillance include the receipt of keystrokes, call durations, emotional tone, and adherence to scripts from their supervisors, creating an environment that describes as a "virtual panopticon" - a place where the authority exercised by algorithms is met with immediately delivered feedback and predictive correction. Over time, this data-driven form of regulation has produced an alternate form of workplace visibility that is considered rational and efficient; however, it conceals the various hierarchical levels of trust, power, and exclusion that exist within this system (Moore, 2018; Delfanti, 2021). Thus, the governance exercised by algorithms is indicative of a technological shift, but it also manifests a substantial alteration in ideology at the workplace.

Digital Despotism and Power Asymmetry

Digital despotism refers to the concentration of authority within invisible computational infrastructures rather than visible human agents. Unlike traditional authoritarian management, which operates through explicit hierarchical structures, digital despotism embeds command into data systems, rendering power diffuse, automated, and seemingly objective (Zuboff, 2019; Delfanti, 2021). Moore (2023) describes this phenomenon as *invisible management*, wherein employees are subjected to constant surveillance while the governing systems that regulate them remain opaque.

Zuboff's (2019) theory of surveillance capitalism situates this asymmetry within a broader economic logic in which human behavior is extracted as raw material for predictive modeling and monetization. When applied to workplaces, this logic transforms workers' bodies, emotions, time, and interactions into data streams for extraction and optimization. Algorithmic systems thus produce anticipatory obedience, as workers preemptively align their behavior with machine expectations to avoid penalties or negative evaluations (Kellogg, Valentine, & Christin, 2020).

This form of power operates not through direct coercion but through predictive conditioning and self-regulation.

Power asymmetries are particularly pronounced in digital workplaces across the Global South. Research from Asia and Latin America demonstrates that global firms embed algorithmic standards that privilege Western norms of communication, timing, and comportment, a phenomenon increasingly described as digital colonialism (Couldry & Mejias, 2019). For example, call center workers in India are often evaluated based on accent neutrality, emotional tone, and conversational pacing aligned with Western customer expectations, leading to penalization of culturally situated communication styles (D'Cruz & Noronha, 2016). This produces compliance with deviant normative codes that erode authenticity and cultural identity, legitimized through algorithmic "objectivity." Digital despotism thus functions as an ideological regime that normalizes control by conflating surveillance with accountability and productivity with compliance.

Algorithmic Surveillance and Worker Psychosocial Impacts

A significant amount of literature has now emerged around the psychological and emotional aspects of algorithmic surveillance. Parent-Rocheleau and Parker (2023) describe algorithmic surveillance as fostering "quantified anxiety," where workers internalize the knowledge that they are under constant evaluation as part of self-worth. This form of constant evaluation enables self-surveillance, which can be understood in relation to Foucault's (1977) conceptualization of surveillance as a manifestation of disciplinary power where individuals participate in the control of their own behaviour.

There is also empirical evidence to support these theorizations. Mbare (2024) found in a study of gig workers and remote workers that constant management leads to a decline in intrinsic motivation and increased cognitive fatigue. Likewise, Rosenblat and Stark (2016) show how Uber drivers interpret algorithmic directives as a moral obligation to provide "good service." This interpretation leads to feelings of inadequacy or guilt when drivers do not perform at an "invisible" level. The literature also evidences a gendered aspect to this control, where Costa and Peterson (2023) demonstrate that algorithmic performance affects emotional labour in gendered ways: women's performance is often penalized when it does not meet expected gendered affective norms.

In other regions, including India, algorithmic management takes similar forms in customer services and e-commerce spaces, creating similar psychosocial effects. In those contexts, researchers found that "digital scoring" reduces collective identity and innovation in exchanges with these platforms. Consequently, algorithmic surveillance is not only a technological practice but a psychological regime that disciplines emotion, imagination, and agency within the boundaries of code.

Ideological Reproduction and Bias in Algorithmic Systems

Despite being framed as neutral tools of rationality, algorithms increasingly demonstrate the capacity to reproduce and institutionalize social and organizational biases. Noble's (2018) work on search engines illustrates how algorithmic systems reinforce racial hierarchies, while some researchers document systemic racial and gender bias in facial recognition technologies. In organizational contexts, such biases manifest through automated hiring systems, productivity scoring tools, and sentiment analysis platforms that privilege Western linguistic norms and penalize neurodivergent or culturally diverse communication styles (Ajunwa, 2020).

Some argue that these biases reflect deeper epistemic politics rather than surface-level design flaws. Algorithms encode the worldviews, assumptions, and priorities of their designers, privileging certain identities while marginalizing others. Within organizational settings, this process materializes as digital favoritism, wherein algorithmic systems disproportionately reward those who conform to dominant normative standards while disponating others under the guise of objectivity. Digital favoritism operates precisely because algorithmic decisions are framed as neutral, scientific, and beyond contestation, thereby naturalizing unequal outcomes.

Eubanks (2018) further demonstrates how algorithmic systems enforce inequality by translating subjective assumptions into formalized mathematical rules, producing discrimination in statistical form. The Indian and Southeast Asian service sectors show that algorithmic evaluation systems reinforce Global North norms of competence, professionalism, and emotional expression, marginalizing localized forms of care, relational labor, and cultural expression. These dynamics exemplify a form of digital imperialism, whereby cultural biases are exported through technological infrastructures and normalized as universal standards.

Collectively, the literature calls for a deeper ideological critique of algorithms—not as neutral tools, but as instruments of power that reproduce hierarchies of race, gender, geography, and ability under the veneer of rationality and efficiency.

Towards Digital Humanism and Ethical Resistance

Recent scholarship has increasingly proposed Digital Humanism as a normative and practical alternative to algorithmic dominance (Floridi et al., 2018). Rooted in human-centered design, ethical governance, and critical post-humanist theory, Digital

Humanism seeks to orient technological development toward human flourishing rather than surveillance and control.

Researchers argue for embedding principles of explainability, fairness, and accountability within algorithmic architectures to re-establish moral agency in socio-technical systems. Crawford (2021) advances the concept of algorithmic transparency, which requires that systems make their reasoning processes accessible and intelligible to users. For example, in workplace performance evaluation systems, transparency would involve allowing workers to understand how scores are generated, which data are used, and how errors or biases can be challenged (Wachter, Mittelstadt, & Floridi, 2017).

Policy frameworks increasingly reflect this shift. The European Commission's *Ethics Guidelines for Trustworthy AI* (2021) promote human-centered design, participatory oversight, and worker inclusion in algorithmic governance. Similarly, emerging Indian policy discourse emphasizes algorithmic literacy, worker rights to explanation, and ethical AI deployment in workplaces.

Digital Humanism also functions as a form of ideological resistance. It contends that reasserting the ethical nature of technology requires not only technical reform but also ideological critique—challenging the assumption that optimization, efficiency, and automation are inherently desirable. This literature converges on the view that the future of work does not require abandoning algorithms but humanizing algorithms. This can be achieved by designing hybrid governance systems where algorithmic outputs are subject to human review, worker participation, and ethical deliberation. For example, instead of fully automated disciplinary systems, organizations can implement co-governed decision processes where workers, managers, and technologists jointly interpret data and assess outcomes.

Through such practices, Digital Humanism transforms the algorithmic gaze from a mechanism of surveillance into a framework of collaboration, shared agency, and ethical accountability.

OBJECTIVES

The intention of this chapter is to analyze the ways in which algorithmic systems are altering power, control, and human agency within the digital workplace. Informed by theoretical frameworks of algorithmic governance, digital despotism, and recent periodizations of digital humanism, this chapter attempts to unpack the ideological, psychological, and structural dimensions of technology-driven management. Accordingly, the objectives of the research study include the following:

- To conceptualize algorithmic governance as a new regime of control in the workplace

This chapter aim is to define algorithmic governance as an emergent managerial paradigm beyond data-driven decision making towards a system of embedded authority. It seeks to explain how algorithms act as organizational actors that are implementing behavioral changes, normative performance, and altered hierarchical structures via coded rules, metrics, and automated evaluations.

- To analyze the power asymmetries and digital despotism produced by algorithmic management systems

This objective encompasses understanding how algorithmic infrastructures are economically centralizing control, disguising accountability, and producing asymmetries of visibility because, while workers are monitored in totality, algorithms stricken the systems that disciplines visibility will not be visible. This chapter evaluates the power asymmetries as they reconfigure authority and affect autonomy.

- To evaluate the psychosocial, emotional, and behavioral effects of algorithmic surveillance on workers

In addition to considering the impact of ongoing digital surveillance, performance ratings, and predictive analytics on stress, self-image, identity formation, and motivation. The chapter utilizes current research to demonstrate the ways in which algorithmic supervision creates anxiety, precarity, and new strategies of self-surveillance.

- To investigate how algorithmic systems reproduce bias, ideology, and cultural stratification within workplace systems

This objective examines how algorithms encode beliefs, perpetuate structural inequity, and legitimize favoritism through ostensibly neutral computational actions. The chapter discusses the socio-technical reproduction of race, gender, class, and geographic bias within hiring processes, appraisals, and workflow automation.

- To develop a human-centered and ethical-resistance based framework that looks forward

The chapter intends to sketch the outline for a conceptual framework that integrates transparency, fairness, worker agency, and participatory governance into algorithmic management systems. It will look to articulate pathways for human-centered actions, collective resistance, and ethical redesign efforts that could lead to more just, accountable, and humane digital workplaces.

- To suggest potential actions to policymakers, leaders of organizations, and designers of technologies

The chapter ends with concrete recommendations around managing algorithm systems, creating a workplace social contract, designing ethical AI rules, and creating organizational cultures based on dignity, autonomy, and democratic participation in the time of digital management.

CASE STUDY ANALYSIS

Algorithmic management now structures work across service industries, platform labour, finance, and logistics. Despite using different tools—such as Electronic Performance Monitoring (EPM), emotion-recognition AI, and algorithmic scheduling—these systems share a common effect: the reorganization of managerial power. Control shifts from human discretion to automated systems that continuously observe, evaluate, and discipline or reward workers.

This chapter examined three empirical cases—call centres, fintech, and European logistics, to show how algorithmic systems reshape labour processes, worker subjectivity, and forms of resistance. These cases reveal persistent tensions between efficiency-driven digital control and the ethical, psychological, and democratic demands of algorithmic governance.

Case 1: Algorithmic Taylorism – The Mechanization of Trust

Algorithmic Taylorism refers to the extension of scientific management into digital systems, where labor is disaggregated into measurable units and governed through continuous algorithmic surveillance rather than human supervision (Moore, 2018; Delfanti, 2021; Kellogg, Valentine, & Christin, 2020). Unlike classical Taylorism, which relied on supervisors to observe and discipline workers, Algorithmic Taylorism embeds control into software infrastructures, producing a regime of automated managerial authority.

In multinational customer service outsourcing firms such as Teleperformance, Concentrix, Alorica, and cloud-based centres leveraging Amazon Connect, algorithmic monitoring has become central to performance governance. Electronic Performance Monitoring (EPM) systems collect data on keystrokes, idle time, call duration, biometric voice patterns, and screen activity, producing continuous streams of behavioural data (Moore, 2018). These data are integrated into algorithmic dashboards that determine worker rankings, contract renewals, coaching interventions, and automated disciplinary actions.

Policy and Managerial Logic

The managerial philosophy governing these environments exemplifies what Moore (2018) terms automated managerialism—a shift in which software, rather than supervisors, becomes the primary arbiter of legitimacy and performance. Based on fieldwork in Teleperformance centres in the United Kingdom, Philippines, and India, Moore documents how managers increasingly rely on algorithmic rankings to assess "productive minutes," "schedule adherence," and "behavioural consistency."

This approach replaces relational trust with computational trust. Workers are no longer evaluated through contextual judgment or interpersonal knowledge but through their ability to conform to algorithmic expectations. Deviations—regardless of situational context—are treated as objective evidence of underperformance. In this way, algorithmic systems redefine legitimacy as compliance with machine-generated norms rather than with human judgment, thereby institutionalizing a form of depersonalized managerial authority (Kellogg et al., 2020; Delfanti, 2021).

Worker Subjectivity and Digital Conformism

Empirical research on call centre workers in India and the Philippines shows that workers internalize algorithmic discipline and modify their behaviour in response to machine expectations. Agents frequently monitor dashboards more closely than supervisors, limit restroom breaks to avoid being classified as "non-productive time," and adjust speech patterns to satisfy voice-analytics technologies.

This behaviour reflects what Kellogg et al. (2020) describe as anticipatory conformity, whereby workers preemptively align their actions with algorithmic standards to minimize risk and maximize evaluation scores. This produces the phenomenon of Digital Conformism—a form of self-regulation in which workers actively monitor their own surveillance and adjust conduct to conform to algorithmic norms (Moore, 2018). Digital Conformism thus extends Foucault's notion of disciplinary power into computational infrastructures, transforming surveillance into an internalized mode of governance.

Outcomes and Psychosocial Strain

Extensive research links exposure to EPM systems with heightened stress, anxiety, emotional exhaustion, and burnout (Moore, 2019; Wood et al., 2021; Parent-Rocheleau & Parker, 2023). Because algorithmic systems lack contextual understanding, non-workplace factors—such as hostile customers, technical failures, network instability, or caregiving responsibilities—are frequently categorized as efficiency failures.

Over time, continuous monitoring blurs the distinction between meaningful labour and machine-induced compliance. Performance is no longer evaluated based on service quality, relational competence, or ethical judgment, but on adherence to algorithmic metrics. In this sense, Algorithmic Taylorism operates as a form of digital despotism—a technologically intensified labor discipline regime that eliminates relational judgment in favor of computational authority (Delfanti, 2021; Zuboff, 2019).

Case 2: Digital Meritocracy – Algorithmic Bias in the Ideology of Efficiency

Digital Meritocracy refers to the belief that algorithmic systems objectively identify talent and performance, thereby producing fair, merit-based outcomes (Ajunwa, 2020). This ideology assumes data-driven evaluations eliminate human bias, positioning algorithms as neutral arbiters. However, scholarship shows that such systems frequently reproduce cultural, cognitive, and neurotypical biases embedded in their design and training data (Noble, 2018).

AI-driven evaluation tools—such as HireVue, Pymetrics, and sentiment-analysis software—are widely used in fintech, consulting, and global HR systems, yet studies demonstrate that these technologies disproportionately disadvantage women, racial minorities, neurodivergent individuals, and non-Western communication styles (Ajunwa, 2020).

These systems enforce a narrow definition of "merit" privileging speed, assertiveness, and emotional neutrality while marginalizing relational labour and culturally diverse expressions of competence . Consequently, Digital Meritocracy operates as an ideological mechanism that masks structural inequality under the rhetoric of objectivity and efficiency.

The Ideology of Algorithmic Objectivity

The appeal of algorithmic evaluation stems from the belief that computation eliminates human bias. Yet empirical audits reveal that facial-analysis and emotion-recognition models struggle to accurately classify darker skin tones, non-Western facial expressions, and neurodivergent behavioural cues . Linguistic-analytics tools similarly favour Western speech patterns over Indian, Filipino, or African English (Mollick & Nanda, 2021). The ideology of "digital meritocracy" thus disguises structural bias under the veneer of scientific precision. Instead of leveling the playing field, algorithms reflect the cultural assumptions coded into their datasets.

Digital Favoritism and the Production of Homogeneity

When algorithmic scores become central to hiring, internal mobility, and engagement assessment, organisations begin privileging workers whose natural behaviours align with machine norms. Studies show that emotion-recognition systems reward constant positivity, extroversion, and neurotypical facial affect, while penalising culturally varied or understated communication styles (Bogen & Rieke, 2018). This produces Digital Favoritism, where only certain behavioural identities are privileged. Over time, organisational cultures become homogenized, suppressing diversity of personality, communication, and cultural identity in favour of machine-legible behaviour.

Psychosocial Risks, Identity Strain, and Trust Erosion

AI-based evaluation introduces psychological risks by pressuring employees to perform artificial versions of themselves. Remote workers report anxiety that sentiment-analysis models may misinterpret fatigue or stress as disengagement (Ajunwa, 2020). Neurodivergent employees often feel mischaracterised or penalised due to misalignment with AI-defined norms. As trust in algorithmic fairness erodes, workers view evaluation systems as opaque and unchallengeable, leading to disengagement and reduced organisational commitment (Wood et al., 2021). Digital meritocracy thus becomes a self-defeating system—promising neutrality while deepening existing inequities.

Case 3: Digital Humanism – Resistance and Accountability

Unlike the first two cases, which focus on algorithmic control, this case demonstrates how workers, unions, and regulatory bodies can challenge and reshape algorithmic governance. Across European logistics and delivery networks—including Amazon Europe, DPD, UPS, DHL, and Deliveroo—worker movements and institutional interventions have created new frameworks for algorithmic transparency and labour rights.

The Fight for Algorithmic Transparency

Investigations by worker councils and unions revealed that Amazon's productivity-tracking algorithms frequently misreported errors and assigned unrealistic workloads (Cant, 2021). At Deliveroo and DPD, algorithmic route assignment often ignored environmental or safety conditions, penalising workers for delays beyond their control (Tassinari & Maccarrone, 2020). These revelations led workers to demand transparency regarding the models, data inputs, error rates, and decision logic behind algorithmic evaluations.

Collective Agency and Ethical Governance

Through strikes, collective bargaining, GDPR-based data access requests, and multi-country union alliances, workers secured significant changes. Under pressure, companies were required to implement mandatory human review for algorithmic disciplinary decisions and provide explanations and appeal pathways for automated sanctions). These victories illustrate the emergence of ethical algorithmic governance, where workers actively shape the systems that evaluate them.

Policy and Regulatory Outcomes

Worker resistance has significantly influenced European digital labour governance. The EU Platform Work Directive and the European Union Artificial Intelligence Act mandate transparency, contestability, and meaningful human oversight in algorithmic decision-making affecting workers . Furthermore, Article 22 of the General Data Protection Regulation (GDPR) prohibits solely automated decisions that produce significant effects on individuals without meaningful human intervention.

These regulatory developments demonstrate that algorithmic management is not technologically inevitable but politically negotiable. Algorithmic governance emerges not as a neutral technical system but as a socio-technical construct shaped by legal frameworks, labour movements, and democratic processes. This case illustrates the practical realization of Digital Humanism, where technology is reoriented toward accountability, worker dignity, and shared governance.

Comparative Insights

Taken together, the three cases reveal how algorithmic governance restructures labour, redistributes managerial authority, and redefines workplace identity. The call-centre case illustrates how algorithmic Taylorism intensifies surveillance and quantification, transforming work into a data-driven disciplinary regime. The fintech case demonstrates how AI systems embed cultural and neurotypical bias under the rhetoric of objectivity, reinforcing workplace inequalities. The logistics case reveals that algorithmic control can be resisted and re-regulated through institutional, legal, and collective action. Across all cases, the key themes include the reshaping of worker subjectivity, the redefinition of organisational fairness, and the emergence of new governance structures to manage digital power.

Synthesis

These case studies show that algorithmic management is not merely a technical tool but a sociopolitical architecture that governs how labour is valued, monitored, and controlled. Algorithmic Taylorism substitutes relational confidence with continual digital monitoring; digital meritocracy promotes cultural and cognitive injustices under the pretense of being efficient; and digital humanism shows that democracy can adapt an algorithmic community (including its accountability) to operate through algorithmic systems in a new way.

The future of algorithmically created jobs depends on the balance of efficiency against dignity, automation against fairness, and data-driven reasoning against human value by organisations, government and workers together.

DISCUSSION AND FRAMEWORK

Algorithmic management has now changed the way organizations in service, fintech, and logistics operate through the reshaping of power, authority, and labour. Algorithmic management not only automates the work process of workers but also provides mechanisms for monitoring, making decisions, and defining efficiency. This includes a spectrum of control such as increased monitoring in call centres, bias in digital hiring processes and worker-led resistance in the logistical industry of Europe.

Algorithmic governance serves as more than just a technology innovation; it functions as a socio-political system wherein power is transferred from people to machines. Unlike traditional models of supervision and management that provide accountability through human interaction, algorithmic governance executes all three levels of management (monitoring, decision-making and defining efficiency) through a continuous cycle of collecting data, monitoring behaviour and utilizing predictive models to enforce employee discipline through the use of data systems as opposed to human relationships.

The findings from this study show that algorithms are not neutral or predetermined. These algorithms encode priorities for the organization (e.g., efficiency, standardization) and thus help shape individual worker outcomes (Kellogg, Valentine, & Christin, 2020; Moore, 2018). For example, a call centre dashboard prioritizes speed over emotional labour resulting in increased levels of stress experienced by employees, whereas fintech hiring tools have disadvantages based on neurodiversity and cultural differences (Ajunwa, 2020).Conversely, the logistics case shows that collective action and regulation can render algorithmic management contestable .

Overall, algorithmic management is a negotiated system, not a technological destiny. Ethical and equitable outcomes depend on how institutions regulate, monitor, and resist these systems, as developed through the thematic analysis and ethical governance framework.

Thematic Analysis

Algorithmic Power, Policy Alignment, and Regulatory Gaps

Algorithmic power refers to the capacity of automated systems to structure behavior, allocate resources, and define legitimacy within organizations, often without transparency or accountability (Katzenbach & Ulbricht, 2019). Algorithmic management tends to flourish in environments where regulatory protections are weak, outdated, or unenforced.

Technologies such as digital surveillance, biometric monitoring, sentiment analysis, and automated decision-making systems extend managerial control into workers' bodies, emotions, and cognitive rhythms, often without meaningful consent or recourse (Moore, 2018). In the call center case, algorithmic policies operated as managerial directives without regulatory review, allowing employers to monitor keystrokes, voice tone, and emotional states with minimal accountability .

Similarly, in fintech recruitment, AI-driven hiring systems were framed as a "digital meritocracy," presenting algorithmic decisions as objective even when they reproduced racial, cultural, and neurotypical biases (Ajunwa, 2020). The absence of enforceable standards for explainability and contestability allowed organizations to deploy opaque models without institutional oversight.

In contrast, European logistics firms operated within stronger regulatory ecosystems. Frameworks such as the GDPR, EU Labour Directives, and worker council laws constrain algorithmic power through rights to explanation, institutionalized human oversight, and data transparency (Wachter, Mittelstadt, & Floridi, 2017). These examples illustrate that algorithmic governance is always situated within a policy environment, and ethical outcomes depend on anticipatory regulation rather than reactive correction after harm occurs.

Governance Architectures and the Algorithmic Redistribution of Authority

Traditional workplace governance structures revolve around human managers who interpret context, negotiate expectations, and exercise discretion. Algorithmic systems disrupt this architecture by reallocating authority from supervisors to data infrastructures. Performance dashboards, behavioural scores, and automated warnings become the new arbiters of workplace legitimacy.

In the case of Teleperformance and Concentrix call centres, supervisors defer to algorithmic rankings rather than their own evaluations. The authority to assess performance is silently transferred to algorithmic systems that quantify behaviour continuously. This leads to a scenario where workers negotiate primarily with software rather than human managers.

Fintech hiring systems further institutionalise this shift: AI platforms evaluate candidate "potential," "fit," and "emotional stability" using computational models. Decisions that once required judgment are outsourced to black-box algorithms trained on historical patterns and biased data.

In contrast, the logistics sector case demonstrated that governance structures can be redesigned. Worker councils negotiated hybrid systems where algorithms provide data, but human managers retain authority over disciplinary actions. This hybrid governance—where AI informs but does not dominate—presents a more democratic model of algorithmic management.

Technological Infrastructures and the Logics of Algorithmic Control

Algorithmic systems do not merely monitor work; they reshape how work is organised. Each case illustrates a different technological logic:

- Call centres: real-time biometric and behavioural monitoring creates a regime of micro-discipline.
- Fintech and corporate hiring: facial analytics, speech pattern analysis, cognitive games, and sentiment detection enforce narrow behavioural norms.
- Logistics platforms: route optimisation algorithms, productivity trackers, and automated shift allocation dictate work pace, rest breaks, and workload distribution.

The unifying logic is behavioural standardisation: algorithms use historical patterns to prescribe optimal behaviour and penalise deviation. This produces a workplace where conformity to machine expectations becomes a condition for survival. Yet this logic can be disrupted when workers demand algorithmic transparency, as seen in the logistics case, leading to recalibration of the technologies themselves.

Organisational Risk, Economic Incentives, and the Efficiency Imperative

The adoption of algorithmic systems is primarily driven by organizational imperatives such as cost reduction, error minimization, and productivity optimization (Delfanti, 2021; Kellogg et al., 2020). Employers often view AI as a means to enforce efficiency without the relational complexities of human supervision.

- In call centers, automated dashboards reduce managerial workload while intensifying worker discipline (Moore, 2018).
- In fintech recruitment, efficiency is framed as rapid filtering of large candidate pools, even when such filtering reproduces bias (Ajunwa, 2020).
- In logistics, algorithmic shift allocation and productivity metrics minimize idle time and operational uncertainty but generate unsustainable workloads .

However, worker resistance in Europe demonstrates that efficiency cannot serve as the sole metric of organizational success. Organizations that neglect organizational risk—including reputational damage, regulatory sanctions, and long-term declines in worker well-being—face significant institutional consequences (Crawford, 2021). Ethical algorithmic governance, therefore, requires balancing efficiency with accountability, fairness, and human dignity (Floridi et al., 2018).

Worker Agency, Stakeholder Inclusion, and the Social Legitimacy of Algorithms

The three cases demonstrate that workers are not passive recipients of algorithmic power. Their reactions range from compliance and self-discipline (Digital Conformism) to active contestation (Digital Humanism).

- Call-centre workers internalise algorithmic expectations, often modifying speech, emotions, and behaviour to align with machine scoring.
- Fintech employees adapt by masking cultural identity or suppressing emotional variability to avoid penalisation.
- Logistics workers collectively resisted opaque algorithms, demanding transparency and fairness through union action.

Social legitimacy depends on whether workers feel they are active participants in algorithmic governance rather than objects of surveillance. Systems that exclude workers from design, oversight, and contestation inevitably generate mistrust. Ethical algorithmic workplaces must create channels for worker voice, human review, and participatory governance.

Framework For Ethical And Accountable Algorithmic Governance

Drawing on the thematic analysis, this framework outlines the necessary components for designing, implementing, and supervising algorithmic systems in workplaces. It emphasises transparency, accountability, human dignity, and democratic oversight.

Regulatory Anchoring and Worker Rights Protection

Ethical algorithmic systems are those that operate within enforceable legal boundaries that protect workers from invasive surveillance, discriminatory scoring models, and automated penalties (Floridi et al., 2018; Wachter et al., 2017). Such systems must guarantee:

- The right to explanation, allowing workers to understand how algorithmic decisions are made.
- Informed consent, particularly in relation to biometric, emotional, and behavioral monitoring.
- Limits on surveillance, including restrictions on continuous biometric tracking and affective analytics.
- Prohibitions on fully automated disciplinary actions, ensuring meaningful human oversight.

These protections institutionalize accountability and prevent the normalization of opaque digital control .

Transparent Governance and Hybrid Human–AI Oversight

Algorithms should inform, not replace, managerial decision-making. Hybrid governance ensures human review of automated flags, contextual interpretation of data, and prevention of machine-determined punishment. For trust,transparency about data use and scoring logic is essential.

Ethical System Design and Explainable Algorithmic Architecture

Ethical design requires bias audits, representative training datasets, and mechanisms to understand how decisions are made.

Explainable AI (XAI) empowers workers, managers, and regulators to interrogate algorithmic reasoning rather than accept it as unquestionable.

Risk-Aware Implementation and Socio-Technical Impact Assessment

Before deployment, algorithmic systems must undergo socio-technical impact assessments that evaluate psychosocial harm, cultural and cognitive bias, data inaccuracies, and long-term behavioral effects (Crawford, 2021). These assessments are necessary because algorithmic systems not only process data but reshape workplace norms, identities, and power relations.

For example, continuous performance scoring may lead to anxiety, burnout, and disengagement, while biased recruitment algorithms may systematically exclude marginalized groups (Parent-Rocheleau & Parker, 2023; Ajunwa, 2020). Risk-aware implementation ensures that organizations anticipate not only technical failures but the human consequences of digital control.

Inclusive Participation and Collective Bargaining

Workers must be active stakeholders, not passive subjects. Participatory mechanisms—worker councils, consultation committees, and union involvement—ensure algorithms reflect diverse needs and values. Inclusion reduces resistance and increases legitimacy.

Continuous Auditing, Monitoring, and Accountability Loops

Algorithmic systems evolve over time through model updates, data drift, and organizational adaptation. Ethical governance therefore requires continuous auditing, including periodic fairness assessments, real-time feedback mechanisms, evaluation of unintended effects, and accessible channels for workers to contest algorithmic decisions (Wachter et al., 2017).

Such accountability loops transform algorithmic governance from a static technical system into a dynamic, adaptive, and socially responsive process. Continuous oversight ensures that algorithms remain aligned with evolving ethical standards, legal frameworks, and worker needs.

CHALLENGES & IMPLICATIONS

As algorithmic systems become embedded across workplaces, they introduce new forms of managerial power that reshape labour relations, organisational governance, and worker autonomy. While these technologies promise efficiency, consistency, and data-driven decision-making, they also generate structural challenges affecting fairness, legitimacy, and the long-term sustainability of digital workplaces. Understanding these challenges is essential for regulators, organisations, unions, and civil society actors seeking to promote ethical and accountable algorithmic governance.

Governance Complexity and Algorithmic Accountability

A central challenge lies in the governance complexity created by algorithmic systems. Unlike traditional management, algorithmic decision-making diffuses authority across multiple layers—data collection tools, predictive models, proprietary scoring systems, and human supervisors who rely on software-generated dashboards (Katzenbach & Ulbricht, 2019). Because these systems are often designed by external vendors but deployed internally, responsibility becomes fragmented.

Workers who receive automated warnings or performance penalties frequently cannot identify whether accountability lies with:

1. the algorithm designer,
2. the employer deploying the tool,
3. the external vendor, or
4. the manager interpreting the output.

This fragmentation produces what scholars describe as accountability gaps, where harmful decisions occur without a clear locus of responsibility (Wachter, Mittelstadt, & Floridi, 2017; Pasquale, 2015). From the employee perspective, this opacity creates feelings of powerlessness, procedural injustice, and mistrust. Without transparent governance structures and appeal mechanisms, organizations risk unjust outcomes, workflow disruptions, and declining organizational legitimacy.

Implication: Organizations must establish clear accountability frameworks, define responsibility across the algorithmic lifecycle, and ensure accessible grievance and appeal systems for workers.

Misaligned Institutional Goals and the Ideology of Efficiency

Another challenge arises from the misalignment between technological logics and human-centred organizational values. Algorithmic systems are typically built around optimization principles—speed, accuracy, standardization, and continuous productivity (Delfanti, 2021; Kellogg, Valentine, & Christin, 2020). These priorities often conflict with broader workplace objectives such as fairness, inclusion, well-being, and psychological safety.

For example:

- In fintech hiring systems, efficiency-driven screening excludes culturally diverse and neurodivergent candidates (Ajunwa, 2020).
- In call-centre dashboards, real-time monitoring enhances productivity but undermines autonomy and mental health (Moore, 2019).
- In logistics routing systems, optimization prioritizes delivery speed at the expense of worker fatigue and safety.

From the employee perspective, this produces a sense that organizational values prioritize performance metrics over human dignity. The dominance of efficiency ideology weakens trust, erodes morale, and contributes to burnout and disengagement.

Implication: Ethical governance requires recalibrating organizational success metrics to include fairness, well-being, and sustainability alongside efficiency.

Risk, Bias, and the Fragility of Algorithmic Decision-Making

Algorithmic systems carry significant risks that organizations often underestimate. These include:

- Bias and discrimination embedded in training data, disproportionately affecting racial, linguistic, cultural, and neurodivergent groups (Noble, 2018).
- Technical errors, such as faulty emotion recognition, sensor inaccuracies, or data drift (Crawford, 2021).
- Context-blind metrics that fail to account for situational factors such as network failures, caregiving demands, or emotional strain (Moore, 2018).
- Single points of failure, where algorithmic misclassifications cascade into disciplinary action, deactivation, or job loss (Eubanks, 2018).

Because many systems function as black boxes, risks often remain invisible until harm has occurred. For employees, this fragility produces chronic stress, job insecurity, and a sense of algorithmic vulnerability, where livelihoods depend on opaque computational scores (Parent-Rocheleau & Parker, 2023).

Implication: Organizations must implement robust risk assessment, bias auditing, and human review mechanisms to prevent harm before deployment.

Worker Participation, Power Imbalances, and the Legitimacy Gap

Algorithmic systems are frequently designed and implemented without meaningful worker participation, producing a legitimacy gap in which employees feel acted upon rather than included in decisions shaping their labour (Aloisi & De Stefano, 2022). When workers lack voice:

- systems reflect managerial assumptions rather than lived workplace realities;
- surveillance becomes normalized without ethical justification;
- resistance manifests as burnout, disengagement, or subtle non-cooperation;
- digital despotism becomes entrenched as a governing norm.

From the employee perspective, exclusion from governance processes exacerbates power imbalances and weakens trust in organizational authority. The logistics case illustrates that worker participation—through unions, works councils, and algorithm audits—can rebalance power and enhance legitimacy . However, in many regions, weak labour protections and asymmetric power relations prevent such democratic engagement.

Implication: Sustainable algorithmic governance requires institutionalized worker participation in design, deployment, and oversight processes.

Policy and Practice Implications

These challenges carry significant implications for how institutions should design and regulate algorithmic workplaces. Ethical and sustainable governance requires anticipatory action across Two domains:

Policy Implications

Regulators must adopt frameworks that address automated decision-making, worker data rights, transparency obligations, and protections against algorithmic discrimination. Policies such as GDPR Article 22, algorithmic transparency, and algorithmic transparency EU platform directives mandates early models, but global expansion is needed to safeguard workers in diverse socio-economic contexts.

Organisational Practice Implications

Firms must shift from viewing algorithmic systems as tools for optimisation to viewing them as socio-technical infrastructures requiring ethical stewardship. This includes hybrid human–algorithm decision processes, explainable scoring systems, independent audits, and continuous oversight of psychosocial impacts.

Organisations that ignore these imperatives risk counter reputational damage, employee attrition, and legal challenges.

KEY FINDINGS

The assessment of algorithmic governance across diverse industries demonstrates that digital systems are fundamentally transforming how work is organized, monitored, and evaluated. What initially appeared as a technological upgrade for efficiency has evolved into a deeper restructuring of managerial authority and labor relations (Kellogg, Valentine, & Christin, 2020; Moore, 2018). Algorithms now function as workplace regulators—defining performance norms, directing behavior, and shaping access to opportunities. These findings confirm that algorithmic systems are not neutral tools but powerful infrastructures that govern work through data-driven logics, behavioral standardization, and subtle forms of control (Zuboff, 2019; Delfanti, 2021).

Algorithms Intensify Surveillance and Managerial Control

Across call centres, gig platforms, and logistics environments, algorithmic monitoring captures nearly every aspect of worker activity—voice tone, keystrokes, facial expressions, micro-pauses, and interaction patterns. This creates a workplace governed by constant visibility, where workers must perform according to machine-calibrated metrics. Supervisory discretion decreases, while algorithmic assessments gain authority.

The overall effect is a sharp intensification of surveillance and a shift towards highly granular, automated control.

Bias and Inequality Persist Under the Appearance of "Objectivity"

Despite claims of fairness, algorithmic systems frequently produce biased outcomes. Hiring tools may favour certain communication styles, cultural expressions, or personality traits. Behavioral analytics often misinterpret diverse emotional cues or linguistic patterns.

The appearance of neutrality makes these systems more powerful because workers cannot easily challenge their decisions—leading to a digital form of meritocracy that appears scientific but often reinforces existing social hierarchies.

Algorithmic Regimes Generate Psychosocial Stress and Self-Monitoring

The constant evaluation by algorithms creates heightened psychological pressure. Workers internalise the system's expectations, monitoring themselves to avoid penalties, warnings, or automatic ranking drops. Many suppress emotional variability, adapt speech patterns, limit breaks, and adjust behaviour to align with algorithmic norms.

This leads to chronic stress, identity strain, and a deep merging of work performance with digital evaluation, blurring the boundaries between genuine effort and machine-demanded conformity.

Opaque Algorithms Increase Workplace Power Imbalances

Employees often receive scores and decisions without understanding the underlying logic. Algorithmic opacity—how the system evaluates, classifies, or penalises—magnifies managerial authority. Workers cannot negotiate with the algorithm, appeal decisions effectively, or contextualize their performance.

This places employees at a structural disadvantage and deepens power asymmetry in the workplace, concentrating decision-making within the technological system and those who control it.

Forms of Digital Resistance Are Emerging in Response

Despite their structural power, algorithmic systems are not uncontested. Workers, unions, and advocacy groups within logistics networks, platform work, and service industries have begun demanding transparency, oversight, and human review. In some workplaces, collective action has forced organisations to redesign their monitoring systems, revise automated disciplinary tools, or introduce human intervention points.

This marks the emergence of a new phase—where digital management meets organised resistance.

Algorithmic Management Reflects Ideological, Not Neutral, Priorities

The spread of algorithmic workplace systems reflects more than technological progress; it reflects a managerial ideology centred on efficiency, quantification, behaviour standardisation, and predictive control.

These systems prioritise uniformity, measurable outputs, and behavioural consistency over creativity, emotional labour, and human variability.

The logic of the algorithm becomes the logic of the organisation itself, shaping workplace culture in profound ways.

Human-Centred Governance Is Necessary for Sustainable Digital Workplaces

The findings consistently show that algorithmic governance requires stronger oversight, transparency safeguards, and accountability mechanisms. Without these protections, algorithmic control can quickly shift toward excessive surveillance, discrimination, or unilateral power.

Human-centred governance, through clear policies, ethical guidelines, participatory and audits—is essential to balance technological efficiency with worker dignity and organisational fairness.

CONCLUSION

The rise of algorithm-based governance has deeply transformed how work is organized and experienced. What began as simple digital tools to improve efficiency has now become a powerful system that shapes how employees are managed, evaluated, and even understood. Human decisions are increasingly replaced by automated ones, and workers' actions, attitudes, and performance are often reduced to numbers, scores, and data points. As a result, many employees no longer feel seen as individuals but rather as measurable outputs, with little control over how their work is judged.

While organizations benefit from greater speed, consistency, and scalability, these gains often come at a human cost. Many workers experience increased stress, reduced autonomy, and fewer opportunities for self-expression. This highlights an important truth: algorithmic systems do not operate in isolation. They are built on assumptions about productivity, communication, and behavior that often reflect cultural and cognitive biases. Although algorithms are frequently presented as neutral, they can reinforce existing social hierarchies by favoring certain behaviors while marginalizing others.

At the same time, the chapter points to a hopeful development through digital humanism. Across Europe's logistics and platform labor sectors, workers and regulators are demanding greater transparency, accountability, and human oversight of algorithmic systems. This movement shows that algorithmic governance is not fixed—it can be shaped through collective action, regulation, and ethical design.

Ultimately, algorithmic governance stands at a crossroads. It has the potential to improve efficiency and collaboration, but without strong ethical safeguards, it risks creating workplaces marked by excessive surveillance, inequality, and loss of worker autonomy. The future of work depends on whether technology is used to control workers or to support them.

The chapter concludes that algorithms should not replace human judgment but work alongside it. When organizations combine innovation with fairness, transparency, and respect for human complexity, digital management can empower rather than dominate workers. The choices made today will determine whether future workplaces become more democratic and inclusive—or more restrictive and dehumanizing.

RECOMMENDATIONS / POLICY DIRECTIONS

As algorithmic systems reshape organisational structures, worker experience, and managerial authority, the need for coherent policy direction becomes increasingly urgent. Effective governance of algorithmic management requires a shift from reactive regulation to proactive, human-centred frameworks that align technological innovation with ethical, social, and organisational responsibilities. The following recommendations propose a structured set of interventions for policymakers, organisations, and regulatory bodies.

Strengthening Algorithmic Transparency and Explainability

A central policy priority is the establishment of strong transparency requirements for algorithmic management. As digital systems increasingly dictate hiring outcomes, productivity ratings, behavioural assessments, and disciplinary decisions, organisations must be obligated to disclose how these algorithms operate. Transparency should include clear explanations of the variables used to evaluate workers, the logic behind ranking models, and the specific data sources informing decision-making. When algorithms operate as opaque black boxes, they reinforce asymmetries of power and prevent workers from understanding or challenging unfair outcomes. By embedding transparency, organisations not only increase accountability but also build a more trustworthy digital work environment where employees can interact with algorithmic systems with clarity rather than uncertainty.

Embedding Meaningful Human Oversight

Algorithmic governance must incorporate human review at every stage of consequential decision-making. Automated systems should never serve as the sole authority for termination, performance warnings, hiring or promotion decisions. Human managers must retain interpretive authority to contextualize algorithmic outputs and evaluate whether machine-generated decisions align with organisational values and ethical norms. This form of oversight is not merely procedural; it protects against errors, biases, and misinterpretations that arise when complex human behaviour is assessed through digital proxies. By ensuring that managers critically assess algorithmic recommendations rather than accepting them as absolute, organisations preserve human agency within technologically mediated workplaces.

Reducing Algorithmic Bias and Ensuring Fairness

A key policy direction involves formalising mechanisms to detect, measure, and correct algorithmic bias. Many systems—especially those used for hiring, sentiment analysis, productivity scoring, and behavioural monitoring—are trained on datasets that encode cultural, racial, linguistic, and neurotypical biases. Without deliberate corrective measures, these biases become institutionalised as "digital objectivity." Organisations must, therefore, adopt regular bias audits, fairness validation protocols, and institutional review processes that identify discriminatory patterns in algorithmic outcomes. Ensuring fairness is more than a technical requirement—it is a crucial ethical obligation that determines whether digital workplaces reinforce inequity or move toward more inclusive models of governance.

Protecting Worker Data Rights and Privacy

As algorithmic systems increasingly rely on biometric data, emotional analytics, keystroke tracking, webcam surveillance, and behavioural profiling, protecting worker data rights becomes essential. Workers should have clear rights to access, understand, delete, or correct the data collected about them. Policies must restrict the use of intrusive monitoring tools, especially in remote-work environments where personal boundaries are already strained. Establishing strong consent standards, limiting data retention, and preventing repurposing of behavioural data for unrelated managerial decisions are critical steps. Protecting data rights is not only a matter of privacy but also a foundation for maintaining dignity, autonomy, and psychological safety in algorithmically monitored workplaces.

Building Participatory Governance and Worker Voice

Integrating participatory structures into algorithmic decision-making is essential for ethical and democratic governance. Workers must be consulted before algorithmic systems are introduced and continuously engaged throughout their deployment. This includes forming joint review committees, worker councils, or representative bodies that can evaluate system impacts, report problems, and suggest improvements. Participatory governance ensures that algorithmic management evolves through lived workplace realities rather than strictly technological assumptions. When workers have a meaningful voice, organisations benefit from nuanced insights that lead to safer, more equitable, and more effective digital systems.

Sector-Specific Regulatory Standards

Different industries experience algorithmic management in distinct ways, making sector-specific regulations crucial. High-surveillance sectors such as call centres, warehousing, transport, gig platforms, and fintech require specialised guidelines that address their unique risks. For instance, call centres may need restrictions on continuous biometric monitoring; logistics networks require safeguards against unrealistic algorithmic productivity benchmarks; and gig platforms need oversight to prevent opaque automated deactivation. Tailoring regulatory expectations to each sector ensures that governance frameworks remain grounded in operational realities rather than generic policy principles.

Advancing Algorithmic Literacy for Workers and Managers

A sustainable digital workplace requires improved algorithmic literacy among both workers and managers. Employees need to understand how performance metrics are generated, how behavioural analytics interpret their actions, and what rights they have when interacting with automated tools. Managers, in turn, must be trained to interpret algorithmic outputs critically and ethically, rather than treating software-generated scores as neutral facts. Building algorithmic literacy helps prevent misinformation, reduces fear and uncertainty, and encourages more balanced interactions between humans and machines.

Strengthening Public–Private Collaboration for Ethical AI Governance

Finally, long-term governance requires coordinated collaboration among governments, researchers, civil society organisations, unions, and private firms. Multi-stakeholder partnerships can support the creation of ethical certification systems, regulatory sandboxes, algorithmic audit infrastructures, and national oversight bodies. These collaborations ensure that algorithmic governance evolves with scientific evidence, labour rights principles, and technological innovation in balance. Rather than restricting innovation, such frameworks create a stable and ethical digital environment where efficiency and human dignity can coexist.

REFERENCES

Ajunwa, I. (2020). The automated video interview as a platform for systemic discrimination. *Harvard Law & Policy Review, 15*, 269–315. DOI: 10.15779/Z38RX93F1Q

Aloisi, A., & De Stefano, V. (2022). *Your boss is an algorithm: Artificial intelligence, platform work and labour*. Bloomsbury Publishing. DOI: 10.5040/9781509953219

Beer, D. (2017). The social power of algorithms. *Information Communication and Society*, *20*(1), 1–13. DOI: 10.1080/1369118X.2016.1216147

Bogen, M., & Rieke, A. (2018). *Help wanted: An examination of hiring algorithms, equity, and bias*. Upturn.https://www.upturn.org/reports/2018/help-wanted/

Cant, C. (2021). *Riding for Deliveroo: Resistance in the new economy*. Polity Press.

Costa, J. P., & Peterson, M. (2023). Artificial intelligence and the future of work: Ethical issues and policy challenges. *Ethics and Information Technology*, *25*(1), 1–12.

Couldry, N., & Mejias, U. A. (2019). *The costs of connection: How data is colonizing human life and appropriating it for capitalism*. Stanford University Press.

Crawford, K. (2021). *The atlas of AI: Power, politics, and the planetary costs of artificial intelligence*. Yale University Press., DOI: 10.56315/PSCF3-22Crawford

Curchod, C., Patriotta, G., Cohen, L., & Neysen, N. (2020). Working for an algorithm: Power asymmetries and agency in online labor markets. *Administrative Science Quarterly*, *63*(3), 643–676. DOI: 10.1177/0001839219867024

Delfanti, A. (2021). *The warehouse: Workers and robots at Amazon*. Pluto Press.16. Ethics Guidelines for Trustworthy AI. (2021). *High-Level Expert Group on Artificial Intelligence*. European Commission. DOI: 10.2307/j.ctv2114fnm

Eubanks, V. (2018). *Automating inequality: How high-tech tools profile, police, and punish the poor*. St. Martin's Press.

Floridi, L., Cowls, J., Beltrametti, M., Chatila, R., Chazerand, P., Dignum, V., . . . Vayena, E. (2018). AI4People—An ethical framework for a good AI society: Opportunities, risks, principles, and recommendations. *Minds and Machines, 28*(4), 689–707.s11023-018-9482-5

Foucault, M. (1977). *Discipline and punish: The birth of the prison*. Pantheon Books.

Katzenbach, C., & Ulbricht, L. (2019). Algorithmic governance. *Internet Policy Review*, *8*(4), 1–18. DOI: 10.14763/2019.4.1424

Kellogg, K. C., Valentine, M. A., & Christin, A. (2020). Algorithms at work: The new frontier of control in organizations. *The Academy of Management Annals*, *14*(1), 366–410. DOI: 10.5465/annals.2018.0174

Moore, P. V. (2018). *The quantified self in precarity: Work, technology and what counts*. Routledge.

Newlands, G. (2021). Algorithmic surveillance in the gig economy: The organization of work through Lefebvrian conceived space. *Organization Studies*, *42*(5), 719–737. DOI: 10.1177/0170840620937900

Noble, S. U. (2018). *Algorithms of oppression: How search engines reinforce racism*. New York University Press. DOI: 10.18574/nyu/9781479833641.001.0001

Parent-Rocheleau, X., & Parker, S. K. (2023). Algorithmic management: A review and research agenda. *Journal of Management*, *49*(1), 332–365. DOI: 10.1016/j.hrmr.2021.100838

Pasquale, F. (2015). *The black box society: The secret algorithms that control money and information*. Harvard University Press. DOI: 10.4159/harvard.9780674736061

Rosenblat, A., & Stark, L. (2016). Algorithmic labor and information asymmetries: A case study of Uber's drivers. *International Journal of Communication*, *10*, 3758–3784. https://ijoc.org/index.php/ijoc/article/view/4892

Sadowski, J. (2020). *Too smart: How digital capitalism is extracting data, controlling our lives, and taking over the world.* MIT Press., DOI: 10.7551/mitpress/12240.001.0001

Tassinari, A., & Maccarrone, V. (2020). The mobilisation of gig economy workers: A comparison of food delivery workers in Italy and the UK. *Industrial Relations Journal*, *51*(4), 350–371. DOI: 10.1111/irj.12292

Wachter, S., Mittelstadt, B., & Floridi, L. (2017). Why a right to explanation of automated decision-making does not exist in the General Data Protection Regulation. *International Data Privacy Law*, *7*(2), 76–99. DOI: 10.1093/idpl/ipx005

Wood, A. J., Graham, M., Lehdonvirta, V., & Hjorth, I. (2019). Good gig, bad gig: Autonomy and algorithmic control in the global gig economy. *Work, Employment and Society*, *33*(1), 56–75. DOI: 10.1177/0950017018785616 PMID: 30886460

Zuboff, S. (2019). *The age of surveillance capitalism: The fight for a human future at the new frontier of power*. PublicAffairs.

Chapter 12
Present but Withheld:
Everyday Practices of Digital Minimalism in Academic WhatsApp

Harika Suklun
http://orcid.org/0000-0003-1016-268X
Batman University, Turkey

ABSTRACT

This chapter explores how academics in Turkey use WhatsApp groups in ways that reduce visibility and interaction, forming a subtle practice of digital minimalism. These groups often encourage openness and responsiveness, yet many members stay silent, do not upload photos, use vague or symbolic names, and avoid status updates. While such behavior may seem passive, it often reflects a deliberate strategy to manage emotional effort, presence, and exposure in academic communication. Rather than interpreting this as disengagement, the chapter sees it as a meaningful form of agency. Drawing on observations from student, research, and professional WhatsApp groups, the chapter identifies patterns such as passive membership, minimal identity disclosure, and limited availability. These strategies show how users handle group norms while preserving boundaries. By viewing these behaviors through communication culture and institutional dynamics, the chapter reframes digital silence as an intentional form of participation on one's own terms.

INTRODUCTION

In contemporary academic life, WhatsApp groups have become central tools of coordination, collaboration, and community. They mediate communication between

DOI: 10.4018/979-8-3373-4531-4.ch012

students and instructors, enable research teams to organize tasks, and sustain informal networks among colleagues. Yet, behind the constant stream of messages and digital connectivity, a quieter set of practices exists: those of withdrawal, silence, or minimal presence. This chapter investigates these subtle yet significant behaviors through the lens of digital minimalism, focusing on how academic users in Turkey negotiate visibility, availability, and attention in WhatsApp group settings.

As mobile messaging applications become increasingly embedded in the fabric of academic work and sociality, users are expected to be constantly reachable, responsive, and expressive. These expectations are not simply social but are structurally embedded in what has been termed algorithmic culture, an environment where engagement is not only encouraged but normalized through technical affordances such as read receipts, online status indicators, and ranking algorithms (Striphas, 2015; Bucher, 2020). In such environments, refusal to engage, or the choice to remain digitally silent, can be interpreted as deviant, inattentive, or even antisocial.

However, this chapter argues that digital silence and minimalism should not be dismissed as mere neglect or personal idiosyncrasy. Rather, they can be understood as everyday tactics of resistance, self-preservation, and meaning-making. Drawing on Goffman's (1959) theory of self-presentation, Scott's (1985) notion of infrapolitics, and Bauman's (2000) insights into the liquid conditions of modern identity, digital minimalism appears not as disengagement per se, but as a recalibration of engagement. Users are not absent; they are present but withheld, strategically choosing when and how to signal their participation.

Beyond mere identity management, digital minimalism in professional contexts often manifests as strategic silence, a deliberate act of non-participation that carries pragmatic significance (Dakoru, 2025). Unlike physical silence, digital silence is a timestamped and socially legible act that allows users to navigate high-stress academic environments by managing emotional regulation and boundary setting (Ali et al., 2024). This form of 'withheld presence' acts as a resource-saving mechanism where silence is reimagined as a strategic communicative tool shaped by institutional power dynamics.

In the Turkish academic context, where both institutional and cultural expectations shape communicative behavior, these choices become especially nuanced. Academic WhatsApp groups often blur the boundaries between professional obligations and personal space, between peer collaboration and hierarchical surveillance. As such, practices like using a flower emoji instead of a personal photo, maintaining a blank status message, or muting notifications for months at a time, emerge not simply as practical decisions but as ideological gestures, ways of reclaiming autonomy in hyperconnected spaces.

This chapter builds on emerging scholarship in digital sociology and media studies that emphasizes how silence, invisibility, and minimal engagement function within platformized systems of labor and communication (Gray & Suri, 2020; Karppi, 2018). It positions digital minimalism as an ideological practice, a patterned response to the structural pressures of platform-based communication. Through ethnographic and observational analysis of academic WhatsApp groups in Turkey, the chapter reveals how minimalism functions as a cultural logic that redefines what it means to be "active," "present," or "engaged" in digital environments.

LITERATURE REVIEW

The increasing entanglement of everyday academic life with digital technologies has transformed not only the pace but also the expectations of presence and responsiveness among academic users. Messaging platforms such as WhatsApp now serve as ambient infrastructures of communication and coordination (Selwyn, 2016), especially within higher education ecosystems where formal and informal boundaries frequently collapse. Recent scholarship has examined WhatsApp's utility in education, highlighting its roles in knowledge sharing, coordination, and social presence (Baishya & Maheshwari, 2020; Cetinkaya, 2017). However, these studies primarily focus on visible interaction such as message exchanges, group activities, and learning outcomes while neglecting the invisible, affectively charged work of disengagement or selective non-participation.

As digital technologies increasingly mediate professional relationships, a new body of literature has turned toward digital withdrawal, platform resistance, and selective participation. For instance, Brubaker (2020) explores how individuals engage in "strategic ignorance" by muting notifications or archiving group threads as a form of self-protection in overloaded digital environments. This framing resonates with Baumer et al.'s (2014) concept of non-use, which is not simply technological abstention but a reflexive, contextually grounded choice shaped by socio-cultural and institutional conditions. Moreover, the concept of digital minimalism, often discussed in popular discourse (Newport, 2019), has gained academic attention as a framework for analyzing intentional reductions in digital engagement. Within the academic context, this practice is not merely about individual preference but reflects negotiations of power, hierarchy, and emotional labor (Gill, 2009; Svelch, 2023). Quietness, then, becomes a meaningful communicative strategy, particularly in group settings where continuous visibility is subtly demanded but rarely mandated.

In the context of Türkiye, studies by Durgungöz (2022) and Minlo (2024) have explored WhatsApp as a professional tool used by educators, emphasizing its perceived immediacy, accessibility, and emotional burdens. These studies underline how regional academic cultures shape digital expectations differently, often amplifying silent tensions between obligation and burnout. However, none of these studies directly examine the profile-level self-presentation or the symbolic meanings encoded in non-verbal participation cues like display pictures, names, and "About" statuses. This chapter builds on these works by introducing a novel methodological lens: analyzing WhatsApp profile data, including user images, pseudonyms, and personal slogans, to uncover silent practices of presence and withdrawal. Unlike traditional content analysis of chat transcripts, this approach foregrounds the ways users curate identity and visibility in passive forms, offering a fresh perspective on ambient digital subjectivity in academic life.

By foregrounding quiet or semi-visible practices such as selective profile curation, ambiguous self-identification, or muted presence within WhatsApp academic groups, this chapter expands the conceptual terrain of digital minimalism. These behaviors, often overlooked in studies focused on overt content or platform metrics, are reinterpreted here as culturally meaningful acts of communicative restraint. Building on the literature above, the following section outlines the methodological approach employed to explore how such practices are enacted and interpreted within a specific academic WhatsApp group in Türkiye.

THEORETICAL FRAMEWORK

Digital minimalism is often positioned in mainstream discourse as a self-improvement strategy, a productivity tool designed to help individuals reduce screen time and reclaim attention (Newport, 2019). While this framing emphasizes personal agency, it overlooks the structural, cultural, and institutional forces that shape how individuals relate to digital environments. This chapter reframes digital minimalism not as a lifestyle choice but as an ideological and culturally embedded practice, emerging at the intersection of digital labor, platform surveillance, and academic stratification. To explore this complexity, we draw on an interdisciplinary range of sociological, cultural, and media theories, which allow us to interpret muted participation, ambiguous digital presence, and intentional silence as meaningful social actions within contextually specific academic communities.

Identity and Power in Digital Spaces

Erving Goffman's (1959) dramaturgical approach to self-presentation provides a foundation for understanding identity performance in WhatsApp groups. Here, the front stage is curated through profile pictures, emojis, and message tone, while backstage behaviors are masked by silence or minimal engagement. What is withheld can be as communicative as what is expressed.

Michel Foucault's (1988) concept of technologies of the self-expands on this, illustrating how individuals internalize institutional norms, like constant availability or performative enthusiasm, and discipline themselves accordingly. Digital minimalism, in this light, becomes a micro-political act: the refusal to over-perform in spaces of soft surveillance.

Zygmunt Bauman's (2000) idea of liquid modernity reminds us that in today's unstable environments, especially in academia, users are reluctant to overinvest in relationships or networks that may be temporary. Digital silence may represent relational caution in liquid institutions.

Scott (1990) offers a vocabulary of everyday resistance to understand these behaviors as low-risk, symbolic deflections of institutional expectations. Muted notifications, absence of profile images, or the use of default statuses all function as subtle refusals of imposed digital norms.

Cultural Logics Across Academic Subgroups

To understand how digital minimalism varies between faculty, graduate students, and undergraduates, we must consider the cultural hierarchies and symbolic boundaries embedded in academic life. For this, several cultural theorists are helpful:

Geert Hofstede: Power Distance and Uncertainty Avoidance

Hofstede's cultural dimensions' theory (2001) helps explain how power distance and uncertainty avoidance manifest in digital interactions. Faculty members may maintain greater distance through minimalist practices as a way to assert status, whereas graduate students, positioned between authority and dependency, may engage in selective visibility as a way to navigate both upward and downward social expectations. Undergraduates, often uncertain of norms, may oscillate between over-participation and withdrawal as they negotiate belonging and evaluation.

Clifford Geertz: Thick Description and Local Meaning

Drawing from Clifford Geertz's (1973) interpretive anthropology, this chapter treats minimalist practices not as universal behaviors but as culturally meaningful acts. What counts as "engagement" or "silence" varies by group norms. For instance, using a flower emoji instead of a real photo may signal modesty or playfulness among undergraduates but might be read as strategic ambiguity among graduate students or quiet dissent among faculty.

Mary Douglas: Group and Grid

Mary Douglas's (1978) group-grid theory helps to analyze WhatsApp group cultures as micro-communities with distinct orientations to authority and individualism. Faculty groups may reflect high-grid/high-group dynamics (structured roles, strong norms), while student groups may be more fluid or fragmented. Digital minimalism in each setting is thus not only a personal stance but a cultural adaptation to group logic.

Symbolic Capital and Platform Governance

Pierre Bourdieu's (1986) concept of symbolic capital explains how visibility, such as being "seen" by superiors in group chats, can contribute to one's academic reputation. The choice to remain less visible, then, is not merely passive but a withholding of symbolic capital, especially among those already secure in their status (e.g., tenured faculty). Zuboff (2019) push us further into questions of data ethics and platform capitalism. If every click, view, and reply is potentially commodified, then choosing not to engage or to do so obliquely is a tactic of data resistance. Bucher (2018) emphasizes that users act based on algorithmic imaginaries, their perceptions of how the system might interpret or rank their actions. For example, some graduate students may mute groups to avoid emotional overload but still feel pressure to "check in" so as not to fall behind. van Dijck (2013) frames this within platformed sociality, where interpersonal communication is shaped by corporate infrastructures.

BRIDGING THEORY AND EMPIRICAL ANALYSIS

These theoretical insights collectively allow us to reframe digital minimalism as a culturally situated, power-conscious, and context-specific practice. By comparing its enactment across faculty, graduate students, and undergraduates, we uncover not only different tactics of withdrawal but different logics of engagement rooted in status, role, and group belonging. The following empirical sections explore how these logics play out across academic WhatsApp groups in Turkey, focusing on modes of symbolic resistance, boundary-making, and selective visibility.

BACKGROUND AND RATIONALE

WhatsApp groups have become an integral part of academic life, functioning as informal digital infrastructures where coordination, resource sharing, peer support, and professional updates routinely occur. From student cohorts to departmental teams, these messaging platforms operate as semi-private spaces that blend formal obligations with social dynamics. Unlike highly visible practices on public-facing platforms such as Twitter or LinkedIn, WhatsApp interactions are governed by ambient expectations of participation, attention, and affective presence.

However, the dominance of "always-on" communication obscures another layer of behavior: intentional silence, partial withdrawal, and strategic invisibility. While the digitalization of academia has been widely discussed in terms of connectivity, productivity, and platform dependency (Selwyn, 2016; Williamson, 2017), relatively little attention has been paid to how academic users actively resist, negotiate, or restructure their communicative behaviors within these systems. This chapter responds to that gap by exploring digital minimalism as practiced in academic WhatsApp groups in Türkiye, a context where global techno-cultural norms intersect with local academic hierarchies. Defined here as a deliberate and mindful reduction of digital engagement, digital minimalism is positioned not as neglect, but as a culturally meaningful and ideologically informed stance.

Unlike previous studies that focus primarily on message content, engagement metrics, or usage frequency, this study employs profile-level analysis, specifically examining users' about sections, profile photos, and name formats. These elements are understood as ambient signals through which individuals curate their identity, signal availability, or assert distance.

The enactment of these minimalist strategies is inextricably tied to platform affordances, the action possibilities provided by the digital environment (Bucher & Helmond, 2018). WhatsApp's 'architecture of availability,' characterized by features such as 'last seen' timestamps and 'read receipts,' creates an environment of ambient visibility that demands constant responsiveness. When users adopt minimalist profiles, they are actively resisting these social affordances to reclaim agency over their digital rhythm and limit the platform's intrusive reach.

In many cases, users insert personal mottos, job titles, or abstract reflections into the "About" section, offering a form of passive self-presentation. By focusing on how users modulate their presence, often choosing to be "present but withheld," this chapter sheds light on the cultural and emotional dimensions of quiet digital practices in academic group communication. It aims to uncover how power dynamics, institutional expectations, and emotional labor are negotiated through selective participation and curated silence.

RESEARCH QUESTIONS

While much has been written about the affordances and intensities of digital communication in academic settings, the practices of intentional silence, symbolic disengagement, and digital boundary-making remain underexplored. This chapter seeks to investigate these practices through the lens of digital minimalism, specifically within academic WhatsApp groups in Türkiye. The inquiry is guided by the following research questions:

- How do academic users; faculty, graduate students, and undergraduates engage in selective participation or conscious silence within WhatsApp groups?
- What every day self-presentation strategies signal a digital minimalist stance in academic messaging environments?
- How are power dynamics, institutional expectations, and emotional labor negotiated through "present but withheld" behaviors across academic subgroups?

By addressing these questions, the study aims to uncover the cultural logic behind minimalist digital practices and their broader implications for identity, autonomy, and resistance in platform-mediated academic life.

METHODOLOGY AND ETHICAL CONSIDERATIONS

This study adopts a qualitative, interpretive methodology to explore how digital minimalism is practiced and signified in academic WhatsApp groups in Türkiye. A qualitative approach is appropriate for this research because the goal is not to quantify usage patterns, but to understand the meaning, context, and intent behind practices of silence, non-responsiveness, or low visibility phenomena often overlooked in studies that focus solely on active engagement or message content (Silverman, 2020; Denzin & Lincoln, 2018). By focusing on visual and textual cues embedded in profile data and group interaction environments, this study treats WhatsApp as a socio-cultural space where digital subjectivity and resistance are enacted. To operationalize this approach, the data were analyzed using a thematic coding approach, where profile elements such as usernames and status messages were categorized into recurring patterns of digital minimalism. This manual coding process enabled a nuanced understanding of the symbolic, cultural, and ideological meanings embedded in low-participation or low-visibility behaviors (Saldaña, 2021).

Cultural Logics Across Academic Subgroups

To understand how digital minimalism varies between faculty, graduate students, and undergraduates, we must consider the cultural hierarchies and symbolic boundaries embedded in academic life. For this, several cultural theorists are helpful:

Data Collection and Scope

Although there are many academic WhatsApp groups with large memberships, such as *Management Science* (650 members), *Academic Publication Announcements* (1,024 members), and *Project Announcements* (1,024 members), individuals often belong to multiple groups simultaneously. For this study, the *Academic Survey Sharing Group* was selected due to its moderate size and focused purpose. The dataset comprises three WhatsApp groups commonly used in academic contexts.

Academic Survey Sharing Group

A large-scale national WhatsApp group with 722 members, primarily composed of academics and graduate students from various universities across Türkiye. For this study, a subset of 565 profiles, those listed in alphabetical order from A to M, was analyzed. This partial dataset was selected due to WhatsApp's security and display limitations, which restricted the ability to load the full member list at once.

Graduate Academic Writing and Presentation Course Group

A closed class group with 33 members, used for coordination and academic communication in the MBA course.

Undergraduate Sociology Course Group

A classroom WhatsApp group with 44 undergraduate students, used for announcements, peer interaction, and informal discussion.

A total of 642 publicly visible WhatsApp profiles were systematically analyzed. Profile data included: Usernames (e.g., real names, initials, pseudonyms), Profile photos (e.g., personal photos, symbolic images, blank avatars), and About messages (e.g., quotes, greetings, religious expressions, blank). Data were collected through systematic screenshotting conducted over several sessions between June and August 2025, using a consistent protocol. Screenshots were then sanitized by manually removing phone numbers, institutional affiliations, and any sensitive or personally identifiable information. This process was critical for maintaining participant confidentiality, especially in large groups where individuals might not be aware they are under observation, despite their information being publicly visible to fellow members.

The resulting profiles were then categorized into thematic clusters reflecting different digital self-presentation strategies (e.g., symbolic images, anonymity, professional branding, religious identifiers, or complete minimalism). This manual coding process enabled a nuanced understanding of the symbolic, cultural, and ideological meanings embedded in low-participation or low-visibility behaviors (Saldaña, 2021).

Justification for Method

The choice to study profile metadata, rather than message content, was deliberate. In academic WhatsApp groups, especially those with hierarchical or cross-institutional structures, much of the communicative power lies in presence, visibility, and identity signaling rather than frequent verbal participation. By focusing on profile configurations, this research captures subtle yet potent forms of digital expression and resistance that align with the chapter's theoretical grounding in everyday resistance (Scott, 1990), digital self-presentation (Goffman, 1959), and surveillance capitalism (Zuboff, 2019). This also aligns with visual and cultural methods that emphasize interpretation of semiotic choices in online environments (Rose, 2016; Kozinets, 2020). Such practices often signal membership, status, or intentional ambiguity, and are particularly meaningful when viewed through the lens of platformed academic culture.

Ethical Considerations

Although all data were collected from publicly visible group content, this research adheres to key ethical principles outlined in qualitative and internet research guidelines (British Psychological Society, 2021; Eynon, Fry, & Schroeder, 2008). Consent was not individually obtained from participants, given that: The study did not involve any private messaging or direct interaction. Following the Ethical Guidelines 3.0 set by the Association of Internet Researchers (Franzke et al., 2020), this study prioritized the protection of 'digital subjectivity' even when dealing with technically accessible profile data. Recognizing that WhatsApp groups are 'semi-public' spaces where users may retain an expectation of privacy, the research utilized a 'minimization of harm' approach. This involved not only anonymization but also an analytical focus on metadata and visual patterns rather than private conversational content, ensuring the research remained within ethical standards (Rogers, 2021).

No personal identifiers or contact information were retained. The analysis focused on aggregated patterns, not individual profiles, and the WhatsApp groups analyzed were pre-existing and not created for research purposes. Still, the analysis recognizes the sensitivity of visibility in closed digital spaces. All efforts were made to anonymize findings, present aggregated results, and avoid profiling specific individuals. The study aims not to evaluate user behavior, but to interpret collective patterns of digital cultural resistance and adaptation.

Profile-Based Digital Minimalism: Naming, Visibility, and Self-Presentation

This section explores how academic users construct their digital identities on WhatsApp through naming practices, visibility choices, and self-presentation strategies. Given the differing institutional positions, communicative expectations, and identity performances between faculty members and students, the analysis is conducted in two parts. Faculty and student profiles are examined separately to better capture role-based nuances in digital minimalism, including the use of symbolic names, professional identifiers, profile photos, and expressive "About" messages. The separation allows for a more precise understanding of how academic hierarchy intersects with digital visibility and participation practices.

Faculty Members' Digital Presence

In analyzing the profiles of 565 members from the Academic Survey Sharing Group (Akademik Anket Paylaşım Grubu), we identified key patterns of digital minimalism enacted through profile elements such as usernames, profile photos, and status messages. These patterns offer valuable insights into how academic users negotiate visibility, identity, and participation.

Symbolic and Ambiguous Usernames

As detailed in Table 1, a substantial number of participants opted for symbolic identifiers over recognizable names. This patterns suggests a 'shadow presence' where the user maintains group access while intentionally obscuring their searchable identity to minimize social accountability.

Table 1. Symbolic and ambiguous usernames

Profile Type	Count Approx.	Percentage
Full Name Displayed	~158	28%
First Name Only	~198	35%
Initials or Abbreviations	~124	22%
No Name (emoji, number, etc.)	~85	15%

Naming Practices and Partial Visibility

The naming practices captured in Table 2 highlight what appears to be a tension between professional integration and personal privacy. While a minority maintained full-name visibility, the prevalence of first-name-only or initial-based profiles may suggest a cautious navigation of the 'ambient visibility' inherent in academic WhatsApp groups

Table 2. Naming practices and partial visibility

Description	Count	Percentage (Approx.)
Real name and a profile photo (usually a portrait)	88	16%
First name only (without last name)	112	20%
e.g., "MY", "AB", or nicknames	53	9%
Phone numbers only (WhatsApp default display)	49	9%
Default icon, no photo set	121	21%
Pets, scenery, flowers, objects	89	16%
Short textual expressions	53	9%

This table likely reflects a broad range of self-presentation strategies, many of which align with identity theories in digital sociology. For example, the use of names, academic cues, and expressive quotes may serve as identity signals, which could be linked to the frequency of group engagement (e.g., active sharers vs. silent members).

Profile Photos and Emotional Distance

Visual data in Table 3 reveals that nearly a third of participants utilized 'visual shields' either blank avatars or non-human imagery to maintain emotional distance. This strategy effectively reduces the user's digital footprint and discourages informal interpersonal overtures within the professional group

Table 3. Profile photos and emotional distance

Picture Type	Notable Examples	Interpretation
Personal portraits	Selfies, headshots	Traditional self-representation; more likely to engage
Pets	Cats, dogs	Emotional expression, often humorous or intimate
Nature/scenery	Forest, oceans, sunsets	Projecting serenity, values, or mood
Academic symbols	Books, diplomas, lecture halls	Strong identification with profession
Artistic/abstract	Color shapes, symbols	Visual ambiguity; indirect self-presentation

By contrast, members who used personal or professional headshots tended to also include informative or expressive status messages, an indicator of stronger digital presence.

"About" Section as Reflective Boundary-Making

Rather than the more dynamic WhatsApp Status feature, many participants appear to utilize the static "About" section (Table 4). While some used professional identifiers like "Asst. Prof. Dr.," others inserted existential or philosophical quotes, such as: "*Ölümün olduğu yerde daha ciddi ne olabilir ki*" ("What could be more serious than death?"). These choices may suggest that for some users, even minimal platform affordances like the "About" section can become vital tools for narrative construction and identity signaling. Such expressions could be interpreted as a poetic or emotionally introspective form of visibility that exists alongside more formal academic markers.

Table 4. About section as reflective boundary-making

Original (TR)	English Translation	Interpretation
Ölümün olduğu yerde daha ciddi ne olabilir ki...	"What could be more serious than death..."	Existential, possibly melancholic tone
Bilgi paylaştıkça çoğalır	"Knowledge grows when shared"	Collaborative mindset, academic alignment
Elhamdülillah	"Praise be to God"	Religious identity or gratitude expression
Hayat kısa, kuşlar uçuyor	" Life is short, the birds are flying"	Poetic, fleetingness of life
Asst. Prof. Dr. – Sociology – Nowhere University		Institutional and academic identity signaling
…… or blank		Possibly passive or privacy-conscious

These expressions may suggest a poetic, emotionally introspective identity, indicating that for some users, even minimal platform affordances like the "About" section can become tools for narrative construction and identity signaling. Those who shared such reflective quotes seemed more likely to use formal names and profile photos, and were more frequently observed participating in group discussions.

Passive Membership and Participation Gaps

Although all group members are technically allowed to post, most do not. Members who used symbolic usernames or blank about sections were less likely to initiate or engage in conversations, aligning with prior observations that limited self-disclosure often correlates with silent participation (Turkle, 2011; Lomborg, 2017). Professional anxieties, fear of being judged, or the hierarchical nature of academic culture in Türkiye may also inhibit participation.

Strategic Status Messaging and Temporal Boundaries

A smaller group of users expressed temporal withdrawal through their status messages. For example:

"Please do not write unless urgent"

"I will respond after New Year"

Graduate Students' Digital Presence

Graduate students, like faculty members, exhibit a wide range of digital minimalism behaviors on WhatsApp. Their profile choices often reflect transitional professional identities, balancing academic aspirations with social boundaries. The following analysis is structured in parallel to the categories used for faculty members.

Naming Practices and Visibility

Among the 33 graduate student profiles analyzed, only 9 profiles (27%) displayed full names, while others opted for first names only, initials, or even non-identifiable symbols. Some examples include single letters or decorative icons in place of names. This mirrors the cautious self-disclosure strategies observed among junior academics. Profiles with full names were more likely to contain academic titles such as "Res. Asst." or "M.A. Candidate," suggesting alignment with professional identity.

Profile Photo Use

Roughly 15 students (45%) used a personal photograph, while the remaining students opted for scenic images, objects, pets, or no image at all (default silhouette). Like faculty members, those who included personal photos often had stronger academic signals in their usernames or statuses, pointing to a more integrated or publicly confident digital identity. Those without personal photos generally displayed lower group engagement.

Status Message Content

The "About" section revealed varied approaches to self-expression. Some students included motivational phrases such as:

"Dream big, work hard"

"You exist as much as you are free"

"Exam season, don't expect a reply soon"

Others left this section entirely blank or retained WhatsApp's default message. Profiles with quotes tended to use them for boundary-setting (e.g., limiting communication) or identity signaling (philosophical/reflective stance).

Symbolic Profiles and Anonymity

Approximately 30% of the students used usernames that were either non-verbal, symbolic, or incomplete. Many of these users had no profile photo and an empty "About" section, creating a triple-layered anonymity. These profiles reflected a strong form of digital minimalism, signaling presence without identity, echoing theories of strategic invisibility in mediated academic life.

Silent Participation Patterns

As demonstrated in Table 5, in the WhatsApp group with 33 graduate students, only a handful regularly contributed messages or initiated discussions. The majority were passive observers. While everyone had access to post, participation appeared constrained by academic hierarchy, uncertainty, or norms of silence. Users with anonymous profiles tended to be the most silent, reinforcing the correlation between low profile disclosure and minimal group visibility.

Table 5. Silent participation patterns

Category	# of Students	Percentage %
Full Name	9	27
Partial Name (First name, initials, etc.)	15	45
Symbolic or Unidentifiable Names	9	27
Personal Photo	15	45
Non-personal Photo (Scenery, Object, etc.)	10	30
No Photo	8	24
Motivational/Philosophical Status	11	33
Default/Empty Profiles	22	67
Symbolic/Empty Profiles	10	30
Active Participants	5	15
Silent Observers	28	85

Note: Although the graduate group consisted of 33 enrolled students, some categories in the table may reflect totals greater than 33 due to overlapping characteristics or temporary group membership fluctuations (e.g., students leaving and rejoining, or the presence of teaching assistants). Individual profiles were coded across multiple dimensions (e.g., name format, photo type, status), so one user may appear in more than one category.

The table above provides a categorized breakdown of self-presentation strategies among graduate students in the academic WhatsApp group. While the visibility patterns mirror those of faculty members in some respects, key differences emerge. A significant portion of graduate students use only their first names or initials, suggesting a cautious engagement with academic identity. Symbolic or ambiguous usernames, such as emojis, punctuation marks, or motivational phrases, also appear frequently, reflecting a personalized yet withdrawn digital presence. Compared to faculty members, fewer graduate students display full academic titles or formal profile photos, which may indicate transitional identity positions within the academic hierarchy. Notably, a large number of students leave their "About" section empty or include quotes that hint at emotional fatigue, disillusionment, or a desire for autonomy. These minimalist choices suggest a nuanced balancing act between visibility and privacy, and between professional aspiration and emotional distancing within academic digital spaces.

Undergraduate Students' Digital Presence

The undergraduate student profiles reveal a clear trend toward informal and semi-anonymous digital self-presentation. The majority of users either used only their first name or opted for nicknames, emojis, or symbolic characters. Full names were rare, suggesting a reluctance to fully associate one's formal identity with the WhatsApp group space. Profile pictures followed a similar pattern, with many displaying pets, cartoons, or aesthetic imagery rather than professional photos. "About" sections were often left blank, or included humorous or inspirational quotes, reflecting an expressive but non-academic orientation. This indicates that undergraduates approach group membership with a more playful or passive stance, possibly viewing the group as a secondary communication channel rather than a formal academic space. Those with minimal or symbolic profiles were also less visible in the group's message history, reinforcing the connection between reduced self-disclosure and digital minimalism. These findings align with previous studies on youth digital culture, where selective participation is used as a strategy to balance privacy, identity experimentation, and social belonging.

Cross-Group Comparison

Across all three groups, faculty members, graduate students, and undergraduate students, distinct patterns of digital self-presentation emerged, revealing a spectrum of visibility, identity signaling, and minimalist practices (Table 6.) Faculty members exhibited the most formal and professional presence, often including full names, academic titles, and profile photos that reflect their institutional roles. Their "About" sections frequently conveyed philosophical or professional messages, indicating a deliberate construction of identity.

Table 6. Cross-group comparison

Category	Faculty Members	Graduate Students	Undergraduate Students
Use of Full Name	High (many include academic titles)	Moderate (some use full name or initials)	Low (mostly first names, nicknames, or symbols)
Use of Professional Title	Common ("Dr.", "Assoc. Prof.", etc.)	Rare	None
Profile Photo (Professional)	Common (formal portraits, academic settings)	Limited (mixed with casual images)	Rare (mostly non-human images or empty)
Profile Photo (Symbolic/Fun)	Minimal	Moderate	High (cartoons, pets, landscapes, etc.)
"About" Section Content	Academic or philosophical quotes	Short quotes, emojis, or empty	Mostly empty or humorous quotes
Participation in Group Messages	Higher among full-name & title users	Mixed; correlates with fuller profiles	Generally low, especially with anonymous profiles
Signs of Digital Minimalism	Strategic, boundary-setting silence	Passive participation or time-based boundaries	Semi-anonymous presence, rarely posting

The comparison across subgroups (Table 6) demonstrates that digital minimalism is statistically more prevalent among undergraduates and graduate students than faculty. While faculty members utilize their profiles as 'digital business cards' to assert institutional status, students utilize 'symbolic anonymity' to manage the pressures of academic hierarchy. This suggests that the higher the power distance, the more likely a subordinate member is to adopt a 'present but withheld' stance to protect their digital autonomy.

DISCUSSION

This section interprets the empirical findings through the lens of digital minimalism, identity signaling, and power asymmetries within academic WhatsApp groups. Drawing on theories of self-presentation, boundary work, resistance, and affective labor, it explores how everyday decisions, such as name formatting, profile picture selection, or passive membership function as strategies for navigating the structural and emotional demands of academic life.

Digital Identity and Boundary Management

Across all three groups, users appear to treat WhatsApp profiles not merely as labels, but as curated digital surfaces points of entry into their academic identity. Faculty members most frequently displayed full names and professional titles (e.g., "Dr. Amber Rackers," "Assoc. Prof. John T."), often paired with formal or institutional photographs. These choices may reinforced professional credibility and could be seen as conforming to academic hierarchies. Graduate students showed a more ambiguous stance, they often used initials, partial names, or neutral images like books or landscapes, suggesting a transitional identity negotiating both deference to authority and self-branding. Undergraduates more frequently opted for emojis, nicknames, or symbolic avatars (e.g., nature photos, K-pop stars, or abstract art), potentially signaling a desire for playfulness, privacy, or resistance to formality.

This gradient of visibility, from faculty's public-facing personas to undergraduates' ambiguous profiles, appears to illustrate what Gieryn (1983) terms boundary work, the strategic delineation of personal and professional space. WhatsApp, though private in architecture, fosters ambient visibility (Leonardi, 2014), where users are always potentially seen. This likely drives participants to fine-tune their self-disclosures, using names and images to modulate access to their identities while maintaining group membership.

Faculty members tended to use full names and professional titles, may serve to reinforce a public-facing academic persona. This gradient of visibility, from full-name professionalism to symbolic anonymity, likely reflects not only identity negotiation but also the distribution of symbolic capital (Bourdieu, 1986), where name recognition and academic rank appear to shape digital authority. The minimalist strategies observed among Turkish academics can be further understood through Bourdieu's concept of *habitus*—the internalized structures that govern behavior. In the Turkish academic field, the 'digital habitus' is increasingly defined by a tension between traditional hierarchical respect and the modern affordances of instant messaging. When a faculty member or student chooses a minimalist profile, they are practicing a form of 'strategic disposition' that aligns with their position in the academic hierarchy. This 'logic of practice' ensures that while the digital space is informal, the underlying power structures remain intact. Such behaviors suggest that digital silence is not a void, but a sophisticated manifestation of professional habitus in a high-power-distance culture. In these academic WhatsApp groups, symbolic capital manifests not only in message content but in how individuals present themselves. Faculty members, by displaying credentials, may assert institutional legitimacy, while students might opt for anonymity or informality as a way to potentially resist hierarchical visibility or preserve a sense of privacy.

Across all three groups, users treat WhatsApp profiles not merely as functional labels but as curated digital surfaces, points of entry into their academic identity. Faculty members most frequently displayed full names and professional titles (e.g., "Dr. Ayşe Kaya," "Assoc. Prof. Mehmet T."), often paired with formal or institutional photographs. These choices reinforce professional credibility and reflect academic hierarchies. Graduate students adopted more ambiguous strategies: initials, partial names, or neutral images (books, landscapes), signaling a transitional identity, balancing deference to authority with emerging professional self-branding. Undergraduates more commonly used emojis, nicknames, or symbolic avatars (e.g., nature photos, K-pop stars, abstract art), expressing playfulness, privacy, or resistance to formality.

These self-presentation choices appear to reflect the uneven distribution of symbolic capital (Bourdieu, 1986). Name recognition and academic titles may function as markers of authority within digital hierarchies. Faculty appear to possess more capital to "display," while students, especially undergraduates, seem to navigate this field with less institutional legitimacy, leading to what could be interpreted as cautious or playful identity performances.

Silence as a Meaningful Act

The prevalence of silent participation, especially among graduate and undergraduate users, should not necessarily be mistaken for apathy. Drawing on Scott's (1990) concept of everyday resistance, these acts of digital silence may represent micro-political refusal strategies aimed at preserving autonomy and emotional energy within demanding academic cultures (Ali et al., 2024). Similarly, Zuboff's (2019) critique of surveillance capitalism suggests that even non-action constitutes data.

Similarly, Zuboff's (2019) critique of surveillance capitalism suggests that even non-action constitutes data; therefore, choosing not to post could potentially serve as a way to shield one's behavioral surplus from algorithmic capture.

Many users adopted what could be interpreted as symbolic silence, maintaining vague or poetic status messages like "One day at a time," "Text only if urgent," or "Just passing through." These phrasings appear to allow users to express availability boundaries without direct confrontation. Such behaviors might also be shaped by the conditions of liquid modernity (Bauman, 2000), where communication must often balance the need for connection with the desire for protection.

Silence, in this sense, appears to function as a mode of presence management. Instead of logging off entirely, users stay available but inert, a stance akin to what Goffman (1959) might describe as backstage behavior occurring within the front stage. From a Foucauldian perspective (1988), this could be described as a technology of the self, a reflexive practice of self-discipline performed under the pressure of ambient social norms.

Emotional Labor and Institutional Hierarchies

The asymmetry of emotional labor across user groups appears to be striking. Faculty members, often utilizing identifiable titles and formal photos, tended to engage more actively by posting reminders, comments, or resources. This level of participation may reflect both institutional authority and the performance of availability as a form of leadership. For this group, visibility could be interpreted as a strategic and professional choice.

In contrast, graduate students seemed to exhibit a sense of performance fatigue, potentially feeling an expectation to appear responsive, collegial, and competent even in high-traffic groups. Many appeared to respond by retreating into monitored silence checking messages without replying or using polite emojis instead of verbal commentary. This behavior aligns with Hochschild's (1983) theory of emotional labor, where the suppression or modulation of emotion appears to become a necessary part of role performance.

Undergraduate students, potentially facing the double pressure to remain included while avoiding negative judgment, frequently used ambiguity and delay as a form of protection. Their silence may be less about direct resistance and more about navigating uncertainty and perceived social risk. While they are expected to participate, they may feel they lack the power or clarity to do so safely. These patterns suggest that while WhatsApp groups appear structurally flat, they remain likely coded with academic hierarchies. In this context, titles, names, and silence all appear to communicate status, intent, and vulnerability.

Cultural and Platform-Specific Dynamics

Set in the context of Türkiye, these findings appear to be shaped by both local academic culture and the global affordances of WhatsApp. Turkish academic norms often emphasize respect for hierarchy, status signaling, and indirectness in communication. The widespread use of titles like "Dr." or "Asst. Prof." and philosophical quotes in status fields likely reflects a broader cultural preference for symbolic and respectful communication.

WhatsApp, unlike institutional platforms like Moodle or university email, affords an informal yet persistent presence. Its interface provides the action possibilities for minimalist self-presentation; users can hide their photos, leave their status blank, or mute group notifications. These technical affordances appear to create a space for strategic non-engagement a form of "digital slow resistance" that may be less possible on more bureaucratic or strictly monitored platforms.

Moreover, WhatsApp's mobile-first design appears to contribute to asynchronous rhythms of participation. Delayed responses, ghost participation (reading without reacting), and muted notifications could be interpreted as temporal strategies ways to manage digital overwhelm without formally exiting the group. These practices suggest that users are not simply being passive, but are actively utilizing the platform's specific design features to navigate the tension between institutional belonging and personal privacy.

Beyond Participation: Toward Digital Cultural Logic

Ultimately, the minimalist strategies observed in this study appear to signal more than just personal preference; they may reflect a cultural logic of boundary-setting, soft resistance, and identity curation within academic digital life. In this context, silence should not necessarily be viewed as absence, and ambiguity may not equate to disengagement. Instead, these practices appear to reflect a growing tension between institutional demands for responsiveness and individual needs for privacy, autonomy, and self-preservation.

Rather than viewing these behaviors as deviant or disruptive, they could be understood as part of a broader negotiation with digital culture—one that is likely informed by power dynamics, cultural values, emotional labor, and the specific design affordances of communication platforms. By interpreting these minimalist acts as a legitimate form of digital subjectivity, we can begin to see how users navigate the complexities of being "present but withheld" in an era of hyperconnectivity.

REFLECTIONS ON PRACTICE

The findings of this study suggest recurring tensions in how informal digital platforms, especially user-initiated WhatsApp groups, are utilized within academic life. These groups often fall outside institutional oversight, yet they appear to significantly shape communication between students, instructors, and peers. This creates a "grey zone" where personal digital expression coexists with professional expectations, often without clearly defined shared norms.

One persistent challenge concerns naming and profile practices. Faculty members may occasionally encounter students whose profiles show only a phone number, an emoji, or a culturally playful nickname. While these choices are entirely voluntary, they can potentially make it difficult to maintain clarity, formality, or relational coherence in instructional contexts. When the act of addressing a student becomes ambiguous, the tension between personal expression and academic interaction becomes apparent.

Although this study is based on the analysis of one survey-sharing group, it is informed by broader participation in a wide range of academic WhatsApp groups. These experiences suggest that platform norms and identity management vary significantly across participant roles. From a practical standpoint, academic administrators and course coordinators could address these tensions by establishing clear digital communication protocols. Rather than mandating profile visibility, departments might consider implementing "digital office hours" or guidelines for group interactions that respect the need for "withheld presence" while maintaining functional academic clarity.

Why Faculty Engagement Still Matters

While participation in such groups is voluntary, faculty often join at the invitation of students or in response to coordination needs. Once present, they appear to be implicitly expected to contribute, lead, or respond, especially in groups related to coursework or institutional tasks. The lack of identifiable names or structured norms may create interactional uncertainty, potentially hindering relational dynamics and contributing to digital fatigue. These challenges might not fall under formal job descriptions, but they arguably become part of the hidden emotional labor of academic life in platform-mediated spaces.

The author has encouraged students in course-related WhatsApp groups to use identifiable names or clear profile information to support respectful and efficient communication. While many complied, others maintained anonymous or symbolic profiles. This underscores what appears to be the voluntary and uneven nature of digital identity management in informal academic settings and highlights the importance of framing such suggestions as dialogic rather than prescriptive. Cultivating shared digital norms in hybrid academic spaces likely requires ongoing, relational negotiation, rather than top-down regulation.

Instead of proposing rigid solutions, these observations call for institutional awareness of how informal digital spaces shape academic relationships. While universities may choose not to regulate these environments, they could acknowledge their influence and foster critical conversations around digital identity, boundary-setting, and communication fatigue. In hybrid academic ecologies, the tension between autonomy and coherence may remain unresolved, but it appears to deserve recognition rather than dismissal.

To effectively manage these tensions, academic administrators and course coordinators should consider establishing clear digital communication protocols. Rather than assuming constant availability, departments could implement 'digital office hours' or 'no-response weekends' to legitimize disengagement. Recognizing that profile-level minimalism is often a protective strategy against emotional labor, instructors should ideally avoid penalizing students for low digital visibility, instead fostering environments where 'withheld presence' is respected as a valid boundary-setting practice.

CONCLUSION

This chapter has examined how digital minimalism manifests in the ambient, semi-private spaces of academic WhatsApp groups in Türkiye. Through profile-based analysis of faculty members, graduate students, and undergraduates, the study highlights how identity, participation, and silence are negotiated in subtle but symbolically powerful ways. Rather than framing non-participation as mere absence or disengagement, the findings reveal a spectrum of strategic digital behaviors, from the selective use of profile photos and names to the adoption of poetic, ironic, or vague status messages.

By focusing on self-presentation rather than message content, this study contributes to a deeper understanding of how academic users curate visibility and manage emotional labor within platform-mediated group communication. Even in low-interaction environments, where users may not post or comment, digital subjectivities are actively constructed. Especially among students, the minimalist approach reflects both an internalized caution about hierarchy and a broader cultural adaptation to the "always-on" pressures of academic life.

Furthermore, the study demonstrates that WhatsApp, despite its simplicity, functions as a layered social interface where presence, withdrawal, and identity signaling coexist. The act of remaining silent while customizing one's profile becomes a form of "present but withheld" participation, a communicative stance that challenges dominant narratives of digital hypervisibility and productivity.

The patterns observed in WhatsApp profile presentation, ranging from ambiguous naming to silent participation, are best understood not merely as individual quirks but as socially embedded practices shaped by academic power relations. Drawing on Goffman's (1959) dramaturgical theory, these behaviors illustrate the backstage management of digital selves in contrast to frontstage expectations of constant visibility. Similarly, Foucault's (1988) concept of technologies of the self helps explain how users curate or withdraw their presence as a means of exercising agency within surveillance-laden environments (Zuboff, 2019). The presence of veiled dissent through profile quotes resonates with Scott's (1990) notion of hidden transcripts, signaling subtle resistance to academic norms and platform expectations.

In addition to identity-focused frameworks, cultural dimensions further illuminate the variations in self-presentation and engagement across user groups. Drawing on Hofstede's (2001) dimensions, the high power distance and uncertainty avoidance embedded in Turkish academic culture may contribute to restrained participation and anonymized profiles. Hall's (1976) concept of high-context communication helps explain the use of indirect cues, such as poetic quotes or vague status messages, as meaningful acts of positioning. Furthermore, Trompenaars and Hampden-Turner's (1998) framework on particularism suggests that users modulate their digital behavior based on relational proximity and situational context, rather than universal norms. Together, these theories suggest that what appears as digital minimalism may, in fact, be a culturally embedded form of strategic engagement.

These findings also hold significance for the study of organizational behavior and institutional communication. In particular, the digital minimalist practices observed in academic WhatsApp groups reveal how knowledge workers manage boundary work and emotional labor within informal yet highly consequential communication environments. WhatsApp groups, though often outside official institutional channels, function as ambient workspaces where expectations of visibility, responsiveness, and collegiality persist. Faculty members' curated digital presence and students' strategic silence mirror broader dynamics in organizational life, where status, identity, and labor are continuously negotiated under conditions of soft surveillance. These practices resonate with established concerns in management literature around communication overload, role ambiguity, and the emotional cost of digital availability (Hochschild, 1983; Mazmanian et al., 2013). Importantly, they suggest that institutions should reflect on the unintended burdens of digital communication culture and reconsider norms of constant accessibility, especially for precarious or junior members of academic communities.

In conclusion, this profile-level examination contributes to emerging debates in digital sociology, platform studies, and academic communication by foregrounding the aesthetics and politics of digital quietness. It argues that digital minimalism, as observed in WhatsApp-based academic groups, is an emerging cultural logic shaped by the overload and overexposure of algorithmic life. It functions as a non-confrontational form of agency, a way for users to say "I am here, but on my own terms." In an era where digital participation is often equated with self-disclosure, such quiet practices deserve deeper theoretical and empirical attention as legitimate forms of resistance, identity management, and cultural adaptation.

LIMITATIONS AND FUTURE RESEARCH

Like all qualitative inquiries, this study has its limitations. First, the analysis is based exclusively on publicly visible WhatsApp profile metadata, such as usernames, profile pictures, and status messages. While these offer rich symbolic insight, they do not capture private messaging behaviors, lurking practices, or interpretive intentions behind minimalist choices. Future studies could incorporate interviews or ethnographic observation to better understand how users conceptualize their own digital self-presentation and silence.

Second, the sample is drawn from a specific national and cultural context, Türkiye, and from academic groups with varying internal hierarchies. While the findings offer culturally grounded insights, generalizability to other professional or regional contexts remains limited. Comparative studies across countries or disciplines could illuminate how digital minimalism manifests differently depending on institutional norms, platform ecologies, and cultural expectations of visibility.

Third, this study focuses on WhatsApp, a platform with limited expressive affordances compared to alternatives like Slack, Discord, or Telegram. Each platform carries its own communicative logic and expectations of presence. Future research could explore how minimalist practices differ across platforms, particularly in relation to interface design, data visibility, and social incentives for participation.

While this study provides insights into the Turkish academic context, characterized by high power distance and specific hierarchical structures, the findings may differ in more horizontal or Westernized academic cultures. Future research should examine how varying degrees of institutional hierarchy influence the necessity for 'symbolic anonymity' and whether these minimalist tactics are as prevalent in fields with different professional norms

Finally, this chapter primarily examines profile-level phenomena. A more comprehensive study might analyze the temporal rhythms of participation (e.g., response time, muting habits, reaction use) or investigate the gendered and classed dimensions of digital silence within academic communication networks. These avenues offer fertile ground for expanding our understanding of digital discretion, agency, and resistance in professional life.

Ultimately, this study suggests that digital minimalism in academic WhatsApp groups is not merely a personal preference, but a reactive strategy to the blurring of professional and private boundaries. As digital ideologies continue to prioritize 'engagement' and 'transparency,' the value of withheld presence, or symbolic anonymity, becomes a critical site of agency. By choosing to remain silent or maintain a low-visibility profile, academics in Türkiye are navigating a complex field of power, preserving their focus and autonomy in an increasingly noisy digital landscape. Future institutional policies must recognize these practices not as disengagement, but as a deliberate and necessary management of one's professional digital footprint.

REFERENCES

Ali, A., ... (2024). When silence hurts: A conservation of resources perspective on digital disengagement. *Online Information Review*. https://www.emerald.com/oir/article/doi/10.1108/OIR-12-2024-0789

Baishya, A., & Maheshwari, S. (2020). WhatsApp groups in academic context: Exploring the academic uses of WhatsApp groups among the students. *Contemporary Educational Technology*, *11*(1), 71–83. DOI: 10.30935/cet.6271

Bauman, Z. (2000). *Liquid modernity*. Polity Press.

Baumer, E. P. S., Adams, P., Khovanskaya, V. D., Liao, T. C., Smith, M. E., Schwanda Sosik, V., & Williams, K. (2014). Limiting, leaving, and (re)lapsing: An exploration of Facebook non-use practices and experiences. *Proceedings of the SIGCHI Conference on Human Factors in Computing Systems*, 3257–3266. https://doi.org/ DOI: 10.1145/2556288.2557096

Bourdieu, P. (1986). The forms of capital. In Richardson, J. G. (Ed.), *Handbook of theory and research for the sociology of education* (pp. 241–258). Greenwood.

British Psychological Society. (2021). *Ethics guidelines for internet-mediated research (INF294/04.2021)*. https://www.bps.org.uk/news-and-policy/ethics-guidelines-internet-mediated-research-2021

Brubaker, J. R. (2020). Strategic ignorance in digital communication. *Social Media + Society*, *6*(1). Advance online publication. DOI: 10.1177/2056305120903402

Bucher, T. (2018). *If... then: Algorithmic power and politics*. Oxford University Press. DOI: 10.1093/oso/9780190493028.001.0001

Bucher, T. (2020). Nothing to disconnect from? Being singular plural in an age of machine learning. *Media Culture & Society*, *42*(4), 610–617. DOI: 10.1177/0163443720914028

Bucher, T., & Helmond, A. (2018). *The affordances of social media platforms*. The SAGE Handbook of Social Media. https://journals.sagepub.com/doi/10.1177/1461444816644424

Cetinkaya, L. (2017). The impact of WhatsApp use on success in education process. *International Review of Research in Open and Distance Learning*, *18*(7), 59–74. DOI: 10.19173/irrodl.v18i7.3279

Dakoru, A. (2025). Digital silence as a pragmatic strategy: An intercultural qualitative study of online group chats. *ResearchGate*. https://www.researchgate.net/publication/394378314_Digital_silence_as_a_pragmatic_strategy

Denzin, N. K., & Lincoln, Y. S. (Eds.). (2018). *The SAGE handbook of qualitative research* (5th ed.). SAGE Publications.

Douglas, M. (1978). *Implicit meanings: Essays in anthropology* (2nd ed.). Routledge.

Durgungöz, A. (2022). WhatsApp and educational communication in Türkiye: A case study on mathematics teachers. *Journal of Teacher Education and Lifelong Learning*, *4*(2), 13–27.

Eynon, R., Fry, J., & Schroeder, R. (2008). The ethics of internet research. In Fielding, N., Lee, R. M., & Blank, G. (Eds.), *The SAGE handbook of online research methods* (pp. 23–41). SAGE Publications., DOI: 10.4135/9780857020055.n2

Foucault, M. (1988). *Technologies of the self: A seminar with Michel Foucault*. University of Massachusetts Press.

Franzke, A. S., ... (2020). Internet Research: Ethical Guidelines 3.0. *Association of Internet Researchers*. https://aoir.org/reports/ethics3.pdf

Geertz, C. (1973). *The interpretation of cultures: Selected essays*. Basic Books.

Gieryn, T. F. (1983). Boundary-work and the demarcation of science from non-science: Strains and interests in professional ideologies of scientists. *American Sociological Review*, *48*(6), 781–795. DOI: 10.2307/2095325

Gill, R. (2009). Breaking the silence: The hidden injuries of neo-liberal academia. In Gill, R., & Donaghue, R. (Eds.), *The Handbook of Gender and Communication* (pp. 228–245). Palgrave Macmillan.

Goffman, E. (1959). *The presentation of self in everyday life*. Anchor Books.

Gray, M. L., & Suri, S. (2020). *Ghost work: How to stop Silicon Valley from building a new global underclass*. Houghton Mifflin Harcourt.

Hall, E. T. (1976). *Beyond culture*. Anchor Books.

Hochschild, A. R. (1983). *The managed heart: Commercialization of human feeling*. University of California Press.

Hofstede, G. (2001). *Culture's consequences: Comparing values, behaviors, institutions, and organizations across nations* (2nd ed.). SAGE.

Karppi, T. (2018). *Disconnect: Facebook's affective bonds*. University of Minnesota Press. DOI: 10.5749/j.ctv65sz27

Kozinets, R. V. (2020). *Netnography: The essential guide to qualitative social media research* (3rd ed.). SAGE Publications. DOI: 10.4135/9781036233846

Leonardi, P. M. (2014). Social media, knowledge sharing, and innovation: Toward a theory of communication visibility. *Information Systems Research*, *25*(4), 796–816. DOI: 10.1287/isre.2014.0536

Lomborg, S. (2017). *Social media, social genres: Making sense of the ordinary*. Routledge.

Mazmanian, M., Orlikowski, W. J., & Yates, J. (2013). The autonomy paradox: The implications of mobile email devices for knowledge professionals. *Organization Science*, *24*(5), 1337–1357. DOI: 10.1287/orsc.1120.0806

Minlo, A. (2024). Academics' dependence on WhatsApp and its impact on social and educational learning. *International Journal of Educational Technology Studies*, *7*(1), 45–59. DOI: 10.2139/ssrn.384239993

Newport, C. (2019). *Digital minimalism: Choosing a focused life in a noisy world*. Portfolio.

Rogers, R. (2021). Visual media analysis for Instagram and other online platforms. *Big Data & Society*. https://journals.sagepub.com/doi/10.1177/20539517211022370

Rose, G. (2016). *Visual methodologies: An introduction to researching with visual materials* (4th ed.). SAGE Publications.

Saldaña, J. (2021). *The coding manual for qualitative researchers* (4th ed.). SAGE Publications.

Scott, J. C. (1985). *Weapons of the weak: Everyday forms of peasant resistance*. Yale University Press.

Scott, J. C. (1990). *Domination and the arts of resistance: Hidden transcripts*. Yale University Press.

Selwyn, N. (2016). *Education and technology: Key issues and debates*. Bloomsbury Academic.

Silverman, D. (2020). *Qualitative research* (5th ed.). SAGE Publications.

Striphas, T. (2015). Algorithmic culture. *European Journal of Cultural Studies*, *18*(4–5), 395–412. DOI: 10.1177/1367549415577392

Svelch, J. (2023). Disconnection, resistance, and avoidance: Non-use as a meaningful practice in digital labor. *New Media & Society*, *25*(6), 1213–1229. DOI: 10.1177/14614448221088939

Trompenaars, F., & Hampden-Turner, C. (1998). *Riding the waves of culture: Understanding diversity in global business*. McGraw-Hill.

Turkle, S. (2011). *Alone together: Why we expect more from technology and less from each other*. Basic Books.

van Dijck, J. (2013). *The culture of connectivity: A critical history of social media*. Oxford University Press. DOI: 10.1093/acprof:oso/9780199970773.001.0001

Williamson, B. (2017). Big data in education: The digital future of learning, policy and practice. *Sage (Atlanta, Ga.)*. Advance online publication. DOI: 10.4135/9781529714920

Zuboff, S. (2019). *The age of surveillance capitalism: The fight for a human future at the new frontier of power*. PublicAffairs.

Chapter 13
The Digital Panopticon at Work:
Authority and Influence in Remote Organizations

Begüm Kanat Tiryaki
http://orcid.org/0000-0001-7410-1216
Ege University, Turkey

Nazlı Ayşe Ayyıldız Ünnü
http://orcid.org/0000-0002-8427-5727
Ege University, Turkey

ABSTRACT

The pandemic has reshaped organizational practices by accelerating digital transformation and embedding remote work into everyday operations. This chapter examines how influence tactics and organizational authority are redefined under these conditions, where traditional face-to-face control is replaced by digital visibility. Drawing on maximum diversity sampling, interviews with 12 participants from different sectors and levels were analyzed with MAXQDA 2024. Findings indicate that remote work challenges authority structures, compelling subordinates to adapt their strategies. A notable trend is the increased reliance on rational and communication-based tactics, while subordinates strengthen their social presence in digital environments to shape decisions. At the same time, the absence of nonverbal cues limits the expression of authority and influence. Interpreted through digital panopticism, these dynamics highlight how remote work transforms power: authority and influence are mediated and disciplined by constant online monitoring.

DOI: 10.4018/979-8-3373-4531-4.ch013

1. INTRODUCTION

The selection and utilization of influence tactics by leaders, managers, and subordinates are associated with a wide range of organizational outcomes, including organizational commitment, job satisfaction, organizational justice, absenteeism, burnout, self-efficacy, productivity, and efficiency (Elias, 2008). Previous studies have consistently demonstrated that organizational power bases and influence tactics play a central role in shaping these outcomes (Meydan et al., 2018; Bocchiaro & Zamperini, 2012; Guérin et al., 2013; Bélanger, 2016). Collectively, this body of research indicates that influence tactics are not peripheral managerial practices but constitute a critical domain with direct implications for multiple dimensions of organizational life.

From a sociological perspective, Giddens (1979) argues that when individuals act collectively within organizations, they actively produce meaning, power, and norms, which form the core elements of social interaction (Melin & Axelsson, 2005). Accordingly, power and influence remain persistent and relevant organizational phenomena, regardless of changing work conditions. Building on this view, French and Raven (1959) conceptualize power and influence around two fundamental questions: what determines the behavior of the actor exercising power, and what shapes the response of the individual subject to that influence.

While power and influence have been extensively examined in traditional organizational settings, research focusing on remote work contexts remains comparatively limited and is predominantly quantitative in nature (Panteli & Tucker, 2009; Steizel & Rimbau-Gilabert, 2013; Wadsworth & Blanchard, 2015). As a result, there is still a lack of in-depth understanding of how influence processes are experienced, interpreted, and enacted in digitally mediated work environments. Adopting an exploratory qualitative approach, this study seeks to address this gap by providing a more nuanced examination of influence dynamics in remote work.

To achieve this aim, the chapter examines changing influence processes in remote work environments through the lens of digital panopticism. Drawing on Foucault's metaphor of the Panopticon (Foucault, 1977), digital panopticism highlights how visibility functions as a disciplinary mechanism. In contemporary remote work settings, constant visibility is produced through digital tools such as cameras, online meetings, shared calendars, status indicators, and routine reporting practices. These mechanisms not only enable managerial oversight but also foster self-regulation among employees.

Within this context, both managers and employees adapt their influence tactics to the logic of remote work. Authority is increasingly exercised through rational, communicative, and evidence-based strategies, while employees develop social presence cues to maintain visibility and agency. The absence of traditional social context cues, combined with intensified digital surveillance, reshapes established hierarchies of influence. Accordingly, this study aims to explore how authority and influence are redefined in remote working environments under conditions of digital panopticism.

2. ORGANIZATIONAL POWER, INFLUENCE AND AUTHORITY

The use of social power and influence processes has long occupied an important place in the social sciences, particularly within organizational and social psychology. At the interpersonal level, early research largely focused on the the followers, who are influenced rather than on the influencer. However, since the 1980s, a growing interest in the power-holder has shifted scholarly attention toward leaders, their influence styles, and the personality traits and situational factors shaping these behaviors (Falbo, 1977; Goodstadt & Hjelle, 1973; Kipnis, Schmidt & Wilkinson, 1980; Instone et al., 1983). Within this perspective, power and influence are not considered as interchangeable terms but as distinct processes. Influence involves both the agent, who seeks to affect others and the target who responds, and this relationship may unfold vertically (top-down or bottom-up) or horizontally.

A thorough review of the literature reveals the existence of numerous studies addressing the classification of influence tactics (see Kipnis et al., 1980; Jones & Pittman, 1982; Kipnis & Schmidt, 1988; Yukl & Falbe, 1990; Yukl et al., 2005). A substantial body of research has emerged from the seminal study conducted by Kipnis et al. (1980), with subsequent studies building upon the findings and methodologies established in that seminal work. The classification proposed by them, which has garnered the most acceptance within the extant literature. This research identified eight distinct influence tactics that employees utilize when attempting to exert influence over superiors, subordinates, and co-workers. The following terms are defined as follows: favouritism, rationality, assertiveness, sanctions, exchange of interests, appeal to a superior, obstruction, and coalitions. Later studies expanded this framework. For instance, Yukl and Falbe (1990) introduced inspirational appeals and consultation as additional tactics, while Yukl et al. (2005) expanded the taxonomy further with "collaboration" and "debriefing."

Together, these contributions illustrate that influence is a multidimensional process shaped by both relational dynamics and organizational context.

This evolution also reflects a broader transformation in how authority and power are conceptualized within organizations. At the beginning of the 20th century, the prevailing concept of authority in business organisations was rooted in property rights or a managerial position. As Follett (1949) observed, this model often relied on issuing orders and demanding obedience, which could lead to arbitrary decisions, suppress employee initiative and diminish individuals' self-confidence and self-esteem (Melé & Rosanas, 2003).

The literature has consistently argued that authority is effective only when it is recognized as legitimate by others. In this sense, authority is not merely imposed; it is co-constructed through meaning-making and communicative practices (Haugaard, 2010). Foucault (1982) similarly argued that power is exercised through everyday mechanisms such as education, division of labour, and hierarchical structures, which both discipline and enable actors.

While authority figures may occasionally misuse power through coercion or symbolic violence, Haugaard (2010) emphasizes that the stability of organizational systems depends on actors generally refraining from such abuses. Authority is sustainable only when it is accountable—that is, when those in positions of power can justify their actions in ways consistent with prevailing local norms and circumstances.

In organizational studies, scholars generally distinguish power, authority, and influence as related but distinct concepts. Thus, power refers to the capacity of an individual or group to affect the behavior, beliefs, or actions of others, even in the absence of formal approval or agreement. Power can be coercive, reward-based, expert, referent, or legitimate (French & Raven, 1959). It is often exercised through both visible mechanisms (e.g., hierarchical decision-making) and subtle processes (e.g., shaping norms or organizational culture).

Authority is the legitimate right to make decisions, command resources, and enforce compliance within a given organizational framework. Unlike power, authority is recognized and accepted by others as appropriate; it is not only imposed (Follett, 1949; Haugaard, 2010).

Influence is the social process through which individuals intentionally affect the thoughts, behaviors, or attitudes of others. It involves both the agent (the influencer) and the target (the influenced), and can occur vertically (top-down or bottom-up) or horizontally (peer-to-peer). It is enacted through various tactics such as rational persuasion, inspirational appeals, collaboration, or sanctions and is shaped by relational and situational factors (Kipnis et al., 1980; Yukl & Fu, 2000).

As defined before power represents the potential to affect others, authority is the legitimate and recognized right to make decisions, and influence is the active process through which actors shape behavior or attitudes. While closely intertwined, these concepts differ in scope, legitimacy, and enactment: power can exist without recognition, authority depends on legitimacy, and influence depends on relational and situational dynamics. Grasping these distinctions provides a foundation for analyzing how organizational actors exercise control, guide decisions, and interact with one another. Importantly, it sets the stage for examining how these processes evolve under contemporary conditions such as remote work and digital communication, where traditional mechanisms of power, authority, and influence may manifest differently.

Influence itself is a social act, and its meaning depends on perspective (Kipnis & Schmidt, 1985). Deutsch and Gerard (1955) distinguished two classic forms of social influence: normative and informational. Normative influence arises from social dependence and the desire for approval or rewards, often resulting in superficial conformity without deep internalization. Informational influence, by contrast, emerges when individuals facing uncertainty rely on others' perspectives to interpret reality; this tends to produce genuine internalization. While different, both forms of influence involve psychological dependence on others (Simon & Oakes, 2006).

Revisiting influence tactics, Kipnis et al. (1980, 1984) found that assertiveness, sanctions, ingratiation, and rational persuasion appeared consistently across hierarchical levels. Other tactics, such as upward appeals and coalitions, varied by whether the target was a superior or a subordinate. Yukl and colleagues later extended this research by identifying additional strategies: inspirational appeals, consultation, collaboration, and apprising (Yukl & Michel, 2006). These tactics highlight the importance of values, participation, and personal benefits in shaping influence outcomes. Yukl and Fu (2000) further systematized behavioral forms of influence into rational persuasion, exchange, upward appeals, ingratiation, and pressure, showing the wide range of approaches that actors employ in organizational life (see Table 1).

Table 1. Influence tactics

Kipnis et al. (1980, 1984)	**Influence Tactics**
	Rational Persuasion, Inspirational Appeals, Consultation, Ingratiation, Exchange, Personal Appeals, Coalition, Pressure, Legitimating
Fu & Yukl (2000)	**Behavioural Forms Of Influence Tactics**
	Rational Persuasion, Exchange, Upward Appeals, Ingratiation, Pressure
Yukl & Michel (2006)	**Extended Influence Tactics**
	Rational Persuasion, Inspirational Appeals, Consultation, Ingratiation, Exchange, Personal Appeals, Coalition, Pressure, Legitimating, Collaboration, Apprising

Source: Kipnis et al. (1980, 1984), Fu & Yukl (2000), Yukl & Michel (2006)

Taken together, this literature demonstrates that organizational power, influence, and authority are intertwined yet distinct dimensions of social interaction. Influence is enacted through a variety of tactics that evolve over time, authority is legitimized through communication and recognition, and power operates both visibly and subtly through organizational structures.

While these classifications emerged in face-to-face organizational contexts, the rise of remote work and digital monitoring requires re-examining how these tactics are deployed and perceived. These dynamics form the theoretical foundation for examining how influence processes are reshaped under conditions of remote work and digital mediation.

3. COMPUTER-MEDIATED COMMUNICATION AND REMOTE WORK MODELS

The pandemic has had a profound impact on conventional behaviours and practices, leading to irreversible changes in lifestyles. The productive and transformative nature of this pandemic has resulted in significant social and economic repercussions (both direct and indirect) across different businesses and sectors globally (Kamal, 2020). The dynamism, uncertainty and complexity of contemporary work environments, including the disruptive change that occurred in the aftermath of the pandemic, can be identified as the primary catalysts that initiated the transformation to digital business, computer mediated communication and remote work models (Priyono et al., 2020).

3.1. From Computerization to Communication Systems

A review of the literature shows that computerization is conceptualized as a generic information system or a combination of processing systems, office systems, management information systems, electronic mail systems, etc. These systems may consist of mainframes and microcomputers, or they may have workstations and a stand-alone or networked configuration (Leifer, 1988).

Building on this foundation, computer-based communication systems have been developed to reduce the costs of coordination and increase the associated benefits. For example, document sharing and electronic mail can increase the efficiency of reports, ensure that materials reach the right people quickly, and also enable materials to be easily stored and retrieved (Desanctis & Jackson, 1994).

Electronic communication can take many forms, including e-mail, group decision support systems, shared database applications and desktop video conferencing. These systems differ in a number of key respects, including the synchronization and interaction structure and the channels available for information flow (Straus, 1997). More specifically, Computer mediated communication systems (CMCS) are sociotechnical systems that support and enhance the communication-related activities of team members participating in computer-supported collaborative work. Teams using CMCS may collaborate synchronously or asynchronously, and they can be either physically co-located or geographically dispersed. The technology may support tasks at both the individual and group level (Warkentin et al., 1997).

3.2. Benefits and Challenges of Electronic Communication

Electronic communication systems improve the frequency and impact of information exchange, as well as its accessibility and speed. Remote working for employees and their mobilization, communication of organizational culture, dissemination of policies and procedures are more easily achieved through e-mail (i.e. computer-based communication). It also encourages the dissemination of internal decisions and the consolidation of ideas. Electronic communication can be described as more informal, relaxed and generally more frank and conversational than traditional organizational communication (Sproull & Kiesler, 1991).

However, research has emphasized that the absence of non-verbal cues is a critical factor influencing the relational tone of CMC. This limitation can make interactions seem impersonal or task-oriented. Yet, longitudinal findings suggest that individuals gradually form impressions of others by accumulating cues embedded in CMC messages. These impressions eventually support relationship development and allow the exchange of multidimensional messages through textual strategies (Walther, 1992).

For managers, the expansion of communication technologies has created both opportunities and challenges. With e-mail, managers can reach remote partners more efficiently than via telephone, and teleconferencing reduces the need for costly travel while enabling real-time group meetings. Still, the proliferation of communication alternatives also brings confusion. Selecting the most appropriate medium is neither straightforward nor trivial, as media choice critically shapes communication effectiveness. Mistakes in media selection may not only hinder effectiveness but also produce negative consequences (Trevino et al., 1990).

3.3. Media Richness and Managerial Communication

Media Richness Theory provides an important framework for understanding managerial choices in communication. Daft et al. (1987) demonstrated that media differ in their capacity to transmit information cues. Managers tend to prefer rich media for ambiguous communication and less rich media for sensitive communication. The data suggest that high- performing managers are more sensitive to the correlation between message ambiguity and media richness than low-performing managers.

Complementary evidence shows the complex outcomes of computer-mediated communication. For instance, Straus and McGrath (1994) found that Computer Mediated (CM) groups had lower levels of productivity and lower levels of task satisfaction than Face-to-Face (FtF) groups. Further analysis revealed that CM groups experienced reduced coherence, although they achieved greater equality of participation and lower rates of disagreement. Interestingly, contrary to earlier claims that electronic communication depersonalizes interaction, Straus (1997) found that CM groups engaged in higher levels of supportive communication and avoided aggressive behaviors.

Additional studies highlight the contrasts between CM and FtF groups. Findings of these studies show that computer-mediated groups make better decisions, generate more ideas and are happier than face-to-face groups (Valacich et al., 2002). Thus, while the absence of non-verbal cues may create challenges, CMC also fosters distinct advantages in terms of inclusivity, creativity, and decision quality.

Overall, the literature illustrates that computerization and CMC systems are not only tools for efficiency; they fundamentally reshape the dynamics of organizational communication. Managers are now required to navigate a complex environment of multiple communication channels, making media choice a strategic decision. Moreover, while CMC reduces reliance on traditional cues, it simultaneously enables new forms of relational and task-oriented communication that, under certain conditions, may outperform face-to-face interaction.

3.4. Remote Work and Organizational Implications

In light of the widespread adoption of remote working models, it is imperative to examine the implications of these models on the contemporary workplace. Remote working is closely associated with numerous concepts in organisational behaviour, including power, influence, and authority, as well as communication processes.

Since computer-mediated communication (CMC) has become an indispensable tool in remote work, theories addressing the absence of non-verbal cues and their effects on communication, such as Media Richness Theory, Social Presence Theory, Social Context Cues Theory, Social Impact Model of Technology Use, and the Hyperpersonal Model have gained increasing importance in understanding organisational interactions in general and organisational power, influence, and authority in spesific.

3.4.1. Theoretical Perspectives on Computer-Mediated Communication

The Social Presence Theory highlights the extent to which a communication medium allows participants to experience each other as psychologically close or present. Biocca (1997) defines social presence as occurring when users perceive access to another's intelligence, intentions, and impressions. Early studies (Short et al., 1976; Fulk & Boyd, 1991) emphasised that different media vary in the cues they provide, and that individuals' perceptions of these cues shape their behaviour. However, later work (Walther, 1992) pointed out that research in CMC often assumed, rather than empirically verified, that social presence depends primarily on media characteristics.

Another communication theory is the Social Context Cues Theory. According to this theory, the social context of a communication is interpreted through both static and dynamic cues. People's gaze and factors such as a clock, a private office, a large desk and a personal secretary provide static cues. Non-verbal cues that change during an interaction, such as nodding in agreement and frowning in disapproval, are examples of dynamic cues. As people observe social context cues, they may generate or elicit cognitive interpretations as well as simultaneous emotional responses. Individuals change the target, tone and verbal substance of their speech depending on how they identify and interpret the situation. When social context cues are strong, behavior is typically focused on others, differentiated and regulated. People's sense of anonymity tends to create especially egocentric and disorganized behavior when social context cues are weak (Sproull & Kiesler, 1986).

The psychological distance between a communicator and the listener of messages, expressed in speech and accompanying verbal, textual, non-verbal and other cues, is referred to as directness. Members' perceptions of social context indicators such as eye contact, proximity, personal space and demeanour are referred to as proximity effects (Baskin et al., 2004). Social context cues determine directness and proximity; learning encounters frame learning relationships; and communication patterns feed into (and generate) social context cues. Each is related and interconnected. Directness has a positive impact on various knowledge creation processes.

Many different studies have been conducted and various theories have been developed over time to examine and demonstrate the ways in which communicators adapt computer generated signals for the purposes of relational effects. According to the social context cues theory, a literature has been developed to signal hierarchical positions of electronic communicators in line with relational dominance and status cues that are assumed to be absent in CMC (Walther, 1992). To sum up, social context cues affect directness and proximity, thereby influencing knowledge creation, relational dynamics, and authority signalling (Baskin et al., 2004; Walther, 1992).

In the context of previous studies and theories (Social Context Theory, Social Presence Theory and Media Wealth Theory), Culnan and Markus (1987) conceptualised the cue-filtered approach, arguing that CMC inevitably reduces socio-emotional content due to the absence of cues, rendering it less personal than face-to-face communication. Rice and Love (1987) supported this view, suggesting that computer-based communication is perceived as impersonal and lacking normative reinforcement due to the absence of auditory or visual cues, so there will be less socio-emotional content exchange. However, Walther, with the Hyperpersonal Model he developed, argues and defends the opposite of the findings generally put forward by these approaches and theories. He argues that in computer-mediated communication there are sub-processes related to receivers, senders, channels and feedback aspects that can improve impressions and interpersonal interactions.

To address how CMC can influence cognitive and communication processes related to message creation and reception, the model follows four common components of the communication process: (1) effects arising from receiver processes, (2) effects between message senders, (3) channel attributes, and (4) feedback effects (Walther, 2011). While exchanges over time are key parts of the communication process, a classical model of communication includes feedback between sender and receiver. In CMC, attractive impressions and intimacy can begin through the sender and receiver mechanisms described here, but reciprocal influence exerted through a process known as behavioral confirmation has the ability to significantly enhance these benefits (Walther, 1996).

Collectively, Hyperpersonal Theory can be defined as a theoretical framework that attempts to elucidate the mechanisms through which human-to-human interaction with the help of computer-mediated communication or other electronic devices can rapidly become intimate or promote the perception of intimacy. And unlike previous theories, it suggests that CMC is richer than face-to-face communication. In summary, while early theories depicted CMC as inherently impoverished, later perspectives demonstrated that its relational potential depends on user adaptation, cognitive framing, and the dynamic use of communication channels. These insights provide an essential foundation for understanding how remote work reshapes organisational dynamics.

3.4.2. Remote Working Models

The concept of remote working first emerged in the 1970s as a response to the US oil crisis. At that time, the aim was to move work to workers rather than workers to work, in order to reduce traffic congestion and energy use. Soon after, state governments began to fund and support projects to investigate the feasibility and effectiveness of telework, making it more widespread (Allen et al., 2015). Since then, remote working has become increasingly adopted by organisations with the spread of information and communication technologies in the late 20th century. Finally, the COVID-19 pandemic forced many organisations to adopt remote working methods on a compulsory basis, embedding these practices more permanently into business life (ILO, 2021).

Long before laptops, mobile phones, and wireless internet transformed airports and hotels into workstations, teleworkers were already working at home, reshaping perceptions of how and where work could be done. This development forced managers to rethink how to evaluate and supervise employees, while also heralding changes in the psychological contract between individuals and organisations (Bailey & Kurland, 2002).

Employees, who work from home, can be defined as those who provide services or produce goods for a certain fee, following the instructions given by the employer. Although the concept of remote working and housework did not attract much attention for a long time due to being carried out within the private sphere of the home, it has in fact always existed throughout history. Such work includes a wide range of activities, from sewing, embroidery, and assembly to various administrative and professional services that can be conducted remotely using available technologies (ILO, 2021).

Over the past twenty years, organisations have increasingly made use of remote working models enabled by computer-based communication. With the pandemic in 2020, these models became even more significant and have continued to persist in work life thereafter. However, the literature presents diverse and sometimes conflicting definitions of remote working. These conceptual differences create a challenge for synthesising scientific findings. Remote working is variously referred to as telecommuting, working from home, dispersed working, virtual working, flexible working, and flexplace. While these terms overlap to a large extent, they represent different perspectives on the same phenomenon. Even among studies that use the same label (e.g., "telework"), definitions differ, which affects study designs, examples, and comparability of findings. As a result, a fragmented literature has emerged across disciplines such as transportation, information systems, management, communication, and psychology, often without reference to each other's work (Allen et al., 2015).

One of the earliest models is telecommuting, also referred to as telework. Olson (1983) defined teleworking as organisational work that takes place outside a specific location and beyond traditional time and space constraints. In general, telework is defined as remote work involving the use of information and communication technologies (ICT) (Sullivan, 2003). Telework can also be understood as an arrangement that blurs the boundaries between workplace and residence through telecommunication tools (Alizadeh, 2013).

Telework and remote work share similarities but also differ in important respects. Teleworkers are expected to be online during normal business hours according to their employer's time zone, and communication is predominantly synchronous. Remote workers, in contrast, often rely on asynchronous communication and can be located anywhere in the world. While teleworkers usually reside close to the central office for occasional face-to-face meetings or gatherings, remote workers are more geographically flexible (Prasad et al., 2020).

Information technologies have created new organisational structures that challenge traditional management thinking. Virtual organisations lack centralised facilities and traditional hierarchies, but individuals work together for a common purpose (Staples et al., 1999). Akuta and Carley (1998) define a virtual organisation as "a geographically distributed organisation whose members are bound by a long-term common interest or goal and communicate and coordinate through information technology." The literature highlights that virtual organisations tend to be non-hierarchical (Mills, 1991; Drucker, 1988) and decentralised.

Virtual teams, as a subset of virtual organisations, consist of members spread across various organisations, time zones, locations, and cultures, collaborating through IT (Huang et al., 2010: 1098). They are characterised by fluid structures, cross-boundary collaboration, and temporal flexibility. Often, they form to address specific tasks and disband once objectives are achieved (Powell et al., 2004).

3.4.3. Remote Working in Practice

Remote working more broadly is defined as "a flexible working arrangement in which employees work in locations far from their head offices or production facilities, without personal contact with their colleagues there, but with the ability to communicate with them using technology" (Wang et al., 2021). Similarly, Elshaiekh et al. (2018) describe it as a scheme in which employees fulfil duties and responsibilities from an approved site outside the traditional workplace. In practice, this means work activities are not tied to a single physical location, allowing tasks to be completed without commuting (Prasad et al., 2020).

Since face-to-face meetings are rare in remote work, digital communication technologies are the main medium of interaction with management and coworkers. This increases the risk of isolation and reduces opportunities for informal consultation. As a result, remote workers' performance may rely more heavily on their self-motivation and self-efficacy than employees in traditional office environments (Staples et al., 1999).

Building on these definitions, the following section outlines common remote work arrangements in practice:

- Full-time remote work: employees work entirely offsite.
- Part-time or hybrid work: time is divided between home, office, or client locations.
- Ad hoc remote work: occasional work from home, for example during illness or childcare.
- Telecommuting: working from home exclusively for a single employer.
- Freelance remote work: working remotely for multiple employers simultaneously (Nakrošienė et al., 2019).

All these models, telework, remote work, working from home (WFH), or even working from anywhere (WFA), illustrate a significant transformation in work practices worldwide. Innovations in information and computer-mediated communication technologies have enabled organisations to adopt these flexible models on a large scale. If managed properly, remote work can become a "win-win" arrangement, providing both employers and employees with benefits (Popovici & Popovici, 2020).

Nevertheless, remote work also presents managerial challenges. Since teleworkers operate outside the direct reach of supervisors, they are monitored and evaluated differently than traditional staff (Elshaiekh et al., 2018). For this reason, impression management strategies can be useful. Exemplification and self-promotion, for example, may help teleworkers demonstrate dedication and competence (Jones & Pittman, 1982). Recent research indicates that remote workers adopt various influence tactics to convince managers, colleagues, and clients of their legitimacy and productivity in virtual environments (Haddon, 1998; Johnson, 1998; Bailey & Kurland, 2002).

4. DIGITAL PANOPTICSM IN THE CONTEXT OF REMOTE WORKING

The global trend of remote working, accelerated by the pandemic, has redefined workplace surveillance. Building on Jeremy Bentham's Panopticon and Michel Foucault's subsequent developments, digital panopticism now operates in the digital space through pervasive data capture, algorithmic monitoring, and automated control mechanisms (Ansorge, 2011). This advanced version of Foucault's panopticon metaphor permeates remote work environments through monitoring tools, algorithmic management systems, and constant data collection. This framework reshapes power dynamics and managerial relations, eroding worker autonomy and promoting self-discipline.

In the context of remote work, digital panopticism refers to a situation where employees are subject to continuous, real-time, and pervasive monitoring through digital tools and algorithms, even though they are not physically present in an office (Baiocco et. al., 2022). This concept is also referred to as the "algorithmic panopticon" in today's business world and represents a structure where data is transformed into an absolute tool of control (Benlian et. al., 2022).

In this context, digital panopticism is technologically enabled surveillance that constantly monitors activities and directs power relations through algorithmic processes. Constant surveillance, therefore, replaces traditional visibility and trust, reshaping formal and informal working relationships.

The pandemic, coupled with the shift to working from home, has caused a massive surge in the use of surveillance software (De Stefano & Taes, 2023). Although these tools are often justified as being necessary for productivity, they erode privacy and cause stress and burnout (Aloisi & De Stefano, 2022). Unlike the architectural panopticon, where an invisible guardian regulates behaviour, the digital panopticon extends visibility, discipline and normalisation into everyday life and work. Through databases, biometric systems, and algorithmic processes, it distributes surveillance across platforms, centralising information and generating new forms of power and control (Bashir, 2021). It is argued that digital data collected, especially in the business world, is a "simulation" or illusion that does not reflect real human actions, and that it serves "surveillance capitalism" by reducing individuals to data (York, 2021).

This shift enables behaviours to be regulated not by visible authority, but by the implicit awareness of constant observation, recording and analysis (Hyslop-Margison & Rochester, 2020). Thus, while digital monitoring can promote accountability, it can at the same time breed distrust and self-censorship (Duke, 2022). The opacity of algorithms exacerbates the imbalance between employer control and employee autonomy (Hafermalz, 2021). Indeed, Foucault's insights into the power of discipline are directly applicable: Knowing that one is constantly monitored necessitates self-regulation (Manokha, 2018; Andrejevic & Volcic, 2021).

Remote technologies capture detailed data, often without clear boundaries as to when and where monitoring occurs (East, 2021). However, it is also highlighted as an important point that, like the "impartial spectator" concept, it promotes ethical individual growth and serves as a resistance against this new generation of digital encroachment, particularly artificial intelligence and algorithms (Rathbone, 2022). As a result, surveillance is shifting from overt surveillance to subtle, algorithmically mediated control.

By tracking keystrokes, applications, and biometrics, tools generate a "data copy" of employees. These profiles are then used for predicting and tracking performance, aiming to discipline non-compliant behaviour. While teleworking offers some flexibility, invisible surveillance can restrict freedom through self-monitoring. The widespread adoption of remote working models during the pandemic, for instance, has encouraged the use of advanced monitoring software that records digital actions and extends the workplace to homes. These technologies use artificial intelligence to interpret productivity data and predict behaviour (Girona, 2024). Moreover, algorithmic management systems not only assign tasks and evaluate performance but also determine pay and access to future work. Consequently, this ambiguous power dynamic places oversight beyond the grasp of employees and into black-box algorithms (De Vaujany et al., 2021).

Surveillance mechanisms also involve connection monitoring, geolocation and biometric scanning (Bashir, 2021). In practice, remote workers experience "electronic sweatshop"', facing pressure to maintain their online presence and constant productivity (Duke, 2022). Such mechanisms inevitably erode trust. Managers who rely on data-driven supervision undermine professional autonomy. Employees, in turn, internalise surveillance, self-censorship and self-discipline in order to conform to institutional expectations (Hafermalz, 2021). However, this constant vigilance can lead to increased anxiety, stress and burnout. Many employees report feelings of vulnerability and a loss of privacy when their activities are monitored without recourse (Leclercq-Vandelannoitte, 2022). These situations not only reduce job satisfaction and impair mental health (Manning & Stern, 2018) but also disrupt team cohesion and collaboration.

When surveillance extends into the home, the boundaries between the personal and professional spheres become blurred, forcing employees to adapt their private routines to align with employer expectations (Manokha, 2018; De Moya & Pallud, 2020). Thus, remote working relations are profoundly reshaped by pervasive institutional control (Nemorin, 2017).

Against this backdrop, ethical concerns are of great importance. Surveillance that is justified on the grounds of necessity often constitutes an unprecedented encroachment on autonomy and dignity. The expansion into private spheres has therefore led to calls for stronger regulatory frameworks and ethical guidelines (Hafermalz, 2021). Yet, as the GDPR and other legislation struggle to keep pace with rapid innovation, proposals for AI regulations and platform directives continue to emerge as possible solutions. Nevertheless, opaque data collection and algorithmic decision-making present challenges to traditional legal principles such as privacy and consent (Andrejevic & Volvic, 2021). Accordingly, policy recommendations emphasise transparency, communication, and worker participation in monitoring decisions. In this regard, social dialogue and collective bargaining are vital to redressing asymmetrical power dynamics, while digital literacy enables workers to understand and negotiate surveillance terms (Girona, 2024).

Importantly, workers also resist surveillance. They are developing coping strategies and informal norms to counter the dominant logic of monitoring. Practices such as "strategic inconspicuousness" (minimising their digital footprint) reflect an attempt to reclaim privacy and resist algorithmic control (Girona, 2024). Furthermore, digital panopticism has fostered solidarity networks that criticise and respond collectively to surveillance practices (De Vaujany et al., 2021). Some scholars even argue that digital panopticism can paradoxically promote empowerment by encouraging self-regulation and the development of skills to manage digital visibility (Bashir, 2021). However, this empowerment is ambivalent: The same mechanisms can also reinforce excessive accountability and performance anxiety, trapping workers in cycles of self-surveillance and self-censorship (Duke, 2022).

Consequently, digital panopticism in remote work restructures power relations through constant monitoring, algorithmic management, and data-driven surveillance. Although it promises accountability and efficiency, it also erodes trust, autonomy, and well-being, while extending institutional control into private spheres. Transparent practices, robust regulation and collective resistance are vital in overcoming these challenges. Remote workers are both subjects of surveillance and instruments of compliance, thereby shaping the future evolution of digital power in the world of work.

5. METHODOLOGY

5.1. Research Aim and Design

This study employed a qualitative research design to investigate how influence tactics and organizational authority are experienced and reshaped in remote working environments. The inquiry was guided by the conceptual lens of digital panopticism, which provided a framework for interpreting how constant digital visibility transforms organizational power dynamics. A qualitative approach was deemed appropriate given the exploratory nature of the research and the need to capture participants' subjective meanings and lived experiences in understanding authority and influence under remote and hybrid work models.

This study aims to examine power and influence processes in remote work environments through the lens of digital panopticism by adopting an exploratory qualitative approach. While the existing literature demonstrates that influence tactics and power bases are closely associated with key organizational outcomes such as organizational commitment, job satisfaction, productivity, and burnout, research addressing these processes specifically within remote work contexts remains limited. Moreover, the majority of existing studies rely predominantly on quantitative methods, offering limited insight into how these dynamics are experienced and interpreted by employees in digitally mediated work settings. By focusing on remote work environments and employing a qualitative methodology, this study seeks to address this gap in the literature and contribute a deeper, context-sensitive understanding of how power and influence are reshaped under conditions of digital surveillance.

5.2. Sampling and Participants

In line with qualitative research principles, the adequacy of the sample size in this study was determined not by numerical representativeness but by analytical depth and theoretical saturation. A thematic analysis was conducted following Braun and Clarke's (2006) systematic approach, including familiarization with the data, initial coding, theme development, and interpretation. To enhance the trustworthiness of the findings, strategies such as member checking, peer debriefing, and the maintenance of an audit trail were employed in accordance with the criteria proposed by Lincoln and Guba (1988). Data collection continued until no new codes or themes emerged during the analysis, indicating that theoretical saturation had been reached, a criterion widely recognized as sufficient for determining sample size adequacy in qualitative studies.

A purposive sampling strategy was adopted with the aim of including diverse participants, who could provide rich insights into organizational power relations, within remote work contexts. Maximum variation was sought in terms of sector, role, and level of organizational responsibility, thereby enhancing the depth and breadth of perspectives. The use of maximum variation sampling enabled the inclusion of participants with diverse organizational backgrounds, allowing for the identification of both shared patterns and contextual differences in perceptions of organizational power and influence.

The final sample comprised 12 participants, the majority of whom were women, aged between 25 and 38. Most held a bachelor's degree, while one participant had completed a master's program. Their professional backgrounds spanned several industries, including fast-moving consumer goods, logistics, energy, automotive, and banking. Participants' roles varied, with finance, supply chain management, and logistics being the most common. While all participants working remote, two reported working fully remotely from home. Work experience ranged from 1.5 to 14 years, with the majority having between one and three years of experience in remote or hybrid models. This profile reflects a predominance of early- and mid-career professionals, who have accumulated experience across different sectors, while adapting to remote work practices.

5.3 Data Collection

Data were collected through semi-structured interviews, selected for their capacity to elicit in-depth accounts of influence strategies, authority relations, and perceptions of digital visibility. The interview protocol was developed on the basis of the research questions, which were first translated into thematic areas and subsequently refined into open-ended questions. The draft protocol was reviewed by a panel of experts, and adjustments were made in response to their feedback.

Pilot interviews were conducted with two professionals, one from the fast-moving consumer goods sector and another from the logistics sector, who had prior experience with hybrid and remote working models. Feedback from these pilot sessions, particularly regarding the clarity and precision of the questions, informed further revisions to the interview guide. The finalized protocol was then used for the main round of interviews.

All interviews were conducted online, recorded with participant consent, and transcribed verbatim. This process ensured both accuracy and completeness in capturing participants' accounts.

5.4. Data Analysis

The interview data were analyzed using MAXQDA 2024, following the principles of thematic content analysis. MAXQDA 2024 was selected due to its capacity to facilitate systematic coding, support theme development, and ensure transparent data organization, thereby enhancing the rigor and reliability of the qualitative analysis process. The analysis proceeded iteratively, beginning with open coding and progressing toward the identification of categories and themes. Codes were developed both deductively, drawing from existing literature on influence tactics and authority and inductively, emerging directly from the participants' narratives.

Analytic procedures included the use of MAXMaps, hierarchical code–subcode modeling, cross-tabulation and code maps. These tools facilitated a deeper exploration of relationships between themes, as well as the visualization of influence dynamics across different participants and contexts.

Several strategies were adopted to ensure the trustworthiness of the study. Credibility was enhanced through pilot testing of the interview guide and the use of expert feedback during its development. Dependability was strengthened through the systematic documentation of analytic decisions and the maintenance of analytic memos throughout the coding process. Transferability was supported by providing a detailed account of the sampling strategy and participant characteristics, enabling readers to assess the applicability of findings to other contexts. Finally, reflexivity was maintained by the researcher's critical engagement with personal assumptions and their potential impact on interpretation.

6. FINDINGS

The findings of this study point to the central role of influence in shaping how it is used and perceived in organisations, particularly in remote working conditions. Of the various tactics discussed, rational persuasion was identified as the most effective and frequently employed. Participants often shared how using data, facts and solid evidence strengthened their influence when trying to gain approval or influence decisions. Subordinates, in particular, said they relied on rational persuasion to sway their managers, generally seeing this as a successful approach. Many also emphasised the importance of backing up claims with proof rather than opinions. When examining what motivates individuals to comply with requests or decisions, the results consistently emphasised the importance of effective communication: the clearer and more thoughtful the communication, the greater the likelihood of success. Conversely, behaviours that sparked resistance were also tied to communication; however, these were often related to attitudes or behaviours that created tension or eroded trust. The study also highlights an important point for today's digital workplace. The results show that, in order to leverage influence in computer-mediated communication, one must pay attention not only to the message, but also to the social context, subtle cues and overall tone. Strengthening these elements can help organisations to use influence more effectively and to make power dynamics work more smoothly.

The findings are based on a qualitative sample and reflect participants' subjective perceptions within a specific remote work context. Therefore, the results should be interpreted as context-dependent and may not be fully generalizable to other organizational settings or work arrangements.

The table below (see Table 2) shows the themes identified in the content analysis, along with the three most frequently occurring subcodes related to these codes. These codes and subcodes are then explained in detail using discourse examples.

Table 2. Code list

Row	Code Name	Most Frequent Sub-Codes
1	Influence tactics	Rational persuasion
		Keeping good relations
		Transparency
2	Behaviors that increase the likelihood of successful influence attempts	Speaking based on evidence
		Conducting one-on-one interviews
		Giving feedback
3	Behaviors that increase the likelihood of unsuccessful influence attempts	Manipulation
		Not being convincing
		Being inexperienced
4	Determinants of influence tactics	Manager's management style
		Departmental culture
		Organizational culture
5	Differences in the use of influence tactics	The use of emojis and GIFs
		Waiting for a face-to-face meeting
		Making small talk
6	Advantages in influencing and communication when working remotely	Being able to hide negative emotions

continued on following page

Table 2. Continued

Row	Code Name	Most Frequent Sub-Codes
		More accessibility of superiors
		Ensuring sustainable managerial communication
7	Disadvantages in influencing and communication when working remotely	Lack of social context cues
		Longer access time
		Fewer non-work conversations
8	Definition of influence	High performance
		Making a good impression on the manager
		Communicating well

6.1. Influence Tactics: Rational Persuasion as the Dominant Strategy

According to the findings, rational persuasion was the most frequently mentioned influence tactic by subordinates. The participants mentioned that they utilized rational persuasion tactic the most in influencing managers and that this tactic was successful. At this point, they also mentioned the importance of speaking based on evidence. The examination of influence tactics shows that employees often use them to shape how they are perceived by their managers. Beyond the well-documented strategies in the literature (Kipnis et al., 1980), our qualitative content analysis points to additional themes, most notably transparency, efforts to sustain positive relations, and reliance on intermediaries. Examples of discourse illustrating these themes are presented below.

> *"My manager likes to talk with data when it comes to persuasion. Actually, the more data I bring to managers and the more they can see the big picture, the more clearly they are persuaded." (Interview 12, Male, 27, Human Resources Assistant Specialist)*
>
> *"I can influence my boss more easily when working remotely, in line with what I say and what I want. I feel more confident because my performance is measured much better, as what I do can be seen transparently." (Interview 1, Female, 30, Supply Chain Specialist)*

6.2. Behaviors Increasing the Likelihood of Successful Influence Attempts

Consistent with the category of behaviors that increase the likelihood of successful influence attempts (Table 2), participants most frequently emphasized the importance of supporting their arguments with evidence. This was seen as a way to compensate for the lack of social context cues such as body language or gestures in remote communication. Speaking with data, presenting concrete proof, conducting one-on-one interviews, giving feedback, opening the camera during online meetings, using moderate language, and demonstrating high performance were repeatedly cited as strategies to enhance persuasiveness. These findings suggest that successful influence attempts are closely tied to communication-oriented actions that strengthen social presence, echoing concepts from Social Presence Theory (Short, Williams, & Christie, 1976). At this point, it can be concluded that reinforcing social presence positively affects compliance. Discourse examples illustrating this theme are presented below.

"I need to go to my manager with evidence. I need to show him that we are having problems with this person from Kenya for these reasons. For example, I need to go with something like, 'In the last operation, he created such and such a problem because he sent the documents too late,' or I need to go considering all the cases. To convince him." (Interview 5, Female, 38, Supply Chain Specialist)

"I think the one-on-one meetings we hold every month are very important at this point. Every month, we take notes on the important events of that month and talk to our manager. I did this and that this month, I struggled with this this month, you reacted like this to me here, which I didn't like very much. We have to say these things. We give feedback to our manager not to blame each other but to find solutions, for example, 'You couldn't help me here, you didn't have time, what can we do about this?'. This is the company culture. Every month, the manager has to listen to you for an hour. At the end of the year, when performance is evaluated, the notes taken during one-on-one meetings are also evaluated. It's like your diary. I did these things, I had problems here, this was the cause of the crisis, and because this was the cause, the solution could be this. Your manager can say, "Okay, I was also at fault in this matter," or give you negative feedback". (Interview 1, Female, 30, Supply Chain Specialist)

6.3. Behaviors Increasing the Likelihood of Unsuccessful Influence Attempts

As for the behaviors that increase the likelihood of unsuccessful influence attempts, it is seen that subordinates, do not hesitate to share negative examples. At this point, two of the most frequently mentioned behaviors were manipulation and not being convincing. They mentioned that employees who manipulate cannot deceive managers and that managers lose their sincerity towards them because they are not successful in manipulating them. Being unconvincing also includes not showing evidence. Participants identified the absence of evidence-based communication as a key reason for lacking credibility, alongside factors such as inexperience, ineffective delegation, the use of inappropriate language, and attempts at self-promotion. Behaviors associated with resistance were likewise communication-oriented, but more closely tied to employees' attitudes and negatively perceived personal characteristics within the organization. To illustrate these findings, a representative participant statement is provided below.

"We have a colleague on the team who, despite somehow managing to get their work done, is constantly demanding and manipulative. They lie. They deliberately fail to complete assigned tasks by the deadline, and they do this repeatedly. They are likely doing this to show that they don't know or respect their manager. He manipulates the manager's sincerity; for example, the manager extends his deadline by three days. Then, in front of our manager's superior, he makes statements like deadlines are never taken seriously or adhered to anyway, and no one pays attention to deadlines. If you do this, you undermine the manager's trust in you, and whatever you ask for later, you will never get it accepted. Those who try to manipulate are usually weeded out and cannot stay in the organization." (Interview 10, Male, 28, Financial Accounting Analyst)

6.4. Determinants of Influence Tactics: Managerial Style and Organizational Culture

When asked about the factors shaping their choice of influence tactics, participants in subordinate positions emphasized the manager's management style, which they assessed by observing the manager's character, attitudes, and behaviors. They noted that no single tactic, or fixed combination of tactics, is universally effective, as the choice varies from one manager to another. In addition, both organizational and departmental culture were highlighted as key determinants, with culture more broadly emerging as a central element in influence processes. Overall, the findings suggest that managerial leadership style and cultural context directly shape and constrain the use of influence tactics. The following quotations from participants provide illustrative examples of the theme.

"So, both at my previous company and at my current company, my managers are actually very reasonable people. Therefore, they are very open to hearing ideas. When there is an issue that challenges us in any operation, as I said, they are very open about everything from changing the meeting to the way a job is done. They are eager to fix it in the way that suits us best." (Interview 11, Female, 29, Financial Accounting Analyst)

"Actually, this also depends on the communication style of this organization, that is, this department of the global company. This is a package that was already prepared for me, as I said, and is outside of my own preferences. Rather than

proceeding by email, we talk to get faster results, discuss the pros and cons, and if there's anything else on their mind, we discuss the details, clarify them, come to a decision that way, and close it that way. This is actually something that comes with the structure. I can say it's a tool, a method." (Interview 4, Female, 35, Product Manager)

6.5. Differences in Influence Tactics in Computer-Mediated Communication

In computer-mediated communication, the most striking difference in the use of influence tactics was the use of emojis and GIFs. Participants noted that these tools were helpful in expressing emotions and opinions to the other party. Other differences in the use of influence tactics included waiting for a face-to-face meeting, making small talk, connecting through different channels, differentiating and choosing the means of communication, using the manager's calendar, paying attention to written language, showing evidence, paying attention to appearance in video meetings, and sharing screens. Participants' accounts also indicated that employees sought to strengthen social context cues and enhance social presence in communication. Some further emphasized efforts to address the lack of intimacy and disconnection associated with remote work by increasing the frequency or depth of communication, or by waiting for face-to-face interaction. Representative discourse illustrating these differences are provided below.

"I use a lot of emojis, by the way, because you can say 'good evening,' for example, or send a good evening smiley, a flower, something like that, and then you show that you have a more positive attitude. So emojis take up a lot of space in your life." (Interview 11, Female, 29, Financial Accounting Analyst)

"I use emojis a lot, meaning that with coworkers I've reached a certain level of intimacy with, I communicate as if on a personal phone call. Sometimes, for example, I'm waiting for a task from a friend, and I don't want to pressure them, but I need the document to be completed. So I send them the 'You're not coming anymore' song. It creates a great environment to sweetly wrap things up, like 'what's going on with my work?' I think it's really nice." (Interview 8, Female, 33, Logistics Specialist)

6.6. Advantages of Influencing and Communication in Remote Work

In computer-mediated communication, participants most frequently mentioned the advantage of being able to hide negative emotions. This is inherent to the nature of distance communication and can be considered a significant benefit in online meetings or computer-mediated interactions. Participants also highlighted that the increased accessibility of their superiors, the maintenance of clear and unbroken communication with managers, and the visibility of their work offer various advantages in the application of influence tactics. These advantages appear to facilitate and enhance effective relationship management with managers. Moreover, some participants who identified as introverted or experiencing social anxiety reported that remote working models and computer-mediated communication allowed them to influence their managers more effectively. The following exemplary participant statements illustrate these points.

"Sometimes, for example, when you're working remotely and you really panic and get scared, or when you're worried about something, I think it's a good thing that you don't immediately go over to the other side. So, let's say you realize you might have done something wrong while talking to your boss. You want to check on them right then and there. But because you don't react immediately, you calmly finish talking to the other person and then turn around and think, 'Did I do that? If I did, I'll fix it,' and so on. Actually, it can be good, I think, because not immediately showing your emotions to the other person is also an advantage; it makes you more professional. Because, for example, in my early years, when I was a recent graduate, I cried a lot. Go to the bathroom and cry. When you came back with a red face, people might think you're very sensitive, but in remote work, I think it's better." (Interview 6, Female, 31, Financial Analyst)

"Being able to hide negative emotions is a huge plus. You get angry, you get upset, but the screen is always on, yet you don't get what the other person is saying directly from the screen, and you don't get those bad feelings as much. The other side may be less affected in a way; it doesn't fully reach us. The relationship is less distorted. When negative emotions are involved, remote work can have a slightly more protective effect, I think." (Interview 3, Female, 26, Strategic Planning and Efficiency Specialist)

6.7. Disadvantages of Influencing and Communication in Remote Work

As a disadvantage, the lack of cues about the social context was most frequently mentioned. This can be considered a handicap of computer-mediated communication, but it is also evident from the interviews that organizations have not taken much action to overcome this problem. Other disadvantages identified included longer access time, fewer non-work conversations, technical problems, reduced visibility of achievements, cultural differences, and easy accessibility. The decrease in non-work conversations was reported to lead to lower motivation and a reduced sense of belonging to the job. Similarly, the other disadvantages mentioned are consistently associated with the characteristics of computer-mediated communication tools. Participants who highlighted the decrease in off-work conversations also emphasized its impact on their motivation and job engagement. It can be argued that practitioners should focus on mitigating these disadvantages in order to improve the quality of communication in the context of power and influence in remote work. Additionally, while participants acknowledged multiple advantages of computer-mediated communication, most noted that distance communication cannot fully replace face-to-face interaction. The following exemplary participant statements illustrate these points.

"When working remotely, for example, I'm talking normally, my facial expression is actually very normal, but my voice doesn't come across that way to the other person, and I always get questions like, 'Are you unhappy? ' I hear things like that a lot. So, actually, if they could see my face, I'm not in that kind of place, but just because they're making assumptions based on my voice, I've had many moments where I've fallen into negativity. Then it immediately occurs to me: wait a minute, you can't use your facial expressions right now, so use your voice like an expression and adjust the end accordingly." (Interview 11, Female, 29, Financial Accounting Analyst)

"The face-to-face interaction that used to exist is gone. The person in front of you can no longer see your facial expressions, or rather, it's not just facial expressions. It's like this: you're a kind, sympathetic person who can get things done through human relationships, and you use that. It's one of your characteristics. You could use it when you were face-to-face, but you can't use it when you're at home. If you work hybrid, you need to show and introduce this trait on office days to evoke sympathy or build the relationship on those days, or you will have to try to do the same thing in writing, which is more difficult." (Interview 1, Female, 30, Supply Chain Specialist)

6.8. Definitions of Influence and Perceived Sources of Power

When participants were asked to define the concept of influence, the majority defined it in terms of high performance. In addition, influence was defined as making the manager think well of you, communicating well, changing opinions, gaining trust, marketing yourself effectively, exercising informational power, being appreciated and taking initiative at the right moment. Considering these definitions, it is evident that the concept of influence is framed around the qualities or competencies required to be influential or effective. The following exemplary participant statements illustrate these points.

"Making an impact on my work actually means exceeding performance expectations. Doing work beyond my role in different departments, making their jobs

easier, and ensuring they receive positive feedback from their own managers." (Interview 9, Female, 26, Robotics Process Automation Specialist)

"Generally, making them think that I am a high-performing employee." (Interview 2, Female, 25, Business Analyst)

When the participants were asked about their views on the sources of power that they considered effective, the most frequently mentioned source was rational persuasion. Participants also indicated that they found referent power, reward power, and legitimate power effective, in that order. This suggests that hard power sources are generally not perceived as effective in computer-mediated communication, whereas softer power sources are considered more influential. The sources of power that were deemed ineffective were identified by participants only as legitimate power, with the observation that legitimate power alone is insufficient. They noted that legitimate power can be effective when combined with other sources of power. It is evident that participants differentiated between legitimate and coercive power, considering only authority-based power less effective. The following exemplary participant statements illustrate these points.

"When someone asks me for something, I don't want them to be left hanging. So if I can explain my work to someone in a way that leaves no questions in their mind, I want them to explain things to me in the same way. This is an important factor for me." (Interview 10, Male, 28, Financial Accounting Analyst)

"Why does it have to be so official, important, and formal? Why does it have to take so long? I need to be convinced, I need to find it meaningful, you know, to be convinced." (Interview 6, Female, 31, Financial Analyst)

6.9. Similarities with Previous Studies

The findings of this study are consistent with prior research on power and influence tactics in remote and computer-mediated work contexts. In particular, the prominence of rational persuasion as the most effective influence tactic aligns with the findings of Steizel and Rimbau-Gilabert (2013), who showed that lower-status members in virtual teams frequently rely on rationality and mediation to influence superiors. Similarly, Wadsworth and Blanchard (2015) identified rational persuasion as one of the most commonly used influence tactics in virtual teams. The emphasis on evidence-based communication and transparency observed in this study also supports Boughton's (2011) conclusion that knowledge, expertise, and task-related competence are more effective sources of influence than formal authority in virtual settings. In addition, Sherblom's (1988) analysis of email signatures as symbolic influence cues resonates with the present findings regarding the importance of visibility, transparency, and communicative form in shaping influence within digitally mediated environments.

6.10. Differences from Previous Research and Emerging Contributions

Despite the similarities, the present study extends the literature in several important ways. While earlier research has primarily focused on structural, task-related, or relational aspects of influence in virtual teams (Ferguson, 2004; Panteli & Tucker, 2009), this study foregrounds the role of digital panopticism by highlighting constant visibility, self-regulation, and communicative discipline as central mechanisms shaping influence processes. Moreover, the identification of emojis and GIFs as deliberate strategies to humanize digital communication represents a departure from prior studies, which have largely overlooked informal and affective communication cues. In doing so, the study contributes a more nuanced understanding of how power and influence are reconfigured under conditions of digital surveillance.In doing so, the study contributes a more nuanced understanding of how power and influence are reconfigured under conditions of digital surveillance.

7. DISCUSSION

Examining the findings reveals the strong effect of digital panopticism on the use of influence tactics by individuals within the framework of remote work. Especially under remote work conditions, employees increasingly avoid reliance on authority for the approval of their ideas; rather, they are progressively inclined to employ data, factual evidence, and logical reasoning. This phenomenon is closely connected to the widespread feeling of "constant visibility" created by digital surveillance mechanisms.

It is observed that employees are careful not only regarding the content of their communications but also in relation to their delivery, tone, and way of expressing to effectively sway their superiors. Consequently, the dynamics of influence and persuasion occur in a more rational, transparent, and evidence-based environment, aligning with the themes of rational persuasion and behaviors that increase successful influence attempts identified in the study (Table 2, Rows 1 and 2).

Nonetheless, this constant visibility, manifested through frequent reporting and the encouragement for employees to activate their cameras during virtual meetings, creates a dilemma within organizational relationships. While it promotes reliable, data-driven discourse, it simultaneously imposes undue pressure and can elicit reactions from managers marked by lack of trust or passive resistance. Hence, digital panopticism emerges as a mechanism that disciplines employees and fosters evidence-based communication, although with the inherent risk of creating tension and resistance within interpersonal relationships. As a result, power relations in contemporary digital contexts are established not solely on the basis of "what is articulated" but also on "how and with what proof it is articulated"; this complexity renders workplace interactions both more detailed and more transparent.

The actions taken by participants to reduce the coldness of remote communication through the inclusion of emojis and GIFs can be seen as a human strategy devised to balance out the controlling and distancing sides of digital panopticism. Nonetheless, their capacity to obscure negative emotions in computer-mediated communication underscores the reality that panoptic surveillance strengthens the way of self-control; individuals tend to present themselves in a more careful way under the widespread feeling of surveillance, thereby slowing down the decline of interpersonal relationships.

The observation that individuals possessing superior communication skills are regarded as effective, whereas those who exhibit controlling behaviors or lack communication proficiency are perceived as ineffective, indicates that power within the panoptic framework is based on not only hierarchical status but also on the quality of communication and planned visibility (Table 2, Rows 1, 2, and 3). Therefore, digital panopticism compels employees to present themselves in an acceptable manner; communication evolves into a domain of power and influence not solely through message content but also via tonal qualities, form, and perceived authenticity.

The lack of social signals in remote work diminishes the quality of interactions within digital communication and creates cracks in trust dynamics (Table 2, Row 7). Within the context of digital panopticism, this compels employees to articulate their thoughts in a more controlled and data-oriented manner, aware of their perpetual surveillance. Thus, communication diverges from spontaneous human engagement, adopting a more mechanical, measurable, and disciplined character. This evolution illustrates the two-sided nature of the panoptic order, which simultaneously fosters transparency while limiting the quality of communication.

Research findings also indicate that digital panopticism alters both personal communication strategies and organisational culture (Table 2, Row 4). Over time, the transition of employees towards evidence-based discourse fosters a heightened valuation of data and transparency within the institution. However, constant monitoring and evaluation strengthen the self-discipline mechanisms among employees, with individuals regulating their own conduct and communication in accordance with an established comprehension of surveillance. This leads to a dual effect within organisations, increasing productivity whilst constraining individual creativity and originality. Ultimately, digital panopticism can be characterized as both a modality of surveillance in contemporary work environments and a comprehensive social and technical system that maintains workplace regulations and power dynamics.

8. CONCLUSION

This study examined power and influence processes in remote work environments through the lens of digital panopticism, with a particular focus on how influence tactics are exercised and perceived under conditions of computer-mediated communication. The findings demonstrate that rational persuasion emerges as the most prominent and effective influence tactic in remote work settings, largely driven by the heightened visibility and accountability created by digital surveillance mechanisms. Employees increasingly rely on data, evidence, and logical reasoning rather than authority-based power to influence managerial decisions. Moreover, the results highlight that influence in remote contexts is not determined solely by message content, but also by communication tone, delivery, visibility management, and the ability to compensate for the absence of social context cues.

Overall, the study reveals the dual nature of digital panopticism in contemporary organizations. While constant visibility and monitoring foster transparency, performance orientation, and evidence-based communication, they simultaneously generate pressure, trust-related tensions, and constraints on spontaneity and creativity. The increased use of strategies such as emojis and controlled emotional expression illustrates employees' efforts to humanize digital interactions and manage relational dynamics under surveillance. These findings suggest that influence in remote work environments are increasingly shaped by communicative competence and planned visibility rather than formal hierarchical authority, underscoring the transformative impact of digital surveillance on organizational relationships.

9. MANAGERIAL IMPLICATIONS

The findings of this study offer several important implications for organizations operating in remote and digitally monitored work environments. First, the widespread use of digital surveillance and performance monitoring systems has certain consequences for trust-building processes between managers and employees. While transparency and data-driven evaluation can enhance the perception of fairness and accountability, excessive monitoring risks undermining psychological safety and employee well-being. In this context, ethical leadership becomes critical; leaders must balance control with autonomy and clearly define the purpose, scope, and limitations of digital monitoring practices. Additionally, the sustainability of remote work arrangements depends not only on technological efficiency but also on organizations' ability to maintain organizational justice, emotional well-being, and trust over time. Practices that accept employee consent, protect confidentiality, and encourage supportive communication can help mitigate the negative effects of constant visibility and create more resilient and sustainable remote work cultures.

10. LIMITATIONS AND FUTURE RESEARCH

Despite its contributions, this study has several limitations that should be acknowledged. First, the qualitative nature of the research and the relatively small sample size limit the generalizability of the findings. In addition, the study is based on participants' self-reported perceptions, which may be influenced by subjective interpretations and contextual factors. The focus on remote work settings also restricts the applicability of the results to hybrid or fully office-based work arrangements. Future research could address these limitations by employing mixed-methods or quantitative designs with larger and more diverse samples, as well as by comparing influence dynamics across different work modalities and cultural contexts. Longitudinal studies may further enhance understanding of how digital panopticism and influence strategies evolve over time in organizations.

ACKNOWLEDGEMENTS

This study is derived from the Doctoral thesis titled "A research for understanding the nature of organizational power and influence in the context of new working models", completed by Dr. Begüm Kanat Tiryaki under the supervision of Prof. Dr. Nazlı Ayşe Ayyıldız Ünnü at the Department of Business Administration, Graduate School of Social Sciences, Ege University.

REFERENCES

Alizadeh, T. (2013). Planning implications of telework: A policy analysis of the Sydney metropolitan strategy. *Australian Plants*, *50*(4), 304–315. DOI: 10.1080/07293682.2013.764906

Allen, T. D., Golden, T. D., & Shockley, K. M. (2015). How effective is telecommuting? Assessing the status of our scientific findings. *Psychological Science in the Public Interest*, *16*(2), 40–68. DOI: 10.1177/1529100615593273 PMID: 26403188

Aloisi, A., & De Stefano, V. (2022). Essential jobs, remote work and digital surveillance: Addressing the COVID-19 pandemic panopticon. *International Labour Review*, *161*(2), 289–314. DOI: 10.1111/ilr.12219 PMID: 34548685

Andrejevic, M., & Volcic, Z. (2021). Pandemic lessons: Total surveillance and the post-trust society. *The Political Economy of Communication*, *9*(1), 4–12.

Bailey, D. E., & Kurland, N. B. (2002). A Review of Telework Research: Findings, New Directions, and Lessons for the Study of Modern Work. *Journal of Organizational Behavior*, *23*(4), 383–400. DOI: 10.1002/job.144

Baiocco, S., Fernández-Macías, E., Rani, U., & Pesole, A. (2022). *The algorithmic management of work and its implications in different contexts* (No. 2022/02). JRC Working Papers Series on Labour, Education and Technology.

Bashir, M. (2021). Surveillance and panopticism in the digital age. *Qlantic Journal of Social Sciences and Humanities*, *2*(1), 11–16. DOI: 10.55737/qjssh.779670819

Baskin, C., Barker, M., & Woods, P. (2004). Scoping social presence and social context cues to support knowledge construction in an ICT rich environment. In *Proceedings of 2004 AARE conference*.

Bélanger, J. J., Pierro, A., Barbieri, B., De Carlo, N. A., Falco, A., & Kruglanski, A. W. (2016). One size doesn't fit all: The influence of supervisors' power tactics and subordinates' need for cognitive closure on burnout and stress. *European Journal of Work and Organizational Psychology*, *25*(2), 287–300. DOI: 10.1080/1359432X.2015.1061999

Benlian, A., Wiener, M., Cram, W. A., Krasnova, H., Maedche, A., Möhlmann, M., Recker, J., & Remus, U. (2022). Algorithmic management: Bright and dark sides, practical implications, and research opportunities. *Business & Information Systems Engineering*, *64*(6), 825–839. DOI: 10.1007/s12599-022-00764-w

Biocca, F. (1997). The cyborg's dilemma: Progressive embodiment in virtual environments. *Journal of Computer-Mediated Communication*, *3*(2), JCMC324. DOI: 10.1111/j.1083-6101.1997.tb00070.x

Bocchiaro, P., & Zamperini, A. (2012). Conformity, obedience, disobedience- The power of the situation. Psychology–Selected papers, 275, 294.

Culnan, M. J., Markus, M. L., Jablin, F. M., Putnam, L. L., Roberts, K. H., & Porter, L. W. (1987). Handbook of organizational communication: An interdisciplinary perspective.

Daft, R. L., Lengel, R. H., & Trevino, L. K. (1987). Message Equivocality, Media Selection, and Manager Performance: Implications for Information Systems. *Management Information Systems Quarterly*, *11*(3), 355–366. DOI: 10.2307/248682

De Moya, J. F., & Pallud, J. (2020). From panopticon to heautopticon: A new form of surveillance introduced by quantified-self practices. *Information Systems Journal*, *30*(6), 940–976. DOI: 10.1111/isj.12284

De Stefano, V., & Taes, S. (2023). Algorithmic management and collective bargaining. *Transfer: European Review of Labour and Research*, *29*(1), 21–36. DOI: 10.1177/10242589221141055

De Vaujany, F. X., Leclercq-Vandelannoitte, A., Munro, I., Nama, Y., & Holt, R. (2021). Control and surveillance in work practice: Cultivating paradox in 'new' modes of organizing. *Organization Studies*, *42*(5), 675–695. DOI: 10.1177/01708406211010988

DeSanctis, G., Jackson, B. M., (1994). Coordination of Information Technology Management: Team-Based Structures and Computer-Based Communication Systems, Source: Journal of Management Information Systems, Spring, 1994, Vol. 10, No. 4 (Spring, 1994), 85-110.

Deutsch, M., & Gerard, H. B. (1955). A study of normative and informational social influences upon individual judgment. *Journal of Abnormal and Social Psychology*, *51*(3), 629–636. DOI: 10.1037/h0046408 PMID: 13286010

Drucker, P. F. (1988). The coming of the new organization. *Harvard Business Review*, *66*, 45–53.

Duke, B. (2022). 24/7 Digital work-based spy: The effects of technological panopticism on workers in the digital age. *Journal of Labor and Society*, *25*(4), 520–558. DOI: 10.1163/24714607-bja10068

East, Emma E., "THE EFFECTS OF VIRTUAL PANOPTICISM" (2021). *Selected Honors Theses*. 140.

Elias, S. (2008). Fifty years of influence in the workplace: The evolution of the French and Raven power taxonomy. *Journal of Management History*, *14*(3), 267–283. DOI: 10.1108/17511340810880634

Elshaiekh, N. M., Alghafri, F. S. S., Alsakeiti, F. S. S., & Aziza, C. H. (2018). The impact of information technology on SMEs in Oman. *Compusoft*, *7*(10), 2843–2845.

Foucault, M. (1982). The Subject and Power, Source: Critical Inquiry, Vol. 8, No. 4, 777-795 Published by: The University of Chicago Press, https://www.jstor.org/stable/1343197

French, J. R. P. Jr., Raven, B. (1959). The bases of social power. In D. Cartwright (Ed.), Studies in Social Power, 150–167.

Fu, P. P., & Yukl, G. (2000). Perceived effectiveness of influence tactics in the United States and China. *The Leadership Quarterly*, *11*(2), 251–266. DOI: 10.1016/S1048-9843(00)00039-4

Fulk, J., & Boyd, B. (1991). Emerging theories of communication in organizations. *Journal of Management*, *17*(2), 407–446. DOI: 10.1177/014920639101700207

Giddens, A. (1979). *Central problems in social theory: Action, structure, and contradiction in social analysis* (Vol. 241). Univ of California Press. DOI: 10.1007/978-1-349-16161-4

Girona, A. E. (2024). *Navigating Trust, Privacy, and Mental Health: Remote Workers' Experiences During the COVID-19 Pandemic—A Textual Analysis of Reddit Data*. The Pennsylvania State University.

Goodstadt, B. E., & Hjelle, L. A. (1973). Power To The Powerless: Locus Of Control And The Use Of Power. *Journal of Personality and Social Psychology*, *27*(2), 190–196. DOI: 10.1037/h0034784 PMID: 4723967

Guérin, I., Agier, I., & Kumar, S. (2013). Women's Empowerment: Power to Act or Power over Other Women? Lessons from Indian Microfinance. *Oxford Development Studies*, *41*(sup1), 76–94. DOI: 10.1080/13600818.2013.781147

Hafermalz, E. (2021). Out of the panopticon and into exile: Visibility and control in distributed new culture organizations. *Organization Studies*, *42*(5), 697–717. DOI: 10.1177/0170840620909962

Haugaard, M. (2010). Democracy, Political Power, and Authority, Social Research, Vol. 77, No. 4, From Impunity to Accountability: Africa's Development in the 21st Century, 1049-1074.

Hyslop-Margison, E., & Rochester, R. (2020). Assessment or Surveillance? Panopticism and Higher Education. *Philosophical Inquiry in Education.*, *24*(1), 102–109. DOI: 10.7202/1070559ar

Instone, D., Major, B., & Bunker, B. B. (1983). Gender, self confidence, and social influence strategies: An organizational simulation. *Journal of Personality and Social Psychology*, *44*(2), 322–333. DOI: 10.1037/0022-3514.44.2.322

International Labour Organization. (2021). *Teleworking for Workers and Employers in the ICTS and Financial Services Sectors*. https://www.ilo.org/sites/default/files/wcmsp5/groups/public/%40ed_dialogue/%40sector/documents/meetingdocument/wcms_547099.pdf

Jones, E. E., Pittman, T.S., (1982). Toward A General Theory Of Strategic Self-Presentation.

Kamal, M. M. (2020). The triple-edged sword of COVID-19: Understanding the use of digital technologies and the impact of productive, disruptive, and destructive nature of the pandemic. *Information Systems Management*, *37*(4), 310–317. DOI: 10.1080/10580530.2020.1820634

Kipnis, D., & Schmidt, S. (1985). The language of persuasion. *Psychology Today*, *19*(4), 40.

Kipnis, D., Schmidt, S. M., Swaffin-Smith, C., & Wilkinson, I. (1984). Patterns of managerial influence: Shotgun managers, tacticians, and bystanders. *Organizational Dynamics*, *12*(3), 58–67. DOI: 10.1016/0090-2616(84)90025-1

Kipnis, D., Schmidt, S. M., & Wilkinson, I. (1980). Intraorganizational influence tactics: Explorations in getting one's way. *The Journal of Applied Psychology*, *65*(4), 440–452. DOI: 10.1037/0021-9010.65.4.440

Leclercq-Vandelannoitte, A. (2022). Is employee technological "ill-being" missing from corporate responsibility? The Foucauldian ethics of ubiquitous IT uses in organizations. In *Business and the ethical implications of technology* (pp. 33–55). Springer Nature Switzerland. DOI: 10.1007/978-3-031-18794-0_3

Leifer, R. (1988). Matching Computer-Based Information Systems with Organizational Structures. *Management Information Systems Quarterly*, *12*(1), 63–73. DOI: 10.2307/248805

Lincoln, Y. S., & Guba, E. G. (1988). Criteria for Assessing Naturalistic Inquiries as Reports.

Manokha, I. (2018). Surveillance, panopticism, and self-discipline in the digital age. *Surveillance & Society*, *16*(2), 219–237. DOI: 10.24908/ss.v16i2.8346

Melé, D., & Rosanas, J. M. (2003). Power, Freedom and Authority in Management: Mary Parker Follett's 'Power- With'. *Philosophy of Management*, *3*(2), 35–46. DOI: 10.5840/pom20033221

Melin, U., & Axelsson, K. (2005). Understanding Organizational Coordination and Information Systems : Mintzberg's Coordination Mechanisms Revisited and Evaluated. *Proceedings of the 13th European Conference on Information Systems*, 1634–1644.

Meydan, C., Dirik, D., & Eryılmaz, İ. (2018). Liderin Güç Kaynakları Ve İş Performansı Arasındaki İlişkide Pelz Etkisinin Düzenleyici Rolü, Yönetim ve Ekonomi. *Celal Bayar Üniversitesi İktisadi ve İdari Bilimler Fakültesi Dergisi*, *25*(1), 75–92.

Mills, D. Q. (1991). *Rebirth of the corporation*. Wiley.

Nakrošienė, A., Bučiūnienė, I., & Goštautaitė, B. (2019). Working from home: Characteristics and outcomes of telework. *International Journal of Manpower*, *40*(1), 87–101. DOI: 10.1108/IJM-07-2017-0172

Nemorin, S. (2017). Post-panoptic pedagogies: The changing nature of school surveillance in the digital age. *Surveillance & Society*, *15*(2), 239–253. DOI: 10.24908/ss.v15i2.6033

Olson, M. H. (1983). Remote office work: Changing work patterns in space and time. *Communications of the ACM*, *26*(3), 182–187. DOI: 10.1145/358061.358068

Panteli, N., & Tucker, R. (2009). Power and trust in global virtual teams. *Communications of the ACM*, *52*(12), 113–115. DOI: 10.1145/1610252.1610282

Popovici, V., & Popovici, A. L. (2020). Remote work revolution: Current opportunities and challenges for organizations. Ovidius University Annals. *Economic Sciences Series*, *20*, 468–472.

Powell, A., Piccoli, G., & Ives, B. (2004). Virtual teams: A review of current literature and directions for future research. *The Data Base for Advances in Information Systems*, *35*(1), 6–36. DOI: 10.1145/968464.968467

Prasad, D. K., Mangipudi, D. M. R., Vaidya, D. R., & Muralidhar, B. (2020). Organizational climate, opportunities, challenges and psychological wellbeing of the remote working employees during COVID-19 pandemic: A general linear model approach with reference to information technology industry in Hyderabad. [IJARET]. *International Journal of Advanced Research in Engineering and Technology*, *11*(4).

Priyono, A., Moin, A., & Putri, V. N. A. O. (2020). Identifying Digital Transformation Paths in the Business Model of SMEs during the COVID-19 Pandemic. *Journal of Open Innovation*, *6*(4), 104. DOI: 10.3390/joitmc6040104

Rathbone, M. (2022). Panopticism, impartial spectator and digital technology. *The Indo-Pacific Journal of Phenomenology*, *22*(1), e2064720. DOI: 10.1080/20797222.2022.2064720

Rice, R. E., & Love, G. (1987). Electronic emotion: Socioemotional content in a computer-mediated communication network. *Communication Research*, *14*(1), 85–108. DOI: 10.1177/009365087014001005

Short, J., Williams, E., & Christie, B. (1976). *The social psychology of telecommunications*. John Wiley & Sons.

Simon, B., & Oakes, P. (2006). Beyond dependence: An identity approach to social power and domination. *Human Relations*, *59*(1), 105–139. DOI: 10.1177/0018726706062760

Sproull, L., & Kiesler, S. (1991). Connections: New Ways of Working in the Networked Organization. *Administrative Science Quarterly*, •••, 37.

Staples, D. S., Hulland, J. S., & Higgins, C. A. (1999). A self-efficacy theory explanation for the management of remote workers in virtual organizations. *Organization Science*, *10*(6), 758–776. DOI: 10.1287/orsc.10.6.758

Steizel, S., & Rimbau-Gilabert, E. (2013). Upward influence tactics through technology-mediated communication tools. *Computers in Human Behavior*, *29*(2), 462–472. DOI: 10.1016/j.chb.2012.04.024

Straus, S. G. (1997). Technology, group process, and group outcomes: Testing the connections in computer-mediated and face-to-face groups. Human–Computer Interaction, 12(3), 227-266, https-//DOI: 10.1207/s15327051hci1203_1

Straus, S. G., & McGrath, J. E. (1994). Does the medium matter? The interaction of task type and technology on group performance and member reactions. *The Journal of Applied Psychology*, *79*(1), 87–97. DOI: 10.1037/0021-9010.79.1.87 PMID: 8200874

Sullivan, C. (2003). What's in a name? Definitions and conceptualisations of teleworking and homeworking. *New Technology, Work and Employment*, *18*(3), 158–165. DOI: 10.1111/1468-005X.00118

Teboho Ansorge, J. (2011). Digital power in world politics: Databases, panopticons and Erwin Cuntz. *Millennium*, *40*(1), 65–83. DOI: 10.1177/0305829811409178

Trevino, L. K., Daft, R. L., & Lengel, R. H. (Eds.). (1990). Understanding managers' media choices- A symbolic interactionist perspective. SAGE Publications, Inc., https-//DOI: <ALIGNMENT.qj></ALIGNMENT>10.4135/9781483325385.pdf

Valacich, J. S., Sarker, S., Pratt, J., & Groomer, M. (2002, January). Computer-mediated and face-to-face groups: who makes riskier decisions? In *Proceedings of the 35th Annual Hawaii International Conference on System Sciences* (pp. 133-142). IEEE. DOI: 10.1109/HICSS.2002.993870

Wadsworth, M. B., & Blanchard, A. L. (2015). Influence tactics in virtual teams. *Computers in Human Behavior*, *44*, 386–393. DOI: 10.1016/j.chb.2014.11.026

Walther, J. B. (1992). Interpersonal Effects in Computer-Mediated Interaction: A Relational Perspective [CR]. *Communication Research*, *19*(1), 52–90. DOI: 10.1177/009365092019001003

Walther, J. B. (1996). Computer-Mediated Communication: Impersonal, Interpersonal, and Hyperpersonal Interaction [CR]. *Communication Research*, *23*(3), 3–43. DOI: 10.1177/009365096023001001

Walther, J. B. (2011). Theories of computer-mediated communication and interpersonal relations. The handbook of interpersonal communication, 4, 443-479.

Wang, B., Liu, Y., Qian, J., & Parker, S. K. (2021). Achieving effective remote working during the COVID-19 pandemic: A work design perspective. *Applied Psychology*, *70*(1), 16–59. DOI: 10.1111/apps.12290 PMID: 33230359

Warkentin, M. E., Sayeed, L., & Hightower, R. (1997). Virtual teams versus face-to-face teams: An exploratory study of a web-based conference system. *Decision Sciences*, *28*(4), 975–996. DOI: 10.1111/j.1540-5915.1997.tb01338.x

York, E. J. (2021). Digital surveillance in online writing instruction: Panopticism and simulation in learning management systems. *Computers and Composition*, *62*, 102680. DOI: 10.1016/j.compcom.2021.102680

Yukl, F., Chavez, C., & Seifert, C. F. (2005). Assessing the construct validity and utility of two new influence tactics. *Journal of Organizational Behavior*, *26*(6), 705–725. DOI: 10.1002/job.335

Yukl, G., & Falbe, C. M. (1990). Influence Tactics and Objectives in Upward, Downward, and Lateral Influence Attempts. *The Journal of Applied Psychology*, *75*(2), 132–140. DOI: 10.1037/0021-9010.75.2.132

Yukl, G., & Falbe, C. M. (1990). Influence Tactics and Objectives in Upward, Downward, and Lateral Influence Attempts. *The Journal of Applied Psychology*, *75*(2), 132–140. DOI: 10.1037/0021-9010.75.2.132

Yukl, G., & Michel, J. W. (2006). Proactive influence tactics and leader member exchange. *Power and influence in organizations*, 87-103.

Yukl, G., & Tracey, J. B. (1992). Consequences of Influence Tactics Used With Subordinates, Peers, and the Boss. *The Journal of Applied Psychology*, *77*(4), 525–535. DOI: 10.1037/0021-9010.77.4.525

Chapter 14
The Fungible Archive: Digital Repatriation and the Illusion of Archival Restitution

L. S. Ascensão de Macedo
http://orcid.org/0000-0001-7251-7314
Centro de Estudos Clássicos, Faculdade de Letras, Universidade de Lisboa, Portugal

ABSTRACT

This chapter examines three cases—the Ndembu Archives, the documentary heritage of Madeira, and the Lúcio Costa collection—to show how digitisation has functioned as symbolic compensation that substitutes for, without resolving, the issue of material restitution. The Ndembu Archives, removed from their African political context in 1934 and now largely held by the Overseas Historical Archive, illustrate how joint digitisation and inscription in UNESCO's Memory of the World Register operate as postcolonial legitimising devices, recasting acts of documentary appropriation as shared heritage. Similar dynamics appear in the archival centralisation exercised by the National Archive of Portugal regarding Madeira, and in the transfer of the Lúcio Costa archive to the Casa da Arquitectura in Portugal. The chapter concludes by advancing a neo-custodial perspective that acknowledges the historicity of archival displacement, rejects digital fungibility as a final solution, and recentres material restitution within archival justice.

INTRODUCTION

The increasing use of digitisation as a response to claims for archival restitution or repatriation[1] has generated significant debate within Information Science, Archival Studies, and heritage and memory research. So-called digital repatriation/restitution

DOI: 10.4018/979-8-3373-4531-4.ch014

is often presented as a conciliatory solution—much as microfilming was in the 1970s and 1980s (Kecskeméti, 2009; Kecskeméti & van Laar, 1981). In this model, access for claimant communities is ensured through the provision of surrogates in the form of digital copies, while the originals remain in the holding institutions.

Nevertheless, the use of digitisation as a substitute for physical restitution creates an ambivalent situation: while, in some cases, the physical return becomes unfeasible for claimant communities due to the often prohibitive costs of preserving the holdings, in others—where all conditions for receiving the documents are in place—the originals remain intentionally retained by the holding institution, thereby perpetuating the dispute over their custody.

Surrogating technologies were initially designed to ensure both access and preservation, by allowing fragile or hard-to-reach documents to be digitised or otherwise reproduced. The aim was to guarantee their long-term preservation without compromising their use by the communities concerned. The adoption of digital technologies has provided not only broader access but also the possibility of virtually reunifying fragmented collections—often sharing the same provenance—across multiple holding institutions (Punzalan, 2014[a]; Punzalan, 2014b). However, these technologies have consistently served the interests of holding institutions, which rely on surrogates and invoke the argument of fungibility, presenting it as a solution that ensures access without requiring the physical return of the originals to the claimant community. This pragmatic and, to some extent, compensatory approach tends to diminish or delegitimise the claims of communities insisting on physical restitution/repatriation, to the point that the supposed fungibility of substitutes becomes the only—albeit always provisional—avenue for resolving disputes.

This type of dispute arises primarily within the broader phenomenon of *displaced archives*. The most widely accepted definition is found in the report submitted to the EGSAH – Expert Group on Shared Archival Heritage of the International Council on Archives, which describes them as "archives removed from the place of their creation, where the ownership of the archives is disputed by two or more parties" (International Council on Archives, 2020, p. 5). This designation coexists with others — *removed*, *disputed*, *seized*, *migrated*, *expatriated*, *estray archives* — each pointing to more specific causal contexts, yet all functioning as hyponyms of the broader category of displaced archives (Lowry, 2019). Contemporary understanding of this phenomenon is largely indebted to international surveys conducted by Bautier (1963), Auer (1998), and Lowry (2020), which identified not only cross-national cases but also subnational or intranational ones (Fishman, 2010)[2]. Given the periodic nature of these surveys, it is particularly challenging today to determine which cases have been resolved, which remain active, or which are dormant but may be reactivated at any moment. In both international and intranational contexts, digitisation appears at times as a fungible solution and, at others, as a neocolonial approach—this time mediated by technology.

In this chapter, "digital fungibility" is not treated as a generic claim about the usefulness of digital copies, but as a specific normative move in restitution debates. It refers to the assumption that a digital surrogate can stand in for the material record in ways that are not merely practical (access, preservation, virtual reunification) but also political and ethical, as if digitisation could discharge the obligations of return. In other words, the digital is framed not as mediation but as closure, shifting the dispute from custody and documentary sovereignty to technical provision and remote consultation. It is precisely this conflation—between facilitating access and settling claims—that the chapter interrogates.

The fundamental question may be formulated as follows: can archival restitution be legitimately and fully replaced by digital repatriation, or does the latter constitute merely a provisional — and potentially ideological — mechanism that does not dispense with the material return of the archives?

To address this question, the chapter adopts a multiple-case study approach (Stake, 2006; Yin, 1984), centred on Portugal, enabling a comparative analysis of digital repatriation/restitution across intranational, post-colonial, and transnational contexts. It examines three cases—the Madeira archipelago dispute with the National Archives of Portugal *Torre do Tombo*, the *Ndembu* Archives divided between Portugal and Angola, and the Lúcio Costa collection transferred to *Casa da Arquitectura* despite Brazilian opposition—showing how digital strategies are used to retain or symbolically reconfigure documentary sovereignty. The chapter first outlines the conceptual bases of digital fungibility and archival restitution, then analyses the three cases, and concludes by proposing a neo-custodial framework that re-centres archival materiality and affirms restitution as essential to archival justice.

DIGITAL FUNGIBILITY IN ARCHIVAL REPATRIATION/ RESTITUTION: LIMITS, CONTRADICTIONS, AND MATERIAL JUSTICE

The digitisation of archival materials has long been recognised as both a tool for democratising access and a strategy for preservation. In addition, it is frequently promoted as a desirable practice for fostering intercultural dialogue and supporting communities of origin. This logic is far from new. From the second half of the twentieth century onwards, microform technologies were presented as substitutes for original records, premised on the idea that access could be secured while reducing the need for physical restitution or circulation of the documents. Digital technologies inherited and expanded this paradigm, amplifying the ideological claim that copies may serve as adequate replacements for displaced archives.

As Auer notes, the "exchange of quality microform or digital copies and their finding aids" (2017, p. 123) was considered a potential means of resolving contested claims over archival fonds, positioned as an alternative to physical return—while simultaneously acknowledging that such measures "would not be an equally satisfactory means of resolving such disputed claims" (2017, p. 123). Mnjama and Lowry (2017) similarly recognise that microform surrogates offered a fungible solution when physical repatriation to former British colonies in Africa was deemed impossible. Yet their significant limitations—political, financial, infrastructural, technological, and, crucially, related to archival sovereignty—generated new injustices, thereby transforming these substitutes into instruments that defer restitution while reproducing colonial relations of authority.

From this perspective, microforms were undeniably useful for reconstructing dispersed series and facilitating research; however, they neither resolved the historical injustice of dispossession nor replaced the need for physical repatriation.

Digitisation and web-based access have been increasingly mobilised by memory institutions as instruments of heritage mediation in disputes over the return of displaced archives. Presented as a mechanism capable of combining public access, preservation, and knowledge sharing, this practice has been praised as a technological response for contexts in which physical restitution proves politically contentious or logistically complex (Huebner & Marr, 2019). However, the rhetoric of digital repatriation often rests on a problematic premise: the presumed fungibility between the material record and its digital surrogate. Evidence from practice and recent scholarship suggests that this premise is, at best, insufficient—and, in some cases, serves to perpetuate colonial asymmetries under the guise of openness and democratisation (Macedo et al., 2022b).

For example, Punzalan (2014; 2014b) values virtual reunification as a collaborative strategy to restore dispersed documentary contexts and to strengthen access and participation among source communities, highlighting its potential for identity reconstruction and cultural mediation. Yet, although he acknowledges technical and institutional challenges, he avoids directly addressing the issue of digital fungibility and does not fully consider the possibility that digitisation may be used as a substitute for physical restitution. His framework thus privileges relational and access-oriented dimensions while paying limited attention to material sovereignty and archival justice. As a result, virtual reunification—presented as a solution—may in practice perpetuate the retention of originals and the historical asymmetries associated with the colonial displacement of archives.

Linebaugh and Lowry (2021) are particularly forceful in this critique. While they acknowledge that post-custodialism and digitisation have expanded the circulation of archival content, they emphasise that the same logic has been used to suggest that digital surrogates can "resolve" disputes over documentary custody. The outcome, they argue, is the preservation of structural inequality: the digital image circulates, but the archive remains physically captive. They therefore reject the very notion of equivalence between original and reproduction. Digital repatriation, they conclude, must be dismissed as a solution to archival displacement in colonial contexts, because originals belong in the places and communities where they were created. When digitisation is deployed as an end rather than a means, it becomes a mechanism for extending colonial violence by consolidating symbolic and legal authority within the holding institution.

This perspective aligns with Krupa and Grimm (2021), who explicitly recognise that digitisation and digital return have often been mobilised as institutional practices that, although presented as reparatory or inclusive, may operate as extensions of colonial power structures. By reinforcing the perception that the "natural" place of the records is the institution that retains them, the fungibility argument positions digital surrogates as simulacra of restitution/repatriation.

In a convergent line of argument, Griffin (2022) observes that digitisation projects promoted by European institutions rarely amount to genuine restitution. In practice, many digitisation initiatives involving displaced collections — whether or not they are subject to formal claims — are carried out within the walls of the holding institution, typically without participatory processes involving claimant communities. Moreover, these digitised records are made available within the institution's own systems of knowledge organisation, monopolising not only their representation but also their descriptive frameworks, metadata schemes, classification and indexing. Such systems rely on professional "literary warrants" (standards, technical guidelines, procedural manuals) as legitimising devices that consolidate institutional control over the custodial narrative.

Digital repatriation, as described by Griffin, thus operates as an illusory technology of substitution which, despite the rhetoric of openness, reinforces the monopoly of materiality. Without physical transfer or archival sovereignty, the digital process does not compensate for historical loss; it merely dampens — temporarily — the reparative impulse. For example, in the case of the records removed from the United States Virgin Islands, extensively studied by Bastian (2006, 2007), Agostinho (2019) notes that digital access constitutes an important vector for the reconstruction of historical and identity bonds among claimant communities, enabling encounters with documentary fragments previously inaccessible and allowing the symbolic reinscription of narratives disrupted by colonial displacement and appropriation. Nevertheless, the author considers this structurally insufficient, noting that "digitization alone does not resolve and may in fact entrench: language barriers, unequal digital infrastructures, insufficient or inadequate metadata, [and] radically incommensurate experiences of colonialism that dictate radically different ways of engaging with archival material" (2019, p. 162).

The argument is further developed by Linebaugh (2022) in another study, where she analyses the discourse of shared heritage. The notion of shared heritage, here critically examined, operates as a rhetorical tool that dilutes responsibility and legitimises the retention of archives: by invoking ideas of reciprocity and common ownership, the discourse diverts attention from the forced extraction and the power structures underpinning colonial possession. Within this discursive regime, digitisation becomes a mechanism of "technical cooperation" that paradoxically freezes the status of the displaced archive, transforming what was coercively seized into an object of controlled circulation. It is a "solution" that deactivates restitution/repatriation by recoding plunder, theft, or appropriation — even when legally sanctioned — as simple acquisition.

These contributions converge on a fundamental point: the digital, although valuable, is not fungible with the original, especially in contexts of archival decolonization. Digitisation does not erase the legal, political, or affective significance of material custody, nor does it replace its role in historical repair. When presented as a definitive solution, it operates as:

- a mechanism for maintaining institutional power and authority;
- a contemporary form of symbolic and epistemic extraction;
- a device of discursive pacification that postpones demands for justice;
- a strategy that preserves the cultural and scientific capital of dominant institutions.

By contrast, experiences such as the digitisation of the Koori photographic archives held at the University of Melbourne Archives (Huebner & Marr, 2019), or the digital return associated with the Maya manuscript *Popol Vuh* (Espinosa de los Monteros, 2019), show that technology can, when governed by principles of reciprocity and community sovereignty, create space for identity reconstruction, Indigenous participation in custodianship, and narrative rebalancing. Even so, these cases reveal the fundamentally transitional nature of the digital: a useful instrument, but not a substitute for physical return.

Similarly, the physical repatriation of colonial archives to Suriname by the Netherlands shows — among the few known cases of actual archival repatriation — that even when digitisation is presented as a modern solution for access and preservation, it does not replace the political, symbolic, and historical necessity of returning the originals. In this case, digitisation functioned as a precondition imposed by the holding institution, ensuring that "the Surinamese archive material does not go out the door without duplicates being made beforehand" (Dijk et al., 2022, p. 297), which reveals the persistence of logics of control and asymmetry. Surinamese, however, insisted that the archives "belong to Suriname" (Dijk et al., 2022, p. 282) and that their repatriation was essential for the country's historical dignity and archival sovereignty. The process resulted in the restitution of the originals and the creation of millions of digital copies for consultation. In this paradigmatic example, the digital appears as a complement rather than a substitute, and material restitution emerges as an indispensable condition for genuine post-colonial justice.

At the level of information representation in the finding aids, the authors show that the inherited descriptions of Surinamese records reproduced the dominant colonial perspective. This aligns with Olson's (2002) argument on *surrogates of knowledge* and the power to name, insofar as the finding aids were constructed entirely from the viewpoint of the colonisers. Repatriation allowed for the reconfiguration of this mediating layer, enabling Surinamese archivists to recentre the narrative on historically silenced subjects, supported by handwritten-text OCR technologies to reveal the data and information contained in the documents, while explicitly rejecting the hegemony of the metadata produced by Dutch institutions.

Yet the descriptive gains observed in these "successful" cases should not be mistaken for a broadly replicable template: physical repatriation is not, from the outset, a franchisable solution, since its feasibility is shaped primarily by political and ideological considerations—an asymmetry that helps explain why, in restitution debates, archives often remain less visible than museums and libraries (Grimsted, 1998, 2010).

Time also plays a decisive role in the physical restitution/repatriation of archives. It is not uncommon for entities that reject the custodial claims of communities of origin to benefit from, or even encourage, an induced forgetting on the part of those communities. The archives confiscated by Napoleonic forces from the *Archivo General de Simancas* (Spain) were returned only a few years after Bonaparte's exile (Galland, 2019). Yet in many other cases, as we shall see, commemorative contexts can both reactivate dormant restitution/repatriation claims and deepen intergenerational fractures inherited from the original displacement.

The core issue is not technological but ethical and ideological: digital access may broaden the circulation of memory, but only material restitution can address the historical realities of dispossession. Digital repatriation is, at best, an interim measure — a bridge rather than an endpoint. When the digital surrogate is treated as equivalent to the original, a new layer of technical coloniality emerges, keeping archives in the places to which they were displaced while offering only their images to the communities of origin.

Thus, debates on archival justice must recognise that digitisation does not remedy the conditions that produced archival displacement; it merely exposes them more clearly. Digital initiatives hold value when they restore voice and agency, but they fail when proposed as substitutes for the return of the physical substance of memory, which remains essential for any meaningful postcolonial reparation.

QUESTIONING INSTITUTIONAL ARCHIVAL CANONS

One way to understand disputes over the custody of archives is through the lens of the archival canon. The acquisition of fonds and collections by an archival institution is often grounded in juridical concepts that, while ostensibly neutral, may obscure contentious origins and acquisition processes—even when these are legally sanctioned. Beyond the presence or absence of conflict, the incorporation of archival fonds into an institution is neither random nor neutral (Cox, 2004).

Although the notion of an archival canon was popularised as a transposition from Literary Studies—within the broader *archival turn*—to the context of postmodern archival theory (Harris, 2004; Trace & Ovalle, 2012), largely to analyse the most influential authors in archival literature and their impact on institutional practices, Lappin (2022) identifies the coexistence of two distinct canons: a scientific-administrative one, grounded in technical neutrality and the management of documentary systems, and a critical-postmodern one, more attuned to questions of power, identity and social justice. While the postmodern canon has gained prominence within academic settings, the technical canon remains dominant within institutions, shaping the ways in which they respond to claims for restitution/repatriation.

To question the institutional archival canon is to interrogate the principles, authorities, and practices that define, legitimise, and reproduce particular conceptions of the archive, of custody, and of documentary sovereignty. The canon determines who is authorised to produce memory, which records are attributed value, and which narratives are granted visibility. More than a sanctioned *corpus* of permanently preserved materials, it functions as a normative framework that shapes the very conditions of interpretation and action: through processes of archival appraisal and reappraisal, it selects what will count as memory; it structures who is allowed to speak and which memories are recognised as worthy of preservation; it delineates who will be represented and who will remain marginalised; and it constrains the range of solutions deemed legitimate when negotiating the custody of a *fonds*.

Harris (2004) deepens this problem by demonstrating that the Anglophone archival canon was historically shaped by "the voices of Western white men," a condition that demands a critical effort of deconstruction and an openness to alterity. For Harris, reading the canon should not be treated as a ritual of disciplinary veneration but rather as a hermeneutic practice oriented towards exposing silences, limits, and exclusions. This proposal for *decanonisation* aligns with contemporary decolonial approaches that call for the restoration of intellectual and cultural authority to communities affected by historical displacements of archives, differing only in the recognition that not all archival removals occurred under the sign of colonialism.

For example, Macedo, Silva and Freitas (2022b) identify several cases in the literature on digital reunification projects involving dispersed archival materials organised under Latinised ethnonymic labels such as *Rossica*, *Hungarica*, *Polonica*, *Ucrainica*, and *Baltica*, which are presented as emblematic forms of archival canonisation through acts of naming and identity aggregation. By classifying dispersed documentary sets under these categories, institutions seek to symbolically reconstruct a lost archival unity, reinscribing these *fonds* within a national and cultural genealogy. These terms therefore operate as markers of belonging and patrimonial legitimacy, elevating certain archives to the status of canonical national memory, even when they remain physically scattered or under contested custody.

However, the authors emphasise that such operations, though often motivated by reparative intentions, are far from neutral: they may reproduce disputes over documentary sovereignty, reinforce state-driven projects of historical identity, and crystallise cultural boundaries around *fonds* whose trajectories were shaped by forced migration, armed conflict, shifting borders, and imperial dynamics. Canonisation through labels such as *Rossica* or *Hungarica* thus emerges as a double gesture—simultaneously a symbolic claim and an act of power—revealing how, in the case of displaced archives, representation and classification remain central arenas for the contestation and reconfiguration of collective memory.

It is within this horizon that the contribution of Assmann and of those who respond to her must be situated. Assmann (2008) argues that cultural memory is historically organised around a tension between *active memory* (the canon—what a society chooses to highlight, celebrate, and transmit) and *storage memory* (the archive—where non-activated traces remain, often forgotten or silenced). However, Youngman, Modrow and Meth (2024) challenge the rigidity of this dichotomy, contending that the archive is not a passive repository but a central actor in the process of canon formation: by selecting, preserving, and describing documents, the archive directly shapes what is recognised as memory and as legitimate for social circulation. Thus, far from being confined to the conservation of the past, archival practice participates in the active construction of collective memory and cultural hierarchies; it may reproduce structures of power and exclusion, or—under a critical and reparative approach—open space for historically marginalised voices and narratives, thereby reconfiguring the canon and rendering it more plural and participatory.

Pushing the argument further, Matienzo (2008) radicalises and complexifies this relationship by demonstrating that canonisation within the archival field cannot be understood as an exclusively literary or academic process; rather, it has a direct analogue in what Ketelaar (1999) defined as *archivalization*, the social and cultural process that determines what is deemed worthy of being archived. Matienzo therefore introduces the concept of *archivicity* to denote the set of abstract attributes that qualify a document as "archivable," emphasising that such attributes are socially constructed and embedded in dynamics of power and legitimacy. Just as the literary canon is institutionally mediated by academia, the archival canon is shaped by archival institutions and the professional traditions that structure them—traditions that reflect competing and often hierarchical paradigms, ranging from cultural-humanistic perspectives to technocratic models centred on evidence and administrative functionality.

By bringing debates on literary canon formation into dialogue with the archival practices of selection, preservation, and exclusion, Matienzo demonstrates that the archive, like the canon, is not a neutral space but an active mechanism of cultural valuation, ideological reproduction, and potential exclusion of voices, documentary forms, and memories deemed peripheral or "non-archivable." At the same time, he points to pathways for a critical reconfiguration of this framework, highlighting participatory and community-driven approaches that can "open the archives" and expand the scope of what may be recognised as legitimate documentary heritage, aligned with a reparative and plural archival practice.

In the case analysed by Lowry and Harris (2022), the archive of the colonial state does not function as a neutral repository but as a constitutive device of sovereignty and legitimacy, producing and imposing an administrative canon that naturalises power relations, defines the legitimate subjects of history, and circumscribes the very field of what is "documentable." Confronting the Jenkinsonian canon reveals that, despite contemporary reinterpretations, conceptual structures persist that privilege institutional authority, proclaimed impartiality, and the centrality of the state as the arbiter of authenticity. As the authors note, attempts at reconciliation often remain within the boundaries of the hegemonic disciplinary tradition, emerging as forms of "colonially settled rapprochements" that acknowledge past violence without relinquishing the assumptions that underpinned it.

Hence, critique of the canon cannot be limited to terminological revisions or the inclusive expansion of the theoretical corpus; it requires a radical denaturalisation of the epistemology of the state archive, recognition of indigenous and community-based documentary ontologies, and the reconfiguration of appraisal, description, and custodial practices in ways that displace—rather than merely mitigate—historical hierarchies of authority and assimilation. Within this framework, the archive ceases to be conceived as latent memory awaiting canonical activation and is instead understood as an active locus of political contestation.

These perspectives converge on the need for approaches to archival *decanonisation* (Macedo et al., 2022b), of which archival decolonisation constitutes only one dimension. *Decanonisation* seeks to destabilise institutional criteria of value and authority, reopening the definition of what counts as an archive, who holds legitimacy to narrate it, and which documentary forms may be recognised as legitimate memory. Such an approach requires a re-examination of traditional principles—provenance, original order, integrity—not to reject them, but to recover their reparative and reunifying potential when applied in dialogue with claimant communities, particularly in contexts of forced displacement of archival holdings. The form of *decanonisation* that emerges here is not destructive but transformative: it consists of rethinking the canon from the standpoint of historical justice, informational sovereignty, and the right to memory, especially for communities affected by processes of archival displacement.

The following section shifts from conceptual discussion to a comparative, Portugal-centred set of three case studies, showing how claims of digital fungibility are mobilised as practical and rhetorical instruments of non-return. Across intranational, post-colonial, and transnational settings, these cases illustrate how digitisation and "digital return" are invoked to retain originals and to symbolically reconfigure documentary sovereignty—moves that, in turn, are stabilised by the defence of institutional archival canons and their accompanying narratives of legitimacy.

CASE STUDY I: AUTONOMOUS REGION OF MADEIRA VERSUS THE NATIONAL ARCHIVES *TORRE DO TOMBO*

The intranational Madeira Island – *Torre do Tombo* case, and the rhetoric of "digital return," offers a testing ground for this chapter's central argument: a copy is not equivalent to an original, and its absolutisation tends to transform restitution into a simulacrum. On 12 January 2017, the Legislative Assembly of Madeira unanimously approved Resolution No. 3/2017/M (Assembleia Legislativa da Região Autónoma da Madeira, 2017), recommending the transfer to the Region of five *fonds* described as Madeiran — *Cabido da Sé do Funchal* [Chapter of the Cathedral of Funchal], *Convento da Santa Clara* [Convent of Santa Clara], *Convento da Encarnação* [Convent of the Incarnation], *Provedoria da Real Fazenda* [Royal Treasury Administration], and *Alfândega do Funchal* [Customs House of Funchal]. This decision marked a moment of public reactivation of a long and intermittent dispute over archival custody in an intranational context — that is, one occurring within the same country.

However, archival analysis of contemporary finding aids shows that the custodial reality was broader than the resolution acknowledged: a survey of the National Archives' systems identified, at the time, eleven Madeiran fonds held at *Torre do Tombo*. This discrepancy is plausibly explained by the legislative process having relied on descriptive instruments produced before 2000, and thus misaligned with the reorganisations and individualisations carried out in the early twenty-first century (Macedo et al., 2022a). In the divergence between five and eleven fonds, a first practical effect of the problem becomes clear: political decision-making continues to operate on incomplete informational maps, thereby reproducing asymmetries between what is known, what is described, and what could, in principle, be restituted.

The custodial history of the disputed sets of records confirms the complexity of the phenomenon. Between 1886 and 1894, official missions transferred documentation from Funchal to Lisbon, invoking—within contemporaneous instruments—the Decree of 2 October 1862 (Ministério da Justiça, 1862) and a Ordinance of the Ministry of the Kingdom of 9 June 1886, repeatedly cited in reports and inventories and described by Machado (1935) as a "deaf ordinances," that is, orders repeatedly invoked yet absent from the official record. The absence of this order in the official record does not invalidate the legality of actions carried out under the 1862 decree; rather, it exposes the performative power of archival description. By reproducing an unverified legal basis, finding aids and inventories become agents of legitimation, stabilising narratives about the "natural destiny" of the records. The problem is not merely legal but archival: when descriptive mediation is left unscrutinised, it crystallises particular versions of custodial history that shape present and future decisions regarding restitution.

From an early stage, Madeiran voices denounced the material consequences of the displacement. The *Elucidário Madeirense* (Silva & Menezes, 1921), written a decade before the establishment of the *Arquivo Distrital do Funchal* [Funchal District Archive], lamented the dispossession of the archive of the *Cabido da Sé do Funchal* [Chapter of the Cathedral of Funchal] and the inaccessibility of a "precious ore" of manuscripts concentrated in Lisbon, bereft of descriptive instruments for those researching the history of the archipelago, which was then commemorating 500 years of settlement. The critique highlighted a break in continuity between the communities of origin and their documentary bodies, exacerbated by distance and by the absence of adequate description.

In the 1930s, the newly created *Arquivo Distrital do Funchal* sought to reverse this estrangement by formally requesting restitution; the supervising authority, the *Inspeção Superior de Bibliotecas e Arquivos* [Higher Inspectorate of Libraries and Archives], refused, asserting that the *Torre do Tombo* functioned as the general archive of the country. In 1937, remnants of the same record groups removed to Lisbon were rediscovered in the archipelago, raising the problem of reunification not only at the physical level but also in terms of intellectual representation. During that same decade, the journal *Arquivo Histórico da Madeira* published several lists of document sets held at the national archive, once again making visible material that had "fallen out of sight"—a movement that linked political claim-making, descriptive reconstruction, and the dignity of local access (Macedo et al., 2022a). These episodes demonstrate that disputes over displaced archives are also disputes over the institutional canon: between a centralising vision that naturalises incorporation and a reparative vision that claims local reintegration within its symbolic territory.

It is in this context that digitisation emerged as a "conciliatory" response. For example, part of the Madeiran *fonds* held at the *Torre do Tombo* — the Funchal Customs House, the Royal Treasury of Funchal, the Cathedral Chapter, and the Convents — was microfilmed and, in some cases, digitised from the microfilm, a process carried out in coordination with regional and national services during the 1990s. The immediate outcome was broader access and the mitigation of consultation barriers; the structural outcome was the preservation of physical custody in Lisbon and the consolidation of a logic of substitution: the image circulates, while the documentary body remains captive in Lisbon. The regional project that supported digital dissemination has meanwhile been discontinued due to technological obsolescence; in current portals, descriptions and inventories predominate, rarely accompanied by full digital representations. The technological "bridge" did not lead to a restorative "shore"; on the contrary, it served as a provisional solution, functional in terms of public service yet insufficient in terms of material justice.

However, in more recent stages, a discursive shift has become visible on the part of the island authorities who initiated the claim: what had been a demand for physical restitution turns into a matter of facilitating consultation; the historical dispute over documentary custody becomes a problem of digital accessibility. The central issue, therefore, does not lie in the efficiency of the technology, but in its political instrumentalisation: to what extent does the acceptance of the digital not amount to a tacit renunciation—almost a silent capitulation—of the autonomic principles that justified the initial claim for the physical return of the displaced archives to Lisbon more than a century ago? Instead of asserting the Region's right to recover the material possession of documentation produced in its territory—especially since the documentation would not leave national borders—the digital solution tends to reposition the claim on gentler, institutionally comfortable ground, aligned with the State's centralising narrative.

In this sense, the Madeiran case illustrates how digital fungibility can function as a mechanism for neutralising and pacifying conflict: the political dimension of restitution is hollowed out, reduced to a form of public service provision — "guaranteed" access from the mainland, yet dematerialised, which preserves intact the original geography of archival inequalities. Restitution ceases to be conceived as a reparative act, linked to the affirmation of historical and territorial autonomy, and becomes instead a modality of technocratic concession. It is not merely a matter of symbolic substitution: it is an inversion of the logic of the claim, in which institutional satisfaction replaces historical right — and technological convenience takes the place of material justice.

The concrete data reinforce this reading. In the case of the documentary fonds of the Funchal Customs House (Arquivo Nacional da Torre do Tombo, 2008; Arquivo Regional e Biblioteca Pública da Madeira, 1990), only about 4.6% of the storage units are held at the *Torre do Tombo* — predominantly documentation from the fifteenth and eighteenth centuries — while 95.4% remain at the Regional Archive and Public Library of Madeira, mostly referring to the nineteenth and twentieth centuries. Yet the *Torre do Tombo* makes available online around 98% of the portion it holds, whereas the documentation preserved in Madeira lacks updated access tools and any unified digital representation. The same pattern can be observed in other Madeiran fonds under the custody of the *Torre do Tombo*. This asymmetry points to a structural paradox in which the central institution, while holding only a fraction of the heritage, projects a narrative of completeness, whereas the regional institution, with more limited resources, sees its capacity to represent and disseminate its own holdings constrained.

The historical division of the fonds illustrates the structural dilemma of displaced archives: physical dispersion fractures organicity, while intellectual reunification, when reduced to digital substitution, crystallises custodial imbalance. Digitisation recomposes series, but when taken as a final solution, it reopens the wound of displacement by instituting a new intranational centralism, in which technology pacifies inequalities under the appearance of access.

Thus, in sum, the present case demonstrates how digital fungibility operates in practice: not as a neutral resource, but as a response canonically shaped by a national-archive imaginary that absorbs the regional exception (Macedo et al., 2022a). When material restitution is indefinitely postponed, technique replaces reparation. Archival justice values the digital but rejects the idea that it can close the conflict. In the Portuguese context, a solution requires revisiting the legal narrative that legitimised the transfers; ensuring an interoperable descriptive reunification between the *Torre do Tombo* and the ABM; and taking political decisions on models of return — total, partial, rotational, or shared — that recognise the symbolic and legal significance of the presence of documents in their places of origin.

CASE STUDY II: THE *NDEMBU* ARCHIVES (ANGOLA *VERSUS* PORTUGAL)

The *Ndembu* Archives, currently under divided custody between the *Arquivo Histórico Ultramarino* [Overseas Historical Archive, henceforth AHU] in Lisbon and the *Arquivo Nacional de Angola* [National Archive of Angola, ANA] in Luanda, constitute one of the most paradigmatic cases, in the Lusophone world, of the phenomenon of migrated archives: records produced by autonomous African political entities, later removed from their territory of origin and unilaterally reinscribed into the archival system of the former colonial power, after having been concealed from public knowledge for many decades and revealed only in a post-colonial context (Badger, 2012; Banton, 2009, 2012).

The documentation known as the *Ndembu* Archives results from the governmental activity of the African authorities of the *Ndembu* or *Dembos*, in northern Angola—politically organised ethnic communities that, between the seventeenth and twentieth centuries, developed their own practices of administrative, diplomatic, and legal writing, produced in Portuguese, Kimbundu and, occasionally, Kikongo and Latin.

These records document inter-sovereign relations between *sobados*[3], diplomatic ties with the Kingdom of Kongo, regular communication with Portuguese colonial authorities, judicial proceedings, mechanisms for the election and succession of leaders, trade routes, taxation practices, dynamics of war and peace, as well as modes of teaching writing, document authentication and the preservation of political memory. The archival description provided by the AHU (2024) summarises the extent of this *corpus*: approximately 1,867 documents, distributed across twelve boxes, produced between 1677 and 1920. A particularly relevant dimension lies in the presence of hybrid linguistic structures, bearing witness to the local appropriation of Portuguese by Kimbundu-oral-tradition communities. On the Angolan side, only a single codex survives — Codex 240, containing the register of letters sent by colonial authorities to the *sobados* between 1798 and 1854 — highlighting the profound custodial asymmetry that characterises this archive.

The displaced condition of the *Ndembu* Archives does not result from any administrative or diplomatic transfer process. The breaking point occurred in 1934, when António de Almeida (1900–1984), a Portuguese physician and physical anthropologist, collected the documentation during a scientific mission organised within the framework of the *Escola Superior Colonial* [Colonial School of Higher Education] and funded by the *Junta de Educação Nacional* [National Board of Education] (Almeida, 1938), both public institutions of the *Estado Novo* regime.

Until then, the archives had remained in the *banza*[4] of Caculo Cacahenda, preserved by the authorities that had produced and accumulated them over centuries (Santos, 2009). The mission — focused on anthropometry and ethnography — appropriated the *corpus* without any negotiation with local authorities, inscribing it into colonial scientific agendas aimed at collecting, classifying, and reinterpreting African materials according to metropolitan epistemologies. This was not an act of preservation, but an operation of documentary capture typical of colonial power, grounded in the conviction that scientific authority legitimised the removal of the archives to the metropole. The subsequent incorporation of the *corpus* into the AHU between 2006 and 2009, and the additional purchase of 96 documents in 2014, reinforced — already in full post-colonial context — this process of extraction, which is today reproduced in the archival description itself, where the acquisition is mentioned but the circumstances and conditions under which these documents came into Portuguese possession are not transparently explained.

The inscription of this *corpus* in UNESCO's Memory of the World Register in 2011 introduces, however, an additional layer of complexity. The nomination, submitted jointly by Angola and Portugal, emphasises the "universal importance" of the archive, the uniqueness of the African appropriation of Portuguese writing, the symbolic value of the shared heritage, and its potential for historical, anthropological and linguistic research. Yet the Memory of the World programme privileges heritage visibility and technical preservation, without considering the political dimension of colonial displacement. Its criteria — significance, integrity, rarity, management — exclude any principle of reunification, reparation or restitution.

Thus, the inscription ultimately legitimises the post-colonial arrangement: Portugal retains nearly two thousand documents, Angola only one codex, but the programme presents this asymmetry as "shared heritage". Colonial extraction is reinterpreted as cooperation, and historical imbalance as intercultural dialogue, turning monumentalisation into a form of consecration of inequalities.

It is in this context that the critique of digital fungibility becomes central. The digitisation of the *Ndembu* Archives — promoted as a joint project and as an example of cooperation between Angola and Portugal — is often presented as a solution to address the custodial imbalance. To date, the AHU (2024) has digitised the entirety of the *corpus* under its custody, and no action of this kind is known on the part of the ANA. Remote access to digital images, in the Portuguese case, would thus be equivalent to access to the original sources, mitigating the physical absence of the documents from Angolan territory.

However, as argued by Linebaugh and Lowry (2021) and Mnjama and Lowry (2017), this logic constitutes one of the most recurrent mechanisms of symbolic substitution: digitisation transforms material restitution into a mere representation, creating the illusion of heritage justice while archival power remains unchanged — the copy circulates, the original remains withheld. In the *Ndembu* Archives, this mechanism functions as technological pacification, offering a simulacrum of belonging while the *corpus* remains in Lisbon. The belief that the image replaces the document — or that access substitutes sovereignty — reinforces a new archival coloniality mediated by technology. Even so, no Angolan claim is known, despite long-standing — and never clarified — suspicions of documents having left the country in the late nineteenth century, indicating an inherited and naturalised archival imaginary (Dulley, 2017).

The Memory of the World Register, in celebrating digitisation as a model of cooperation, proves largely insensitive to the politics of displacement. Operating within a universalist heritage grammar that overlooks historical asymmetries, it helps stabilise an unequal post-colonial arrangement. The inscription of the *Ndembu* Archives reinforces a narrative of shared heritage while obscuring the central fact that an African archive, produced by African authorities and removed under colonial rule, remains mostly outside Angola. Digitisation does not correct this imbalance; it conceals it. The result is a convergence of international heritage-making and digital fungibility that turns restitution into a deferred promise and material justice into mere remote access.

CASE STUDY III: "VOLUNTARILY" DISPLACED ARCHIVES: THE LÚCIO COSTA CASE (BRAZIL *VERSUS* PORTUGAL)

The recent agreement signed between the *Casa da Arquitectura* – Portuguese Centre for Architecture (Portugal) and the Public Archive of the Federal District of Brasília (Brazil) for the digital sharing of the Lúcio Costa collection raises important questions about the dynamics of documentary sovereignty, control over historical memory, and the mechanisms of cultural preservation. The collection of the Brazilian architect Lúcio Costa (1902–1998), which includes approximately 11,000 documents, comprises plans, sketches, correspondence and photographs related to the urban planner responsible for Brasília's Pilot Plan — a legacy whose significance extends beyond architecture, touching essential aspects of Brazil's history. Although the agreement aims at preserving and disseminating his legacy, the transfer of this collection to a Portuguese institution may be seen as raising critical questions regarding the limits of exporting cultural assets from one country to another.

Casa da Arquitectura, located in Matosinhos (Portugal), received the donation in 2021 and has held the collection ever since, following the heirs' claim that preservation could not be guaranteed by any Brazilian memory institution, especially the *Instituto Antônio Carlos Jobim* [Antônio Carlos Jobim Institute] in Rio de Janeiro, which had held the collection for more than two decades and had initiated a deaccessioning process (Rodrigues, 2021). The donation made by the heirs to *Casa da Arquitectura* grants the institution both possession of and ownership over the documentation.

The justification that the preservation and digitisation conditions at *Casa da Arquitectura* were, in the heirs' view, better suited to ensuring the longevity of the documents cannot, however, dismiss the broader implications. The transfer to a foreign institution raises questions concerning Brazil's cultural sovereignty and the loss of control over a body of heritage that is profoundly significant for the country. Although the intention behind the transfer appears to be the guarantee of proper preservation, one cannot overlook the symbolic and political implications of this decision.

In this context, the *Fórum de Entidades em Defesa do Patrimônio Cultural Brasileiro* [Forum of Entities for the Protection of Brazilian Cultural Heritage], in its January 2025 statement, brought to the forefront concerns about a symbolic neocolonisation of Brazilian architectural collections (Fórum de Entidades em Defesa do Patrimônio Cultural Brasileiro, 2025), highlighting the export of cultural heritage of great historical value and the complacency of both national and foreign institutions in relation to this phenomenon. The transfer of collections belonging to prominent figures such as Lúcio Costa and Paulo Mendes da Rocha (1928–2021) to institutions abroad constitutes a loss that is not only material but also symbolic. It severs the direct link between Brazil and its cultural heritage, particularly in the preservation of the built environment, whose original documents come to be managed and safeguarded outside the country's borders.

In this context, the digitisation of the Lúcio Costa collection, while expanding access and enhancing the visibility of the material, does not resolve the central issue of cultural sovereignty. The idea that digitisation can replace the physical custody of the collection has become a *locus communis* for the non-repatriation of holdings. Although digital representations may provide broader access and facilitate the dissemination of knowledge, they do not capture the full meaning or the symbolic value of a physical document.

The critique of the concept of digital fungibility suggests that it does not resolve the dispute over material possession, which inherently involves physical custody. Digitisation does not eliminate the need for physical restitution, nor does it replace the symbolic and political function of holding an archive. On the contrary, digitisation reappropriates not only the collection but also its very representation, as Olson (2002) has pointed out.

The institutional discourse of *Casa da Arquitectura*, in presenting the incorporation of the Lúcio Costa collection, mobilises a vocabulary of honour, distinction and responsibility, through which the institution self-inscribes as the legitimate guardian of a foreign heritage (Casa da Arquitectura & Centro Português de Arquitectura, 2025). This rhetoric, typical of institutions seeking to consolidate status through cultural internationalism (Merryman, 2005), operates simultaneously as an instrument of symbolic legitimisation and as a mechanism for naturalising the transfer.

In this case, as in many others, digitisation emerges as a necessary "complement" but not as a definitive solution. Digital access may facilitate research and preservation, but the implications for cultural sovereignty and the recognition of historical justice bring to the forefront the question of the physical return of cultural heritage. Thus, although the digitisation of the Lúcio Costa collection brings benefits in terms of preservation and accessibility, the central issue of cultural sovereignty and historical justice remains unresolved.

Lima's doctoral thesis (2023), which focuses on the study of the Lúcio Costa collection at *Casa da Arquitectura* in Portugal, does not problematise the question of dispute. On the contrary, it recognises in the custodial institution a role of mediation and internationalisation of Brazilian architectural memory, functionally corresponding to the idea of an international mediator of modern Brazilian architectural heritage.

This case is not unique, given that the Portuguese architect Siza Vieira has distributed his collection both within and outside the country (Seccareccia et al., 2021), to the point where the donor himself embraces digital fungibility — from the perspective of virtual reunification — as a means of promoting access to the documentary *corpora*.

In response to the concerns raised by the Forum and other entities, several Brazilian academic and institutional bodies are calling for an urgent public policy to safeguard Brazil's cultural sovereignty and protect national collections. Such a response may be crucial to preventing the dispersal of cultural heritage and to minimising the unanticipated removal of documentary holdings from the country.

CONCLUSION: TOWARDS A NEO-CUSTODIAL APPROACH

The comparative analysis of the cases examined in this chapter — Madeira Island, the *Ndembu* Archives and Lúcio Costa collection — among many other cases that could be illustrated, reveals the persistence of a problematic axis that cuts across, in a transversal manner, colonial, post-colonial and intranational contexts: the mobilisation of digitisation as an instrument of symbolic substitution for material restitution. This conceptual shift — from restitution to access, from documentary sovereignty to the circulation of images — relies on the assumption of digital fungibility, whose critique, developed by Linebaugh, Lowry and Mnjama, allows us to understand how technological mediation simultaneously produces visibility and concealment, symbolic proximity and material distance.

In the case of the *Ndembu* Archives, this mechanism becomes particularly clear. The collection carried out by António de Almeida in 1934, within the framework of a colonial scientific mission, constituted an originating act of extraction and decontextualisation, through which archives produced by autonomous African political entities were removed from their own administrative circuit and reinscribed within a colonial epistemic matrix. The subsequent incorporation into the AHU, consolidated by late accessions between 2006 and 2009 and by the acquisition of loose items in 2014, confirms the continuity of a logic of documentary appropriation even in a post-colonial context.

The inscription of the *corpus* in UNESCO's Memory of the World Register, often celebrated as recognition of its "universal importance", nonetheless operates a semantic displacement that warrants scrutiny. The heritage programme privileges criteria of significance, integrity and cultural value, but ignores structural dimensions such as custodial inequality, lack of reunification and the historicity of extraction practices. The logic of shared heritage — ostensibly cooperative — thus tends to neutralise the condition of the displaced archive, recoding a process of colonial capture as a technical-institutional partnership. Joint digitisation, when presented as a satisfactory solution, reinforces this dynamic: it suggests an equivalence between digital presence and restitution, obscuring the political implications of the continued physical custody of the documents in Portugal.

The Madeiran case, although not colonial, demonstrates the reproduction of analogous patterns. The digitisation of the fonds held at the *Torre do Tombo* has been mobilised as a sufficient response to autonomic claims and as a substitute for any discussion of material restitution. Thus, even in an intranational state context, digitisation operates as a mechanism of discursive pacification, shifting the debate from dynamics of historical centralisation to the seemingly neutral terrain of public service and access.

The Lúcio Costa case, in turn, illustrates the persistence of similar logics in the contemporary circulation of personal archives. The transfer of the collection to *Casa da Arquitectura*, legitimised by technical arguments of preservation and institutional capacity, is inscribed within a symbolic economy that privileges entities with technical and infrastructural capital, naturalising displacement through the promise of digitisation and international dissemination. Here too, access is presented as a form of compensation, while the physical displacement remains unquestioned. Digitisation appears once again as a technocratic mediation that depoliticises the issue of cultural sovereignty.

From these three cases, it becomes evident that digitisation, when promoted as a definitive solution, operates not merely as a technology of access but as a mechanism for stabilising historical inequalities. The digital copy, by offering an image of restitution, dilutes the demand for physical return and reinforces a geography of power that concentrates originals in historically hegemonic institutions. However broad its circulation may be, the circulation of the image does not alter the structure of authority that derives from material possession.

For lack of space, many other cases could be examined here. Although several public historical archives were established in Portugal's colonial territories during the *Estado Novo*—such as in Angola (1930), Mozambique (1934), Macao (1952), Cape Verde (1958), and São Tomé and Príncipe (1969)—their creation did not entail the restitution of archival holdings. On the contrary, major colonial fonds, including those of the *Governo Geral de Angola* (1676-1975), *Governo Geral da Guiné* (1822-1935), *Governo Geral de Moçambique* (1693-1897), and *Governo Geral de São Tomé e Príncipe* (1608-1871), remain in metropolitan custody at the AHU. Similarly, the archives of the political police (PIDE–DGS) from Angola, Mozambique, Cape Verde, and other former territories were transferred to Portugal (1974-1975) during decolonisation and are now preserved at the *Torre do Tombo*, limiting possibilities for transitional justice. Corporate archives followed comparable paths, as illustrated by the donation of the *Companhia de Moçambique* records to the *Torre do Tombo* despite recovery efforts by the *Arquivo Histórico de Moçambique* (Tembe, 2006). Thus, these states seek digital access agreements with Portugal, prompting questions about whether this recognizes or obscures the fungibility of archival repatriation.

The discussion on shared archival heritage shows that responses to the historical displacement of archives have largely favoured diplomatic and technological solutions, rarely oriented toward physical restitution. In the Luso-Brazilian context, projects such as *COLUSO*, *Projeto Resgate Barão do Rio Branco*, and *Projeto Reencontro* exemplify this approach: through multilateral agreements, extensive Brazilian documentary collections held in Portugal were microfilmed and digitised, significantly expanding access while leaving the custody of the originals unchanged. Similar initiatives can be observed in the treatment of the *Official Records of Macao During the Qing Dynasty (1693–1886)*, inscribed on the UNESCO Memory of the World Register between Portugal and Macao (China), as well as in the *Casa Comum* platform, which provides remote access to fonds from former Portuguese colonies, yet without facilitating the virtual reunification of scattered holdings.

Another illustrative case is the *Centro Audiovisual Max Stahl Timor-Leste* (CAMSTL), hosted by the University of Coimbra (Portugal) since 2016. The partnership enabled preservation and digital dissemination of a collection central to Timorese memory, but relies on digital surrogates and online access rather than restitution. These examples show that shared heritage prioritises digital circulation, consolidating custodial geographies and reframing sovereignty as technological mediation, while underscoring the need for archival justice and material restitution.

Despite these cases, a central question remains: why is the physical restitution of archives so difficult, particularly when compared with the recent advances in the repatriation of museum artefacts? Disputes over archival custody are largely shaped by entrenched archival canons that naturalise the authority of institutions that historically accumulated these collections, thereby marginalising claims grounded in sovereignty, cultural continuity, and post-colonial reparation.

Within this framework, a neo-custodial perspective emerges as a necessary response to the limits of both classical custodialism, focused on institutional sovereignty, and technological post-custodialism, which reduces archives to the mere circulation of information. A neo-custodial approach begins with full recognition of the historicity of displacement, including a critical analysis of the scientific, administrative, or voluntary mechanisms of appropriation that produced the current unequal distribution of archives. On that basis, it reasserts the centrality of material restitution as a guiding principle, particularly in cases where records were removed through colonial asymmetries, extractive practices, or processes of state centralisation. At the same time, it calls for an epistemological reconfiguration of archival description so as to incorporate local documentary ontologies and to make visible the trajectory of dispossession, resisting the technicist neutralisation often embedded in contemporary access tools. Digitisation, in turn, must be integrated critically and treated as an instrument of mediation rather than a substitute—capable of supporting democratic access, but not of resolving inequalities of sovereignty. Finally, a neo-custodial approach requires the revision of international heritage regimes, such as the Memory of the World Register, so that they include criteria of archival justice, reunification of fonds, and physical return, thereby preventing global recognition from legitimising asymmetrical post-colonial configurations.

This neo-custodial perspective shifts the focus from the archive as a technical object to the archive as a political space. It asserts that archival justice cannot be achieved through the image but through restitution; not through technological accessibility but through the reconstitution of material and jurisdictional bonds; not through symbolic heritage-making but through the reorganisation of the geographies of power that structure the circulation of documents. While digitisation is vital for democratising access, it does not, in itself, address questions of historical reparation. Physical restitution remains essential to restore documentary sovereignty and advance archival justice in contexts of displacement.

REFERENCES

Agostinho, D. (2019). Archival encounters: Rethinking access and care in digital colonial archives. *Archival Science, 19*(2), 141–165. DOI: 10.1007/s10502-019-09312-0

Almeida, A. de. (1938). *Relações com os Dembos: Das cartas do Dembado de Kakulu-Kahenda*. [s.n.].

Arquivo Histórico Ultramarino. (2024). *Dembos—AHU – Digitarq*. DIGITARQ. https://digitarq.arquivos.pt/documentDetails/381e8e909f864a7089972d159f54d1e7

Arquivo Nacional da Torre do Tombo. (2008). *Alfândega do Funchal*. DigitArq. https://digitarq.arquivos.pt/details?id=4205154

Arquivo Regional e Biblioteca Pública da Madeira. (1990). *Alfândega do Funchal: Inventário (Instrumentos Descritivos IDD 3)*.

Assmann, A. (2008). Canon and archive. In Erll, A., & Nünning, A. (Eds.), *Cultural Memory Studies* (pp. 97–108). Walter de Gruyter., DOI: 10.1515/9783110207262.2.97

Auer, L. (1998). *Disputed archival claims: Analysis of an international survey: A RAMP study*. https://academic.microsoft.com/paper/589670184

Auer, L. (2017). Auer, L. (2017). Displaced Archives in the Wake of Wars. In Lowry, J. (Ed.), *Displaced Archives* (pp. 114–129). Routledge., DOI: 10.4324/9781315577609-9

Badger, A. (2012). Historians, a legacy of suspicion and the "migrated archives". *Small Wars & Insurgencies, 23*(4–5, SI), 799–807. https://doi.org/DOI: 10.1080/09592318.2012.709761

Banton, M. (2009). "Expatriate" or "migrated" archives: The role of the UK archivist. *Archives, 34*(121), 14–24.

Banton, M. (2012). 'Lost' and 'found': The concealment and release of the Foreign and Commonwealth Office "migrated archives". *Comma* (2012), 33–46. https://doi.org/DOI: 10.3828/comma.2012.1.04

Bastian, J. A. (2006). Reading colonial records through an archival lens: The provenance of place, space and creation. *Archival Science, 6*(3–4), 267–284. DOI: 10.1007/s10502-006-9019-1

Bastian, J. A. (2007). A question of custody: The colonial archives of the United States Virgin Islands. *The American Archivist, 64*(1), 96–114. DOI: 10.17723/aarc.64.1.h6k872252u2gr377

Bautier, R.-H. (1963). Les archives et le droit international. In Samaran, C. (Ed.), *Les Archives dans la Vie Internationale* (pp. 11–56). Direction des Archives de France.

Casa da Arquitectura & Centro Português de Arquitectura. (2025). *Casa da Arquitectura e Arquivo Público do Distrito Federal de Brasília unem esforços para partilha de acervo digital de Lúcio Costa*. https://casadaarquitectura.pt/pt/noticias/casa-da-arquitectura-e-arquivo-publico-do-distrito-federal-de-brasilia-unem-esforcos-para-partilha-de-acervo-digital-de-lucio-costa-2025-02-19/

Cornu, M., & Renold, M.-A. (2010). New developments in the restitution of cultural property: Alternative means of dispute resolution. *International Journal of Cultural Property, 17*(1), 1–31. DOI: 10.1017/S0940739110000044

Cox, R. (2004). *No innocent deposits: Forming archives by rethinking appraisal*. Scarecrow Press.

Dulley, I. (2017). Fontes e contextos do Arquivo Nacional de Angola: Entrevista com Alexandra Aparício. *Revista do Arquivo Geral da Cidade do Rio de Janeiro, 12*, 229–245.

Espinosa de los Monteros, P. (2019). Decolonial information practices: Repatriating and stewarding the *Popol Vuh* online. *Preservation. Digital Technology & Culture, 48*(3–4), 107–119. DOI: 10.1515/pdtc-2019-0009

Fishman, J. (2010). Locating the international interest in intranational cultural property disputes. *The Yale Journal of International Law, 35*(2), 347–404.

Fórum de Entidades em Defesa do Patrimônio Cultural Brasileiro. (2025, January 9). *Contra a neocolonização e a evasão dos acervos brasileiros de arquitetura*. https://forumpatrimoniobr.wordpress.com/2025/01/08/contra-a-neocolonizacao-e-a-evasao-dos-acervos-brasileiros-de-arquitetura/

Galland, B. (2019). Les archives de Simancas: De la saisie napoléonienne à la restitution de Pétain. In V. Laniol & A. Sumpf (Eds.), *Saisies, spoliations, restitutions: Archives et bibliothèques au XXe siècle* (pp. 199–212). Presses universitaires de Rennes. https://books.openedition.org/pur/130275

Griffin, S. H. (2022). Value Displaced, Value Re/Claimed: Reparations, Shared Heritage and Caribbean Archival Records. In Lowry, J. (Ed.), *Disputed Archival Heritage* (pp. 304–331). Routledge., DOI: 10.4324/9781003057765-17

Grimsted, P. K. (1998). "Trophy" archives and non-restitution. *Problems of Post-Communism, 45*(3), 3–. https://doi.org/DOI: 10.1080/10758216.1998.11655785

Grimsted, P. K. (2010). Why do captured archives go home? Restitution achievements under Russian law. *International Journal of Cultural Property, 17*(2), 291–333. DOI: 10.1017/S0940739110000123

Harris, V. (2004). Concerned with the writings of others: Archival canons, discourses and voices. *Journal of the Society of Archivists, 25*(2), 211–220. DOI: 10.1080/0037981042000271529

Huebner, S., & Marr, S. (2019). Between policy and practice: Archival descriptions, digital returns and a place for coalescing narratives. *Archives and Manuscripts, 47*(1), 113–130. DOI: 10.1080/01576895.2018.1552161

International Council on Archives. (2020). *Disputed Archival Claims: An International Survey 2018/2019*. https://www.ica.org/sites/default/files/disputed_archival_claims_an_international_survey_2018_2019.pdf

Kecskeméti, C. (2009). Displaced European archives: Is it time for a post-war settlement? *The American Archivist, 55*(1), 132–140. DOI: 10.17723/aarc.55.1.g15783l74577780t

Kecskeméti, C., & van Laar, E. (1981). *Model bilateral and multicultural agreements and conventions concerning the transfer of archives*. UNESCO. https://unesdoc.unesco.org/ark:/48223/pf0000046909_fre

Ketelaar, E. (1999). Archivalisation and archiving. *Archives & Manuscripts*, 54–61. https://publications.archivists.org.au/index.php/asa/article/view/8759

Krupa, K. L., & Grimm, K. T. (2021). Digital repatriation as a decolonizing practice in the archaeological archive. *Across the Disciplines, 18*, 47–58.

Lappin, J. (2022). Two archival canons. *Archives and Records (Abingdon, England), 43*(2), 180–187. DOI: 10.1080/23257962.2022.2051457

Linebaugh, R. (2022). "Joint heritage": Provincializing an archival ideal. In Lowry, J. (Ed.), *Disputed Archival Heritage* (pp. 19–48). Routledge., DOI: 10.4324/9781003057765-4

Linebaugh, R., & Lowry, J. (2021). The archival colour line: Race, records and post-colonial custody. *Archives and Records (Abingdon, England), 42*(3), 284–303. DOI: 10.1080/23257962.2021.1940898

Lowry, J. (2019). "Displaced archives": Proposing a research agenda. *Archival Science, 19*(4), 349–358. DOI: 10.1007/s10502-019-09326-8

Lowry, J., & Harris, V. (2022). Settler to settler (Reading "Remnants of Jenkinson"). *Archives and Records (Abingdon, England)*, *43*(2), 161–163. DOI: 10.1080/23257962.2022.2040455

Macedo, L. S. A. de,, , da Silva, C. G., & de Freitas, M. C. V. (2022a). Below the nation state: Power asymmetry and jurisdictional boundaries around the archives of Madeira Archipelago. In Lowry, J. (Ed.), *Contested Archival Heritage* (pp. 137–170). Routledge. DOI: 10.4324/9781003057765-9

Macedo, L. S. A. de,, , da Silva, C. G., & de Freitas, M. C. V. (2022b). Information representation in displaced archives: A meta-synthesis. *Knowledge Organization*, *49*(5), 329–351. DOI: 10.5771/0943-7444-2022-5-329

Matienzo, M. A. (2008). Canonization, archivalization, and the "archival imaginary". *Archive Fervour/Archive Further: Literature, Archives, and Literary Archives*, Aberystwyth, 9–11 July. http://hdl.handle.net/10150/216929

Merryman, J. H. (2005). Cultural property internationalism. *International Journal of Cultural Property*, *12*(1), 11–39. DOI: 10.1017/S0940739105050046

Mnjama, N., & Lowry, J. (2017). A proposal for action on African archives in Europe. In Lowry, J. (Ed.), *Displaced Archives* (pp. 101–113). Routledge., DOI: 10.4324/9781315577609-8

Olson, H. A. (2002). *The Power to Name: Locating the Limits of Subject Representation in Libraries*. Springer. DOI: 10.1007/978-94-017-3435-6

Punzalan, R. (2014a). Barriers and challenges to virtual reunification. *Proceedings of the American Society for Information Science and Technology*, *51*(1), 1–8. DOI: 10.1002/meet.2014.14505101041

Punzalan, R. (2014b). Understanding virtual reunification. *The Library Quarterly*, *84*(3), 294–323. DOI: 10.1086/676489

Rodrigues, A. K. (2021, October 19). *Família de Lucio Costa doa acervo de arquiteto brasileiro a Portugal*. Metrópoles. https://www.metropoles.com/distrito-federal/familia-de-lucio-costa-doa-acervo-de-arquiteto-brasileiro-a-portugal

Santos, C. M. (2009). Écrire le pouvoir en Angola: Les archives ndembu (XVIIe–XXe siècles). *Annales*, *64*(4), 767–795. DOI: 10.1017/S0395264900022460

Seccareccia, A., de Vletter, M., Seixas, C., Pereira, E., Garcia, M., & Oliveira, S. (2021). Álvaro Siza Archive – A shared archive. In International Council on Archives & Arquivo Distrital de Braga (Eds.), *Proceedings of the International Congress on Architectural Archives* (pp. 19–30). Arquivo Distrital de Braga.

Silva, F. A., & Menezes, C. A. (1921). *Elucidário madeirense* (Vol. 1–2). Junta Geral do Distrito do Funchal.

Stake, R. E. (2006). *Multiple case study analysis*. Guilford Press.

Tembe, J. (2006). Linking global to local through archives: Some notes on the experiences of Mozambique in sharing memories with global partners. *Comma*, *2006*(3–4), 1–5. DOI: 10.3828/comma.2006.3-4.11

Trace, C. B., & Ovalle, C. J. (2012). Archival reference and access: Syllabi and a snapshot of the archival canon. *The Reference Librarian*, *53*(1), 76–94. DOI: 10.1080/02763877.2011.596364

UNESCO. (2011). *Arquivos dos Dembos / Ndembu Archives – Memory of the World*. https://www.unesco.org/en/memory-world/arquivos-dos-dembos/ndembu-archives

van Dijk, F., & Fooh, R. T. (2022). The repatriation of Surinamese archives from the Netherlands. In Lowry, J. (Ed.), *Disputed Archival Heritage* (pp. 282–303). Routledge., DOI: 10.4324/9781003057765-16

Yin, R. (1984). *Case study research: Design and methods*. Sage Publications.

Youngman, T., Modrow, S., & Meth, I. (2024). Deceiving dichotomies: On the interrelation of the archive and the cultural memory canon. *Proceedings of the Association for Information Science and Technology*, *61*(1), 697–702. DOI: 10.1002/pra2.1082

ENDNOTES

1 For this chapter, following Cornu and Renold (2010), *restitution* refers to the return of items lost through illicit means such as wartime plunder, theft, or other unlawful appropriation. *Return* designates the transfer back of materials removed in colonial settings or through illicit export, even when such removal was legally permitted at the time. *Repatriation* is a particular form of restitution directed not only to States but also to communities or cultural groups, especially Indigenous peoples. Although technically distinct, these terms frequently overlap in practice, with *restitution* often used as a broad label for any process involving the recovery of cultural property. In this chapter, the terms are treated interchangeably and separated by a slash where appropriate.

2 In this study, the term *intranational* is used, even though it is synonymous with *subnational*.

3 *Sobado* is an old administrative and jurisdictional entity found mainly in areas of central-northern Angola (Mbundu, Kimbundu and neighbouring regions).

4 *Banza* refers to the political capital of a *sobado* or of a Central African kingdom, particularly among Kimbundu- and Kikongo-speaking peoples.

Conclusion

The book "Digital Ideologies in the Age of Algorithmic Culture" aims to make a significant contribution to the literature by addressing the ideological dimensions of the digital age with contributions from different disciplines. While a significant portion of studies on digital technologies focus on technical or economic aspects, this book centers on the ideological, cultural, and behavioural impacts of digitalization.

The chapters in the book comprehensively analyse how algorithmic systems restructure power relations, how digital platforms shape public discourse, and how data-driven governance systems affect organizational behaviour. In this respect, the book aims to develop the concept of digital ideologies theoretically and to reveal its reflections across different social spheres.

Furthermore, the study provides an interdisciplinary discussion platform by bringing together new concepts and research areas arising from digitalization. In this context, the book offers new perspectives on academic discussions of digital culture, algorithmic governance, and the platform-based society.

In conclusion, this book aims to provide a comprehensive analysis of the ideological structure of the digital age, making significant contributions to both the academic literature and researchers and practitioners seeking to understand digital transformation.

Compilation of References

AAC (Austrian Academy Corpus). Kraus, K. *Die Fackel*. 1899-1936. www.aac.ac.at/fackel

Abbate, J. (2012). *Recoding gender: Women's changing participation in computing*. MIT Press. DOI: 10.7551/mitpress/9014.001.0001

Abidin, C. (2018). Internet Celebrity and Traditional Media. In *Internet Celebrity: Understanding Fame Online* (pp. 37–69). Emerald Publishing Limited. DOI: 10.1108/978-1-78756-076-520181003

Abidin, C. (2018). *Internet celebrity: Understanding fame online*. Emerald Publishing. DOI: 10.1108/9781787560765

Abidin, C. (2021). Mapping internet celebrity on TikTok: "Understanding Douyin as a technical and social platform.". *International Journal of Communication*, *15*, 3255–3277.

Abramowicz, A. (2018). Sociologia da infância: traçando algumas linhas. *Contemporânea – Revista de Sociologia da UFSCar*, 8(2), 371–383.

Abramowicz, A. (2022). *Estudos da infância no Brasil: encontros e memórias*. EdUFSCar.

Acker, A. (2018). How Fascism Went Digital: A Historian's Perspective on Bolsonaro's Victory in Brazil. *Geschichte und Gegenwart*.

Adams-Prassl, J., Binns, R., & Kelly-Lyth, A. (2022). Directly Discriminatory Algorithms. *The Modern Law Review*, *86*(1), 144–180. DOI: 10.1111/1468-2230.12759 PMID: 37065788

Agostinho, D. (2019). Archival encounters: Rethinking access and care in digital colonial archives. *Archival Science*, *19*(2), 141–165. DOI: 10.1007/s10502-019-09312-0

Ajana, B. (2020). *Governing through biometrics: The biopolitics of identity*. Palgrave Macmillan., DOI: 10.1007/978-3-030-37629-3

Ajunwa, I. (2020). The automated video interview as a platform for systemic discrimination. *Harvard Law & Policy Review, 15*, 269–315. DOI: 10.15779/Z38RX93F1Q

Albrechtslund, A. (2008). Online social networking as participatory surveillance. *First Monday, 13*(3). Advance online publication. DOI: 10.5210/fm.v13i3.2142

Algorithmic Justice League. (2020). *Who audits the auditors? Recommendations from a field scan of the algorithmic auditing ecosystem*. Retrieved from https://www.ajl.org/auditors

Ali, A., ... (2024). When silence hurts: A conservation of resources perspective on digital disengagement. *Online Information Review*. https://www.emerald.com/oir/article/doi/10.1108/OIR-12-2024-0789

Ali, S., & Procter, R. (2022). Algorithmic bias and the marginalization of minority voices in social media. *New Media & Society, 24*(5), 1152–1171.

Alizadeh, T. (2013). Planning implications of telework: A policy analysis of the Sydney metropolitan strategy. *Australian Plants, 50*(4), 304–315. DOI: 10.1080/07293682.2013.764906

Allen, T. D., Golden, T. D., & Shockley, K. M. (2015). How effective is telecommuting? Assessing the status of our scientific findings. *Psychological Science in the Public Interest, 16*(2), 40–68. DOI: 10.1177/1529100615593273 PMID: 26403188

Almeida, A. de. (1938). *Relações com os Dembos: Das cartas do Dembado de Kakulu-Kahenda*. [s.n.].

Aloisi, A., & De Stefano, V. (2022). Essential jobs, remote work and digital surveillance: Addressing the COVID-19 pandemic panopticon. *International Labour Review, 161*(2), 289–314. DOI: 10.1111/ilr.12219 PMID: 34548685

Aloisi, A., & De Stefano, V. (2022). *Your boss is an algorithm: Artificial intelligence, platform work and labour*. Bloomsbury Publishing. DOI: 10.5040/9781509953219

Aloisi, A., & De Stefano, V. (2023). *Your Boss Is an Algorithm: Artificial Intelligence, Platform Work and Labour*. Hart Publishing., DOI: 10.5040/9781509947065

Althusser, L. (1971). Ideology and Ideological State Apparatuses. Lenin and Philosophy and Other Essays, Monthly Review Press. https://www.csun.edu/~snk1966/Lous%20Althusser%20Ideology%20and%20Ideological%20State%20Apparatuses.pdf

Althusser, L. (2020). *On ideology*. Verso Books.

Amoore, L. (2020). *Cloud ethics: Algorithms and the attributes of ourselves and others*. Duke University Press., DOI: 10.1515/9781478007686

Andrade, J. G., & Dias, P. (2022). Crianças no mundo digital: a dinâmica de uma língua portuguesa viva. In *F. Ilharco et al. (orgs.), Em português: falar, viver e pensar no século XXI* (pp. 371–388). Universidade Católica Editora.

Andrae, S. (2026a). A Future of equal rights: An agnostic legal framework for the coexistence of humans and autonomous AI. In Luftman, J., & Tomer, A. (Eds.), *Moral and Legal Aspects of Artificial Intelligence: Machine Bias and Rule of Law* (pp. 33–92). IGI Global Publishing., DOI: 10.4018/979-8-3373-3114-0.ch002

Andrae, S. (2026b). The role of local platforms and Non-Western perspectives on platformization. In Çelik, N., Ateşoğlu, N., & Güner, S. S. (Eds.), *Sociological Dimensions of Platformization: Power, Culture, and Identity in the Digital Age* (pp. 31–70). IGI Global Publishing., DOI: 10.4018/979-8-3373-4267-2.ch002

Andrejevic, M. (2014). Surveillance and alienation in the online economy. *Surveillance & Society*, *12*(3), 381–397. DOI: 10.24908/ss.v8i3.4164

Andrejevic, M., & Volcic, Z. (2021). Pandemic lessons: Total surveillance and the post-trust society. *The Political Economy of Communication*, *9*(1), 4–12.

Angwin, J., Larson, J., Mattu, S., & Kirchner, L. (2016, May 23). Machine bias. *ProPublica*. https://www.propublica.org/article/machine-bias-risk-assessments-in-criminal-sentencing

Angwin, J., Larson, J., Mattu, S., & Kirchner, L. (2016). *Machine bias: There's software used across the country to predict future criminals. And it's biased against blacks*. ProPublica.

Arencón Beltrán, S., Sola Morales, S., & Hernández Conde, M. (2022). Digital Fascism to Block Feminist Participation and Deliberation. Teknokultura. *Journal of Digital Culture and Social Movements*, *19*(2), 123–135. DOI: 10.5209/tekn.81002

Arnold, M., Goldschmitt, M., & Rigotti, T. (2023). Dealing with information overload: A comprehensive review. *Frontiers in Psychology*, *14*, 1122200. DOI: 10.3389/fpsyg.2023.1122200 PMID: 37416535

Arquivo Histórico Ultramarino. (2024). *Dembos—AHU – Digitarq*. DIGITARQ. https://digitarq.arquivos.pt/documentDetails/381e8e909f864a7089972d159f54d1e7

Arquivo Nacional da Torre do Tombo. (2008). *Alfândega do Funchal*. DigitArq. https://digitarq.arquivos.pt/details?id=4205154

Arquivo Regional e Biblioteca Pública da Madeira. (1990). *Alfândega do Funchal: Inventário (Instrumentos Descritivos IDD 3).*

Ashwini, D. Y., Vishwanatha, , & Puneeth, R. P. (2025). Social media as a platform for resistance: Examining the language of dissent in Indian society. *Frontiers in Communication, 10*, 1648587. Advance online publication. DOI: 10.3389/fcomm.2025.1648587

Assmann, A. (2008). Canon and archive. In Erll, A., & Nünning, A. (Eds.), *Cultural Memory Studies* (pp. 97–108). Walter de Gruyter., DOI: 10.1515/9783110207262.2.97

Auer, L. (1998). *Disputed archival claims: Analysis of an international survey: A RAMP study*. https://academic.microsoft.com/paper/589670184

Auer, L. (2017). Auer, L. (2017). Displaced Archives in the Wake of Wars. In Lowry, J. (Ed.), *Displaced Archives* (pp. 114–129). Routledge., DOI: 10.4324/9781315577609-9

Badger, A. (2012). Historians, a legacy of suspicion and the "migrated archives". *Small Wars & Insurgencies, 23*(4–5, SI), 799–807. https://doi.org/DOI: 10.1080/09592318.2012.709761

Bailey, D. E., & Kurland, N. B. (2002). A Review of Telework Research: Findings, New Directions, and Lessons for the Study of Modern Work. *Journal of Organizational Behavior, 23*(4), 383–400. DOI: 10.1002/job.144

Baiocco, S., Fernández-Macías, E., Rani, U., & Pesole, A. (2022). *The algorithmic management of work and its implications in different contexts* (No. 2022/02). JRC Working Papers Series on Labour, Education and Technology.

Baishya, A., & Maheshwari, S. (2020). WhatsApp groups in academic context: Exploring the academic uses of WhatsApp groups among the students. *Contemporary Educational Technology, 11*(1), 71–83. DOI: 10.30935/cet.6271

Bajwa, U., Gastaldo, D., Di Ruggiero, E., & Knorr, L. (2018). The health of workers in the global gig economy. *Globalization and Health, 14*(1), 124. DOI: 10.1186/s12992-018-0444-8 PMID: 30563539

Ball, K. (2021). Workplace surveillance: An overview. *Labor Studies Journal, 46*(3), 244–260. DOI: 10.1177/0160449X21995889

Banet-Weiser, S. (2018). *Empowered: Popular feminism and popular misogyny*. Duke University Press.

Banton, M. (2012). 'Lost' and 'found': The concealment and release of the Foreign and Commonwealth Office "migrated archives". *Comma* (2012), 33–46. https://doi.org/DOI: 10.3828/comma.2012.1.04

Banton, M. (2009). "Expatriate" or "migrated" archives: The role of the UK archivist. *Archives*, *34*(121), 14–24.

Bardall, G. (2016). Automating discrimination? Algorithmic, data, and design-based discrimination in the context of welfare reform in Britain. *New Political Economy*, *21*(4), 530–547.

Bardzell, S. (2010). Feminist HCI: Taking stock and outlining an agenda for design. *Proceedings of the SIGCHI Conference on Human Factors in Computing Systems*, 1301–1310. https://doi.org/DOI: 10.1145/1753326.1753521

Barocas, S., Hardt, M., & Narayanan, A. (2019). *Fairness and machine learning: Limitations and opportunities*. fairmlbook.org.

Bashir, M. (2021). Surveillance and panopticism in the digital age. *Qlantic Journal of Social Sciences and Humanities*, *2*(1), 11–16. DOI: 10.55737/qjssh.779670819

Baskin, C., Barker, M., & Woods, P. (2004). Scoping social presence and social context cues to support knowledge construction in an ICT rich environment. In *Proceedings of 2004 AARE conference*.

Bastian, J. A. (2006). Reading colonial records through an archival lens: The provenance of place, space and creation. *Archival Science*, *6*(3–4), 267–284. DOI: 10.1007/s10502-006-9019-1

Bastian, J. A. (2007). A question of custody: The colonial archives of the United States Virgin Islands. *The American Archivist*, *64*(1), 96–114. DOI: 10.17723/aarc.64.1.h6k872252u2gr377

Batagoda, S. (2024, April 19). Digital inclusion: Bridging communities out of poverty in the global south. *LinkedIn Pulse*. Retrieved from https://www.linkedin.com/pulse/digital-inclusion-bridging-communities-out-poverty-global-batagoda-psukc

Baudrillard, J. (1987). *The Ecstacy of Communication*.

Bauman, Z. (2000). *Liquid modernity*. Polity Press.

Bauman, Z., & Lyon, D. (2013). *Liquid surveillance: A conversation*. Polity Press.

Baumer, E. P. S., Adams, P., Khovanskaya, V. D., Liao, T. C., Smith, M. E., Schwanda Sosik, V., & Williams, K. (2014). Limiting, leaving, and (re)lapsing: An exploration of Facebook non-use practices and experiences. *Proceedings of the SIGCHI Conference on Human Factors in Computing Systems*, 3257–3266. https://doi.org/ DOI: 10.1145/2556288.2557096

Bautier, R.-H. (1963). Les archives et le droit international. In Samaran, C. (Ed.), *Les Archives dans la Vie Internationale* (pp. 11–56). Direction des Archives de France.

Bawa, Z., & Ghatak, S. (2017). Digital colonialism and interventions: India's ban on Free Basics and the politics of the digital divide. *Media Culture & Society*, *39*(7), 1047–1062.

Baym, N. K. (2015). Connect With Your Audience! The Relational Labor of Connection. *Communication Review*, *18*(1), 14–22. DOI: 10.1080/10714421.2015.996401

Bechmann, A., & Kim, J. Y. (2020). Algorithmic bias and gender in digital platforms: Feminist perspectives on artificial intelligence. *Feminist Media Studies*, *20*(6), 887–903. DOI: 10.1080/14680777.2020.1713843

Beer, (2016). The social power of algorithms. Information Communication & Society, 20(1), 1–13. https://doi.org/DOI: 10.1080/1369118x.2016.1216147

Beer, D. (2016). *Metric power*. Routledge.

Beer, D. (2017). The data gaze: Capitalism, power and perception. *Sage (Atlanta, Ga.)*.

Beer, D. (2017). The social power of algorithms. *Information Communication and Society*, *20*(1), 92–109.

Beer, D. (2019). The Data Gaze: Capitalism, Power and Perception. *Sage (Atlanta, Ga.)*. Advance online publication. DOI: 10.4135/9781526463210

Bélanger, J. J., Pierro, A., Barbieri, B., De Carlo, N. A., Falco, A., & Kruglanski, A. W. (2016). One size doesn't fit all: The influence of supervisors' power tactics and subordinates' need for cognitive closure on burnout and stress. *European Journal of Work and Organizational Psychology*, *25*(2), 287–300. DOI: 10.1080/1359432X.2015.1061999

Bender, E. M., Gebru, T., McMillan-Major, A., & Shmitchell, S. (2021). On the dangers of stochastic parrots: Can language models be too big? *Proceedings of the ACM Conference on Fairness, Accountability, and Transparency*, 610–623. DOI: 10.1145/3442188.3445922

Benjamin, R. (2019). *Race after technology: Abolitionist tools for the new Jim Code*. Polity Press.

Benjamin, R. (2019). *Race after technology: Abolitionist tools for the New Jim Code*. Polity Press.

Benkler, Y. (2017). Law, innovation, and collaboration in networked economy. *Annual Review of Law and Social Science, 13*(1), 231–250. DOI: 10.1146/annurev-lawsocsci-110316-113340

Benlian, A., Wiener, M., Cram, W. A., Krasnova, H., Maedche, A., Möhlmann, M., Recker, J., & Remus, U. (2022). Algorithmic management: Bright and dark sides, practical implications, and research opportunities. *Business & Information Systems Engineering*, *64*(6), 825–839. DOI: 10.1007/s12599-022-00764-w

Benvenuto, S. (1995). Freud's Concept of Narcissism. *European Journal of Psychoanalysis, 1*. https://www.journal-psychoanalysis.eu/articles/freuds-concept-of-narcissism/

Berardi, F. (2017). *Futurability: The age of impotence and the horizon of possibility*. Verso.

Berg, J., Furrer, M., Harmon, E., Rani, U., & Silberman, M. S. (2018). *Digital Labour Platforms and the Future of Work*. International Labour Organization. DOI: 10.2139/ssrn.3166150

Berlant, L. (2016). The commons and the infrastructure of emotion. *Critical Inquiry*, *42*(3), 357–381.

Bhat, M. M. (2020). Fighting impunity in hate crime — history, ethics, and the law: An interview with harsh Mander. *Jindal Global Law Review*, *11*(1), 157–179. DOI: 10.1007/s41020-020-00118-1

Biocca, F. (1997). The cyborg's dilemma: Progressive embodiment in virtual environments. *Journal of Computer-Mediated Communication*, *3*(2), JCMC324. DOI: 10.1111/j.1083-6101.1997.tb00070.x

Birhane, A., Prabhu, V. U., & Kahembwe, E. (2021). Multimodal datasets: Misogyny, pornography, and malicious intent. *arXiv preprint arXiv:2110.01963*.

Birhane, A. (2020). Algorithmic colonization of Africa. *Script-ed*, *17*(2), 389–409.

Blackwell, L., Dimond, J., Schoenebeck, S., & Lampe, C. (2019). Classification and its consequences for online harassment. *Proceedings of the ACM on Human-Computer Interaction*, 3(CSCW), 1–25.

Blencowe, C. (2011). *Biopolitical experience: Foucault, power and positive critique*. Springer.

Bocchiaro, P., & Zamperini, A. (2012). Conformity, obedience, disobedience- The power of the situation. Psychology–Selected papers, 275, 294.

Bogen, M., & Rieke, A. (2018). *Help wanted: An examination of hiring algorithms, equity, and bias*. Upturn.https://www.upturn.org/reports/2018/help-wanted/

Bourdieu, P. (1986). The forms of capital. In Richardson, J. G. (Ed.), *Handbook of theory and research for the sociology of education* (pp. 241–258). Greenwood.

Bovens, M., & Zouridis, S. (2002). From Street-Level to System-Level Bureaucracies: How Information and Communication Technology is Transforming Administrative Discretion and Constitutional Control. *Public Administration Review*, *62*(2), 174–184. DOI: 10.1111/0033-3352.00168

Bowker, G. C., & Star, S. L. (1999). *Sorting things out: Classification and its consequences*. MIT Press. DOI: 10.7551/mitpress/6352.001.0001

Boyd, D., & Crawford, K. (2012). Critical questions for big data: Provocations for a cultural, technological, and scholarly phenomenon. *Information Communication and Society*, *15*(5), 662–679. DOI: 10.1080/1369118X.2012.678878

Bozdag, E. (2013). Bias in algorithmic filtering and personalization. *Ethics and Information Technology*, *15*(3), 209–227. 10.1007/s10676-013-9321-6

Brayne, S. (2020). *Predict and surveil: Data, discretion, and the future of policing*. Oxford University Press., DOI: 10.1093/oso/9780190684099.001.0001

British Academy. (2023). *Developing digital inclusion networks and tackling digital inequalities (policy brief)*. Retrieved from https://www.thebritishacademy.ac.uk/documents/5375/Developing-digital-inclusion-networks-tackling-digital-inequalities.pdf

British Psychological Society. (2021). *Ethics guidelines for internet-mediated research (INF294/04.2021)*. https://www.bps.org.uk/news-and-policy/ethics-guidelines-internet-mediated-research-2021

Brito, D. Polifonia e o direito de voz das crianças: diálogos entre a sociologia da infância e a educação musical da infância. 2025. Tese (Doutoramento) –Universidade do Minho, Braga, 2025. Disponível em: https://hdl.handle.net/1822/94998. Acesso em: 10 nov. 2025

Brito, D. D., Andrade, J. G., & Dias, P. (2025). "Musicmedia" in childhood: the impact of digital platforms of the musical preferences of lusophone children. In Duarte, A., Andrade, J. G., & Dias, P. (Eds.), *Digital tools and platforms for effective and personalized learning* (pp. 311–336). IGI Global Publishing., DOI: 10.4018/979-8-3373-6013-3.ch011

Browley, J. (2022, June 4). *Report: Gen Z Increasingly Turning Their Passion into Side Hustle*. Essence. https://www.essence.com/news/money-career/gen-z-willing-to-work-more-than-millennials/

Brown, J. M. (2021). Twitter and Tear Gas: The Power and Fragility of Networked Protest Twitter and Tear Gas: The Power and Fragility of Networked Protest, by Zeynep Tufekci, New Haven, Yale University Press, 2017, 360 pp., available through Digital Commons at http://www.twitterandteargas.org. Terrorism and Political Violence, 33(5), 1139–1140. https://doi.org/10.1080/09546553.2021.1939547

Browne, S. (2015). *Dark matters: On the surveillance of Blackness*. Duke University Press., DOI: 10.1515/9780822375302

Brubaker, J. R. (2020). Strategic ignorance in digital communication. *Social Media + Society*, *6*(1). Advance online publication. DOI: 10.1177/2056305120903402

Brunton, F., & Nissenbaum, H. (2015). *Obfuscation: A user's guide for privacy and protest*. MIT Press., DOI: 10.7551/mitpress/9780262029735.001.0001

Bucher, T., & Helmond, A. (2018). *The affordances of social media platforms*. The SAGE Handbook of Social Media. https://journals.sagepub.com/doi/10.1177/1461444816644424

Bucher, T. (2017). The algorithmic imaginary: Exploring the ordinary affects of Facebook algorithms. *Information Communication and Society*, *20*(1), 30–44. DOI: 10.1080/1369118X.2016.1154086

Bucher, T. (2018). *If... Then: Algorithmic power and politics*. Oxford University Press. DOI: 10.1093/oso/9780190493028.001.0001

Bucher, T. (2018). *If... Then: Algorithmic power and politics*. Oxford University Press.

Bucher, T. (2020). Nothing to disconnect from? Being singular plural in an age of machine learning. *Media Culture & Society*, *42*(4), 610–617. DOI: 10.1177/0163443720914028

Buckingham, D. (2020). *The media education manifesto*. Polity Press.

Buolamwini, J., & Gebru, T. (2018). Gender shades: Intersectional accuracy disparities in commercial gender classification. In *Proceedings of the Conference on fairness, accountability and transparency.* PMLR, 77-91. Available from https://proceedings.mlr.press/v81/buolamwini18a.html

Buolamwini, J., & Gebru, T. (2018). Gender shades: Intersectional accuracy disparities in commercial gender classification. *Proceedings of Machine Learning Research, 81*, 1–15. http://proceedings.mlr.press/v81/buolamwini18a.html

Buolamwini, J., & Gebru, T. (2018). Gender shades: Intersectional accuracy disparities in commercial gender classification. *Proceedings of Machine Learning Research*, *81*, 1–15.

Bureau of Labor Statistics. (2024). *Contingent and Alternative Employment Arrangements Summary*. U.S. Department of Labor.

Cadwalladr, C., & Graham-Harrison, E. (2018, March 17). Revealed: 50 million Facebook profiles harvested for Cambridge Analytica in major data breach. *The Guardian*. https://www.theguardian.com/news/2018/mar/17/cambridge-analytica-facebook-influence-us-election

Cai, W., Grossman, J., Lin, Z. J., Sheng, H., Wei, J. T., Williams, J. J., & Goel, S. (2021). Bandit algorithms to personalize educational chatbots. *Machine Learning*, *110*(9), 2389–2418. DOI: 10.1007/s10994-021-05983-y

Cant, C. (2021). *Riding for Deliveroo: Resistance in the new economy*. Polity Press.

Cant, C. (2024). *The Fast and the Furious: Platform Labour and Protest in the Gig Economy*. Pluto Press., DOI: 10.2307/j.ctv2x0wptf

Capilla, P. (2021). Post-truth as a mutation of epistemology in journalism. *Media and Communication*, *9*(1), 78–88. DOI: 10.17645/mac.v9i1.3529

Carroll, S., Garba, I., Figueroa-Rodriguez, O., Holbrook, J., Lovett, R., Materechera, S., Parsons, M., Raseroka, K., Rodriguez-Lonebear, D., Rowe, R., Sara, R., Walker, J., Anderson, J., & Hudson, M. (2020). The CARE principles for Indigenous data governance. *Data Science Journal*, *19*(1), 43.

Casa da Arquitectura & Centro Português de Arquitectura. (2025). *Casa da Arquitectura e Arquivo Público do Distrito Federal de Brasília unem esforços para partilha de acervo digital de Lúcio Costa*. https://casadaarquitectura.pt/pt/noticias/casa-da-arquitectura-e-arquivo-publico-do-distrito-federal-de-brasilia-unem-esforcos-para-partilha-de-acervo-digital-de-lucio-costa-2025-02-19/

Castells, M. (1996). *The Rise of the Network Society*. Blackwell.

Castells, M. (2009). *Communication Power*. Oxford University Press.

Cetinkaya, L. (2017). The impact of WhatsApp use on success in education process. *International Review of Research in Open and Distance Learning*, *18*(7), 59–74. DOI: 10.19173/irrodl.v18i7.3279

Cheney-Lippold, J. (2017). *We are data: Algorithms and the making of our digital selves*. NYU Press.

Cheney-Lippold, J. (2017). *We Are Data: Algorithms and the Making of Our Digital Selves*. NYU Press. DOI: 10.18574/nyu/9781479888702.001.0001

Chen, J. Y., & Sun, P. (2020). Temporal arbitrage, fragmented rush, and opportunistic behaviors: The labor politics of time in the platform economy. *New Media & Society*, *23*(12), 3487–3506. DOI: 10.1177/1461444820913567

Chen, L., & Yan, S. (2021). Occupational health and safety challenges for gig workers during COVID-19 and beyond. *Journal of Occupational Health*, *63*(1), e12234. DOI: 10.1002/1348-9585.12234 PMID: 33993611

Chen, M. K., Rossi, P. E., Chevalier, J. A., & Oehlsen, E. (2019). The value of flexible work: Evidence from Uber drivers. *Journal of Political Economy*, *127*(6), 2735–2794. DOI: 10.1086/702171

Choudhury, M. (2022). Platform power and caste exclusion: Instagram and vernacular creators in India. *Information Communication and Society*, *25*(9), 1309–1327.

Christensen, P. (2003). Place, space and knowledge: children in the village and the city. In *P. Christensen & M. O'Brien (orgs.), Children in the city: home, neighbourhood and community*. Routledge.

Cinelli, M., Quattrociocchi, W., Galeazzi, A., Valensise, C. M., Brugnoli, E., Schmidt, A. L., Zola, P., Zollo, F., & Scala, A. (2020). The COVID-19 social media infodemic. *Scientific Reports*, *10*(1), 1–10. DOI: 10.1038/s41598-020-73510-5 PMID: 33024152

Citton, Y. (2017). *The ecology of attention*. Polity Press.

CNI. (2023). *Directions in digital scholarship: Support for digital, data-intensive and computational research in academic libraries*. Coalition for Networked Information. Retrieved from https://www.cni.org/events/cni-workshops/directions-in-digital-scholarship-support-for-digital-data-intensive-and-computational-research-in-academic-libraries/report

Cohen, J. E. (2019). *Between truth and power: The legal constructions of informational capitalism*. Oxford University Press.

Coleman, D. (2019). Digital colonialism: The 21st-century scramble for Africa through the extraction and control of user data and the limitations of data protection laws. *Michigan Journal of Race & Law*, *24*, 417–472.

Collins, P. H. (2000). *Black feminist thought* (2nd ed.). Routledge.

Cornu, M., & Renold, M.-A. (2010). New developments in the restitution of cultural property: Alternative means of dispute resolution. *International Journal of Cultural Property*, *17*(1), 1–31. DOI: 10.1017/S0940739110000044

Corsaro, W. A. (2011). *Sociologia da infância*. Artmed.

Costa, J. P., & Peterson, M. (2023). Artificial intelligence and the future of work: Ethical issues and policy challenges. *Ethics and Information Technology*, *25*(1), 1–12.

Costanza-Chock, S., Raji, I. D., & Buolamwini, J. (2022). Who audits the auditors? Recommendations from a field scan of the algorithmic auditing ecosystem. In *Proceedings of the 2022 ACM Conference on Fairness, Accountability, and Transparency*, 1571-1583. https://doi.org/DOI: 10.1145/3531146.3533213

Couldry, N., & Mejias, U. (2019). *The costs of connection: How data is colonizing human life and appropriating it for capitalism*. Stanford University Press.

Couldry, N., & Mejias, U. A. (2019). Data colonialism: Rethinking big data's relation to the contemporary subject. *Television & New Media*, *20*(4), 336–349.

Couldry, N., & Mejias, U. A. (2019). *The costs of connection*. Stanford University Press.

Couldry, N., & Mejias, U. A. (2019). *The costs of connection: How data is colonising human life and appropriating it for capitalism*. Stanford University Press., DOI: 10.1515/9781503609754

Cox, R. (2004). *No innocent deposits: Forming archives by rethinking appraisal*. Scarecrow Press.

Crawford, K., & Joler, V. (2018). *Anatomy of an AI system*. https://anatomyof.ai

Crawford, K. (2021). *Atlas of AI: Power, politics, and the planetary costs of artificial intelligence*. Yale University Press.

Crawford, K. (2021). *The atlas of AI: Power, politics, and the planetary costs of artificial intelligence*. Yale University Press., DOI: 10.56315/PSCF3-22Crawford

Creemers, R. (2018). China's social credit system: An evolving practice of control. SSRN *Electronic Journal*. https://doi.org/DOI: 10.2139/ssrn.3175792

Creemers, R. (2018). China's social credit system: An evolving practice of control. *SSRN.*

Criado-Perez, C. (2019). *Invisible women: Data bias in a world designed for men.* Abrams Press.

Culnan, M. J., Markus, M. L., Jablin, F. M., Putnam, L. L., Roberts, K. H., & Porter, L. W. (1987). Handbook of organizational communication: An interdisciplinary perspective.

Cunningham, S., & Craig, D. (2019). *Social Media Entertainment: the New Intersection of Hollywood and Silicon Valley*. New York University Press.

Curchod, C., Patriotta, G., Cohen, L., & Neysen, N. (2020). Working for an algorithm: Power asymmetries and agency in online labor markets. *Administrative Science Quarterly*, *63*(3), 643–676. DOI: 10.1177/0001839219867024

D'Arcy, J., Polizzi, G., Harris, R., Barrera, P., Yates, S., & Yeoman, F. (2024). *Exploring challenges and best practices in addressing digital inequalities: A UK regional case study approach.* University of Liverpool., Retrieved from https://livrepository.liverpool.ac.uk/3181004/1/01_05_24_BA%20Final%20Report%20Designed.pdf

D'Ignazio, C., & Klein, L. F. (2020). *Data feminism.* MIT Press. DOI: 10.7551/mitpress/11805.001.0001

Daft, R. L., Lengel, R. H., & Trevino, L. K. (1987). Message Equivocality, Media Selection, and Manager Performance: Implications for Information Systems. *Management Information Systems Quarterly*, *11*(3), 355–366. DOI: 10.2307/248682

Dahiya, B. (2023). *Digital colonialism: Neo-colonialism of the Global South.* Global South Studies Series.

Dakoru, A. (2025). Digital silence as a pragmatic strategy: An intercultural qualitative study of online group chats. *ResearchGate.* https://www.researchgate.net/publication/394378314_Digital_silence_as_a_pragmatic_strategy

Dastin, J. (2018, October 10). Amazon scraps secret AI recruiting tool that showed bias against women. Reuters. https://www.reuters.com/article/us-amazon-com-jobs-automation-insight-idUSKCN1MK08G

Daudi, A. (2022). The Culture of Narcissism: A Philosophical Analysis of "Fitspiration" and the Objectified Self. *Physical Culture and Sport Studies and Research*, *94*(1), 46–55. DOI: 10.2478/pcssr-2022-0005

De Moya, J. F., & Pallud, J. (2020). From panopticon to heautopticon: A new form of surveillance introduced by quantified-self practices. *Information Systems Journal, 30*(6), 940–976. DOI: 10.1111/isj.12284

De Stefano, V., & Aloisi, A. (2018). European legal framework for digital labour platforms. European Commission. https://doi.org/DOI: 10.2139/ssrn.3186489

De Stefano, V., & Taes, S. (2023). Algorithmic management and collective bargaining. *Transfer: European Review of Labour and Research, 29*(1), 21–36. DOI: 10.1177/10242589221141055

De Vaujany, F. X., Leclercq-Vandelannoitte, A., Munro, I., Nama, Y., & Holt, R. (2021). Control and surveillance in work practice: Cultivating paradox in 'new' modes of organizing. *Organization Studies, 42*(5), 675–695. DOI: 10.1177/01708406211010988

Deleuze, G. (1992). Postscript on the societies of control. *October, 59*, 3–7. https://www.jstor.org/stable/778828

Delfanti, A. (2021). *The warehouse: Workers and robots at Amazon*. Pluto Press.16. Ethics Guidelines for Trustworthy AI. (2021). *High-Level Expert Group on Artificial Intelligence*. European Commission. DOI: 10.2307/j.ctv2114fnm

Dencik, L., Hintz, A., Redden, J., & Treré, E. (2019). *Data justice and civic technology: Co-creating frameworks for equitable data governance*. Cardiff University. https://datajusticehub.org

Denzin, N. K., & Lincoln, Y. S. (Eds.). (2018). *The SAGE handbook of qualitative research* (5th ed.). SAGE Publications.

DePastino, T. (2021). *Citizen Hobo: How a Century of Homelessness Shaped America*. University of Chicago Press.

DeSanctis, G., Jackson, B. M., (1994). Coordination of Information Technology Management: Team-Based Structures and Computer-Based Communication Systems, Source: Journal of Management Information Systems, Spring, 1994, Vol. 10, No. 4 (Spring, 1994), 85-110.

Deutsch, M., & Gerard, H. B. (1955). A study of normative and informational social influences upon individual judgment. *Journal of Abnormal and Social Psychology, 51*(3), 629–636. DOI: 10.1037/h0046408 PMID: 13286010

Diakopoulos, N. (2016). Accountability in algorithmic decision making. *Communications of the ACM, 59*(2), 56–62.

Diakopoulos, N. (2016). Accountability in algorithmic decision-making. *Communications of the ACM, 59*(2), 56–62. DOI: 10.1145/2844110

Dias, A. F., Dias, P., & Andrade, J. G. (2025). A Geração Alpha e a música: A influência do TikTok no consumo musical. *Revista Opus*, *31*(e253132), 1–22. DOI: 10.20504/opus2025.31.32

Dickinson, E. E. (2019, March 18). *The promise and peril of academia wading into Twitter*. Johns Hopkins Magazine. https://hub.jhu.edu/magazine/2019/spring/more-academics-turn-to-twitter/

Donoghue, R. (2025). Freedom under algorithms: How unpredictable and asocial management erodes free choice. *Frontiers in Artificial Intelligence*, *8*, 1582085. DOI: 10.3389/frai.2025.1582085

Dotson, K. (2018). Accumulating epistemic power: A problem with epistemology. *Philosophical Topics*, *46*(1), 129–154.

Douglas, M. (1978). *Implicit meanings: Essays in anthropology* (2nd ed.). Routledge.

Drucker, P. F. (1988). The coming of the new organization. *Harvard Business Review*, *66*, 45–53.

Dubal, V. B. (2023). The drive to precarity: A political history of work, regulation, & labor advocacy. *Berkeley Journal of Employment and Labor Law*, *38*(1), 73–135. DOI: 10.15779/Z382B8VC7J

Duffy, B. E., & Meisner, C. (2023). Platform governance at the margins: Social media creators' experiences with algorithmic (in)visibility. *Media Culture & Society*, *45*(2), 285–304. DOI: 10.1177/01634437221111923

Duffy, B. E., & Meisner, C. (2024). Platform precarity and the pandemic. *New Media & Society*, *26*(1), 278–297. DOI: 10.1177/14614448211063648

Duffy, B. E., & Wissinger, E. (2017). Mythologies of Creative Work in the Social Media Age: Fun, Free, and "Just Being Me.". *International Journal of Communication*, *11*(11), 4652–4671. https://ijoc.org/index.php/ijoc/article/view/7322

Duke, B. (2022). 24/7 Digital work-based spy: The effects of technological panopticism on workers in the digital age. *Journal of Labor and Society*, *25*(4), 520–558. DOI: 10.1163/24714607-bja10068

Dulley, I. (2017). Fontes e contextos do Arquivo Nacional de Angola: Entrevista com Alexandra Aparício. *Revista do Arquivo Geral da Cidade do Rio de Janeiro*, *12*, 229–245.

Durgungöz, A. (2022). WhatsApp and educational communication in Türkiye: A case study on mathematics teachers. *Journal of Teacher Education and Lifelong Learning*, *4*(2), 13–27.

East, Emma E., "THE EFFECTS OF VIRTUAL PANOPTICISM" (2021). *Selected Honors Theses*. 140.

Eatwell, R., & Goodwin, M. (2018). *National Populism: The Revolt Against Liberal Democracy*. Penguin Books.

El Informante [@elinformante84]. (2025, March 28). *Los vínculos de @LuisaGonzalezEc con el #Narcotráfico saldrán a la luz, lo dijo hoy @DanielNoboaOk. Luisa realizó 24 viajes internacionales en el avión presidencial a PARAÍSOS FISCALES, SIN MANIFIESTO DE PASAJEROS Y SIN CONTROL DE CARGA. Lavó del narcotráfico y utilizó fondos del Estado* [Post]. X. https://x.com/elinformante84/status/1905679440899604861

El Universo. (2025, January 15). Candidato vicepresidencial Diego Borja insiste en que son calumnias las denuncias sobre manejo de recursos de proveedora de Petroecuador. *El Universo*. https://www.eluniverso.com/noticias/politica/candidato-vicepresidencial-diego-borja-rc-fideicomiso-gesticon-contrato-petroecuador-downhole-tools-nota/

Elias, S. (2008). Fifty years of influence in the workplace: The evolution of the French and Raven power taxonomy. *Journal of Management History*, *14*(3), 267–283. DOI: 10.1108/17511340810880634

Ellison, N. B., Steinfield, C., & Lampe, C. (2007). The benefits of Facebook "Friends:" social capital and college students' use of online social network sites. *Journal of Computer-Mediated Communication*, *12*(4), 1143–1168. https://doi.org/10.1111/j.1083-6101.2007.00367.x

Elshaiekh, N. M., Alghafri, F. S. S., Alsakeiti, F. S. S., & Aziza, C. H. (2018). The impact of information technology on SMEs in Oman. *Compusoft*, *7*(10), 2843–2845.

Ensmenger, N. (2010). *The computer boys take over*. MIT Press. DOI: 10.7551/mitpress/9780262050937.001.0001

Espinosa de los Monteros, P. (2019). Decolonial information practices: Repatriating and stewarding the *Popol Vuh* online. *Preservation. Digital Technology & Culture*, *48*(3–4), 107–119. DOI: 10.1515/pdtc-2019-0009

Eubanks, V. (2018). *Automating inequality*. St. Martin's Press.

Eubanks, V. (2018). *Automating inequality: How high-tech tools profile, police, and punish the poor*. St. Martin's Press.

Eynon, R., Fry, J., & Schroeder, R. (2008). The ethics of internet research. In Fielding, N., Lee, R. M., & Blank, G. (Eds.), *The SAGE handbook of online research methods* (pp. 23–41). SAGE Publications., DOI: 10.4135/9780857020055.n2

Federici, S. (2012). *Revolution at point zero*. PM Press.

Ferguson, A. G. (2017). *The rise of big data policing: Surveillance, race, and the future of law enforcement*. NYU Press.

Fernandes, F. (1979). As trocinhas do Bom Retiro: contribuição ao estudo folclórico e sociológico dos grupos infantis. In F. Fernandes, *Folclore e mudança social na cidade de São Paulo* (2.ª ed.). Petrópolis: Vozes.

Fernandes, N., & Marchi, R. de C. (2020). A participação das crianças nas pesquisas: Nuances a partir da etnografia e na investigação participativa. *Revista Brasileira de Educação, 25*, e250024. DOI: 10.1590/s1413-24782020250024

Fielitz, M., & Marcks, H. (2020). *Digitaler Faschismus: Die sozialen Medien als Motor des Rechtsextremismus*. Dudenverlag.

Fishman, J. (2010). Locating the international interest in intranational cultural property disputes. *The Yale Journal of International Law*, *35*(2), 347–404.

Flaxman, S., Goel, S., & Rao, J. M. (2016). Filter bubbles, echo chambers, and online news consumption. *Public Opinion Quarterly*, *80*(S1), 298–320. DOI: 10.1093/poq/nfw006

Fleming, P. (2017). The human capital hoax: Work, debt and insecurity in the era of Uberization. *Organization Studies*, *38*(5), 691–709. DOI: 10.1177/0170840616686129

Florida, R. L. (2004). *The rise of the creative class : and how it's transforming work, leisure, community and everyday life*. Basic Books.

Floridi, L., Cowls, J., Beltrametti, M., Chatila, R., Chazerand, P., Dignum, V., . . . Vayena, E. (2018). AI4People—An ethical framework for a good AI society: Opportunities, risks, principles, and recommendations. *Minds and Machines, 28*(4), 689–707.s11023-018-9482-5

Floridi, L. (2011). *The philosophy of Information*. Oxford University Press. DOI: 10.1093/acprof:oso/9780199232383.001.0001

Foong, E., Vincent, N., Hecht, B., & Gerber, E. M. (2018). Women (still) ask for less: Gender differences in hourly rate. *Proceedings of the ACM on Human-Computer Interaction*, 2(CSCW), 1-21. DOI: 10.1145/3274322

Fórum de Entidades em Defesa do Patrimônio Cultural Brasileiro. (2025, January 9). *Contra a neocolonização e a evasão dos acervos brasileiros de arquitetura.* https://forumpatrimoniobr.wordpress.com/2025/01/08/contra-a-neocolonizacao-e-a-evasao-dos-acervos-brasileiros-de-arquitetura/

Foucault, M. (1982). The Subject and Power, Source: Critical Inquiry, Vol. 8, No. 4, 777-795 Published by: The University of Chicago Press, https://www.jstor.org/stable/1343197

Foucault, M. (1971). The order of discourse. In Young, R. (Ed.), *Untying the text: A post-structuralist reader* (pp. 48–78). Routledge.

Foucault, M. (1977). *Discipline and punish.* Pantheon.

Foucault, M. (1977). *Discipline and punish: The birth of the prison.* Pantheon Books.

Foucault, M. (1982). The subject and power. *Critical Inquiry*, *8*(4), 777–795. DOI: 10.1086/448181

Foucault, M. (1988). *Technologies of the self: A seminar with Michel Foucault.* University of Massachusetts Press.

Fraher, A. L. (2015). Technology-push, market-demand and the missing safety-pull: A case study of American Airlines Flight 587. *New Technology, Work and Employment*, *30*(2), 109–127. DOI: 10.1111/ntwe.12050

Franzke, A. S., ... (2020). Internet Research: Ethical Guidelines 3.0. *Association of Internet Researchers.* https://aoir.org/reports/ethics3.pdf

French, J. R. P. Jr., Raven, B. (1959). The bases of social power. In D. Cartwright (Ed.), Studies in Social Power, 150–167.

Freud, S. (1914). *On Narcissism.*

Fromm, E. (1976). *Haben oder Sein : die seelischen Grundlagen einer neuen Gesellschaft.* Deutschet Taschenbuch Verlag. https://www.lyrik-klinge.de/wp-content/uploads/Haben_oder_Sein__Fromm.pdf

Fromm, E. (1977). *El Miedo A La Libertad (Fear of Freedom)* (G. Germani, Ed.). Paidos. https://conductitlan.org.mx/13_psicologiasocial/Materiales/L_FROMM_El%20Miedo%20A%20La%20Libertad.pdf

Fromm, E. (1978). *Tener Y Ser.* Fondo de cultura economica. https://consumoetico.webs.uvigo.es/textos/tener_ser.pdf

Fromm, E. (2000). *El Arte de Amar*. Martins Fontes. https://share.google/C3UCmvwDeIDN6Qr5u Fromm, E. (2023, May 30). *The Psychology of Narcissism - Erich Fromm's Video Essay*. Youtube. https://youtu.be/V9Pz9VZhbL8?si=gcZWkjitr1kd9S-I

Fromm, E. (2024, July 21). *The Art of Loving - Erich Fromm's Video Essay*. Youtube. https://youtu.be/iagSm_E_thk?si=Kx4KDRZh1m4ibodc

Fromm, E. (1956). *Psicoanálisis de la sociedad contemporánea Hacia una sociedad sana* (6th ed.). Fondo de Cultura Economica., https://ayudacontextos.wordpress.com/wp-content/uploads/2018/04/erich_fromm-psicoanalisis_de_la_sociedad_contemporanea.pdf

Fuchs, C. (2011). Web 2.0, prosumption, and surveillance. *Surveillance & Society*, *8*(3), 288–309. DOI: 10.24908/ss.v8i3.4165

Fuchs, C. (2025). What is Digital Fascism? *St. Antony's International Review*, *20*(1), 26–39.

Fulk, J., & Boyd, B. (1991). Emerging theories of communication in organizations. *Journal of Management*, *17*(2), 407–446. DOI: 10.1177/014920639101700207

Fundo das Nações Unidas para a Infância (UNICEF). (2012). *Crianças em um mundo urbano*. New York: UNICEF.

Fu, P. P., & Yukl, G. (2000). Perceived effectiveness of influence tactics in the United States and China. *The Leadership Quarterly*, *11*(2), 251–266. DOI: 10.1016/S1048-9843(00)00039-4

Galeano, E., & Allende, I. (1997). *Open veins of Latin America: Five centuries of the pillage of a continent*. Monthly Review Press.

Galič, M., Timan, T., & Koops, B. J. (2017). Bentham, Deleuze and beyond: An overview of surveillance theories from the Panopticon to participation. *Philosophy & Technology*, *30*(1), 9–37. DOI: 10.1007/s13347-016-0219-1

Galland, B. (2019). Les archives de Simancas: De la saisie napoléonienne à la restitution de Pétain. In V. Laniol & A. Sumpf (Eds.), *Saisies, spoliations, restitutions: Archives et bibliothèques au XXe siècle* (pp. 199–212). Presses universitaires de Rennes. https://books.openedition.org/pur/130275

Galloway, A. (2012). The Interface Effect. *Polity*.

Gandini, A. (2019). Labour process theory and the gig economy. *Human Relations*, *72*(6), 1039–1056. DOI: 10.1177/0018726718790002

García-Villar, C. (2021). A critical review on altmetrics: Can we measure the social impact factor? *Insights Into Imaging*, *12*(1), 92. DOI: 10.1186/s13244-021-01033-2 PMID: 34215935

Geertz, C. (1973). *The interpretation of cultures: Selected essays*. Basic Books.

Giddens, A. (1979). *Central problems in social theory: Action, structure, and contradiction in social analysis* (Vol. 241). Univ of California Press. DOI: 10.1007/978-1-349-16161-4

Gieryn, T. F. (1983). Boundary-work and the demarcation of science from non-science: Strains and interests in professional ideologies of scientists. *American Sociological Review*, *48*(6), 781–795. DOI: 10.2307/2095325

Gillespie, T. (2014). The Relevance of Algorithms. In T. Gillespie, P. Boczkowski, & K. Foot (Eds.), Media Technologies Essays on Communication, Materiality, and Society (pp. 185–193). Cambridge, MA MIT Press. - References - Scientific Research Publishing. (n.d.). https://www.scirp.org/reference/referencespapers?referenceid=2798839

Gillespie, T. (2014). The relevance of algorithms. *Media technologies: Essays on communication, materiality, and society, 167*(2014), 167. https://doi.org/DOI: 10.7551/mitpress/9780262525374.003.0009

Gillespie, T. (2014). The relevance of algorithms. In Gillespie, T., Boczkowski, P. J., & Foot, K. A. (Eds.), *Media technologies* (pp. 167–194). MIT Press.

Gillespie, T. (2014). The relevance of algorithms. In Gillespie, T., Boczkowski, P., & Foot, K. (Eds.), *Media technologies: Essays on communication, materiality, and society* (pp. 167–194). MIT Press. DOI: 10.7551/mitpress/9042.003.0013

Gillespie, T. (2018). *Custodians of the internet: Platforms, content moderation, and the hidden decisions that shape social media*. Yale University Press.

Gillespie, T. (2018). *Custodians of the Internet: Platforms, Content Moderation, and the Hidden Decisions That Shape Social Media*. Yale University Press.

Gill, R. (2009). Breaking the silence: The hidden injuries of neo-liberal academia. In Gill, R., & Donaghue, R. (Eds.), *The Handbook of Gender and Communication* (pp. 228–245). Palgrave Macmillan.

Gill, R., & Orgad, S. (2018). The shifting terrain of sex and power: From the "sexualization of culture" to #MeToo. *Sexualities*, *21*(8), 1313–1324. DOI: 10.1177/1363460718794647

Gilmore, G. (2022). *Hobohemia: Emma Goldman, Lucy Parsons, and the Culture of Revolutionary Dissent*. University of California Press.

Girona, A. E. (2024). *Navigating Trust, Privacy, and Mental Health: Remote Workers' Experiences During the COVID-19 Pandemic—A Textual Analysis of Reddit Data*. The Pennsylvania State University.

Gleim, M. R., & Lawson, S. J. (2022). The sharing economy: Carving out an identity in a crowded field. *Journal of the Association for Consumer Research*, *7*(1), 1–5. DOI: 10.1086/717515

Glissant, É. (1997). *Poetics of relation* (Wing, B., Trans.). University of Michigan Press. DOI: 10.3998/mpub.10257

Goffman, E. (1959). *The presentation of self in everyday life*. Anchor Books.

Gogoi, G. S., & Bora, S. (2021). Challenges of online learning: Digital inequality in the context of India. *Players-Palarch's Journal of Archaeology of Egypt/Egyptology, 18*(4), 4234-4239.

Gomes Nascimento, L., & Nabarrete Bastos, P. (2024). Platformized intellectual: theoretical contributions, scope and digital limits of praxis. *Correspondencias & análisis*, (19), 196-220. https://doi.org/DOI: 10.24265/cian.2024.n19.08

Gonçalves, J., Weber, I., Masullo, G. M., Da Silva, M. T., & Hofhuis, J. (2021). Common sense or censorship: How algorithmic moderators and message type influence perceptions of online content deletion. *New Media & Society*, *25*(10), 2595–2617. DOI: 10.1177/14614448211032310

González, M. (2025, January 10). Ecuador cerró el 2024 con la segunda tasa de muertes violentas más alta de su historia, pese a una reducción importante. *Primicias*. https://www.primicias.ec/seguridad/ecuador-2024-tasa-muertes-violendas-segunda-peor-historia-87118/

Goodman, E. P., & Trehu, J. (2022). Algorithmic auditing: Chasing AI accountability. *Santa Clara High-Technology Law Journal*, *39*(3), 289–332. DOI: 10.2139/ssrn.4227350

Goods, C., Veen, A., & Barratt, T. (2019). "Is your gig any good?" Analysing job quality in the Australian platform-based food-delivery sector. *The Journal of Industrial Relations*, *61*(4), 502–527. DOI: 10.1177/0022185618817069

Goodstadt, B. E., & Hjelle, L. A. (1973). Power To The Powerless: Locus Of Control And The Use Of Power. *Journal of Personality and Social Psychology*, *27*(2), 190–196. DOI: 10.1037/h0034784 PMID: 4723967

Graham, M., Hjorth, I., & Lehdonvirta, V. (2021). Digital labour and development: Impacts of global digital labour platforms. *Transfer: European Review of Labour and Research, 23*(2), 135–162. DOI: 10.1177/1024258916687250 PMID: 28781494

Gramsci, A. (1971). *Selections from the Prison Notebooks*. International Publishers.

Gray, M. L. (2020). *Ghost work: How to stop Silicon Valley from building a new global underclass*. Houghton Mifflin Harcourt.

Gray, M. L., & Suri, S. (2019). *Ghost Work: How to Stop Silicon Valley from Building a New Global Underclass*. Houghton Mifflin Harcourt.

Greenwald, G. (2014). *No place to hide: Edward Snowden, the NSA, and the U.S. surveillance state*. Metropolitan Books.

Griffin, S. H. (2022). Value Displaced, Value Re/Claimed: Reparations, Shared Heritage and Caribbean Archival Records. In Lowry, J. (Ed.), *Disputed Archival Heritage* (pp. 304–331). Routledge., DOI: 10.4324/9781003057765-17

Grimsted, P. K. (1998). "Trophy" archives and non-restitution. *Problems of Post-Communism, 45*(3), 3–. https://doi.org/DOI: 10.1080/10758216.1998.11655785

Grimsted, P. K. (2010). Why do captured archives go home? Restitution achievements under Russian law. *International Journal of Cultural Property*, *17*(2), 291–333. DOI: 10.1017/S0940739110000123

Grosfoguel, R. (2011). Decolonizing postcolonial studies and paradigms of political-economy: Transmodernity, decolonial thinking, and global coloniality. *Transmodernity*, *1*(1), 1–38.

Guamán, A., Aragoneses, A., & Martín, S. (Eds.). (2019). *Neofascismo: La Bestia Neoliberal*. Siglo XXI.

Guenther, L., Wilhelm, C., Oschatz, C., & Brück, J. (2023). Science communication on Twitter: Measuring indicators of engagement and their links to user interaction in communication scholars' Tweet content. *Public Understanding of Science (Bristol, England), 32*(7), 860–869. DOI: 10.1177/09636625231166552 PMID: 37132036

Guérin, I., Agier, I., & Kumar, S. (2013). Women's Empowerment: Power to Act or Power over Other Women? Lessons from Indian Microfinance. *Oxford Development Studies*, *41*(sup1), 76–94. DOI: 10.1080/13600818.2013.781147

Gurumurthy, A., & Chami, N. (2016). Digital India through the looking glass of net neutrality. *International Journal of Communication*, *10*, 4282–4302.

Habgood-Coote, J. (2021). *A global charter for truth: Social epistemology for the internet age* (IYTT Working Paper No. 2). International Youth Think Tank. Retrieved from https://iythinktank.com/wp-content/uploads/2021/06/iytt-working-paper-no-2-june-2021.pdf

Hafermalz, E. (2021). Out of the panopticon and into exile: Visibility and control in distributed new culture organizations. *Organization Studies*, *42*(5), 697–717. DOI: 10.1177/0170840620909962

Haggerty, K. D., & Ericson, R. V. (2000). The surveillant assemblage. *The British Journal of Sociology*, *51*(4), 605–622. DOI: 10.1080/00071310020015280 PMID: 11140886

Hailu, M., & Wu, J. (2021). The use of academic social networking sites in scholarly communication: Scoping review. *Data and Information Management*, *5*(2), 277–298. DOI: 10.2478/dim-2020-0050

Hall, E. T. (1976). *Beyond culture*. Anchor Books.

Han, B.-C. (2010). *The Burnout Society* (Butler, E., Ed.). Stanford University Press.

Han, B.-C. (2013). *Schwarm*. Ansichten des Digitalen. Matthes & Seitz.

Han, B.-C. (2017). *Psychopolitics: Neoliberalism and new technologies of power*. Verso.

Haraway, D. (1988). Situated knowledges. *Feminist Studies*, *14*(3), 575–599. DOI: 10.2307/3178066

Haraway, D. (1991). *A cyborg manifesto: Science, technology, and socialist-feminism in the late twentieth century*. Routledge.

Haraway, D. (2016). A cyborg manifesto: Science, technology, and socialist-feminism in the late twentieth century. In *Manifestly Haraway* (pp. 5–90). University of Minnesota Press., DOI: 10.5749/minnesota/9780816650477.003.0001

Harcourt, B. E. (2015). *Exposed: Desire and disobedience in the digital age*. Harvard University Press.

Harding, S. (1986). *The science question in feminism*. Cornell University Press.

Hargittai, E., & Walejko, G. (2008). The participation divide: Content creation and sharing in the digital age. *Information Communication and Society*, *11*(2), 239–256. DOI: 10.1080/13691180801946150

Harris, V. (2004). Concerned with the writings of others: Archival canons, discourses and voices. *Journal of the Society of Archivists*, *25*(2), 211–220. DOI: 10.1080/0037981042000271529

Hars, A. (2000). Web Based Knowledge Infrastructures for the Sciences: An Adaptive document. *Communications of the Association for Information Systems*, *4*. Advance online publication. DOI: 10.17705/1cais.00401

Haugaard, M. (2010). Democracy, Political Power, and Authority, Social Research, Vol. 77, No. 4, From Impunity to Accountability: Africa's Development in the 21st Century, 1049-1074.

Heidegger, M. (1954). *Die Frage nach der Technik*. Klostermann.

Helberger, N. (2016). Policy implications from algorithmic profiling and the changing relationship between newsreaders and the media. Javnost - the Public, 23(2), 188–203. https://doi.org/10.1080/13183222.2016.1162989

Held, V. (2006). *The ethics of care*. Oxford University Press.

Herari, N., Waluyo, W., & Rubiyanto, R. (2024). Self-Directed Visionaries: Evolutionize the Passion Economy through Digital Entrepreneurship on Instagram. In U. Yunus & et al (Eds.) (Eds.), *Proceeding Book of The International Conference on Communication and Business. Strengthening ASEAN's Leadership in Sustainable Business and Advanced Comunication, Volume 2. The Intersection of Communication and Business in the Pursuit of Sustainability* (pp. 14–14). LSPR Publishing. https://www.researchgate.net/publication/377964759_Self-Directed_Visionaries_Evolutionize_the_Passion_Economy_through_Digital_Entrepreneurship_on_Instagram

Herari, N. (2025). Piramida Kebutuhan dan Passion Economy, Pemenuhan Kebutuhan Diri melalui Media Digital di Indonesia. In Rosanah, R., Berto, A. R., Yuniarti, T., Lestari, A., Safrudiningsih, S., Ramonita, L., & Arifah, A. (Eds.), *Transformasi Komunikasi Digital Menuju Indonesia Berkelanjutan: Komunikasi Digital dan Inovasi Bagi Masyarakat* (1st ed., pp. 128–143). PT Elex Media Komputindo., https://www.researchgate.net/publication/390760825_Piramida_Kebutuhan_dan_Passion_Economy_Pemenuhan_Kebutuhan_Diri_melalui_Media_Digital_di_Indonesia

Herari, N., & Waluyo, W. (2023). Instagram Business Coach sebagai Penggerak Passion Economy dalam Perspektif Islam. *Warta ISKI*, *6*(1), 32–47. DOI: 10.25008/wartaiski.v6i1.201

Herari, N., Waluyo, W., & Rubiyanto, R. (2025). Leading Alone, Leading Forward: Solopreneurs and the Quiet Power of the Passion Economy. In Paradiso-Testa, M. (Ed.), *The Purpose of Passion in Leadership* (1st ed.). IGI Global. DOI: 10.4018/979-8-3373-2404-3.ch012

Herrera, S., & Macasoff, A. (2023). Daniel Noboa and the Exercise of "Landowner Power". *Ecuador Debate*, (20), 135–153.

Hicks, M. (2017). *Programmed inequality*. MIT Press.

Hochschild, A. R. (1983). *The managed heart*. University of California Press.

Hochschild, A. R. (1983). *The managed heart: Commercialization of human feeling*. University of California Press.

Hofstede, G. (2001). *Culture's consequences: Comparing values, behaviors, institutions, and organizations across nations* (2nd ed.). SAGE.

Holmes, H., & Burgess, G. (2022). Digital exclusion and poverty in the UK: How structural inequality shapes experiences of getting online. *Digital Geography and Society*, *3*, 100041. DOI: 10.1016/j.diggeo.2022.100041

Huebner, S., & Marr, S. (2019). Between policy and practice: Archival descriptions, digital returns and a place for coalescing narratives. *Archives and Manuscripts*, *47*(1), 113–130. DOI: 10.1080/01576895.2018.1552161

Huggett, J. (2019). Resilient scholarship in the digital age. *Journal of Computer Applications in Archaeology*, *2*(1), 25. DOI: 10.5334/jcaa.25

Hussaini, U., & Dikko, M. U. (2025). Impact of Digital Financial Inclusion on Poverty Reduction in North-Western Nigeria. *African Journal of Management and Business Research*, *20*(1), 390–411. DOI: 10.62154/ajmbr.2025.020.01031

Huws, U., Spencer, N. H., Syrdal, D. S., & Holts, K. (2017). *Work in the European gig economy*. Foundation for European Progressive Studies.

Hyslop-Margison, E., & Rochester, R. (2020). Assessment or Surveillance? Panopticism and Higher Education. *Philosophical Inquiry in Education.*, *24*(1), 102–109. DOI: 10.7202/1070559ar

IDW. (2021). *Christopher Lasch - The Culture of Narcissism*. YouTube. https://www.youtube.com/watch?v=6dR2ghd8rmg

Ihde, D. (1990). *Technology and the lifeworld: From garden to Earth*. Indiana University Press. DOI: 10.2979/3108.0

Instone, D., Major, B., & Bunker, B. B. (1983). Gender, self confidence, and social influence strategies: An organizational simulation. *Journal of Personality and Social Psychology*, *44*(2), 322–333. DOI: 10.1037/0022-3514.44.2.322

International Council on Archives. (2020). *Disputed Archival Claims: An International Survey 2018/2019*. https://www.ica.org/sites/default/files/disputed_archival_claims_an_international_survey_2018_2019.pdf

International Labour Organization. (2021). *Teleworking for Workers and Employers in the ICTS and Financial Services Sectors*. https://www.ilo.org/sites/default/files/wcmsp5/groups/public/%40ed_dialogue/%40sector/documents/meetingdocument/wcms_547099.pdf

International Labour Organization. (2024). *World Employment and Social Outlook: Trends 2024*. ILO Publications.

International Telecommunication Union. (2024). *Measuring digital development: Facts and figures 2024*. Retrieved from https://www.itu.int/en/ITU-D/Statistics/Pages/facts/default.aspx

Introna, L. D., & Nissenbaum, H. (2000). Shaping the Web: Why the politics of search engines matters. *The Information Society*, *16*(3), 169–185.

Jabagi, N., Croteau, A. M., Audebrand, L. K., & Marsan, J. (2019). Gig-workers' motivation: Thinking beyond carrots and sticks. *Journal of Managerial Psychology*, *34*(4), 192–213. DOI: 10.1108/JMP-06-2018-0255

James, A., & Prout, A. (1997). *Constructing and reconstructing childhood: contemporary issues in the sociological study of childhood*. RoutledgeFalmer.

Jane, E. A. (2016). *Online misogyny and feminist digital media studies*. Routledge.

Jenkins, H. (2009). *Confronting the challenges of participatory culture: Media education for the 21st century*. The MIT press., Retrieved from https://library.oapen.org/bitstream/handle/20.500.12657/26083/1004003.pdf DOI: 10.7551/mitpress/8435.001.0001

Jhaver, S., Birman, I., Gilbert, E., & Bruckman, A. (2019). Human evaluation of content moderation algorithms: Accuracy, biases, and the role of augmentations. In *CHI Conference* proceedings.

Johnston, A. (2022, December 24). *Jacques Lacan*. Stanford Encyclopedia of Philosophy. https://plato.stanford.edu/entries/lacan/

Johnston, H., & Land-Kazlauskas, C. (2021). Organizing on-demand: Representation, voice, and collective bargaining in the gig economy. *ILO Working Paper*, 94. https://doi.org/DOI: 10.2139/ssrn.3788600

Jones, E. E., Pittman, T.S., (1982). Toward A General Theory Of Strategic Self-Presentation.

Jordan, K., & Weller, M. (2018). Academics and social networking sites: Benefits, problems and tensions in professional engagement with online networking. *Journal of Interactive Media in Education*, *2018*(1), 1. Advance online publication. DOI: 10.5334/jime.448

Kalleberg, A. L., & Vallas, S. P. (2018). Probing precarious work: Theory, research, and politics. *Research in the Sociology of Work*, *31*, 1–30. DOI: 10.1108/S0277-283320170000031017

Kamal, M. M. (2020). The triple-edged sword of COVID-19: Understanding the use of digital technologies and the impact of productive, disruptive, and destructive nature of the pandemic. *Information Systems Management*, *37*(4), 310–317. DOI: 10.1080/10580530.2020.1820634

Kamande, E. (2025). *Digital governance in action: Success stories and lessons from global leaders*. TheFutureList. Retrieved from https://www.thefuturelist.com/digital-governance-in-action-success-stories-and-lessons-from-global-leaders/

Karppi, T. (2018). *Disconnect: Facebook's affective bonds*. University of Minnesota Press. DOI: 10.5749/j.ctv65sz27

Katzenbach, C., & Ulbricht, L. (2019). Algorithmic governance. *Internet Policy Review*, *8*(4). Advance online publication. DOI: 10.14763/2019.4.1424

Kearns, M., & Roth, A. (2019). *The ethical algorithm: The science of socially aware algorithm design*. Oxford University Press.

Kecskeméti, C., & van Laar, E. (1981). *Model bilateral and multicultural agreements and conventions concerning the transfer of archives*. UNESCO. https://unesdoc.unesco.org/ark:/48223/pf0000046909_fre

Kecskeméti, C. (2009). Displaced European archives: Is it time for a post-war settlement? *The American Archivist*, *55*(1), 132–140. DOI: 10.17723/aarc.55.1.g1578317457778 0t

Kellogg, K. C., Valentine, M. A., & Christin, A. (2019). Algorithms at Work: The new contested terrain of control. *The Academy of Management Annals*, *14*(1), 366–410. DOI: 10.5465/annals.2018.0174

Kelly, J. (2021). Algorithmic content moderation: Technical, political, and legal challenges. *Social Media + Society*, *7*(3).

Kenney, M., & Zysman, J. (2021). The platform economy: Restructuring the space of capitalist accumulation. *Cambridge Journal of Regions, Economy and Society*, *13*(1), 55–76. DOI: 10.1093/cjres/rsaa001

Keskin, B. (2018) "Van Dijk, Poell, and de Wall, The Platform Society: Public Values in a Connective World (2018)," Markets, Globalization & Development Review: Vol. 3: No. 3, Article 8.

Ketelaar, E. (1999). Archivalisation and archiving. *Archives & Manuscripts*, 54–61. https://publications.archivists.org.au/index.php/asa/article/view/8759

Khera, R. (2019). *Dissent on Aadhaar: Big data meets big brother*. Orient BlackSwan.

Kim, Y. (2021). *The Soft Power of The Korean Wave; Parasite, BTS and Drama* (1st ed.). Routledge., https://www.routledge.com/ DOI: 10.4324/9781003102489

Kipnis, D., & Schmidt, S. (1985). The language of persuasion. *Psychology Today*, *19*(4), 40.

Kipnis, D., Schmidt, S. M., Swaffin-Smith, C., & Wilkinson, I. (1984). Patterns of managerial influence: Shotgun managers, tacticians, and bystanders. *Organizational Dynamics*, *12*(3), 58–67. DOI: 10.1016/0090-2616(84)90025-1

Kipnis, D., Schmidt, S. M., & Wilkinson, I. (1980). Intraorganizational influence tactics: Explorations in getting one's way. *The Journal of Applied Psychology*, *65*(4), 440–452. DOI: 10.1037/0021-9010.65.4.440

Kitchin, R. (2014). The data revolution: Big data, open data, data infrastructures and their consequences. *Sage (Atlanta, Ga.)*. Advance online publication. DOI: 10.4135/9781473909472

Kitchin, R. (2017). Thinking critically about and researching algorithms. *Information Communication and Society*, *20*(1), 14–29.

Knipp, R. (2024). Digital Scholarship from the Periphery: Insights from Researchers in Chile on Academia.edu and ResearchGate. *Journal of Interactive Media in Education, 2024*(1). https://doi.org/DOI: 10.5334/jime.856

Kostka, G. (2019). China's social credit systems and public opinion: Explaining high levels of approval. *New Media & Society*, *21*(7), 1565–1593. DOI: 10.1177/1461444819826402

Kozinets, R. V. (2020). *Netnography: The essential guide to qualitative social media research* (3rd ed.). SAGE Publications. DOI: 10.4135/9781036233846

Krieger, D. J. (2025). *Informational Pragmatism: Towards a Philosophy of Digital Transformation*. Ethics Press.

Kroll, J. A., Huey, J., Barocas, S., Felten, E. W., Reidenberg, J. R., Robinson, D. G., & Yu, H. (2017). Accountable algorithms. *University of Pennsylvania Law Review, 165*(3), 633–705.

Krupa, K. L., & Grimm, K. T. (2021). Digital repatriation as a decolonizing practice in the archaeological archive. *Across the Disciplines, 18*, 47–58.

Kukutai, T., & Taylor, J. (2016). *Indigenous data sovereignty: Toward an agenda*. ANU Press.

Kumar, S. S., & Jie, Q. (2023). Exploring the role of financial inclusion in poverty reduction: An empirical study. *World Development Sustainability, 3*, 100103. DOI: 10.1016/j.wds.2023.100103

Kwet, M. (2019). Digital colonialism: US empire and the new imperialism in the Global South. *Race & Class, 61*(1), 14–28.

La Posta [@LaPosta_Ecu]. (2025, August 8). *¡Las muertes violentas no bajan! Ecuador registró 4.619 homicidios entre enero y junio de 2025, una cifra histórica, según el Observatorio Ecuatoriano de Crimen Organizado. La cifra aumentó un 47% frente a 2024. Además, los asesinatos de menores de 10 a 19 años aumentaron un 68%, al pasar de 300 a 504 casos* [Post]. X. https://x.com/LaPosta_Ecu/status/1953819952147783791

Lacan, J. (1936). *Lacan - Mirror Stage*.

Lappin, J. (2022). Two archival canons. *Archives and Records (Abingdon, England), 43*(2), 180–187. DOI: 10.1080/23257962.2022.2051457

Lasch, C. (1979). *The Culture of Narcissism*. W.W.Norton & Company.

Latour, B. (1993). *We Have Never Been Modern*. Harvard University Press.

Latour, B. (2005). *Reassembling the Social: An Introduction to Actor-Network-Theory*. Oxford University Press. DOI: 10.1093/oso/9780199256044.001.0001

Leclercq-Vandelannoitte, A. (2022). Is employee technological "ill-being" missing from corporate responsibility? The Foucauldian ethics of ubiquitous IT uses in organizations. In *Business and the ethical implications of technology* (pp. 33–55). Springer Nature Switzerland. DOI: 10.1007/978-3-031-18794-0_3

Lefebvre, H. (2003). *The urban revolution*. U of Minnesota Press.

Lehdonvirta, V., Kässi, O., Hjorth, I., Barnard, H., & Graham, M. (2019). The global platform economy: A new offshoring institution. *Journal of Management*, *45*(2), 567–599. DOI: 10.1177/0149206318786781 PMID: 30774168

Leifer, R. (1988). Matching Computer-Based Information Systems with Organizational Structures. *Management Information Systems Quarterly*, *12*(1), 63–73. DOI: 10.2307/248805

Leonardi, P. M. (2014). Social media, knowledge sharing, and innovation: Toward a theory of communication visibility. *Information Systems Research*, *25*(4), 796–816. DOI: 10.1287/isre.2014.0536

Lessig, L. (1999). *Code and Other Laws of Cyberspace*. Basic Books.

Levy, K. E., & Barocas, S. (2024). Designing against discrimination in online markets. *Berkeley Technology Law Journal*, *32*(3), 1183–1237. DOI: 10.15779/Z38N873094

Liang, F., Das, V., Kostyuk, N., & Hussain, M. M. (2018). Constructing a data-driven society: China's social credit system as a state surveillance infrastructure. *Policy and Internet*, *10*(4), 415–453. DOI: 10.1002/poi3.183

Licitra Rosa, C., Antonucci, C., Siracusano, A., & Centonze, D. (2021). From the Imaginary to Theory of the Gaze in Lacan. *Frontiers in Psychology*, *12*, 578277. Advance online publication. DOI: 10.3389/fpsyg.2021.578277 PMID: 33859589

Lincoln, Y. S., & Guba, E. G. (1988). Criteria for Assessing Naturalistic Inquiries as Reports.

Linebaugh, R., & Lowry, J. (2021). The archival colour line: Race, records and post-colonial custody. *Archives and Records (Abingdon, England)*, *42*(3), 284–303. DOI: 10.1080/23257962.2021.1940898

Lippincott, J. (2023). *Directions in Digital Scholarship: Support for Digital, Data-Intensive, and Computational Research in Academic Libraries*. Coalition for Networked Information., DOI: 10.56561/ULHJ1168

Littler, J. (2013). Book Review Authentic TM: The Politics of Ambivalence in a Brand Culture. *International Journal of Communication*, *7*, 1156–1158. https://ijoc.org/index.php/ijoc/article/view/2229/917

Livingstone, S. (2013). Children's internet culture: power, change and vulnerability in twenty-first century childhood. Taylor & Francis., Disponível em http://eprints.lse.ac.uk/63975/, Retrieved January 9, 2025, from.

Livingstone, S., Jessen, R. S., Stoilova, M., Stänicke, L. I., Graham, R., Staksrud, E., & Jensen, T. (2025). Can platform literacy protect vulnerable young people against the risky affordances of social media platforms? *Information Communication and Society*, •••, 1–18. DOI: 10.1080/1369118X.2025.2518254

Lombardinilo, A. (2017). Baudrillard between Benjamin and McLuhan: "The narcissistic seduction" of the media society. *Italian Sociological Review, 7*(4), 499–524. DOI: 10.13136/isr.v7i4.208

Lomborg, S. (2017). *Social media, social genres: Making sense of the ordinary*. Routledge.

Lowry, J. (2019). "Displaced archives": Proposing a research agenda. *Archival Science, 19*(4), 349–358. DOI: 10.1007/s10502-019-09326-8

Lowry, J., & Harris, V. (2022). Settler to settler (Reading "Remnants of Jenkinson"). *Archives and Records (Abingdon, England), 43*(2), 161–163. DOI: 10.1080/23257962.2022.2040455

Lozano, D. (2025, February 11). Noboa vincula al correísmo con la banda Los Lobos. *El Mundo*.

Lucy, L., & Bamman, D. (2021). Gender and representation bias in GPT-3. *Proceedings of NLP4PI*.

Luhmann, N. (1997). *Die Gesellschaft der Gesellschaft*. Suhrkamp.

Lung, C., AbuHilal, I., Blackburn, J., De Cristofaro, E., Zannettou, S., & Stringhini, G. (2021). Dissecting the Meme Magic: Understanding Indicators of Virality in Image Memes. *24th ACM Conference on Computer-Supported Coop- Erative Work and Social Computing (CSCW 2021)*. https://arxiv.org/abs/2101.06535 DOI: 10.1145/3449155

Lupton, D. (2016). *The quantified self*. Polity Press.

Lyon, D. (2018). *The culture of surveillance: Watching as a way of life*. Polity Press.

Ma, A. (2024). Regulation in pursuit of artificial intelligence (AI) sovereignty: China's mix of restrictive and facilitative modalities. [AJIC]. *The African Journal of Information and Communication, 34*, 1–16. https://doi.org/10.23962/ajic.i34.20103

Macedo, L. S. A. de,, , da Silva, C. G., & de Freitas, M. C. V. (2022a). Below the nation state: Power asymmetry and jurisdictional boundaries around the archives of Madeira Archipelago. In Lowry, J. (Ed.), *Contested Archival Heritage* (pp. 137–170). Routledge. DOI: 10.4324/9781003057765-9

Macedo, L. S. A. de,, , da Silva, C. G., & de Freitas, M. C. V. (2022b). Information representation in displaced archives: A meta-synthesis. *Knowledge Organization, 49*(5), 329–351. DOI: 10.5771/0943-7444-2022-5-329

Macey, D. (2009). Rethinking biopolitics, race and power in the wake of Foucault. *Theory, Culture & Society, 26*(6), 186–205.

MacKinnon, R. (2012). *Consent of the networked: The worldwide struggle for Internet freedom*. Basic Books.

Madiega, T. (2020). *Data localisation measures and their implications on the free flow of data*. European Parliamentary Research Service.

Maier, C., & Ruthven, I. (2024). Gamification in crowdsourcing: A review. *Technological Forecasting and Social Change, 188*, 122239. DOI: 10.1016/j.techfore.2022.122239

Malafouris, L. (2013). *How Things Shape the Mind: A Theory of Material Engagement*. MIT Press. DOI: 10.7551/mitpress/9476.001.0001

Manokha, I. (2018). Surveillance, panopticism, and self-discipline in the digital age. *Surveillance & Society, 16*(2), 219–237. DOI: 10.24908/ss.v16i2.8346

Manzar, A. (2023, January 27). *Empowering women in the digital age: India's digital inclusion journey*. Global Digital Inclusion. Retrieved from https://globaldigitalinclusion.org/2023/01/27/empowering-women-in-the-digital-age-indias-digital-inclusion-journey/

Margolis, J., & Fisher, A. (2003). *Unlocking the clubhouse*. MIT Press.

Maricato, E. (2003). Metrópole, legislação e desigualdade. *Estudos Avançados, 17*(48), 151–166. DOI: 10.1590/S0103-40142003000200013

Marker, S. L., Verstergaard, M., & Hendricks, V. F. (2019). Digital colonialism on the African continent. *African Statistical Newsletter, 10*, 6–9.

Marwala, T. (2025, January 23). *The algorithmic problem in artificial intelligence governance*. United Nations University. Retrieved from https://unu.edu/article/algorithmic-problem-artificial-intelligence-governance

Marwick, A. E., & Boyd, D. (2011). I tweet honestly, I tweet passionately: Twitter users, context collapse, and the imagined audience. *New Media & Society, 13*(1), 114–133. DOI: 10.1177/1461444810365313

Marx, K., & Engels, F. (1845/1846). *Die deutsche Ideologie*.

Marx, K., & Engels, F. (1973). *Karl Marx on society and social change: With selections by Friedrich Engels*. University of Chicago Press.

Mason, P. (2015). *Postcapitalism: A guide to our future*. Penguin.

Mastrangelo, F. (2021). *Theorizing #Girlboss Culture: Mediated Neoliberal Feminisms from Influencers t om Influencers to Multi-le o Multi-level Mark el Marketing Schemes eting Schemes* [Virginia Commonwealth University]. https://scholarscompass.vcu.edu/cgi/viewcontent.cgi?article=7768&context=etd

Matienzo, M. A. (2008). Canonization, archivalization, and the "archival imaginary". *Archive Fervour/Archive Further: Literature, Archives, and Literary Archives*, Aberystwyth, 9–11 July. http://hdl.handle.net/10150/216929

Mazmanian, M., Orlikowski, W. J., & Yates, J. (2013). The autonomy paradox: The implications of mobile email devices for knowledge professionals. *Organization Science*, *24*(5), 1337–1357. DOI: 10.1287/orsc.1120.0806

McChesney, R. W. (2013). *Digital disconnect: How capitalism is turning the Internet against democracy.*

McCrindle, M., & Fell, A. (2021). *Generation Alpha: understanding our children and helping them thrive*. Hachette.

McKelvey, F. (2018). A brief history of Internet.org: The life and death of Facebook's connectivity project. *Internet Policy Review*, *7*(4).

McPhail, T. (1981). Electronic colonialism: The future of international broadcasting and communication. *Sage (Atlanta, Ga.)*.

McRae, R. (2019). Queer digital feminisms: Challenging binary classifications online. *Feminist Media Studies*, *19*(4), 523–538.

Mejias, U. A., & Couldry, N. (2025) Data grab. University of Chicago Press. https://press.uchicago.edu/ucp/books/book/chicago/D/bo216184200.html

Melé, D., & Rosanas, J. M. (2003). Power, Freedom and Authority in Management: Mary Parker Follett's 'Power- With'. *Philosophy of Management*, *3*(2), 35–46. DOI: 10.5840/pom20033221

Melin, U., & Axelsson, K. (2005). Understanding Organizational Coordination and Information Systems : Mintzberg's Coordination Mechanisms Revisited and Evaluated. *Proceedings of the 13th European Conference on Information Systems*, 1634–1644.

Méndez-Domínguez, P., Muñoz, C., Raya, D., Díez, E., & De Castillo, J. (2023). Digital inclusion for social inclusion: Case study on digital literacy. *Frontiers in Communication*, *8*, 1191995. DOI: 10.3389/fcomm.2023.1191995

Merryman, J. H. (2005). Cultural property internationalism. *International Journal of Cultural Property*, *12*(1), 11–39. DOI: 10.1017/S0940739105050046

Meydan, C., Dirik, D., & Eryılmaz, İ. (2018). Liderin Güç Kaynakları Ve İş Performansı Arasındaki İlişkide Pelz Etkisinin Düzenleyici Rolü, Yönetim ve Ekonomi. *Celal Bayar Üniversitesi İktisadi ve İdari Bilimler Fakültesi Dergisi*, *25*(1), 75–92.

Miessler, D. (2023, September 28). *Extracted Wisdom Series: Achievement Society and the Rise of Narcissism, Depression, and Anxiety*. Danielmiessler.Com. https://danielmiessler.com/blog/extracted-wisdom-series-achievement-society-and-the-rise-of-narcissism-depression-and-anxiety

Mignolo, W. D. (2011). *The darker side of Western modernity: Global futures, decolonial options*. Duke University Press.

Mills, D. Q. (1991). *Rebirth of the corporation*. Wiley.

Minlo, A. (2024). Academics' dependence on WhatsApp and its impact on social and educational learning. *International Journal of Educational Technology Studies*, *7*(1), 45–59. DOI: 10.2139/ssrn.384239993

Mirzoeff, N. (2011). *The right to look: A counterhistory of visuality*. Duke University Press., DOI: 10.2307/j.ctv1134d5q

Möhlmann, M., & Zalmanson, L. (2017). Hands on the wheel: Navigating algorithmic management and Uber drivers' autonomy. *Proceedings of the International Conference on Information Systems*, 1-17.

Mol, A., Moser, I., & Pols, J. (Eds.). (2010). *Care in practice: On tinkering in clinics, homes and farms*. Transcript Verlag., DOI: 10.14361/9783839414477

Molina Ramón, J. A., & Moncada Landeta, K. T. (2024). Energy Crisis, Necropolitics and Simulacrum: The Ecuadorian Situation under the Daniel Noboa Administration. *Revista Veritas De Difusão Científica*, *5*(3), 1651–1673. DOI: 10.61616/rvdc.v5i3.304

Molina Ramón, J. A., Moncada Landeta, K. T., & Torres Merino, J. F. (2025). Authoritarian Neoliberalism and Patrimonialism in the Daniel Noboa Azín Government. *Revista Veritas De Difusão Científica*, *6*(1), 2796–2838. https://doi.org/10.61616/rvdc.v6i1.547

Moore, P. V. (2018). *The quantified self in precarity: Work, technology and what counts*. Routledge., DOI: 10.4324/9781315231997

Moore, P. V., & Robinson, A. (2016). The quantified self: What counts in the neoliberal workplace. *New Media & Society*, *18*(11), 2774–2792. DOI: 10.1177/1461444815604328

Murphy, M., & Costa, C. (2019). Digital scholarship, higher education and the future of the public intellectual. *Futures*, *111*, 205–212. DOI: 10.1016/j.futures.2018.04.011

Nakamura, L. (2013). *Cybertypes*. Routledge. DOI: 10.4324/9780203699188

Nakrošienė, A., Bučiūnienė, I., & Goštautaitė, B. (2019). Working from home: Characteristics and outcomes of telework. *International Journal of Manpower*, *40*(1), 87–101. DOI: 10.1108/IJM-07-2017-0172

Napoli, P. M. (2019). *Social media and the public interest: Media regulation in the disinformation age*. Columbia University Press. DOI: 10.7312/napo18454

Nemorin, S. (2017). Post-panoptic pedagogies: The changing nature of school surveillance in the digital age. *Surveillance & Society*, *15*(2), 239–253. DOI: 10.24908/ss.v15i2.6033

Newlands, G. (2021). Algorithmic surveillance in the gig economy: The organization of work through Lefebvrian conceived space. *Organization Studies*, *42*(5), 719–737. DOI: 10.1177/0170840620937900

Newport, C. (2019). *Digital Minimalism: Choosing A Focused Life in A Noisy World*.

Newport, C. (2019). *Digital minimalism: Choosing a focused life in a noisy world*. Penguin.

Nguyen-Hoang, T. A., Hoang, N. C., Hua, P. T., Thi, M. T. N., Ta, T. T., Nguyen, T., & Nguyen, H. T. (2024). *Advancing scholarship management: A blockchain-enhanced platform with privacy-secure identities and ai-driven recommendations*. IEEE., DOI: 10.1109/ACCESS.2024.3486078

Noble, S. U. (2018). *Algorithms of oppression: How search engines reinforce racism*. NYU Press.

Nothias, T. (2025). An intellectual history of digital colonialism. *Journal of Communication*.

O'Callaghan, D., Greene, D., Conway, M., Carthy, J., & Cunningham, P. (2015). Down the (white) rabbit hole: The extreme right and online recommender systems. *Social Science Computer Review*, *33*(4), 459–478.

O'Neil, C. (2016). *Weapons of math destruction: How big data increases inequality and threatens democracy*. Crown.

Obermeyer, Z., Powers, B., Vogeli, C., & Mullainathan, S. (2019). Dissecting racial bias in an algorithm. *Science*, *366*(6464), 447–453. DOI: 10.1126/science.aax2342 PMID: 31649194

O'Brien, M.; Rustin, M.; Jones, D.; Sloan, D. (2000). 'Children's Independent Spatial Mobility in the Urban Public Realm' Childhood. *A Global Journal of Child Research (Special issue of children's geographies)*, *7*(3), 257-277. http://dx.doi.org/ DOI: 10.1177/0907568200007003002

Ocran, T., Barfi, K. A., Kodua-Ntim, K., Kwafoa, P. N. Y., & Filson, C. K. (2023). Leveraging social media in digital scholarship: Perspective from developing country students. *PLoS One*, *18*(9), e0291334. DOI: 10.1371/journal.pone.0291334 PMID: 37738249

Octavia, S., & Sari, W. P. (2024). Persepsi Generasi Z dengan Pernyataan "Kerja Sesuai Passion" dalam Menentukan Profesi. *Koneksi*, *8*(1), 25–33. DOI: 10.24912/kn.v8i1.21659

OECD. (2023). *Algorithmic transparency recording standard*. OECD Observatory of Public Sector Innovation. Retrieved from https://oecd-opsi.org/innovations/algorithmic-transparency-standard/

Olson, H. A. (2002). *The Power to Name: Locating the Limits of Subject Representation in Libraries*. Springer. DOI: 10.1007/978-94-017-3435-6

Olson, M. H. (1983). Remote office work: Changing work patterns in space and time. *Communications of the ACM*, *26*(3), 182–187. DOI: 10.1145/358061.358068

OpenMined. (2023). Open source privacy tech.

Orlando [@Orlando62183489]. (2025, March 17). *Los lobos, latin king, choneros, cartel de nueva generación, cartel de sinaloa, cartel colombiano, far, eln, maduro, cristina, castro, ortega, ESTÁN HACIENDO CAMPAÑA POR LUISA GONZÁLEZ* [Post]. X. https://x.com/Orlando62183489/status/1901542085859098968

Panteli, N., & Tucker, R. (2009). Power and trust in global virtual teams. *Communications of the ACM*, *52*(12), 113–115. DOI: 10.1145/1610252.1610282

Parent-Rocheleau, X., & Parker, S. K. (2023). Algorithmic management: A review and research agenda. *Journal of Management*, *49*(1), 332–365. DOI: 10.1016/j.hrmr.2021.100838

Pariser, E. (2011). *The Filter Bubble: What the Internet Is Hiding from You.* https://bvbr.bib-bvb.de:443/F?func=service&doc_library=BVB01&local_base=BVB01&doc_number=022632142&sequence=000002&line_number=0001&func_code=DB_RECORDS&service_type=MEDIA

Pariser, E. (2011). *The filter bubble: What the internet is hiding from you.* Penguin Press.

Pariser, E. (2011). *The filter bubble: What the Internet is hiding from you.* Penguin.

Parrott, J. A., & Reich, M. (2020). *A minimum compensation standard for Seattle TNC drivers.* Center on Wage and Employment Dynamics Policy Brief.

Pasquale, F. (2015). *The black box society: The secret algorithms that control money and information.* Harvard University Press.

Pasquale, F. (2015). *The Black Box Society: The Secret Algorithms That Control Money and Information.* Harvard University Press. DOI: 10.4159/harvard.9780674736061

Paula, L. (2015). Da "questão do menor" à garantia de direitos: Discursos e práticas sobre o envolvimento de adolescentes com a criminalidade urbana. *Civitas, 15*(1), 27–43. DOI: 10.15448/1984-7289.2015.1.16937

Paxton, R. O. (2007). *The Anatomy of Fascism.* Alfred A. Knopf.

Percy-Smith, B., & Thomas, N. (2010). *A handbook of children and young people's participation: perspectives from theory and practice.* Routledge.

Pereira da Silva, S. L. (2022). *O Irracionalismo de Conveniência: Ensaio Sobre Pós-Verdade, Fake News e a Psicopolítica do Fascismo Digital.* Editora Appris.

Pinto, R. A. (2018). *Digital sovereignty or digital colonialism?* Sur – International Journal on Human Rights.

Plantin, J.-C. (2019). Data cleaners for pristine datasets: Visibility and invisibility of data processors in social science. *Science, Technology & Human Values, 44*(1), 52–73.

Plantin, J.-C., Lagoze, C., Edwards, P., & Sandvig, C. (2018). Infrastructure studies meet platform studies in the age of Google and Facebook. *New Media & Society, 20*(1), 293–310. DOI: 10.1177/1461444816661553

Plant, S. (1997). *Zeros + ones: Digital women + the new technoculture.* Doubleday.

Popovici, V., & Popovici, A. L. (2020). Remote work revolution: Current opportunities and challenges for organizations. Ovidius University Annals. *Economic Sciences Series, 20,* 468–472.

Powell, A., Piccoli, G., & Ives, B. (2004). Virtual teams: A review of current literature and directions for future research. *The Data Base for Advances in Information Systems, 35*(1), 6–36. DOI: 10.1145/968464.968467

Prado, R. L. C. (2014). *A participação de crianças em pesquisas brasileiras das ciências sociais e humanas* [Tese de Doutoramento, Universidade de São Paulo]. São Paulo: USP. Disponível em: https://www.teses.usp.br/teses/disponiveis/47/47131/tde-27112014-103246/pt-br.php. Acesso em: 9 jan. 2025.

Prasad, D. K., Mangipudi, D. M. R., Vaidya, D. R., & Muralidhar, B. (2020). Organizational climate, opportunities, challenges and psychological wellbeing of the remote working employees during COVID-19 pandemic: A general linear model approach with reference to information technology industry in Hyderabad. [IJARET]. *International Journal of Advanced Research in Engineering and Technology, 11*(4).

Privacy International. (2019). *No body's business but mine: How companies are profiling us through period-tracking apps.*

Priyono, A., Moin, A., & Putri, V. N. A. O. (2020). Identifying Digital Transformation Paths in the Business Model of SMEs during the COVID-19 Pandemic. *Journal of Open Innovation, 6*(4), 104. DOI: 10.3390/joitmc6040104

Punzalan, R. (2014a). Barriers and challenges to virtual reunification. *Proceedings of the American Society for Information Science and Technology, 51*(1), 1–8. DOI: 10.1002/meet.2014.14505101041

Punzalan, R. (2014b). Understanding virtual reunification. *The Library Quarterly, 84*(3), 294–323. DOI: 10.1086/676489

Quan-Haase, A., Martin, K., & McCay-Peet, L. (2015). Networks of digital humanities scholars: The informational and social uses and gratifications of Twitter. *Big Data & Society, 2*(1), 2053951715589417. Advance online publication. DOI: 10.1177/2053951715589417

Quijano, A. (2000). Coloniality of power and Eurocentrism in Latin America. *International Sociology, 15*(2), 215–232.

Raghavan, M., Barocas, S., Kleinberg, J., & Levy, K. (2020). Mitigating bias in algorithmic hiring: Evaluating claims and practices. *Proceedings of the ACM on Human-Computer Interaction, 4*(CSCW2), 1–27. https://doi.org/DOI: 10.1145/3351095.3372828

Raji, I. D., (2020). Saving face: Investigating facial recognition performance. *AAAI/ACM Conference on AI Ethics and Society*. DOI: 10.1145/3375627.3375820

Rakotondrazaka, T. H., & Velomasy, Y. G. (2024). Digital economy and poverty reduction in Africa: The role of governance quality. *European Journal of Business and Management Research*, *9*(4), 1–7. DOI: 10.24018/ejbmr.2024.9.4.2372

Rao, U. (2019). Biometric citizenship. *Social Anthropology*, *27*(2), 174–188. DOI: 10.1111/1469-8676.12620

Rathbone, M. (2022). Panopticism, impartial spectator and digital technology. *The Indo-Pacific Journal of Phenomenology*, *22*(1), e2064720. DOI: 10.1080/20797222.2022.2064720

Reich, J., Buttimer, C. J., Coleman, D., Colwell, R. D., Faruqi, F., & Larke, L. R. (2020). What's lost, what's left, what's next: Lessons learned from the lived experiences of teachers during the 2020 novel coronavirus pandemic. Retrieved from https://edarxiv.org/8exp9 DOI: 10.35542/osf.io/8exp9

Reid, A., & Thomas, S. L. (2022). The health impacts of precarious employment among workers in industrialized countries. *Journal of Public Health*, *44*(2), e203–e215. DOI: 10.1093/pubmed/fdab077 PMID: 34604905

Reisman, D., Schultz, J., Crawford, K., & Whittaker, M. (2018). Algorithmic impact assessments: a practical Framework for Public Agency. *AI Now, 9*. Retrieved from https://ainowinstitute.org/wp-content/uploads/2023/04/aiareport2018.pdf

Restrepo Echavarría, R., & Oliván López, F. (2025). The Citizens' Revolution in Ecuador: A comparative history of political ideas, processes, and outcomes. *Humanities & Social Sciences Communications*, *12*, 1696. Advance online publication. https://doi.org/10.1057/s41599-025-05077-5

Ribeiro, M. H., Ottoni, R., West, R., Almeida, V. A. F., & Meira, W.Jr. (2020). Auditing radicalization pathways on YouTube. *Proceedings of the ACM on Human-Computer Interaction, 4*(CSCW3), 1–27.

Rice, R. E., & Love, G. (1987). Electronic emotion: Socioemotional content in a computer-mediated communication network. *Communication Research*, *14*(1), 85–108. DOI: 10.1177/009365087014001005

Richardson, R., Schultz, J. M., & Crawford, K. (2019). Dirty data, bad predictions: How civil rights violations impact police data, predictive policing systems, and justice. *NYU Law Review*, *94*, 192.

Roberts, S. T. (2019). *Behind the screen*. Yale University Press.

Roberts, S. T. (2019). *Behind the screen: Content moderation in the shadows of social media*. Yale University Press.

Rodrigues, A. K. (2021, October 19). *Família de Lucio Costa doa acervo de arquiteto brasileiro a Portugal*. Metrópoles. https://www.metropoles.com/distrito-federal/familia-de-lucio-costa-doa-acervo-de-arquiteto-brasileiro-a-portugal

Rodrigues, M. G. (2024). Digital Fascism and School Violence: Subjective Deformation of Contemporary Neoliberalism? *Estilos da Clínica*, *29*(3), 359–377.

Rogers, R. (2021). Visual media analysis for Instagram and other online platforms. *Big Data & Society*. https://journals.sagepub.com/doi/10.1177/20539517211022370

Rosa, H., & Jonathan, T.H. (2015). *Social Acceleration: A New Theory of Modernity*. Columbia University Press.

Rose, G. (2016). *Visual methodologies: An introduction to researching with visual materials* (4th ed.). SAGE Publications.

Rosemberg, F., & Mariano, C. S. (2010). A Convenção Internacional sobre os Direitos da Criança: Debates e tensões. *Cadernos de Pesquisas*, *40*(141), 693–728. DOI: 10.1590/S0100-15742010000300003

Rosenblat, A. (2018). *Uberland: How Algorithms Are Rewriting the Rules of Work*. University of California Press., DOI: 10.1525/9780520970632

Rosenblat, A., & Stark, L. (2016). Algorithmic labor and information asymmetries: A case study of Uber's drivers. *International Journal of Communication*, *10*, 3758–3784. https://ijoc.org/index.php/ijoc/article/view/4892

Rouvroy, A., & Berns, T. (2013). Algorithmic governmentality and prospects of emancipation. *Réactivation du concept de biopolitique*, 1–20. https://hal.archives-ouvertes.fr/hal-00739755

Rouvroy, A.; Berns, T. (2013). Algorithmic governmentality and prospects of emancipation. *Réactivation des pouvoirs critiques face à la gouvernance algorithmique. Le Sujet dans la Cité*, 5, 163–180.

Rupert, M. (2009). Antonio Gramsci. In *Critical theorists and international relations* (pp. 190–200). Routledge.

Sachs, G. (2023, April 19). *The creator economy could approach half-a-trillion dollars by 2027*. GoldmanSachs.Com. https://www.goldmansachs.com/insights/articles/the-creator-economy-could-approach-half-a-trillion-dollars-by-2027

Sadowski, J. (2019). When data is capital: Datafication, accumulation, and extraction. *Big Data & Society*, *6*(1), 1–12. DOI: 10.1177/2053951718820549

Sadowski, J. (2020). *Too smart: How digital capitalism is extracting data, controlling our lives, and taking over the world.* MIT Press., DOI: 10.7551/mitpress/12240.001.0001

Safatle, V., da Silva Júnior, N., & Dunker, C. (2020). *Neoliberalismo como Gestão do Sofrimento Psíquico*. Autêntica.

Saldaña, J. (2021). *The coding manual for qualitative researchers* (4th ed.). SAGE Publications.

Sanders, C. K., & Scanlon, E. (2021). The Digital Divide Is a Human Rights Issue: Advancing Social Inclusion Through Social Work Advocacy. *Journal of Human Rights and Social Work*, *6*(2), 130–143. DOI: 10.1007/s41134-020-00147-9 PMID: 33758780

Sanders, C., & Sheptycki, J. (2017). Policing, crime and 'big data'; towards a critique of the moral economy of stochastic governance. *Crime, Law, and Social Change*, *68*(1–2), 1–15. DOI: 10.1007/s10611-016-9678-7

Sandoval, M. (2020). Entrepreneurial activism? Platform cooperativism between subversion and co-optation. *Critical Sociology*, *46*(6), 801–817. DOI: 10.1177/0896920519870577

Santos, C. M. (2009). Écrire le pouvoir en Angola: Les archives ndembu (XVIIe–XXe siècles). *Annales*, *64*(4), 767–795. DOI: 10.1017/S0395264900022460

Sarmento, M. J. (2021). Culturas infantis / Children's culture. In C. Tomás et al. (orgs.), *Conceitos-chave em Sociologia da Infância: perspetivas globais* (pp. 179–186). Braga: UMinho Editora.

Sarmento, M. J. (2007). Visibilidade social e estudo da infância. In *V. M. R. Vasconcellos & M. J. Sarmento (orgs.), Infância (in)visível* (pp. 25–49). Junqueira & Marin.

Sarmento, M. J. (2008). Sociologia da infância: correntes e confluências. In *M. J. Sarmento & M. C. S. Gouvea (orgs.), Estudos da infância: educação e práticas sociais* (pp. 17–39). Vozes.

Sarmento, M. J. (2018). Infância e cidade: Restrições e possibilidades. *Educação*, *41*(2), 232–240.

Schiller, H. I. (1969, 1989). *Mass communication and American empire*; *Culture, Inc.: The corporate takeover of public expression*. Oxford University Press.

Scholz, T. (2016). *Platform Cooperativism: Challenging the Corporate Sharing Economy*. Rosa Luxemburg Foundation.

Schor, J. B., Attwood-Charles, W., Cansoy, M., Ladegaard, I., & Wengronowitz, R. (2021). Dependence and precarity in the platform economy. *Theory and Society, 49*(5-6), 833–861. DOI: 10.1007/s11186-020-09408-y PMID: 32836676

Schwellnus, C., Geva, A., Pak, M., & Veiel, R. (2019). Gig economy platforms: Boon or bane? *OECD Economics Department Working Papers*, 1550. DOI: 10.1787/18151973

Scott, J. C. (1985). *Weapons of the weak: Everyday forms of peasant resistance*. Yale University Press.

Scott, J. C. (1990). *Domination and the arts of resistance: Hidden transcripts*. Yale University Press.

Seaver, N. (2017). Algorithms as culture: Some tactics for the ethnography of algorithmic systems. *Big Data & Society, 4*(2), 1–12.

Seaver, N. (2019). Captivating algorithms: Recommender systems as traps. *Journal of Material Culture, 24*(4), 421–436.

Seccareccia, A., de Vletter, M., Seixas, C., Pereira, E., Garcia, M., & Oliveira, S. (2021). Álvaro Siza Archive – A shared archive. In International Council on Archives & Arquivo Distrital de Braga (Eds.), *Proceedings of the International Congress on Architectural Archives* (pp. 19–30). Arquivo Distrital de Braga.

Selbst, A. D., boyd, d., Friedler, S. A., Venkatasubramanian, S., & Vertesi, J. (2019). Fairness and abstraction in sociotechnical systems. In *Proceedings of the Conference on Fairness, Accountability, and Transparency* (pp. 59–68).

Selwyn, N. (2016). *Education and technology: Key issues and debates*. Bloomsbury Academic.

Senft, T. M. (2013). Microcelebrity and the Branded Self. In *A Companion to New Media Dynamics* (pp. 346–354). Wiley., DOI: 10.1002/9781118321607.ch22

Shahrzadi, L., Mansouri, A., Alavi, M., & Shabani, A. (2024). Causes, consequences, and strategies to deal with information overload: A scoping review. *International Journal of Information Management Data Insights, 4*(2), 100261. DOI: 10.1016/j.jjimei.2024.100261

Sharma, S. (2014). *In the Meantime: Temporality and Cultural Politics*. Duke University Press.

Sharon, T. (2016). The Googlization of health research. *Medicine, Health Care, and Philosophy, 19*(4), 587–598. PMID: 29754546

Sherman Center for Digital Scholarship. (2025). What is digital scholarship? McMaster University. Retrieved from https://scds.ca/what-is-ds/

Short, J., Williams, E., & Christie, B. (1976). *The social psychology of telecommunications*. John Wiley & Sons.

Silva, F. A., & Menezes, C. A. (1921). *Elucidário madeirense* (Vol. 1–2). Junta Geral do Distrito do Funchal.

Silverman, D. (2020). *Qualitative research* (5th ed.). SAGE Publications.

Simon, B., & Oakes, P. (2006). Beyond dependence: An identity approach to social power and domination. *Human Relations*, *59*(1), 105–139. DOI: 10.1177/0018726706062760

Simonsen, J., & Robertson, T. (Eds.). (2012). *Routledge international handbook of participatory design*. Routledge.

Sproull, L., & Kiesler, S. (1991). Connections: New Ways of Working in the Networked Organization. *Administrative Science Quarterly*, •••, 37.

Srnicek, N. (2017). *Platform capitalism*. Polity Press.

Srnicek, N. (2021). *Platform Capitalism*. Polity Press. DOI: 10.17323/978-5-7598-2561-6

Stake, R. E. (2006). *Multiple case study analysis*. Guilford Press.

Stalder, F. (2016). *Kultur der Digitalität*. Suhrkamp.

Stanley, J. (2020). *How Fascism Works: The Politics of Us and Them*. Random House.

Staples, D. S., Hulland, J. S., & Higgins, C. A. (1999). A self-efficacy theory explanation for the management of remote workers in virtual organizations. *Organization Science*, *10*(6), 758–776. DOI: 10.1287/orsc.10.6.758

Star, S. L. (1999). The ethnography of infrastructure. *The American Behavioral Scientist*, *43*(3), 377–391.

Star, S. L., & Ruhleder, K. (1996). Steps toward an ecology of infrastructure: Design and access for large information spaces. *Information Systems Research*, *7*(1), 111–134.

Steizel, S., & Rimbau-Gilabert, E. (2013). Upward influence tactics through technology-mediated communication tools. *Computers in Human Behavior*, *29*(2), 462–472. DOI: 10.1016/j.chb.2012.04.024

Stiegler, B., & Ross, D. (2015). *Automatic Society 1: The Future of Work-Introduction*. https://archive.wired.com/science/discoveries/magazine/16-07/pb_theory

Stiegler, B., & Rossouw, J. (2011). *Suffocated Desire, or How the Cultural Industry Destroys the Individual: Contributon to A Theory of Mass Consumption.*

Stiegler, B. (2010). *Taking care of youth and the generations.* Stanford University Press.

Stinson, C. (2021). Algorithms are not neutral: Bias in collaborative filtering. *ArXiv.* 10.48550/arXiv.2105.01031

Straus, S. G. (1997). Technology, group process, and group outcomes: Testing the connections in computer-mediated and face-to-face groups. Human–Computer Interaction, 12(3), 227-266, https-//DOI: 10.1207/s15327051hci1203_1

Straus, S. G., & McGrath, J. E. (1994). Does the medium matter? The interaction of task type and technology on group performance and member reactions. *The Journal of Applied Psychology, 79*(1), 87–97. DOI: 10.1037/0021-9010.79.1.87 PMID: 8200874

Striphas, T. (2015). Algorithmic culture. *European Journal of Cultural Studies, 18*(4–5), 395–412. DOI: 10.1177/1367549415577392

Suchman, L. A. (2007). *Human–machine reconfigurations: Plans and situated actions* (2nd ed.). Cambridge University Press.

Sullivan, C. (2003). What's in a name? Definitions and conceptualisations of teleworking and homeworking. *New Technology, Work and Employment, 18*(3), 158–165. DOI: 10.1111/1468-005X.00118

Sustainability Directory. (2025). Algorithmic epistemology. Retrieved from https://climate.sustainability-directory.com/term/algorithmic-epistemology/

Svelch, J. (2023). Disconnection, resistance, and avoidance: Non-use as a meaningful practice in digital labor. *New Media & Society, 25*(6), 1213–1229. DOI: 10.1177/14614448221088939

Sweeney, L. (2013). Discrimination in online ad delivery. SSRN Electronic Journal, 11(3), 10–29. https://doi.org/DOI: 10.2139/ssrn.2208240

Tassinari, A., & Maccarrone, V. (2020). The mobilisation of gig economy workers: A comparison of food delivery workers in Italy and the UK. *Industrial Relations Journal, 51*(4), 350–371. DOI: 10.1111/irj.12292

Taylor, L., & Richter, C. (2015). Data justice and data citizenship. *Open Data and the Knowledge Society Conference Proceedings.* https://doi.org/DOI: 10.2139/ssrn.2656787

Teboho Ansorge, J. (2011). Digital power in world politics: Databases, panopticons and Erwin Cuntz. *Millennium, 40*(1), 65–83. DOI: 10.1177/0305829811409178

Tembe, J. (2006). Linking global to local through archives: Some notes on the experiences of Mozambique in sharing memories with global partners. *Comma, 2006*(3–4), 1–5. DOI: 10.3828/comma.2006.3-4.11

Thaler, R. H., & Sunstein, C. R. (2008). *Nudge: Improving decisions about health, wealth, and happiness.* Yale University Press.

This, P. (2023, October 4). *Episode #189 - Transcript.* Philosophize This! https://www.philosophizethis.org/transcript/episode-189-transcript

Trace, C. B., & Ovalle, C. J. (2012). Archival reference and access: Syllabi and a snapshot of the archival canon. *The Reference Librarian, 53*(1), 76–94. DOI: 10.1080/02763877.2011.596364

Traverso, E. (2019). *The New Faces of Fascism: Populism and the Far Right.* Verso.

Trevino, L. K., Daft, R. L., & Lengel, R. H. (Eds.). (1990). Understanding managers' media choices- A symbolic interactionist perspective. SAGE Publications, Inc., https-//DOI: <ALIGNMENT.qj></ALIGNMENT>10.4135/9781483325385.pdf

Trevisan, G., Bento, G., Carvalho, M., Silva, C., & Sarmento, M. J. (2022). Infância, espaço público e participação: a abordagem do território de aprendizagem. In M. Gobbi et al. (orgs.), *O direito das crianças à cidade: perspetivas desde Portugal e o Brasil* (pp. 35–58). São Paulo: FEUSP. https://doi.org/DOI: 10.11606/9786587047317

Trevisan, G. P. (2014). *'Somos as pessoas que temos de escolher, não são as outras pessoas que escolhem por nós': infância e cenários de participação pública: uma análise sociológica de condecisão das crianças na escola e na cidade* [Tese de Doutoramento, Universidade do Minho, Instituto de Educação]. Universidade do Minho.

Trompenaars, F., & Hampden-Turner, C. (1998). *Riding the waves of culture: Understanding diversity in global business.* McGraw-Hill.

Tronto, J. (1993). *Moral boundaries.* Routledge.

Tufekci, Z. (2015). Algorithmic harms beyond Facebook and Google: Emergent challenges of computational agency. *Colorado Technology Law Journal, 13*(1), 203–218. Retrieved from https://ctlj.colorado.edu/wp-content/uploads/2015/08/Tufekci-final.pdf

Tufekci, Z. (2015). Algorithmic harms beyond Facebook and Google: Emergent challenges of computational agency. *Colorado Technology Law Journal, 13*, 203–218.

Tufekci, Z. (2017). *Twitter and Tear Gas: The Power and Fragility of Networked Protest*. Yale University Press.

Tufekci, Z. (2018). *Twitter and tear gas: The power and fragility of networked protest*. Yale University Press.

Turkle, S. (2011). *Alone together: Why we expect more from technology and less from each other*. Basic Books.

Turow, J. (2017). *The aisles have eyes: How retailers track your shopping, strip your privacy, and define your power*. Yale University Press.

UNESCO. (2011). *Arquivos dos Dembos / Ndembu Archives – Memory of the World*. https://www.unesco.org/en/memory-world/arquivos-dos-dembos/ndembu-archives

United Nations Development Programme. (2024, September 30). Seven inspiring stories of people who acquired digital skills at an older age. Retrieved from https://www.undp.org/ukraine/stories/seven-inspiring-stories-people-who-acquired-digital-skills-older-age

Urman, A., Makhortykh, M., & Hannak, A. (2024). Mapping the Field of Algorithm Auditing: A Systematic Literature Review Identifying Research Trends, Linguistic and Geographical Disparities. Retrieved from https://arxiv.org/html/2401.11194v1

Usera, D., & Durham, N. (2025). What Predicts Engagement on LinkedIn? Engagement-Boosting Strategies for Professionals. *Business and Professional Communication Quarterly*, *0*(0), 23294906251336710. Advance online publication. DOI: 10.1177/23294906251336710

Valacich, J. S., Sarker, S., Pratt, J., & Groomer, M. (2002, January). Computer-mediated and face-to-face groups: who makes riskier decisions? In *Proceedings of the 35th Annual Hawaii International Conference on System Sciences* (pp. 133-142). IEEE. DOI: 10.1109/HICSS.2002.993870

van Dijck, J. (2013). *The culture of connectivity: A critical history of social media*. Oxford University Press. DOI: 10.1093/acprof:oso/9780199970773.001.0001

Van Dijck, J. (2014). Datafication, dataism and dataveillance: Big Data between scientific paradigm and ideology. *Surveillance & Society*, *12*(2), 197–208. https://doi.org/10.24908/ss.v12i2.4776

Van Dijck, J., Poell, T., & De Waal, M. (2018). *The Platform Society*. https://doi.org/10.1093/oso/9780190889760.001.0001

Veale, M., Van Kleek, M., & Binns, R. (2018). Fairness and accountability design needs for algorithmic support in high-stakes public sector decision-making. *Proceedings of the ACM on Human-Computer Interaction, 2*(CSCW), 1–20.

Veletsianos, G., & Kimmons, R. (2012). Networked participatory scholarship: Emergent techno-cultural pressures toward open and digital scholarship in online networks. *Computers & Education, 58*(2), 766–774. DOI: 10.1016/j.compedu.2011.10.001

Verbeek, P.-P. (2005). *What Things Do: Philosophical Reflections on Technology, Agency, and Design*. Penn State University Press.

Wachter, S., Mittelstadt, B., & Floridi, L. (2017). Why a right to explanation of automated decision-making does not exist in the General Data Protection Regulation. *International Data Privacy Law, 7*(2), 76–99. DOI: 10.1093/idpl/ipx005

Wadsworth, M. B., & Blanchard, A. L. (2015). Influence tactics in virtual teams. *Computers in Human Behavior, 44*, 386–393. DOI: 10.1016/j.chb.2014.11.026

Wajcman, J. (1991). *Feminism confronts technology*. Penn State Press.

Wajcman, J. (2004). *Technofeminism*. Polity Press.

Waldman, A. E. (2018). *Privacy as trust: Information privacy for an information age*. Cambridge University Press. DOI: 10.1017/9781316888667

Walther, J. B. (2011). Theories of computer-mediated communication and interpersonal relations. The handbook of interpersonal communication, 4, 443-479.

Walther, J. B. (1992). Interpersonal Effects in Computer-Mediated Interaction: A Relational Perspective [CR]. *Communication Research, 19*(1), 52–90. DOI: 10.1177/009365092019001003

Walther, J. B. (1996). Computer-Mediated Communication: Impersonal, Interpersonal, and Hyperpersonal Interaction [CR]. *Communication Research, 23*(3), 3–43. DOI: 10.1177/009365096023001001

Wang, B., Liu, Y., Qian, J., & Parker, S. K. (2021). Achieving effective remote working during the COVID-19 pandemic: A work design perspective. *Applied Psychology, 70*(1), 16–59. DOI: 10.1111/apps.12290 PMID: 33230359

Warkentin, M. E., Sayeed, L., & Hightower, R. (1997). Virtual teams versus face-to-face teams: An exploratory study of a web-based conference system. *Decision Sciences, 28*(4), 975–996. DOI: 10.1111/j.1540-5915.1997.tb01338.x

Weiskopf, R., & Hansen, H. K. (2022). Algorithmic governmentality and the space of ethics: Examples from 'People Analytics.'. *Human Relations*, *76*(3), 483–506. DOI: 10.1177/00187267221075346

Wells, G., Horwitz, J., & Seetharaman, D. (2021). Facebook knows Instagram is toxic for teen girls, company documents show. *The Wall Street Journal, 14*. Retrieved from https://www.wsj.com/tech/personal-tech/facebook-knows-instagram-is-toxic-for-teen-girls-company-documents-show-11631620739

Whittaker, M.. (2018). *AI Now Report 2018*. AI Now Institute.

Wikipedia contributors. (2003, May 14). Intellectual. In *Wikipedia*. Retrieved April 2025, from https://en.wikipedia.org/wiki/Intellectual

Williamson, B. (2017). Big data in education: The digital future of learning, policy and practice. *Sage (Atlanta, Ga.)*. Advance online publication. DOI: 10.4135/9781529714920

Wood, A. J., Graham, M., Lehdonvirta, V., & Hjorth, I. (2019). Good gig, bad gig: Autonomy and algorithmic control in the global gig economy. *Work, Employment and Society*, *33*(1), 56–75. DOI: 10.1177/0950017018785616 PMID: 30886460

Yeung, K. (2018). 'Hypernudge': Big data as a mode of regulation by design. *Information Communication and Society*, *20*(1), 118–136.

Yilmaz, Ö. (2024). The origins of digital colonialism. *İmgelem, 16, 321-344. https://doi.org/*DOI: 10.53791/imgelem.1636282

Yin, R. (1984). *Case study research: Design and methods*. Sage Publications.

York, E. J. (2021). Digital surveillance in online writing instruction: Panopticism and simulation in learning management systems. *Computers and Composition*, *62*, 102680. DOI: 10.1016/j.compcom.2021.102680

Youngman, T., Modrow, S., & Meth, I. (2024). Deceiving dichotomies: On the interrelation of the archive and the cultural memory canon. *Proceedings of the Association for Information Science and Technology*, *61*(1), 697–702. DOI: 10.1002/pra2.1082

Yukl, G., & Michel, J. W. (2006). Proactive influence tactics and leader member exchange. *Power and influence in organizations*, 87-103.

Yukl, F., Chavez, C., & Seifert, C. F. (2005). Assessing the construct validity and utility of two new influence tactics. *Journal of Organizational Behavior*, *26*(6), 705–725. DOI: 10.1002/job.335

Yukl, G., & Falbe, C. M. (1990). Influence Tactics and Objectives in Upward, Downward, and Lateral Influence Attempts. *The Journal of Applied Psychology*, *75*(2), 132–140. DOI: 10.1037/0021-9010.75.2.132

Yukl, G., & Tracey, J. B. (1992). Consequences of Influence Tactics Used With Subordinates, Peers, and the Boss. *The Journal of Applied Psychology*, *77*(4), 525–535. DOI: 10.1037/0021-9010.77.4.525

Zeiher, H. (2003). Shaping daily life in urban environments. In *Children in the City* (pp. 84–99). Routledge.

Ziewitz, M. (2016). Governing algorithms: Myth, mess, and methods. *Science, Technology & Human Values*, *41*(1), 3–16.

Zuboff, S. (2019). *The age of surveillance capitalism: the fight for a human future at the new frontier of power*. Profile Books.

Zuboff, S. (2019). *The age of surveillance capitalism: The fight for a human future at the new frontier of power*. PublicAffairs.

Zuboff, S. (2023). The age of surveillance capitalism. In *Social theory re-wired* (pp. 203–213). Routledge. DOI: 10.4324/9781003320609-27

Zuboff, S., Möllers, N., Wood, D. M., & Lyon, D. (2019). Surveillance capitalism: An interview with Shoshana Zuboff. *Surveillance & Society*, *17*(1/2), 257–266. DOI: 10.24908/ss.v17i1/2.13238

Zuiderveen Borgesius, F., Trilling, D., Möller, J., Bodó, B., De Vreese, C., & Helberger, N. (2016). Should we worry about filter bubbles? *Internet Policy Review*, *5*(1). Advance online publication. DOI: 10.14763/2016.1.401

About the Contributors

Esra Gökçen Kaygisiz is an Associate Professor of the Department of Business at the Faculty of Economics and Administrative Sciences, University of Giresun, since 2014. She graduated from the Computer Teaching Program at Fırat University. Kaygisiz completed a master's program at Bilgi University and a doctorate in Business Management at Selçuk University. During her master's and doctoral studies, she served as an instructor in the Computer Programming Program at Gaziantep University. She has a lot of research and conference papers at the international and national levels. Her research interests include knowledge and wisdom management, human resource management, women, reputation, and entrepreneurship studies with a focus on IT and digital transformation.

***

Babita is an Assistant Professor teaching at CHRIST (Deemed to be University) specializing in Finance & Account where she has a profound knowledge in economic growth corporate finance & international trade. A UGC NET/JRF-qualified scholar, she has done her Ph.D. in Management Studies from Guru Jambheshwar University of Science and Technology, Hisar, Haryana. Dr. Chaudhary has a diverse academic background in both Finance and Human Resource Management coupled with prior corporate experience of two years. She has published in various international journals such as IFI, ABDC, SAGE, and Inderscience Apart from research, she has presented papers in many national/ international conferences. Dr. Babita's research at present explores the effects of consumer ethnocentrism on purchase behaviors within the context of OTT platforms, considering important consumer behavior domains within a more globalized media environment. Dr. Babita Chaudhary works as an Assistant Professor in School of Business and Management of CHRIST (Deemed to be University) Indore Campus, India., she holds Ph.D., UGC NET-JRF completed her MBA in Human Resource and Finance.

Palak Aggarwal is a third-year Bachelor of Business Administration student specializing in Finance and Marketing Analytics at Christ (Deemed to be) University, Delhi NCR. Her academic interests include Finance, data analytics, consumer behavior, and the integration of gamification in educational contexts. Beyond academics, Palak is an active contributor to university life, serving in student leadership roles, including the creative leader, creatively supporting institutional events, event organizer, and leading teams in cultural and academic initiatives. Her research reflects a critical and interdisciplinary approach, combining managerial insight with contemporary socio-technological perspectives to examine how digital systems shape organizational behavior, accountability, and human agency.

José Gabriel Andrade is a researcher and professor on media, marketing and communication at the University of Minho. José holds a European PhD in Communication Sciences from the Catholic University of Portugal with the support of the Portuguese Foundation for Science and Technology, Fundação para a Ciência e a Tecnologia (FCT) and a Master in Communication Sciences: Communication, Organization and New Technologies from the Portuguese Catholic University, Universidade Católica Portuguesa - UCP, with the support of the high level scholarship Program of the European Union for Latin America (Alban). He coordinated the Master in Digital Communication and integrated the structure responsible for quality management, internships, communication and interface with the University community, actively participating in the professional and personal development of students. He is the director of the Casa do Conhecimento Cultural Unit of the University of Minho.

L. S. Ascensão de Macedo, PhD, is an integrated researcher at the Centre for Classical Studies, School of Arts and Humanities, University of Lisbon, and holds a doctorate in Information Science from the University of Coimbra. He currently serves as Head of the Division of General Archives and Planning within the Regional Directorate for Budget and Treasury of the Regional Government of Madeira. He is also a visiting lecturer at the Universidade Autónoma de Lisboa and an active member of both the Portuguese Association of Librarians, Archivists, Information and Documentation Professionals (BAD) and the Iberian Chapter of ISKO. He presently assumes the role of Chair of the Expert Group on Shared Archival Heritage (EGSAH) of the International Council on Archives (ICA).

Ayyıldız Ünnü received her Ph.D. in Business Administration from the Institute of Social Sciences at Ege University in 2012. She has been a faculty member at the Faculty of Economics and Administrative Sciences since 2006, where she was promoted to Professor and currently serves as Chair of the International Management

Department. In addition, she has served as Coordinator of the university's Human Resources Unit and as Departmental Coordinator for the Erasmus+ Program for four years. She has been part of many consultancy projects in her home country such as reorganization of a Family-Owned Business (FOB), and Designing Human Resources Management System. Her scholarly interests range widely, from management and organization generally to Human Resources Management, Leadership, Gender Roles, Decision Making, Innovation and Entrepreneurship specifically. She has presented many papers at both international and national conferences and all of her papers have been published as proceedings. Besides, she has articles published in national and international refereed journals. She and her colleagues got Best Paper Award with the paper titled "Management Fads and Fashion In Turkey: Role of Consulting Firms on Dissemination Process of Strategic Management Tools", presented at International Strategic Management Conference in 2007. She got Young Academician Incentive Award, 2015, which is given based on the academic performance annually by a Scientific Committee at Ege University, Faculty of Economics & Administrative Sciences. Her recent research, conducted in collaboration with two colleagues, titled "Gender of Turkish Academia" was also awarded by Turkish Researchers' Association (https://tuad.org.tr/en) in 2016. Finally, she was awarded a three-month scholarship, funded by DAAD (Deutscher Akademischer Austauschdienst- German Academic Exchange Service) to conduct a research project, entitled "The Dynamics of Academic Employment in The Light of Gender Roles: A Comparative Perspective on German and Turkish Universities". Her Academic Contact was "Prof. Dr. Katrin Muehlfed, Chair of Management, Organisation und Personal (muehlfeld@uni-trier.de)", at Trier University. The research project was finalized successfully.

Rino F. Boer is an expert in Management Communication with extensive academic and professional experience in higher education. He earned his Doctorate in Communication Science (S3) from Universitas Indonesia in 2013, a Master's degree in Management (S2) from Universitas Gadjah Mada in 2000, and Bachelor's degrees in Law from Universitas Padjadjaran (1999) and Economics from Universitas Katolik Parahyangan (1997). Since January 2014, Dr. Boer has served as Director of the Postgraduate Program at the London School of Public Relations (LSPR) Jakarta. With more than a decade of leadership experience, he is actively involved in developing postgraduate education, advancing management communication practices, and strengthening the link between academic insight and professional application in Indonesia.

Fernando Casado Gutierrez holds a Law Degree from the University of Granada (Spain), a Master's in Human Rights and Democratization from the

European Inter-University Centre in Venice (Italy) in 2004, and a Ph.D. in Social Communication from the Faculty of Communication at the University of La Laguna (Spain) in 2012. He has worked at various universities in Latin America and Spain, including the Bolivarian University of Ecuador and the Technical University of Manabí in Ecuador, the International University of Communications in Venezuela, and the Universities of Cádiz and Lleida in Spain.

Dhemy de Brito is a researcher and Assistant Professor on sociology of childhood and music education of childhood at the University of Minho. Dhemy holds a PhD in Child Studies (specialization in Childhood, Culture and Society) from the University of Minho, with the support of the Portuguese Foundation for Science and Technology, Fundação para a Ciência e a Tecnologia (FCT) and a Master in Music from the State University of Santa Catarina, Universidade do Estado de Santa Catarina - UDESC, with the support onf the Coordination for the Improvement of Higher Education Personnel, Coordenação de Aperfeiçoamento de Pessoal de Nível Superior (CAPES). He is a member of the Research Centre on Child Studies (CIEC) and of mei – the research group on music, education and childhood, affiliated with PPGMUS/UDESC. In 2020, he published the book "O Coro Infantil e as Crianças: por quê e para quem elas cantam," with Paco Editorial.

Shashi Kant Dikshit, with more than 24 years in academia and practice, focuses on project management, business analytics, and contemporary operations strategy. As an assistant professor and industry consultant, he is known for designing scenario-based learning modules, assessment tools, and skill-oriented curriculum innovations. His research output includes empirical studies and application-driven frameworks for supply chain and operational performance, with a particular interest in the role of AI and agility in management. Dr Dikshit is respected for fostering knowledge transfer and advancing employability through experiential education.

Balaji Gopalan is a leader in curriculum innovation and assessment within MBA education. With extensive experience designing and evaluating courses aligned to market needs, he excels at creating assessment tools and scenario-based modules that support experiential learning. Dr Gopalan's efforts have greatly contributed to advancing employability for MBA graduates both in India and internationally. His approach emphasizes the development of practical skills, industry-aligned learning outcomes, and robust frameworks for measuring academic achievement.

Deepak Gupta is a distinguished academician with over 20 years of teaching experience and expertise in Computer Science and Engineering. He holds a Ph.D. in Computer Engineering and has an extensive research portfolio, including many international journal papers, multiple conference proceedings, and several books.

His research interests span machine learning, artificial intelligence, and data mining. Currently, Dr. Gupta serves as an Associate Professor and Head of Department of CSE (Emerging Branches) at ITM Gwalior, MP, India. He has also contributed significantly to the field through patents and copyrights and actively engages as a reviewer, conference chair and editor.

Noprita Herari, M.I.Kom is a communication scholar and lecturer at Universitas Negeri Jakarta, Indonesia. Her academic work focuses on digital communication, the passion economy, and humanistic approaches to algorithmic culture. She is actively engaged in interdisciplinary research on digital labor, identity, and ethics, with particular attention to how platforms reshape subjectivity, creativity, and social relations. Noprita has contributed to several international edited volumes and journals, and she combines scholarly inquiry with practical engagement in creative and digital entrepreneurship. Her work seeks to bridge critical theory and contemporary digital realities, emphasizing the importance of humanistic communication in the age of algorithms.

Amit Kumar Jain is a distinguished academic and researcher in Electronics and Communication Engineering with a PhD from Poornima University (2025), an M.Tech in VLSI, and a B.Tech in ECE. With over 14 years of teaching experience, he currently serves as an Associate Professor at Poornima University, Jaipur. He has taught a range of subjects including Microwave Engineering, Analog Electronics, and Microprocessors, and has significantly contributed to engineering education through textbooks and numerous research publications in reputed SCOPUS and ABDC-indexed journals. Dr. Jain's research interests include wireless networks, machine learning, and sensor networks. He has presented his work at both national and international conferences. In addition to academics, he plays a pivotal role in institutional operations, managing CRM systems and admission analytics, and leading large administrative teams. His dedication to teaching, research, and university development continues to make a lasting impact in the field of technical education.

Kanat Tiryaki received her Ph.D. in Business Administration from the Institute of Social Sciences at Ege University in 2024. She has been a faculty member at the Faculty of Economics and Administrative Sciences since 2020. She also served as Departmental Vice Coordinator for the Erasmus+ Program since 2021. She participated in the Erasmus Program during both her undergraduate and doctoral studies. During her doctoral studies, she worked as a visiting researcher at the University of Oviedo for two months. Her research focuses on digital transformation in organizations, human resource management, and organizational power. She has published several articles and is currently involved in ongoing research projects.

Najmi Nuji is a seasoned Public Relations Lecturer at the Faculty of Communication and Media Studies, UiTM Shah Alam, where he has been contributing for over a decade. He holds a Bachelor of Mass Communication (Hons) in Public Relations and has furthered his academic journey with a Master of Social Sciences (Communication Management) and a Master of Mass Communication, and is currently furthering his PhD in Communication and Information Technology, focusing on Digital Public Relations, AI adoption, and Youth Entrepreneurship. With a specialization in Public Relations in Government and Diplomacy, Najmi's professional background includes serving at the National Anti-Drugs Agency under the Ministry of Home Affairs, where he honed his expertise in public sector communications. Currently, he holds the position of Honorary Secretary at the Institute of Public Relations Malaysia (IPRM) and has earned the prestigious Accreditation in Public Relations (APR). Najmi has been recognized for his excellence in public speaking and thought leadership, winning the Best Presenter Award at both the 5th International Conference on Communication & Business (2023) and the World Public Relations Forum (2024) during the Global Communications Knowledge Conference, where he contributed to discussions on Purposeful Influence for the Common Good and recently in 2025 he won best presenter awards at the 7th International Conference on the roles of the Humanities and Social Sciences in Engineering 2025 (ICoHSE7) held at World Trade Centre, Kuala Lumpur.

Diksha Pandey is an accomplished academician and practitioner specializing in Design Thinking, sustainable management, and innovation. She serves as an Assistant Professor at Christ University, Delhi NCR, where she spearheads curriculum development and teaches subjects like Lean Startup Principles, Global Business, and Personality Development. A University Topper in her MBA from Ramaiah Institute of Management, Bangalore, Ms. Pandey is also a certified Design Thinking trainer with extensive experience conducting workshops globally. She is a prolific author with notable contributions, including a book titled Design Thinking & I and several book chapters on disruptive innovation and sustainability. Her research explores organizational preparedness, sustainable energy solutions, and the integration of AI in resource management. Prof. Pandey is a co-founder of Grokalp Limited, where she applied Design Thinking to solve complex business challenges. She has received prestigious awards for her contributions to design thinking and innovation.

Koteshwar Ramesh Rakesh is a psychologist and educator with expertise in cognitive science, behavioral analysis, and emerging technologies. He holds a PhD in Psychology from Jamia Millia Islamia and brings a decade of academic experience teaching and conducting research across premier institutions. Currently, Dr. Rakesh serves as Senior Researcher at Synapse International and Associate Editor at Scientific Navigations. His research interests include cognitive biases, artificial intelligence in education, and sustainable technology. He has published in peer-reviewed journals, authored three books, and received the "Best Innovation in Teaching using Technology" Award (2024). Based in New Delhi, he is committed to bridging psychology with digital innovation and advancing equitable knowledge ecosystems.

Yogananthan S brings over 26 years of experience as a senior faculty member in operations management. Renowned for his research and teaching excellence, he specializes in supply chain strategy, project management, and business analytics. Dr Yogananthan has developed and delivered MBA-level courses and executive workshops addressing operational transformation, digitalization, and performance measurement. His work bridges academic rigor with practical challenges faced by modern organizations, earning recognition for his mentoring and curriculum innovation within business education.

Ravishankar S Ulle has authored and co-authored numerous papers published in esteemed Scopus and Web of Science–indexed journals, such as Production and Operations Management, International Journal of Operations & Production Management, and Project Management Journal. His scholarly activity encompasses empirical investigations in industrial settings, designing novel operational frameworks, and producing case studies that unite theory with practice. Dr Ulle's ongoing commitment to collaborative research advances understanding in the areas of manufacturing efficiency, supply chain resilience, and project execution.

Bharath Sampath is an accomplished academic and industry expert with over 19 years of experience in operations management, project delivery, and supply chain analytics. He integrates AI-driven solutions, digital transformation, and agile frameworks into teaching and research. Actively involved in international conferences and academic reviewing, Dr Sampath's career spans teaching at leading institutions and contributing innovative curricula for MBA and executive education. His collaborative research advances operational excellence and connects theory to industry needs, preparing students for complex business challenges.

Rebeca Sánchez Professor at the Universidad Bolivariana de Ecuador. Sociologist graduated at the Central University of Venezuela in 2004. Master on

Research on Latin American Studies & International Relations in the Simon Bolívar University (2014-2016). Member of the Research Team in Critical Studies for Social Justice at the Technical University of Manabí. PhD Student at the Universidad Rey Juan Carlos in Spain

Charu Sehgal is currently an assistant professor at CHRIST (Deemed to be University), Delhi NCR Campus.

Harika Suklun completed her associate degree in Science in 1997 and her undergraduate education in 1998. In 2000, she earned her master's degree in Business Administration from Western Kentucky University. She completed her Doctorate in Business Administration with a focus on Conflict Management at Sullivan University in 2014. Dr. SUKLUN carried out academic and professional work in the United States for nearly thirty years. After returning to Turkey in 2017, she served as an Assistant Professor at Abdullah Gül University, where she also held the position of Head of the Business Administration Department. Since March 2023, she has continued her academic work at Batman University. Her research interests include migration, women's studies, conflict management, organizational behavior, and communication. She has published various national and international articles, book chapters, and conference papers in these fields.

Somesh Varandani is a dynamic communication professional with a strong foundation in journalism, mass communication, event management, and organizational operations. He holds a Master's degree in Journalism and Mass Communication, along with a Post-Graduate Diploma in the same field from Indira Gandhi National Open University. Additionally, he completed a PGDEM in Event Management and PR from the National Academy of Event Management & Development, Jaipur, reflecting his diverse academic background and keen interest in media and events. Somesh has built a multifaceted career across education, banking, media, and event industries. He is currently serving as an Admission & Outreach Associate at Poornima University, Jaipur, where he specializes in admissions counseling, outreach coordination, student engagement, and promotional communication. Previously, he worked as a Training & Placement Officer at Poornima Group, handling placement coordination, student interactions, reporting, and academic activity management. Before joining the education sector, Somesh gained significant experience in the banking industry as a Branch Digital Officer and Branch Money Officer with AU Small Finance Bank, where he developed expertise in customer services, digital banking systems, telesales, and operational management. His media journey includes roles as an Assistant Producer at IBA News Network and a legal trainee at News India 24x7, where he honed his skills in news writing, scripting, anchoring, interviews, and video editing. Parallel to his professional roles, Somesh has actively contributed to major national-level events, film festivals, weddings, and expos through extensive freelancing projects. A passionate learner and creative communicator, he continues to expand his expertise in media, management, and public engagement.

Kirti Varandani is a visionary architect and academician based in Jaipur, Rajasthan, whose work reflects a deep commitment to sustainable design and innovative urban development. With over eight years of combined experience in architecture, interior design, and academia, she has established herself as a thoughtful designer and educator dedicated to creating spaces that blend functionality, aesthetics, and environmental responsibility. Kirti completed her Master of Design (M.Des.) in Sustainable Design from Vivekananda Global University, Jaipur (2019–2021), where she specialized in sustainable architectural practices and green building concepts. She also holds a Post-Graduate Diploma in Urban Planning and Development from Indira Gandhi National Open University (IGNOU) and a Bachelor of Architecture (B.Arch.) from Jagannath University, Jaipur (2009–2014). Her academic foundation has been enriched through various professional training programs, workshops, and certifications focused on sustainable architecture, daylight optimization, and green building standards. Currently, Kirti serves as an Assistant Professor (Guest Faculty) at the Faculty of Design, Banasthali Vidyapith, where she teaches design subjects in the Interior Design Department. Previously, she held faculty positions at Vivekananda Global University (VGU), Jaipur, and the Apex Group of Institutions, Jaipur, where she taught architecture and interior design. Her teaching philosophy centers on encouraging students to approach design as a social, cultural, and ecological process—aimed at improving human well-being and environmental health. Before entering academia, Kirti gained substantial professional experience in architectural practice. She worked as an Architect with SNG Group, Jaipur, where she was responsible for preparing architectural and landscape drawings, designing internal services, and overseeing large residential projects such as Samriddhi, Krishnangan, Shree Enclave, Shivangan, and Dusad Garden. She also worked as a Trainee Architect at Sanidhya Design Consultancy Pvt. Ltd., Jaipur, collaborating on residential and commercial projects for prominent developers such as Dhanuka Group, Anukampa Group, and Pink City Consortium. Her earlier professional experiences at Design Core Consultancy and Khilnani Associates helped her refine her technical proficiency and design sensibility. Kirti's portfolio includes a wide range of architectural and interior projects—residences, educational institutions, offices, and hospitality spaces. Some notable works include the Residence cum Hospital at Jaipur, Boys' Hostel at MPUAT Bhilwara, Dev Group of Colleges at Jaipur, and Landscape proposals for farmhouses and resorts across

Rajasthan. Her commitment to sustainable architecture is evident in her research publications, including papers in the EPRA Journal (2021) on Optimization of Daylight in Museums and Art Galleries and Impact of Green Roofs on Heating and Cooling in Different Climatic Zones of India. An active learner and researcher, Kirti has participated in numerous professional development programs, including workshops on Griha Rating and Certification, Affordable Housing, and Daylighting Simulation by ECBC. She was also recognized with the Built Today Architectural Journalism Award (2010) for her contribution to architectural writing. Beyond her professional achievements, Kirti finds inspiration in teaching, continuous learning, and sustainable innovation. Her vision is to contribute to the development of eco-conscious design education and to inspire the next generation of architects to create spaces that harmonize human needs with environmental balance.

Index

A

C

D

E

F

G

H

I

K

M

N

O

P

R

S

T

www.ingramcontent.com/pod-product-compliance
Ingram Content Group UK Ltd.
Pitfield, Milton Keynes, MK11 3LW, UK
UKHW050843101026
15624UKWH00018B/457

9 798337 345314